An Introduction to
Community
Health

Fifth Edition

James F. McKenzie
PhD, MPH, CHES

Robert R. Pinger
PhD

Jerome E. Kotecki
HSD

BALL STATE UNIVERSITY

JONES AND BARTLETT PUBLISHERS
Sudbury, Massachusetts
BOSTON   TORONTO   LONDON   SINGAPORE

We would like to dedicate this book to our students.

World Headquarters
Jones and Bartlett Publishers
40 Tall Pine Drive
Sudbury, MA 01776
978-443-5000
info@jbpub.com
www.jbpub.com

Jones and Bartlett Publishers Canada
2406 Nikanna Road
Mississauga, ON L5C 2W6
CANADA

Jones and Bartlett Publishers International
Barb House, Barb Mews
London W6 7PA
UK

Library of Congress Cataloging-in-Publication Data

McKenzie, James F., 1948–
    An introduction to community health / James F. McKenzie, Robert R. Pinger,
    Jerome E. Kotecki.—5th ed.
    p. ; cm.
    Includes bibliographical references and index.
    ISBN 10: 0-7637-2953-1
    ISBN 13: 978-0-7637-2953-0
    1. Community health services—United States. 2. Public health—United States.
    3. Medical care—United States. 4. Environmental health—United States.
    [DNLM: 1. Community Health Services—United States. 2. Delivery of Health Care—United States.
    3. Environmental Health—United States. 4. Public Health—United States. WA 546 AA1 M47i 2005]
    I. Pinger, R. R. II. Kotecki, Jerome Edward. III. Title.
RA445.M29 2005   2004021978
362.12—dc22
6048

Chief Executive Officer: Clayton Jones
Chief Operating Officer: Don W. Jones, Jr.
President, Higher Education and Professional Publishing: Robert Holland
V.P., Design and Production: Anne Spencer
V.P., Manufacturing and Inventory Control: Therese Bräuer
Acquisitions Editor: Jacqueline A. Mark
Production Editor: Julie C. Bolduc
Associate Editor: Nicole Quinn
Associate Marketing Manager: Wendy Thayer
Photo Researcher: Kimberly Potvin
Composition: Interactive Composition Corporation
Printing and Binding: DB Hess Company
Cover Printing: DB Hess Company
Cover Design: Hannus Design Associates

Printed in the United States of America
08 07 06   10 9 8 7 6 5 4 3

CONTENTS

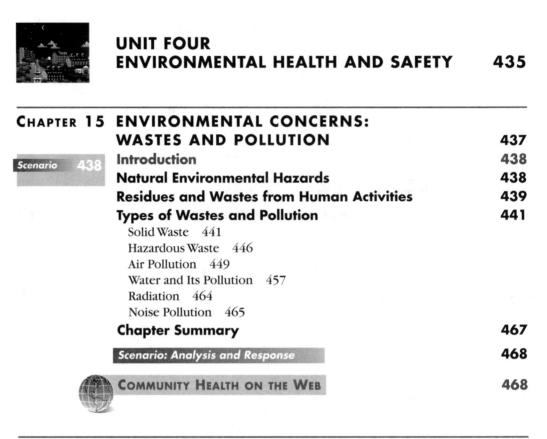

PREFACE
For the Fifth Edition

As its title suggests, *An Introduction to Community Health* was written to introduce students to community health. It is a textbook that combines the power of today's electronic technology, via the Internet, with the traditional textbook presentation. We believe that your students will find *An Introduction to Community Health* easy to read, understand, and use. If they read the chapters carefully and make an honest effort to answer the review questions and to complete some of the activities, we are confident that students will gain a good understanding of the realm of community health. *An Introduction to Community Health* incorporates a variety of pedagogical elements that assist and encourage students to understand complex community health issues. Each chapter of the book includes (1) chapter objectives, (2) a scenario, (3) an introduction, (4) content, (5) marginal definitions of key terms, (6) a chapter summary, (7) a scenario analysis and response, (8) review questions, (9) activities, (10) information about Web activities, and (11) references. In addition, many figures, tables, boxes, and photos have been presented to clarify and illustrate the concepts presented in the text. Selected content in each chapter is related to the *Healthy People 2010* goals and objectives. A glossary of key terms used throughout the text is also included.

Chapter Objectives

The chapter objectives identify the content and skills that should be mastered through reading the chapters, answering the end-of-chapter questions, and completing the activities. To use the objectives effectively, it is suggested that they be reviewed before and after reading the chapters. This review will help your students focus on the major points in each chapter and facilitate answering the questions and completing the activities at the end of each chapter.

Scenarios

Short scenarios are presented at the beginning of each chapter. The purpose of these scenarios is to bridge the gap between your students' personal experiences and ideas discussed within the chapter. The chapter content will enable your students to propose solutions to the community health problem posed in the scenario.

Introduction

Each chapter begins with a brief introduction that informs the reader of the topics to be presented and explains how these topics relate to others in the book.

Marginal Definitions

Key terms are introduced in each chapter of the textbook. These terms are important to the understanding of the chapter. Such terms are presented in boldface type within each chapter, and the definitions are presented in the margins (marginal definitions). Before reading the chapter, it is suggested that the student skim the chapters, paying particular attention to the key terms. This should provide greater understanding of the content. The boldfaced terms, including those defined in the margin, appear in the glossary at the end of the book. In addition, some words in the textbook have been italicized for emphasis, and are often key terms that have been defined either in another chapter or the glossary.

Content

Although each chapter in the textbook could be expanded and, indeed, there are entire books written on many of the topics we cover, we believe each chapter contains the essential material needed to introduce your students to the issues related to community health. To enhance and facilitate learning, the chapters are organized in four units: Foundations of Community Health, The Nation's Health, Health Care Delivery, and Environmental Health and Safety.

Chapter Summary

At the end of each chapter, the reader will find several bulleted points that review the major concepts contained in each chapter.

Scenario: Analysis and Response

Following the chapter summary, students are provided with an opportunity to respond to the scenario presented earlier in the chapter. The content presented in the chapter will help the students to formulate their responses or solutions.

Review Questions

The purpose of the questions at the end of each chapter is to provide the readers with feedback regarding their mastery of the chapter's content. The questions reinforce the chapter objectives and key terms.

Activities

The activities at the end of each chapter provide an opportunity for students to apply their new knowledge in a meaningful way. The activities, which are presented in a variety of formats, should appeal to the varying learning styles of your students.

Community Health on the Web (health.jbpub.com/communityhealth/5e)

The Internet contains a wealth of information about community and public health. The Web activities are presented to encourage students to further explore the chapter's content by visiting relevant Web sites. These activities recap three concepts or issues from the text in each chapter. The starting point for these activities is Jones and Bartlett's own exclusive Community Health Web page (health.jbpub.com/communityhealth/5e).

Once students have connected to the designated community health link through the Jones and Bartlett Community Health home page, they will be provided with activity instructions for further exploration of the Web site. Animated flashcards, an interactive glossary, and crossword puzzles are also available online. When more up-to-date information becomes available at an assigned site, the authors are able to immediately edit the exercise to reflect the most recent material.

The Web activities bring to life the theory presented in the text, thus giving students a real-world context for understanding community health concepts and issues. The intent of including Web activities in the textbook is to inspire the students, in real time, to authentically assess and to critically think about what they have just read in the text by asking them thought-provoking questions related to the assigned Web site. By integrating the Web into the text, we have created a dynamic learning environment that is as up-to-date as today's newspaper.

What Is New to This Edition?

Although the format of this edition is similar to the previous edition, much has changed. First, the content and statistics have been reviewed and updated with the latest information. New tables, figures, boxes, and photographs have been added. Second, the *Healthy People 2010* boxes that were a part of each chapter in the previous edition of the textbook now include, where available, data that show the status of each objective with regard to meeting the 2010 target figure. Third, the Web activities at the end of each chapter have been revised and updated. Instructors and students alike will find that these activities greatly expand the usefulness of the textbook. And fourth, two new individuals have brought their expertise to the writing team. Denise M. Seabert, PhD, CHES, Assistant Professor in the Department of Physiology and Health Science at Ball State University, completed the revisions for Chapter 6 (The School Health Program: A Component of Community Health) and Chapter 8 (Adolescents, Young Adults, and Adults). David A. Haber, PhD, the John and Janice Fisher Distinguished Professor and Associate Director of the Fisher Institute for Wellness and Gerontology at Ball State University, was responsible for the revisions to Chapter 9 (Elders). Their expertise is greatly welcomed.

Accompanying Ancillaries

Repetition is often the key to learning; in the fifth edition we offer the *Student Note Taking Guide,* which allows students to revisit key topics discussed in the text. This edition is also accompanied by several ancillaries including a lecture outline and PowerPoint presentation for each chapter as well as a computerized TestBank. These products are available free to adopters of the text. We thank Jamie Johnson, PhD, at Western Illinois University for updating the ancillary material. For more information about these ancillary products, please contact your sales representative at Jones and Bartlett Publishers.

ACKNOWLEDGMENTS

A project of this nature could not be completed without the assistance and understanding of a number of individuals. First, we would like to thank all of our past and present students and professional colleagues who have inspired us to produce a better community health textbook. Second, we would like to thank several colleagues for their contributions. They include Dale B. Hahn, PhD, Department of Physiology and Health Science, Ball State University, for encouraging us to take on this project; David V. Perkins, PhD, Department of Psychological Sciences, Ball State University, for his review of and suggestions for Chapter 11; the staff of the High Library, especially Acting Director Sylvia T. Morra, at Elizabethtown College, Elizabethtown, Pennsylvania, for their assistance in making this project possible; and Billie Kennedy and Ruth Ann Duncan for their support and friendship.

Third, we would like to express our appreciation to those professionals who took the time and effort to review and provide feedback for this edition. They include John B. Amadio, PhD, Brigham Young University; Steve G. Gabany, PhD, Indiana State University; Regina Galer-Unti, PhD, CHES, Purdue University; Stephen Hohman, PhD, RN, Ohio University; and Nancy Parsons, PhD, MPH, CHES, Western Illinois University.

Fourth, we would like to acknowledge those professionals who reviewed the previous editions of the text. They include John Amadio, Brigham Young University; Amy Bernard, University of Cincinnati; Jim Broadbear, Illinois State University; Daniel Cabrera, Northern Illinois University; A. Davanni, California State University–Sacramento; Donald Ensley, East Carolina University; Mariane Fahlman, Wayne State University; Donna Gates, University of Cincinnati Medical Center; Claudia S. Goggins, University of North Texas Health Science Center at Fort Worth; Mary Hawk, Western Washington University; Stephen Hohman, Ohio University; Joseph Hudak, Ohio Eastern University; Gay James, South West Texas State University; Marshall Meyer, Portland Community College; Marilyn Morton, State University of New York—Plattsburgh; Kay Mueggenburg, Indiana University-Bloomington; Carol M. Parker,

University of Central Oklahoma; Jane Petrillo, Western Kentucky University; Carl Peter, Western Illinois University; Jacquie Rainey, University of Central Arkansas; Janet Reis, University of Illinois–Urbana/Champaign; Gayle Schmidt, Texas A & M University; J. L. Sexton, Fort Hays State University; Green Waggener, College of Charleston; Bob Walsh, Idaho State University; and Kathleen Welshimer, Southern Illinois University.

Fifth, we would like to thank all of the employees of Jones and Bartlett Publishers. Their hard work and confidence in us was most helpful in creating this edition. Specifically, we would like to thank Jacqueline Mark, Acquisitions Editor; Julie Bolduc, Production Editor; and Nicole Quinn, Associate Editor. Finally, we would like to thank our families for their support, encouragement, and tolerance of the time that writing takes away from family activities.

James F. McKenzie, PhD, MPH, CHES
Robert R. Pinger, PhD
Jerome E. Kotecki, HSD

U N I T
O N E

FOUNDATIONS OF COMMUNITY HEALTH

Chapter 1

Community Health: Yesterday, Today, and Tomorrow

Chapter Objectives

After studying this chapter, you will be able to:

1　Accurately define the terms of *health, community, community health, population health,* and *public health.*

2　Explain the difference between personal and community health activities.

3　List and discuss the factors that influence a community's health.

4　Briefly relate the history of community/public health, including the recent U.S. history of community and public health in the twentieth century.

5　Provide a brief overview of the current health status of Americans.

6　Describe the status of efforts to improve world health and list some plans for the future.

7　Describe the purpose of the *Healthy People 2010* goals and objectives as they apply to the planning process of the health of Americans.

8　Briefly describe the impact terrorism has on community/public health.

SCENARIO

Amy and Eric are a young working couple who are easing into a comfortable lifestyle. They have good-paying jobs, drive nice cars, are buying a home in a good neighborhood, and have two healthy preschool children. When Amy picked her children up from day care earlier in the day she learned from the head teacher that another parent had reported that his child was diagnosed with hepatitis. This news frightened Amy and made her begin to question the quality of the day care center. Amy told Eric of this situation when he got home from work. As the couple discussed whether or not they should take their children to day care as usual the following day, they discovered that they have many unanswered questions. How serious is hepatitis? What is the likelihood that their children will be at serious risk for getting the disease? What steps are being taken to control the outbreak? Is any state or local agency responsible for standardizing health practices at private day care centers in the community? Does the city, county, or state carry out any type of inspection when they license these facilities? And, if the children do not attend day care, which parent will stay home with them?

INTRODUCTION

In reflecting on the twentieth century, it is easy to point to the tremendous progress that was made in the health and life expectancy of many people of the world. Infant mortality dropped, many of the infectious diseases have been brought under control, and better family planning became available. However, there is still room for improvement! Individual health behaviors, such as the use of tobacco, poor diet, and physical inactivity, have given rise to an unacceptable number of cases of illness and death from noninfectious diseases such as cancer and heart disease. New and emerging infectious diseases, such as severe acute respiratory syndrome (SARS) and those caused by drug-resistant pathogens, are stretching resources available to control them. And the events stemming from the attacks on the World Trade Center in New York, the Pentagon in Washington, DC, and the failed terrorist attack on a third site that ended with the crash of the airliner in western Pennsylvania on September 11, 2001 (now commonly referred to as 9/11) and the subsequent anthrax mailings have caused us to refocus our priorities. Even with all that has happened in recent years in the United States and around the world, the achievement of good health remains a worldwide goal of the twenty-first century. Governments, private organizations, and individuals throughout the world are working to improve health. Although individual actions to improve one's own personal health certainly contribute to the overall health of the community, organized community actions are often necessary when health problems exceed the resources of any one individual. When such actions are not taken, the health of the entire community is at risk.

This chapter introduces the concepts and principles of community health, explains how community health differs from personal health, and provides a brief history of community health. Some of the key health problems facing Americans are also described, and an outlook for the twenty-first century is provided.

Definitions

The word *health* means different things to different people. Similarly, there are other words that can be defined in various ways. Some basic terms we will use in this book are defined in the following paragraphs.

Health

The word *health* is derived from *hal,* which means "hale, sound, whole." When it comes to the health of people, the word *health* has been defined in a number of different ways—often in its social context, as when a parent describes the health of a child or when an avid fan defines the health of a professional athlete. Until the beginning of the health promotion era in the mid-1970s, the most widely accepted definition of health was the one published by the World Health Organization in 1947. That definition states that "health is a state of complete physical, mental, and social well-being and not merely the absence of disease and infirmity."[1] However, in more recent times, the word has taken on a more holistic approach; Payne, Hahn, and Mauer describe health in terms of six interacting and dynamic dimensions—physical, emotional, social, intellectual, spiritual, and occupational.[2] We have chosen to combine these definitions of health and create our own. Thus, we define **health** as a dynamic state or condition that is multidimensional in nature and results from a person's adaptations to his or her environment. It is a resource for living and exists in varying degrees. "Many persons enjoy a state of well-being even though they may be classed as unhealthy by others."[3]

health
a dynamic state or condition that is multidimensional in nature and results from a person's adaptations to his or her environment; it is a resource for living and exists in varying degrees

Community

Traditionally, a community has been thought of as a geographic area with specific boundaries—for example, a neighborhood, city, county, or state. However, in the context of community health, a **community** is "a group of people who have common characteristics; communities can be defined by location, race, ethnicity, age, occupation, interest in particular problems or outcomes, or common bonds."[4] Communities are characterized by the following elements:

(1) membership—a sense of identity and belonging; (2) common symbol systems—similar language, rituals, and ceremonies; (3) shared values and norms; (4) mutual influence—community members have influence and are influenced by each other; (5) shared needs and commitment to meeting them; and (6) shared emotional connection—members share common history, experiences, and mutual support.[5]

community
a group of people who have common characteristics; communities can be defined by location, race, ethnicity, age, occupation, interest in particular problems or outcomes, or other common bonds

Examples of communities include the people of the city of Columbus (location), the Asian community of San Francisco (race), the Hispanic community of Miami (ethnicity), seniors in the church (age), the business or the banking communities (occupation), the homeless of Indiana (specific problem), those on welfare in Ohio (particular outcome), or local union members (common bond). A community may be as small as the group of people who live on a residence hall floor or as large as all of the individuals who make up a nation. "A healthy community is a place where people provide leadership in assessing their own resources and needs, where public health and social infrastructure and policies support health, and where essential public health services, including quality health care, are available."[6]

community health
the health status of a defined group of people and the actions and conditions, both private and public (governmental), to promote, protect, and preserve their health

Community Health

Community health refers to the health status of a defined group of people and the actions and conditions, both private and public (governmental), to promote, protect, and preserve their health. For example, the health status of the people of Muncie, Indiana, and the private and public actions taken to promote, protect, and preserve the health of these people, would constitute community health.

Population Health

The term *population health,* which is similar to *community health,* has emerged in recent years. The primary difference between these two terms is the degree of organization or identity of the people. **Population health** refers to the health status of people who are not organized and have no identity as a group or locality and the actions and conditions to promote, protect, and preserve their health. Men under fifty, adolescents, prisoners, and white collar workers are all examples of populations.[7]

population health
the health status of people who are not organized and have no identity as a group or locality and the actions and conditions to promote, protect, and preserve their health

Public Health

Public health refers to the health status of a defined group of people and the governmental actions and conditions to promote, protect, and preserve their health.

Community Health Versus Personal Health

To further clarify the definitions presented in this chapter, it is important to distinguish between the terms *personal health* and *community health activities*.

Personal Health Activities

Personal health activities are individual actions and decision making that affect the health of an individual or his or her immediate family members. These activities may be preventive or curative in nature but seldom directly affect the behavior of others. Choosing to eat wisely, to regularly wear a safety belt, and to visit the physician are all examples of personal health activities.

Community Health Activities

Community health activities are activities that are aimed at protecting or improving the health of a population or community. Maintenance of accurate birth and death records, protection of the food and water supply, and participating in fund drives for voluntary health organizations such as the American Lung Association are examples of community health activities.

Within this book, you will be introduced to the many community health activities and to the organizations that are responsible for carrying them out. The following are some of the key topics that are covered in this text:

- Organizations that contribute to community health
- How communities measure health, disease, injury, and death
- Control of communicable and noncommunicable diseases
- How communities organize to solve health problems
- Community health in schools
- Community health needs of people at different stages of life
- Community health needs of special populations
- Community mental health
- Abuse of alcohol, tobacco, and other drugs
- The health care delivery system
- Environmental health problems
- Intentional and unintentional injuries
- Occupational safety and health

FIGURE 1.1

Factors that affect the health of a community.

Physical factors

Social and cultural factors

Health of the community

Community organization

Individual behaviors

Factors That Affect the Health of a Community

There are a great many factors that affect the health of a community. As a result, the health status of each community is different. These factors may be physical, social, and/or cultural. They also include the ability of the community to organize and work together as a whole as well as the individual behaviors of those in the community (see Figure 1.1).

Physical Factors

Physical factors include the influences of geography, the environment, community size, and industrial development.

Geography

A community's health problems can be directly influenced by its altitude, latitude, and climate. In tropical countries where warm, humid temperatures and rain prevail throughout the year, parasitic and infectious diseases are a leading community health problem (see Figure 1.2). In many tropical countries, survival from these diseases is made more difficult because poor soil conditions result in inadequate food production and malnutrition. In temperate climates with fewer parasitic and infectious diseases and a more than adequate food supply, obesity and heart disease are important community health problems.

Environment

The quality of our environment is directly related to the quality of our stewardship over it. Many experts believe that if we continue to allow uncontrolled population growth and continue to deplete nonrenewable natural resources, succeeding generations will inhabit communities that are less desirable than ours. Many feel that we must accept responsibility for this stewardship and drastically reduce the rate at which we foul the soil, water, and air.

Community Size

The larger the community, the greater its range of health problems and the greater its number of health resources. For example, larger communities have more health professionals and better health facilities than smaller communities. These resources are often needed because communicable diseases can spread more quickly and environmental problems are often more severe in densely populated areas. For example, the amount of trash generated by the approximately 8+ million people in New York City is many times greater than that generated by the entire state of Wyoming, with its population of about 501,000.

It is important to note that a community's size can impact both positively and negatively on that community's health. The ability of a community to effectively plan, organize, and utilize its resources can determine whether its size can be used to good advantage.

FIGURE 1.2

In tropical countries, parasitic and infectious diseases are a leading community health problem.

Industrial Development

Industrial development, like size, can have either positive or negative effects on the health status of a community. Industrial development provides a community with added resources for community health programs, but it may bring with it environmental pollution and occupational illnesses. Communities that experience rapid industrial development must eventually regulate the way in which industries (1) obtain raw materials, (2) discharge by-products, (3) dispose of wastes, (4) treat and protect their employees, and (5) clean up environmental accidents. Unfortunately, many of these laws are usually passed only after these communities have suffered significant reductions in the quality of their life and health.

Social and Cultural Factors

Social factors are those that arise from the interaction of individuals or groups within the community. For example, people who live in urban communities, where life is fast-paced, experience higher rates of stress-related illnesses than those who live in rural communities, where life is more leisurely. On the other hand, those in rural areas may not have access to the same quality or selection of health care (i.e., providers, hospitals, or medical specialists) that is available to those who live in urban communities.

Cultural factors arise from guidelines (both explicit and implicit) that individuals "inherit" from being a part of a particular society. Culture "teaches us what to fear, what to respect, what to value, and what to regard as relevant in our lives."[8] Some of the factors that contribute to culture are discussed in the following sections.

Beliefs, Traditions, and Prejudices

The beliefs, traditions, and prejudices of community members can affect the health of the community. The beliefs of those in a community about such specific health behaviors as exercise and smoking can influence policy makers on whether or not they will spend money on bike trails and no-smoking ordinances. The traditions of specific ethnic groups can influence the types of food, restaurants, retail outlets, and services available in a community. Prejudices of one specific ethnic or racial group against another can result in acts of violence and crime. Racial and ethnic disparities will continue to put certain groups, such as black Americans or certain religious groups, at greater risk.

Economy

Both national and local economies can affect the health of a community through reductions in health and social services. An economic downturn means lower tax revenues (fewer tax dollars) and fewer contributions to charitable groups. Such actions will result in fewer dollars being available for programs such as welfare, food stamps, community health care, and other community services. This occurs because revenue shortfalls cause agencies to experience budget cuts. With less money, these agencies often must alter their eligibility guidelines, thereby restricting aid to only the neediest individuals. Obviously, many people who had been eligible for assistance before the economic downturn become ineligible.

Employers usually find it increasingly difficult to provide health benefits for their employees as their income drops. The unemployed and underemployed face poverty and deteriorating health. Thus, the cumulative effect of an economic downturn significantly affects the health of the community.

Politics

Those who happen to be in political office, either nationally or locally, can improve or jeopardize the health of their community by the decisions they make. In the most general terms, the argument is over greater or lesser governmental participation in health issues. For example, there has been a long-standing discussion in the United States on the extent to which the government should involve itself in health care. Historically, Democrats have been in favor of such action while Republicans have been against it. However, as the cost of health care continues to grow, both sides see the need for some kind of increased regulation. Local politicians also influence the health of their communities each time they vote on health-related measures brought before them.

Religion

A number of religions have taken a position on health care. For example, some religious communities limit the type of medical treatment their members may receive. Some do not permit immunizations; others do not permit their members to be treated by physicians. Still others prohibit certain foods. For example, Kosher dietary regulations permit Jews to eat the meat only of animals that chew cud and have cloven hooves and the flesh only of fish that have both gills and scales, while still others, like the Native American Church of the Morning Star, use peyote, a hallucinogen, as a sacrament.

Some religious communities actively address moral and ethical issues such as abortion, premarital intercourse, and homosexuality. Still other religions teach health-promoting codes of living to their members. Obviously, religion can affect a community's health positively or negatively (see Figure 1.3).

Social Norms

The influence of social norms can be positive or negative and can change over time. Cigarette smoking is a good example. During the 1940s, 1950s, and 1960s, it was socially acceptable to

FIGURE 1.3
Religion can affect a community's health either positively or negatively.

smoke in most settings. As a matter of fact, in 1960, 53% of American men and 32% of American women smoked. Thus, in 1960 it was socially acceptable to be a smoker, especially if you were male. Now, early in the twenty-first century, those percentages have dropped to 25.2% (for males) and 20.7% (for females), and in most public places it has become socially unacceptable to smoke.[9] The lawsuits against tobacco companies by both the state attorneys general and private citizens provide further evidence that smoking has fallen from social acceptability. Because of this change in the social norm, there is less secondhand smoke in many public places, and in turn the health of the community has improved.

Unlike smoking, alcohol consumption represents a continuing negative social norm in America, especially on college campuses. The normal expectation seems to be that drinking is fun (and almost everyone wants to have fun). Despite the fact that most college students are too young to drink legally, 85% to 90% of college students drink.[2] It seems fairly obvious that the American alcoholic-beverage industry has influenced our social norms.

Socioeconomic Status (SES)
"In both the United States and Western Europe, the gap in health status and mortality between those commanding, and those who lack, economic power and social resources continues to widen. These parallel trends—of growing economic inequalities and growing social inequalities in health—reflect, in part, the relationship between people's socioeconomic position as consumers and employers or employees and their social, biological, and mental well-being."[10] That is, those in the community with the lowest socioeconomic status also have the poorest health and the most difficulty in gaining access to health care. The point of entry into the health care system for most Americans is the family doctor. The economically disadvantaged seldom have a family doctor. For them, the point of entry is the local hospital emergency room. In addition to health care access, higher incomes enable people to afford better

housing, live in safer neighborhoods, and increase the opportunity to engage in health-promoting behaviors.[11]

Community Organizing

community organizing
a process through which communities are helped to identify common problems or goals, mobilize resources, and in other ways develop and implement strategies for reaching their goals they have collectively set

The way in which a community is able to organize its resources directly influences its ability to intervene and solve problems, including health problems. **Community organizing** "is a process through which communities are helped to identify common problems or goals, mobilize resources, and in other ways develop and implement strategies for reaching their goals they have collectively set."[12] It is not a science but an art of building consensus within a democratic process.[13] If a community can organize its resources effectively into a unified force, it "is likely to produce benefits in the form of increased effectiveness and productivity by reducing duplication of efforts and avoiding the imposition of solutions that are not congruent with the local culture and needs."[6] For example, many communities in the United States have faced community-wide drug problems. Some have been able to organize their resources to reduce or resolve these problems while others have not. (See Chapter 5 for a full explanation of community organizing.)

Individual Behavior

herd immunity
the resistance of a population to the spread of an infectious agent based on the immunity of a high proportion of individuals

The behavior of the individual community members contributes to the health of the entire community. It takes the concerted effort of many—if not most—of the individuals in a community to make a program work. For example, if each individual consciously recycles his or her trash each week, community recycling will be successful. Likewise, if each occupant would wear a safety belt, there could be a significant reduction in the number of facial injuries and deaths from car crashes for the entire community. In another example, the more individuals who become immunized against a specific disease, the slower the disease will spread and the fewer people will be exposed. This concept is known as **herd immunity.**

FIGURE 1.4
Archeological findings reveal community health practices of the past.

A Brief History of Community and Public Health

The history of community and public health is almost as long as the history of civilization. This brief summary provides an account of some of the accomplishments and failures in community and public health. It is hoped that a knowledge of the past will enable us to better prepare for future challenges to our community's health.

Earliest Civilizations

In all likelihood, the earliest community health practices went unrecorded. Perhaps these practices involved taboos against defecation within the tribal communal area or near the source of drinking water. Perhaps they involved rites associated with burial of the dead. Certainly, the use of herbs for the prevention and curing of diseases and communal assistance with childbirth are practices that predate archeological records.

Ancient Societies (Before 500 B.C.)

Excavations at sites of some of the earliest known civilizations have uncovered evidence of community health activities (see Figure 1.4). Archeological findings from the Indus Valley of northern India, dating from about 2000 B.C., provide evidence of bathrooms and drains in homes and sewers below street level. Drainage systems have also been discovered among the ruins of the Middle Kingdom of ancient

Egypt (2700–2000 B.C.). The Myceneans, who lived on Crete in 1600 B.C., had toilets, flushing systems, and sewers.[14] Written medical prescriptions for drugs have been deciphered from a Sumerian clay tablet dated at about 2100 B.C. By 1500 B.C. more than 700 drugs were known to the Egyptians.[15]

Perhaps the earliest written record concerning public health is the Code of Hammurabi, the famous king of Babylon, who lived 3900 years ago. Hammurabi's code of conduct included laws pertaining to physicians and health practices (see Figure 1.5). The Bible's Book of Leviticus, written about 1500 B.C., provides guidelines for personal cleanliness, sanitation of campsites, disinfection of wells, isolation of lepers, disposal of refuse, and the hygiene of maternity.[16]

Classical Cultures (500 B.C.–A.D. 500)

During the thirteenth and twelfth centuries B.C., the Greeks began to travel to Egypt and continued to do so over the next several centuries. Knowledge from the Babylonians, Egyptians, Hebrews, and other peoples of the eastern Mediterranean was included in the Greeks' philosophy of health and medicine.[15] During the "Golden Age" of ancient Greece (in the sixth and fifth centuries B.C.), men participated in physical games of strength and skill and swam in public facilities. There is little evidence that this emphasis on fitness and on success in athletic competition was imparted equally to all members of the community.[17] Participation in these activities was not encouraged or even permitted for women, the poor, or slaves.

The Greeks were also active in the practice of community sanitation. They supplemented local city wells with water supplied from mountains as far as 10 miles away. In at least one city, water from a distant source was stored in a cistern 370 feet above sea level.[14]

The Romans improved upon the Greek engineering and built aqueducts that could transport water for many miles. Evidence of some 200 Roman aqueducts remains today, from Spain to Syria and from northern Europe to northern Africa. The Romans also built sewer systems and initiated other community health activities, including the regulation of building construction, refuse removal, and street cleaning and repair.[16]

FIGURE 1.5

The Code of Hammurabi included laws pertaining to physicians and health practices.

The Roman Empire was the repository for Greek medical ideas, but with few exceptions, the Romans did little to advance medical thinking. However, they did make one important contribution to medicine and health care—the hospital. Although the first hospitals were merely infirmaries for slaves, before the end of the Roman era, Christians had established public hospitals as benevolent charitable organizations.[15] When the Roman Empire eventually fell in A.D. 476, most of the public health activities ceased.

Middle Ages (A.D. 500–1500)

The period from the end of the Roman Empire in the West to about 1500 has become known as the Middle Ages. The Eastern Roman Empire (the Byzantine Empire), with its capital in Constantinople, continued until 1453. While the Greco-Roman legacy of society was largely preserved in the Eastern Roman Empire, it was lost to most of western Europe. Most of what knowledge remained was preserved only in the churches and monasteries.

The medieval approach to health and disease differed greatly from that of the Roman Empire. During this time, there was a growing revulsion for Roman materialism and a growth of spirituality. Health problems were considered to have both spiritual causes and spiritual solutions.[14] This was especially true at the beginning of the Middle Ages, during a period known as the Dark Ages (500–1000). Both pagan rites and Christian beliefs blamed disease on supernatural causes. St. Augustine, for example, taught that diseases were caused by demons sent to torment the human spirit, and most Christians generally believed that disease was a punishment for sins.[15]

The failure to take into account the role of the physical and biological environment in the causation of communicable diseases resulted in the failure to control the unrelenting epidemics during this **spiritual era of public health.** These epidemics were responsible for the suffering and death of millions. One of the earliest recorded epidemic diseases was leprosy. It has been estimated that by 1200, there were 19,000 leper houses and leprosaria in Europe.[14]

The deadliest of the epidemic diseases of the period was the plague. It is hard for us, living here in the twenty-first century, to imagine the impact of plague on Europe. Three great epidemics of plague occurred: The first began in A.D. 543, the second in 1348, and the last in 1664. The worst epidemic occurred in the fourteenth century, when the disease became known as the "black death." An estimated 25 million people died in Europe alone. This is more than the total number of people who live in the states of Ohio and Pennsylvania today. Half of the population of London was lost, and in some parts of France only 1 in 10 survived.[16]

The Middle Ages also saw epidemics of other recognizable diseases, including smallpox, diphtheria, measles, influenza, tuberculosis, anthrax, and trachoma. Many other diseases, unidentifiable at the time, took their toll. The last epidemic disease of this period was syphilis, which appeared in 1492. This, like the other epidemics, killed thousands.

spiritual era of public health
a time during the Middle Ages when the causation of communicable disease was linked to spiritual forces

Renaissance and Exploration (1500–1700)

The Renaissance period was characterized by a rebirth of thinking about the nature of the world and of humankind. There was an expansion of trade between cities and nations and an increase in population concentrations in large cities. This period was also characterized by exploration and discovery. The travels of Columbus, Magellan, and many other explorers eventually ushered in a period of colonialism. The effects of the Renaissance on community health were substantial. A more careful accounting of disease outbreaks during this period revealed that diseases such as the plague killed saints and sinners alike. There was a growing belief that diseases were caused by environmental, not spiritual, factors. For example, the term *malaria,* meaning bad air, is a distinct reference to the humid or swampy air that often harbors mosquitoes that transmit malaria.

More critical observations of the sick led to more accurate descriptions of symptoms and outcomes of disease. These observations led to the first recognition of whooping cough, typhus, scarlet fever, and malaria as distinct and separate diseases.[14]

Epidemics of smallpox, malaria, and plague were still rampant in England and throughout Europe. In 1665, the plague took 68,596 lives in London, which at the time had a population of 460,000 (a population loss of almost 15%). Explorers, conquerors, and merchants and their crews spread disease to colonists and indigenous people throughout the New World. Smallpox, measles, and other diseases ravaged the unprotected natives.

The Eighteenth Century

The eighteenth century was characterized by industrial growth. In spite of the beginnings of recognition of the nature of disease, living conditions were hardly conducive to good health. Cities were overcrowded, and water supplies were inadequate and often unsanitary. Streets were usually unpaved, filthy, and heaped with trash and garbage. Many homes had unsanitary dirt floors.

Workplaces were unsafe and unhealthy. A substantial portion of the work force was made up of the poor, which included children, who were forced to work long hours as indentured servants. Many of these jobs were unsafe or involved working in unhealthy environments, such as textile factories and coal mines.

One medical advance, made at the end of the eighteenth century, deserves mention because of its significance for public health. In 1796, Dr. Edward Jenner successfully demonstrated the process of vaccination as a protection against smallpox. He did this by inoculating a boy with material from a cowpox (*Vaccinia*) pustule. When challenged later with material from a smallpox (*Variola*) pustule, the boy remained healthy.

Dr. Jenner's discovery remains as one of the great discoveries of all time for both medicine and for public health. Prior to Dr. Jenner's discovery, millions died or were severely disfigured by smallpox (see Figure 1.6). The only known prevention had been "variolation," inoculation with smallpox material itself. This was a risky procedure because people sometimes became quite ill with smallpox. Nonetheless, during the American Revolution, General George Washington ordered the Army of the American Colonies "variolated." He did this so that he could be sure an epidemic of smallpox would not wipe out his colonial forces.[14] Interestingly enough, the average age at death for one living in the United States during this time was 29 years.

Following the American Revolution, George Washington ordered the first U.S. census for the purpose of the apportionment of representation in the House of Representatives. The census, first taken in 1790, is still conducted every 10 years and serves as an invaluable source of information for community health planning.

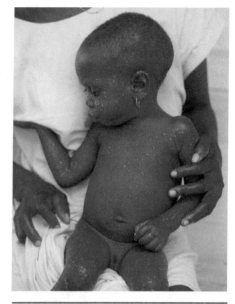

FIGURE 1.6

Prior to the elimination of smallpox, millions died or were severely disfigured by the disease.

As the eighteenth century came to a close, a young United States faced numerous disease problems, including continuing outbreaks of smallpox, cholera, typhoid fever, and yellow fever. Yellow fever outbreaks usually occurred in port cities such as Charleston, Baltimore, New York, and New Orleans, where ships arrived to dock from tropical America. The greatest single epidemic of yellow fever in America occurred in Philadelphia in 1793, where there were an estimated 23,000 cases, including 4,044 deaths in a population estimated at only 37,000.[18]

In response to these continuing epidemics and the need to address other mounting health problems, such as sanitation and protection of the water supply, several governmental health agencies were created. In 1798, the Marine Hospital Service (forerunner to the U.S. Public Health Service) was formed to deal with disease that was occurring onboard water vessels. By 1799, several of America's largest cities, including Boston, Philadelphia, New York, and Baltimore, also had founded municipal boards of health.

The Nineteenth Century

During the first half of the nineteenth century, few remarkable advancements in public health occurred (see Figure 1.7). Living conditions in Europe and England remained unsanitary, and industrialization led to an even greater concentration of the population within cities. However, better agricultural methods led to improved nutrition for many.

During this period, America enjoyed westward expansion, characterized by a spirit of pioneering, self-sufficiency, and rugged individualism. The federal government's approach to health problems was characterized by the French term *laissez faire,* meaning noninterference. There were also few health regulations or health departments in rural areas. Health quackery thrived; this was truly a period when "buyer beware" was good advice.

Epidemics continued in major cities in both Europe and America. In 1849, a cholera epidemic struck London. Dr. John Snow studied the epidemic and hypothesized that the disease was being caused by the drinking water from the Broad Street pump. He obtained permission

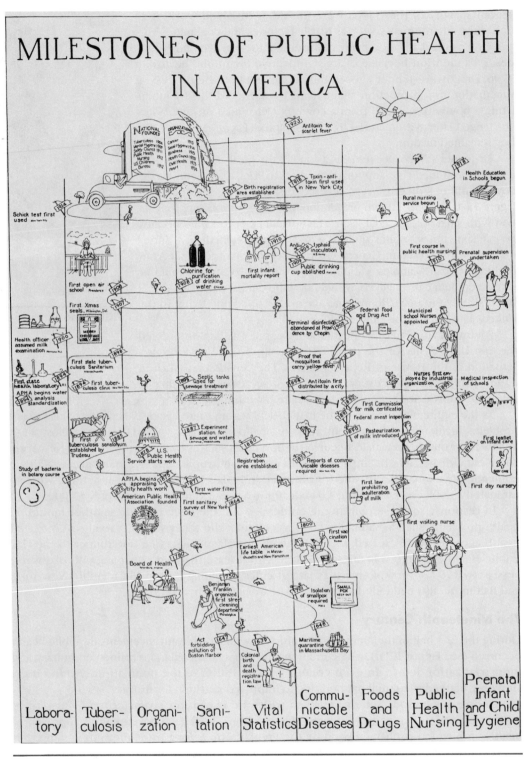

FIGURE 1.7

Milestones of public health in America.

Source: American Public Health Association. Copyright © 1926, 1985. Reprinted with permission.

to remove the pump handle, and the epidemic was abated (see Figure 1.8). Snow's action was remarkable because it predated the discovery that microorganisms can cause disease. The predominant theory of contagious disease at the time was the "miasmas theory." According to this theory, vapors, or miasmas, were the source of many diseases. The miasmas theory remained popular throughout much of the nineteenth century.

In the United States in 1850, Lemuel Shattuck drew up a health report for the Commonwealth of Massachusetts that outlined the public health needs for the state. It included recommendations for the establishment of boards of health, the collection of vital statistics, the implementation of sanitary measures, and research on diseases. Shattuck also recommended health education and controlling exposure to alcohol, smoke, adulterated food, and nostrums (quack medicines).[16] Although some of his recommendations took years to implement (the Massachusetts Board of Health was not founded until 1869), the significance of Shattuck's report is such that 1850 is a key date in American public health; it marks the beginning of the **modern era of public health.**

Real progress in the understanding of the causes of many communicable diseases occurred during the last quarter of the nineteenth century. One of the obstacles to progress was the theory of spontaneous generation, the idea that living organisms could arise from inorganic or nonliving matter. Akin to this idea was the thought that one type of contagious microbe could change into another type of organism.

In 1862, Louis Pasteur of France proposed his germ theory of disease. Throughout the 1860s and 1870s, he and others carried out experiments and made observations that supported this theory and disproved spontaneous generation. Pasteur is generally given credit for providing the death blow to the theory of spontaneous generation.

It was the German scientist Robert Koch who developed the criteria and procedures necessary to establish that a particular microbe, and no other, causes a particular disease. His first demonstration, with the anthrax bacillus, was in 1876. Between 1877 and the end of the century, the identity of numerous bacterial disease agents was established, including those that caused gonorrhea, typhoid fever, leprosy, tuberculosis, cholera, diphtheria, tetanus, pneumonia, plague, and dysentery. This period (1875–1900) has come to be known as the **bacteriological period of public health.**

Although most scientific discoveries in the late nineteenth century were made in Europe, there were significant public health achievements occurring in America as well. The first law prohibiting the adulteration of milk was passed in 1856, the first sanitary survey was carried out in New York City in 1864, and the American Public Health Association was founded in 1872. The Marine Hospital Service gained new powers of inspection and investigation under the Port Quarantine Act of 1878.[16] In 1890 the pasteurization of milk was introduced, and in 1891 meat inspection began. It was also during this time that nurses were first hired by industries (in 1895) and schools (in 1899). Also in 1895, septic tanks were introduced for sewage treatment. In 1900, Major Walter Reed of the U.S. Army announced that yellow fever is transmitted by mosquitoes.

FIGURE 1.8

In London, England, 1849, John Snow interrupted a cholera epidemic by removing the handle from this pump, located on Broad Street.

modern era of public health
the era of public health that began in 1850 and continues today

bacteriological period of public health
the period of 1875–1900, during which the causes of many bacterial diseases were discovered

The Twentieth Century

As the twentieth century began, life expectancy was still less than 50 years.[19] The leading causes of death were communicable diseases—influenza, pneumonia, tuberculosis, and infections of the gastrointestinal tract. Other communicable diseases, such as typhoid fever, malaria, and diphtheria, also killed many people.

There were other health problems as well. Thousands of children were afflicted with conditions characterized by noninfectious diarrhea or by bone deformity. Although the symptoms of pellagra and rickets were known and described, the causes of these ailments remained a mystery at the turn of the century. Discovery that these conditions resulted from vitamin deficiencies was slow because some scientists were searching for bacterial causes.

Vitamin deficiency diseases and one of their contributing conditions, poor dental health, were extremely common in the slum districts of both European and American cities. The unavailability of adequate prenatal and postnatal care meant that deaths associated with pregnancy and childbirth were also high.

Health Resources Development Period (1900–1960)

health resources development period
the years of 1900–1960, a time of great growth in health care facilities and providers

Much growth and development took place during the 60-year period from 1900 to 1960. Because of the growth of health care facilities and providers, this period of time is referred to as the **health resources development period.** This period can be further divided into the reform phase (1900-1920), the 1920s, the Great Depression and World War II, and the postwar years.

The Reform Phase (1900-1920)

By the beginning of the twentieth century, there was a growing concern about the many social problems in America. The remarkable discoveries in microbiology made in the previous years had not dramatically improved the health of the average citizen. By 1910, the urban population had grown to 45% of the total population (up from 19% in 1860). Much of the growth was the result of immigrants who came to America for the jobs created by new industries (see Figure 1.9). Northern cities were also swelling from the northward migration of black Americans from the southern states. Many of these workers had to accept poorly paying jobs involving hard labor and low wages. There was also a deepening chasm between the upper and lower classes, and social critics began to clamor for reform.

reform phase of public health
the years of 1900–1920, characterized by social movements to improve health conditions in cities and in the workplace

The years 1900 to 1920 have been called the **reform phase of public health.** The plight of the immigrants working in the meat packing industry was graphically depicted by Upton Sinclair in his book *The Jungle.* Sinclair's goal was to draw attention to unsafe working conditions. What he achieved was greater governmental regulation of the food industry through the passage of the Pure Food and Drugs Act of 1906.

The reform movement was broad, involving both social and moral as well as health issues. Edward T. Devine noted in 1909 that "Ill health is perhaps the most constant of the attendants of poverty."[19] The reform movement finally took hold when it became evident to the majority that neither the discoveries of the causes of many communicable diseases nor the continuing advancement of industrial production could overcome continuing disease and poverty. Even by 1917, the United States ranked fourteenth of sixteen "progressive" nations in maternal death rate.[19]

Although the relationship between occupation and disease had been pointed out 200 years earlier in Europe, occupational health in America in 1900 was an unknown quantity. However, in 1910 the first International Congress on Occupational Diseases was held in Chicago.[20] That same year, the state of New York passed a tentative Workman's Compensation Act, and over the next 10 years most other states passed similar laws.[20] Also in 1910, the U.S. Bureau of Mines was created and the first clinic for occupational diseases was established in New York at Cornell Medical College.[19] By 1910, the movement for healthier conditions in the workplace was well established.

This period also saw the birth of the first national-level volunteer health agencies. The first of these agencies was the National Association for the Study and Prevention of Tuberculosis, which was formed in 1902. It arose from the first local voluntary health agency, the Pennsylvania Society for the Prevention of Tuberculosis, organized in 1892.[21] The

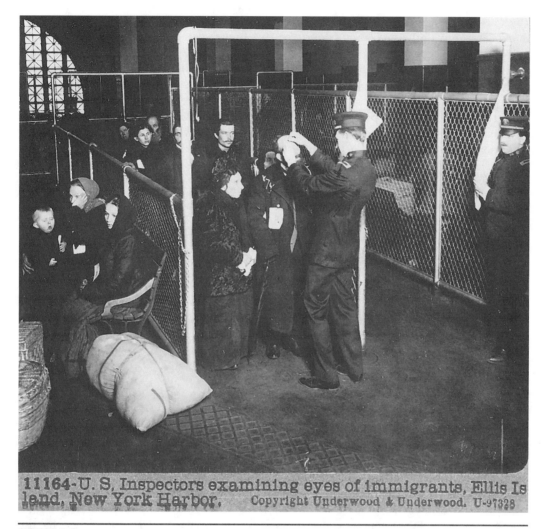

11164-U. S. Inspectors examining eyes of immigrants, Ellis Island, New York Harbor.   Copyright Underwood & Underwood. U-97328

FIGURE 1.9

Ellis Island immigration between 1860 and 1910 resulted in dramatic increases in the urban population in America.

American Cancer Society, Inc., was founded in 1913. That same year, the Rockefeller Foundation was established in New York. This philanthropic foundation has funded a great many public health projects, including work on hookworm and pellagra, and the development of a vaccine against yellow fever.

Another movement that began about this time was that of public health nursing. The first school nursing program was begun in New York City in 1902. In 1918, the first School of Public Health was established at Johns Hopkins University in Baltimore. This was followed by establishment of another school at Harvard University in 1923. Also in 1918 was the birth of school health instruction as we know it today.

These advances were matched with similar advances by governmental bodies. The Marine Hospital Service was renamed the Public Health and Marine Hospital Service in 1902 in keeping with its growing responsibilities. In 1912, it became the U.S. Public Health Service.[16]

By 1900, 38 states had state health departments. The rest followed during the first decades of the twentieth century. The first two local (county) health departments were established in 1911, one in Guilford County, North Carolina, and the other in Yakima County, Washington.

The 1920s

In comparison with the preceding period, the 1920s represented a decade of slow growth in public health, except for a few health projects funded by the Rockefeller and Millbank foundations. Prohibition resulted in a decline in the number of alcoholics and alcohol-related deaths. While the number of county health departments had risen to 467 by 1929, 77% of the rural population still lived in areas with no health services.[21] However, it was during this period in 1922 that the first professional preparation program for health educators was begun at Columbia University by Thomas D. Wood, M.D., whom many consider the father of health education. The life expectancy in 1930 had risen to 59.7 years.

The Great Depression and World War II

Until the Great Depression (1929–1935), individuals and families in need of social and medical services were dependent on friends and relatives, private charities, voluntary agencies, community chests, and churches. By 1933, after three years of economic depression, it became evident that private resources could never meet the needs of all the people who needed assistance. The drop in tax revenues during the Depression also reduced health department budgets and caused a virtual halt in the formation of new local health departments.[21]

Beginning in 1933, President Franklin D. Roosevelt created numerous agencies and programs for public works as part of his New Deal. Much of the money was used for public health, including the control of malaria, the building of hospitals and laboratories, and the construction of municipal water and sewer systems.

The Social Security Act of 1935 marked the beginning of the government's major involvement in social issues, including health. This act provided substantial support for state health departments and their programs, such as maternal and child health and sanitary facilities. As progress against the communicable diseases became visible, some turned their attention toward other health problems, such as cancer. The National Cancer Institute was formed in 1937.

America's involvement in World War II resulted in severe restrictions on resources available for public health programs. Immediately following the conclusion of the war, however, many of the medical discoveries made during wartime made their way into civilian medical practice. Two examples are the antibiotic penicillin, used for treating pneumonia, rheumatic fever, syphilis, and strep throat, and the insecticide DDT, used for killing insects that transmit diseases.

During World War II, the Communicable Disease Center was established in Atlanta, Georgia. Now called the Centers for Disease Control and Prevention (CDC), it has become the premier epidemiological center of the world.

The Postwar Years

Following the end of World War II, there was still concern about medical care and the adequacy of the facilities in which that care could be administered. In 1946, Congress passed the National Hospital Survey and Construction Act (the Hill-Burton Act). The goal of the legislation was to improve the distribution of medical care and to enhance the quality of hospitals. From 1946 through the 1960s, hospital construction occurred at a rapid rate with relatively little thought given to planning. Likewise, attempts to set national health priorities or to establish a national health agenda were virtually nonexistent.

The two major health events in the 1950s were the development of a vaccine to prevent polio and President Eisenhower's heart attack. The latter event helped America to focus on its Number 1 killer, heart disease. When the president's physician suggested exercise, some Americans heeded his advice and began to exercise on a regular basis.

Period of Social Engineering (1960–1973)

The 1960s marked the beginning of a period when the federal government once again became active in health matters. The primary reason for this involvement was the growing realization that many Americans were still not reaping any of the benefits of 60 years of medical advances. These Americans, most of whom were poor or elderly, either lived in under-served areas or simply could not afford to purchase medical services.

In 1965, Congress passed the Medicare and Medicaid bills (amendments to the Social Security Act of 1935). **Medicare** assists in the payment of medical bills for the elderly and certain people with disabilities, and **Medicaid** assists in the payment of medical bills for the poor. These pieces of legislation helped provide medical care for millions who would not otherwise have received it, and this legislation also improved standards in health care facilities. Unfortunately, the influx of federal dollars accelerated the rate of increase in the cost of health care for everyone. As a result, the 1970s, 1980s, and the 1990s saw repeated attempts and failures to bring the growing costs of health care under control.

Period of Health Promotion (1974–present)

By the mid-1970s, it had become apparent that the greatest potential for saving lives and reducing health care costs in America was to be achieved through means other than health care.

> Most scholars, policymakers, and practitioners in health promotion would pick 1974 as the turning point that marks the beginning of health promotion as a significant component of national health policy in the twentieth century. That year Canada published its landmark policy statement, *A New Perspective on the Health of Canadians.*[22] In the United States, Congress passed PL 94-317, the Health Information and Health Promotion Act, which created the Office of Health Information and Health Promotion, later renamed the Office of Disease Prevention and Health Promotion.[23]

In the late 1970s, the Centers for Disease Control conducted a study that examined premature deaths (defined then as deaths prior to age 65, but now as deaths prior to age 75) in the United States in 1977. That study revealed that approximately 48% of all premature deaths could be traced to one's lifestyle or health behavior—choices that people make. Lifestyles characterized by a lack of exercise, unhealthy diets, smoking, uncontrolled hypertension, and the inability to control stress were found to be contributing factors to premature mortality.[24] This led the way for the U.S. government's publication *Healthy People: The Surgeon General's Report on Health Promotion and Disease Prevention.*[25] "This document brought together much of what was known about the relationship of personal behavior and health status. The document also presented a 'personal responsibility' model that provided Americans with the prescription for reducing their health risks and increasing their chances for good health."[26]

Healthy People was then followed by the release of the first set of health goals and objectives for the Nation, called *Promoting Health/Preventing Disease: Objectives for the Nation.*[27] These goals and objectives, now in their third edition called *Healthy People 2010,*[11] have defined the Nation's health agenda and guided its health policy since their inception. And, in part, they have also kept the importance of good health visible to all Americans (see Box 1.1).

Community Health in the Early 2000s

Early in the new millennium, it is widely agreed that while decisions about health are an individual's responsibility to a significant degree, society has an obligation to provide an environment in which the achievement of good health is possible and encouraged. Furthermore, many recognize that certain segments of our population whose disease and death rates exceed the general population may require additional resources, including education, in order to achieve good health.

The American people face a number of serious public health problems. These problems include the continuing rise in health care costs, growing environmental concerns, the ever-present lifestyle diseases, emerging and re-emerging communicable diseases, serious substance abuse problems, and now terrorism. In the paragraphs that follow, we have elaborated on each of these problems briefly because they seem to represent a significant portion of the community health agenda for the years ahead.

Medicare
government health insurance for the elderly and those with certain disabilities

Medicaid
government health insurance for the poor

Healthy People 2010
the third set of health goals and objectives for the U.S that defines the Nation's health agenda and guides its health policy

BOX
1.1
A LOOK BACK ON THE TWENTIETH CENTURY IN THE UNITED STATES

As the twentieth century came to a close, the overall health status and life expectancy in the United States were at all-time highs. Since 1900, the average lifespan of people in the United States had lengthened by more than 30 years; 25 of these years have been attributed to advances in public health.[29] There were many public health achievements that can be linked to this gain in life expectancy, however. The Centers for Disease Control and Prevention (CDC), the U.S. government agency charged with protecting the public health of the Nation, singled out the "Ten Great Public Health Achievements" in the United States between 1900 and 1999. Some of these achievements will be discussed in greater detail in other chapters of this book where they are more relevant to the content being presented. Here is the entire list:[30]

1. *Vaccination.* Vaccines are now available to protect children and adults against 15 life-threatening or debilitating diseases. Rates of all vaccine-preventable diseases are down more than 97% from peak levels before vaccines were available.[31]

2. *Motor vehicle safety.* A number of advances over the years, including safety belts, air bags, safer cars and roads, and enforcement of drunk driving and other laws, have saved many lives.[31]

3. *Safer workplaces.* A number of voluntary and mandatory practices in the workplace have created a much safer work environment. In the early 1900s, the work-related death rate was about 21 per 100,000. By the mid-1990s, that number had dropped to about 4 per 100,000.[32]

4. *Control of infectious diseases.* At the beginning of the century, the leading causes of death were infectious diseases, but by mid-century many of these diseases were under control. This control can be attributed to cleaner water, improved sanitation, and antibiotics.

5. *Decline of deaths from coronary heart disease and stroke.* While these remain the leading causes of death, significant progress has been made in reducing the death rates since 1950. This progress can be attributed to the identification and modification of risk factors such as smoking and high blood pressure, and the improved access to early detection and better treatment.

6. *Safer and healthier foods.* Over the century much of the microbial contamination of food has been significantly reduced, and the nutritional value of foods has been greatly enhanced.

7. *Healthier mothers and babies.* Infant and maternal mortality rates have decreased 90% and 99%, respectively. This can be attributed to advances in hygiene, nutrition, antibiotics, medical technology, and access to health care.

8. *Family planning.* Advances in family planning and contraceptive services have provided for greater health benefits for mothers and babies, and have reduced the transmission of several sexually transmitted diseases.

9. *Fluoridation of drinking water.* Though fluoridation of water only began in mid-century, it has played an important role in the reduction of both tooth decay and tooth loss.

10. *Recognition of tobacco use as a health hazard.* Recognition of tobacco as the single most preventable cause of death in the United States has saved the lives and suffering of millions of people in this country.

Health Care Delivery

Arguably, health care delivery continues to be the single greatest community health challenge in the United States. The exorbitant cost of health care is impacting the entire economy in America. Even though the annual growth rate in national health expenditure slowed during the late 1990s due primarily to the advent of managed care, the United States continues to spend more money on health care than any other industrialized country. In 2002, health care expenditures made up about 14.9% of America's gross domestic product, up from 10.2% in 1985. Also in 2002, national health care expenditures totaled $1.553 trillion, an average of more than $5,540 per person.[28] If left unchecked, it is estimated that the cost of health care will continue to rise faster than the rate of inflation. It was estimated that total health care expenditures would reach $1.9 trillion in 2005 and $2.7 trillion by 2010.[28]

If the costs of health care were not enough, there is still a significant portion of the U.S. population without health care insurance. In 2002, the proportion of the population without health care insurance (either public or private) was approximately 17%. In other words, more than 43 million Americans were uninsured throughout 2002. Another 12 million lacked health insurance coverage for shorter periods during that year.[33]

Environmental Problems

Millions of Americans live in communities where the air is unsafe to breathe, the water is unsafe to drink, or solid waste is disposed of improperly. With a few minor exceptions, the rate at which we pollute our environment continues to increase. Many Americans still believe that our natural resources are unlimited and that their individual contributions to the overall pollution are insignificant. In actuality, we must improve upon our efforts in resource preservation and energy conservation if our children are to enjoy an environment as clean as ours. These environmental problems are compounded by the fact the world population continues to grow; it is now over 6.2 billion people and expected to reach 7 billion by the year 2013.[34]

Lifestyle Diseases

The leading causes of death in the United States today are not the communicable diseases that were so feared 100 years ago but chronic illnesses resulting from unwise lifestyle choices. "The prevalence of obesity and diseases like diabetes are increasing."[6] The four leading causes of death in the early 2000s are heart disease, cancer, stroke, and chronic lower respiratory diseases.[35] Although it is true that everyone has to die from some cause sometime, too many Americans die prematurely because of their unhealthy lifestyles. In the latter part of the twentieth century, it was known that better control of behavioral risk factors alone—such as lack of exercise, poor diet, use of tobacco and drugs, and alcohol abuse—could prevent between 40% and 70% of all premature deaths, one-third of all acute disabilities, and two-thirds of chronic disabilities.[36] As we begin the twenty-first century, behavior patterns continue to "represent the single most prominent domain of influence over health prospects in the United States."[37] (See Table 1.1.)

Communicable Diseases

While communicable (infectious) diseases no longer constitute the leading causes of death in the United States, they remain a concern for several reasons. First, they are the primary reason for days missed at school or at work. The success in reducing the life-threatening nature of these diseases has made many Americans complacent about obtaining vaccinations or taking other precautions against contracting these diseases. With the exception of smallpox, none of these diseases has been eradicated when several should have been, such as measles.

Table 1.1
Comparison of Most Common Causes of Death and Actual Causes of Death

Most Common Causes of Death, United States, 2000	Actual Causes of Death, United States, 2000
1. Diseases of the heart	1. Tobacco
2. Malignant neoplasms (cancers)	2. Poor diet and physical inactivity
3. Cerebrovascular diseases (stroke)	3. Alcohol consumption
4. Chronic lower respiratory diseases	4. Microbial agents
5. Unintentional injuries (accidents)	5. Toxic agents
6. Diabetes mellitus	6. Motor vehicles
7. Influenza and pneumonia	7. Firearms
8. Alzheimer's disease	8. Sexual behavior
9. Nephritis, nephrotic syndrome, and nephrosis	9. Illicit drug use
10. Septicemia	

Sources: Minino, A. M., and B. L. Smith (2001). "Deaths: Preliminary Data for 2000." *National Vital Statistics Report,* 49(12); and Mokdad, A. H., J. S. Marks, D. F. Stroup, and J. L. Gerberding (2004). "Actual Causes of Death in the United States, 2000." *Journal of the American Medical Association,* 291(10): 1238–1245.

Second, as new communicable diseases continue to appear, old ones re-emerge, sometimes in drug-resistant forms like tuberculosis, demonstrating that communicable diseases still represent a serious community health problem in America. Legionnaires' disease, toxic shock syndrome, Lyme disease, acquired immunodeficiency syndrome (AIDS), and severe acute respiratory syndrome (SARS) are diseases that were unknown only 30 years ago. The first cases of AIDS were reported in June 1981.[38] By August 1989, 100,000 cases had been reported[39] and it took only an additional two years to report the second 100,000 cases.[40] By December 2002, 859,000 cases of the disease had been reported to the CDC.[41] (See Figure 1.10.)

Third, and maybe the most disturbing, is the use of communicable diseases for bioterrorism. **Bioterrorism** involves "the threatened or intentional release of biological agents (virus, bacteria, or their toxins) for the purpose of influencing the conduct of government or intimidating or coercing a civilian population to further political or social objectives. These agents can be released by way of the air (as aerosols) food, water or insects."[4] Concern in the United States over bioterrorism was heightened after 9/11 and the subsequent intentional distribution of *Bacillus anthracis* spores through the U.S. postal system (the anthrax mailings). The anthrax mailings resulted in 22 people developing anthrax, 5 of whom died. In addition, thousands more were psychologically impacted, and between 10 and 20 thousand people were advised to take postexposure prophylactic treatment because they were at known or potential risk for inhalational anthrax.[42]

Alcohol and Other Drug Abuse
"Abuse of legal and illegal drugs has become a national problem that costs this country thousands of lives and billions of dollars each year. Alcohol and other drugs are often associated

bioterrorism
the threatened or intentional release of biological agents for the purpose of influencing the conduct of government or intimidating or coercing a civilian population to further political or social objectives

FIGURE 1.10
AIDS is one of the most feared communicable diseases today.

with unintentional injuries, domestic violence, and violent crimes."[43] Federal, state, and local governments as well as private agencies are attempting to address the supply and demand problems associated with the abuse of alcohol and other drugs, but a significant challenge remains for America.

Terrorism

Mention was made earlier of the use of a communicable disease as part of terrorism. However, in fact there are a number of agents that could be used as part of terrorism. Since the anthrax mailings, community and public health professionals have focused on the possibility that future terrorism could include chemical, nuclear/radiological, and/or biological (CNB) agents, resulting in mass numbers of casualties. Such concern led to an evaluation of community and public health emergency preparedness and response. "Determining the level of state and local health departments' emergency preparedness and response capacities is crucial because public health officials are among those, along with firefighters, emergency medical personnel, and local law enforcement personnel, who serve on 'rapid response' teams when large-scale emergency situations arise"[6] (see Figure 1.11). Results of that evaluation showed that the

FIGURE 1.11

News media ad early in 2002 promoting health infrastructure as a front-line defense against bioterrorism.

Source: Trust for America's Health, 2002. Reprinted with permission.

Table 1.2
The FDA's Five Broad Strategies for Terrorism

- *Awareness:* Increasing awareness through collecting, analyzing, and spreading information and knowledge.
- *Prevention:* Identifying specific threats or attacks that involve biological, chemical, radiological, or nuclear attacks.
- *Preparedness:* Developing and making available medical countermeasures such as drugs, devices, and vaccines.
- *Response:* Ensuring rapid and coordinated response to any terrorist attacks.
- *Recovery:* Ensuring rapid and coordinated treatment for any illness that may result from a terrorist attack.

Source: Meadows, M. (2004). "The FDA and the Fight Against Terrorism." *FDA Consumer,* 38(1): 21.

---

public health infrastructure was not where it should be to handle large-scale emergencies, as well as a number of more common public health concerns.

> The . . . public health infrastructure has suffered from political neglect and from the pressure of political agendas and public opinion that frequently override empirical evidence. Under the glare of a national crisis, policy makers and the public became aware of vulnerable and out-dated health information systems and technologies, an insufficient and inadequately trained public health workforce, antiquated laboratory capacity, a lack of real-time surveillance and epidemiological systems, ineffective and fragmented communications networks, incomplete domestic preparedness and emergency response capabilities, and communities without access to essential public health services.[6]

Many efforts, including the creation of the Department of Homeland Security and special activities by a number of different governmental agencies (see Table 1.2), have been and continue to be made to improve the United States' preparedness for terrorism. However, there is still much work to be done.

Outlook for Community Health in the Twenty-First Century

So far in this chapter we have discussed community health, past and present. Now we will describe what community health leaders in the United States and elsewhere in the world hope to achieve in the coming years.

World Planning for the Twenty-First Century

World health leaders recognized the need to plan for the twenty-first century at the thirtieth World Health Assembly of the World Health Organization (WHO), held in 1977. At that assembly, delegations from governments around the world set as a target "that the level of health to be attained by the turn of the century should be that which will permit all people to lead a socially and economically productive life."[44] This target goal became known as "Health for All by the Year 2000." The following year in Alma-Ata, U.S.S.R., the joint WHO/UNICEF (United Nations Children's Fund) International Conference adopted a Declaration on Primary Health Care as the key to attaining the goal of "Health for All by the Year 2000." At the thirty-fourth World Health Assembly in 1981, delegates from the member nations unanimously adopted a "Global Strategy for Health for All by the Year 2000." That same year, the United Nations General Assembly endorsed the "Global Strategy" and urged other international organizations concerned with community health to collaborate with WHO. The underlying concept of "Health for All by the Year 2000" was that health resources should be distributed in such a way that essential health care services are accessible to everyone.

As we now know, the lofty goal of health for all around the world by the year 2000 was not reached. That does not mean that the goal was abandoned. With the passing into a new century, the program was renamed Health for All (HFA). HFA continues to seek "to create the conditions where people have, as a fundamental human right, the opportunity to reach and

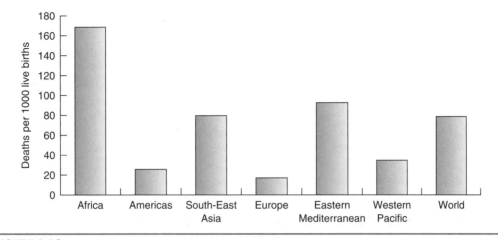

FIGURE 1.12

Child mortality in the six World Health Organization regions, 2002.

Source: World Health Organization (2003). *World Health Report 2003: Shaping the Future.* Geneva, Switzerland: Author, 8. Used with permission of the World Health Organization.

maintain the highest level of health. The vision of a renewed HFA policy builds on the WHO Constitution, the experience of the past and the needs for the future."[45]

Even though the "Health for All by the Year 2000" goal was not reached, some progress was made. Overall global health, as measured by life expectancy at birth, did improve. In 1955 life expectancy worldwide was 46.5 years, while in 2002 it increased to 65.2 years.[45] Yet, many do not have a longer life expectancy or enjoy better health. There is evidence of widening gaps in health worldwide between the very poorest developing countries and all other countries. For example, in 2002 while life expectancy at birth for women from developed countries reached 78 years, it fell back to less than 46 years for men in sub-Saharan Africa, and the chances of children in Africa surviving until their fifth birthday were less than they were a decade earlier[45] (see Figure 1.12). Much of the widening health gap is a result of the continuing impact of communicable diseases, especially HIV/AIDS. However, global increases in noncommunicable diseases (especially from tobacco use) and unintentional injuries (primarily from road traffic crashes) are simultaneously occurring, adding to the daunting challenges facing developing countries.[45]

The challenges[46] of the twenty-first century that need to be addressed in order to improve the world's health include:

1. Greatly reducing the burden of excess mortality and morbidity suffered by the poor. This means shifting the ways in which governments all over the world use their resources. It also means focusing on those interventions that enable the greatest health gain possible with the available resources so that the diseases that disproportionately affect the poor, like tuberculosis, malaria, and HIV/AIDS, can be less of a burden.

2. Countering the potential threats to health resulting from economic crises, unhealthy environments, or risky behaviors. Stable economic growth throughout the world, environments with clean air and water, adequate sanitation, healthy diets, safer transportation, and the reductions in risky behaviors, such as tobacco use, will go a long way in creating a healthier world.

3. Developing more effective health systems. The goals of these systems should be to improve health status, reduce health inequalities, enhance responsiveness to legitimate expectations, increase efficiency, protect people from financial loss, and enhance fairness in the financing and delivery of health care.

4. Investing in the expanding knowledge base. The increased knowledge base of the twentieth century did much to improve health. The search for new knowledge must continue because it benefits all humanity. Two areas that need special attention are infectious diseases that overwhelmingly affect the poor, and information that will help shape future health systems.

As can be seen from the above stated challenges, much of the attention for improved world health in the twenty-first century is focused on the less developed and poorer countries of the world. The plan for tackling these global health challenges and other non-health-related global challenges of the twenty-first century is guided by the *United Nations Millennium Declaration,*[47] which was adopted at the United Nations' Millennium Summit in September 2000. More information about the declaration is presented in Chapter 2 in the section that discusses the WHO.

The United States' Planning for the Twenty-First Century

In addition to its participation in WHO's plans for the twenty-first century, the United States has created its own plans. The United States has decided to develop its planning process around 10-year blocks of time. The current plan is called *Healthy People 2010.*[11] As noted earlier in this chapter, *Healthy People 2010* and its two predecessor editions do in fact outline the health agenda of the Nation. Some have referred to the *Healthy People* documents as the health blueprint of the Nation. Each of these documents obviously is created on the best available data at the time, but all have been structured in a similar way. All three editions have included several overarching goals and many supporting objectives for the Nation's health. The goals provide a general focus and direction, while the objectives are used to measure progress within a specified period of time.[11] For example, in 2001 when the *Healthy People 2000 Final Review* document was released, it showed that 21% of the year 2000 objectives met their targets, 41% showed movement toward their targets, 11% showed mixed results, 2% showed no movement from the baseline, 15% moved away from their targets, and 10% could not be assessed because of a lack of data.[48] Based upon this measured progress and other available data, the *Healthy People 2010* document was created.

Healthy People 2010 is the most sophisticated Healthy People planning document to date, which is reflective of the planning that went into creating it. The *Healthy People 2010* document is composed of three parts. *Healthy People 2010: Understanding and Improving Health,* the first part, provides a history of *Healthy People 2010* and the overall Healthy People initiative. This section also presents the Determinants of Health model (see Figure 1.13) on which Healthy People is based, describes how to use Healthy People as a systematic approach to health improvement, and defines the Leading Health Indicators (LHIs). The LHIs are new to the *Healthy People* document and were created to provide a snapshot of the health of the Nation. *Healthy People 2010* identifies 10 LHIs: physical activity, overweight and obesity, tobacco use, substance abuse, responsible sexual behavior, mental health, injury and violence, environmental quality, immunization, and access to health care. The LHIs highlight major health priorities for the Nation and include the individual behaviors, physical and social environmental factors, and health system issues that affect the health of individuals and communities. Each of the 10 LHIs has one or more Healthy People measures associated with it and will be used to measure progress throughout the decade.[11]

The second part of the document, *Healthy People 2010: Objectives for Improving Health,* contains the two overarching goals and detailed descriptions of 467 objectives to improve health. The two overarching goals for *Healthy People 2010* are as follows:

1. Increase quality and years of healthy life.
2. Eliminate health disparities.

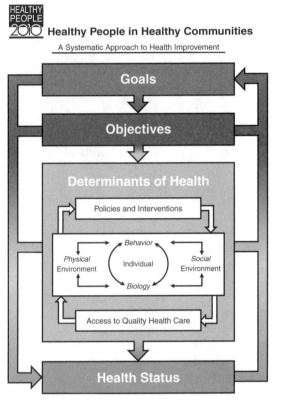

FIGURE 1.13
Healthy people in healthy communities.
Source: U.S. Department of Health and Human
Services. *Healthy People 2010.* Available at
http://www.healthypeople.gov.

The first goal is a carryover from the *Healthy People 2000* goals and has the aim to help individuals of all ages increase the quality and years of healthy life, while the second strengthens a previous goal by using the words "eliminate health disparities" instead of the previous wording of "reduce health disparities." These two goals are supported by specific objectives in 28 focus areas (see Table 1.3).

Table 1.3
***Healthy People 2010* Focus Areas**

1. Access to Quality Health Services	15. Injury and Violence Prevention
2. Arthritis, Osteoporosis, and Chronic Back Conditions	16. Maternal, Infant, and Child Health
3. Cancer	17. Medical Product Safety
4. Chronic Kidney Disease	18. Mental Health and Mental Disorders
5. Diabetes	19. Nutrition/Overweight
6. Disability and Secondary Conditions	20. Occupational Safety and Health
7. Educational and Community-based Programs	21. Oral Health
8. Environmental Health	22. Physical Activity and Fitness
9. Family Planning	23. Public Health Infrastructure
10. Food Safety	24. Respiratory Diseases
11. Health Communication	25. Sexually Transmitted Diseases
12. Heart Disease and Stroke	26. Substance Abuse
13. HIV	27. Tobacco Use
14. Immunization and Infectious Diseases	28. Vision and Hearing

Source: U.S. Department of Health and Human Services. *Healthy People 2010.* Available at http://www.healthypeople.gov.

In the document, each focus area is presented as a chapter. Each chapter contains a concise goal statement that frames the overall purpose of the area, an overview of the health issue that provides the context and background for the objectives, an interim progress report on progress toward the year 2000 objectives, and the 2010 objectives. There are two types of objectives—measurable and developmental. The measurable objectives provide direction for action and include national baseline data from which the 2010 target was set. The developmental objectives provide a vision for a desired outcome or health status. The purpose of developmental objectives is to identify areas of emerging importance and to drive the development of data systems to measure them. National surveillance systems for tracking these objectives were not available in 2000, but it was expected that such would be in place for most of the objectives by 2004.[11]

The third part of the document, *Tracking Healthy People 2010,* provides a comprehensive review of the statistical measures that will be used to evaluate progress. The purpose of this third part is to provide technical information so that others will be able to understand how the data are derived and the major statistical issues affecting the interpretation of the statistics. This is the first set of Healthy People objectives to have such a section.[11]

When *Healthy People 2010* was written, no one envisioned what would transpire on 9/11 and in the years to follow. Thus, the threats of terrorism and bioterrorism are not specifically reflected in the *Healthy People* document. It was not until a year after 9/11 that the Homeland Security Act of 2002 was passed. It was that legislation that created the Department of Homeland Security (DHS).[49] It was felt that a new federal agency was needed to provide the unifying core for the vast national network of organizations and institutions involved in efforts to secure the Nation.[50] The daily operations of the DHS are guided by its strategic planning document, *Securing Our Nation.*[51] (See Table 1.4 for the vision and mission statements and the strategic goals of the DHS.) Only time will tell how effective this new department will be in providing a secure Nation.

Table 1.4
Vision, Mission, and Strategic Goals of the Department of Homeland Security

Vision
Preserving our freedoms, protecting America . . . we secure our homeland.

Mission
We will lead the unified national effort to secure America. We will prevent and deter terrorist attacks and protect against and respond to threats and hazards to the nation. We will ensure safe and secure borders, welcome lawful immigrants and visitors, and promote the free flow of commerce.

Strategic Goals
Awareness: Identify and understand threats, assess vulnerabilities, determine potential impacts and disseminate timely information to our homeland security partners and the American public.
Prevention: Detect, deter and mitigate threats to our homeland.
Protection: Safeguard our people and their freedoms, critical infrastructure, property, and the economy of our Nation from acts of terrorism, natural disasters, or other emergencies.
Response: Lead, manage and coordinate the national response to acts of terrorism, natural disasters, or other emergencies.
Recovery: Lead national, state, local and private sector efforts to restore services and rebuild communities after acts of terrorism, natural disasters, or other emergencies.
Service: Serve the public effectively by facilitating lawful trade, travel and immigration.
Organizational Excellence: Value our most important resource, our people. Create a culture that promotes a common identity, innovation, mutual respect, accountability and teamwork to achieve efficiencies, effectiveness, and operational synergies.

Source: U.S. Department of Homeland Security (DHS). (2004). *DHS Organization.* Available at
http://www.dhs.gov/dhspublic/theme_home1.jsp.

As can be seen from the previous discussion, much planning and work have taken place to improve the health and safety of populations in the twenty-first century. Yet,

> The systems and the entities that protect and promote the public's health, already challenged by problems like obesity, toxic environments, a large uninsured population, and health disparities, must also confront emerging threats, such as antimicrobial resistance and bioterrorism. The social, cultural, and global contexts of the nation's health are also undergoing rapid and dramatic change. Scientific and technological advances, such as genomics and informatics, extend the limits of knowledge and human potential more rapidly than their implications can be absorbed and acted upon. At the same time, people, products, and germs migrate and the nation's demographics are shifting in ways that challenge public and private resources.[6]

Even with so much change and the many uncertainties about the future, we must stay focused on what is necessary to gain and maintain health for all. There is still much work ahead!

CHAPTER SUMMARY

- A number of key terms are associated with the study of community health, including *health, community, community health, population health*, and *public health*.

- The four factors that affect the health of a community are physical (e.g., community size), social and cultural (e.g., religion), community organization, and individual behaviors (e.g., exercise and diet).

- It is important to be familiar with and understand the history of community health in order to be able to deal with the present and future community health issues.

- The earliest community health practices went unrecorded; however, archeological findings of the ancient societies (before 500 B.C.) show evidence of concern for community health. There is evidence during the time of the classical cultures (500 B.C.–A.D. 500) that people were interested in physical strength, medicine, and sanitation.

- The belief of many living during the Middle Ages (A.D. 500–1500) was that health and disease were associated with spirituality. Many epidemics were seen during this period.

- During the Renaissance period (A.D. 1500–1700), there was a growing belief that disease was caused by the environment, not spiritual factors.

- The eighteenth century was characterized by industrial growth. Science was being used more in medicine and it was during this century that the first vaccine was discovered.

- The nineteenth century ushered in the modern era of public health. The germ theory was introduced during this time, and the last fourth of the century is known as the bacteriological period of public health.

- The twentieth century can be divided into several periods. The health resources development period (1900–1960) was a time when many public and private resources were used to improve health. The period of social engineering (1960–1973) saw the U.S. government's involvement in health insurance through Medicare and Medicaid. The health promotion period began in 1974 and continues today.

- Great concern still exists for health care, the environment, diseases caused by an impoverished lifestyle, the spread of communicable diseases (such as AIDS, Legionnaires' disease, toxic shock syndrome, and Lyme disease), the harm caused by alcohol and other drug abuse, and terrorism.

- Both the WHO and the U.S. government continue to plan for the health of humanity. The planning of the United States is reflected in the *Healthy People* documents, the health agenda for the Nation.

- The threat of terrorism, both in the United States and worldwide, has created many new challenges for those trying to provide improved health for all.

REVIEW QUESTIONS

1. How does the 1947 WHO definition of health differ from the one offered by Payne, Hahn, and Mauer?[2]

2. What is the difference between community health and public health? Community health and population health?

3. What is the difference between personal health activities and community health activities?

4. Define the term *community*.

5. What are four major factors that affect the health of a community? Provide an example of each.

SCENARIO: ANALYSIS AND RESPONSE

The Internet has many sources of information that could help Amy and Eric with the decisions that they will have to make about the continued use of the day care center for their children. Use a search engine (e.g., Google, Excite, Lycos) and enter (a) hepatitis, and (b) hepatitis and day care centers. Print out the information that you find and use it in answering the following questions.

1. Based upon the information you found from the Web, if you were Amy or Eric would you take your children to the day care center the next day? Why or why not?

2. Do you feel the hepatitis problem in day care centers is a personal health concern or a community health concern? Why?
3. Which of the factors noted in this chapter that affect the health of a community play a part in the hepatitis problem faced by Amy and Eric?
4. Why does the hepatitis problem remind us of the health problems faced by people in this country prior to 1900?
5. Under which of the focus areas in the *Healthy People 2010* would hepatitis fall? Why?

6. Identify some of the major events of community health in each of the following periods of time:

   Early civilizations (prior to A.D. 500)

   Middle Ages (A.D. 500–1500)

   Renaissance and Exploration (A.D. 1500–1700)

   The eighteenth century

   The nineteenth century

7. Provide a brief explanation of the origins from which the following twentieth-century periods get their names:

   Health resources development period

   Period of social engineering

   Period of health promotion

8. What are the major community health problems facing the United States in the twenty-first century?

9. How is the world planning for the health of people in the twenty-first century?

10. What significance do the *Healthy People* documents play in community health development in recent years?

11. What significance do you think *Healthy People 2010* will play in the years ahead?

12. How has the United States organized to deal with the threat of terrorism?

ACTIVITIES

1. Write your own definition for health.

2. In a one-page paper, explain why heart disease can be both a personal health problem and a community health problem.

3. Select a community health problem that exists in your hometown, then using the factors that affect the health of a community noted in this chapter, analyze and

discuss in a two-page paper at least three factors that contribute to the problem in your hometown.

4. Select one of the following individuals (all have been identified in this chapter), go to the library and do some additional reading or find two reliable Web sites, and then write a two-page paper on the person's contribution to community health.

   Dr. Edward Jenner

   Dr. John Snow

   Lemuel Shattuck

   Louis Pasteur

   Robert Koch

   Major Walter Reed

5. Locate a copy of *Healthy People 2010*. (It is available on the Web.) Then, set up a time to talk with an administrator in your hometown health department. Find out which of the objectives the health department has been working on as priorities. Summarize in a paper what the objectives are, what the health department is doing about them, and what it hopes to accomplish by the year 2010.

COMMUNITY HEALTH ON THE WEB

The Internet contains a wealth of information about community and public health. Increase your knowledge of some of the topics presented in this chapter by accessing the Jones and Bartlett Publishers Web site at **health.jbpub.com/communityhealth/5e** and follow the links to complete the following Web activities.

• Healthy People 2010

• Schools of Public Health

• The International History of Public Health

REFERENCES

1. World Health Organization (1947). "Constitution of the World Health Organization." *Chronicle of the World Health Organization 1.*

2. Payne, W. A., D. B. Hahn, and E. B. Mauer (2005). *Understanding Your Health,* 8th ed. Boston: McGraw-Hill.

3. Thomas, C. L., ed. (1989). *Taber's Cyclopedic Medical Dictionary.* Philadelphia, PA: F. A. Davis Company.

4. Turnock, B. J. (2004). *Public Health: What It Is and How It Works,* 3rd ed. Sudbury, MA: Jones and Bartlett Publishers.

5. Israel, B. A., B. Checkoway, A. Schulz, and M. Zimmerman (1994). "Health Education and Community Empowerment: Conceptualizing and Measuring Perceptions of Individual, Organizational, and Community Control." *Health Education Quarterly,* 21(2): 149-170.

6. Institute of Medicine (2003). *The Future of the Public's Health.* Washington, DC: The National Academies Press.

7. Green, L. W., and J. F. McKenzie (2002). "Community and Population Health." In L. Breslow, ed., *Encyclopedia of Public Health.* New York: Macmillan Reference USA.

8. Association for the Advancement of Health Education (1994). *Cultural Awareness and Sensitivity: Guidelines for Health Educators.* Reston, VA: Author.

9. American Cancer Society (2004). *Cancer Facts and Figures—2004.* Atlanta, GA: Author.

10. Moss, N., and N. Krieger (1995). "Measuring Social Inequalities in Health: Report on the Conference of the National Institutes of Health." *Public Health Reports,* 110(3): 302-305.

11. U.S. Department of Health and Human Services. *Healthy People 2010.* Available at http://www.healthypeople.gov.

12. Minkler, M. (1997). "Introduction and Overview." In M. Minkler, ed., *Community Organizing and Community Building for Health.* New Brunswick, NJ: Rutgers University Press, 3-19.

13. Ross, M. G. (1967). *Community Organization: Theory, Principles, and Practice.* New York: Harper & Row.

14. Rosen, G. (1958). *A History of Public Health.* New York: MD Publications.

15. Burton, L. E., H. H. Smith, and A. W. Nichols (1980). *Public Health and Community Medicine,* 3rd ed. Baltimore, MD: Williams & Wilkins.

16. Pickett, G., and J. J. Hanlon (1990). *Public Health: Administration and Practice,* 9th ed. St. Louis, MO: Times Mirror/Mosby.

17. Legon, R. P. (1986). "Ancient Greece." *World Book Encyclopedia.* Chicago, IL: World Book.

18. Woodruff, A. W. (1977). "Benjamin Rush, His Work on Yellow Fever and His British Connections." *Amer. J. Trop. Med. Hyg.* 26(5): 1055-1059.

19. Rosen, G. (1975). *Preventive Medicine in the United States, 1900-1975.* New York: Science History Publications.

20. Smillie, W. G. (1955). *Public Health: Its Promise for the Future.* New York: Macmillan.

21. Duffy, J. (1990). *The Sanitarians: A History of American Public Health.* Chicago, IL: Univ. of Illinois Press.

22. Lalonde, M. (1974). *A New Perspective on the Health of Canadians: A Working Document.* Ottawa, Canada: Minister of Health.

23. Green, L. W. (1999). "Health Education's Contributions to the Twentieth Century: A Glimpse through Health Promotion's Rearview Mirror." In J. E. Fielding, L. B. Lave, and B. Starfield, eds., *Annual Review of Public Health.* Palo Alto, CA: Annual Reviews, 67-88.

24. U.S. Dept. of Health and Human Services, Public Health Service (1980). *Ten Leading Causes of Death in the United States, 1977.* Washington, DC: U.S. Government Printing Office.

25. U.S. Dept. of Health, Education, and Welfare (1979). *Healthy People: The Surgeon General's Report on Health Promotion and Disease Prevention* (DHEW pub. no. 79-55071). Washington, DC: U.S. Government Printing Office.

26. McKenzie, J. F., B. L. Neiger, and J. L. Smeltzer (2005). *Planning, Implementing, and Evaluating Health Promotion Programs: A Primer,* 4th ed. San Francisco: Benjamin Cummings.

27. U.S. Dept. of Health and Human Services (1980). *Promoting Health/Preventing Disease: Objectives for the Nation.* Washington, DC: U.S. Government Printing Office.

28. U.S. Census Bureau (2003). *Statistical Abstract of the United States: 2003,* 123rd ed. Washington, DC: Author.

29. Bunker, J. P., H. S. Frazier, and F. Mosteller (1994). "Improving Health: Measuring Effects of Medical Care." *Milbank Quarterly,* 72: 225-258.

30. Centers for Disease Control (1999). "Ten Great Public Health Achievements—United States, 1900-1999." *Morbidity and Mortality Weekly Report,* 48(12): 241-243.

31. Koplan (2000). *21st Century Health Challenges: Can We All Become Healthy, Wealthy, and Wise?* Atlanta, GA: Centers for Disease Control and Prevention.

32. National Safety Council (1997). *Accident Facts, 1997 Edition.* Itasca, IL: Author.

33. Institute of Medicine (2004). *Insuring America's Health: Principles and Recommendations.* Available at http://www.iom.edu/Object.File/Master/17/732/0.pdf.

34. U.S. Census Bureau (2004). *Global Population at a Glance: 2002 and Beyond.* Available at http://www.census.gov/ipc/www/wp02.html.

35. Kochanek, K. D., and B. L. Smith (2004). "Deaths: Preliminary Data for 2002," *National Vital Statistics Reports,* 52(13).

36. U.S. Dept. of Health and Human Services (1990). *Prevention '89/'90.* Washington, DC: U.S. Government Printing Office.

37. McGinnis, J. M., P. Williams-Russo, and J. R. Knickman (2002). "The Case for More Active Policy Attention to Health Promotion." *Health Affairs,* 21(2): 78-93.

38. Centers for Disease Control (1981). "Pneumocystis Pneumonia—Los Angeles." *Morbidity and Mortality Weekly Report,* 30: 250-252.

39. Centers for Disease Control (1989). "First 100,000 Cases of Acquired Immunodeficiency Syndrome—United States." *Morbidity and Mortality Weekly Report,* 38: 561-563.

40. Centers for Disease Control (1992). "The Second 100,000 Cases of Acquired Immunodeficiency Syndrome—United States, June 1981-December 1991." *Morbidity and Mortality Weekly Report,* 42(2): 28-29.

41. Centers for Disease Control and Prevention (2003). *Cases of HIV Infection and AIDS in the United States, 2002.* Available at http://www.cdc.gov/hiv/stats/hasr1402.htm.

42. Gerberding, J. L., J. M. Hughes, and J. P. Koplan (2003). "Bioterrorism Preparedness and Response: Clinicians and Public Health Agencies as Essential Partners." In P. R. Lee and C. L. Estes, eds., *The Nation's Health.* Sudbury, MA: Jones & Bartlett Publishers, 305-309.

43. Pinger, R. R., W. A. Payne, D. B. Hahn, and E. J. Hahn (1998). *Drugs: Issues for Today,* 3rd ed. Boston: WCB McGraw-Hill.

44. World Health Organization (1990). *Facts about WHO.* Geneva, Switzerland: Author.

45. World Health Organization (2003). *World Health Report 2003: Shaping the Future.* Geneva, Switzerland: Author.

46. World Health Organization (1999). *The World Health Report 1999: Making a Difference.* Geneva, Switzerland: Author.

47. United Nations (2000). *United Nations Millennium Declaration.* New York: Author.

48. National Center for Health Statistics (2001). *Healthy People 2000 Final Review.* Hyattsville, MD: Public Health Service.

49. U.S. Department of Homeland Security (DHS) (2004). *DHS Organization.* Available at http://www.dhs.gov/dhspublic/display?theme=59&content=411.

50. U.S. Department of Homeland Security (DHS) (2004). *DHS Organization.* Available at http://www.dhs.gov/dhspublic/theme_home1.jsp.

51. U.S. Department of Homeland Security (DHS) (2004). *Securing Our Homeland.* Available at http://www.dhs.gov/interapp/editorial/editorial_0413.xml.

Chapter 2

Organizations That Help Shape Community Health

Chapter Outline

Chapter Objectives

1 Explain the need for organizing to improve community health.

2 Explain what a governmental health organization is and give an example of one at each of the following levels—international, national, state, and local.

3 Explain the role the World Health Organization (WHO) plays in community health.

4 Briefly describe the structure and function of the United States Department of Health and Human Services (HHS).

5 State the three core functions of public health.

6 List the 10 essential public health services.

7 Explain the relationship between a state and local health department.

8 Explain what is meant by the term *coordinated school health program*.

9 Define the term *quasi-governmental* and explain why some health organizations are classified under this term.

10 List the four primary activities of most voluntary health organizations.

11 Explain the purpose of a professional health organization/association.

12 Explain how philanthropic foundations contribute to community health.

13 Discuss the role that service, social, and religious organizations play in community health.

14 Identify the major reason why corporations are involved in community health and describe some corporate activities that contribute to community health.

SCENARIO

Mary and Bill are average, hardworking Americans who hope to make a better future for their children. Mary is a secretary in a company that is well known for its high-quality glass products. Bill has just been promoted to foreman after having worked on the "line" for 17 years at his company. Their combined income puts them in the middle income bracket. Through their respective employers, both Mary and Bill have benefit packages that include good health insurance programs.

For the past few months, Bill has not felt 100% healthy, so he made an appointment to see his physician.

After checking Bill over, his doctor referred him to a specialist, who told Bill that he has cancer. His years on the line at the factory may have contributed to his illness, but no one can be sure. The specialist told Bill that the cancer is still in its early stages and that he has a good chance of beating it.

Battling a serious disease like cancer often requires a great many personal and family resources as well as support from the community. The result can be financial and social devastation. Are there any organizations in the community to which Mary and Bill can turn for help?

INTRODUCTION

As noted in Chapter 1, the history of community health dates to antiquity. For much of that history, community health issues were addressed only on an emergency basis. For example, if a community faced a drought or an epidemic, a town meeting would be called to deal with the problem. It has been only in the last 100 years or so that communities have taken explicit actions to deal aggressively with health issues on a continual basis.

Today's communities differ from those of the past in several important ways. Although individuals are better educated, more mobile, and more independent than in the past, communities are less autonomous and are more dependent on state and federal funding for support. Contemporary communities are too large and complex to respond effectively to sudden health emergencies or to make long-term improvements in public health without community organization and careful planning. Better community organizing and careful long-term planning are essential to ensure that a community makes the best use of its resources for health, both in times of emergency and over the long run.

The ability of today's communities to respond effectively to their own problems is hindered by the following characteristics: (1) highly developed and centralized resources in our national institutions and organizations, (2) continuing concentration of wealth and population in the largest metropolitan areas, (3) rapid movement of information, resources, and people made possible by advanced communication and transportation technologies that eliminate the need for local offices where resources were once housed, (4) the globalization of health, (5) limited horizontal relationships between/among organizations, and (6) a system of **top-down funding** (money that comes from either the federal or state government to the local level) for many community programs.[1]

In this chapter, we discuss organizations that help to shape a community's ability to respond effectively to health-related issues by protecting and promoting the health of the community and its members. These community organizations can be classified as governmental, quasi-governmental, and nongovernmental—according to their sources of funding, responsibilities, and organizational structure.

GOVERNMENTAL HEALTH AGENCIES

Governmental health agencies are part of the governmental structure (federal, state, or local). They are funded primarily by tax dollars and managed by government officials. Each

top-down funding
a method of funding in which funds are transmitted from federal or state government to the local level

governmental health agencies
health agencies that are part of the governmental structure (federal, state, or local) and that are funded primarily by tax dollars

FIGURE 2.1

The emblem of the World Health Organization.

Source: World Health Organization. Used with permission.

governmental health agency is designated as having authority over some geographic area. Such agencies exist at the four governmental levels—international, national, state, and local.

International Health Agencies

The most widely recognized international governmental health organization today is the **World Health Organization (WHO)** (see Figure 2.1). Its headquarters is located in Geneva, Switzerland, and there are six regional offices around the world. The names, acronyms, and cities and countries of location for WHO regional offices are as follows: Africa (AFRO), Harare, Zimbabwe; Americas/Pan American Health Organization (AMRO/PAHO), Washington, DC, United States; Eastern Mediterranean (EMRO), Cairo, Egypt; Europe (EURO), Copenhagen, Denmark; South-East Asia (SEARO), New Delhi, India; and Western Pacific (WPRO) Manila, Philippines.[2]

Although the WHO is now the largest international health organization, it is not the oldest. Among the organizations (listed with their founding dates) that predate WHO are the International D'Hygiene Publique (1907), which was absorbed by the WHO; the Health Organization of the League of Nations (1919), which was dissolved when WHO was created; the United Nations Relief and Rehabilitation Administration (UNRRA); the United Nations Children's Fund (UNICEF) (1946), which was formerly known as the United Nations International Children's Emergency Fund; and the Pan American Health Organization (PAHO) (1902), which is still an independent organization but is integrated with WHO in a regional office. Because the WHO is the largest and most visible international health agency, it is discussed at greater length in the following sections.

History of WHO

Planning for WHO began when a charter of the United Nations was adopted at an international meeting in 1945. Contained in the charter was an article calling for the establishment of a health agency with wide powers. In 1946, at the International Health Conference, representatives from all of the countries in the United Nations succeeded in creating and ratifying the constitution of the WHO. However, it was not until April 7, 1948, that the constitution went into force and the organization officially began its work. In recognition of this beginning, April 7 is commemorated each year as World Health Day.[2]

Organization of WHO

Membership in WHO is open to any nation that has ratified the WHO constitution and receives a majority vote of the World Health Assembly. At the beginning of 2004, 192 countries were members. The **World Health Assembly** comprises the delegates of the member

World Health Organization (WHO) the most widely recognized international governmental health organization

World Health Assembly a body of delegates of the member nations of the WHO

nations. This assembly, which meets in general sessions annually and in special sessions when necessary, has the primary tasks of approving the WHO program and the budget for the following biennium and deciding major policy questions.[2]

The WHO is administered by a staff that includes a director-general and nine assistant directors-general. Great care is taken to ensure political balance in staffing WHO positions, particularly at the higher levels of administration.

Purpose and Work of WHO

The primary objective of WHO as stated in the constitution is the attainment by all peoples of the highest possible level of health.[2] The WHO has six core functions:[2]

- Articulating consistent, ethical and evidence-based policy and advocacy positions
- Managing information by assessing trends and comparing performance; setting the agenda for, and stimulating research and development
- Catalyzing change through technical and policy support, in ways that stimulate cooperation and action and help to build sustainable national and inter-country capacity
- Negotiating and sustaining national and global partnerships
- Setting, validating, monitoring and pursuing the proper implementation of norms and standards
- Stimulating the development and testing of new technologies, tools and guidelines for disease control, risk reduction, health care management, and service delivery

The work of WHO is financed by its member nations, each of which is assessed according to its ability to pay; the wealthiest countries contribute the greatest portion of the total budget.

Although WHO has sponsored and continues to sponsor many worthwhile programs, we want to mention one that is especially noteworthy. This was the work of WHO in helping to eradicate smallpox. In 1967, smallpox was active in 31 countries. During that year, 10 to 15 million people contracted the disease, and of those, approximately 2 million died and many millions of others were permanently disfigured or blinded. The last known case of smallpox was diagnosed on October 26, 1977, in Somalia.[2] In 1980, the World Health Assembly declared the global eradication of this disease. Using the smallpox mortality figures from 1967, it can be estimated that well over 40 million lives have been saved since the eradication (see Box 2.1).

As noted in Chapter 1, the current work of WHO is guided by the *United Nations Millennium Declaration,* which was adopted at the Millennium Summit in 2000.[3] The declaration set out principles and values in seven areas (peace, security, and disarmament; development and poverty eradication; protecting our common environment; human rights, democracy, and good governance; protecting the vulnerable; meeting special needs of Africa; and strengthening the United Nations) that should govern international relations in the twenty-first century.[3] Following the summit, the *Road Map* was prepared, which established goals and targets to be reached by 2015 in each of the seven areas.[4] The resulting eight goals in the area of development and poverty eradication are now referred to as the Millennium Development Goals (MDGs). More specifically, the MDGs are aimed at reducing poverty and hunger, tackling ill-health, gender inequality, lack of education, lack of access to clean water, and environmental degradation.

As can be seen from this description, the MDGs are not exclusively aimed at health, but there are interactive processes between health and economic development that create a crucial link. That is, better health is "a prerequisite and major contributor to economic growth and social cohesion. Conversely, improvement in people's access to health technology is a good indicator of the success of other development processes."[5] As such, "three of the eight goals, eight of the 18 targets required to achieve them, and 18 of the 48 indicators of progress are health-related"[5] (see Table 2.1).

BOX 2.1	THE KINDEST CUT

Once I was in Geneva at the World Health Organization researching a book on communicable diseases. I met Donald Henderson, M.D., director of the smallpox eradication effort.

Not long ago, smallpox was one of the worst diseases anyone could have. About six of every ten who contracted it died. In the United States, even a single known case was regarded as an epidemic.

There is no smallpox known anywhere today. Credit the WHO smallpox vaccination effort. There is still no cure, only prevention; that is, vaccination. At that time, WHO was ready to vaccinate the world, if necessary, to eradicate the disease.

Henderson had been in one high-incidence smallpox region in South America. But few people there were coming to the WHO field station for vaccinations. The warnings about this disease were ho-hum, even though people were seeing smallpox deaths every day.

So, Henderson said, they tried bribery. Not money or goods. They substituted ordinary sewing needles for the standard stainless steel stylets, used to prick under the skin. Then the WHO people spread the word that anyone who came for immunization could keep the needle. Women wanted them for sewing and working of cloth. Men saw them as fine tips for hunting darts.

The sudden fervor and turnout for vaccination rivaled that at any Christmas Eve mass at St. Patrick's Cathedral in New York. Henderson's lesson in resourcefulness for the common good did indeed involve some low-road seduction with rewards, but it was a clear lesson, and one with merit. "Get people to come in for vaccination any way you can. But get them," he said that day in Geneva. "First get them healthy. Then there's time enough to try to educate them about staying healthy."

Source: Gallagher, R. (1993). "Resourcerer's Apprentice." *Living: The Magazine of Life,* 22(3): 12.

To date, progress on the MDGs has been slow, and it appears that many of the targets will not be reached by 2015. There are several reasons for this, including, but not limited to, the changing world climate since 9/11, the political processes associated with developed countries helping developing countries (e.g., providing expensive drugs to fight HIV/AIDS to those who cannot afford to pay for them), and the lack of national ownership of the MDGs.[5] To accelerate the progress toward reaching the MDGs will take the work of many international organizations, not just the United Nations and its health arm, the WHO.

To do its part in reaching the MDGs, the WHO's work will be guided by three principles.

> First, WHO will work with countries to help them develop and work towards a more complete set of health goals that are relevant to their particular circumstances. Second, WHO will give special priority to helping countries develop goals and plans to ensure that deprived groups share fully in progress towards the health-related MDGs (by, for example, ensuring that the percentage improvement in conditions among people below the country's poverty line is at least as large as the percentage improvement in the national average). Third, at the global level, WHO will vigorously advocate that developed countries live up to their part of the compact, especially by acting on those elements of Goal 8 that are of central importance to the MDGs.[5]

Much work lies ahead, by all people of the world, to improve the health of those most in need.

National Health Agencies

Each national government has a department or agency that has the primary responsibility for the protection of the health and welfare of its citizens. These national health agencies meet their responsibilities through the development of health policies, the enforcement of health regulations, the provision of health services and programs, the funding of research, and the support of their respective state and local health agencies.

In the United States, the primary national health agency is the Department of Health and Human Services (HHS). HHS "is the United States government's principal agency for

Table 2.1
Health-Related Millennium Development Goals, Targets, and Indicators

Goal: 1. Eradicate Extreme Poverty and Hunger
Target: 2. Halve, between 1990 and 2015, the proportion of people who suffer from hunger
   Indicator: 4. Prevalence of underweight children under five years of age
                  5. Proportion of population below minimum level of dietary energy consumption[a]

Goal: 4. Reduce Child Mortality
Target: 5. Reduce by two-thirds, between 1990 and 2015, the under-five mortality rate
   Indicator: 13. Under-five mortality rate
                  14. Infant mortality rate
                  15. Proportion of 1-year-old children immunized against measles

Goal: 5. Improve Maternal Health
Target: 6. Reduce by three-quarters, between 1990 and 2015, the maternal mortality ratio
   Indicator: 16. Maternal mortality ratio
                  17. Proportion of births attended by skilled health personnel

Goal: 6. Combat HIV/AIDS, Malaria, and Other Diseases
Target: 7. Have halted by 2015 and begun to reverse the spread of HIV/AIDS
   Indicator: 18. HIV prevalence among young people aged 15 to 24 years[b]
                  19. Condom use rate of the contraceptive prevalence rate
                  20. Number of children orphaned by HIV/AIDS
Target: 8. Have halted by 2015 and begun to reverse the incidence of malaria and other major diseases
   Indicator: 21. Prevalence and death rates associated with malaria
                  22. Proportion of population in malaria-risk areas using effective malaria prevention and
                      treatment measures
                  23. Prevalence and death rates associated with tuberculosis
                  24. Proportion of tuberculosis cases detected and cured under Directly Observed
                      Treatment, Short-course (DOTS)

Goal: 7. Ensure Environmental Sustainability
Target: 9. Integrate the principles of sustainable development into country policies and programmes and reverse
                  the loss of environmental resources
   Indicator: 29. Proportion of population using solid fuel
Target: 10. Halve by 2015 the proportion of people without sustainable access to safe drinking-water
   Indicator: 30. Proportion of population with sustainable access to an improved water source, urban
                      and rural
Target: 11. By 2020 to have achieved a significant improvement in the lives of at least 100 million slum dwellers
   Indicator: 31. Proportion of urban population with access to improved sanitation

Goal: 8. Develop a Global Partnership for Development
Target: 17. In cooperation with pharmaceutical companies, provide access to affordable essential drugs in
                  developing countries
   Indicator: 46. Proportion of population with access to affordable essential drugs on a sustainable basis

[a]Health-related indicator reported by the Food and Agriculture Organization only.
[b]Indicators from the MDG list reformulated by WHO and United Nations General Assembly Special Session on HIV/AIDS.

Source: World Health Organization (2003). *World Health Report 2003: Shaping the Future.* Geneva, Switzerland: Author, 28. Used
with permission of the World Health Organization.

protecting the health of all Americans and providing essential human services, especially
for those who are least able to help themselves."[6] It is important to note, however, that other
federal agencies also contribute to the betterment of our Nation's health. For example, the
Department of Agriculture inspects meat and dairy products and coordinates the Women,
Infants, and Children (WIC) food assistance program; the Environmental Protection Agency
(EPA) regulates hazardous wastes; the Department of Labor houses the Occupational
Safety and Health Administration (OSHA), which is concerned with safety and health in the
workplace; the Department of Commerce, which includes the Bureau of the Census, collects

much of the national data that drives our Nation's health programs; and the Department of Homeland Security (DHS) deals with all aspects of terrorism within the United States. While information about the DHS was presented in Chapter 1, each of these other departments or agencies will be discussed in greater detail in later chapters. A detailed description of the Department of Health and Human Services follows.

Department of Health and Human Services (HHS)

The Department of Health and Human Services (HHS) is headed by the Secretary of Health and Human Services, who is appointed by the President and is a member of his/her cabinet. The Department of Health and Human Services was formed in 1980 (during the administration of President Jimmy Carter), when the Department of Health, Education, and Welfare (HEW) was divided into two new departments, HHS and the Department of Education. HHS is the department most involved with the Nation's human concerns. In one way or another it touches the lives of more Americans than any other federal agency. It is literally a department of people serving people, from newborn infants to persons requiring health services to our most elderly citizens. With an annual budget in excess of approximately $548 billion (representing about 25% of the federal budget), HHS is the largest department in the federal government, and it spends approximately $150 billion more per year than the Department of Defense.[6,7]

Since its formation, HHS has undergone several reorganizations. Some of the more recent changes have been the addition of the Center for Faith-Based and Community Initiatives and an Assistant Secretary for Public Health Emergency Preparedness. Currently, the HHS is organized into 12 operating divisions (see Figure 2.2) whose heads report directly to the Secretary. In addition, the HHS has 10 regional offices located throughout the United States (see Table 2.2). These offices serve as representatives of the Secretary of HHS in direct, official dealings with the state and local governmental organizations.

Although in reviewing Figure 2.2 it appears that the Public Health Service (PHS), a long-standing federal health agency (see Chapter 1), was eliminated from HHS, this is not the case. Eight of the 12 operating divisions of HHS now constitute the PHS (see Table 2.3). Another three operating divisions (CMS, ACF, and AoA) comprise the human services operating divisions. The following is a brief description of all the operating divisions comprising the HHS.

Administration on Aging (AoA)

This division of HHS is the principal agency designated to carry out the provisions of the Older Americans Act of 1965. (See Chapter 9 for more information on this act.) This agency tracks the characteristics, circumstances, and needs of older people; develops policies, plans, and programs to promote their welfare; administers grant programs to benefit older Americans; and administers training, research, demonstration programs, and protective services for older Americans. One exemplary program supported by the AoA is Meals on Wheels.

Administration for Children and Families (ACF)

The ACF is comprised of a number of smaller agencies and is responsible for providing direction and leadership for all federal programs for needy children and families. One of the better known programs originating out of this division is Head Start, which serves more than 900,000 preschool children. Other programs are aimed at family assistance, refugee resettlement, and child support enforcement.

Agency for Healthcare Research and Quality (AHRQ)

Prior to 1999 this division of HHS was called the Agency for Health Care Policy and Research, but its name was changed as part of the Healthcare Research and Quality Act of 1999. AHRQ is "the Nation's lead Federal agency for research on health care quality, costs, outcomes, and patient safety."[8] AHRQ sponsors and conducts research that provides evidence-based information on health care outcomes; quality; and cost, use, and access. The information helps health care decision makers—patients and clinicians, health system leaders, and policy makers—make more informed decisions and improve the quality of health care services.

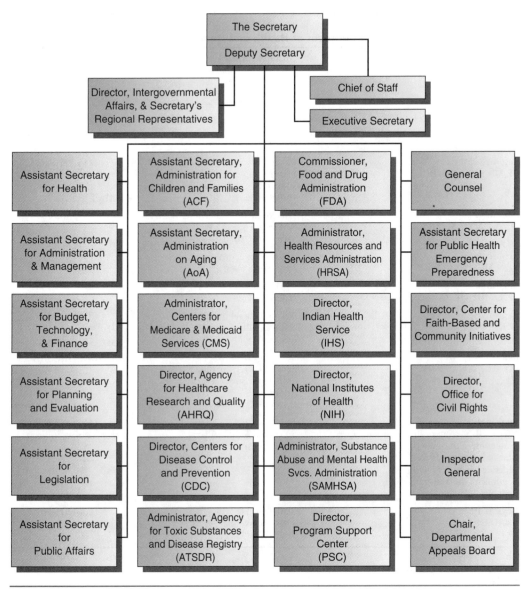

FIGURE 2.2

Organizational chart for the U.S. Department of Health and Human Services (HHS).

Source: U.S. Department of Health and Human Services (2003). *U.S. Department of Health and Human Services Organizational Chart.* Available at http://www.hhs.gov/about/orgchart.html.

Agency for Toxic Substances and Disease Registry (ATSDR)

This agency was created by the **Superfund legislation** (Comprehensive Environmental Response, Compensation, and Liability Act) in 1980. This legislation was enacted to deal with the cleanup of hazardous substances in the environment. ATSDR's mission "is to serve the public by using the best science, taking responsive public health actions, and providing trusted health information to prevent harmful exposures and disease related to toxic substances."[9] To carry out its mission and to serve the needs of the American public, ATSDR evaluates information on hazardous substances released into the environment in order to assess the impact on public health; conducts and sponsors studies and other research related to hazardous substances and adverse human health effects; establishes and maintains registries

Superfund legislation legislation enacted to deal with the clean-up of hazardous substances in the environment

Table 2.2
Regional Offices of the U.S. Department of Health and Human Services

Region/Areas Served	Office Address	Telephone Number
Region 1: CT, MA, ME, NH, RI, VT	John F. Kennedy Bldg. Government Center Boston, MA 02203	(617) 565-1500
Region 2: NJ, NY, Puerto Rico, Virgin Islands	Jacob K. Javits Federal Bldg. 26 Federal Plaza New York, NY 10278	(212) 264-4600
Region 3: DE, MD, PA, VA, WV, DC	Public Ledger Building 150 S. Independence Mall West Suite 436 Philadelphia, PA 19106	(215) 861-4633
Region 4: AL, FL, GA, KY, MS, NC, SC, TN	Sam Nunn, Atlanta Federal Center 61 Forsyth Street, SW Atlanta, GA 30303	(404) 562-7888
Region 5: IL, IN, MI, MN, OH, WI	233 N. Michigan Avenue Chicago, IL 60601	(312) 353-5160
Region 6: AR, LA, NM, OK, TX	1301 Young Street Dallas, TX 75202	(214) 767-3301
Region 7: IA, KS, MO, NE	Bolling Federal Building 601 East 12th Street Kansas City, MO 64106	(816) 426-2821
Region 8: CO, MT, ND, SD, UT, WY	Bryon G. Rogers Federal Office Building 1961 Stout Street Room 1076 Denver, CO 80294	(303) 844-3372
Region 9: AZ, CA, HI, NV, American Samoa, Guam, Commonwealth of the Northern Mariana Islands, Federated States of Micronesia, Republic of the Marshall Islands, Republic of Palau	Federal Office Building 50 United Nations Plaza San Francisco, CA 94102	(415) 437-8500
Region 10: AK, ID, OR, WA	Blanchard Plaza Bldg. 2201 6th Avenue Seattle, WA 98121	(206) 615-2010

Table 2.3
Agencies of the Public Health Service

Agency for Healthcare Research and Quality (AHRQ)
Agency for Toxic Substances and Disease Registry (ATSDR)
Centers for Disease Control and Prevention (CDC)
Food and Drug Administration (FDA)
Health Resources and Services Administration (HRSA)
Indian Health Service (IHS)
National Institutes for Health (NIH)
Substance Abuse and Mental Health Services Administration (SAMHSA)

of human exposure (for long-term follow-up) and complete listings of areas closed to the public or otherwise restricted in use due to contamination; summarizes and makes data available on the effects of hazardous substances; and provides consultations and training to ensure adequate response to public health emergencies. Although ATSDR has been responding to chemical emergencies in local communities across the country for the last 25 years, like many of the other federal health agencies its work has taken on new meaning since 9/11. For example, some of the projects the agency's staff have worked on or continue to work on include sampling dust in New York City residences after 9/11; working with New York health agencies to create a registry of people who lived or worked near the World Trade Center (WTC) on 9/11 to collect health information on those most heavily exposed to smoke, dust, and debris from the collapse of the WTC; conducting environmental sampling at anthrax-contaminated buildings; and disseminating critical information to agencies and organizations with a role in terrorism preparedness and response.[10] (Note: At the time this book was being written, new organization plans were announced by the Centers for Disease Control and Prevention that would include ATSDR as part of one of the CDC coordinating centers beginning October 2005. See the discussion of the CDC that follows.)

Centers for Disease Control and Prevention (CDC)
The CDC, located in Atlanta, Georgia (see Figure 2.3), "is recognized as the lead federal agency for protecting the health and safety of people—at home and abroad, providing credible information to enhance health decisions, and promoting health through strong partnerships."[11] CDC serves as the national focus for developing and applying disease prevention (including bioterrorism) and control, environmental health, and health promotion and education activities designed to improve the health of the people of the United States.[11] Once known solely for its work to control communicable diseases, the CDC now also maintains records, analyzes disease trends, and publishes epidemiological reports on all types of diseases, including those that result from lifestyle, occupational, and environmental causes. Beyond its own specific responsibilities, the CDC also supports state and local health departments and cooperates with similar national health agencies from other WHO member nations.

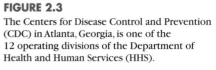

FIGURE 2.3

The Centers for Disease Control and Prevention (CDC) in Atlanta, Georgia, is one of the 12 operating divisions of the Department of Health and Human Services (HHS).

To better meet the challenges of public health for the twenty-first century, in 2003 the CDC began a strategic planning process called the *Futures Initiative.*[11] As a part of the Futures Initiative, the CDC adopted new overarching health protection goals and a new organizational structure. The goals that were adopted included the following:

- *Preparedness:* People in all communities will be protected from infectious, environmental, and terrorist threats.

- *Health promotion and prevention of disease, injury, and disability:* All people will achieve their optimal lifespan with the best possible quality of health in every stage of life.

The reorganization of the CDC created Coordinating Centers, the Office of Global Health, and the Office of Terrorism Preparedness and Emergency Response, whose directors report directly to the director of the CDC. The new Coordinating Centers are as follows:

- Coordinating Center for Infectious Disease: Includes the National Center for Infectious Diseases (NCID); the National Immunization Program (NIP); and the National Center for HIV, STD, and TB Prevention (NCHSTP).

- Coordinating Center for Health Promotion: Includes the National Center for Chronic Disease Prevention and Health Promotion (NCCDPHP); the National Center for Birth Defects and Developmental Disabilities (NCBDDD); and Genomics.

- Coordinating Center for Environmental Health, Injury Prevention, and Occupational Health: Includes the National Center for Environmental Health (NCEH)/Agency for Toxic Substances and Disease Registry (ATSDR); the National Center for Injury Prevention and Control (NCIPC); and the National Institute for Occupational Safety and Health (NIOSH).
- Coordinating Center for Public Health Information and Services: Includes the National Center for Health Statistics (NCHS); a new National Center for Health Marketing, and a new center for public health information.

Food and Drug Administration (FDA)

The FDA touches the lives of virtually every American every day. It "is responsible for protecting the public health by assuring the safety, efficacy, and security of human and veterinary drugs, biological products, medical devices, our nation's food supply, cosmetics, and products that emit radiation. The FDA is also responsible for advancing the public health by helping to speed innovations that make medicines and foods more effective, safer, and more affordable; and helping the public get the accurate, science-based information they need to use medicines and foods to improve their health."[12] Much of this work revolves around regulatory activities and the setting of health and safety standards as spelled out in the Federal Food, Drug, and Cosmetic Act and other related laws. However, due to the complex nature of its standards and the agency's limited resources, enforcement of many FDA regulations is left to other federal agencies and to state and local agencies. For example, the Department of Agriculture is responsible for the inspection of many foods, such as meat and dairy products. Restaurants, supermarkets, and other food outlets are inspected by state and local public health agencies.

Centers for Medicare and Medicaid Services (CMS)

Established as the Health Care Financing Administration (HFCA) in 1977, the CMS is responsible for overseeing the Medicare program (health care for the elderly and the disabled), the federal portion of the Medicaid program (health care for low-income individuals), and the related quality assurance activities. Both Medicare and Medicaid were created in 1965 to ensure that the special groups covered by these programs would not be deprived of health care because of cost. In 2004, about 85 million Americans were covered by these programs.[6] In 1997, the State Children's Health Insurance Program (SCHIP) also became the responsibility of the CMS. Medicare, Medicaid, and SCHIP are discussed in greater detail in Chapter 14.

Health Resources and Services Administration (HRSA)

The HRSA is the principal primary health care service agency of the Federal Government that provides access to essential health care services for people who are low-income, uninsured, or who live in rural areas or urban neighborhoods where health care is scarce.[6] Its "mission is to improve and expand access to quality health care for all."[13] HRSA "helps prepare the nation's health care system and providers to respond to bioterrorism and other public health emergencies, maintains the National Health Service Corps and helps build the health care workforce through many training and education programs. HRSA administers a variety of programs to improve the health of mothers and children and serves people living with HIV/AIDS through the Ryan White CARE Act programs. HRSA also oversees the nation's organ transplantation system."[6]

Indian Health Service (IHS)

The goal of the IHS is to raise the physical, mental, social, and spiritual health of American Indians and Alaska Natives to the highest level.[14] To attain its goal, the IHS:

1. Assists Indian tribes develop their health programs through activities such as health management training, technical assistance, and human resource development.
2. Facilitates and assists Indian tribes coordinate health planning, in obtaining and using health resources available through federal, state, and local programs, and in operating comprehensive health care services and health programs.

3. Provides comprehensive health care services, including hospital and ambulatory medical care, preventive and rehabilitative services, and development of community sanitation facilities.
4. Serves as the principal federal advocate in the health field for Indians to ensure comprehensive health services for American Indian and Alaska Native people.[14]

Though health services have been provided sporadically by the United States government since the early nineteenth century, it was not until 1989 that the IHS was elevated to an agency level; prior to that time it was a division in HRSA. (See Chapter 10 for more information on the IHS.)

National Institutes of Health (NIH)

Begun as a one-room Laboratory of Hygiene in 1887, the NIH today is one of the world's foremost medical research centers, and the Federal focal point for medical research in the United States.[15] The mission of the NIH "is to uncover new knowledge that will lead to better health for everyone."[15] Although a significant amount of research is carried out by NIH scientists at NIH laboratories in Bethesda and elsewhere, a much larger portion of this research is conducted by scientists at public and private universities and other research institutions. These scientists receive NIH funding for their research proposals through a competitive, peer-review grant application process. Through this process of proposal-review by qualified scientists, NIH seeks to ensure that federal research monies are spent on the best conceived research projects. Table 2.4 provides a listing of all the institutes and centers located in NIH.

Table 2.4
Units within the National Institutes of Health (NIH)

National Cancer Institute (NCI)
National Eye Institute (NEI)
National Heart, Lung, and Blood Institute (NHLBI)
National Human Genome Research Institute (NHGRI)
National Institute on Aging (NIA)
National Institute on Alcohol Abuse and Alcoholism (NIAAA)
National Institute of Allergy and Infectious Diseases (NIAID)
National Institute of Arthritis and Musculoskeletal and Skin Diseases (NIAMS)
National Institute of Biomedical Imaging and Bioengineering (NIBIB)
National Institute of Child Health and Human Development (NICHD)
National Institute on Deafness and Other Communication Disorders (NIDCD)
National Institute of Dental and Craniofacial Research (NIDCR)
National Institute of Diabetes and Digestive and Kidney Diseases (NIDDK)
National Institute on Drug Abuse (NIDA)
National Institute of Environmental Health Sciences (NIEHS)
National Institute of General Medical Sciences (NIGMS)
National Institute of Mental Health (NIMH)
National Institute of Neurological Disorders and Stroke (NINDS)
National Institute of Nursing Research (NINR)
National Library of Medicine (NLM)
Warren Grant Magnuson Clinical Center (CC)
Center for Information Technology (CIT)
National Center for Complementary and Alternative Medicine (NCCAM)
National Center on Minority Health and Health Disparities (NCMHD)
National Center for Research Resources (NCRR)
John E. Fogarty International Center (FIC)
Center for Scientific Review (CSR)

Source: National Institutes of Health. (2004). *Institutes, Centers & Offices.* Available at http://www.nih.gov/icd/.

Program Support Center (PSC)

The PSC became a new component of HHS in 1995. Its mission is to provide "customer-focused administrative services and products for the Department of Health and Human Services."[16] The formation of the PSC resulted from the HHS's efforts to streamline and minimize duplication of functions in providing administrative services to the HHS components and other federal agencies. Products and services provided by the PSC focus primarily on "the following areas: Human Resources; Financial Management; Administrative Operations; Health Resources; Strategic Acquisition and Human Resources Center."[16]

Substance Abuse and Mental Health Services Administration (SAMHSA)

The SAMHSA is the primary federal agency responsible for ensuring that up-to-date information and state-of-the-art practice is effectively used for the prevention and treatment of addictive and mental disorders. "SAMHSA is the Federal agency charged with improving the quality and availability of prevention, treatment, and rehabilitation services in order to reduce illness, death, disability, and cost to society resulting from substance abuse and mental illnesses."[17] Within SAMHSA, there are three centers—the Center for Substance Abuse Treatment (CSAT), the Center for Substance Abuse Prevention (CSAP), and the Center for Mental Health Services (CMHS). Each of these centers has its own set of missions that contribute to the overall mission of SAMHSA (see Chapter 11 and Chapter 12 for more information on SAMHSA).

State Health Agencies

All 50 states have their own state health departments (see Figure 2.4). Although the names of these departments may vary from state to state (e.g., Ohio Department of Health, Indiana State Department of Health), their purposes remain the same: to promote, protect, and maintain the

FIGURE 2.4

Each of the 50 states has its own health department.

health and welfare of their citizens. These purposes are represented in the **core functions of public health,** which include *assessment* of information on the health of the community, comprehensive public health *policy development,* and *assurance* that public health services are provided to the community.[18] These core functions have been defined further with the following 10 essential public health services.[19]

> **core functions of public health**
> assessment, policy development, and assurance

1. Monitor health status to identify community health problems.
2. Diagnose and investigate health problems and health hazards in the community.
3. Inform, educate, and empower people about health issues.
4. Mobilize community partnerships to identify and solve health problems.
5. Develop policies and plans that support individual and community health efforts.
6. Enforce laws and regulations that protect health and ensure safety.
7. Link people to needed personal health services and assure the provision of health care when otherwise unavailable.
8. Ensure a competent public health and personal health care workforce.
9. Evaluate effectiveness, accessibility, and quality of personal- and population-based health services.
10. Research for new insights and innovative solutions to health problems (see Figure 2.5).

FIGURE 2.5

Core functions of public health and the 10 essential services.

Adopted: Fall 1994. *Source:* Public Health Functions Steering Committee, Members (July 1995): American Public Health Association • Association of Schools of Public Health • Association of State and Territorial Health Officials • Environmental Council of the States • National Association of County and City Health Officials • National Association of State Alcohol and Drug Abuse Directors • National Association of State Mental Health Program Directors • Public Health Foundation • U.S. Public Health Service—*Agency for Health Care Policy and Research • Centers for Disease Control and Prevention • Food and Drug Administration • Health Resources and Services Administration • Indian Health Service • National Institutes of Health • Office of the Assistant Secretary for Health • Substance Abuse and Mental Health Services Administration*

Source: Office of Disease Prevention and Health Promotion (2004). *Public Health in America.* Available at http://web.health.gov/phfunctions/public.htm.

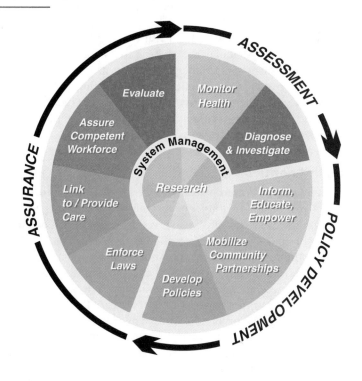

The head of the state health department is usually a medical doctor, appointed by the governor, who may carry the title of director, commissioner, or secretary. However, due to the political nature of the appointment, this individual may or may not have extensive experience in community or public health. Unfortunately, political influence sometimes reaches below the level of commissioner to the assistant commissioners and division chiefs; it is the commissioner, assistant commissioners, and division chiefs who set policy and provide direction for the state health department. Middle- and lower-level employees are usually hired through a merit system and may or may not be able to influence health department policy. These employees, who carry out the routine work of the state health department, are usually professionally trained health specialists such as microbiologists, engineers, sanitarians, epidemiologists, nurses, and health educators.

Most state health departments are organized into divisions or bureaus that provide certain standard services. Typical divisions include Administration, Communicable Disease Prevention and Control, Chronic Disease Prevention and Control, Vital and Health Statistics, Environmental Health, Health Education or Promotion, Health Services, Maternal and Child Health, Mental Health, Occupational and Industrial Health, Dental Health, Laboratory Services, Public Health Nursing, Veterinary Public Health, and most recently, a division of Public Health Preparedness to deal with bioterrorism issues.

In promoting, protecting, and maintaining the health and welfare of their citizens, state health departments play many different roles. They can establish and promulgate health regulations that have the force and effect of law throughout the state. The state health departments also provide an essential link between federal and local (city and county) public health agencies. As such, they serve as conduits for federal funds aimed at local health problems. Federal funds come to the states as block grants. Funds earmarked for particular health projects are distributed to local health departments by their respective state health departments in accordance with previously agreed upon priorities. State health departments may also link local needs with federal expertise. For example, epidemiologists from CDC are sometimes made available to investigate local disease outbreaks at the request of the state health department. And, state health departments usually must approve appointments of local health officers and can also remove any local health officers who neglect their duties.

The resources and expertise of the state health department are also at the disposal of local health departments. One particular area where the state health departments can be helpful is laboratory services; many modern diagnostic tests are simply too expensive for local health departments. Another area is environmental health. Water and air pollution problems usually extend beyond local jurisdictions, and their detection and measurement often require equipment too expensive for local governments to afford. This equipment and expertise are often provided by the state health department.

Local Public Health Agencies

Local-level governmental health organizations, referred to as local public health agencies (LPHAs) are usually the responsibility of the city or county governments. In large metropolitan areas, community health needs are usually best served by a city health department. In smaller cities with populations of up to 75,000, people often come under the jurisdiction of a county health department. In some rural counties where most of the population is concentrated in a single city, an LPHA may have jurisdiction over both city and county residents. In sparsely populated rural areas, it is not uncommon to find more than one county served by a single health department. In 2000, there were approximately 2,912 LPHAs; of that number, 60% were located in nonmetropolitan areas, while the other 40% were in metropolitan areas[20] (see Figure 2.6).

It is through LPHAs that health services are provided to the people of the community. A great many of these services are mandated by state laws, which also set standards for health and safety. Examples of mandated local health services include the inspection of restaurants,

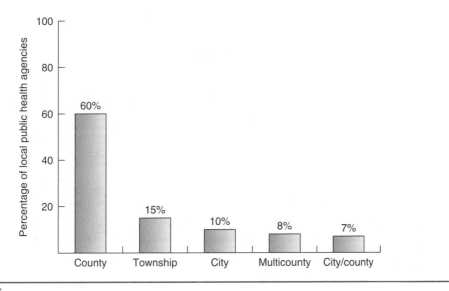

FIGURE 2.6

Type of local public health agencies ($n = 694$).

Source: Adapted from Hajat, A., C. K. Brown, and M. R. Fraser (2001). *Local Public Health Infrastructure: A Chartbook.* Washington, DC: National Association of County and City Health Officials, 11. Used with permission of the National Association of County and City Health Officials.

public buildings, and public transportation systems, the detection and reporting of certain diseases, and the collection of vital statistics such as births and deaths. Other programs such as safety belt programs and immunization clinics may be locally planned and implemented. In this regard, local health jurisdictions are permitted (unless pre-emptive legislation is in place) to enact ordinances that are stricter than those of the state, but these jurisdictions cannot enact codes that fall below state standards. It is at this level of governmental health agencies that sanitarians implement the environmental health programs, nurses and physicians offer the clinical services, and health educators present health education and promotion programs.

Organization of Local Public Health Agencies

Each LPHA is headed by a health officer/administrator/commissioner (see Figure 2.7). In most states, there are laws that prescribe who can hold such a position. Those often noted are physicians, dentists, veterinarians, or individuals with a master's or doctoral degree in public health. If the health officer is not a physician, then a physician is usually hired on a consulting basis to advise as needed. Usually, this health officer is appointed by a board of health, the members of which are themselves appointed by officials in the city or county government or, in some situations, elected by the general public. The health officer and administrative assistants may recommend which programs will be offered by the LPHAs. However, they may need final approval from a board of health. Although it is desirable that those serving on the local board of health have some knowledge of community health programs, most states have no such requirement. Oftentimes, politics plays a role in deciding the make-up of the local board of health.

The local health officer, like the state health commissioner, has far-reaching powers including the power to arrest someone who refuses to undergo treatment for a communicable disease (tuberculosis, for example) and who thereby continues to spread disease in the community. The local health officer has the power to close a restaurant on the spot if it has serious health law violations or to impound a shipment of food if it is contaminated. Because many local public health agencies cannot afford to employ a full-time physician, the health officer is usually hired on a part-time basis. In such cases, the day-to-day activities of the LPHA

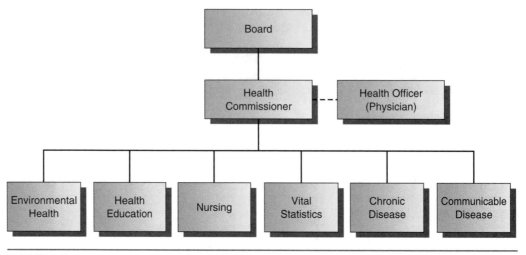

FIGURE 2.7
Organizational chart of a local public health agency.

are carried out by an administrator trained in public health. The administrator is also hired by the board of health based upon qualifications and the recommendation of the health officer.

About half of the funding for the programs and services of the LPHAs comes from the state (30%) and federal (19%) governments, while most of the other half (44%) comes from local property taxes.[20] A limited number of LPHA services are provided on a "fee-for-service" basis. For example, there is usually a fee charged for birth and death certificates issued by the LPHA. Also, in some communities, minimal fees are charged to offset the cost of providing immunizations, lab work, or inspections. Seldom do these fees cover the actual cost of the services provided. Therefore, income from service fees usually makes up a very small portion of any LPHA budget. And, it is not unusual to find that many LPHAs use a **sliding scale** to determine the fee for a service.

sliding scale
the scale used to determine the fee for services based on ability to pay

Coordinated School Health Programs

Few people think of public schools as governmental health organizations. Consider, however, that schools are funded by tax dollars, are under the supervision of an elected school board, and include as a part of their mission the improvement of the health of those in the school community. Because school attendance is required throughout the United States, the potential for school health programs to make a significant contribution to community health is enormous. In fact, Allensworth and Kolbe have stated that schools "could do more perhaps than any other single agency in society to help young people, and the adults they will become, to live healthier, longer, more satisfying, and more productive lives."[21] Yet coordinated school health programs have faced a number of barriers, including the following:[22]

1. Insufficient local administrative commitment
2. Inadequately prepared teachers
3. Too few school days to teach health in the school year
4. Inadequate funding
5. The lack of credibility of health education as an academic subject
6. Insufficient community/parental support
7. Concern for the teaching of controversial topics (i.e., sex education)

If communities were willing to work to overcome these barriers, the contribution of coordinated school health programs to community health could be almost unlimited.

PUBLIC HEALTH IN THE UNITED STATES

Governmental health agencies at the local, state, and national levels make up the backbone of the public health system. The system is there to (1) prevent epidemics and the spread of disease, (2) protect against environmental hazards, (3) prevent injuries, (4) promote and encourage healthy behaviors, (5) respond to disasters and assist communities in recovery, and (6) assure the quality and accessibility of health services.[19] It is a system that has been taken for granted by most Americans, including those who fund it. As Noreen M. Clark, Dean of the School of Public Health at the University of Michigan, stated, "often when public health works effectively, it is invisible. . . . public health is the disease you *didn't* get, the epidemic that *didn't* spread, the environmental disaster that *didn't* occur."[23]

However, the events of 9/11 "highlighted the state of the infrastructure with unprecedented clarity to the public and policy makers: outdated and vulnerable technologies; a public health workforce lacking training and reinforcements; antiquated laboratory capacity; lack of real-time surveillance and epidemiological systems; ineffective and fragmented communications networks; incomplete domestic preparedness and emergency

response capabilities; and communities without access to essential public health services."[24] Yet, if the public health system is to be improved, government health agencies cannot do it alone. They will need to partner "with other organizations and sectors of society, working closely with communities and community based organizations, the health care delivery system, academia, business, and the media."[24]

Building on the vision articulated by *Healthy People 2010*—healthy people in healthy communities—the Committee on Assuring the Health of the Public in the 21st Century of the Institute for Medicine has developed 34 recommendations for assuring population health in the United States. The committee's recommendations revolve around (1) adopting a focus on population health that includes multiple determinants of health, (2) strengthening the public health infrastructure, (3) building partnerships, (4) developing systems of accountability, (5) emphasizing evidence, and (6) improving communications. More specifics about the committee's recommendations can be found at the Institute for Medicine's Web site (www.iom.edu).

What exactly is meant by coordinated school health? Prior to 1998, a coordinated school health program was commonly referred to as a "comprehensive school health program." However, it was commonly confused with "comprehensive health education." To eliminate this confusion, the term "coordinated" school health program is used. A coordinated school health program is defined as "an organized set of policies, procedures, and activities designed to protect, promote, and improve the health and well-being of students and staff, thus improving a student's ability to learn. It includes but is not limited to comprehensive school health education; school health services; a healthy school environment; school counseling; pyschological and social services; physical education; school nutrition services; family and community involvement in school health; and school-site health promotion for staff."[25]

As previously stated, there are three essential components in every coordinated school health program—health education, a healthy school environment, and health services. Health instruction should be based on a well-conceived, carefully planned curriculum that has an appropriate scope (coverage of topics) and logical sequencing. Instructional units should include cognitive (knowledge), affective (attitudes), and psychomotor (behavioral) components. The healthy school environment should provide a learning environment that is both physically and mentally safe and healthy. Finally, each school's health program should provide the essential health services, from emergency care through health appraisals, to ensure that students will be healthy learners. These topics and others will be discussed in much greater detail in Chapter 6.

QUASI-GOVERNMENTAL HEALTH ORGANIZATIONS

The **quasi-governmental health organizations**—organizations that have some official health responsibilities but operate, in part, like voluntary health organizations—make important contributions to community health. Although they derive some of their funding and

quasi-governmental health organizations organizations that have some responsibilities assigned by the government but operate more like voluntary agencies

FIGURE 2.8

The American Red Cross was founded by Clara Barton in 1881.

legitimacy from governments, and carry out tasks that may be normally thought of as government work, they operate independently of government supervision. In some cases, they also receive financial support from private sources. Examples of quasi-governmental agencies are the American Red Cross (ARC), the National Science Foundation, and the National Academy of Sciences.

The American Red Cross

The ARC, founded in 1881 by Clara Barton (see Figure 2.8), is a prime example of an organization that has quasi-governmental status. While it has certain "official" responsibilities placed on it by the federal government, it is funded by voluntary contributions. "Official" duties of the ARC include (1) providing relief to victims of natural disasters such as floods, tornadoes, hurricanes, and fires (Disaster Services), and (2) serving as the liaison between members of the active armed forces and their families during emergencies (Services to the Armed Forces and Veterans). In this latter capacity, the ARC can assist active-duty members of the armed services in contacting their families in case of an emergency, or vice versa.

In addition to these "official" duties, the ARC also engages in many nongovernmental services. These include blood drives, safety services (including water safety, first aid, CPR, and HIV/AIDS instruction), nursing and health services, youth services, community volunteer services, and international services.

The ARC was granted a charter by Congress in 1900, and the ARC and the federal government have had a special relationship ever since. The President of the United States is the honorary chairman of the ARC. The U.S. Attorney General and Secretary of the Treasury are honorary counselor and treasurer, respectively.

The Red Cross idea was not begun in the United States. It was begun in 1863 by five Swiss men in Geneva, Switzerland, who were concerned with the treatment provided to the wounded during times of war. The group, which was called the International Committee for the Relief to the Wounded, was led by Henry Dunant. With the assistance of the Swiss government, the International Committee brought together delegates from 16 nations in 1864 to the Geneva Convention for the Amelioration of the Condition of the Wounded in Armies in the Field (now known as the first Geneva Convention) to sign the Geneva Treaty.

The efforts of Henry Dunant and the rest of the International Committee led to the eventual establishment of the International Committee of the Red Cross (ICRC). The ICRC, which still has its headquarters in Geneva and is still governed by the Swiss, continues to work today during times of disaster and international conflict. It is the organization that visits prisoners of war to ensure they are being treated humanely.[26,27]

Today, the international movement of the Red Cross comprises the Geneva-based ICRC, the International Federation of Red Cross and Red Crescent Societies (the red crescent emblem is used in Moslem countries), and the 181 National Red Cross and Red Crescent Societies.[26] There are a number of other countries that believe in the principles of the Red Cross Movement, but have not officially joined because the emblems used by the movement are offensive. Thus, the ICRC has been working to create a third emblem that meets all the criteria for use as a protective device and at the same time is free of any national, political, or religious connotations. At the time this book was being written, the design that was being considered was composed of a red frame in the shape of a square on the edge of a white background. The name that was being considered for this distinctive emblem was "red crystal," to signify purity.[27]

Other Quasi-Governmental Organizations

Two other examples of quasi-governmental organizations in the United States are the National Science Foundation (NSF) and the National Academy of Sciences (NAS). The purpose of NSF is the funding and promotion of scientific research and the development of individual scientists. NSF receives and disperses federal funds but operates independently of governmental supervision. Chartered by Congress in 1863, the NAS acts as an advisor to the government on questions of science and technology. Included in its membership are some of America's most renowned scientists. Although neither of these agencies exists specifically to address health problems, both organizations fund projects, publish reports, and take public stands on health-related issues.

NONGOVERNMENTAL HEALTH AGENCIES

Nongovernmental health agencies are funded by private donations or, in some cases, by membership dues. There are thousands of these organizations that all have one thing in common: They arose because there was an unmet health need. For the most part, the agencies operate free from governmental interference as long as they meet Internal Revenue Service guidelines with regard to their specific tax status. In the following sections, we discuss the following types of nongovernmental health agencies—voluntary, professional, philanthropic, service, social, religious, and corporate.

Voluntary Health Agencies

Voluntary health agencies are an American creation. Each of these agencies was created by one or more concerned citizens who felt that a specific health need was not being met by existing governmental agencies. In a sense, these new voluntary agencies arose by themselves, in much the same way as a "volunteer" tomato plant arises in a vegetable garden. New voluntary agencies continue to be born each year. Examples of recent additions to the perhaps 100,000 agencies already in existence are the Alzheimer's Association and the Sudden Infant Death Syndrome Alliance. A discussion of the commonalities of voluntary health agencies follows.

> **voluntary health agencies** nonprofit organizations created by concerned citizens to deal with a health need not met by governmental health agencies

Organization of Voluntary Health Agencies

Most voluntary agencies exist at three levels—national, state, and local. At the national level, policies that guide the agency are formulated. A significant portion of the money raised locally is forwarded to the national office, where it is allocated according to the agency's budget. Much of the money is designated for research. By funding research, the agencies hope to discover the cause of and cure for a particular disease or health problem. There have been some major successes. The March of Dimes, for example, helped to eliminate polio as a major disease problem in the United States through its funding of immunization research.

There is not always a consensus of opinion about budget decisions made at the national level; some believe that less should be spent for research and more for treating those afflicted with the disease. Another common internal disagreement concerns how much of the funds raised at the local level should be sent to the national headquarters instead of being retained for local use. Those outside the agency sometimes complain that when an agency achieves success, as the March of Dimes did in its fight against polio, it should dissolve. This does not usually occur; instead, successful agencies often find a new health concern. The March of Dimes now fights birth defects; and when tuberculosis was under control, the Tuberculosis Society changed its name to the American Lung Association in order to fight all lung diseases.

The state-level offices of voluntary agencies are analogous to the state departments of health in the way that they link the national headquarters with local offices. The primary work at this level is to coordinate local efforts and to ensure that policies developed at the national headquarters are carried out. The state-level office may also provide training services for employees and volunteers of local-level offices and are usually available as consultants and problem solvers. In recent years, some voluntary agencies have been merging several state offices into one to help reduce overhead expenses.

The local-level office of each voluntary agency is usually managed by a paid staff worker who has been hired either by the state-level office or by a local board of directors. Members of the local board of directors usually serve in that capacity on a voluntary basis. Working under the manager of each agency are local volunteers, who are the backbone of voluntary agencies. It has been said that the local level is where the "rubber meets the road." In other words, this is where most of the money is raised, most of the education takes place, and most of the service is rendered. Volunteers are of two types, professional and lay. Professional volunteers have had training in a medical profession, while lay volunteers have had no medical training. The paid employees help facilitate the work of the volunteers with expertise, training, and other resources.

Purpose of Voluntary Health Agencies

Voluntary agencies share four basic objectives: (1) to raise money to fund their programs with the majority of the money going to fund research, (2) to provide education both to professionals and to the public, (3) to provide service to those individuals and families that are afflicted with the disease or health problem, and (4) to advocate for beneficial policies, laws, and regulations that impact the work of the agency and in turn the people they are trying to help.

Fund-raising is a primary activity of many voluntary agencies. While in the past this was accomplished primarily by door-to-door solicitations, today mass-mailing and telephone solicitation are more common. In addition, most agencies sponsor special events like golf outings, dances, or dinners. One type of special event that is very popular today is the "a-thon." The term "a-thon" is derived from the name of the ancient Greek city Marathon, and usually signified some kind of "endurance" event. Examples include bike-a-thons, rock-a-thons, telethons, skate-a-thons, and dance-a-thons. These money-making "a-thons" seem to be limited in scope only by the creativity of those planning them. In addition, some of these agencies have become United Way agencies and receive some funds derived from the annual United Way campaign, which conducts fund-raising efforts at worksites. The three largest (in terms of dollars raised) voluntary agencies in the United States today (see Figure 2.9) are the American Cancer Society (see Box 2.3), the American Heart Association, and the American Lung Association.

Over the years, the number of voluntary agencies formed to help meet special health needs has continually increased. Due to the growth in the number of new agencies, several consumer "watch dog" groups have taken a closer look into the practices of the agencies. A major concern of these consumer groups has been the amount of money that the voluntary agencies spend on the cause (e.g., cancer, heart disease, AIDS, etc.) and how much they spend on fund-raising and overhead (e.g., salaries, office furniture, leasing of office space). Well-run agencies will spend less than 15% of what they raise on fund-raising. Some of the not so well-run agencies spend as much as 80% to 90% on fund-raising. All consumers should ask agencies how they spend their money prior to contributing.

FIGURE 2.9

Voluntary health organizations, such as those represented in this figure, make significant contributions to community health.

BOX **2.3**	A CLOSER LOOK AT ONE VOLUNTARY HEALTH AGENCY: THE AMERICAN CANCER SOCIETY

The American Cancer Society (ACS) was founded in 1913 by 10 physicians and five laymen. At that time, it was known as the American Society for the Control of Cancer. Today, with offices throughout the country and approximately two million volunteers, ACS is one of our largest voluntary health organizations. In spite of its success, its mission has remained constant since its founding. It is "dedicated to eliminating cancer as a major health problem by preventing cancer, saving lives, and diminishing suffering from cancer, through research, education, advocacy and service."[28]

The mission of ACS includes both short- and long-term goals. Its short-term goals are to save lives and diminish suffering. This is accomplished through education, advocacy, and service. Its long-term goal, the elimination of cancer, is being approached through the society's support of cancer research.

The American Cancer Society's educational programs are targeted at two different groups—the general public and the health professionals who treat cancer patients. The public education program promotes the following skills and concepts to people of all ages: (1) taking the necessary steps to prevent cancer, (2) knowing the seven warning signals, (3) understanding the value for regular checkups, and (4) coping with cancer. The society accomplishes this by offering free public education programs, supported by up-to-date literature and audiovisual materials, whenever and wherever they may be requested. These programs may be presented in homes, worksites, churches, clubs, organizations, and schools. A few of their better-known programs include "I Can Cope," "Reach to Recovery," and "Man to Man."[28] From time to time, the society also prepares public service messages for broadcasting or televising.

The Society's professional education program is aimed at the professionals who work with oncology patients. The objective of this program is to motivate "medical and allied health professionals to use the latest and best possible cancer detection, diagnostic, and patient management techniques."[29] Such education is provided through professional publications, up-to-date audiovisual materials, conferences, and grants that fund specialized education experiences.

The ACS offers patient service and rehabilitation programs that ease the impact of cancer on those affected. The services offered include information and referral to appropriate professionals, home care supplies and equipment for the comfort of patients, transportation of patients to maintain their medical and continuing care programs, and specialized education programs for cancer patients to help them cope and feel better about themselves. There are also rehabilitation programs that provide social support for all cancer patients and specific programs for those who have had a mastectomy, laryngectomy, or ostomy.

The ACS is the largest source of private, not-for-profit cancer research funds in the United States, second only to the federal government in total dollars spent. Since 1946, when the ACS first started awarding grants, it has invested over $2.5 billion in cancer research. The research program consists of three components: extramural grants, intramural epidemiology and surveillance research, and the intramural behavioral research center."[28] The most recent addition to the work of the ACS is in the area of advocacy. Specifically, the ACS works to (1) support cancer research and programs to prevent, detect, and treat cancer; (2) expand access to quality cancer care, prevention, and awareness; (3) reduce cancer disparities in minority and medically underserved populations; and (4) reduce and prevent suffering from tobacco-related illnesses.[28]

All ACS programs—education, service, research, and advocacy—are planned primarily by the society's volunteers. However, the society does employ staff members to carry out the day-to-day operations and to help advise and support the work of the volunteers. This arrangement of volunteers and staff working together has created a very strong voluntary health agency.

Professional Health Organizations/Associations

Professional health organizations and associations are made up of health professionals who have completed specialized education and training programs and have met the standards of registration, certification, and/or licensure for their respective fields. Their mission is to promote high standards of professional practice for their specific profession, thereby improving the health of society by improving the people in the profession. Professional organizations are funded primarily by membership dues. Examples of such organizations are the American Medical Association, the American Dental Association, the American Nursing Association, the

American Public Health Association, the American Association for Health Education, and the Society for Public Health Education, Inc.

Although each professional organization is unique, most provide similar services to their members. These services include the certification of continuing-education programs for professional renewal, the hosting of annual conventions where members share research results and interact with colleagues, and the publication of professional journals and other reports. Some examples of journals published by professional health associations are the *Journal of the American Medical Association,* the *American Journal of Public Health,* and *The American Journal of Health Education.*

Like voluntary health agencies, another important activity of some professional organizations is advocating on issues important to their membership. The American Medical Association, for example, has a powerful lobby nationally and in some state legislatures. Their purpose is to affect legislation in such a way as to benefit their membership and their profession. Many professional health organizations provide the opportunity for benefits, including group insurance and discount travel rates. There are hundreds of professional health organizations in the United States, and it would be difficult to describe them all here.

Philanthropic Foundations

philanthropic foundation
an endowed institution that donates money for the good of humankind

Philanthropic foundations have made and continue to make significant contributions to community health in the United States and throughout the world. These foundations support community health by funding programs and research on the prevention, control, and treatment of many diseases. Foundation directors, sometimes in consultation with a review committee, determine the types of programs that will be funded. Some foundations fund an array of health projects, while others have a much narrower scope of interests. Some foundations, such as the Rockefeller Foundation, fund international health projects, while others restrict their funding to domestic projects. The geographical scope of domestic foundations can be national, state, or local. Local foundations may restrict their funding to projects that only benefit local citizens.

The activities of these foundations differ from those of the voluntary health agencies in two important ways. First, foundations have money to give away, and therefore no effort is spent on fund-raising. Second, foundations can afford to fund long-term or innovative research projects, which might be too risky or expensive for voluntary or even government-funded agencies. The development of a vaccine for yellow fever by a scientist funded by the Rockefeller Foundation is an example of one such long-range project.

Some of the larger foundations, in addition to the Rockefeller Foundation, that have made significant commitments to community health are the Commonwealth Fund, which has contributed to community health in rural communities, improved hospital facilities, and tried to strengthen mental health services; the Ford Foundation, which has contributed greatly to family-planning efforts throughout the world; the Robert Wood Johnson Foundation, which has worked to improve access to medical and dental care throughout the United States and lessen the impact of tobacco on health; the Henry J. Kaiser Family Foundation, which has supported the development of health maintenance organizations (HMOs) and community health promotion; the W. K. Kellogg Foundation, which has funded many diverse health programs that address human issues and provide a practical solution; and the Milbank Memorial Fund, which has primarily funded preventive-medicine projects.

Service, Social, and Religious Organizations

Service, social, and religious organizations have also played a part in community health over the years (see Figure 2.10). Examples of service and social groups involved in community health are the Jaycees, Kiwanis Club, Fraternal Order of Police, Rotary Club, Elks, Lions, Moose,

FIGURE 2.10
Community service groups contribute needed resources for the improvement of the health of the community.

Shriners, American Legion, and Veterans of Foreign Wars. Members of these groups enjoy social interactions with people of similar interests in addition to fulfilling the groups' primary reason for existence—service to others in their communities. Although health may not be the specific focus of their mission, several of these groups make important contributions in that direction by raising money and funding health-related programs. Sometimes, their contributions are substantial. Examples of such programs include the Shriners' children's hospitals and burn centers, the Lions' contributions to pilot (lead) dog programs and other services for those who are visually impaired, such as the provision of eyeglasses for school-aged children unable to afford them, and the Lions' contributions to school health programs via the educational program named "Quest: Skills for Living."

The contributions of religious groups to community health have also been substantial. Such groups also have been effective avenues for promoting health programs because (1) they have had a history of volunteerism and pre-existing reinforcement contingencies for volunteerism, (2) they can influence entire families, and (3) they have accessible meeting-room facilities.[30] One way in which these groups contribute is through donations of money for missions for the less fortunate. Examples of religious organizations that solicit donations from their members include the Protestants' One Great Hour of Sharing, the Catholics' Relief Fund, and the United Jewish Appeal. Other types of involvement in community health by religious groups include (1) the donation of space for voluntary health programs such as blood donations, Alcoholics Anonymous, and other support groups, (2) the sponsorship of food banks and shelters for the hungry, poor, and homeless, (3) the sharing of the doctrine of good personal health behavior, and (4) allowing community health professionals to deliver their programs through the congregations. This latter contribution has been especially useful in black American communities because of the importance of churches in the culture of this group of people.

In addition, it should be noted that some religious groups have hindered the work of community health workers. Almost every community in the country can provide an example where a religious organization has protested the offering of a school district's sex education program, picketed a public health clinic for providing reproductive information or services to women, or has spoken out against homosexuality.

Corporate Involvement in Community Health

From the way it treats the environment by its use of natural resources and the discharge of wastes, to the safety of the work environment, to the products and services it produces and provides, to the provision of health care benefits for its employees, corporate America is very much involved in community health. Though each of these aspects of community health is important to the overall health of a community, because of the concern for the "bottom line" in corporate America, it is the provision of health care benefits that often receives the most attention. In fact, many corporations today find that their single largest annual expenditure behind salaries and wages is for employee health care benefits. Consider, for example, the cost of manufacturing a new car. The cost of health benefits for those who build the car now exceeds the cost of the raw materials for the car itself.

In an effort to keep a healthy workforce and reduce the amount paid for health care benefits, many companies support health-related programs both at and away from the worksite. Worksite programs aimed at trimming employee medical bills have been expanded beyond the traditional safety awareness programs and first aid services to include such programs as substance abuse counseling, nutrition education, smoking cessation, stress management, physical fitness, and disease management. Many companies also are implementing health promotion policies and enforcing state and local laws that prohibit (or severely restrict) smoking on company grounds or that mandate the use of safety belts at all times in all company-owned vehicles. (See Chapter 18 for more on safety and health in the workplace.)

CHAPTER SUMMARY

- Contemporary society is too complex to respond effectively to community health problems on either an emergency or a long-term basis. This fact necessitates organizations and planning for health in our communities.

- The different types of organizations that contribute to the promotion, protection, and maintenance of health in a community can be classified into three groups according to their sources of funding and organizational structure—governmental, quasi-governmental, and nongovernmental.

- Governmental health agencies exist at the local, state, federal, and international levels and are funded primarily by tax dollars.

- WHO is the largest and most visible governmental health agency on the international level.

- The Department of Health and Human Services (HHS) is the U.S. government's principal agency for the protection of the health of all Americans and for providing essential human services, especially for those who are least able to help themselves.

- The core functions of public health include the assessment of information on the health of the community, comprehensive public health policy development, and assurance that public health services are provided to the community.

- Quasi-governmental agencies, such as the American Red Cross, share attributes with both governmental and nongovernmental agencies.

- Nongovernmental organizations include voluntary and professional associations, philanthropic foundations, and service, social, and religious groups.

- Corporate America has also become more involved in community health, both at the worksite and within the community.

REVIEW QUESTIONS

1. What characteristics of modern society necessitate planning and organization for community health?

2. What is a governmental health agency?

3. What is the World Health Organization (WHO) and what does it do?

4. What federal department in the United States is the government's principal agency for protecting the health of all Americans and for providing essential human services, especially to those who are least able to help themselves? What major services does this department provide?

5. What are the three core functions of public health?

6. What are the 10 essential public health services?

7. How do state and local health departments interface?

8. What is meant by the term *coordinated school health program?* What are the major components of it?

9. What is meant by the term *quasi-governmental agency?* Name one such agency.

10. Describe the characteristics of a nongovernmental health agency.

11. What are the major differences between a governmental health organization and a voluntary health agency?

12. What does a health professional gain from being a member of a professional health organization?

13. How do philanthropic foundations contribute to community health? List three well-known foundations.

14. How do service, social, and religious groups contribute to the health of the community?

15. Why has corporate America become involved in community health?

SCENARIO: ANALYSIS AND RESPONSE

After having read this chapter, please respond to the following questions in reference to the scenario at the beginning of the chapter.

1. What type of health agency do you think will be of most help to Mary and Bill?

2. If this scenario were to happen to someone in your community, what recommendations would you give to him or her on seeking help from health agencies?

3. The Internet has many sources of information that could help Mary and Bill. Use a search engine (e.g., Google, Excite, or Lycos) and enter the word "cancer." Find the Web site of one governmental health agency at the national level and one voluntary health agency that might be able to help them. Explain how these agencies could be of help.

4. If Mary and Bill do not have Internet access, how would you suggest they find out about local health agencies in their area that could help them?

ACTIVITIES

1. Using a local telephone book, list all the health-related organizations that service your community. Divide your list by the three major types of health organizations noted in this chapter.

2. Make an appointment to interview someone at one of the organizations identified in Activity 1. During your visit, find answers to the following questions:

   a. How did the organization begin?

   b. What is its mission?

   c. How is it funded?

   d. How many people (employees and volunteers) work for the organization, and what type of education/training do they have?

   e. What types of programs/services does the organization provide?

3. Obtain organizational charts from the U.S. Department of Health and Human Services (a copy is in this chapter), your state department of health, and your local health department. Compare and contrast these charts and describe their similarities and differences.

4. Call a local voluntary health organization in your community and ask if you could volunteer to work 10 to 15 hours during this academic term. Then volunteer those hours and keep a journal of your experience.

5. Carefully review your community newspaper each day for an entire week. Keep track of all articles or advertisements that make reference to local health organizations. Summarize your findings in a one-page paper. (If you do not subscribe to your local paper, copies are available in libraries.)

COMMUNITY HEALTH ON THE WEB

The Internet contains a wealth of information about community and public health. Increase your knowledge of some of the topics presented in this chapter by accessing the Jones and Bartlett Publishers Web site at **health.jbpub.com/communityhealth/5e** and follow the links to complete the following Web activities.

- World Health Organization
- Department of Health and Human Services
- Association of State and Territorial Health Officials

REFERENCES

1. Green, L. W. (1990). "The Revival of Community and the Public Obligation of Academic Health Centers." In R. E. Bulger and S. J. Reiser, eds. *Integrity in Institutions: Humane Environments for Teaching, Inquiry and Healing.* Iowa City: Univ. of Iowa Press, 163–180.

2. World Health Organization (2004). *World Health Organization.* Available at http://www.who.int/about/en/.

3. United Nations (2000). *United Nations Millennium Declaration.* New York: Author.

4. United Nations (2002). *Road Map Towards the Implementation of the United Nations Millennium Declaration.* New York: Author.

5. World Health Organization (2003). *World Health Report 2003: Shaping the Future.* Geneva, Switzerland: Author.

6. U.S. Department of Health and Human Services (2004). *United States Department of Health and Human Services.* Available at http://www.hhs.gov/about/whatwedo.html.

7. U.S. Bureau of Census (2003). *Statistical Abstract of the U.S., 2003,* 123rd ed. Washington, DC: Author.

8. Agency for Healthcare Research and Quality (2004). *What Is AHRQ?* Available at http://www.ahrq.gov/about/Whatis.htm.

9. Agency for Toxic Substances and Disease Registry (2004). *About the Agency for Toxic Substances and Disease Registry.* Available at http://www.atsdr.cdc.gov/about.html.

10. Falk, H. (2003). "A message from Dr. Henry Falk, ATSDR Assistant Administrator." *Public Health and the Environment,* 2(1/2):1.

11. Centers for Disease Control and Prevention (2004). *Centers for Disease Control and Prevention.* Available at http://www.cdc.gov/.

12. U.S. Food and Drug Administration (2004). *FDA's Mission Statement.* Available at http://www.fda.gov/opacom/morechoices/mission.html.

13. Health Resources and Services Administration (2004). *About HRSA.* Available at http://www.hrsa.gov/about.htm.

14. Indian Health Service (2004). *Indian Health Service Fact Sheet.* Available at http://www.ihs.gov/PublicInfo/PublicAffairs/Welcome_Info/ThisFacts.asp.

15. National Institutes for Health (2004). *Questions and Answers about NIH.* Available at http://www.nih.gov/about/Faqs.htm#NIH.

16. Program Support Center (2004). *Administrative Operations.* Available at http://www.psc.gov/aos/business/gpra/gpra05/index.html.

17. Substance Abuse and Mental Health Services Administration (2004). *SAMSHA: Who Are We?* Available at http://www.samhsa.gov/about/about.html.

18. National Academy of Sciences, Institute of Medicine (1988). T*he Future of Public Health.* Washington, DC: National Academy Press.

19. Office of Disease Prevention and Health Promotion (2004). *Public Health in America.* Available at http://web.health.gov/phfunctions/public.htm.

20. Hajat, A., C. K. Brown, and M. R. Fraser (2001). *Local Public Health Infrastructure: A Chartbook.* Washington, DC: National Association of County and City Health Officials.

21. Allensworth, D. D., and L. J. Kolbe (1987). "The Comprehensive School Health Program: Exploring an Expanded Concept." *The Journal of School Health,* 57(10): 409–412.

22. Butler, S. C. (1993). "Chief State School Officers Rank Barriers to Implementing Comprehensive School Health Education." *The Journal of School Health,* 63(3): 130–132.

23. Clark, N. M. (2002). *A Letter from the Dean.* Ann Arbor, MI: University of Michigan, School of Public Health.

24. Institute of Medicine (2003). *The Future of the Public's Health.* Washington, DC: The National Academies Press.

25. Joint Committee on Health Education and Promotion Terminology (2001). "Report of the 2000 Joint Committee on Health Education and Promotion Terminology." *American Journal of Health Education,* 32(2): 89–103.

26. American Red Cross (2004). *Frequently Asked Questions.* Available at http://www.redcross.org/faq.

27. International Committee of the Red Cross (2004). *About the Red Cross/Red Crescent Emblem: Questions and Answers.* Available at http://www.icrc.org/Web/eng.

28. American Cancer Society (2004). *Cancer Facts and Figures—2004.* Atlanta, GA: Author.

29. American Cancer Society (1986). *American Cancer Society: What Is It, What It Does, How It Began, Who Directs It, Where Is It Going.* New York: Author.

30. Lasater, T. M., B. L. Wells, R. A. Carleton, and J. P. Elder (1986). "The Role of Churches in Disease Preventive Research Studies." *Public Health Report,* 101(2): 125–131.

Chapter 3

Epidemiology: The Study of Disease, Injury, and Death in the Community

Chapter Outline

Chapter Objectives

After studying this chapter you will be able to:

1   Define the terms *epidemic, epidemiology,* and *epidemiologist,* and explain their importance in community health.

2   List some diseases that caused epidemics in the past and some that are causing epidemics today.

3   Discuss how the practice of epidemiology has changed since the days of Benjamin Rush and John Snow.

4   Explain why rates are important in epidemiology and list some of the commonly used rates.

5   Define incidence and prevalence rates and provide examples of each.

6   Calculate a variety of rates from the appropriate data.

7   Discuss the importance of disease reporting to a community's health and describe the reporting process.

8   Define the following standardized measurements of health status—life expectancy, years of potential life lost (YPLL), disability-adjusted life years (DALYs), disability-adjusted life expectancy (DALEs), and health-adjusted life expectancy (HALE).

9   Identify sources of standardized data used by epidemiologists, community health workers, and health officials and list the types of data available from each source.

10 List and describe the three types of epidemiological studies and explain the purpose of each.

SCENARIO

John thought about this afternoon's picnic. Everyone had a blast. For a while it had seemed almost too warm, but plenty of cold drinks were available, and by late afternoon it had become quite pleasant. The games were fun too . . . frisbee, soccer, softball, and volleyball. Then there was the picnic itself—turkey, potato salad, bread and butter, milk, and dessert—served about noon.

It was now 8 P.M. that same night, and instead of studying as he had planned, John was lying on his bed with a bad stomachache. He was experiencing severe diarrhea and had made several hurried trips to the bathroom in the last half-hour.

The telephone rang, and it was Michael, John's roommate. He had gone to his girlfriend's house after the picnic to work on a class project with her. He and Caroline were both sick with stomach cramps and diarrhea, and Michael was calling to ask whether John was sick too. As John was answering, he realized that he needed to run to the bathroom again. He quickly hung up, promising to call back soon. Moments later as he returned to his bedroom, John began to think about what a coincidence it was that all three of them were sick with the same symptoms at about the same time. Could they have become ill from food they ate at the picnic? There were about 50 people at the picnic; how many others might also be sick? Was it the heat? Was it the food? Was this an epidemic? A half-hour later, John

called Michael back to tell him that he had decided to go to the campus health center.

Elsewhere . . .

This had turned out to be an interesting volunteer experience. As a requirement for her community health class, Kim had agreed to volunteer at the local health department. The spring semester was almost over now, and she was writing a final report of her activities. During the term, she had spent her Friday afternoons accompanying a sanitarian on his inspections of restaurants and retail food stores. She also had helped him complete his reports on substandard housing and malfunctioning septic tanks.

Dr. Turner, the health officer, had given Kim permission to use one of the department's personal computers for preparing her final report. Because it was Sunday evening, she was alone in the health department office when the telephone rang. She briefly considered not answering it but finally picked up the receiver. It was Dr. Lee from the University Health Center. He said he was calling in the hope that someone might be there because he needed to reach Dr. Turner immediately. He said that he had admitted six students to the infirmary with severe stomach cramps, vomiting, and diarrhea. The students had been at a picnic earlier, and he thought they could have food poisoning. He called to ask Dr. Turner to investigate this outbreak and asked Kim to try to reach him as soon as possible.

INTRODUCTION

When you become ill and visit a doctor, the first thing the physician does is take measurements and collect information. The measurements include your temperature, heart rate, and blood pressure. The information includes time of onset of your illness, where you have traveled, and what you might have eaten. Next, you may be given a physical examination and asked to provide a specimen such as urine or blood for laboratory examination. The information gathered helps the physician understand the nature of your illness and prescribe an appropriate treatment.

While a primary care physician is concerned with the course of disease in an individual patient, an epidemiologist is concerned with the course of disease in a population. When illness, injury, or death occur at unexpected or unacceptable levels in a community or population, epidemiologists seek to collect information about the disease status of the community. First, epidemiologists want to know *how many* people are sick. Second, they want to know *who* is sick—the old? the young? males? females? rich? poor? They also want to know *when* the people became sick, and finally, *where* the sick people live or have traveled. In summary, epidemiologists want to know what it is that the sick people have in common. For this reason, epidemiology is sometimes referred to as *population medicine*.

Epidemiology is one of the community health activities "aimed at protecting or improving the health of a population or community" discussed in Chapter 1. Information gathered from epidemiological studies assists community decision makers to make the best use of the community's human and financial health resources. Data gathered at local, state, and national levels can be used not only to prevent disease outbreaks or control those that are in progress, but also to assess whether an ongoing disease prevention program is effective.

Definition of Epidemiology

Before we discuss the types of questions an epidemiologist asks, we need to define the term *epidemiology*. **Epidemiology** is "the study of the distribution and determinants of diseases and injuries in human populations."[1] The term *epidemiology* is derived from Greek words that can be translated into the phrase "the study of that which is upon the people." The goal of epidemiology is to limit disease, injury, and death in a community by intervening to prevent or limit outbreaks or epidemics of disease and injury. This is accomplished by describing outbreaks and designing studies to analyze them and to validate new approaches to prevention, control, and treatment. Through these practices, epidemiologists contribute to our knowledge of how diseases begin and spread through populations, and how they can be prevented, controlled, and treated.

The question might be asked, how many cases are required before a disease outbreak is considered an epidemic—10 cases? 100 cases? 1,000 cases? The answer is that it depends upon the disease and the population, *but any unexpectedly large number of cases of a disease* in a particular population at a particular time and place can be considered an **epidemic.** Some recent epidemics in the United States are presented in Table 3.1.

The question might be asked, what are diseases called that occur regularly in a population but are not epidemic? These diseases are referred to as **endemic diseases.** Whether a disease is epidemic or endemic depends on the disease and the population. Heart disease is endemic in America, while in many regions of equatorial Africa, malaria is endemic.

While an **epidemiologist** studies outbreaks of disease, injury, and death in human populations (*epidemics*), an *epizootiologist* studies disease outbreaks in animal populations (*epizootics*). Some diseases, such as bubonic plague and St. Louis encephalitis, may begin as epizootics but later become epidemics. When both animals and humans are involved in a disease outbreak, the term *epizoodemic* is appropriate. Occasionally, an epidemic will spread over a wide area, perhaps even across an entire continent or around the world. Such a widespread epidemic is termed a **pandemic.** The influenza pandemic of 1918 is an example

epidemiology
the distribution and determinants of diseases and injuries in human populations

epidemic
an unexpectedly large number of cases of disease in a particular population

endemic disease
a disease that occurs regularly in a population as a matter of course

epidemiologist
one who practices epidemiology

pandemic
an outbreak of disease over a wide geographical area such as a continent

Table 3.1
Recent Epidemics in the United States

Disease	Cases in Previous Years	Epidemic Period	Number of Cases
St. Louis encephalitis	5–72	1975	1,815 [3]
Legionnaires' disease	Unknown	1976	235 [4]
Toxic shock syndrome	11–272	1980	877 [5]
AIDS	Unknown	1981–2002	886,575 [6]
Lyme disease	Unknown	1990–2002	181,173 [7]
Plague	13–19	1983	40 [4]
West Nile virus	Unknown	1999–2003	13,217 [8]
Severe acute respiratory syndrome (SARS)	Unknown	2003	192 [9]
Monkey pox	0	2003	37 [10]

FIGURE 3.1
More than 25 million people died during the influenza pandemic of 1918-1919.

(see Figure 3.1). This disease spread from France to Spain and then to England and the rest of Europe. It then spread to China and West Africa and eventually reached the United States, Australia, and New Zealand. An estimated 25 million people died over several years as a result of this pandemic. The current outbreak of acquired immunodeficiency syndrome (AIDS) is another example of a pandemic. During 2003, an estimated 3 million people died of AIDS worldwide.[2]

History of Epidemiology

If one searches diligently, it is possible to trace the roots of epidemiological thinking back to the "Father of Medicine," Hippocrates, who as early as 300 B.C. suggested a relationship between the occurrence of disease and the physical environment.[11] For example, cases of a disease fitting the description of malaria were found to occur in the vicinity of marshes and swamps.

With the fall of the classical civilizations of Greece and Rome and the return in Europe to a belief in spiritual causes of disease, few advances were made in the field of epidemiology. As a result, epidemics continued to occur. There were three waves of plague—one in 542-543, one in 1348-1349, and another in 1664-1665.[12] There were also epidemics of leprosy, smallpox, malaria, and, later, syphilis and yellow fever.

Epidemics occurred in the New World as well. One such epidemic of yellow fever struck Philadelphia in 1793, causing the death of 4,044 people. Yellow fever was epidemic again in

Philadelphia in 1797, 1798, and in 1803.[13] Dr. Benjamin Rush, a prominent Philadelphia physician and signatory of the Declaration of Independence, was able to trace the cases of yellow fever to the docks where ships arrived from tropical ports. However, his conclusion that the disease was caused by vapors arising from decaying coffee beans in port warehouses was incorrect. He could not have known that yellow fever is caused by a virus and is carried by the yellow fever mosquito, *Aedes aegypti*. These facts were discovered by Major Walter Reed of the U.S. Army and his associates a century later.

In 1849, some 50 years after the yellow fever outbreaks in Philadelphia, cholera became epidemic in London. A prominent physician, John Snow, investigated the outbreak by interviewing numerous victims and their families. He concluded that the source of the epidemic was probably water drawn from a particular communal well located on Broad Street. Snow extinguished the epidemic when he removed the pump handle from the Broad Street pump, thus forcing people to obtain their water elsewhere.[14]

John Snow's quashing of the London cholera epidemic in 1849 is a classic example of how epidemiological methods can be used to limit disease and deaths. His achievement was even more remarkable because it occurred 30 years before Louis Pasteur proposed his "germ theory of disease." It was not until 1883 that Robert Koch discovered the organism that causes cholera, *Vibrio cholerae*.

From its early use for the description and investigation of communicable diseases, epidemiology has developed into a sophisticated field of science. Epidemiological methods are used to evaluate everything from the effectiveness of vaccines to the possible causes of occupational illnesses and unintentional injury deaths.

Knowledge of epidemiology is important to the community health worker who wishes to establish the presence of a set of needs or conditions for a particular health service or program or to justify a request for funding. Likewise, epidemiological methods are used to evaluate the effectiveness of programs already in existence and to plan to meet anticipated needs for facilities and personnel.

THE IMPORTANCE OF RATES

Epidemiologists are concerned with numbers. Of prime importance is the number of **cases** (people who are sick) and, of course, the number of deaths. These numbers alone, however, are not enough to provide a description of the extent of the disease in a community. Epidemiologists must also know the total number in the susceptible population so that rates can be calculated. A **rate** is the number of events (births, cases of disease, or deaths) in a given population over a given period or at a given point in time. Three general categories of rates are **natality (birth) rates, morbidity (sickness) rates,** and **mortality or fatality (death) rates.**

Why are rates important? Why not simply enumerate the sick or dead? The answer is that rates enable one to compare outbreaks that occur at different times or in different places. For example, by using rates it is possible to determine whether there are more cases of gonorrhea per capita this year than there were last year or whether there are more homicides per capita in City A than in City B.

For example, suppose you wish to compare transportation deaths associated with travel by autos and airplanes. To examine this hypothetical situation, consider that for a given time period, 1,000 people died in auto crashes while 50 people died in airplane crashes. Without calculating rates, one might assume that auto travel is more dangerous than air travel. However, if you knew the population exposed (100,000 people for auto travel versus 1,000 people for air travel), you could calculate fatality rates, the number of deaths divided by the population, for each mode of travel.[15] (See Table 3.2.) These rates have greater meaning because they are based upon the **population-at-risk,** those who are susceptible to disease

cases
people afflicted with a disease

rate
the number of events that occur in a given population in a given period of time

natality (birth) rate
the number of live births divided by the total population

morbidity rate
the rate of illness in a population

mortality (fatality) rate
the number of deaths in a population divided by the total population

population-at-risk
those in the population who are susceptible to a particular disease or condition

Table 3.2
Number of Deaths and Death Rates for Two Modes of Travel

	Source of Fatalities	
	Auto	Airplane
Number of fatalities per year	1,000	50
Number exposed to risk	100,000	1,000
Rate of fatality	0.01 (1/100)	0.05 (5/100)

incidence rate
the number of new cases of a disease in a population-at-risk during a particular period of time, divided by the total number in that same population

or death from a particular cause. In this case, the fatality rates are 1/100 for autos and 5/100 for airplanes, thus indicating that in this hypothetical example air travel is five times more dangerous than auto travel.

Incidence, Prevalence, and Attack Rates

acute disease
a disease that lasts three months or less

Three important types of morbidity rates are incidence rates, prevalence rates, and attack rates. An **incidence rate** is defined as the number of new cases of a disease in a population-at-risk (those in the population who are susceptible to the disease) in a given time period—the number of *new* cases of influenza in a community over a week's time, for example. Those who became ill with influenza during the previous week and remain ill during the week in question are not counted in an incidence rate. Incidence rates are important in the study of **acute diseases,** diseases in which the peak severity of symptoms occurs and subsides within days or weeks. These diseases usually move quickly through a population. Examples of acute diseases are the common cold, influenza, chicken pox, measles, and mumps.

prevalence rate
the number of new and old cases of a disease in a population in a given period of time, divided by the total number in that population

Prevalence rates are calculated by dividing *all* current cases of a disease (*old and new*) by the total population. Prevalence rates are useful for the study of **chronic disease,** diseases that usually last three months or longer. In these cases, it is more important to know how many people are currently suffering from a chronic disease—such as arthritis, heart disease, cancer, or diabetes—than it is to know when they became afflicted. Furthermore, with many chronic diseases, it is difficult or impossible to determine the date of onset of disease. Because a preponderance of health services and facilities are used for the treatment of persons with chronic diseases and conditions, prevalence rates are more useful than incidence rates for the planning of public health programs, personnel needs, and facilities.

chronic disease
a disease or health condition that lasts longer than three months

An **attack rate** is a special incidence rate calculated for a particular population for a single disease outbreak and expressed as a percentage. For example, suppose a number of people who traveled on the same airline flight developed a similar illness, and epidemiologists suspected that the cause of this illness was associated with the flight itself. An attack rate could be calculated for the passengers on that flight to express the percentage who became ill. Furthermore, attack rates could be calculated for various subpopulations, such as those seated at various locations in the plane, those who selected specific entrees from the menu, those of particular age groups, or those who boarded the flight at specific stops. Differences in attack rates for different subpopulations might indicate to the epidemiologists the source or cause of the illness.

attack rate
an incidence rate calculated for a particular population for a single disease outbreak and expressed as a percentage

Crude and Age-Adjusted Rates

crude rate
a rate in which the denominator includes the total population

Incidence and prevalence rates can be expressed in two forms—crude and specific. **Crude rates** are those in which the denominator includes the total population. The most important of these are the crude birth rate and the crude death rate. The **crude birth rate** is the number of live births in a given year, divided by the midyear population. The **crude death rate** is the total number of deaths in a given year from all causes, divided by the midyear

Table 3.3
Crude Rates

Name of Rate		Definition of Rate		Multiplier
Crude birth rate	=	Number of live births / Estimated midyear population	×	1,000
Crude death rate	=	Number of deaths (all causes) / Estimated midyear population	×	1,000

Table 3.4
Crude and Age-Adjusted Mortality Rates for Alaska and Florida, 2001

State	Number of Deaths	Crude Death Rate*	Age-Adjusted Death Rate*
Alaska	2,571	469.4	825.8
Florida	158,167	1,021.6	799.7

*Deaths per 100,000 population.

Source: Arias, E., R. N. Anderson, K. Hsiang-Ching, et al. (2003). "Deaths: Final Data for 2001." *National Vital Statistics Reports,* 52(3): 1–116.

population (see Table 3.3). Crude rates are relatively easy to obtain and are useful when comparing similar populations. But they can be misleading when populations differ by age structure or by some other attribute. For example, crude birth rates are normally higher in younger populations, which have a higher proportion of people of reproductive age, than in populations with more elderly people. Conversely, crude death rates are normally higher in older populations. This makes it difficult to use crude rates to compare the risk of death in different populations, such as those of the states of Florida and Alaska. To show what the level of mortality would be if the age composition of different populations were the same, epidemiologists use **age-adjusted rates.** For example, because of its larger senior population, Florida has a higher crude death rate (1,021.6 per 100,000) compared to Alaska's (469.4 per 100,000), where the population is younger. However, when these death rates are adjusted for differences in the age structures of the populations of these two states, one can see that the death rate in Florida (799.7 per 100,000) compares favorably with the death rate in Alaska (825.8 per 100,000). See Table 3.4.[16] Methods for calculating age-adjusted rates can be found in standard epidemiology textbooks.

Specific Rates

Specific rates measure morbidity and mortality for particular populations or for particular diseases. One could, for example, calculate the age-specific mortality rate for a population of 35- to 44-year-olds by dividing the number of deaths in that age group by the midyear population of 35- to 44-year-olds. Similarly, one could calculate race- and sex-specific mortality rates.

A very important specific rate is the **cause-specific mortality rate (CSMR),** which measures the death rate for a specific disease. This rate can be calculated by dividing the number of deaths due to a particular disease by the total population. One could also calculate an age-specific, cause-specific mortality rate. Because fewer people can be expected to die from each cause than to die from all causes, CSMRs are usually reported per 100,000 population. Table 3.5 lists some important rates used in epidemiology, defines them, and gives an example of each.

crude birth rate
the number of live births per 1,000 in a population in a given period of time

crude death rate (CDR)
the number of deaths (from all causes) per 1,000 in a population in a given period of time

age-adjusted rates
rates used to make comparisons of relative risks across groups and over time when groups differ in age structure

specific rate
a rate that measures morbidity or mortality for particular populations or diseases

cause-specific mortality rate (CSMR)
the death rate due to a particular disease

Table 3.5
Important Rates in Epidemiology

Rate		Definition		Multiplier	Examples (U.S. 2001)[16,18]
Crude birth rate	=	$\dfrac{\text{Number of live births}}{\text{Estimated midyear population}}$	×	1,000	14.5/1000
Crude death rate	=	$\dfrac{\text{Number of deaths (all causes)}}{\text{Estimated midyear population}}$	×	1,000	8.5/1000
Age-specific death rate	=	$\dfrac{\text{Number of deaths, 15--24}}{\text{Estimated midyear population, 15--24}}$	×	100,000	80.7/100,000
Infant mortality rate	=	$\dfrac{\text{Number of deaths under 1 year of age}}{\text{Number of live births}}$	×	100,000	683.4/100,000
Neonatal mortality rate	=	$\dfrac{\text{Number of deaths under 28 days of age}}{\text{Number of live births}}$	×	100,000	450/100,000
Cause-specific death rate	=	$\dfrac{\text{Number of deaths (diabetes mellitus)}}{\text{Estimated midyear population}}$	×	100,000	25.1/100,000
Age-specific, cause-specific death rate	=	$\dfrac{\text{Number of deaths, 15--24 (motor vehicles)}}{\text{Estimated midyear population}}$	×	100,000	26.8/100,000

case fatality rate (CFR)
the percentage of cases of a particular disease that result in death

Two other important measures of disease are the **case fatality rate (CFR)** and the **proportionate mortality ratio (PMR).**[17] The CFR is simply the percentage of cases that result in death. It is a measure of the severity of a disease and is directly related to the virulence of the disease agent. It is calculated by dividing the number of deaths from a particular disease in a specified period of time by the number of cases of that same disease in the same time period. The resulting fraction is multiplied by 100 and is reported as a percentage. For example, if there were 200 cases of a severe illness and 10 of them resulted in death, the CFR would be 10 ÷ 200 × 100 = 5%.

proportionate mortality ratio (PMR)
the percentage of overall mortality in a population that is attributable to a particular cause

The PMR describes the relationship between the number of deaths from a specific cause to the total number of deaths attributable to all causes. It is calculated by dividing the number of deaths attributed to a particular disease by the total number of deaths from all causes in the same population during the same period of time. This rate is also reported as a percentage. For example, in the United States, there were 700,142 deaths due to diseases of the heart in 2001, and 2,416,425 total deaths reported that same year.[16] Thus, the PMR for cardiovascular disease can be calculated as follows: 700,142 ÷ 2,416,425 × 100 = 29%. In other words, in the United States, heart disease was responsible for 29% of all deaths in 2001.

REPORTING OF BIRTHS, DEATHS, AND DISEASES

notifiable diseases
infectious diseases for which health officials request or require reporting for public health reasons

It is important to epidemiologists that births, deaths, and cases of diseases be recorded promptly and accurately. Physicians, clinics, and hospitals are required by law to report all births and deaths as well as all cases of certain **notifiable diseases** to their local health departments. Notifiable diseases are infectious diseases that can become epidemic and for which health officials maintain weekly records. The Centers for Disease Control and Prevention (CDC) issues a list of notifiable diseases for which they request reports from each state health department. This list is revised periodically. In 2002, CDC designated nearly 60 diseases as notifiable at the national level (see Table 3.6). Several diseases caused by possible

Table 3.6
Reported Cases of Notifiable Diseases, United States, 2002

Disease	Total	Disease	Total
AIDS[†]	42,745	Hepatitis C/non-A, non-B	1,853
Anthrax	2	Legionellosis	1,321
Botulism, foodborne	28	Listeriosis	665
Infant	69	Lyme disease	23,763
Other (includes wound)	21	Malaria	1,430
Brucellosis	125	Measles	44
Chancroid[§]	67	Meningococcal disease	1,814
Chlamydia[§¶]	834,555	Mumps	270
Cholera	2	Pertussis	9,771
Coccidioidomycosis**	4,968	Plague	2
Cryptosporidiosis	3,016	Psittacosis	18
Cyclosporiasis	156	Q fever	61
Diphtheria	1	Rabies, animal	7,609
Ehrlichiosis, human granulocytic	511	Rabies, human	3
Human monocytic	216	Rocky Mountain spotted fever	1,104
Encephalitis/meningitis,		Rubella	18
arboviral California serogroup	164	Rubella, congenital syndrome	1
Eastern equine	10	Salmonellosis	44,264
Powassan	1	Shigellosis	23,541
St. Louis	28	Streptococcal disease, invasive, group A	4,720
West Nile	2,840	Streptococcal toxic-shock syndrome	118
Escherichia coli, enterohemorrhagic		*Streptococcus pneumoniae,*	
(EHEC) O157:H7	3,840	invasive, drug-resistant,	2,546
EHEC, serogroup non-O157	194	Streptococcus pneumoniae, invasive, <5 yrs	513
EHEC, not serogrouped	60	Syphilis, total (all stages)[§]	32,871
Giardiasis	21,206	Congenital (age <1 yr)[§]	412
Gonorrhea[§]	351,852	Primary and secondary[§]	6,862
Haemophilus influenzae, invasive disease	1,743	Tetanus	25
Age <5 yrs, serotype b	34	Toxic-shock syndrome	109
Age <5 yrs, non-serotype b	144	Trichinosis	14
Age <5 yrs, unknown serotype	153	Tuberculosis[††]	15,075
Hansen disease	96	Tularemia	90
Hantavirus pulmonary syndrome	19	Typhoid fever	321
Hemolytic uremic syndrome, postdiarrheal	216	Varicella[§§]	22,841
Hepatitis A, acute	8,795	Varicella deaths	9
Hepatitis B, acute	7,996	Yellow fever	1

*No cases of western equine encephalitis or paralytic poliomyelitis were reported in 2002.
[†]Total number of acquired immunodeficiency syndrome (AIDS) cases reported to the Division of HIV/AIDS Prevention—Surveillance and Epidemiology, National Center for HIV, STD, and TB Prevention (NCHSTP), through December 31, 2002.
[§]Totals reported quarterly to the Division of Sexually Transmitted Diseases Prevention, NCHSTP, as of May 2, 2003.
[¶]Chlamydia refers to genital infections caused by *C. trachomatis.*
**Notifiable in <40 states.
[††]Totals reported to the Division of Tuberculosis Elimination, NCHSTP, as of March 28, 2003.
[§§]Although varicella (chickenpox) is not a nationally notifiable disease, the Council of State and Territorial Epidemiologists recommends reporting cases of this disease to CDC.

Source: Centers for Disease Control and Prevention (2004). "Summary of Notifiable Diseases—United States, 2002." *MMWR,* 51(53): 16–17.

bioterrorism agents, such as anthrax and Q fever, were added. Individual states may require the reporting of additional diseases that are of local public health concern. Local health departments are required by their respective state health departments to summarize all records of births (see Figure 3.2), deaths, and notifiable diseases, and to report them. State health departments summarize these reports and relay them to the CDC through the

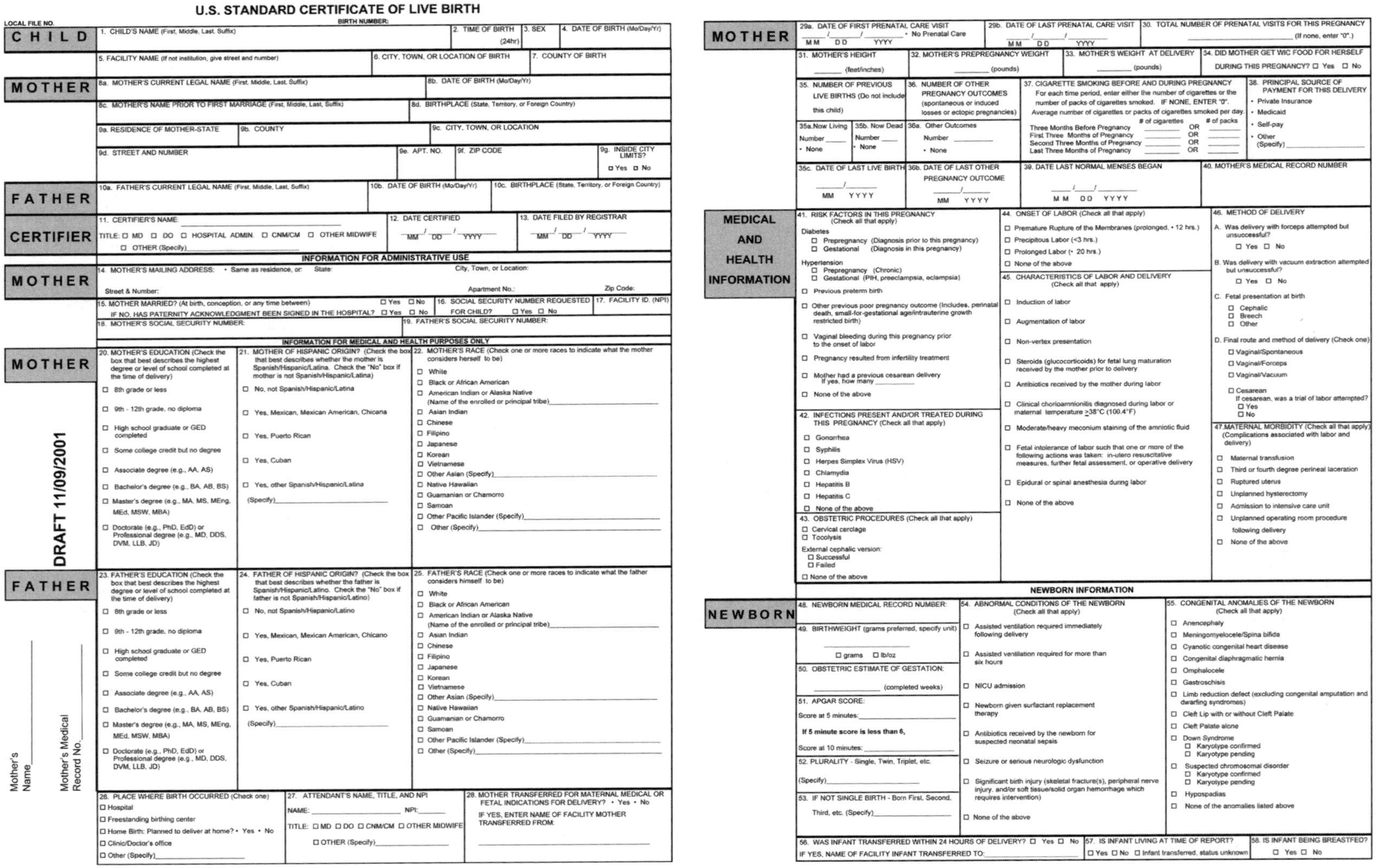

FIGURE 3.2
Birth certificates are issued by local health departments that have jurisdiction where the birth occurred.

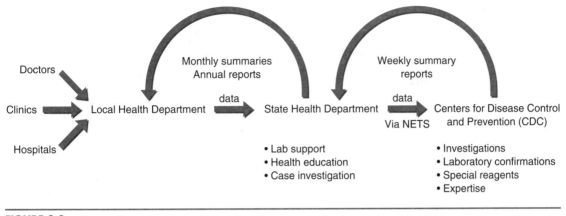

FIGURE 3.3
Scheme for the reporting of notifiable diseases.

National Electronic Telecommunications System (NETS). The reporting scheme for notifiable disease is shown in Figure 3.3.

The CDC summarizes state and territorial data and uses it to plan epidemiological research, conduct investigations, and issue reports. One series of reports, published weekly by the CDC, is called the *Morbidity and Mortality Weekly Report* (MMWR). MMWRs are available to the public at the CDC Web site www.cdc.gov/mmwr. Paper copies can usually be found in the government documents areas of certain larger libraries.

Unfortunately, the information reported is not always as good as it should be. One study estimated that local health departments may receive notification of only 35% of the cases of some communicable diseases and that many physicians are not familiar with the requirement of reporting. Clinics may not report each and every case of measles or gonorrhea. Doctors' offices and clinics may be understaffed or simply too busy to keep up with reporting. In other cases, patients recover—with or without treatment—before a diagnosis is confirmed. Also, changes in local and state government administration or other key personnel often interfere with the timely reporting of disease data. The accuracy of disease reporting also depends on the type of disease. In this regard, serious diseases are more likely to be reported than milder ones. Rabies cases, for example, are almost 100% reported while German measles cases may be only 80% to 90% reported. Therefore, morbidity data—while useful for reflecting disease trends—cannot always be considered to be precise counts of the actual number of cases of diseases.

National Electronic Telecommunications System (NETS) the electronic reporting system used by state health departments and the CDC

STANDARDIZED MEASUREMENTS OF HEALTH STATUS OF POPULATIONS

It is often difficult to precisely measure the level of wellness or, for that matter, ill health. On the other hand, death can be clearly defined. For this reason, mortality statistics continue to be the single most reliable indicator of a population's health status. While mortality statistics do not completely describe the health status of a population, they can be used to calculate other useful measurements; two of these are life expectancy and years of potential life lost. Finally, there are measurements of ill health that, while less precise than mortality, can nonetheless be meaningful. Such measurements are disability-adjusted life years (DALYs), disability-adjusted life expectancy (DALE), and health-adjusted life expectancy (HALE).

Mortality Statistics

In 2001, 2,416,425 deaths were registered in the United States. The crude mortality rate was 848.5 per 100,000. The age-adjusted death rate, which eliminates the effects of the aging population, was 854.5 deaths per 100,000 U.S. standard population. This was a record low.[16] Age-adjusted death rates show what the level of mortality would be if no changes occurred in the age make-up of the population from year to year. Thus, they are a better indicator than unadjusted (crude) death rates for examining changes in the risk of death over a period of time when the age distribution of the population is changing. Death rates and age-adjusted death rates for the 15 leading causes of death for the entire population in the United States in 2001 are presented in Table 3.7.

Naturally, morbidity and mortality rates vary greatly depending on age, sex, race, and ethnicity. For example, while heart disease is the leading cause of death for the general population and especially for seniors (those who have reached 65 years of age), cancer is the leading cause of death for the 45- to 64-years age group, and unintentional injuries are the leading cause of death for all age groups between 1 and 44. (In Chapters 7–10, we will discuss the differences in the health statistics of people in different age, sex, and minority groups.)

A study of the mortality statistics for the twentieth century reveals a shift in the leading causes of death. When the century began, communicable diseases such as pneumonia, tuberculosis, and gastrointestinal infections were the leading causes of death. However, a century of progress in public health practice and in biomedical research has resulted in a significant reduction in the proportion of deaths from communicable diseases, so that the four leading causes of death today are noncommunicable diseases (see Table 3.8). At the beginning of the twenty-first century, the five leading causes of death in the United States—heart disease, cancer, stroke, chronic obstructive pulmonary disease, and unintentional injuries (accidents and adverse effects)—account for about 68% of all deaths (see Table 3.8).[16]

This domination of annual mortality statistics by noncommunicable diseases masks the importance of communicable diseases as causes of deaths in certain age groups. For example, pneumonia and influenza still kill many seniors in this country each year. Also, HIV/AIDS, listed as the eighth overall leading cause of death for Americans as recently as 1996, kills more males than females. Thus, it is important to remember that viewing the leading causes of death for the entire population does not provide a clear picture of the health for any one segment of the population.

Life Expectancy

life expectancy
the average number of years a person from a specific cohort is projected to live from a given point in time

Life expectancy is another standard measurement used to compare the health status of various populations. Also based on mortality, **life expectancy** is defined as the average number of years a person from a specific cohort is projected to live from a given point in time. While life insurance companies are interested in life expectancy at every age, health statisticians are usually concerned with life expectancy at birth, at the age of 65 years, and, more recently, at age 75. It must be remembered that life expectancy is an average for an entire cohort (usually of a single birth year) and is not necessarily a useful prediction for any one individual. Moreover, it certainly cannot describe the quality of one's life. However, the ever-increasing life expectancy for Americans suggests that, as a country, we have managed to control some of those factors that contribute to early deaths.

Table 3.9 provides a summary of life expectancy figures for the United States from 1900 to 2000. The data presented indicate that the overall life expectancy at birth, at 65 years, and at 75 years has generally increased since 1900. Life expectancies at birth for both sexes rose from 47.3 years in 1900 to 76.9 years in 2000, when the life expectancy of a newborn baby girl was 79.5 years compared with a newborn baby boy—74.1 years.[19]

When compared with the life expectancy figures of other countries (see Table 3.10), the United States figures roughly correspond with those of other countries with well-developed

Table 3.7

Percentage of Total Deaths, Death Rates, and Age-Adjusted Death Rates for 2001, the Percent Change in Age-Adjusted Death Rates from 2000 to 2001, and the Ratio of Age-Adjusted Death Rates by Race and Sex for the 15 Leading Causes of Death for the Total U.S. Population in 2001

Rank*	Cause of Death (Based on the *Tenth Revision, International Classification of Diseases, 1992*)	Number	Percentage of Total Deaths	2001 Crude Death Rate	Age-Adjusted Death Rate				
					2001	Percent Change 2000 to 2001	Ratio Male to female	Ratio Black to white	Ratio Hispanic to white non-Hispanic
...	All causes	2,416,425	100.0	848.5	854.5	−1.7	1.4	1.3	0.8
1	Diseases of heart	700,142	29.0	245.8	247.8	−3.8	1.5	1.3	0.8
2	Malignant neoplasms	553,768	22.9	194.4	196.0	−1.8	1.5	1.3	0.7
3	Cerebrovascular diseases	163,538	6.8	57.4	57.9	−4.9	1.0	1.4	0.8
4	Chronic lower respiratory diseases	123,013	5.1	43.2	43.7	−1.1	1.4	0.7	0.4
5	Accidents (unintentional injuries)	101,537	4.2	35.7	35.7	2.3	2.2	1.0	0.8
6	Diabetes mellitus	71,372	3.0	25.1	25.3	1.2	1.2	2.1	1.7
7	Influenza and pneumonia	62,034	2.6	21.8	22.0	−7.2	1.4	1.1	0.9
8	Alzheimer's disease	53,852	2.2	18.9	19.1	5.5	0.8	0.7	0.5
9	Nephritis, nephrotic syndrome, and nephrosis	39,480	1.6	13.9	14.0	3.7	1.5	2.4	1.0
10	Septicemia	32,238	1.3	11.3	11.4	0.9	1.2	2.3	0.8
11	Intentional self-harm (suicide)	30,622	1.3	10.8	10.7	2.9	4.6	0.5	0.5
12	Chronic liver disease and cirrhosis	27,035	1.1	9.5	9.5	0	2.1	1.0	1.8
13	Assault (homicide)	20,308	0.8	7.1	7.1	20.3	3.3	4.3	2.1
14	Essential (primary) hypertension and hypertensive disease	19,250	0.8	6.8	6.8	4.6	1.0	2.9	1.1
15	Pneumonitis due to solids and liquids	17,301	0.7	6.1	6.1	0	1.8	1.1	0.7
...	All other causes	400,935	16.6	140.8	...	...	...	...	...

*Rank is based on number of deaths.

... Category not applicable.

Note: Death rates are on an annual basis per 100,000 population; age-adjusted rates are per 100,000 U.S. standard population.

Source: Arias, E., R. N. Anderson, K. Hsiang-Ching, et al. (2003). "Deaths: Final Data for 2001." *National Vital Statistics Report*, 52(3): 8.

Table 3.8
Leading Causes of Death in the United States: 1900, 1940, 2001

1900

1.	Pneumonia, influenza
2.	Tuberculosis
3.	Diarrhea
4.	Diseases of the heart
5.	Cerebrovascular diseases (stroke)
6.	Nephritis
7.	Unintentional injuries (accidents)
8.	Malignant neoplasms (cancers)
9.	Senility
10.	Diphtheria

1940

1.	Diseases of the heart
2.	Malignant neoplasms (cancers)
3.	Cerebrovascular diseases (stroke)
4.	Nephritis
5.	Pneumonia, influenza
6.	Unintentional injuries (non-motor vehicle)
7.	Tuberculosis
8.	Diabetes mellitus
9.	Unintentional injuries (motor vehicle)
10.	Premature birth

2001

1.	Diseases of the heart
2.	Malignant neoplasms (cancers)
3.	Cerebrovascular diseases (stroke)
4.	Chronic obstructive pulmonary diseases
5.	Unintentional injuries (all)
6.	Diabetes mellitus
7.	Influenza and pneumonia
8.	Alzheimer's disease
9.	Nephritis (kidney diseases)
10.	Septicemia

Table 3.9
Life Expectancy at Birth, at 65 Years of Age, and at 75 Years of Age According to Sex: In the United States, During the Selected Years 1900–2000

	At Birth			At 65 Years			At 75 Years		
Year	Both Sexes	Male	Female	Both Sexes	Male	Female	Both Sexes	Male	Female
1900	47.3	46.3	48.3	11.9	11.5	12.2	*	*	*
1950	68.2	65.6	71.1	13.9	12.8	15.0	*	*	*
1960	69.7	66.6	73.1	14.3	12.8	15.8	*	*	*
1970	70.8	67.1	74.7	15.2	13.1	17.0	*	*	*
1980	73.7	70.7	77.4	16.4	14.1	18.3	10.4	8.8	11.5
1990	75.4	71.8	78.8	17.2	15.1	18.9	10.9	9.4	12.0
2000	76.9	74.1	79.5	17.9	16.3	19.2	11.3	10.1	12.2

*Data not available.

Source: Adapted from the National Center for Health Statistics (2003). *Health, United States, 2003 with Chartbook on Trends in the Health of Americans.* (HHS pub. no. 2003-1232). Hyattsville, MD: Public Health Service.

Table 3.10
Life Expectancy at Birth for Selected Countries by Sex in 1980 and 2002

	1980	2002
Ethiopia	42	42
Malawi	44	38
India	54	63
Nicaragua	59	69
Ecuador	63	70
Congo, Dem, Rep.	50	45
Thailand	64	69
Poland	70	74
Malaysia	67	73
South Africa	57	46
Brazil	63	69
Latvia	69	70
Korea, Republic of	67	74
Greece	74	78
New Zealand	73	78
United Kingdom	74	77
United States	74	78
Sweden	76	80
Japan	76	81

Source: World Bank (2003). Adapted from www.worldbank.org/data/wdi2003/.

economies. The highest life expectancy figures are reported in Japan (81 years in 2002) while the lowest are reported from countries in Africa.[20] Note that in three African countries— Congo, Malawi, and South Africa—life expectancy has declined since 1980, in part because of HIV/AIDS.

Years of Potential Life Lost

While standard mortality statistics, such as leading causes of death, provide one measure of the importance of various diseases, **years of potential life lost (YPLL)** provides another, different measure. YPLL is calculated by subtracting a person's age at death from his or her life expectancy. Such calculations are difficult because each person may have a different life expectancy at any given time. Thus, the ages 65 years or 75 years are often used in these calculations. For a person who dies at age 59, the YPLL-75 is 16. For many years in the United States, a death prior to 65 years was considered a premature death, perhaps because 65 was the standard age of retirement and when full Social Security payments could begin. Now, however, 75 years of age is increasingly being used to calculate YPLL because the life expectancy for a child born today is about 75 years (see Table 3.9). People are living longer, and many of us know people who continue to work beyond the age of 65; examples include former President Ronald Reagan, his successor, George Bush, and former South Carolina Senator Strom Thurmond, who served as a U.S. Senator into his 90s.

YPLL weights deaths such that the death of a very young person counts more than the death of a very old person. Table 3.11 provides a summary of the age-adjusted YPLL before 75 (YPLL-75) for the 10 leading causes of death in the United States for 1990 and 2000.[19] In examining this table, note that the number of YPLL-75 per 100,000 population was higher for malignant neoplasms (cancer) than for heart disease. Also, YPLL resulting from unintentional injuries was third highest. This is because unintentional injuries and malignant neoplasms (cancer) often kill people when they are young. These differences can also be seen in the two

years of potential life lost (YPLL) the number of years lost when death occurs before the age of 65 or 75

Table 3.11
Age-Adjusted Years of Potential Life Lost Before 75 (YPLL-75) for the 10 Leading Causes of Death, United States, 1990 and 2000

	YPLL per 100,000 Population	
Cause	1990	2000
Diseases of the heart	1,617.7	1,253.0
Malignant neoplasms (cancer)	2,003.8	1,674.1
Cerebrovascular diseases (stroke)	259.6	223.3
Chronic lower respiratory diseases	187.4	188.1
Unintentional injuries	1,162.1	1,026.5
Influenza and pneumonia	141.5	87.1
Diabetes mellitus	155.9	178.4
Human immunodeficiency virus infection (HIV/AIDS)	383.8	147.6
Suicide	393.1	334.5
Homicide and legal intervention	417.4	266.5

Source: Adapted from National Center for Health Statistics (2003). *Health, United States, 2003 with Chartbook on Trends in the Health of Americans* (HHS pub. no. 2003-1232). Hyattsville, MD: Author.

pie charts shown in Figure 3.4. Also, notice that the YPLL-75 per 100,000 population declined for most of the leading causes of death between 1990 and 2000. An important exception is for diabetes mellitus, a disease that is becoming epidemic in the United States.

YPLL from specific causes varies depending upon the gender and face of the subpopulation under consideration. For example, the YPLL-75 per 100,000 population due to unintentional injuries is nearly three times as high for men as it is for women. The YPLL-75 per 100,000 for diseases of the heart for blacks is nearly twice that for whites, and for homicide, it is nearly six times greater.[19]

Disability-Adjusted Life Years (DALYs)

disability-adjusted life years (DALYs)
a measure for the burden of disease that takes into account premature death and loss of healthy life resulting from disability

Mortality does not entirely express the burden of disease. For example, chronic depression and paralysis caused by polio are responsible for great loss of healthy life but are not reflected in mortality tables. Because of this, the World Health Organization (WHO) and the World Bank have developed a measure called the **disability-adjusted life years (DALYs).**[20]

The DALY has emerged as a measure of the burden of disease and it reflects the total amount of healthy life lost, to all causes whether from premature mortality or from some degree of disability during a period of time. These disabilities can be physical or mental. The intended use of the DALY is to assist (i) in setting health service priorities; (ii) in identifying disadvantaged groups and targeting of health interventions; and (iii) in providing a comparable measure of output for intervention, program and sector evaluation and planning.[21]

One DALY is thus one lost year of healthy life. Total DALYs for a given condition for a particular population can be calculated by estimating the total YPLL and the total years of life lived with disability, and then by summing these totals. As an example, the DALYs incurred through firearm injuries in the United States could be calculated by adding the total of YPLL incurred from fatal firearm injuries to the total years of life lived with disabilities by survivors of firearm injuries. Figure 3.5 illustrates the number of DALYs lost per 1,000 in 1990 from eight demographic regions of the world.[20]

Disability-Adjusted Life Expectancy (DALE) and Health-Adjusted Life Expectancy (HALE)

disability-adjusted life expectancy (DALE)
the number of healthy years of life that can be expected on average in a given population

Two other measurements of good health and good health care systems used by the World Health Organization are **disability-adjusted life expectancy (DALE)** and health-adjusted

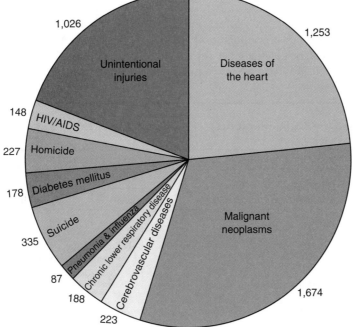

Deaths by Cause, United States, 2000

- 617,316 — All other causes
- 710,760 — Diseases of the heart
- 69,301 — Diabetes mellitus
- 65,313 — Influenza and pneumonia
- 97,900 — Unintentional injuries
- 122,009 — Chronic obstr. lung diseases
- 167,661 — Cerebrovascular diseases
- 553,091 — Malignant neoplasms

YPLL for Leading Causes of Death, 2000

- 1,026 — Unintentional injuries
- 1,253 — Diseases of the heart
- 148 — HIV/AIDS
- 227 — Homicide
- 178 — Diabetes mellitus
- 335 — Suicide
- 87 — Pneumonia & influenza
- 188 — Chronic lower respiratory disease
- 223 — Cerebrovascular diseases
- 1,674 — Malignant neoplasms

FIGURE 3.4

Deaths by cause in the United States, 2000, and the years of potential life lost (YPLL) per 100,000 population for the leading causes of death within the United States, 2000.

Source: National Center for Health Statistics (2003). *Health, United States, 2003 with Chartbook on Trends in the Health of Americans* (HHS pub. no. 2003-1232). Hyattsville, MD: Author.

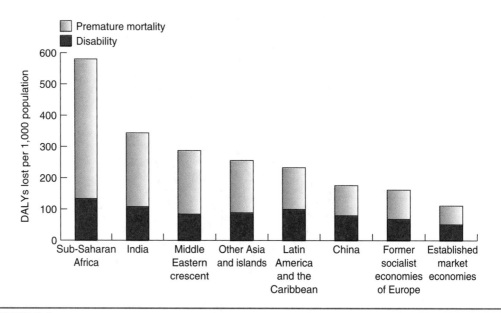

FIGURE 3.5

Burden of disease (disability-adjusted life years lost per 1,000) attributable to premature mortality and disability, by demographic region, 1990.

Source: Murray, D. J., and A. D. Lopez, eds. (1996). *The Global Burden of Disease: A Comprehensive Assessment of Mortality and Disability from Diseases, Injuries and Risk Factors in 1990 and Projected to 2020* (Global Burden of Diseases and Injury, vol. 1). Cambridge, MA: Harvard School of Public Health on behalf of WHO.

life expectancy (HALE). These are estimates of the number of healthy years of life that can be expected on average in a given population. While they are usually calculated at birth (like life expectancy), DALEs can be calculated at any age. DALEs and HALEs have the advantage of capturing all causes of disability across a population and relating them to *life expectancy* as

Table 3.12
Disability-Adjusted Life Expectancy (DALE) for Selected Member Nations of the World Health Organization

		Males		Females	
	Both Sexes	**At Birth**	**At Age 60**	**At Birth**	**At Age 60**
Nation	**At Birth**				
Japan	74.5	71.9	17.5	77.2	21.6
United Kingdom	71.7	69.7	15.7	73.7	18.6
United States	70.0	67.5	15.0	72.6	18.4
Chile	68.6	66.0	14.3	71.3	17.8
Republic of Korea	65.0	62.3	12.1	67.7	15.2
Mexico	65.0	62.4	14.7	67.6	16.8
China	62.3	61.2	11.6	63.3	13.5
Iraq	55.3	55.4	9.2	55.1	8.2
North Korea	52.3	51.4	9.6	53.1	11.6
Congo	45.1	44.3	10.7	45.9	12.8
South Africa	39.8	38.6	6.8	41.0	9.3
Zimbabwe	32.9	33.4	8.8	32.4	10.1
Malawi	29.4	29.3	6.8	29.4	8.3
Sierra Leone	25.9	25.8	6.6	30.1	9.6

Source: Mathers, C. C. , R. Sdana, J. A. Salomon, C. J. L. Murray, and A. D. Lopez (2000). *Estimates of DALE for 191 Countries: Methods and Results* (Global Programme on Evidence for Health Policy Working Paper no. 16). Geneva, Switzerland: World Health Organization. Used with permission of the World Health Organization.

defined by mortality.[22] In 24 countries, DALEs are estimated to equal or exceed 70 years, and in more than half of the countries that belong to WHO, DALEs are equal to or exceed 60 years. In 32 countries, DALEs are estimated to be less than 40 years.[22] DALE and HALE measure approximately the same thing, namely, expected remaining years of healthy life, but they are calculated differently because they differ in the way they measure disability levels.[22] Table 3.12 displays the DALE for selected countries for both sexes at birth and for males and females at birth and at 60 years of age.

Sources of Standardized Data

Because demographic and epidemiological data are used in the planning of public health programs and facilities, students of community health should be aware of the sources of these standardized data. Students can obtain standardized data for use in community health work from the following sources: The U.S. Census, the *Statistical Abstract of the United States,* the *Monthly Vital Statistics Report, Morbidity and Mortality Weekly Report,* the National Health Interview Survey, the National Health and Nutrition Examination Survey, the Behavioral Risk Factor Surveillance System, the Youth Risk Behavior Surveillance System, the National Hospital Discharge Survey, and the National Hospital Ambulatory Medical Care Survey.

Each of these sources of national data has a specific value and usefulness to those in the public health field. Students interested in studying local health problems can obtain data from state and local health departments, hospitals, volunteer agencies, and disease registries. The study and analysis of these data provide a basis for planning appropriate health programs and facilities in your communities.

The U.S. Census

The **U.S. Census,** taken every 10 years, is an enumeration of the population living in the United States. George Washington ordered the first census in 1790 for the purpose of apportioning representation to the House of Representatives. Through the years, the census form has become much more complex than the one filled out 200 years earlier. Data are gathered about income, employment, family size, education, dwelling type, and many other social indicators (see Figure 3.6). Copies of the U.S. Census results are available in most libraries.

U.S. Census
the enumeration of the population of the United States that is conducted every 10 years

Census data are important to health workers because they are used for calculating disease and death rates and for program planning. The U.S. Census is carried out by the Bureau of the Census, located in the U.S. Department of Commerce. Information is available at www.census.gov.

Statistical Abstract of the United States

Another Bureau of the Census publication is the *Statistical Abstract of the United States* (SA). This book, published annually, is the standard summary of statistics on the social, political, and economic organization of the United States. Information is divided into sections under headings such as Population, Vital Statistics, Health and Nutrition, Education, Law Enforcement, Courts and Prisons, and many more. Data contained in the SA are extremely useful and are reasonably up-to-date. (A new edition is published every January and includes data from two years before the publication date.) The SA can be purchased from the Government Printing Office for about $50 and is available in most libraries. Information is also available at www.census.gov/statab/www/.

Monthly Vital Statistics Report

The National Center for Health Statistics (NCHS), one of the Centers for Disease Control and Prevention (CDC), provides the most up-to-date national vital statistics available. These statistics appear in the *Monthly Vital Statistics Report,* published by the NCHS in Hyattsville,

FIGURE 3.6
A census worker collects data used to calculate disease rates.

vital statistics
statistical summaries of records of major life events such as births, deaths, marriages, divorces, and infant deaths

Maryland. **Vital statistics** are statistical summaries of vital records, records of major life events. Listed are live births, deaths, marriages, divorces, and infant deaths. Death rates are also calculated by race and age, and in some issues, by cause. Selected issues also provide mortality data for specific causes (for example, diabetes, drug overdoses, and heart disease). Copies of this publication are available in government document areas of university and large public libraries, on the Web at www.cdc.gov/nchs/, or by writing directly to the NCHS (6525 Belcrest Rd., Hyattsville, MD 20782).

Morbidity and Mortality Weekly Report

Reported cases of specified notifiable diseases are reported weekly in the *Morbidity and Mortality Weekly Report* (MMWR), which lists morbidity and mortality data by state and region of the country. The report is prepared by the Centers for Disease Control and Prevention (CDC) based upon reports from state health departments. This report is printed and distributed through an agreement with the Massachusetts Medical Society, publishers of the *New England Journal of Medicine.* Each weekly issue also contains several reports of outbreaks of disease, environmental hazards, unusual cases, or other public health problems. The MMWR and its annual summary reports are available in larger libraries, on the Web at www.cdc.gov/mmwr, and by subscription from the Massachusetts Medical Society (P.O. Box 9120, Waltham, MA 02254-9120).

National Health Surveys

Another source of standardized data is the National Health Surveys. These surveys are a result of the National Health Survey Act of 1956. This act authorized a continuing survey of the amount, distribution, and effects of illness and disability in the United States. The intent of this act is currently being fulfilled by three types of surveys: (1) health interviews of people; (2) clinical tests, measurements, and physical examinations of people; and (3) surveys of places where people receive medical care, such as hospitals, clinics, and doctors' offices. The following paragraphs describe these surveys. More information about these surveys and results is available at the National Center for Health Statistics Web site, www.cdc.gov/nchs.

National Health Interview Survey

In the *National Health Interview Survey* (NHIS), conducted by the National Center for Health Statistics (NCHS), people are asked numerous questions about their health. One of the questions asks respondents to describe their health status using one of five categories— excellent, very good, good, fair, or poor. Less than 1 in 10 of the respondents in 2001 described their health status as either fair or poor, while 7 in 10 Americans believe they are in very good or excellent health. College graduates (44%) were about three times as likely as persons who had not graduated from high school (16%) to be in excellent health.

Persons with family incomes of $75,000 or more were almost twice as likely as those with incomes of less than $20,000 to be in excellent health (51% vs. 26%).[23]

It is important to remember that these data were generated by self-reported responses to NHIS questions and not by actual examinations objectively generated in a clinic. As such, respondents may over-report good health habits or under-report bad ones. Such reporting is often dependent on the respondent's perceived social stigma or support for a response and the degree to which people's responses are confidential or anonymous. Furthermore, people have widely divergent views on what constitutes poor or good health. For example, many sedentary, cigarette-smoking, high-stress people see themselves as being in good health, while "health nuts" feel their health is deteriorating when they miss a day of exercise. In general, the young assess their health better than the old do, males better than females, whites better than blacks, and those with large family incomes better than those with smaller ones.

National Health and Nutrition Examination Survey

Another of the National Health Surveys is the *National Health and Nutrition Examination Survey* (NHANES). The purpose of the NHANES is to assess the health and nutritional status of the general U.S. population. Using a mobile examination center (see Figure 3.7), the data are collected through direct physical examinations, clinical and laboratory testing, and related procedures on a representative group of Americans. These examinations result in the most authoritative source of standardized clinical, physical, and physiological data on the American people. Included in the data are the prevalence of specific conditions and diseases and data on blood pressure, serum cholesterol, body measurements, nutritional status and deficiencies, and exposure to environmental toxins.

The first series of these surveys, known as *National Health Examination Surveys* (NHES), were carried out during the 1960s. Beginning in the 1970s, nutrition was added as a new focus, and the surveys became known as the *National Health and Nutrition Examination Survey* (NHANES). Three cycles of the NHANES have been conducted by the National Center for Health Statistics. The third (and most recent) cycle (NHANES III) began in 1988 and ended in 1994. During that six-year period, approximately 40,000 persons were examined. A special version of this survey, the *Hispanic Health and Nutrition Examination Survey,* was conducted in 1982 to 1984. This survey provided data on a 12,000-person sample of three subgroups of the Hispanic population: Mexican-Americans in the Southwest; Cubans in Miami (Dade County), Florida; and Puerto Ricans in the New York City area.

Behavioral Risk Factor Surveillance System

The *Behavioral Risk Factor Surveillance System* (BRFSS) is a state-based telephone survey of the civilian, noninstitutional, adult population conducted by the Behavioral Surveillance Branch, a division of Adult and Community Health, National Center for Chronic Disease Prevention and

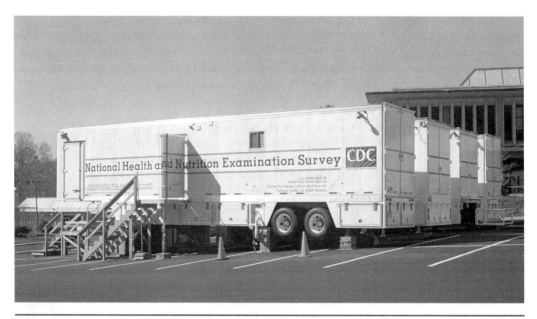

FIGURE 3.7
A National Health and Nutrition Examination Survey (NHANES) mobile examination center.

Health Promotion at the CDC. This survey seeks to ascertain the prevalence of such high-risk behaviors as cigarette smoking, excessive alcohol consumption, and physical inactivity, and the lack of preventive health care such as screening for cancer. These results are published periodically as part of MMWR's *CDC Surveillance Summaries* and are available wherever copies of the CDC MMWR are found. Information is also available at www.cdc.gov/brfss.

Youth Risk Behavior Surveillance System

The *Youth Risk Behavior Surveillance System* (YRBSS) monitors six categories of priority health-risk behaviors among youth and young adults: behaviors that contribute to unintentional and intentional injuries, tobacco use, alcohol and other drug use, sexual behaviors, unhealthy dietary behaviors, and physical inactivity."[24] Included in the YRBSS are three kinds of surveys: (1) high school–based survey, (2) household-based survey of youth (12–21 years of age), and (3) a college-based survey. The YRBSS is conducted by the Division of Adolescent and School Health, National Center for Chronic Disease Prevention and Health Promotion at the Centers for Disease Control and Prevention, and the results are published as part of MMWR's *CDC Surveillance Summaries*. Information is also available at www.cdc.gov/nccdphp/dash/yrbs/.

National Health Care Survey

The *National Health Care Survey* (NHCS) includes about eight different national surveys that gather information on the nation's health care system. Two of the best known health care surveys are the *National Hospital Discharge Survey* (NHDS) and the *National Hospital Ambulatory Medical Care Survey* (NHAMCS). The NHDS provides data on the characteristics of patients discharged from non-federal, short-stay hospitals. These data can be used to examine a variety of important public health issues such as hospitalization rates for selected inpatient surgical procedures, infectious diseases, injuries, substance abuse, and other health problems. It can also be used to estimate costs for public health problems. The NHAMCS gathers and disseminates information about the health care provided by hospital outpatient departments and emergency departments. Summaries of the results of these surveys are published by the National Center for

Health Statistics, Centers for Disease Control and Prevention, and are available at the National Health Care Survey Web site, www.cdc.gov/nchs/nhcs.

EPIDEMIOLOGICAL STUDIES

When disease and/or death occurs in unexpected or unacceptable numbers, epidemiologists may carry out investigations. These investigations may be descriptive, analytical, or experimental in nature, depending upon the objectives of the specific study.

Descriptive Studies

Descriptive studies seek to describe the extent of an outbreak in regard to person, time, and place. These studies are designed to answer the questions *who, when,* and *where*. To answer the first question, epidemiologists first take a "head count" to determine how many cases of a disease have occurred. At this time, they also try to determine who is ill—children, elders, men, women, or both. The data they gather should permit them to develop a summary of cases by age, sex, race, marital status, and type of employment.

To answer the second question (*when*), epidemiologists must determine the time of the onset of illness for each case. The resulting data can be used to prepare an **epidemic curve,** a graphic display of the cases of disease by the time or date of the onset of their symptoms. Three types of epidemic curves are commonly used in descriptive studies—secular, seasonal, and single epidemic curves. The secular display of a disease shows the distribution of cases over many years (e.g., cases of paralytic poliomyelitis for the period 1972 to 2002; see Figure 3.8). Secular graphs illustrate the long-term trend of a disease. A graph of the case data by season or month is usually prepared to show cyclical changes in the numbers of cases of a disease. Cases of arthropod-borne viral infections, for example, peak in the late summer months, following the seasonal rise in populations of the mosquitoes that transmit them (see Figure 3.9).

descriptive study
an epidemiological study that describes an epidemic with respect to person, place, and time

epidemic curve
a graphic display of the cases of disease according to the time or date of onset of symptoms

---

FIGURE 3.8

Vaccine-associated paralytic poliomyelitis: reported cases by year, United States, 1972–2002.

Note: An inactivated poliomyelitis vaccine (IPV) was first licensed in 1955. An oral vaccine was licensed in 1961. No cases of vaccine-associated paralytic poliomyelitis have been reported since the all-IPV schedule was implemented in 2000.

Source: Centers for Disease Control and Prevention (2004). "Summary of Notifiable Diseases—United States, 2002." *MMWR,* 51(53): 1–88.

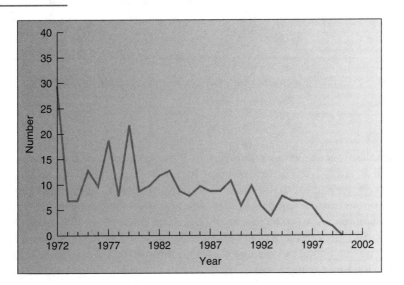

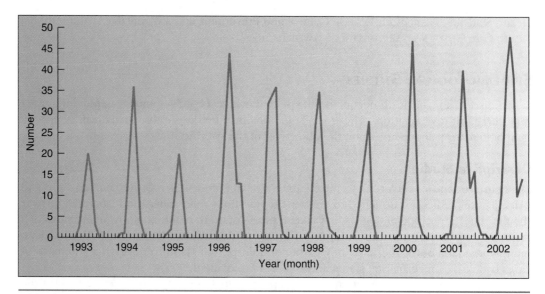

FIGURE 3.9

Encephalitis/meningitis—reported cases of California serogroup viruses by month of onset—United States, 1993–2002.

Source: Centers for Disease Control and Prevention (2004). "Summary of Notifiable Diseases—United States, 2002." *MMWR,* 51(53): 1–88.

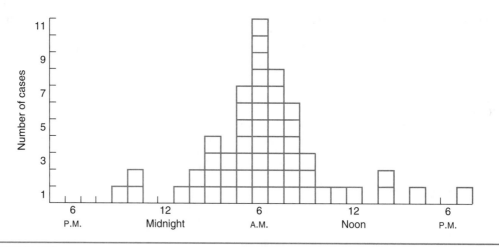

FIGURE 3.10

Point source epidemic curve: Cases of gastroenteritis following ingestion of a common food source.

Source: CDC.

point source epidemic curve
an epidemic curve depicting a distribution of cases which all can be traced to a single source of exposure

Epidemic curves for single epidemics vary in appearance with each disease outbreak; however, two classical types exist. The first is the **point source epidemic curve** (see Figure 3.10). In a point source epidemic, each case can be traced to an exposure to the same source—spoiled food, for example. Because an epidemic curve shows cases of a disease by time or date of the onset of their symptoms, the epidemic curve for a single epidemic can be used to calculate the **incubation period,** the period of time between exposure to an infectious agent and the onset of symptoms. The incubation period, together with the symptoms, can often help epidemiologists determine the cause of the disease.

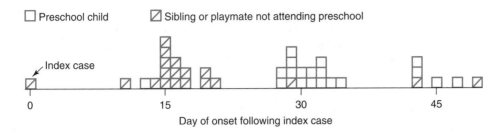

FIGURE 3.11

Propagated epidemic curve: Cases of chickenpox during April through June.

Source: CDC.

The second type of epidemic curve for a solitary outbreak is a **propagated epidemic curve.** In this type of epidemic, primary cases appear first at the end of the incubation period following exposure to an infected source. *Secondary cases* arise after a second incubation period, and they represent exposure to the primary cases; *tertiary cases* appear even later due to exposure to secondary cases, and so on. Because new cases give rise to more new cases, this type of epidemic is termed a *propagated epidemic*. Epidemics of communicable diseases like chickenpox follow this pattern (see Figure 3.11).

Finally, epidemiologists must determine *where* the outbreak occurred. To determine where the illnesses may have originated, the residential address and travel history of each case are recorded. This information provides a geographic distribution of cases and helps to delineate the extent of the outbreak. By plotting cases on a map, along with natural features such as streams and human-made structures such as factories, it is sometimes possible to learn something about the source of the disease.

A descriptive study is usually the first epidemiological study carried out on a disease. Detectable patterns of cases may provide investigators with ideas that can lead to a hypothesis about the cause or source of a disease.

As important and useful as they are, descriptive studies have limited usefulness. Results from descriptive studies are usually not applicable to outbreaks elsewhere. Also, the investigation of a single epidemic cannot provide information about disease trends. Lastly, with few exceptions, descriptive studies by themselves rarely identify with certainty the cause of an outbreak.

Analytical Studies

A second type of epidemiological study is the **analytical study.** The purpose of analytical studies is to test hypotheses about relationships between health problems and possible **risk factors,** factors that increase the probability of disease. While front-line community health workers usually do not conduct analytical studies, it is important that students of community health understand how they are carried out and what kinds of data they generate. Only through such an understanding can those who work in community health interpret the findings of these studies to others in the community, who may then apply the knowledge to improve their own health and that of the community.

An example of an analytical study might be one designed to discover whether diabetes (health problem) is associated with obesity (possible risk factor), or whether lung cancer (health problem) is associated with cigarette smoking (possible risk factor). It is important to remember that the associations discovered through analytical epidemiological studies are not always cause-and-effect associations.

There are two types of analytical studies—retrospective and prospective. **Retrospective studies** are epidemiological studies that compare people with disease (cases) to healthy

incubation period
the period between exposure to a disease and the onset of symptoms

propagated epidemic curve
an epidemic curve depicting a distribution of cases traceable to multiple sources of exposure

analytical study
an epidemiological study aimed at testing hypotheses

risk factors
factors that increase the probability of disease, injury, or death

retrospective study (case/control study)
a study that seeks to compare those diagnosed with a disease with those who do not have the disease for prior exposure to specific risk factors

people of similar age, sex, and background (controls), with respect to prior exposure to possible risk factors. These **case/control studies** are aimed at identifying familial, environmental, or behavioral factors that are more common or more pronounced in the case group than in the control group. Such factors could be associated with the disease under study. For example, epidemiologists might wish to study the factors associated with cervical cancer in women.

To carry out this study, epidemiologists would identify a number of women with cervical cancer (cases) and an equal or larger number of healthy women (controls). Medical histories for each group would be obtained and compared. In this hypothetical example, an examination of the histories suggests that cigarette smoking is more prevalent in the case group. If exposure to the possible risk factor (smoking) is significantly greater in the cases (of cervical cancer) than in the controls, an association is said to exist. Note that this association may or may not be one of cause and effect. Further studies are usually necessary to confirm initial findings. Retrospective studies almost never prove causation by themselves. Instead, they usually indicate the direction for future studies.

Prospective studies or **cohort studies** are epidemiological studies in which the researcher selects a **cohort,** a large number of healthy subjects that share a similar experience such as year of birth or high school graduation. Subjects in this cohort are then classified on the basis of their exposure to one or more possible causative factors such as cigarette smoking, dietary habits, or other factors. The entire cohort is then observed for a number of years to determine the rate at which disease develops in each subgroup that was classified by exposure factor.

It is important to note the difference in the type of results obtained from retrospective and prospective studies and the advantages and disadvantages of each type of study. In retrospective studies, results obtained are not true incidence rates because disease was already present at the beginning of the study; that is, there were cases and controls to begin with, rather than a population-at-risk. For this reason, retrospective studies can only provide a probability statement about the association between factor and disease. This probability statement can be stated mathematically as an odds ratio. The following is a hypothetical example of such a probability statement: Lung cancer patients have a probability of having smoked cigarettes that is 11 times greater than that of the control group. The **odds ratio** in this case is 11:1. (For a more detailed description of how to calculate an odds ratio and relative risk, see Appendix 1.)

In prospective studies, one begins with a population-at-risk, and therefore is able to calculate the risk for developing disease associated with each examined factor. This **relative risk** states the relationship between the risk for acquiring the disease in the presence of the risk factor to the risk of acquiring the disease in the absence of the risk factor. An example of a relative risk statement is: Smokers are 11 times more likely to develop lung cancer than are nonsmokers.

Although prospective studies yield a relative risk, they have three distinct disadvantages: (1) they are expensive, (2) they usually take many years to complete, and (3) they are not very useful for studying rare diseases because the disease may not develop in the cohort. Retrospective studies, on the other hand, are less expensive to carry out, can be completed more quickly, and are useful for studying rare diseases because one can select the cases. Unfortunately, they cannot yield a true risk for acquiring a disease.

Experimental Studies

Experimental studies are carried out in order to identify the cause of a disease or to determine the effectiveness of a vaccine, therapeutic drug, or surgical procedure. The central feature of experimental studies is the *control of variables* surrounding the experimental subjects. These subjects may be humans but more often are animals such as laboratory mice, rats, or monkeys. The use of research animals in experimental studies is necessary to determine the safety and effectiveness of new therapeutic agents or medical procedures with minimum risk to human health.

Whether animals or humans are used, every effort is made to reduce unwanted variability associated with the experimental subjects. In the case of animal studies, the variables over which the experimenter may wish to exert control include age, sex, diet, and environmental conditions. In addition to controlling variables, three other principles are essential to properly designed experimental studies—*control groups, randomization,* and *blindness.*

The use of *control groups* means that the experimental treatment (intervention) such as drug, vaccine, smoke-free environment, or special diet, is withheld from a portion of the subjects. These subjects belong to the control group, which receives blank doses or treatments, called **placebos.** In order for a treatment regimen to be considered effective or for a factor to be considered causally related, it must significantly affect the *treatment group* differently (usually determined using a statistical test) from the control group.

placebo
a blank treatment

Randomization refers to the practice of assigning subjects to treatments or control groups in a completely random manner. This can be accomplished by assigning numbers to subjects and then having numbers selected randomly. Numbers can be selected randomly from a table of random numbers, by drawing lots, or by using a computer-generated list of random numbers. Thus, each research subject, human or animal, has an equal chance of being placed in the treatment group.

Blindness refers to the practice in which the researcher remains uninformed and unaware of the identities of treatment and control groups throughout the period of experimentation and data gathering. This prevents the researcher from looking favorably or unfavorably on the responses of any particular subject or group while gathering data during the experiment. Thus, the researcher can remain unbiased.

When studies involve human subjects, it is important that the subjects also remain uninformed as to whether they have been placed in the treatment group or control (placebo) group. Such a procedure is referred to as *double blind* (neither researcher nor subjects know who is receiving the treatment), and it often involves the use of a placebo, such as a saline (salt-water) injection or sugar pill. The use of a placebo prevents subjects from determining by observation whether or not they are receiving treatment. This is important because human thought processes are such that some people begin to feel better if they believe they have received a treatment. In order for a vaccine or therapeutic drug to be labeled as effective, it must consistently perform better than a placebo.

An example of just such an experiment was performed by Tonnesen and his colleagues, who studied the effectiveness of a 16-hour nicotine patch on smoking cessation.[25] They used a double-blind randomized design to compare the effects of a nicotine skin patch with those of a placebo skin patch. Subjects were assigned to the active treatment or the placebo according to computer-generated random numbers. There were 145 subjects who received a nicotine patch and 144 who received the placebo. Subjects were scheduled for visits 1, 3, 6, 12, 26, and 52 weeks after the first visit—the day smoking cessation was to begin. Table 3.13 presents the results of cessation for each group 6, 12, 26, and 52 weeks after the study began. The results of this study indicated that there was a significant difference between the effectiveness of the nicotine patch and the placebo patch with regard to smoking cessation.

Controlling variables, the use of treatment and control groups, randomization, and blindness are techniques aimed at ensuring objectivity and avoiding bias in experimental studies. Through strict adherence to these principles, researchers hope to achieve experimental results that accurately reflect what occurs in a natural setting.

Table 3.13
Percentage of Subjects Abstaining from Smoking 6, 12, 26, and 52 Weeks after the Start of the Program

Week Number	Percentage of People Remaining Abstinent	
	Nicotine Patch	Placebo Patch
6	53	17
12	41	10
26	24	5
52	17	4

Source: Tonnesen, P., J. Norregaard, K. Simonsen, and U. Sawe (1991). "A Double-Blind Trial of a 16-Hour Transdermal Nicotine Patch in Smoking Cessation." *New England Journal of Medicine,* 325(5): 311–315.

By carrying out carefully planned descriptive studies, epidemiologists define outbreaks of disease, injury, and death in specific populations and develop hypotheses about the causes of these outbreaks. By designing and carrying out analytical and experimental studies, epidemiologists test these hypotheses. In the next chapter, we will examine how this knowledge is used to prevent and control diseases in the community.

Chapter Summary

- Epidemiology is the study of the distribution and determinants of disease and injuries in the community. It is an old science that has become more sophisticated in recent years.

- Rates of birth, death, injury, and disease are essential tools for epidemiologists.

- Incidence rates are a measurement of the number of new cases of disease, injury, or death in a population over a given period of time, while prevalence rates measure all cases. An attack rate is a special kind of incidence rate used for a single outbreak.

- Cases of certain diseases, called notifiable or reportable diseases, are reported by doctors, clinics, and hospitals to local health agencies. These agencies then report them to state health agencies, who then forward the data on to the CDC. These reports assist epidemiologists who study disease trends.

- The health status of a population or community can be measured in a number of different ways, including mortality statistics, life expectancy, years of potential life lost (YPLL), disability-adjusted life years (DALYs), disability-adjusted life expectancy (DALE), and health-adjusted life expectancy (HALE).

- Epidemiologists also consult the data available from the U.S. Census, the *Statistical Abstract of the United States,* the *Monthly Vital Statistics Report,* the *Morbidity and Mortality Weekly Report,* and a variety of national health surveys.

- Epidemiologists conduct three general types of studies to learn about disease and injury in populations—descriptive studies, analytical studies, and experimental studies.

- Descriptive studies describe the extent of outbreaks in regard to person, place, and time.

- Analytical studies test hypotheses regarding associations between diseases and risk factors.

- Experimental studies examine the effects of specific factors under carefully controlled conditions.

- The purpose of each of these studies is to help determine the cause of disease, injury, and death in the community and to provide information that will assist in controlling current outbreaks and preventing future ones.

Review Questions

1. What is an epidemic? A pandemic? Name some diseases that caused epidemics in the past. Name some diseases that are epidemic today.

2. Why are epidemiologists sometimes interested in epizootics?

3. What does the term *endemic disease* mean? Give examples of such diseases.

4. What is the difference between natality, morbidity, and mortality?

5. Why are rates important in community health?

6. What is the difference between crude and specific rates?

7. Why are prevalence rates more useful than incidence rates for measuring of chronic diseases?

SCENARIO: ANALYSIS AND RESPONSE

Assume that you were Kim and you were able to reach Dr. Turner, the local health officer. He then asked whether you would like to help in the investigation of the food-borne outbreak mentioned in the scenario. You agreed to help. So far, you have learned that on Sunday, May 28, 49 people were at a picnic where they had eaten, beginning about noon. People began to report their illnesses later that night. Dr. Turner developed a food-borne outbreak investigation worksheet, which you helped to complete by making numerous phone calls and house visits with the public health nurse. The histories of people attending the picnic appear in Table 3.14.

Using Table 3.15, the Epidemic Curve Tally Sheet, you tally the cases by hour of onset of illness. Using the results of the tally, you establish the incubation period—the range of hours (after the meal) over which symptoms started. Next, you prepare a graph to illustrate the epidemic curve of the outbreak. Try to answer the following questions:

1. What is the incubation period?
2. Does the curve you prepared suggest a single- or multiple-exposure epidemic?
3. Based solely on the incubation period, can you make a guess as to the cause of the outbreak?

Table 3.14
Histories Obtained from Persons Eating Picnic Lunch

Person No.	Bread	Butter	Turkey	Potato Salad	Milk	Jell-O	Ill*	Not Ill
1			X	X	X		7:30	
2	X	X		X	X			X
3	X	X	X	X	X	X	8:00	
4			X		X	X		X
5			X	X	X		9:15	
6			X	X	X		7:40	
7	X	X		X	X			X
8	X	X	X	X	X	X	8:10	
9			X		X	X		X
10			X	X	X	X	10:15	
11	X			X		X		X
12	X	X	X	X	X	X	8:30	
13			X		X			X
14	X	X	X	X	X	X	9:30	
15	X	X		X	X	X		X
16	X			X		X		X
17	X	X	X	X	X	X	8:35	
18			X		X			X
19	X	X	X	X	X	X	10:05	
20	X	X		X	X	X		X
21			X		X	X	9:15	
22	X	X		X	X	X		X
23	X	X			X	X	8:30	
24	X	X			X	X		X
25	X	X	X	X	X	X	12:30 A.M.	
26			X		X	X	9:20	
27	X	X		X	X	X		X
28	X	X	X		X	X	8:40	
29	X	X			X	X		X
30	X	X	X	X	X		12:15 A.M.	
31			X	X	X		7:30	
32	X	X		X	X			X
33	X	X	X	X	X	X	8:00	
34			X		X	X		X
35			X	X	X		10:30	

(continued)

Table 3.14 (continued)

Person No.	Bread	Butter	Turkey	Potato Salad	Milk	Jell-O	Ill*	Not Ill
36			x	x	x		7:30	
37	x	x		x	x			x
38	x	x	x	x	x	x	8:05	
39			x		x	x		x
40			x	x	x	x	9:45	
41	x			x		x		x
42	x	x	x	x	x	x	8:30	
43			x		x			x
44	x	x	x	x	x	x	9:30	
45	x	x		x	x	x		x
46	x			x		x		x
47	x	x	x	x	x	x	8:30	
48			x		x	x		x
49	x	x	x	x	x	x	10:10	

*All time is p.m. unless otherwise indicated.

Table 3.15
Epidemic Curve Tally Sheet

Time of Onset	Tally	Number	Incubation Period
7:00–7:59			
8:00–8:59			
9:00–9:59			
10:00–10:59			
11:00–11:59			
12:00–12:59			

Unfortunately, by the time the investigation began, all the picnic food had been discarded, and no samples were available for laboratory testing. In order to determine which food at the picnic might have caused the outbreak, you need to calculate attack rates for people eating each food as well as for people not eating each food. Using Table 3.16, the Attack Rate Work Sheet, calculate the attack rates for those who ate and did not eat each food served.

1. Which food would you most suspect of causing the illness?
2. Based on this information, what might the causative agent have been?
3. How could the Internet be of assistance to health department officials in this situation?

Table 3.16
Attack Rate Work Sheet

Food	Persons Eating Food				Persons Not Eating Food			
	Total	Ill	Well	Attack Rate	Total	Ill	Well	Attack Rate
Bread								
Butter								
Turkey								
Potato salad								
Milk								
Jell-O								

8. What is an infant mortality rate? Why is it such an important rate in community health?

9. What are notifiable diseases? Give some examples.

10. In general, contrast the leading causes of death in the United States in 1900 with those in 2000. Comment on the differences.

11. At what ages is life expectancy calculated? What does it tell us about a population? Which country has the longest life expectancy?

12. What are years of potential life lost (YPLL)? How does calculating YPLL change the way we think about the leading causes of death?

13. How would you define disability-adjusted life years (DALYs)? How would you define disability-adjusted life expectancy (DALE)?

14. What is the U.S. Census? How often is it conducted? What types of data does it gather?

15. What types of information can you find in the *Statistical Abstract of the United States*?

16. What kinds of data would you expect to find in the Centers for Disease Control and Prevention's *Morbidity and Mortality Weekly Report*?

17. List five important national health surveys that are valuable sources of data about the health and health care of our population.

18. What can be said about the reliability of self-reported health data?

19. What is the National Health Care Survey? Why is it carried out?

20. In a descriptive epidemiological study, what types of information does the epidemiologist gather?

21. What is the purpose of an analytical study? Contrast retrospective and prospective studies in regard to methodology and usefulness.

22. How do experimental studies differ from analytical studies? What value do they have in epidemiology? To what four principles must researchers adhere in order to properly carry out an experimental study?

ACTIVITIES

1. When you hear the word *epidemic,* what disease comes to your mind first? Ask this question of 10 people you know, allowing them time to think and give you an answer. Try to find people of different ages as you complete your informal poll. List their answers on paper. Are there any answers that surprise you? Does your list include both classic and contemporary epidemic diseases?

2. Look at the data in Table 3.17. What conclusion can you draw about the risk for acquiring tuberculosis for

Table 3.17
Reported Tuberculosis Cases, by Age Group, Low Socioeconomic Area, City of Dixon, 1960

Age Group in Years	Number of Cases	Age Group in Years	Number of Cases
0-4	7	35-44	6
5-14	7	45-54	9
15-24	6	55-64	8
25-34	10	65+	7

Table 3.18
Reported Tuberculosis Cases and Incidence Rates per 100,000, Low Socioeconomic Area, City of Dixon, 1960

Age Group in Years	Number of Cases	Population of Age Group	Rate*
0-4	7	8,638	81.0
5-14	7	13,098	53.4
15-24	6	10,247	58.5
25-34	10	8,680	115.2
35-44	6	7,528	79.7
45-54	9	6,736	133.6
55-64	8	4,534	176.4
65+	7	4,075	171.8
Total	60	63,536	94.4

*Example: 7 cases ÷ 8,638 population × 100,000 = 81.0.

populations in each age group? Write down your answer. Now examine Table 3.18. Which age groups exhibit the highest disease rates? Explain why it is important to calculate rates to report disease outbreaks accurately.

3. There are 346 students at Hillside School. During March and April, 56 pupils were absent with chickenpox. What is the attack rate for chickenpox at Hillside School? The 56 pupils who were absent had 88 brothers and sisters at home. Of the 88 siblings, 19 developed chickenpox. What was the attack rate among these children? Of the 75 total cases of chickenpox, one child died. Calculate the case fatality rate for chickenpox in this epidemic.

4. In an epidemic in Sample City (population 100,000—60,000 males and 40,000 females), there were 600 cases (350 males, 250 females) of a severe disease. There were 70 deaths (all males) due to this disease and 880 deaths due to causes other than the specific disease. Calculate the following—crude death rate, cause-specific mortality rate, case fatality rate, cause-specific morbidity rate for females, and case fatality rate for males.

5. Visit, call, or write your state or local health department. Ask for the total number of birth and death

certificates issued for the latest year for which complete data are available. Assuming no migration into or out of your state or county occurred, what is the natural rate of population increase (number of births minus number of deaths)? Try to obtain an estimate of the total population of the state or county for that same year. Calculate a crude birth rate and a crude death rate (number of births and deaths) per 1,000 population.

6. Using the data presented in Table 3.9, estimate (as best you can) the life expectancy of your siblings, parents, and grandparents at birth. If your grandparents are older than 65, determine what their life expectancies were when they turned 65. If you were to fulfill your life expectancy exactly, in what year can you expect to die?

7. Visit your campus library and locate the *American Journal of Epidemiology*. Examine several recent issues, taking note of the different types of articles as they appear in the Table of Contents. Select six articles and read the abstracts. On a piece of paper, list the titles of these articles. Were these descriptive, analytical, or experimental studies? After each title that you have listed, put either the letter D (descriptive), A (analytical), or E (experimental) to denote the type of study that you examined.

 ## COMMUNITY HEALTH ON THE WEB

The Internet contains a wealth of information about community and public health. Increase your knowledge of some of the topics presented in this chapter by accessing the Jones and Bartlett Publishers Web site at **health.jbpub.com/communityhealth/5e** and follow the links to complete the following activities.

- Epidemiology Program Office
- Morbidity and Mortality Weekly Report
- National Center for Health Statistics

REFERENCES

1. Mausner, J. S., and S. Kramer (1985). *Epidemiology: An Introductory Text.* Philadelphia: WB Saunders, 1.

2. United Nations Programme on HIV/AIDS (2004). *AIDS Epidemic Update 2003.* Available at http://www.unaids.org/en/Resources/Publications.

3. Monath, T. P. (1980). *St. Louis Encephalitis.* Washington, DC: American Public Health Association, 240.

4. Centers for Disease Control and Prevention (2003). "Summary of Notifiable Diseases—United States, 2001." *Morbidity and Mortality Weekly Report,* 50(53): 1-108.

5. Centers for Disease Control and Prevention (1981). "Toxic Shock Syndrome—United States, 1970-1980." *Morbidity and Mortality Weekly Report,* 30(3): 25-33.

6. Centers for Disease Control and Prevention (2003). *HIV/AIDS Surveillance Report, Basic Statistics—Cumulative Cases.* Available at http://www.cdc.gov/hiv/stats.htm.

7. Centers for Disease Control and Prevention (2004). "Lyme Disease: Epidemiology." Available at http://www.cdc.gov/ncidod/dvbid/lyme/epi.htm.

8. Centers for Disease Control and Prevention (2004). "West Nile Virus." Available at http://www.cdc.gov/ncidod/dvbid/westnile/index.htm.

9. Centers for Disease Control and Prevention (2004). "Severe Acute Respiratory Syndrome (SARS)." Available at http://www.cdc.gov/ncidod/sars/factsheet.htm.

10. Centers for Disease Control and Prevention (2004). "Monkeypox: Report of Cases in the United States." Available at http://www.cdc.gov/od/oc/media/mpv/cases.htm.

11. Markellis, V. C. (December 1985-January 1986). "Epidemiology: Cornerstone for Health Education." *Health Education,* 15-17.

12. Gale, A. H. (1959). *Epidemiologic Disease.* London: Pelican Books, 25.

13. Woodruff, A. W. (1977). "Benjamin Rush, His Work on Yellow Fever and His British Connections." *American Journal of Tropical Medicine and Hygiene,* 26(5): 1055-1059.

14. Snow, J. (1963). "The Broad Street Pump." In: B. Rouche, ed., *Curiosities of Medicine.* Boston: Little, Brown.

15. Mausner, J. S., and S. Kramer (1985). *Epidemiology: An Introductory Text.* Philadelphia: WB Saunders, 5.

16. Arias, E., R.N. Anderson, K. Hsiang-Ching, S.L. Murphy, and K.D. Kochanek (2003). "Deaths: Final Data for 2001." *National Vital Statistics Report,* 52(3): 8.

17. Morton, R. F., J. R. Hebel, and R. J. Carter (2000). *A Study Guide to Epidemiology and Biostatistics,* 5th ed. Gaithersburg, MD: Aspen Publishers, 21.

18. Martin, J.A., B. E. Hamilton, S. J. Ventura, F. Menacker, M. M. Park, and P. D. Sutton (2002). "Births: Final Data for 2001." *National Vital Statistics Report,* 51(2): 1-104.

19. National Center for Health Statistics (2003). *Health, United States, 2003 with Chartbook on Trends in the Health of Americans* (HHS pub. no. 2003-1232). Hyattsville, MD: Author.

20. Murray, D. J. L., and A. D. Lopez, eds. (1996). *The Global Burden of Disease: A Comprehensive Assessment of Mortality and Disability from Diseases, Injuries and Risk Factors in 1990 and Projected to 2020* (Global Burden of Diseases and Injury, vol. 1). Cambridge, MA: Harvard School of Public Health on behalf of WHO.

21. Homedes, N. (2000). *The Disability-Adjusted Life Year (DALY) Definition, Measurement and Potential Use* (World Bank: Human Capital Development and Operations Policy Working Papers). Available at http://www.worldbank.org/html/extdr/hnp/hddflash/workp/wp_00068.html.

22. Mathers, C. C., R. Sdana, J. A. Salomon, C. J. L. Murray, and A. D. Lopez (2000). *Estimates of DALE for 191 Countries: Methods and Results* (Global Programme on Evidence for Health Policy Working Paper no. 16). Geneva, Switzerland: World Health Organization.

23. Barnes, P. M., P. F. Adams, and J. S. Schiller (2003). "Summary Health Statistics for the U.S. Population: National Health Interview Survey, 2001." *Vital and Health Statistics,* 10(217).

24. Centers for Disease Control and Prevention (June 2002). "Youth Risk Behavior Surveillance—United States, 2001." *MMWR Surveillance Summaries,* 51(SS-4): 1-64.

25. Tonnesen, P., J. Norregaard, K. Simonsen, and U. Sawe (1991). "A Double-Blind Trial of a 16-Hour Transdermal Nicotine Patch in Smoking Cessation." *New England Journal of Medicine,* 325(5): 311-315.

Chapter 4

Epidemiology: Prevention and Control of Diseases and Health Conditions

Chapter Objectives

After studying this chapter you will be able to:

1 Explain the differences between communicable (infectious) and noncommunicable (noninfectious) diseases and between acute and chronic diseases and provide examples of each.

2 Describe and explain communicable and multicausation disease models.

3 Explain how communicable diseases are transmitted in a community using the "chain of infection" model and use a specific communicable disease to illustrate your explanation.

4 Explain why noncommunicable diseases are a community health concern and provide some examples of important noncommunicable diseases.

5 Explain the difference between primary, secondary, and tertiary prevention of disease and provide examples of each.

6 List and explain the various criteria that communities might use in order to prioritize their health problems in preparation for the allocation of prevention and control resources.

7 List and discuss important measures for preventing and controlling the spread of communicable diseases in a community.

8 List and discuss approaches to noncommunicable disease control in the community.

9 Define and explain the purpose and importance of *health screenings*.

10 Outline a chronic, noncommunicable disease control program that includes primary, secondary, and tertiary disease prevention components.

SCENARIO

Bob had always been an active and athletic person. He lettered in three sports in high school and played varsity tennis in college. Following graduation last May, he was lucky enough to land a job with one of the Fortune 500 companies in nearby Indianapolis. He shares an apartment with Chuck, a business colleague, and both work long hours in the hope that hard work will mean success and advancement. Neither seems to find time to exercise regularly, and both rely increasingly on "fast-food" restaurants. Bob's weight is now 12 pounds above his weight at graduation.

Bob is beginning to wonder whether he is compromising his health for financial success. When he first came to the company, he took the stairs between floors two at a time and was never winded, even after climbing several flights. Now he becomes tired after two flights. Also, Bob recently participated in a free serum cholesterol screening. Bob's cholesterol level was 259 mg/dL. Bob decided it was time to have a complete physical examination.

Introduction

In Chapter 3 we discussed the measurement and reporting of disease and the use of rates and ratios to describe disease incidence and prevalence. We then explained how epidemiologists describe disease outbreaks by person, place, and time, and how they search for causal associations through analytical and experimental studies.

In this chapter, we extend our discussion of epidemiology. We begin by describing the different ways to classify diseases and other health conditions. Then, we explain models of communicable and noncommunicable diseases, conceptual frameworks used by epidemiologists to develop prevention and control strategies. We also discuss criteria used by communities to prioritize their health problems and allocate health resources. Finally, we discuss some approaches to disease prevention and control; introduce the concepts of primary, secondary, and tertiary prevention; and provide examples of their application to a communicable and noncommunicable disease.

Classification of Diseases and Health Problems

Diseases and health problems can be classified in several meaningful ways. The public often classifies diseases by organ or organ system, such as kidney disease, heart disease, respiratory infection, and so on. Another method of classification is by causative agent—viral disease, chemical poisoning, physical injury, and so forth. In this scheme, causative agents may be biological, chemical, or physical. Biological agents include viruses, rickettsiae, bacteria, protozoa, fungi, and metazoa (multicellular organisms). Chemical agents include drugs, pesticides, industrial chemicals, food additives, air pollutants, and cigarette smoke. Physical agents that can cause injury or disease include various forms of energy such as heat, ultraviolet light, radiation, noise vibrations, and speeding or falling objects (see Table 4.1). In community health, diseases are usually classified as acute or chronic, or as communicable (infectious) or noncommunicable (noninfectious).

Communicable Versus Noncommunicable Diseases

Another important classification system divides diseases into communicable and noncommunicable diseases. **Communicable (infectious) diseases** are those diseases for which biological agents or their products are the cause and that are transmissible from one individual

communicable disease (infectious disease) an illness caused by some specific biological agent or its toxic products that can be transmitted from an infected person, animal, or inanimate reservoir to a susceptible host

Table 4.1
Causative Agents for Diseases and Injuries

Biological Agents	Chemical Agents	Physical Agents
Viruses	Pesticides	Heat
Rickettsiae	Food additives	Light
Bacteria	Pharmacologics	Radiation
Fungi	Industrial chemicals	Noise
Protozoa	Air pollutants	Vibration
Metazoa	Cigarette smoke	Speeding objects

to another. The disease process begins when the agent is able to lodge and grow or reproduce within the body of the host. The process of lodgment and growth of a microorganism or virus in the host is called *infection*.

Noncommunicable (noninfectious) diseases or illnesses are those that cannot be transmitted from an infected person to a susceptible, healthy one. Delineating the causes of noncommunicable diseases is often more difficult because several, or even many, factors may contribute to the development of a given noncommunicable health condition. These contributing factors may be genetic, environmental, or behavioral in nature. For this reason, many noncommunicable health conditions are called multicausation diseases; an example of such is heart disease. Genetics, environmental factors such as stress, and behavioral choices such as poor diet and lack of exercise can all contribute to heart disease.

noncommunicable disease (noninfectious disease) a disease that cannot be transmitted from infected host to susceptible host

Acute Versus Chronic Diseases and Illnesses

In the acute/chronic classification scheme, diseases are classified by their duration of symptoms. Acute diseases, as defined in Chapter 3, are diseases in which the peak severity of symptoms occurs and subsides within three months (usually sooner) and the recovery of those who survive is usually complete. Examples of acute communicable diseases include the common cold, influenza (flu), chickenpox, measles, mumps, Rocky Mountain spotted fever, and plague. Examples of acute noncommunicable illnesses are appendicitis, injuries from motor vehicle crashes, acute alcohol intoxication or drug overdose, and sprained ankles (see Table 4.2).

Chronic diseases or conditions are those in which symptoms continue longer than three months, and in some cases, for the remainder of one's life (see Figure 4.1). Recovery is slow and sometimes incomplete. These diseases can be either communicable or noncommunicable. Examples of chronic communicable diseases are AIDS, tuberculosis, herpes virus infections, syphilis, and Lyme disease. Chronic noncommunicable illnesses include hypertension, hypercholesterolemia, coronary heart disease, diabetes, and many types of arthritis and cancer.

Table 4.2
Classification of Diseases

Types of Diseases	Examples
Acute Diseases	
Communicable	Common cold, pneumonia, mumps, measles, pertussis, typhoid fever, cholera
Noncommunicable	Appendicitis, poisoning, injury (due to motor vehicle crash, fire, gunshot, etc.)
Chronic Diseases	
Communicable	AIDS, Lyme disease, tuberculosis, syphilis, rheumatic fever following streptococcal infections, hepatitis B
Noncommunicable	Diabetes, coronary heart disease, osteoarthritis, cirrhosis of the liver due to alcoholism

FIGURE 4.1
Arthritis is a noninfectious chronic condition that can persist for one's entire life.

COMMUNICABLE DISEASES

infectivity
the ability of a biological agent to lodge and grow in the host

While **infectivity** refers to the ability of a biological agent to lodge and grow in a host, the term **pathogenicity** refers to an infectious disease agent's ability to produce disease. Selected pathogenic agents and the diseases they cause are listed in Table 4.3. Under certain conditions, pathogenic, biological agents can be transmitted from an infected individual in

pathogenicity
the capability of a communicable disease agent to cause disease in a susceptible host

Table 4.3
Biological Agents of Disease

Types of Agent	Name of Agent	Disease
Viruses	Varicella virus	Chickenpox
	Human immunodeficiency virus (HIV)	Acquired immunodeficiency syndrome (AIDS)
	Rubella virus	German measles
Rickettsiae	*Rickettsia rickettsii*	Rocky Mountain spotted fever
Bacteria	*Vibrio cholerae*	Cholera
	Clostridium tetani	Tetanus
	Yersinia pestis	Plague
	Borrelia burgdorferi	Lyme disease
Protozoa	*Entamoeba histolytica*	Amoebic dysentery
	Plasmodium falciparum	Malaria
	Trypanosoma gambiense	African sleeping sickness
Fungi and yeasts	*Tinea cruris*	Jock itch
	Tinea pedis	Athlete's foot
Nematoda (worms)	*Wuchereria bancrofti*	Filariasis (elephantiasis)
	Onchocerca volvulus	Onchocerciasis (river blindness)

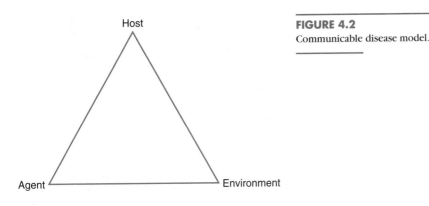

FIGURE 4.2
Communicable disease model.

the community to an uninfected, susceptible one. Noncommunicable diseases are unable to be transmitted as such. Communicable disease agents may be further classified, as will be explained later, according to the manner in which they are transmitted.

The elements of a simplified **communicable disease model**—agent, host, and environment—are presented in Figure 4.2. These three factors seem to sum up the minimal requirements for the occurrence and spread of communicable diseases in a population. In this model, the **agent** is the element that must be present in order for disease to occur. For example, the influenza virus must be present for a person to become ill with influenza (flu). The **host** is any susceptible organism—a single-celled organism, a plant, an animal, or a human—invaded by an infectious agent. The *environment* includes all other factors—physical, biological, or social—that inhibit or promote disease transmission. Communicable disease transmission occurs when a susceptible host and a pathogenic agent exist in an environment conducive to disease transmission.

Chain of Infection

Communicable disease transmission is a complicated but well-studied process that is best understood through a conceptual model known as the **chain of infection** (see Figure 4.3). Using the chain of infection model, one can visualize the step-by-step process by which communicable diseases spread from an infected person to an uninfected person in the community. The *pathogenic* (disease-producing) agent leaves its *reservoir* (infected host) via a *portal of exit*. *Transmission* occurs in either a direct or indirect manner, and the pathogenic agent enters a susceptible host through a *portal of entry* in order to establish disease. For example, let us follow the common cold through the chain of infection. The agent (the cold virus) leaves its reservoir (the throat of an infected person), perhaps when the host sneezes. The portals of exit are the nose and mouth. Transmission may be direct if saliva droplets enter the respiratory tract of a susceptible host at close range, or it may be indirect if droplets dry and

communicable disease model
a visual representation of the interrelationships between causative agent, host, and environment

agent (pathogenic agent)
the cause of the disease or health problem

host
a person or other living organism that affords subsistence or lodgment to a communicable agent under natural conditions

chain of infection
a model to conceptualize the transmission of a communicable disease from its source to a susceptible host

FIGURE 4.3
Chain of infection.

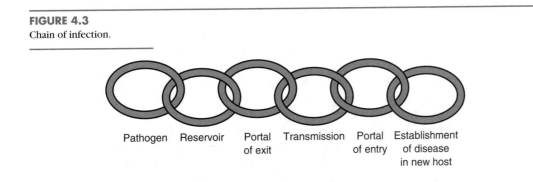

Pathogen   Reservoir   Portal of exit   Transmission   Portal of entry   Establishment of disease in new host

FIGURE 4.4
Portal of exit: The causative agents for many respiratory diseases leave their host via the mouth and nose.

case
a person who is sick with a disease

carrier
a person or animal that harbors a specific communicable agent in the absence of discernible clinical disease and serves as a potential source of infection to others

zoonosis
a communicable disease transmissible under natural conditions from vertebrate animals to humans

anthroponosis
a disease that infects only humans

direct transmission
the immediate transfer of an infectious agent by direct contact between infected and susceptible individuals

indirect transmission
communicable disease transmission involving an intermediate step

become airborne. The portal of entry could be the nose or mouth of a susceptible host. The agent enters, and a new infection is established.

There are many variations in the chain of infection, depending upon the disease agent, environmental conditions, infectivity, and host susceptibility. For example, the reservoir for a disease may be a **case**—a person who has the disease—or a **carrier**—one who is well but infected and is capable of serving as a source of infection. A (disease) carrier could be one who is incubating the disease, such as a person who is HIV positive but has no signs of AIDS, or one who has recovered from the disease (is asymptomatic), as is sometimes the case in typhoid fever. For some diseases, the reservoir is not humans but animals. Diseases for which the reservoir resides in animal populations are called **zoonoses.** Plague, rabies, Rocky Mountain spotted fever, and Lyme disease are zoonoses. Diseases for which humans are the only known reservoir, like measles, are known as **anthroponoses.**

Portals of exit (see Figure 4.4) and entry vary from disease to disease. Natural portals of exit and examples of diseases that use them are the respiratory tract (cold, influenza, measles, tuberculosis, and whooping cough), urogenital tract (gonorrhea, syphilis, herpes, and AIDS), digestive tract (amoebic dysentery, shigellosis, polio, typhoid fever, and cholera), and skin (ringworm and jock itch). The skin is actually a good barrier to infection, but it can be bypassed by a hypodermic needle or when there is an open wound. Blood-sucking insects and ticks make their own portals of entry with mouth parts that penetrate the skin. Finally, many pathogenic agents can cross the placenta from mother to fetus (for example, rubella virus, syphilis spirochetes, and hepatitis B virus).

Modes of Transmission

As noted in the previous paragraphs, communicable disease transmission may be direct or indirect. **Direct transmission** implies the immediate transfer of the disease agent between the infected and the susceptible individuals by direct contact "such as touching, biting, kissing, sexual intercourse, or by direct projection (droplet spread) of droplet spray onto the conjunctiva or onto the mucous membranes of the eye, nose or mouth during sneezing, coughing, spitting, singing or talking (usually limited to a distance of one meter or less)."[1] Examples of diseases for which transmission is usually direct are AIDS, syphilis, gonorrhea, rabies, and the common cold.

Indirect transmission may be one of three types—airborne, vehicleborne, or vectorborne. *Airborne transmission* is the dissemination of microbial aerosols to a suitable portal of entry, usually the respiratory tract. Microbial aerosols are suspensions of dust or droplet nuclei made up wholly or in part of microorganisms. These particles may remain suspended and infective for long periods of time. Tuberculosis, influenza, histoplasmosis, and legionellosis are examples of airborne diseases.

In *vehicleborne transmission,* contaminated materials or objects (fomites) serve as **vehicles**—nonliving objects by which communicable agents are transferred to a susceptible host. The agent may or may not have multiplied or developed on the vehicle. Examples of vehicles include toys, handkerchiefs, soiled clothes, bedding, food service utensils, and surgical instruments. Also considered vehicles are water, milk, food, or biological products such as blood, serum, plasma, organs, and tissues. Almost any disease can be transmitted by vehicles, including those for which the primary mode of transmission is direct, such as dysentery and hepatitis.

Vectorborne transmission is the transfer of disease by a living organism such as a mosquito, fly, or tick. Transmission may be mechanical, via the contaminated mouth parts or feet of the **vector,** or biological, which involves multiplication or developmental changes of the agent in the vector before transmission occurs. In *mechanical transmission,* multiplication and development of the disease organism usually do not occur. For example, organisms that cause dysentery, polio, cholera, and typhoid fever have been isolated from insects such as cockroaches and houseflies and could presumably be deposited on food prepared for human consumption.

FIGURE 4.5

A blacklegged tick, *Ixodes scapularis* (nymph). The nymph is the stage that is responsible for transmitting most of the cases of Lyme disease.

In *biological transmission,* multiplication and/or developmental changes of the disease agent occur in the vector before transmission occurs. Biological transmission is much more important than mechanical transmission in terms of its impact on community health. Examples of biological vectors include mosquitoes, fleas, lice, ticks, flies, and other insects. Mosquitoes are by far the most important vectors of human disease. They transmit the viruses that cause yellow fever and dengue fever as well as more than 200 other viruses, including West Nile fever virus. They also transmit malaria, which infects 100 million people in the world each year (mostly in tropical areas), killing at least 1 million of them. Ticks, another important vector, transmit Rocky Mountain spotted fever, relapsing fever, and Lyme disease (see Figure 4.5). Other insect vectors (and the diseases they transmit) are flies (African sleeping sickness, onchocerciasis, loiasis, and leishmaniasis), fleas (plague and murine typhus), lice (epidemic typhus and trench fever), and kissing bugs (Chagas' disease).

NONCOMMUNICABLE DISEASES

While communicable diseases remain an important concern for communities, certain noncommunicable diseases, such as heart disease, stroke, and cancer, now rank high among the nation's leading causes of death. While these diseases are not infectious, they nonetheless can occur in epidemic proportions. Furthermore, the chronic nature of many of these diseases means that they can deplete a community's resources quite rapidly.

The complex **etiologies** (causes) of many of the noncommunicable diseases, such as coronary heart disease, are best illustrated by the **multicausation disease model** (see Figure 4.6). In this model, the human host is pictured in the center of the environment in which he or she lives. Within the host, there exists a unique genetic endowment that is inalterable. The host exists in an environment comprising a multitude of factors that can contribute to the disease process. These environmental factors may be physical, chemical, biological, or social in nature.

Physical factors include the latitude, climate, and physical geography of where one lives. The major health risks in the tropics—communicable and parasitic diseases—are different

vehicle
inanimate materials or objects that can serve as a source of infection

vector
a living organism, usually an arthropod (e.g., mosquito, tick, louse, or flea), that can transmit a communicable agent to susceptible hosts

etiology
the cause of a disease

multicausation disease model
a visual representation of the host together with various internal and external factors that promote and protect against disease

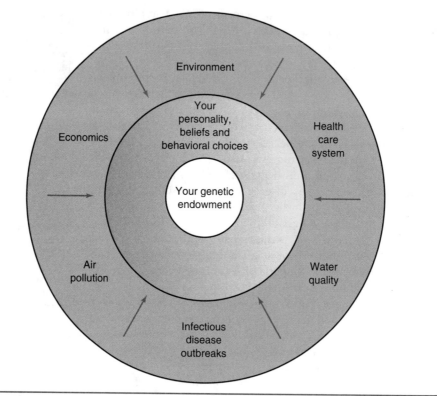

FIGURE 4.6
Multicausation disease model.

from those in temperate regions with cold winters—difficulty in finding food and remaining warm. Chemical factors include not only natural chemical hazards of polluted water and air but also the added pollutants of our modern, industrial society. Biological hazards include communicable disease agents such as pathogenic viruses, bacteria, and fungi. Social factors include one's choice of occupation, recreational activities, and living arrangements. Poor choices in life can increase one's risk factors, which is detrimental to one's health.

Diseases of the Heart and Blood Vessels

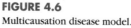

coronary heart disease (CHD) a chronic disease characterized by damage to the coronary arteries in the heart

Diseases of the heart and blood vessels, cardiovascular diseases (CVDs), are a leading cause of death in the United States. **Coronary heart disease (CHD)** is the Number 1 killer of Americans. In 2001 alone, more than 700,000 people died of heart disease in the United States[2] and it was estimated that more than 64 million Americans have one or more types of CVD.[3]

The American Heart Association lists nine types of CVDs: CHD, stroke, high blood pressure, arrhythmias, diseases of the arteries, congestive heart failure, valvular heart disease, rheumatic fever/rheumatic heart disease, and congenital heart defects.[3] CHD causes more than half of all cardiovascular disease deaths. Sometimes called *coronary artery disease,* CHD is characterized by damage to the coronary arteries, the blood vessels that carry oxygen-rich blood to the heart muscle. Damage to the coronary arteries usually evolves from the condition known as *atherosclerosis,* a narrowing of the blood vessels. This narrowing usually results from the build-up of fatty deposits on the inner walls of arteries. When blood flow to the heart muscle is severely reduced or interrupted, a heart attack can occur. If heart damage is severe, the heart may stop beating—a condition known as cardiac arrest.

<table>
<tr><td>BOX
4.1</td><td>TEN GREAT PUBLIC HEALTH ACHIEVEMENTS, 1900–1999: DECLINE IN DEATHS
FROM CORONARY HEART DISEASE AND STROKE</td></tr>
</table>

You Gotta Have Heart

Since 1921, heart disease has been the leading cause of death, and since 1938, stroke has been the third leading cause of death. However, since 1950, age-adjusted death rates from cardiovascular disease (CVD) have declined 60%, representing one of the most important public health achievements in the twentieth century. This decline was made possible through a better understanding of disease epidemiology and advances in prevention techniques, diagnoses, and treatment.

Disease Epidemiology

The risk-factor concept—the idea that particular biologic, lifestyle, and social conditions were associated with an increased risk for specific disease—developed as a result of population-based research into the causes of CVD.

Advances in Prevention, Diagnoses, and Treatment

Prevention efforts and improvements in early detection, treatment, and care have resulted in several beneficial trends that have likely contributed to declines in CVD.

Trends That Have Likely Contributed to Declines in Cardiovascular Disease

- A decline in cigarette smoking among adults
- A decrease in mean blood pressure levels
- A decrease in mean blood cholesterol levels

Over the past 50 years, a more complete understanding of the processes involved in CVDs has resulted in a 56% decline in deaths from heart disease and stroke (see Box 4.1). Numerous *risk factors*—factors that increase the likelihood of experiencing coronary artery disease—have been identified. While some of these factors cannot be altered by changes in lifestyle or behavior, others can. Factors that cannot be altered include one's age, sex, race, and the genetic tendency toward developing the disease. Factors that can be modified include cigarette smoking, high blood pressure, high blood cholesterol, physical inactivity, obesity, diabetes, and stress.

Cerebrovascular disease (stroke) is the third leading cause of death in the United States. Strokes killed more than 163,000 people in 2001.[2] During a stroke, or cerebrovascular accident, the blood supply to the brain is interrupted.

The risk factors for developing cerebrovascular disease are similar to those for CHD and include hereditary, behavioral, and environmental factors. Hypertension and cigarette smoking are especially important risk factors for cerebrovascular disease.

cerebrovascular disease (stroke) a chronic disease characterized by damage to blood vessels of the brain resulting in disruption of circulation to the brain

Malignant Neoplasms (Cancer)

More than 553,000 people died from malignant neoplasms (cancer) in 2001 making it the second leading cause of death in the United States.[2] **Malignant neoplasms** occur when cells lose control over their growth and division. Normal cells are inhibited from continual growth and division by virtue of their contact with adjacent cells. Malignant (cancerous) cells are not so inhibited; they continue to grow and divide, eventually piling up in a "new growth," a neoplasm or tumor. Early-stage tumors or *in situ cancers* are more treatable than later-stage cancers. As tumor growth continues, parts of the neoplasm can break off and be carried to distant parts of the body, where they can lodge and continue to grow. When this occurs, the cancer is said to have **metastasized.** When malignant neoplasms have spread to distant parts of the body and have established new tumors, the cancer is said to be *invasive.*[4] The more the malignancy spreads, the more difficult it is to treat and the lower the survival rates.

Common cancer sites in order of frequency of reported cases and deaths for both men and women are shown in Figure 4.7. Cancer sites with the highest number of reported cases are the prostate gland (men) and breast (women), but cancer frequently occurs in other sites,

malignant neoplasm uncontrolled new tissue growth resulting from cells that have lost control over their growth and division

metastasis the spread of cancer cells to distant parts of the body by the circulatory or lymphatic system

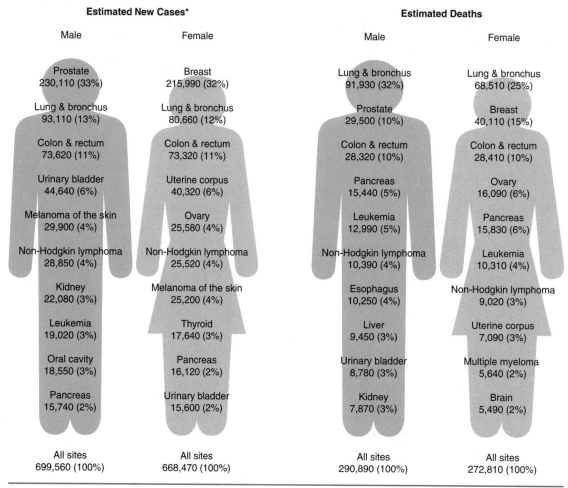

Estimated New Cases*

Male	Female
Prostate 230,110 (33%)	Breast 215,990 (32%)
Lung & bronchus 93,110 (13%)	Lung & bronchus 80,660 (12%)
Colon & rectum 73,620 (11%)	Colon & rectum 73,320 (11%)
Urinary bladder 44,640 (6%)	Uterine corpus 40,320 (6%)
Melanoma of the skin 29,900 (4%)	Ovary 25,580 (4%)
Non-Hodgkin lymphoma 28,850 (4%)	Non-Hodgkin lymphoma 25,520 (4%)
Kidney 22,080 (3%)	Melanoma of the skin 25,200 (4%)
Leukemia 19,020 (3%)	Thyroid 17,640 (3%)
Oral cavity 18,550 (3%)	Pancreas 16,120 (2%)
Pancreas 15,740 (2%)	Urinary bladder 15,600 (2%)
All sites 699,560 (100%)	All sites 668,470 (100%)

Estimated Deaths

Male	Female
Lung & bronchus 91,930 (32%)	Lung & bronchus 68,510 (25%)
Prostate 29,500 (10%)	Breast 40,110 (15%)
Colon & rectum 28,320 (10%)	Colon & rectum 28,410 (10%)
Pancreas 15,440 (5%)	Ovary 16,090 (6%)
Leukemia 12,990 (5%)	Pancreas 15,830 (6%)
Non-Hodgkin lymphoma 10,390 (4%)	Leukemia 10,310 (4%)
Esophagus 10,250 (4%)	Non-Hodgkin lymphoma 9,020 (3%)
Liver 9,450 (3%)	Uterine corpus 7,090 (3%)
Urinary bladder 8,780 (3%)	Multiple myeloma 5,640 (2%)
Kidney 7,870 (3%)	Brain 5,490 (2%)
All sites 290,890 (100%)	All sites 272,810 (100%)

FIGURE 4.7

Leading sites of new cancer cases* and deaths—2004 estimates.

*Excludes basal and squamous cell skin cancer and in situ carcinomas except urinary bladder.

Source: American Cancer Society (2004). *Cancer Facts & Figures* 2004. Atlanta, GA: American Cancer Society. Used with permission from the American Cancer Society. All rights reserved.

including the lung, colon and rectum, pancreas, uterus, ovaries, mouth, bladder, and skin. Lung cancer is the leading cause of cancer deaths in both sexes. There were an estimated 173,770 new cases of lung cancer and an estimated 160,440 lung cancer deaths in 2004 alone. It has been estimated that 87% of these deaths can be attributed to smoking. Alcohol and smokeless tobacco contribute to cancers of the mouth, throat, larynx, esophagus, and liver.[4]

Approximately one million new cases of basal cell or squamous cell skin cancer are detected each year in the United States. Almost all of these cases are attributable to exposure to the sun, and yet many people continue to sunbathe or use tanning salons, believing that a tanned body is a healthy one. The number of cases of nonmelanoma skin cancer is expected to rise as long as the ozone layer in the atmosphere continues to be eroded (see Chapter 16). This is an example of how environmental policy impacts on public health.

Other Noncommunicable Disease Problems

Other noncommunicable diseases of major concern are (1) chronic obstructive pulmonary disease and allied conditions (the fourth leading cause of death), (2) diabetes mellitus (the

Table 4.4
Some Noncommunicable Health Conditions That Affect Americans

Allergic disorders	Epilepsy	Osteoporosis
Arthritis	Fibrocystic breast condition	Premenstrual syndrome
Cerebral palsy	Lower back pain	Sickle cell trait and sickle cell disease
Endogenous depression	Multiple sclerosis	

seventh leading cause of death), and (3) chronic liver disease and cirrhosis (the tenth leading cause of death). Each of these chronic noncommunicable diseases and those listed in Table 4.4 places a burden not only on the afflicted individuals and their families but on the community's health resources as well.

PRIORITIZING PREVENTION AND CONTROL EFFORTS

Communities are confronted with a multitude of health problems—communicable and noncommunicable diseases, unintentional injuries, violence, substance abuse problems, and so on. How can health officials make logical and responsible choices about the allocation of community resources to prevent or control these problems? Which problems are indeed the most urgent? Which problems will benefit the most from a timely intervention? Several criteria are used to judge the importance of a particular disease to a community. Among these are (1) the number of people who die from a disease, (2) the number of years of potential life lost attributable to a particular cause, and (3) the economic costs associated with a particular disease or health condition.

Leading Causes of Death

The National Center for Health Statistics (NCHS) regularly publishes a list of the leading causes of death. For more than 80 years, the leading cause of death in America has been heart disease. Nearly one in every three deaths can be attributed to diseases of the heart. Cancers (malignant neoplasms) represent the second leading killer; nearly one in four deaths is the result of cancer. Cerebrovascular disease (stroke) ranks third, chronic lower pulmonary diseases rank fourth, and unintentional injuries rank fifth (see Table 3.7).[2]

One might prioritize expenditures of health care resources solely on the basis of the number of deaths, but in doing so one would spend about two-thirds of the entire health budget on the four leading health problems alone. Very little or perhaps none of the resources would be available for infant and childhood nutrition programs, for example, which have been shown to prevent more serious health care problems in later life. Nor would there be any funds available for the treatment of those with debilitating, but usually nonfatal, diseases such as chronic arthritis or mental illness.

Years of Potential Life Lost

Another approach toward prioritizing a community's health care problems is by using the *years of potential life lost (YPLL)* statistic described in Chapter 3. Using this approach, diseases that kill people of all ages become as important as those that kill primarily the elderly. Recall, for example, that malignant neoplasms (cancers), are the leading cause of YPLL-75 in the United States and account for 22% of all YPLL-75 compared with CVD, which accounts for only about 16.5%. Unintentional injuries are the third leading cause of YPLL-75, accounting for 13.5% of the total YPLL (refer to Table 3.11 and Figure 3.4).[5]

Economic Cost to Society

Still another way to evaluate the impact of a particular disease or health problem is to estimate the economic cost to the country or community. Economic cost data are hard to come by, and sometimes even experts cannot agree on the estimates obtained. An example of such an estimate is the cost to society resulting from the use and abuse of alcohol and other drugs, a whopping $414 billion annually, more than $1 billion per day.[6] This figure includes not only the cost of treatment and the loss of productivity but also the cost of law enforcement, courts, jails, and social work.

PREVENTION, INTERVENTION, CONTROL, AND ERADICATION OF DISEASES

prevention
the planning for and taking of action to forestall the onset of a disease or other health problem

The goals of epidemiology are to prevent, control, and in rare cases, to eradicate diseases and injuries. **Prevention** implies the planning for and taking of action to prevent or forestall the occurrence of an undesirable event, and is therefore more desirable than **intervention,** the taking of action during an event. For example, immunizing to prevent a disease is preferable to taking an antibiotic to cure one.

intervention
efforts to control a disease in progress

Control is a general term for the containment of a disease and can include both prevention and intervention measures. The term *control* is often used to mean the limiting of transmission of a communicable disease in a population. **Eradication** is the uprooting or total elimination of a disease from the human population. It is an elusive goal, one that is only rarely achieved in public health. Smallpox is the only communicable disease that has been eradicated (see Box 4.2).

eradication
the complete elimination or uprooting of a disease (e.g., smallpox eradication)

LEVELS OF PREVENTION

primary prevention
preventive measures that forestall the onset of illness or injury during the prepathogenesis period

There are three levels of application of preventive measures in disease control—primary, secondary, and tertiary. The purpose of **primary prevention** is to forestall the onset of illness or injury during the prepathogenesis period (before the disease process begins). Examples of primary prevention include health education and health promotion programs, safe-housing projects, and character-building and personality development programs. Other examples are the use of immunizations against specific diseases, the practice of personal hygiene such as hand washing, the use of rubber gloves, and the chlorination of the community's water supply. These are illustrated in Figure 4.8.

Unfortunately, disease or injury cannot always be avoided. Chronic diseases in particular sometimes cause considerable disability before they are detected and treated. In these cases,

---

BOX 4.2

COMMUNITY HEALTH IN YOUR WORLD: SMALLPOX ERADICATION

December 2002 marked 25 years since the last naturally acquired case of smallpox in the world. This last case occurred in Somalia in October 1977.[1] Although two cases of smallpox were reported in the United Kingdom in 1978, these were associated with a research laboratory and did not represent a natural recurrence.

Smallpox is caused by the variola virus. In its severest form, it is a disfiguring and deadly disease. Manifestations of the disease include fever, headache, malaise, and prostration. A rash appears and covers the body, and there is bleeding into the skin, mucous linings, and genital tract.

The circulatory system is also severely affected. Between 15% and 40% of cases die, usually within two weeks. Survivors are terribly scarred for life and are sometimes blinded.

Mass vaccinations and case-finding measures by the World Health Organization (WHO), with financial support from the United States, led to the eradication of smallpox from the world. Why was it possible to eradicate smallpox? Why have we been unable to eradicate any other diseases since 1977? Do you think we will ever be able to do so? If so, what disease will be eliminated next?

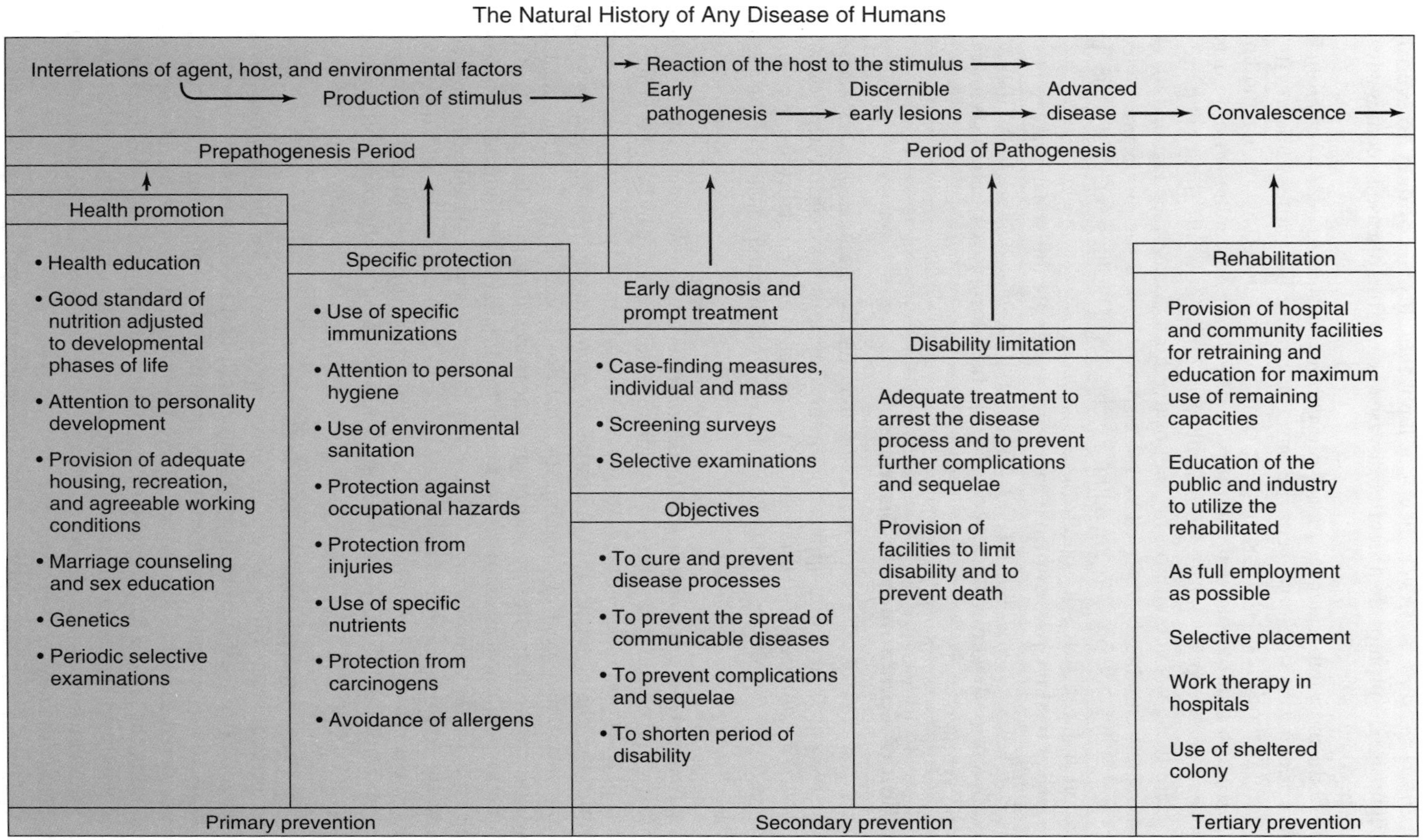

The Natural History of Any Disease of Humans
Interrelations of agent, host, and environmental factors
Production of stimulus
Reaction of the host to the stimulus
Early pathogenesis
Discernible early lesions
Advanced disease
Convalescence
Prepathogenesis Period
Period of Pathogenesis
Health promotion
• Health education
• Good standard of nutrition adjusted to developmental phases of life
• Attention to personality development
• Provision of adequate housing, recreation, and agreeable working conditions
• Marriage counseling and sex education
• Genetics
• Periodic selective examinations
Specific protection
• Use of specific immunizations
• Attention to personal hygiene
• Use of environmental sanitation
• Protection against occupational hazards
• Protection from injuries
• Use of specific nutrients
• Protection from carcinogens
• Avoidance of allergens
Early diagnosis and prompt treatment
• Case-finding measures, individual and mass
• Screening surveys
• Selective examinations
Objectives
• To cure and prevent disease processes
• To prevent the spread of communicable diseases
• To prevent complications and sequelae
• To shorten period of disability
Disability limitation
Adequate treatment to arrest the disease process and to prevent further complications and sequelae
Provision of facilities to limit disability and to prevent death
Rehabilitation
Provision of hospital and community facilities for retraining and education for maximum use of remaining capacities
Education of the public and industry to utilize the rehabilitated
As full employment as possible
Selective placement
Work therapy in hospitals
Use of sheltered colony
Primary prevention
Secondary prevention
Tertiary prevention

FIGURE 4.8
Applications of levels of prevention.

secondary prevention
preventive measures that lead to an early diagnosis and prompt treatment of a disease or injury to limit disability and prevent more severe pathogenesis

prompt *intervention* can prevent death or limit disability. **Secondary prevention** is the early diagnosis and prompt treatment of diseases before the disease becomes advanced and disability becomes severe.

One of the most important secondary prevention measures is *health screenings*. The goal of these screenings is not to prevent the onset of disease but rather to detect its presence during early pathogenesis, thus permitting early intervention (treatment) and limiting disability. It is important to note that the purpose of a health screening is not to diagnose disease. Instead, the purpose is to economically and efficiently sort those who are probably healthy from those who could possibly be positive for a disease (see Figure 4.9). Those who screen positively can then be referred for more specific diagnostic procedures. Screenings for diabetes and high blood pressure are popular examples of health screenings, as are breast self-examination and testicular self-examination.

tertiary prevention
measures aimed at rehabilitation following significant pathogenesis

The goal of **tertiary prevention** is to retrain, re-educate, and rehabilitate the patient who has already incurred a disability. Tertiary preventive measures include those that are applied after significant pathogenesis has occurred. Therapy for a heart patient is an example of tertiary prevention.

Prevention of Communicable Diseases

Prevention and control efforts for communicable diseases include primary, secondary, and tertiary approaches. Successful application of these approaches, particularly primary prevention, resulting in unprecedented declines in morbidity and mortality from communicable diseases, has been one of the outstanding achievements in public health in this century (see Box 4.3).

Primary Prevention of Communicable Diseases

The primary prevention measures for communicable diseases can best be visualized using the chain of infection (see Figure 4.10). In this model, prevention strategies are evident at each link in the chain. Successful application of each strategy can be seen as weakening a link, with the ultimate goal of breaking the chain of infection, or interrupting the disease transmission cycle. Examples of community measures include chlorination of the water supply, the inspection of restaurants and retail food markets, immunization programs that reach all citizens, the maintenance of a well-functioning sewer system, the proper disposal of solid waste, and the control of vectors and rodents. To these can be added personal efforts at primary prevention, including hand washing, the proper cooking of food, adequate clothing and housing, the use of condoms, and obtaining all the available immunizations against specific diseases.

Secondary Prevention of Communicable Diseases

Secondary preventive measures against communicable diseases for the individual involve either (1) self-diagnosis and self-treatment with nonprescription medications or home remedies, or (2) diagnosis and treatment with an antibiotic prescribed by a physician. Secondary preventive measures undertaken by the community against infectious diseases are usually aimed at controlling or limiting the extent of an epidemic. Examples include carefully maintaining records of cases and complying with the regulations requiring the reporting of notifiable diseases (see Chapter 3) and investigating cases and contacts—those who may have become infected through close contact with known cases.

isolation
the separation of infected persons from those who are susceptible

quarantine
limitation of freedom of movement of those who have been exposed to a disease and may be incubating it

Occasionally, secondary disease control measures may include isolation and quarantine. These two practices are quite different from one another and are often confused. **Isolation** is the separation, for the period of communicability, of infected persons or animals from others so as to prevent the direct or indirect transmission of the communicable agent to a susceptible person. **Quarantine** is the limitation of the freedom of movement of well persons or animals that have

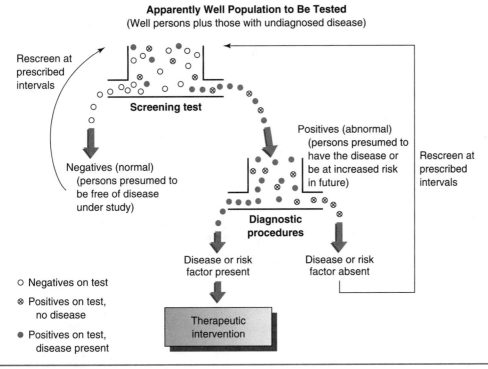

FIGURE 4.9

Flow diagram for a mass screening test.

Source: Mausner, J. S., and S. Kramer (1985). *Epidemiology—An Introductory Text.* Philadelphia: W.B. Saunders Company. Reprinted with permission of Elsevier.

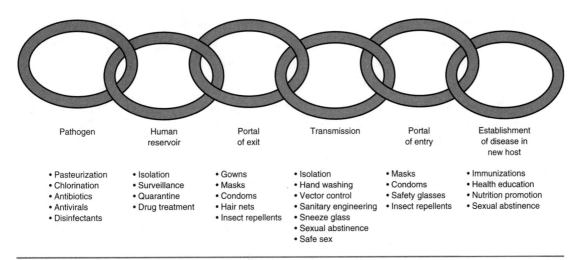

FIGURE 4.10

Chain of infection model showing disease prevention and control strategies.

BOX
4.3
TEN GREAT PUBLIC HEALTH ACHIEVEMENTS, 1900–1999: CONTROL OF INFECTIOUS DISEASES

An Ounce of Prevention Is Worth a Century of Cure

Public health action to control infectious diseases in the twentieth century was founded on the late nineteenth century's discovery of microorganisms as causes of many diseases. Further scientific findings documented the interactions among humans, the environment, and microbes. Improvements in sanitation, hygiene, and food safety; the discovery of antibiotics; and the implementation of universal childhood vaccination programs resulted in the control of many fatal infectious diseases and the global eradication of one disease—smallpox. Scientific and technologic advances played a substantial role in these efforts. Today, those advances are the foundation for the disease surveillance and control systems that are used to combat all infectious diseases.

Sanitation and Hygiene

Early in the twentieth century, infections associated with overcrowding, poor housing, and contaminated water resulted in the transmission of tuberculosis, diptheria, typhoid fever, and dysentery. Improvements in housing and public water supplies—including chlorination and filtration—and waste-disposal systems have resulted in swift progress in disease control.

Antibiotics and Other Antimicrobial Medicines

Antibiotics have been in common use since the 1940s and have saved the lives and health of persons with streptococcal and staphylococcal infections, gonorrhea, syphilis, and other infections. Penicillin was the first of many antibiotics that became widely available to cure previously untreatable bacterial diseases. Drugs also have been developed to treat viral, fungal, and parasitic diseases, but resistance to these miracle drugs is an ever increasing challenge.

Emerging Diseases

For continued success in controlling infectious disease, the U.S. public health system must address such diverse challenges as the emergence of new infectious disease—for example, HIV and Hantavirus—and the re-emergence of old diseases, sometimes in drug-resistant forms—for example, tuberculosis and malaria. Bioterrorism and pandemic influenza are also potential public health crises requiring advance preparedness.

Marvel of Medical Science, Miracle for Mankind

Sometimes a miracle happens and a disease is eradicated. Biomedical science and public health create this miracle when medicines and vaccines are developed that enable disease control and prevention. At the beginning of the twentieth century, few effective treatments and preventive measures existed to prevent infectious diseases. However, vaccines have been developed and are used to prevent many of the infectious diseases that threated our parents, grandparents, and great-grandparents during the twentieth century.

Overall, U.S. vaccination coverage is at record high levels. And up-to-date training for the shot-givers and shot-callers is also at record high levels. Vaccines have the remarkable power to eradicate diseases. However, the combined effort of many partners is needed to achieve the full potential of these miraculous medicines.

---

disinfection
the killing of communicable disease agents outside the host, on counter tops, for example

been exposed to a communicable disease until the incubation period has passed. Further control measures may include **disinfection,** the killing of communicable agents outside of the host, and mass treatment with antibiotics. Finally, public health education and health promotion should be used as both primary and secondary preventive measures.

Tertiary Prevention of Communicable Diseases

Tertiary preventive measures for the control of communicable diseases for the individual include convalescence from infection, recovery to full health, and return to normal activity. In some cases, such as paralytic poliomyelitis, return to normal activity may not be possible even after extensive physical therapy. At the community level, tertiary preventive measures are aimed at preventing the recurrence of an epidemic. The proper removal, embalming, and burial of the dead is an example. Tertiary prevention may involve the re-application of primary and secondary measures in such a way as to prevent further cases. For example, in some countries, such as the Republic of Korea, people with colds or flu wear gauze masks in public to reduce the spread of disease.

Application of Preventive Measures in the Control of a Communicable Disease: AIDS

Acquired immunodeficiency syndrome (AIDS) is a progressive disease that is caused by human immunodeficiency virus (HIV) infection. Individuals can become infected when they come in contact with the virus through sexual activity, intravenous drug use, or blood exposure. It usually takes between two and six months for antibodies to appear in the blood of an infected person. When this happens, these people are referred to as being *HIV positive* or *seropositive*. At some time later (a few months to many years later), as the HIV infection weakens their immune system, they will usually develop signs and symptoms of illnesses caused by opportunistic infections or AIDS indicator infections. Once they do, they are referred to as *HIV positive with symptoms,* and may be diagnosed as having AIDS. Their diagnosis is then referred to as *HIV positive with AIDS.* About half the people with HIV develop AIDS within 10 years after becoming infected (see Figure 4.11).

HIV is responsible for a pandemic of unprecedented size. The WHO estimates that 40 million people are living with HIV/AIDS worldwide. During 2003, 5 million people were newly infected with HIV and 3 million people died of AIDS.[7] In the United States, through December 2002, a cumulative total of 886,575 persons with AIDS were reported to CDC by state and territorial health departments.[8] The reservoir for HIV virus is the infected human population; there are no known animal or insect reservoirs. Referring to the chain of infection, HIV normally leaves its infected host (reservoir) during sexual activity. The portal of exit is the urogenital tract. Transmission is direct and occurs when reproductive fluids or blood are exchanged with the susceptible host. In the case of injection drug users, however, transmission is indirect, by contaminated needles (vehicle). The portal of entry is usually either genital, oral, or anal in direct (sexual) transmission or transdermal in the case of injection drug users or blood transfusion recipients. Transmission can also occur during medical procedures

---

FIGURE 4.11

A time line for untreated HIV infections.

Prepared by Wayne A. Payne.

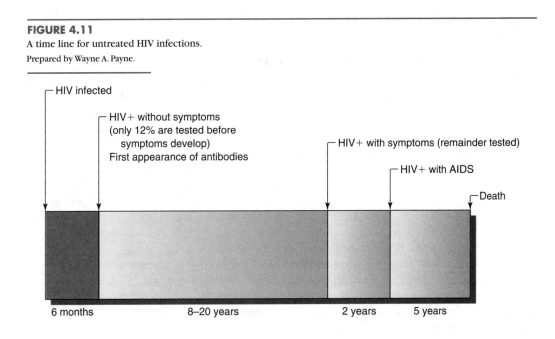

if there is an accidental needle stick or some other type of contamination with blood or other potentially infectious material.

A closer examination of the chain of infection reveals that prevention or control measures can be identified for each link. The pathogen in the diseased host can be held in check by the appropriate drug. Outside the host, measures such as sterilizing needles and other possible vehicles and disinfecting surfaces readily kill the virus and reduce the likelihood of transmission by contamination. The infected host (reservoir) can be identified through blood tests and educated to take precautions against the careless transmission of live virus through unsafe sex and needle sharing. Portals of exit (and entry) can be protected by the use of condoms. Transmission can be stopped by the practice of abstinence or reduced by limiting the number of sexual partners. Urogenital portals of entry can be protected through sexual abstinence and the use of condoms. One of the stated objectives of *Healthy People 2010* is to increase condom use (see Box 4.4). In the case of injection drug users, abstinence from such drug use would preclude transmission by needles and syringes. A more realistic approach to reducing the spread of HIV/AIDS in the injection drug-using population might be a more reasonable syringe sale and possession policy (see Box 4.5).[9]

For those working in the health professions, the risk of acquiring an HIV infection in the workplace is of particular concern. The Occupational Safety and Health Administration (OSHA) estimates that 5.6 million workers in the health care industry and related occupations are at risk of occupational exposure to **bloodborne pathogens,** including HIV, hepatitis B virus (HBV), hepatitis C virus (HCV), and others.[10] In 1991 OSHA, recognizing that workers in the health care industry were at risk of occupational exposure to bloodborne pathogens, issued the Bloodborne Pathogens Standard.

In November 2000, Congress, acknowledging the estimates of 600,000 to 800,000 needlestick and other percutaneous injuries occurring among health care workers annually, passed the Needlestick Safety and Prevention Act.[11] In 2001, in response to the Needlestick Safety and Prevention Act, OSHA revised its **Bloodborne Pathogens Standard.** This revised standard, currently in effect, "clarifies the need for employers to select safer needle devices and to involve employees in identifying and choosing these devices" and to maintain a log of injuries from contaminated sharps.[12] The goal of all of these regulations and standards is to reduce the number of HIV/AIDS cases, as well as cases of other bloodborne diseases, resulting from workplace exposure.

Prevention of Noncommunicable Diseases

Both the individual and the community can contribute substantially to the prevention and control of multicausation diseases. The community can provide a prohealth environment—physical, economic, and social—in which it becomes easier for individuals to achieve a high level of health.

Primary Prevention of Noncommunicable Diseases

Primary preventive measures for noncommunicable diseases include adequate food and energy supplies, good opportunities for education, employment, and housing, and efficient community services. Beyond this foundation, a community should provide health promotion and health education programs, health and medical services, and protection from environmental and occupational hazards.

Individuals can practice primary prevention by obtaining a high level of education that includes a knowledge about health and disease and the history of disease of others in one's family. In particular, the individual should take responsibility for eating properly, exercising adequately, maintaining appropriate weight, and avoiding the overuse of alcohol and other drugs. Individuals can also protect themselves from injury by wearing safety belts, safety goggles, and sunscreen lotions.

---

bloodborne pathogens disease agents, such as HIV, that are transmissible in blood and other body fluids

---

Bloodborne Pathogens Standard a set of regulations promulgated by OSHA that sets forth the responsibilities of employers and employees with regard to precautions to be taken concerning bloodborne pathogens in the workplace

BOX
4.4

HEALTHY PEOPLE 2010: OBJECTIVES

Goal: Prevent HIV infection and its related illness and death.

Target and baseline:

Objective	Increase the proportion of sexually active persons who use condoms.	1995 Baseline	2010 Target
		Percent	
13-6a.	Females aged 18 to 44 years	23	50
13-6b.	Males aged 18 to 49 years	Developmental	

Target setting method: Better than the best.

Data source: National Survey of Family Growth (NSFG), CDC, NCHS.

Unmarried Females 18 to 44 years, 1995	13-6a. Reported Condom Use by Partners*
	Percent
TOTAL	23
Race and ethnicity	
American Indian or Alaska Native	DSU
Asian or Pacific Islander	DSU
Asian	DNC
Native Hawaiian and other Pacific Islander	DNC
Black or African American	22
White	23
Hispanic or Latino	17
Aged 18 to 19 years	16
Aged 20 to 24 years	18
Aged 25 to 29 years	19
Aged 30 to 34 years	22
Aged 35 to 44 years	9
Not Hispanic or Latino	24
Black or African American	22
Aged 18 to 19 years	31
Aged 20 to 24 years	35
Aged 25 to 29 years	23
Aged 30 to 34 years	17
Aged 35 to 44 years	12
White	24
Aged 18 to 19 years	39
Aged 20 to 24 years	29
Aged 25 to 29 years	24
Aged 30 to 34 years	14
Aged 35 to 44 years	18
Family income level	
Poor	16
Near poor	21
Middle/high income	27
Education level (aged 25 to 44 years)	
Less than high school	7
High school	15
At least some college	25
Geographic location	
Urban	24
Rural	18
Sexual orientation	DNC

DNA = Data has not been analyzed. DNC = Data have not been collected. DSU = Data are statistically unreliable.

*Data for both genders and for males currently have not been not collected.

For Further Thought

Unprotected sexual contact, whether homosexual or heterosexual, with a person infected with HIV is one of the most important ways HIV infections are transmitted. An important way to slow the rate of new AIDS cases is to increase the proportion of sexually active females whose partners use condoms. Can you think of other ways to increase the rate of condom use in sexually active persons?

BOX 4.5 INJECTION DRUG USE, HIV/AIDS, AND PUBLIC HEALTH: PROMOTING HEALTH AND SAFETY IN AMERICA THROUGH A REASONABLE SYRINGE SALE AND POSSESSION POLICY

Injection drug use is the second most frequently reported risk factor for AIDS, accounting for 193,527 cases through December 1995. In 2000, 35% of all AIDS cases occurred among injection drug users (IDUs), their heterosexual sex partners, and children whose mothers were IDUs or sex partners of IDUs. Transmission of HIV infection by IDUs occurs primarily through multi-person use of syringes—needle sharing. (In this discussion, the term *syringe* includes both syringes and needles.) When an IDU injects drugs, the syringe becomes contaminated with that person's blood and bloodborne pathogens that can then be transmitted to another IDU who uses the same syringe.

In an effort to control the widespread use of opium, morphine, cocaine, and heroin in the late nineteenth and early twentieth centuries, states passed laws restricting the freedom of physicians to dispense the drugs. These laws also regulated the sale and distribution of syringes. In 1979, the Drug Enforcement Administration wrote the Model Drug Paraphernalia Act (MDPA), versions of which were adopted by many states. These laws were adopted in response to the proliferation of drug paraphernalia industry and the numerous "head shops" operated nationwide. Included as drug paraphernalia are "hypodermic syringes, needles, and other objects used, intended for use, and designed for use in parenterally injecting controlled substances into the human body."

A recent survey reveals that 47 states and the District of Columbia have passed drug paraphernalia statutes. Ten states have laws, regulations, or ordinances that require a prescription for the purchase of syringes and 16 additional states have laws or regulations that can otherwise limit the sale and purchase of syringes. To the extent that these laws, regulations, and ordinances restrict access to sterile syringes, they contribute to the spread of bloodborne diseases among IDUs, their sexual contacts, and their children. Some, but not all of these states, have carved out some provisions to exempt operators and participants of syringe exchange programs (SEPs) from prosecution under these laws.

Pharmacists face substantial legal and professional hurdles if they sell syringes to IDUs. Physicians and other health professionals face potentially dire legal consequences when they prescribe syringes or otherwise directly assist IDUs in obtaining sterile syringes. Criminal and professional sanctions prevent these professionals from providing important HIV prevention services to persons who continue to inject drugs. Most of the laws that restrict the sale, possession, or distribution of syringes were promulgated before the HIV/AIDS epidemic.

The dual epidemics of drug use and the human immunodeficiency virus and acquired immunodeficiency syndrome (HIV/AIDS) are significant burdens on the health and safety of Americans. There are between 1 and 2 million IDUs in the United States who are at risk for acquiring a variety of bloodborne pathogens such as hepatitis B and C, HIV/AIDS, endocarditis, and malaria. Futhermore, illicit drug use results in destruction of families, domestic abuse and neglect, and a variety of social and economic problems. Drug abuse is also associated with higher rates of crime against people and property. The annual cost to society of drug abuse has been estimated at nearly $60 billion.

Many public health, medical, and legal organizations have supported the deregulation of syringes as a strategy to prevent HIV/AIDS and other bloodborne diseases among IDUs. What do you think?

1. What are the legitimate medical (public health) purposes of sterile syringes?
2. Should drug paraphernalia laws be modified?
3. Should syringe prescription laws be changed to exempt authorized use of syringes to prevent multi-person use of syringes in syringe exchange programs, for example?
4. Should pharmacy regulations that prevent pharmacists from dispensing sterile needles to IDUs be repealed?
5. Should there be in-service training for pharmacists and other health professionals and criminal justice personnel so they can advance public health goals?
6. Should states allow local discretion in establishing syringe exchange programs?
7. What kinds of programs should be developed to reduce the number of contaminated syringes in circulation and reduce health risks to the public?

Source: L. O. Gostin, Z. Lazzarini, T. S. Jones, and K. Flaherty (1997). "Prevention of HIV/AIDS and Other Blood-borne Diseases among Injection Drug Users: A National Survey on the Regulation of Syringes and Needles." *JAMA,* 277(1): 53–62.

Secondary Prevention of Noncommunicable Diseases

Secondary preventive measures the community can take include the provision of mass screenings for chronic diseases (see Figure 4.12), case-finding measures, and the provision of adequate health personnel, equipment, and facilities for the community. Secondary prevention responsibilities of individual citizens include personal screenings such as self-examination of

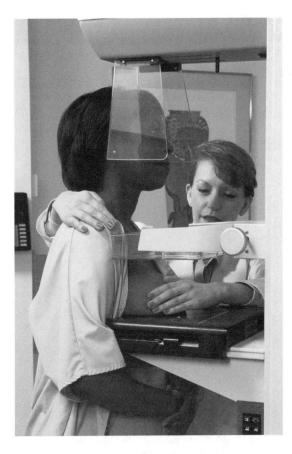

FIGURE 4.12
Mammography, used for screening and early detection of breast cancer, is an example of secondary prevention.

breasts or testes (for cancer of these organs), the hemocult test (for colorectal cancer), and medical screenings such as the Pap test (for cervical cancer), the PSA test for cancer of the prostate, mammography, and screenings for diabetes, glaucoma, or hypertension. Participating in such health screenings and having regular medical and dental checkups represent only the first step in the secondary prevention of noncommunicable diseases. This must be followed by the pursuit of definitive diagnosis and prompt treatment of any diseases detected.

Tertiary Prevention of Noncommunicable Diseases

Tertiary preventive measures for a community include adequate emergency medical personnel, services, and facilities to meet the needs of those citizens for whom primary and secondary preventive measures were unsuccessful. Examples include ambulance services, hospitals, physicians and surgeons, nurses, and other allied health professionals. Interestingly, most communities are doing a more-than-adequate job in tertiary prevention. Many experts feel that most communities in America need to reallocate resources from tertiary prevention to primary and secondary preventive measures.

Tertiary prevention for the individual often requires significant behavioral or lifestyle changes. Examples include strict adherence to prescribed medications, exercise programs, and diet. For example, a heart attack patient could receive nutrition education and counseling and be encouraged to participate in a supervised exercise program, thus maximizing the use of remaining capabilities. This could lead to a resumption of employment and the prevention of a second heart attack. For certain types of noncommunicable health problems, such as those involving substance abuse, regular attendance at support group meetings or counseling sessions may constitute an important part of a tertiary prevention program.

BOX 4.6	HEALTHY PEOPLE 2010: OBJECTIVES

Objective 12.1: Reduce coronary heart disease deaths to 166 deaths per 100,000 population.

Baseline: 208 coronary heart disease deaths per 100,000 in 1998.

Target setting method: 20% improvement.

Data source: National Vital Statistics System (NVSS), CDC, NCHS.

Total Population, 1998	Coronary Heart Disease Deaths Rate per 100,000
TOTAL	203
Race and ethnicity	
American Indian or Alaska Native	148
Asian or Pacific Islander	124
Asian	DNC
Native Hawaiian and other Pacific Islander	DNC
Black or African American	248
White	200
Hispanic or Latino	169
Not Hispanic or Latino	204
Black or African American	250
White	201
Gender	
Female	161
Male	260
Education level (aged 25 to 64 years)	
Less than high school	97
High school graduate	80
At least some college	36

For Further Thought

Important contributing factors to CHD are high blood cholesterol, high blood pressure, and obesity. What is the prevalence of high blood pressure in your community? What is the prevalence of obesity in your state? Do you know your serum cholesterol level?

Application of Preventive Measures in the Control of a Noncommunicable Disease: CHD

Despite considerable progress, CHD remains America's Number 1 killer. Reducing CHD deaths is one of the *Healthy People 2010* objectives (see Box 4.6). Many factors contribute to one's risk of developing this disease. Both the community and the individual can contribute to the prevention of CHD.

The Community's Role

The community must recognize the importance of preventing chronic disease; intervention following a crisis, such as a heart attack, is the least effective and most expensive way to provide help to a CHD patient. While individual behavioral changes hold the best prospects for reducing the prevalence of heart disease in this country, communities can provide a supporting environment for these behavioral changes. For example, the community can support restricting smoking areas and can provide a clear message to youth that smoking is damaging to health. Communities also can provide adequate opportunity for health screening for risk factors such as hypertension and serum cholesterol levels. In particular, schools can permit the administration of Youth Risk Behavior Surveillance System surveys (see Chapter 3) and utilize these occasions as opportunities to teach students about the importance of healthy behavioral choices. Communities also can promote and assist in the development of areas for recreation and exercise, such as safe paths for jogging or cycling and lighted sidewalks for walking. Exercise reduces obesity and increases the high-density lipoproteins (HDLs) in the blood, thereby lowering risk for a heart attack. Finally, communities should promote sound nutrition throughout the lifespan, but particularly in schools.

The Individual's Role

The risk factors for CHD are multiple. Some of these risk factors are unmodifiable, while other risk factors can be modified (reduced) to improve one's health. Each person can increase his or her resistance to CHD by knowing the difference between the types of risk factors and by adopting behaviors that prevent or postpone the onset of CHD.

Each person is endowed with a unique genetic code. An individual's innate resistance or susceptibility to heart disease is encoded in the genes. **Unmodifiable risk factors** for CHD include one's race, gender, personality type, age, and basic metabolic rate. Also inherited is one's baseline serum cholesterol level. That is, children whose parents had high serum cholesterol levels are at risk for those same higher levels, independent of their diet.

Modifiable risk factors for CHD include environmental and behavioral factors over which an individual has some control. Modifiable risk factors that would increase the likelihood of CHD include smoking, a diet too rich in fats, lack of exercise, obesity, uncontrolled hypertension, and too much stress. Although none of these factors alone is likely to cause a premature heart attack, each can contribute to the likelihood of CHD.

> **unmodifiable risk factors**
> factors contributing to the development of a noncommunicable disease that cannot be altered by modifying one's behavior or environment

> **modifiable risk factors**
> factors contributing to the development of a noncommunicable disease that can be altered by modifying one's behavior or environment

CHAPTER SUMMARY

- Diseases can be classified as communicable (infectious) or noncommunicable (noninfectious), and acute or chronic.

- Acute diseases last for less than three months, whereas chronic diseases continue longer than three months.

- Communicable diseases are caused by biological agents and are transmissible from a source of infection to a susceptible host.

- The process of communicable disease transmission is best understood by the chain of infection model, in which the interruption of disease transmission can be visualized as the breaking of one or more links in the chain.

- Noncommunicable diseases are often the result of multiple risk factors that can be genetic, behavioral, and environmental in origin.

- Several of the noncommunicable diseases rank among the leading causes of death in America.

- There are three levels of disease prevention—primary, secondary, and tertiary.

- Primary prevention includes measures that forestall the onset of disease or injury, while secondary prevention encompasses efforts aimed at early detection and intervention to limit disease and disability. Tertiary prevention includes measures aimed at re-education and rehabilitation after significant pathogenesis has occurred.

- Both the spread of communicable diseases and the prevalence of noncommunicable diseases can best be reduced by the appropriate application of primary, secondary, and tertiary preventive measures by the community and the individual.

- The prevention and control of noncommunicable diseases require both individual and community efforts.

REVIEW QUESTIONS

1. What are some of the ways in which diseases and health problems are classified in community health?

2. Contrast the terms *acute disease* and *chronic disease*. Provide three examples of each type of disease.

3. Contrast the terms *communicable disease* and *noncommunicable disease*. Provide three examples of each type of disease.

4. What is the difference between a communicable agent and a pathogenic agent?

5. What are the components of a simplified communicable disease model?

6. List some examples of environmental factors that can influence the occurrence and spread of disease.

7. Draw and explain the model for multicausation diseases.

SCENARIO: ANALYSIS AND RESPONSE

1. If Bob's roommate, Chuck, were to begin to show signs of the flu, what could Bob do to lessen his chances of becoming infected himself? (*Hint:* Think about the chain of infection.)

2. As an accountant, Bob spends most of his day behind a desk. To identify primary, secondary, and tertiary preventive measures Bob should take to reduce his risk for heart disease, visit one governmental and one nongovernmental Web site and find some infor-

mation about prevention of heart disease. For each preventive measure you list, indicate whether it is primary, secondary, or tertiary prevention.

3. In what other health screenings should Bob and Chuck participate? Are there any health screenings available on the Internet?

4. What kinds of thoughts, behaviors, and conditions prevent people from participating in health screenings?

---

8. What is the difference between prevention and intervention?

9. Explain the difference between primary, secondary, and tertiary prevention and provide an example of each.

10. What is the "chain of infection" model of disease transmission? Draw the model and label its parts.

11. Again referring to the chain of infection, indicate how prevention and control strategies could be implemented to interrupt the transmission of gonorrhea. Are most of these strategies primary, secondary, or tertiary prevention measures?

12. Define the following terms—*case, carrier, vector, vehicle.*

13. List five examples each of vectorborne diseases and nonvectorborne diseases.

14. Explain the difference between the public health practices of isolation and quarantine.

15. Apply the principles of prevention and the examples given in this chapter to outline a prevention strategy for breast cancer that includes primary, secondary, and tertiary prevention components.

ACTIVITIES

1. Call your state health department and find out which are the top communicable (infectious) disease problems reported in your state. Which are the rarest? Is Lyme disease reportable?

2. List some of the infections you have had. How were these infections transmitted to you—directly, by vehicle, or by vector? Talk to someone who is very old about diseases they can recall from their youth and how these diseases affected them and their families. Take notes on the response and hand them in or share them orally in class.

3. Look up the disease bubonic plague in an encyclopedia or on the Internet. After reading about the disease, see if you can complete a chain of infection model for plague. Identify the causative agent, the vector, the reservoir, and the mode of transmission. What types of prevention and control strategies were used in the past to stop the spread of this disease? What can be done differently today if there is an epidemic of plague?

4. Think about motor vehicle crashes. List some primary, secondary, and tertiary preventive measures that the community and you can take to reduce the number and seriousness of injuries caused by auto accidents.

COMMUNITY HEALTH ON THE WEB

The Internet contains a wealth of information about community and public health. Increase your knowledge of some of the topics presented in this chapter by accessing the Jones and Bartlett Publishers Web site at **health.jbpub.com/communityhealth/5e** and follow the links to complete the following Web activities.

- National Center for Infectious Diseases
- National Center for Chronic Disease Prevention and Health Promotion
- Epidemic Intelligence Service

REFERENCES

1. Chin, J., ed. (2000). *Control of Communicable Diseases Manual,* 17th ed. Washington, DC: American Public Health Association.

2. Arias, E., R. N. Anderson, K. Hsiang-Ching, S.L. Murphy, and K.D. Kochanek (2003). "Deaths: Final Data for 2001." *National Vital Statistics Report,* 52(3): 1–116.

3. American Heart Association (2003). *2004 Heart Disease and Stroke Statistics—2004 Update.* Dallas, TX: Author.

4. American Cancer Society (2004). *Cancer Facts and Figures—2004.* Atlanta, GA: Author.

5. National Center for Health Statistics (2003). *Health, United States, 2003 with Chartbook on Trends in the Health of Americans.* (HHS pub. no. 2003-1232). Hyattsville, MD: Author.

6. Horgan, C., K. C. Skwara, and G. Strickler (2001). *Substance Abuse: The Nation's Number One Health Problem.* Princeton, NJ: Robert Wood Johnson Foundation.

7. Joint United Nations Programme on HIV/AIDS (UNAIDS) and World Health Organization (WHO) (2003). *AIDS Epidemic Update: 2003.* Available at http://www.who.int/hiv/pub/epidemiology/epi2003/en/.

8. Centers for Disease Control and Prevention, Division of HIV/AIDS Prevention (2003). "Basic Statistics." Available at http://www.cdc.gov/hiv/stats.htm.

9. Gostin, L. O., Z. Lazzarini, T. S. Jones, and K. Flaherty (1997). "Prevention of HIV/AIDS and Other Blood-borne Diseases among Injection Drug Users: A National Survey on the Regulation of Syringes and Needles." *JAMA,* 277(1): 53–62.

10. Occupational Safety and Health Administration (2004). *Bloodborne Pathogens and Needlestick Prevention: Hazard Recognition.* Available at http://www.osha.gov/SLTC/bloodbornepathogens/recognition.html.

11. U.S. Public Law 106-430, 106th Cong. (3 October 2000). "An Act to Require Changes in the Bloodborne Pathogens Standard in Effect under the Occupational Safety and Health Act of 1970." *Congressional Record,* 146.

12. Occupational Safety and Health Administration (2004). "Health and Safety Topics: Bloodborne Pathogens and Needlestick Prevention." Available at http://www.osha.gov/SLTC/bloodbornepathogens/index.html.

Chapter 5

Community Organizing/ Building and Health Promotion Programming

SCENARIO

It was becoming obvious to many that the suburb of Kenzington now had a drug problem, but few wanted to admit it. The community's residents liked their quiet neighborhoods, and most never thought that drugs would be a problem. In fact, the problem really sneaked up on everyone. The town only had one bar, and while occasionally someone drank too much, the bar's patrons usually controlled their drinking and didn't bother anyone. Occasionally, two or three high school seniors would be caught drinking beer purchased at a store in a nearby town. Yet these isolated incidents gave no indication of Kenzington's impending drug problem.

Within the past year, the climate of the town had changed considerably. Incidents of teenagers being arrested for possession of alcohol or even other drugs, such as marijuana, were being reported more regularly in the newspaper. There seemed to be more reports of burglaries, too. There had even been a robbery and two assaults reported within the last month. The population of young adults in the community seemed to be increasing, and many of these seemed to be driving impressive cars and wearing the latest clothes. All of these signs were obvious to a group of concerned citizens in Kenzington and suggested the possibility of a drug problem. So the concerned citizens decided to take their concern to the city council.

INTRODUCTION

In order to deal with the health issues that face many communities, community health professionals must possess specific knowledge and skills. They need to be able to identify problems, develop a plan to attack each problem, gather the resources necessary to carry out that plan, implement that plan, and then evaluate the results to determine the degree of progress that has been achieved. In the previous two chapters, we described epidemiological methods as essential tools of the community health professional. In this chapter, we present two other important capabilities that each successful community health worker must master: the skills to organize a community and to plan a health promotion program.

COMMUNITY ORGANIZING/BUILDING

Community health problems can be small and simple or large and complex. Small, simple problems that are local and involve few people can be solved with the effort of a small group of people and a minimal amount of organization. Large, complex problems that involve whole communities require significant skills and resources for their solution. For these larger problems, a considerable effort must be expended to organize the citizens of the community to work together to implement a lasting solution to their problem. For example:

> The use of community collaborations to prevent violence, rather than relying solely on a law enforcement approach, is a newer strategy gaining widespread acceptance. At the same time, though, those working in this field have to confront a number of pragmatic issues. One is how to integrate this vision of community engagement into their organization's daily efforts. Moreover, the health professional community organizer, or volunteer, who sees promise in addressing the social environment as a means of promoting health may find it necessary to convince others of the usefulness of a particular community-level approach.[1]

"The term *community organization* was coined by American social workers in the late 1880s to describe their efforts to coordinate services for newly arrived immigrants and the poor."[2] More recently, *community organization* has been used by a variety of professionals,

Table 5.1
Terms Associated with Community Organizing

Community capacity	"Community characteristics affecting its ability to identify, mobilize, and address problems"[5]
Community participation	"A process of involving people in the institutions or decisions that affect their lives"[6]
Empowered community	"One in which individuals and organizations apply their skills and resources in collective efforts to meet their respective needs"[7]

community organizing
process through which communities are helped to identify common problems or goals, mobilize resources, and in other ways develop and implement strategies for reaching their goals they have collectively set

including community health workers, and refers to various methods of interventions to deal with social problems. More formally, **community organizing** has been defined as a "process through which communities are helped to identify common problems or goals, mobilize resources, and in other ways develop and implement strategies for reaching their goals they have collectively set."[3] Community organizing is not a science but an art of consensus building within a democratic process[4] (see Table 5.1).

Need for Organizing Communities

In recent years, the need to organize communities seems to have increased. Advances in electronics (television), communications (mobile telephones, fax machines, and the Internet), other household appliances (air conditioners), and increased mobility (automobiles and airplanes) have resulted in a loss of a sense of community. Individuals are much more independent than ever before. The days when people knew everyone on their block are past. Today, it is not uncommon for people to never meet their neighbors (see Figure 5.1). In other cases,

FIGURE 5.1
In today's complex communities, it is not uncommon for people never to meet their neighbors.

people see or talk to their neighbors only once or twice each year. Because of these changes in community social structure, it now takes specific skills to organize a community to act together for the collective good. Note that the usefulness of community organizing skills extends beyond community health.

Assumptions of Community Organizing

According to Ross,[4] those who organize communities do so while making certain assumptions. The assumptions Ross outlines can be summarized as follows:

1. Communities of people can develop the capacity to deal with their own problems.
2. People want to change and can change.
3. People should participate in making, adjusting, or controlling the major changes taking place within their communities.
4. Changes in community living that are self-imposed or self-developed have a meaning and permanence that imposed changes do not have.
5. A "holistic approach" can successfully address problems with which a "fragmented approach" cannot cope.
6. Democracy requires cooperative participation and action in the affairs of the community, and people must learn the skills that make this possible.
7. Frequently, communities of people need help in organizing to deal with their needs, just as many individuals require help in coping with their individual problems.

Community Organizing Methods

There is no single, preferred method for organizing a community. In fact, a careful review reveals that several different approaches have been successful, which led Rothman and Tropman to state, "We would speak of community organization methods rather than the community organization method."[8]

Some of the early methods of formalizing community organization employed revolutionary techniques.[9] In the 1960s, when there was much unrest in America and the target of organizing efforts was authority at every level, revolutionary techniques were appropriate. However, in recent years, three primary methods of community organization have developed—locality development, social planning, and social action.[8] *Locality development* is based on the concept of broad self-help participation from the local community. "It is heavily process oriented, stressing consensus and cooperation aimed at building group identity and a sense of community."[2]

Social planning "is heavily task oriented, stressing rational-empirical problem-solving"[2] and involves various levels of participation from many people and outside planners.

The third method, *social action,* is "both task and process oriented"[2] and has been useful in helping to organize disadvantaged segments of the population. It often involves trying to redistribute power or resources, which enables institutional or community change. This method is not used as much as it once was, but it was useful during the civil rights and gay rights movements and in other settings where people have been oppressed.

Though locality development, social planning, and social action methods have been the primary means by which communities have organized over the years, they do have their limitations. Maybe the greatest limitation is that they are primarily "problem-based and organizer-centered, rather than strength-based and community-centered."[6] Thus, some of the newer models are based more on collaborative empowerment and community building. However, all models—old or new—revolve around a common theme: The work and resources of many have a much better chance of solving a problem than the work and resources of a few.

Minkler and Wallerstein have done a nice job of summarizing the models, old and new, by presenting a typology that incorporates both needs- and strength-based approaches

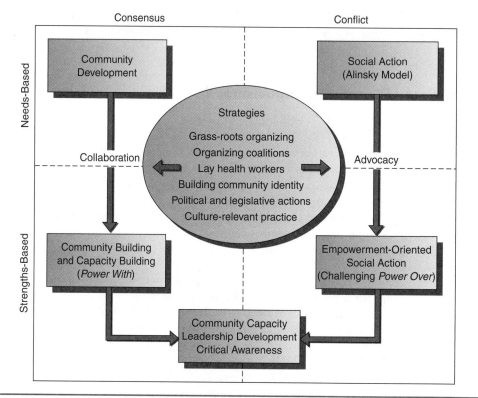

FIGURE 5.2

Community organization and community building typology.

Source: Minkler, M., and N. B. Wallerstein (2002). "Improving Health through Community Organization and Community Building." In K. Glanz, B. K. Rimer, and F. M. Lewis, eds., *Health Behavior and Health Education: Theory, Research, and Practice,* 3rd ed. New York: John Wiley & Sons, 287. Copyright © 2002 by John Wiley & Sons. This material is used by permission of John Wiley & Sons, Inc.

(see Figure 5.2).[5] Their typology is divided into four quadrants, with strength-based and needs-based on the vertical axis and consensus and conflict on the horizontal axis. Though this typology separates and categorizes the various methods of community organizing and building, Minkler and Wallerstein point out that

> Community organizing and community building are fluid endeavors. Although some orga-
> nizing efforts primarily have focused in one quadrant, the majority incorporate multiple ten-
> dencies, possibly starting as a result of a specific need or crisis and moving to a strength-based
> community capacity approach. Different organizing models, such as coalitions, lay health
> worker programs, political action groups, or grassroots organizing may incorporate needs- or
> strength-based approaches at different times as well, depending on the starting place and the
> ever changing social dynamic. It is important, however, that organizing efforts clarify their
> assumptions and make decisions on primary strategies based on skills of group members, his-
> tory of the group, willingness to take risks, or comfort level with different approaches.[5]

THE PROCESS OF COMMUNITY ORGANIZING/BUILDING

It is beyond the scope of this textbook to explain all the approaches to community organizing and building in detail. Instead, we will present a generic approach (see Figure 5.3) created by McKenzie, Neiger, and Smeltzer that draws upon many of these other approaches.[10] The 10 steps of this generic approach are briefly reviewed in the sections that follow.

Recognizing the Issue

The process of community organizing/building begins when someone recognizes that a problem exists in a community and decides to do something about it. This person (or persons) is referred to as the initial organizer. This individual may not be the primary organizer throughout the community organizing/building process. He or she is the one who gets things started. For the purposes of this discussion, let us assume the problem is violence. People in most communities would like to have a violence-free community, but it would be most unusual to live in a community that was without at least some level of violence. How much violence is too much? At what point is a community willing to organize to deal with the problem? In a small-town community, an acceptable level of violence would be very low, while in a large city, an acceptable level would be much higher.

The people, or organizers, who first recognize a problem in the community and decide to act can be members of the community or individuals from outside the community. If those who initiate community organization are members of the community, then the movement is referred to as being **grass-roots,** *citizen initiated,* or organized from the *bottom up.* Community members who might recognize that violence is a problem could include teachers, police officers, or other concerned citizens. When community organization is initiated by individuals from outside of the community, the problem is said to be organized from the *top down* or *outside in.* Individuals from outside the community who might initiate organization could include a judge who presides over cases involving violence, a state social worker who handles cases of family violence, or a politically active group that is against violent behavior wherever it happens. In cases where the person who recognizes the community problem is not a community member, great care must be taken when notifying those in the community that a problem exists. "It is difficult for someone from the outside coming in and telling community members that they have problems or issues that have to be dealt with and they need to organize to take care of them."[10]

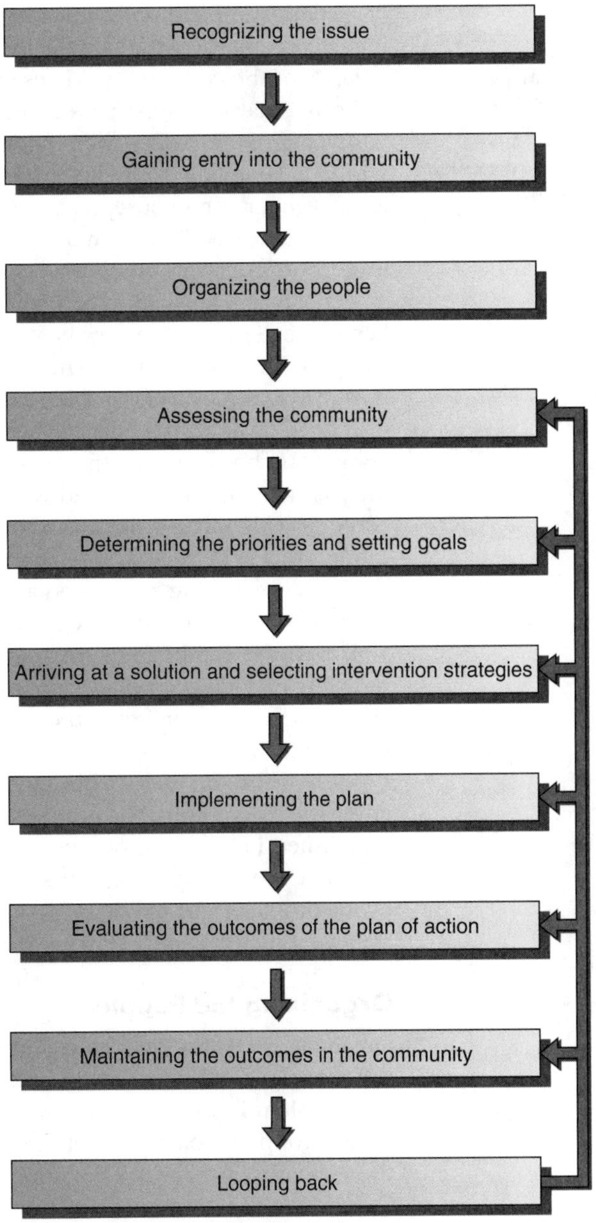

Gaining Entry into the Community

This second step in the community organizing process may or may not be needed, depending on whether the issue in step 1 was identified by someone from within the community or outside. If the issue is identified by someone outside the community, this step becomes a critical step in the process.[10] Gaining entry may seem like a relatively easy matter, but an error by organizers at this step could ruin the chances of successfully organizing the community. This may be the most crucial step in the whole process.

FIGURE 5.3

A summary of steps in community organizing and building.

Source: McKenzie, J. F., B. L. Neiger, and J. L. Smeltzer (2005). *Planning, Implementing, and Evaluating Health Promotion Programs: A Primer,* 4th ed. San Francisco, CA: Benjamin Cummings, 216. Reprinted with permission from Pearson Education, Inc.

grass-roots
a process that begins with those who are affected by the problem/concern

gatekeepers
those who control, both formally and informally, the political climate of the community

Braithwaite and colleagues have stressed the importance of tactfully negotiating entry into a community with the individuals who control, both formally and informally, the "political climate" of the community.[11] These people are referred to as the **gatekeepers.** Thus the term indicates that you must pass through this 'gate' to get to your priority population.[12] These "power brokers" know their community, how it functions, and how to accomplish tasks within it. Long-time residents are usually able to identify the gatekeepers of their community. A gatekeeper can be a representative of an intermediary organization—such as a church or school—that has direct contact with your priority audience.[12] Examples include politicians, leaders of activist groups, business and education leaders, and clergy, to name a few.

Organizers must approach such figures on the gatekeepers' own terms and play the gatekeepers' ball game. However, before approaching these important individuals, organizers must study the community well. They need to know where the power lies, what type of politics must be used to solve a problem, and whether the particular problem they wish to solve has ever been dealt with before in the community.[13] In the violence example, organizers need to know (1) who is causing the violence and why, (2) how the problem has been addressed in the past, (3) who supports and who opposes the idea of addressing the problem, and (4) who could provide more insight into the problem. This is a critical step in the community organization process because failure to study the community carefully in the beginning may lead to a delay in organizing it later and a subsequent waste of time and resources.

Once the organizers have a good understanding of the community, they are then ready to approach the gatekeepers. In keeping with the violence example, the gatekeepers would probably include the police department, elected officials, school board members, social service personnel, members of the judicial system, and possibly some of those who are creating the violence.

When the top-down approach is being used, organizers might find it advantageous to enter the community through a well-respected organization or institution that is already established in the community, such as a church, a service group, or another successful local group. If those who make up such an organization/institution can be convinced that the problem exists and needs to be solved, it can help smooth the way for gaining entry and achieving the remaining steps in the process.

Organizing the People

Obtaining the support of community members to deal with the problem is the next step in the process. It is best to begin by organizing those who are already interested in seeing that the problem is solved. This core group of community members, sometimes referred to as "executive participants,"[14] will become the backbone of the work force and will end up doing the majority of the work. For our example of community violence, the core group could include law enforcement personnel, former victims of violence and their families (or victims' support groups), parent-teacher organizations, and public health officials. It is also important to recruit people from the subpopulation that is most directly affected by the problem. For example, if most of the violence in a community is directed toward teenagers, teenagers need to be included in the core group. If elderly persons are impacted, they need to be included.

"From among the core group, a leader or coordinator must be identified. If at all possible, the leader should be someone with leadership skills, good knowledge of the concern and the community, and most of all, someone from within the community. One of the early tasks of the leader will be to help build group cohesion."[10]

Although the formation of the core group is essential, this group is usually not large enough to do all the work itself. Therefore, one of the core group's tasks is to recruit more members of the community to the cause. This step can take place via a *networking process,* which is when organizers make personal contacts with others who might be interested. Or, the organizers can call an organizing meeting at a local school, community center, or church.

By broadening the constituency, the core group can spread out the workload and generate additional resources to deal with the problem. However, recruiting additional workers can often be difficult. Over the last 30 years, the number of people in many communities interested in volunteering their time has decreased. Today, if you ask someone to volunteer, you may hear the reply, "I'm already too busy." There are two primary reasons for this response. First, there are many families in which both husband and wife work outside the home. And second, there are more single-parent households.

Therefore, when organizers are expanding their constituencies, they should be sure to (1) identify people who are impacted by the problem that they are trying to solve, (2) provide "perks" for or otherwise reward volunteers, (3) keep volunteer time short, (4) match volunteer assignments with the abilities and expertise of the volunteers, and (5) consider providing appropriate training to make sure volunteers are comfortable with their tasks. For example, if the organizers need someone to talk with law enforcement groups, it would probably be a good idea to solicit the help of someone who feels comfortable around such groups and who is respected by them, such as another law enforcement person.

When the core group has been expanded to include these other volunteers, the larger group is sometimes referred to as an *association* or a *task force*. There may even be an occasion where a coalition is formed. A **coalition** is "a formal, long-term alliance among a group of individuals representing diverse organizations, factors or constituencies within the community who agree to work together to achieve a common goal"[15]—often, to compensate for deficits in power, resources, and expertise. A larger group with more resources, people, and energy has a greater chance of solving a community problem than a smaller, less powerful group (see Figure 5.4). "Building and maintaining effective coalitions have increasingly been recognized as vital components of much effective community organizing and community building."[3]

coalition
formal, long-term alliance among a group of individuals representing others within the community who agree to work together to achieve a common goal

---

FIGURE 5.4
Coalition building is often an important step in successful community organization.

Assessing the Community

Earlier in this chapter we referred to Rothman and Tropman's typology for organizing a community—locality development, social planning, and social action.[8] Each of these community organizing strategies operates "from the assumption that problems in society can be addressed by the community becoming better or differently 'organized,' with each strategy perceiving the problems and how or whom to organize in order to address them somewhat differently."[16] In contrast to these strategies is community building. **Community building** "is an orientation to community that is strength-based rather than need-based and stresses the identification, nurturing, and celebration of community assets."[3] Thus, one of the major differences between community organizing and community building is the type of assessment that is used to determine where to focus the community's efforts. In the community organizing approach, the assessment is focused on the needs of the community, while in community building, the assessment focuses on the assets and capabilities of the community. It is assumed that a clearer picture of the community will be revealed and a stronger base will be developed for change if the assessment includes the identification of both needs and assets/capacities and involves those who live in the community. It is from these capacities and assets that communities are built.[17]

In order to determine the needs and assets/capacities of a community, an assessment must be completed. This could include a traditional *needs assessment* and/or a newer technique called *mapping community capacity*. A needs assessment is a process by which data about the issues of concern are collected and analyzed. From the analyzed data, concerns/problems emerge and are prioritized so that strategies can be created to tackle them. (Needs assessment is discussed in greater length in the second half of this chapter, with regard to program planning.)

Mapping community capacity, on the other hand, is a process of identifying community assets, not concerns or problems. It is a process by which organizers literally use a map to identify the different assets of a community. McKnight and Kretzmann[17] have categorized assets into three different groups based upon their availability to the community and refer to them as building blocks. *Primary building blocks* are the most accessible assets. They are located in the neighborhood and are largely under the control of those who live in the neighborhood. Primary building blocks can be organized into the assets of individuals (i.e., skills and talents) and those of organizations or associations (i.e., religious and citizen organizations). The next most accessible building blocks are secondary building blocks. *Secondary building blocks* are assets located in the neighborhood but largely controlled by people outside (i.e., schools, hospitals, and housing structures). The least accessible assets are referred to as potential building blocks. *Potential building blocks* are resources originating outside the neighborhood and controlled by people outside (i.e., welfare expenditures and public information). By knowing both the needs and assets of the community, organizers can work to identify the true concerns/problems of the community and use the assets of the community as a foundation for dealing with the concerns/problems.

Determining the Priorities and Setting Goals

An analysis of the community assessment data should result in the identification of the problems to be addressed. However, more often than not, the resources needed to solve all identified problems are not available. Therefore, the problems that have been identified must be prioritized. This prioritization is best achieved through general agreement or consensus of those who have been organized so that "ownership" can take hold. It is critical that all those working with the process feel that they "own" the problem and want to see it solved. Without this sense of ownership, they will be unwilling to give of their time and energy to solve it. For example, if a few highly vocal participants intimidate people into voting for certain activities to be the top priorities before a consensus is actually reached, it is unlikely that those who disagreed on this assignment of priorities will work enthusiastically to help solve the problem. They may even drop out of the process because they feel they have no ownership in the decision-making process.

Once the problems have been prioritized, goals need to be identified and written that will serve as guides for problem solving. The practice of consensus building should again be employed during the setting of goals. These goals, which will become the foundation for all the work that follows, can be thought of as the "hoped-for end result." In other words, once community action has occurred, what will have changed? In the community where violence is a problem, the goal may be to reduce the number of violent crimes or eliminate them altogether. Sometimes at this point in the process, some members of the larger group drop out because they do not see their priorities or goals included on consensus lists. Unable to feel ownership, they are unwilling to expend their resources on this process. Because there is strength in numbers, efforts should be made to keep them in. One strategy for doing so is to keep the goal list as long as possible.

Arriving at a Solution and Selecting Intervention Strategies

There are alternative solutions for every community problem. The group should examine the alternatives in terms of probable outcomes, acceptability to the community, probable long- and short-term effects on the community, and the cost of resources to solve the problem.[18] A solution involves selecting one or more intervention strategies (see Table 5.2). Each type of intervention strategy has advantages and disadvantages. The group must try to agree upon the best strategy and then select the most advantageous intervention activity or activities. Again, the group must work toward consensus through compromise. If the educators in the group were asked to provide a recommended strategy, they might suggest offering more preventive-education programs; law enforcement personnel might recommend more enforceable laws;

Table 5.2
Intervention Strategies and Example Activities

1. *Health communication strategies:* Mass media, billboards, booklets, bulletin boards, flyers, direct mail, newsletters, pamphlets, posters, and video and audio materials
2. *Health education strategies:* Educational methods (such as lecture, discussion, and group work) as well as audiovisual materials, computerized instruction, laboratory exercises, and written materials (books and periodicals)
3. *Health policy/enforcement strategies:* Executive orders, laws, ordinances, policies, position statements, regulations, and formal and informal rules
4. *Health engineering strategies:* Those that are designed to change the structure of services or systems of care to improve health promotion services, such as safety belts and air bags in cars, speed bumps in parking lots, or environmental cues such as No Smoking signs
5. *Health-related community services:* The use of health risk appraisals (HRAs), community screening for health problems, and immunization clinics
6. Other strategies
   a. *Behavior modification activities:* Modifying behavior to stop smoking, start to exercise, manage stress, and regulate diet
   b. *Community advocacy activities:* Mass mobilization, social action, community planning, community service development, community education, and community advocacy (such as a letter-writing campaign)
   c. *Organizational culture activities:* Activities that work to change norms and traditions
   d. *Incentives and disincentives:* Items that can either encourage or discourage people to behave a certain way, which may include money and other material items or fines
   e. *Social intervention activities:* Support groups, social activities, and social networks
   f. *Technology-delivered activities:* Educating or informing people by using technology (e.g., computers and telephones)

Source: McKenzie, J. F., B. L. Neiger, and J. L. Smeltzer (2005). *Planning, Implementing, and Evaluating Health Promotion Programs: A Primer,* 4th ed. San Francisco, CA: Benjamin Cummings.

judges might want more space in the jails and prisons. The protectionism of the subgroups within the larger group is often referred to as *turfism*. It is not uncommon to have turf struggles when trying to build consensus.

The Final Steps in the Community Organizing/Building Process: Implementing, Evaluating, Maintaining, and Looping Back

The last four steps in this generalized approach to organizing/building a community include implementing the intervention strategy and activities that were selected in the previous step, evaluating the outcomes of the plans of action, maintaining the outcomes over time, and if necessary, going back to a previous step in the process—"looping back"—to modify or restructure the work plan to organize the community.

Implementation of the intervention strategy includes identifying and collecting the necessary resources for implementation and creating the appropriate time line for implementation. Evaluation of the process involves comparing the outcomes of the process to the goals that were set in an earlier step. Maintaining or sustaining the outcomes may be one of the most difficult steps in the entire process. It is at this point that organizers need to seriously consider the need for a long-term capacity for problem solving. And finally, through the steps of implementation, evaluation, and maintenance of the outcomes, organizers may see the need to "loop back" to a previous step in the process to rethink or rework before proceeding onward in their plan.

A Special Note about Community Organizing/Building

Before we leave the processes of community organizing/building, it should be noted that no matter what approach is used in organizing/building a community—locality development, social planning, social action, or the generalized approach outlined here—not all problems can be solved. In other cases, repeated attempts may be necessary before a solution is reached. In addition, it is important to remember that if a problem exists in a community, there are probably some people who benefit from its existence and who may work toward preventing a successful solution to the problem. Whether or not the problem is solved, the final decision facing the organized group is whether to disband the group or to reorganize in order to take on a new problem or attack the first problem from a different direction.

FIGURE 5.5

Healthy People, the 1979 Surgeon General's report on health promotion and disease prevention, charted a new course for community health.

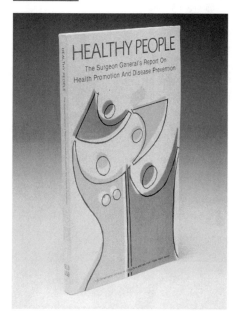

HEALTH PROMOTION PROGRAMMING

In Chapters 2 through 4, we discuss how communities describe, analyze, and intervene to solve existing health problems such as disease outbreaks or other community problems. However, the 1979 Surgeon General's report on health promotion and disease prevention, *Healthy People* (see Figure 5.5), charted a new course for community health—away from curing diseases and toward preventing diseases and promoting health. Health promotion programming has now become an important tool of community health professionals. The second half of this chapter presents the process of health promotion programming.

Basic Understanding of Program Planning

Prior to discussing the process of program planning, two relationships must be presented. These are the relationships between health education and health promotion, and program planning and community organizing/building.

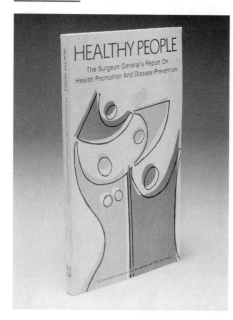

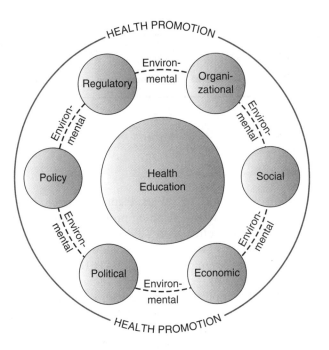

FIGURE 5.6
The relationship of health education and health promotion.

Source: McKenzie, J. F., B. L. Neiger, and J. L. Smeltzer (2005). *Planning, Implementing, and Evaluating Health Promotion Programs: A Primer,* 4th ed. San Francisco, CA: Benjamin Cummings, 4. Reprinted with permission from Pearson Education, Inc.

Health education and *health promotion* are terms that are sometimes used interchangeably. This is incorrect because health education is only a part of health promotion. The Joint Committee on Health Education and Promotion Terminology defined the process of **health education** as "any combination of planned learning experiences based on sound theories that provide individuals, groups, and communities the opportunity to acquire information and the skills to make quality health decisions."[19] The Committee defined **health promotion** as "any planned combination of educational, political, environmental, regulatory, or organizational mechanisms that support actions and conditions of living conducive to the health of individuals, groups, and communities."[19] From these definitions, it is obvious that the terms are not the same and that *health promotion* is a much more encompassing term than *health education.* Figure 5.6 provides a graphic representation of the relationship between the terms.

The first half of this chapter described the process of community organizing/building—the process by which individuals, groups, and organizations engage in planned action to influence social problems. Program planning may or may not be associated with community organizing/building. **Program planning** is a process in which an intervention is planned to help meet the needs of a specific group of people. It may take a community organizing/building effort to be able to plan such an intervention. The anti-violence campaign used earlier in the chapter is such an example, where many resources of the community were brought together in order to create interventions (programs) to deal with the violence problem. However, program planning need not be connected to community organizing/building. For example, a community organizing/building effort is not needed before a company offers a smoking cessation program for its employees or a religious organization offers a stress management class for its members. In such cases, only the steps of the program planning process need to be carried out. These steps are described in the following section.

CREATING A HEALTH PROMOTION PROGRAM

The process of developing a health promotion program, like the process of community organizing/building, involves a series of steps. Success depends upon many factors, including the assistance of a professional experienced in program planning.

health education
any combination of planned learning experiences based on sound theories that provide individuals, groups, and communities the opportunity to acquire information and the skills to make quality health decisions

health promotion
any planned combination of educational, political, environmental, regulatory, or organizational mechanisms that support actions and conditions of living conducive to the health of individuals, groups, and communities

program planning
a process by which an intervention is planned to help meet the needs of a priority population

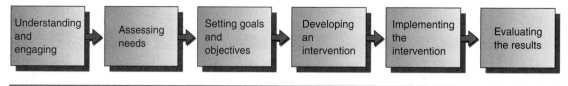

FIGURE 5.7

A generalized model for program planning.

Source: McKenzie, J. F., B. L. Neiger, and J. L. Smeltzer (2005). *Planning, Implementing, and Evaluating Health Promotion Programs: A Primer,* 4th ed. San Francisco, CA: Benjamin Cummings, 16. Reprinted with permission from Pearson Education, Inc.

Experienced program planners use models to guide their work. Planning models are the means by which structure and organization are given to the planning process. Many different planning models exist, some of which are used more often than others.[10] Some of the more frequently used models include the PRECEDE/PROCEED Model,[20] probably the best known and most often used; the Multilevel Approach to Community Health (MATCH);[21] Mobilizing for Action through Planning and Partnership (MAPP);[22] and the more recently developed consumer-based planning models that are based upon health communication and social marketing such as CDCynergy[23] and Social Marketing Assessment and Response Tool (SMART).[24] Each of these planning models has its strengths and weaknesses, and each has distinctive components that makes it unique. In addition, each of the models has been used to plan health promotion programs in a variety of settings, with many successes.

It is not absolutely necessary that the student studying community health for the first time have a thorough understanding of the models mentioned here, but it is important to know the basic steps in the planning process. Therefore, we are presenting a generalized program development model[10] that draws on the major components of these other models. The steps of this generalized model are presented in Figure 5.7 and explained in the following paragraphs.

Understanding the Community and Engaging the Priority Population

priority population (audience)
those whom a program is intended to serve

The first step in the generalized model is to understand the community and engage the **priority population (audience),** those whom the health promotion program is intended to serve. Understanding the community means finding out as much as possible about the priority population and the environment in which it exists. Engaging the priority population means getting those in the population involved in the early stages of the health promotion program planning process. If the priority population was comprised of the employees of a corporation, the planners would want to read all the material they could find about the company, spend time talking with various individuals and subgroups in the company (i.e., new employees, employees who had been with the company for a long time, management, clerical staff, labor representatives, etc.) to find out what they wanted from a health promotion program, and review old documents of the company (i.e., health insurance records, labor agreements, written history of the company, etc.). Also, as a part of this first step, the planners should consider forming a program planning committee with representation from the various subgroups of the work force (i.e., management, labor, and clerical staff). The planning committee can help ensure all segments of the priority population will be engaged in the planning process.

Assessing the Needs of the Priority Population

In order to create a useful and effective program for the priority population, planners, with the assistance of the planning committee, must determine the needs and wants of the priority

FIGURE 5.8
A telephone survey is a common form of data collection for a health needs assessment.

population. This procedural step is referred to as a *needs assessment*. A **needs assessment** is the process of collecting and analyzing information to develop an understanding of the issues, resources, and constraints of the priority population, as related to the development of the health promotion program.[25] The assessment's purpose is to determine whether the needs of the people are being met (see Figure 5.8).

For those interested in a detailed explanation of the process of conducting a needs assessment, extensive accounts are available.[26,27] The following is a simplified six-step approach.[10]

Step 1: Determining the Purpose and Scope of the Needs Assessment

The first step in the needs assessment process is to determine the purpose and the scope of the needs assessment. That is, what is the goal of the needs assessment? What does the planning committee hope to gain from the needs assessment? How extensive will the assessment be? What kind of resources will be available to conduct the needs assessment? Once these questions are answered, the planners are ready to begin gathering data.

Step 2: Gathering Data

The second step in the process is gathering the data that will help to identify the true needs of the priority population. Such data are categorized into two groups—primary and secondary. Primary data are those that are collected specifically for use in this process. An example is having those in the priority population complete a needs assessment questionnaire about their health behavior. Secondary data are data that have already been collected for some other purpose, such as health insurance claims records or BRFSS data. Using both primary and secondary data usually presents the clearest picture of the priority population's needs.

needs assessment
the process of collecting and analyzing information, to develop an understanding of the issues, resources, and constraints of the priority population, as related to the development of the health promotion program

Step 3: Analyzing the Data

Collected data can be analyzed in one of two ways—formally or informally. Formal analysis consists of some type of statistical analysis, assuming that the appropriate statistical criteria have been met. However, a more common means of analysis is an informal technique referred to as "eyeballing the data." With this technique, program developers look for the obvious differences between the health status or conditions of the priority population and the programs and services available to close the gap between what is and what ought to be. Regardless of the method used, data analysis should yield a list of the problems that exist, with a description of the nature and extent of each.

The final part of this step is prioritizing the list of problems. Prioritization must take place because though all needs are important, seldom are there enough resources (money and time) available to deal with all the problems identified. When prioritizing, planners should consider (1) the importance of the need, (2) how changeable the need is, and (3) whether adequate resources are available to deal with the problem.

Step 4: Identifying the Factors Linked to the Health Problem

In this step of the process, planners need to identify and prioritize the risk factors that are associated with the health problem. Thus, if the prioritized health problem identified in step 3 is heart disease, planners must analyze the health behaviors and environment of the priority population for known risk factors of heart disease. For example, higher than expected smoking behavior may be present in the priority population in addition to a community that lacks recreational areas for exercise. Once these risk factors are identified, they also need to be prioritized.

Step 5: Identifying the Program Focus

With risk factors identified and prioritized, planners need to identify those predisposing, enabling, and reinforcing factors that seem to have a direct impact on the targeted risk factors. In the heart disease example, those in the priority population may not (1) have the skills to begin an exercise program (predisposing factor), (2) have access to recreational facilities (enabling factor), or (3) have people around them who value the benefits of exercise (reinforcing factor). "Study of the predisposing, enabling, and reinforcing factors automatically helps the planner decide exactly which of the factors making up the three classes deserve the highest priority as the focus of the intervention. The decision is based on their importance and any evidence that change in the factor is possible and cost-effective."[20]

Step 6: Validating the Prioritized Need

The final step in this process is to double-check or to confirm that the identified need and resulting program focus indeed need to be addressed in the priority population. For example, a limited amount of data may indicate the primary need of the priority group to be one thing—heart disease, for example. However, more extensive data or more comprehensive networking may identify another problem, such as diabetes or malnutrition. Before step 6 is completed, planners must make sure they have indeed identified a true need. In short, all work should be double-checked.

At the conclusion of a needs assessment, planners should be able to answer the following questions:[27]

1. Who is the priority population?
2. What are the needs of the priority population?
3. Which subgroups within the priority population have the greatest need?
4. Where are the subgroups located geographically?
5. What is currently being done to resolve identified needs?
6. How well have the identified needs been addressed in the past?

Setting Appropriate Goals and Objectives

Once the problem has been well defined and the needs prioritized, the planners can set goals and develop objectives for the program. The goals and objectives should be thought of as the foundation of the program. The remaining portions of the programming process—intervention development, implementation, and evaluation—will be designed to achieve the goals by meeting the objectives.

The words *goals* and *objectives* are often used interchangeably, but there is really a significant difference between the two. "A goal is a future event toward which a committed endeavor is directed; objectives are the steps taken in pursuit of a goal."[28] To further distinguish between goals and objectives, McKenzie and colleagues[10] have stated that goals (1) are much more encompassing and global than objectives, (2) are written to cover all aspects of a program, (3) provide overall program direction, (4) are more general in nature, (5) usually take longer to complete, (6) are usually not observed but inferred,[29] and (7) often are not easily measured. Goals are easy to write and include two basic components—who will be affected and what will change because of the program. Here are some examples of program goals:

1. To help employees learn how to manage their stress
2. To reduce the number of teenage pregnancies in the community
3. To help cardiac patients and their families deal with the lifestyle changes that occur after a heart attack

Objectives are more precise and can be considered the steps to achieve the program goals. Because some program goals are more complex than others, the number and type of objectives will vary from program to program. For example, the process of getting a group of people to exercise is a more complex activity than trying to get a group to learn the four food groups. The more complex a program, the greater the number of objectives needed. To deal with these different types of programs, McKenzie and colleagues[10] adapted a hierarchy of program objectives first developed by Deeds[30] and later updated by Cleary and Neiger.[31] Table 5.3 presents the hierarchy and an example of an objective at each of the levels within the hierarchy.

From the examples presented in Table 5.3, it should be obvious that the hierarchy goes from less complex to more complex levels. Thus, it takes less energy and fewer resources to increase awareness in the priority population than to improve its health status. Close examination of the example objectives reveals that the objectives are written in specific terms. They are composed of four parts (who, what, when, and how much) and outline changes that should result from the implementation of the program.[32] As such, the objectives are written so that the level of their attainment is observable and measurable.

One final note about objectives: In Chapter 1, *Healthy People 2010,* the national health goals and objectives of the Nation, was discussed. Selected objectives from this publication are presented in boxes throughout this text (see Box 5.1). These goals and objectives provide a good model for developing goals and objectives for a new program. In fact, these goals and objectives can be adapted for use in most community health promotion programs.

Creating an Intervention That Considers the Peculiarities of the Setting

The next step in the program planning process is to design activities that will help the priority population meet the objectives and, in the process, achieve their goals. These activities are collectively referred to as an **intervention,** or treatment. This intervention or treatment constitutes the program that the priority population will experience.

The number of activities in an intervention may be many or only a few. Although no minimum number has been established, it has been shown that multiple activities are often more effective than a single activity. For example, if the planners wanted to change the attitudes of community members toward a new landfill, they would have a greater chance of doing so by

intervention
an activity or activities designed to create change in people

Table 5.3
Hierarchy of Objectives and Examples of Each

Type of Objective	Program Outcomes	Possible Evaluation Measures	Type of Evaluation	Example Objective
Process/administrative objectives	Activities presented and tasks completed	Number of sessions held, exposure, attendance, participation, staff performance, appropriate materials, adequacy of resources, tasks on schedule	Process (form of formative)	On June 12, 2006, a breast cancer brochure will be distributed to all female customers over the age of 18 at the Ross grocery store.
Learning objectives	Change in awareness, knowledge, attitudes, and skills	Increase in awareness, knowledge, attitudes, and skill development/acquisition	Impact (form of summative)	When asked in class, 50% of the students will be able to list the four principles of cardiovascular conditioning.
Action/behavioral objectives	Change in behavior	Current behavior modified or discontinued, or new behavior adopted	Impact (form of summative)	During a telephone interview, 35% of the residents will report having had their blood cholesterol checked in the last six months.
Environmental objectives	Change in the environment	Protection added to, or hazards or barriers removed from, the environment	Impact (form of summative)	By the end of the year, all senior citizens who requested transportation to the congregate meals will have received it.
Program objectives	Change in quality of life (QOL), health status, or risk, and social benefits	QOL measures, morbidity data, mortality data, measures of risk (e.g., HRA)	Outcome (form of summative)	By the year 2006, infant mortality rates will be reduced to no more than 7 per 1,000 in Franklin County.

Source: Adapted from Deeds, S. G. (1992). *The Health Education Specialist: Self-study for Professional Competence.* Los Alamitos, CA: Loose Canon; Cleary, M. J., and B. L. Neiger (1998). *The Certified Health Education Specialist: A Self-Study Guide for Professional Competence,* 3rd ed. Allentown, PA: National Commission for Health Education Credentialing; and McKenzie, J. F., B. L. Neiger, and J. L. Smeltzer (2005). *Planning, Implementing, and Evaluating Health Promotion Programs: A Primer* (4th ed.). San Francisco, CA: Benjamin Cummings.

distributing pamphlets door to door, writing articles for the local newspaper, and speaking to local service groups, than by performing any one of these activities by itself. "In other words, the size of the 'dose' is important in health promotion programming. Few people change their behavior based on a single exposure (or dose); instead, multiple exposures (doses) are generally needed to change most behaviors. It stands to reason that 'hitting' the priority population from several angles or through multiple channels should increase the chances of making an impact."[10]

The choice of strategies for an intervention depends on a number of variables. McLeroy and colleagues have indicated that the levels of influence need to be considered when developing interventions.[33] These levels of influence are included in the ecological perspective, which "recognizes that health behaviors are part of the larger social system (or ecology) of behaviors and social influences, much like a river, forest or desert is part of a larger biological system (ecosystem), and that lasting changes in health behaviors require supportive changes in the whole system, just as the addition of a power plant, the flooding of a reservoir, or the growth of a city in a desert produce changes in the whole ecosystem."[34] This perspective includes five levels of influence on health-related behaviors and conditions. These levels include:

1. Intrapersonal or individual factors
2. Interpersonal factors
3. Institutional or organizational factors
4. Community factors
5. Public policy factors

Healthy People 2010: Objectives

Educational and Community-Based Programs

7-5. Increase the proportion of worksites that offer a comprehensive employee health promotion program to their employees.

Objective	Increase in Worksites Offering a Comprehensive Employer-Sponsored Health Promotion Program	1999* Baseline	2010 Target
		Percent	
7-5a.	Worksites with <50 employees	Developmental	
7-5b.	Worksites with 50 or more employees	34%	75%
7-5c.	Worksites with 50 to 99 employees	33%	75%
7-5d.	Worksites with 100 to 249 employees	33%	75%
7-5e.	Worksites with 250 to 749 employees	38%	75%
7-5f.	Worksites with 750 or more employees	50%	75%

*No measurement since baseline.

7-6. Increase the proportion of employees who participate in employer-sponsored health promotion activities.

Target: 75 percent.

Baseline: 61 percent of employees aged 18 years and older participated in employer-sponsored health promotion activities in 1994; 1998 status 59%.

7-7. (Developmental) Increase the proportion of health care organizations that provide patient and family education.

7-8. (Developmental) Increase the proportion of patients who report that they are satisfied with the patient education they receive from their health care organization.

7-9. (Developmental) Increase the proportion of hospitals and managed care organizations that provide community disease prevention and health promotion activities that address the priority health needs identified by their community.

7-10. (Developmental) Increase the proportion of tribal and local health service areas or jurisdictions that have established a community health promotion program that addresses multiple *Healthy People 2010* focus areas.

7-11. Increase the proportion of local health departments that have established culturally appropriate and linguistically competent community health promotion and disease prevention programs.

7-12. Increase the proportion of older adults who have participated during the preceding year in at least one organized health promotion activity.

Target: 90 percent.

Baseline: 12 percent of adults aged 65 years and older participated during the preceding year in at least one organized health promotion activity in 1998 (age adjusted to the year 2000 standard population).

For Further Thought

If you had the opportunity to write one more objective dealing with the implementation of health promotion programs for use in *Healthy People 2010,* what would it be? What is your rationale for selecting such an objective?

Thus, interventions can be developed to "attack" a health concern of a priority population at any or all of these levels. The intervention strategies designed to solve problems associated with community organizing/building, as presented in Table 5.2, are the same strategies being discussed here.

Implementing the Intervention

The moment of truth is when the intervention is implemented. **Implementation** is the actual carrying out or putting into practice of the activity or activities that make up the intervention.

implementation
putting a planned program into action

It is at this point that the planners will learn whether the product (intervention) they developed will be useful in producing the measurable changes as outlined in the objectives.

To ensure a smooth-flowing implementation of the intervention, it is wise to pilot test it at least once and sometimes more. A **pilot test** is a trial run. It is when the intervention is presented to just a few individuals who are either from the intended priority population or from a very similar population. For example, if the intervention is being developed for fifth graders in a particular school, it might be pilot tested on fifth graders with similar educational backgrounds and demographic variables but from a different school.

The purpose of pilot testing an intervention is to determine whether there are any problems with it. Some of the more common problems that pop up are those dealing with the design or delivery of the intervention; however, any part of it could be flawed. For example, it could be determined during pilot testing that there is a lack of resources to carry out the intervention as planned or that those implementing the intervention need more training. When minor flaws are detected and corrected easily, the intervention is then ready for full implementation. However, if a major problem surfaces—one that requires much time and many resources to correct—it is recommended that the intervention be pilot tested again with the improvements in place before implementation.

An integral part of the piloting process is collecting feedback from those in the pilot group. By surveying the pilot group, planners can identify popular and unpopular aspects of the intervention, how the intervention might be changed or improved, and whether the program activities were effective. This information can be useful in fine-tuning this intervention or in developing future programs.

Once the intervention has been pilot tested and corrected as necessary, it is ready to be disseminated and implemented. If the program that has been planned is being implemented with a large priority population and there is a lot at stake with the implementation, it is advisable that the intervention be implemented gradually rather than all at once. One way of doing so is by phasing in the intervention. **Phasing in** refers to a step-by-step implementation in which the intervention is introduced first to smaller groups instead of the entire priority population. Common criteria used for selecting participating groups for phasing in include participant ability, number of participants, program offerings, and program location.[10]

The following is an example of phasing in by location. Assume that a local public health agency wants to provide smoking cessation programs for all the smokers in the community (priority population). Instead of initiating one big intervention for all, planners could divide the priority population by residence location. Facilitators would begin implementation by offering the smoking cessation classes on the south side of town during the first month. During the second month, they would continue the classes on the south side and begin implementation on the west side of town. They would continue to implement this intervention until all sections of the town were included.

Evaluating the Results

The final step in the generalized planning model is the evaluation. Although evaluation is the last step in this model, it really takes place in all steps of program planning. It is very important that planning for evaluation occur during the first stages of program development, not just at the end.

Evaluation is the process in which planners determine the value or worth of the objective of interest by comparing it against a **standard of acceptability**.[35] Common standards of acceptability include, but are not limited to, mandates (policies, statues, and laws), values, norms, and comparison/control groups.

Evaluation can be categorized further into summative and formative evaluation. **Formative evaluation** is done during the planning and implementing processes to improve or refine the program. For example, validating the needs assessment and pilot testing are both

pilot test
a trial run of an intervention

phasing in
implementation of an intervention with a series of small groups instead of the entire population

evaluation
determining the value or worth of an objective of interest

standard of acceptability
a comparative mandate, value, norm, or group

formative evaluation
the evaluation that is conducted during the planning and implementing processes to improve or refine the program

forms of formative evaluation. **Summative evaluation** begins with the development of goals and objectives and is conducted after implementation to determine the program's impact on the priority population.

Like other steps in the planning model, this step can be broken down into smaller steps. The mini-steps of evaluation include planning the evaluation, collecting the necessary evaluative data, analyzing the data, and reporting and applying the results.

Planning the Evaluation

As noted earlier, planning for summative evaluation begins with the development of the goals and objectives of the program. These statements put into writing what should happen as a result of the program. Also in this planning mini-step, it should be determined who will evaluate the program—an *internal evaluator* (one who already is involved in the program) or an *external evaluator* (one from outside the program). In addition, this portion of the evaluation process should identify an evaluation design and a time line for carrying out the evaluation.

Collecting the Data

Data collection includes deciding how to collect the data (e.g., with a survey instrument, from existing records, by observation, etc.), determining who will collect them, pilot testing the procedures, and performing the actual data collection.

Analyzing the Data

Once the data are in hand, they must be analyzed and interpreted. Also, it must be decided who will analyze the data and when the analysis is to be completed.

Reporting the Results

Next the evaluation report should be written. Decisions must be made (if they have not been made already) regarding who should write the report, who should receive the report, in what form, and when.

Applying the Results

With the findings in hand, it then must be decided how they will be used. When time, resources, and effort are spent on an evaluation, it is important that the results be useful for reaching a constructive end and for deciding whether to continue or discontinue the program or to alter it in some way.

> **summative evaluation**
> the evaluation that determines the impact of a program on the priority population

CHAPTER SUMMARY

- A knowledge of community organizing and program planning is essential for community health workers whose job it is to promote and protect the health of the community.

- Community organizing is a process through which communities are helped to identify common problems or goals, mobilize resources, and in other ways develop and implement strategies for reaching their goals that they have collectively set.

- Community building is an orientation to community that is strength-based rather than need-based and stresses the identification, nurturing, and celebration of community assets.

- The steps of the general model for community organizing/building include recognizing the issue, gaining entry into the community, organizing the people, assessing the community, determining the priorities and setting goals, arriving at a solution and selecting the intervention strategies, implementing the plan, evaluating the outcomes of the plan of action, maintaining the outcomes in the community, and, if necessary, looping back.

- Program planning is a process in which an intervention is planned to help meet the needs of a priority population (audience).

- The steps in the program planning process include understanding the community and engaging the priority population, assessing the needs of the priority population, setting appropriate goals and objectives, creating an intervention that considers the peculiarities of the setting, implementing the intervention, and evaluating the results.

SCENARIO: ANALYSIS AND RESPONSE

The town of Kenzington sounds like a good candidate for a community organizing/building effort. Assume that Kenzington is the town in which you now live and you belong to the group that has taken the issue to the city council. Based upon what you know about the problem in the scenario and what you know about your town, answer the following questions.

1. What is the real problem?
2. Who do you think the gatekeepers are in the community?
3. What groups of people in the community might be most interested in solving this problem?
4. What groups might have a vested interest in seeing the problem remain unsolved?
5. What interventions would be useful in dealing with the problem?
6. How would you evaluate your efforts to solve the problem?
7. What strategies might you recommend to make the solution lasting?
8. If you were to look for help on the Internet to deal with this problem, what key words would you use to search the Web for help?

REVIEW QUESTIONS

1. What is community organizing?
2. What are the assumptions (identified by Ross) under which organizers work when bringing a community together to solve a problem?
3. What is the difference between top-down and grass-roots community organizing?
4. What is meant by the term *gatekeepers*? Who would they be in your community?
5. Identify the steps in the generalized approach to community organizing/building presented in this chapter.
6. What is meant by community building?
7. What is a needs assessment? Why is it important in the health promotion programming process?
8. What are the six major steps in program development?
9. What are the differences between goals and objectives?
10. What are intervention strategies? Provide five examples.
11. What is meant by the term *pilot testing*? How is it useful when developing an intervention?
12. What is the difference between formative and summative evaluation?
13. Name and briefly describe the five major components of program evaluation.

ACTIVITIES

1. From your knowledge of the community in which you live (or from the yellow pages of the telephone book), generate a list of 7 to 10 agencies that might be interested in creating a coalition to deal with community drug problems. Provide a one-sentence rationale for each why it might want to be involved.

2. Ask your instructor if he or she is aware of any community organizing/building efforts in a local community. If you are able to identify such an effort, make an appointment—either by yourself or with some of your classmates—to meet with the person who is leading the effort and ask the following questions:

   What is the problem that faces the community?

   What is the goal of the group?

   What steps have been taken so far to organize/build the community, and what steps are yet to be taken?

   Who is active in the core group?

   Did the group conduct a community assessment?

   What intervention will be/has been used?

   Is it anticipated that the problem will be solved?

3. Using a smoking cessation program, write one program goal and an objective for each of the levels presented in Table 5.3.

4. Visit a voluntary health agency in your community, either by yourself or with classmates. Ask employees if you may review any of the standard health promotion programs the agency offers to the community. Examine the program materials, locating the six major components of a program development discussed in this chapter. Then, in a two-page paper, summarize your findings.

COMMUNITY HEALTH ON THE WEB

The Internet contains a wealth of information about community and public health. Increase your knowledge of some of the topics presented in this chapter by accessing the Jones and Bartlett Publishers Web site at **health.jbpub.com/communityhealth/5e** and follow the links to complete the following Web activities.

- Public Health Foundation
- Community Health Status Indicators
- Public Health Functions Project

REFERENCES

1. Centers for Disease Control and Prevention/Agency for Toxic Substances and Disease Registry (1997). *Principles of Community Engagement.* Atlanta, GA: Centers for Disease Control and Prevention.

2. Minkler, M., and N. Wallerstein (1997). "Improving Health through Community Organization and Community Building: A Health Education Perspective." In M. Minkler, ed., *Community Organizing and Community Building for Health*. New Brunswick, NJ: Rutgers University Press, 30–52.

3. Minkler, M. (1997). Introduction and Overview. In M. Minkler, ed., *Community Organizing and Community Building for Health*. New Brunswick, NJ: Rutgers University Press, 3–19.

4. Ross, M. G. (1967). *Community Organization: Theory, Principles, and Practice.* New York: Harper and Row, 86–92.

5. Minkler, M., and N. B. Wallerstein (2002). "Improving Health through Community Organization and Community Building." In K. Glanz, B. K. Rimer, and F. M. Lewis, eds., *Health Behavior and Health Education: Theory, Research, and Practice,* 3rd ed. New York: John Wiley and Sons, 279–311.

6. Checkoway, B. (1989). "Community Participation for Health Promotion: Prescription for Public Policy." *Wellness Perspectives: Research, Theory and Practice,* 6(1): 18–26.

7. Israel, B. A., B. Checkoway, A. Schultz, and M. Zimmerman (1994). "Health Education and Community Empowerment: Conceptualizing and Measuring Perceptions of Individual, Organizational, and Community Control." *Health Education Quarterly,* 21(2): 149–170.

8. Rothman, J., and J. E. Tropman (1987). "Models of Community Organization and Macro Practice Perspectives: Their Mixing and Phasing." In F. M. Cox, J. L. Erlich, J. Rothman, and J. E. Tropman, eds., *Strategies of Community Organization: Macro Practice.* Itasca, IL: F. E. Peacock, 3–26.

9. Alinsky, S. D. (1971). *Rules for Radicals: A Pragmatic Primer for Realistic Radicals.* New York: Random House.

10. McKenzie, J. F., B. L. Neiger, and J. L. Smeltzer (2005). *Planning, Implementing, and Evaluating Health Promotion Programs: A Primer,* 4th ed. San Francisco: Benjamin Cummings.

11. Braithwaite, R. L., F. Murphy, N. Lythcott, and D. S. Blumenthal (1989). "Community Organization and Development for Health Promotion within an Urban Black Community: A Conceptual Model." *Health Education,* 20(5): 56–60.

12. Wright, P. A. (1994). "Technical Assistance Bulletin: A Key Step in Developing Prevention Materials Is to Obtain Expert and Gatekeepers' Reviews." Bethesda, MD: Center for Substance Abuse Prevention (CASP) Communications Team, 1–6.

13. Perlman, J. (1978). "Grassroots Participation from Neighborhood to Nation." In S. Langton, ed., *Citizen Participation in America.* Lexington, MA: Lexington Books, 65–79.

14. Brager, G., H. Specht, and J. L. Torczyner (1987). *Community Organizing.* New York: Columbia University Press, 55.

15. Butterfoss, F. D., and M. D. Whitt (2003). "Building and Sustaining Coalitions." In R. J. Bensley and J. Brookins-Fisher, eds., *Community Health Education Methods,* 2nd ed. Boston: Jones and Bartlett Publishers, 325–356.

16. Walter, C. L. (1997). "Community Building Practice: A Conceptual Framework." In M. Minkler, ed., *Community Organizing and Community Building for Health.* New Brunswick, NJ: Rutgers University Press, 68–83.

17. McKnight, J. L., and J. P. Kretzmann (1997). "Mapping Community Capacity." In M. Minkler, ed., *Community Organizing and Community Building for Health.* New Brunswick, NJ: Rutgers University Press, 157–172.

18. Archer, S. E., and R. P. Fleshman (1985). *Community Health Nursing.* Monterey, CA: Wadsworth Health Sciences.

19. Joint Committee on Health Education and Promotion Terminology (2001). "Report of the 2000 Joint Committee on Health Education and Promotion Terminology." *American Journal of Health Education,* 32(2): 89–103.

20. Green, L. W., and M. W. Kreuter (1999). *Health Promotion Planning: An Educational and Ecological Approach,* 3rd ed. Mountain View, CA: Mayfield Publishing Company.

21. Simons-Morton, D. G., W. H. Greene, and N. H. Gottlieb (1995). *Introduction to Health Education and Health Promotion,* 2nd ed. Prospect Heights, IL: Waveland Press.

22. National Association of County and City Health Officials (2001). *Mobilizing for Action through Planning and Partnerships (MAPP).* Washington, DC: Author.

23. Centers for Disease Control and Prevention, U.S. Department of Health and Human Services (2003). *CDCynergy 3.0: Your Guide to Effective Health Communication* [CD-ROM Version 3.0]. Atlanta, GA: Author.

24. Neiger, B. L. (1998). "Social Marketing: Making Public Health Sense." Paper presented at the annual meeting of the Utah Public Health Association, Provo, UT.

25. Anspaugh, D. J., M. B. Dignan, and S. L. Anspaugh (2000). *Developing Health Promotion Programs.* Boston: McGraw-Hill Higher Education.

26. Gilmore, G. D., and M. D. Campbell (2005). *Needs and Capacity Assessment Strategies for Health Education and Health Promotion,* 3rd ed. Sudbury, MA: Jones and Bartlett Publishers.

27. Peterson, D. J., and G. R. Alexander (2001). *Needs Assessment in Public Health: A Practical Guide for Students and Professionals.* New York: Kluwer Academic/Plenum Publishers.

28. Ross, H. S., and P. R. Mico (1980). *Theory and Practice in Health Education.* Palo Alto, CA: Mayfield, 219.

29. Jacobsen, D., P. Eggen, and D. Kauchak (1989). *Methods for Teaching: A Skills Approach,* 3rd ed. Columbus, OH: Merrill.

30. Deeds, S. G. (1992). *The Health Education Specialist: Self-Study for Professional Competence.* Los Alamitos, CA: Loose Canon Publications.

31. Cleary, M. J., and B. L. Neiger (1998). *The Certified Health Education Specialist: A Self-Study Guide for Professional Competence,* 3rd ed. Allentown, PA: National Commission for Health Education Credentialing.

32. McKenzie, J. F. (2004). "Planning and Evaluating Interventions." In J. Kerr, R. Weitkunat, and M. Moretti, eds., *ABC of Behavior Change: A Guide to Successful Disease Prevention and Health Promotion.* Edinburgh, England: Churchill Livingstone, 41–54.

33. McLeroy, K. R., D. Bibeau, A. Steckler, and K. Glanz (1988). "An Ecological Perspective for Health Promotion Programs." *Health Education Quarterly,* 15(4): 351–378.

34. O'Donnell, M. P. (1996). "Editor's Notes." *American Journal of Health Promotion,* 10(4): 244.

35. Green, L. W., and F. M. Lewis (1986). *Measurement and Evaluation in Health Education and Health Promotion.* Palo Alto, CA: Mayfield.

Chapter 6

The School Health Program: A Component of Community Health

Chapter Objectives

After studying this chapter you will be able to:

1 Define *coordinated school health program*.

2 List the ideal members of a school health council.

3 Explain why a school health program is important.

4 Identify the major foundations of a coordinated school health program.

5 Define written *school health policies* and explain their importance to the school health program.

6 Explain processes for developing and implementing school health policies.

7 List the eight components of a coordinated school health program.

8 Describe the role of the school health coordinator.

9 Identify those services offered as part of school health services and explain why schools are logical places to offer such services.

10 Describe three models for offering school health services.

11 Explain what is meant by a *healthy school environment* and discuss the two major environments.

12 Define *school health education*.

13 Identify the seven National Health Education Standards.

14 Explain how a health educator could locate credible health education curricula.

15 Identify and briefly explain four issues that are faced by school health advocates.

SCENARIO

Seldom does an elementary school teacher have a typical day. Each day seems to bring a variety of new experiences. Take, for example, the day Ms. Graff experienced last Wednesday. Even before the first bell at 8:30 A.M. she was summoned to the hallway, where one of her second-graders became ill and threw up. Remembering her teachers' in-service workshop on HIV and AIDS, Ms. Graff put into action her new knowledge of universal precautions for handling blood and body fluids.

After that incident, her day seemed to be going along well until two of Ms. Graff's students began fighting in the lunch room. They were arguing over who had the healthier lunch. It seemed that Billy thought his peanut butter and jelly sandwich was healthier than Tommy's cheese sandwich and bag of potato chips. Ms. Graff was skillful in helping to settle the dispute.

After lunch, Ms. Graff began her lesson on drug education. She wasn't 10 minutes into her lesson when the school nurse stuck her head in the door and asked if Ms. Graff could send five students for their annual vision screening. Reluctantly, Ms. Graff excused five of her students.

During the last half-hour of the school day, Ms. Graff provided the children with quiet time so that they could read or work on some of their homework. Just before the last bell was to ring, Annie came up to Ms. Graff's desk and told her that the girl sitting in front of her kept rubbing her eye and it seemed really red. Annie said, "I think she has pinkeye."

Just another "typical day" for Ms. Graff.

INTRODUCTION

The school health program is an important component of community health. Though the primary responsibility for the health of school-aged children lies with their parents/guardians, the schools have immeasurable potential for affecting the health of children, their families, and the health of the community. Full-service community schools provide a good example of the link between school health and community health. These schools, using an integrated approach, offer a variety of educational, counseling, social, and health services to families in one location. Such schools focus on the well-being of the child and family, and some of their services are available on a 24-hour basis. These school buildings serve as neighborhood hubs and institutions that are safe, attentive, and comfortable.[1,2]

In this chapter, we define *coordinated school health program,* explain who is involved in school health programs, explore the reasons why school health is important, discuss the components of school health, and present some of the issues facing school health programs today.

Coordinated School Health Program Defined

A **coordinated school health program** has been defined as "an organized set of policies, procedures, and activities designed to protect, promote, and improve the health and well-being of students and staff, thus improving a student's ability to learn. It includes, but is not limited to comprehensive school health education; school health services; a healthy school environment; school counseling; psychological and social services; physical education; school nutrition services; family and community involvement in school health; and school-site health promotion for staff."[3] This definition is based on the work of Allensworth and Kolbe[4] and is represented in Figure 6.1.

The school health program has great potential for impacting the health of many. There are over 57 million school-aged children attending over 100,000 schools and 5 million instructional and noninstructional employees in the United States.[5,6] This represents about one-fifth of the entire United States population. "The knowledge, attitudes, behavior, and skills

> **coordinated school health program**
> an organized set of policies, procedures, and activities designed to protect, promote, and improve the health and well-being of students and staff, thus improving a student's ability to learn. It includes, but is not limited to, comprehensive school health education; school health services; a healthy school environment; school counseling; psychological and social services; physical education; school nutrition services; family and community involvement in school health; and school-site health promotion for staff

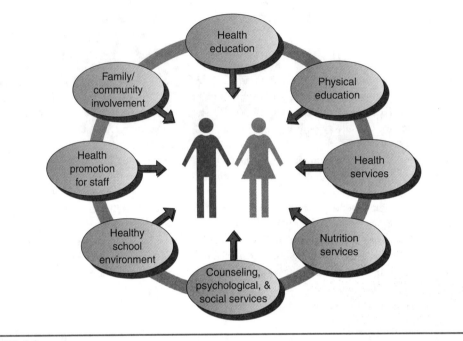

FIGURE 6.1

The coordinated school health program.

Source: Division of Adolescent and School Health, Centers for Disease Control and Prevention (2004). *Coordinated School Health Programs: What Is Coordinated School Health?* Available at http://www.cdc.gov/healthyyouth/CSHP/index.htm.

developed as a result of effective school health programs enable individuals to make informed choices about behavior that will affect their own health throughout their lives, as well as the health of the families for which they are responsible, and the health of the communities in which they live."[7] However, in practice the quality and quantity of coordinated school health programs in school districts throughout the United States vary greatly. In the majority of school districts, school health programs are not well defined or coordinated; "most schools have some elements of a coordinated school health program, few have a health program that includes all components at a full functioning level, and fewer still effectively coordinate all."[8] For example, it is not unusual for a health teacher to be talking about the importance of aerobic exercise but never tell the physical education teacher. Similarly, a science teacher may be teaching about pathogens and the prevention of communicable diseases, but yet the restrooms in a school are not properly equipped for adequate hand washing. Additionally, there is little coordination between school districts and community health agencies to improve the health of the school-aged child. Table 6.1 provides some possibilities for such interaction.

The School Health Council

school health council
individuals from a school or school district and its community who work together to provide advice on aspects of the school health program

In order for coordinated school health programs to fulfill their potential, a great deal of time and effort must be expended by those involved in the program's various components. When these individuals work together to plan and implement a school health program, they are referred to as the **school health council.** The primary role of this council is to provide coordination of the various components of the coordinated school health program to help students reach and maintain high-quality health. An ideal council would include representation from administrators, food service workers, counseling personnel, maintenance workers, medical

Table 6.1
Selected Examples of Exchanges by Functions to Integrate School and Community Programs

Functions	Exchanges		
	One-Way	Two-Way	Three-Way
Information	Distribution of materials produced by voluntary health agencies	Delivery of workshops/seminars on parenting health issues by school and agency experts	Distribution to multiple agencies of newsletters, calendars of events, and/or directory of services
Service	Screening for health problems by volunteer community lay and/or health professionals	Cooperative venture utilizing school setting for training of medical students, nursing students, etc.	Collaborative venture by school and community agencies to provide school clinics
Advising and decision making	Formation of school health advisory council	Collaboration by physician/teacher to improve health status and educational attainment	Formation of an interagency management system
Planning and development	Utilization of school recreational facilities for fitness programs by community residents	Utilization of parents as partners in specific instructional strategies	Development of a consortium to implement a validated curriculum
Research and evaluation	Providing access for researchers from higher educational institutions	Cooperative submission of a grant proposal by schools and community agency	Utilization of multiagency task force to gather specific health, epidemiological, social, and economic data on adolescent health problems
Monitoring and reporting	Citizen monitoring of school desegregation	Monitoring referrals of students between health and social service agencies to ensure continued treatment	Development of Adolescent Services Network to monitor health/educational needs and referral from one agency to another
Training	Utilization of community professionals as consultants for in-service or instructional programs	Utilization of community agencies as learning laboratories for students who serve as volunteers in service/ instructional capacities	Utilization of personnel in Adolescent Health Service Network to provide in-service programs for respective members
Advocacy	Utilization of parents as fund raisers	Initiation and development of a regional school health education coalition by a state health education advocacy network	Formation of a coalition to publicize the benefits of comprehensive school health
Electoral/legislative	Citizen campaigning for individuals running for school board	Campaigning for individual whose platform is supportive of school health	Formation of a coalition to promote legislative mandate

Source: Adapted from Killip, D. C., S. R. Lovick, L. Goldman, and D. D. Allensworth (1987). "Integrated School and Community Programs." *Journal of School Health,* 57(10): 437–444.

personnel (especially a school nurse and school physician), social workers, parents and other caregivers, students, teachers (especially those who teach health, physical education, and family and consumer science classes), and personnel from appropriate community health agencies. From this group must come a leader or coordinator. This coordinator should have an educational background that includes training and certification in school health. In addition, the coordinator should "be able to plan, implement, and evaluate a coordinated school health program; be familiar with existing community resources; and have connections to local, state, and national health and education organizations."[9] Most often the coordinator of the school health council is a health educator or school nurse.

The School Nurse

As previously noted, the school nurse is one of several people who is positioned to provide leadership for a coordinated school health program (Figure 6.2). The nurse not only has medical knowledge, but should also have formal training in health education and an understanding of the health needs of all children in kindergarten through the twelfth grade. Some of the key responsibilities of the school nurse as a member of the school health team include:[10]

1. Providing direct health care to students and staff
2. Providing leadership for the provision of health services
3. Providing screening and referral for health conditions
4. Promoting a healthy school environment
5. Promoting health

FIGURE 6.2

The school nurse is in a good position to guide the school health program.

6. Serving in a leadership role for health policies and programs
7. Serving as a liaison between school personnel, family, community, and health care providers

It should be noted that even though school nurses are in a good position to provide leadership to the school council, there are many school districts that do not have the resources to hire a full-time school nurse. It is not uncommon for a school district to contract with an outside health agency like a local health department for nursing services. When this scenario occurs, it is normal for the contracted nurse to complete only the nursing tasks required by state law and not to take on the leadership responsibilities for the school health council. This task may then be fulfilled by a school health educator. In fact, the health educator may even be responsible when a full-time nurse is present.

The Teacher's Role

Though the school nurse might provide the leadership for a coordinated school health program, the classroom teachers carry a heavy responsibility in seeing that the program works (see Figure 6.3). On the average school day, teachers spend more waking hours with school-aged children than the parents of the children. A teacher may spend six to eight hours a day with any given child, while the parents spend an hour with that child before school and maybe four to five hours with the child after school and before bedtime. Teachers are also in a position to make observations on the "normal and abnormal" behaviors and conditions of children because they are able to compare the students in their classroom each day. Table 6.2 presents a suggested list of competencies for teachers who expect to be active and full participants in a coordinated school health program.

FIGURE 6.3

The classroom teacher's participation is essential for a successful school health program.

Table 6.2
Competencies for Teachers

General

The teacher understands and appreciates

1. The meaning of health as a multidimensional state of well-being, which includes physical, psychological, social, and spiritual aspects
2. That health of individuals is influenced by the reciprocal interaction of the growing and developing organism and environmental factors and is necessary for optimal functioning as productive members of society
3. The significance of children's and youths' health problems on learning
4. The importance and the need for school health programs in today's society
5. The nature of a total school health program
6. The teacher's role in each of the school health program components—services, environment, and instruction
7. The influence on students of teacher health and teacher health habits
8. The need for basic scientific information about a variety of health content areas, including dental health; drugs (alcohol, tobacco, and other drugs); care of eyes, ears, and feet; exercise, fitness, rest, and fatigue; prevention and control of diseases and disorders (communicable and chronic); safety and first aid; family health; consumer health; community health; environmental health; nutrition; mental health; anatomy; and physiology

Health Instruction

The teacher

1. Can identify and use a variety of techniques and procedures to determine the health needs and interests of pupils
2. Is able to organize the health instruction program around the needs and interests of students and can develop effective teaching units for the grade being taught
3. Is able to stress the development of attitudes and behaviors for healthful living based on scientific health information
4. Can distinguish between the various patterns of health instruction and attempts to use the direct approach in teaching whenever possible
5. Realizes that health education must receive time in the school program along with other subject areas
6. Possesses current scientific information about a variety of health content areas
7. Can use a variety of stimulating and motivating teaching techniques derived from fundamental principles of learning
8. Is able to identify and use "teachable moments" or incidents that occur in the classroom, in the school, or in the community
9. Uses a variety of teaching aids within the instructional program and is familiar with their sources
10. Is familiar with the sources of scientific information and the procedures necessary to keep up-to-date with current health information
11. Is able to provide a variety of alternative solutions to health problems to enable students to make wiser decisions
12. Can integrate health into other phases of the curriculum, such as social science, science, and language arts
13. Uses a variety of evaluative procedures periodically to (a) assess the effectiveness of the program on students, and (b) determine the quality and usefulness of teaching aids and materials

Health Services

The teacher

1. Is familiar with the characteristics of the healthy child and can recognize signs and symptoms of unhealthy conditions; refers problems to the school nurse or other appropriate school personnel
2. Is familiar with the variety of health appraisal procedures used in schools and uses them to enrich the health instruction program
3. Acquires limited skills in counseling and guiding students and parents regarding student health problems
4. Understands the value and purposes of teacher-nurse conferences
5. Is familiar with the variety of health personnel found in schools, and their functions, responsibilities, and usefulness
6. Is able to use information contained on health records
7. Can identify and follow the policies and procedures in schools with regard to such matters as emergency care, accidents, disease control, referrals, exclusions, and readmittance of pupils
8. Can administer immediate care when accidents or illnesses to pupils occur or can act promptly to obtain sources of help within the school
9. Is able to adjust the school program according to the individual health needs of students
10. Is able to relate the health services program to the health instruction program

Healthful School Living

The teacher

1. Is familiar with the standards for hygiene, sanitation, and safety needed in schools to provide a safe and healthful environment
2. Is familiar with the physical and emotional needs of students and adjusts the classroom activities to help students satisfy those needs whenever possible
3. Understands the nature and importance of the food service program and is able to relate it to the instructional program
4. Is able to recognize hazardous conditions on the playground, in the classroom, and elsewhere in the school and takes appropriate action to eliminate or correct such conditions

Table 6.2 (continued)

5. Is cognizant of the effect of teacher health, personality, biases, and prejudices on student health and learning and is concerned with the humane treatment of pupils
6. Integrates healthful environmental aspects into the health instruction program

Coordination

The teacher

1. Understands the need for school and community health councils or committees and is willing to participate as a member if requested to do so
2. Realizes the importance of and need for a coordinator, consultant, or a person with administrative responsibility of the school health program

Source: Cornacchia, H. J., L. K. Olsen, and J. M. Ozias (1996). *Health in Elementary Schools*, 9th ed. St. Louis, MO: Mosby, 47–48.

THE NEED FOR SCHOOL HEALTH

The primary role of schools is to educate. However, an unhealthy child has a difficult time learning. Consider, for example, a child who arrives at school with an elevated body temperature, a runny nose, and without adequate sleep. This child will be unable to concentrate on school work and may infect other children. As a reader, you know how difficult it is to study for a test or even to read this textbook when you do not feel well or are sleepy or hungry (see Box 6.1).

"Health of children and their learning are reciprocally related."[11] One cannot exist without the other. That is to say, "education and health for children are inextricably intertwined. A student who is not healthy, who suffers from an undetected vision or hearing

---

BOX **6.1**	IT IS HARDER TO LEARN IF YOU ARE NOT HEALTHY!

It stands to reason that if children are not healthy it is harder for them to concentrate and in turn have a meaningful learning experience. One such example of this has been documented by researchers who have studied the impact of breakfast on learning. Now there is scientific evidence to back the claim that "breakfast may be the most important meal of the day."

It was obvious back in the mid-1960s that millions of children were coming to school hungry and ill prepared to learn. As such, in 1966 Congress authorized a two-year pilot School Breakfast Program (SBP) aimed at children from lower socioeconomic-level families and children who had to travel long distances to school. Congressional amendments extended the SBP through 1975 when it became permanently authorized in PL 94-105. Today, as both a nutrition and education program, the SBP is available to all students nationwide in schools offering the program. In order for schools to receive financial support for the SBP, they must meet the minimal nutritional standards as set forth in the SBP meal pattern established by the U.S. Department of Agriculture's Food and Nutrition Service. The SBP is then offered at no cost, a reduced price, or at full price depending on the students' family size and income.

Because the SBP has been in place for a number of years, several studies have been conducted with those who have participated in SBP. Results of these studies show that students who participate in SBP enhanced their abilities to learn, compared to those who do not. SBP participants showed significantly greater improvements in standardized test scores and decreases in tardiness rates and absenteeism. Beyond the educational benefits, SBP participation has also improved total daily nutrient intake and nutritional status, shown to help control body weight by minimizing impulsive eating, and possibly reducing risk of coronary heart disease by lowering blood cholesterol levels.

The SBP provides a vivid example of (1) how the school acts as a community health service provider, and (2) how school health education can reach beyond the traditional health education classroom.

Source: National Dairy Council (1993). "Breakfast, Its Effects on Health and Behavior." *Dairy Council Digest,* 64(2): 7–12.

BOX
6.2

HEALTHY PEOPLE 2010: OBJECTIVES

7.2 Increase the proportion of middle, junior high, and senior high schools that provide school health education to prevent health problems in the following areas: unintentional injury; violence; suicide; tobacco use and addiction; alcohol and other drug use; unintended pregnancy, HIV/AIDS, and STD infection; unhealthy dietary patterns; inadequate physical activity; and environmental health.

Target, 2000 status, and baseline:

Objective	Schools Providing School Health Education in Priority Areas	1994 Baseline	2000 Status[6]	2010 Target
			Percent	
7-2a.	All components	28	25	70
7-2b.	Unintentional injury	66	68	90
7-2c.	Violence	58	73	80
7-2d.	Suicide	58	59	80
7-2e.	Tobacco use and addiction	86	88	95
7-2f.	Alcohol and other drug use	90	89	95
7-2g.	Unintended pregnancy, HIV/AIDS, and STD infection	65	62	90
7-2h.	Unhealthy dietary patterns	84	84	95
7-2i.	Inadequate physical activity	78	76	90
7-2j.	Environmental health	60	60	80

7-4 Increase the proportion of the nation's elementary, middle, junior high, and senior high schools that have a nurse-to-student ratio of at least 1:750.

Target, 2000 status, and baseline:

Objective	Increase in Schools with Nurse-to-Student Ratio of at Least 1:750	1994 Baseline	2000 Status[6]	2010 Target
			Percent	
7-4a.	All middle, junior high, and senior high schools	28	53	50
7-4a.	Senior high schools	28	26	50
7-4a.	Middle and junior high schools	32	*	50
7-4a.	Elementary schools	Developmental		

* = Data not available.

For Further Thought

Assuming money is available, why doesn't every school district in the nation have a coordinated school health program?

defect, or who is hungry, or who is impaired by drugs or alcohol, is not a student who will profit from the educational process. Likewise, an individual who has not been provided assistance in the shaping of healthy attitudes, beliefs, and habits early in life, will be more likely to suffer the consequences of reduced productivity in later years."[12] A coordinated school health program provides the integration of education and health.

The importance of the school health program is also evident by its inclusion in the national health objectives for the year 2010. Of all the objectives listed in the publication *Healthy People 2010: Understanding and Improving Health,* a significant number can either be directly attained by schools, or their attainment can be influenced in important ways by schools (see Box 6.2).

Nevertheless, a coordinated school health program is not a cure-all. There are no quick and easy solutions to improving the overall health of a community. However, a coordinated school health program provides a strong base upon which to build.

FOUNDATIONS OF THE SCHOOL HEALTH PROGRAM

The true foundations of any school health program are (1) a school administration that supports such an effort, (2) a well-organized school health council that is genuinely interested in providing a coordinated program for the students, and (3) written school health policies. A highly supportive administration is a must for a quality coordinated school health program. In almost all organizations—and schools are no different—the administration controls resources. Without leadership and support from top school administrators, it will be an ongoing struggle to provide a quality program. Furthermore, every effort should be made to employ personnel who are appropriately trained to carry out their responsibilities as members of the school health council. For example, the American Association for Health Education has recommended that the "minimal requirements for school nurses should be state licensure as a registered professional nurse, a baccalaureate degree, with study in school health,"[13] yet many school nurses without college degrees and training in health education are asked to teach. Conversely, certified teachers who lack preparation in health screening procedures are sometimes asked to administer screening tests to students.[14] Qualified personnel are a must.

SCHOOL HEALTH POLICIES

School health policies are written statements that provide a framework[15] to guide all those who work within the program.[14] The written policy also describes the nature of the program and the procedure for its implementation to those outside the program.[16] Well-written school health policies provide a sense of direction and a means of accountability and credibility, and strengthen the possibility that a school health program will become "an institutionalized part of the school culture."[15]

school health policies
written statements that describe the nature and procedures of a school health program

Policy Development

The development of a set of written policies is not an easy task. This challenging and time-consuming task should be executed by the school health council, because the council includes those most knowledgeable about the school health program in addition to representing many different constituencies in the school community.

The policies should cover all facets of the school health program. Table 6.3 provides a checklist that can be used for developing policies. Also, several professional associations that have an interest in school health programs have written a number of policy statements relating to school health issues. A few such associations are the American Academy of Pediatrics (information available at http://www.aap.org/), the American School Health Association (information available at http://www.ashaweb.org), and the American Association for Health Education (information available at http://www.aahperd.org/aahe/template.cfm).

Once the policies have been written, it is important that they receive approval at three levels. Approval should come from (1) the school district's medical advisor, (2) the school administration, and (3) the board of education. The approval process provides credibility to the policies as well as legal protection for those who must implement the policies.[16]

Policy Implementation

The development of written policies is an important step in building a solid base for a coordinated school health program. However, if the policies are never implemented, the school district will be no better off than before their development.

Implementation begins with the distribution of the policies to those who will be affected by them—faculty, staff, students, and parents. Some ideas for carrying out this process include

Table 6.3
A Checklist for Developing Written Policies

	PIP	PN	NA
I. Administration and Organization	███	███	███
A. Duties and Responsibilities of the Coordinator of the School Health Program			
B. Duties and Responsibilities of the School Health Team			
C. Responsibilities of School Health Personnel	███	███	███
1. Medical advisor			
2. School nurse			
3. Health instructors			
4. Other teachers			
5. First-aiders			
6. Other related personnel			
7. Volunteers			
D. School Health Records	███	███	███
1. Recording of health history			
2. Maintenance of school health records			
a. What will be entered (results of screenings and examination, emergency illness/injury)			
b. Who will enter the information			
3. Information for emergency situations			
4. Recording of student immunizations			
E. General School Health Policies	███	███	███
1. Use of prescribed medication in the school			
2. Report of child abuse and neglect			
3. Substance use/abuse			
4. Student health insurance			
5. Home health visits			
6. Health policies for after-school activities (including emergency care)			
7. Sending ill/injured students home			
8. Relationships with community health agencies/organizations			
9. In-service health programs for teachers			
II. School Health Services	███	███	███
A. Emergency Care for Illness/Injury	███	███	███
1. Duties of school employers in the emergency care program			
2. Responsibility for financial charges incurred during the emergency care			
3. Use of emergency care room/health clinic			
4. Purchase and availability of emergency care supplies and equipment			
5. Standing orders for common emergency problems			
6. Notification of personnel needed in an emergency situation			
7. Responsibility for transportation of ill/injured students			
8. Completion and filing of accident reports			
9. Procedure for follow-up inquiry into the post-emergency condition of a student			
10. Procedure for readmission of an injured/ill student to school attendance			
11. Universal Precautions outlined			
B. Students with Special Needs	███	███	███
1. Procedures to adhere to Public Law 94:142			
2. Procedures to adhere to all state laws			
C. Health Appraisal	███	███	███
1. Medical examinations			
a. Financial responsibilities			
b. Who will perform them			
c. When will they be required (including athletic examinations)			
2. Screening programs			
a. Who will perform them			
b. What tests will be given			
c. When will they be given			
d. Follow-up procedures			

Table 6.3 (continued)

	PIP	PN	NA
3. Dental examinations			
a. Who will perform them			
b. Financial responsibilities			
c. When will they be required			
d. Follow-up procedures			
4. Social and psychological evaluations			
a. Who will perform them			
b. Financial responsibilities			
c. When will they be required			
d. Follow-up procedures			
5. Policy for health referrals to parents			
D. Communicable Disease Control			
1. Required immunizations			
2. Student exclusion when the student has measles, German measles, chickenpox, scarlet fever, infectious hepatitis, athlete's foot, impetigo, ringworm, pinkeye, and other communicable diseases			
3. Readmittance policy after a communicable disease			
E. Health Advising			
1. Who will perform it			
2. When will it be performed			
3. Steps in referral			
4. Procedures for follow-up			
III. Healthy School Environment			
A. Safety Program			
1. Responsibilities of school personnel			
2. Expected student classroom conduct			
3. Maintenance of equipment/instructional materials			
4. Reporting of unsafe conditions in school environment			
B. Safety Patrol and Bus Safety			
1. Responsibilities of school personnel			
2. Responsibilities and procedures of students			
C. Emergency Drills (fire, tornado, etc.)			
1. Drill procedures			
2. Emergency exit procedures			
3. Procedure to help individuals with special needs in an emergency situation			
D. Drug-Free Schools			
E. Safe/Violence-Free Schools			
F. Student Discipline			
G. Universal Precautions			
H. Hazardous Materials			
IV. Health Instruction			
A. Procedures for curriculum development and revision			
B. Individual Education Programs for special needs students			
V. School Food Service			
VI. School Counseling			
VII. School Physical Education			
VIII. School-Site Health Promotion for Faculty and Staff			
IX. Integrated School and Community Health Promotion Efforts			

Code: PIP = Policy in place. PN = Policy needed. NA = Not applicable to our district.

Source: Adapted from McKenzie, J. F. (1983). "Written Policies: Developing a Solid Foundation for a Comprehensive School Health Program." *Future Focus: Ohio Journal of Health, Physical Education, Recreation and Dance,* 4(3): 9–11.

(1) distributing the policies with a memorandum of explanation, (2) placing the policies in both faculty/staff and student handbooks, (3) presenting them at a gathering of the different groups (e.g., at staff or PTO meetings, or an open house), (4) holding a special meeting for the specific purpose of explaining the policies, and (5) placing them in the school district newsletter. News releases might even be considered if the policies include major changes. Each school district must decide the best way to disseminate its school health policies.

Monitoring the Status of School Health Policy in the United States

Because school health policy is an important foundation for coordinated school health programs, the Division of Adolescent Health at the Centers for Disease Control and Prevention (CDC) conducts a national survey to assess school health policies and programs at the state, district, school, and classroom levels. The survey, which is titled the School Health Policies and Programs Study (SHPPS), has been conducted twice—in 1994 and 2000. Specifically, SHPPS is used to:[6]

- Monitor the status of the nation's school health policies and programs.
- Describe the professional background of the personnel who deliver each component of the school health program.
- Describe coordination among components of school health programs.
- Describe relationships between state and district policies and school health programs and practices.
- Identify factors that facilitate or impede delivery of effective school health programs.

Results of these national surveys are available at the Division of Adolescent and School Health's Web site.

COMPONENTS OF A COORDINATED SCHOOL HEALTH PROGRAM

If implemented appropriately, a coordinated approach to school health can have a significant positive impact on the overall health status of students, staff, and the community, which, in turn, can be linked to higher academic achievement for students. In order to do so, all eight components illustrated in Figure 6.1 need to be provided. Because of the limitation of space, we will discuss the importance of the administration and organization of the eight components, provide an overview of the three traditional components of the school health program—(1) school health services, (2) healthy school environment, and (3) health education—and provide a brief explanation of the five additional components.

Administration and Organization

school health coordinator
a professional at the district (or school) level responsible for management and coordination of all school health policies, activities, and resources

Effective administration and organization of the school health program ensures that the people and activities that constitute the program work in a coordinated manner to meet the program's goals. As previously noted, the responsibility for coordinating the program in each school district should be delegated to a properly trained and knowledgeable individual. Logical choices for this position of **school health coordinator** would be a trained school nurse or a health educator.[17] While approximately one-half of the states and territories in the United States have school districts who employ school health coordinators, there are only a few states that require such a person.[18]

The American Cancer Society has taken a leadership role in training leaders for school health programs. In 1999 the American Cancer Society conducted the first National School Health Coordinator Leadership Institute, the beginning of a three-year training program for school health coordinators around the United States. As a result of the success of the Institute, a number of replications have been implemented around the country, some as state replication programs and others with specific school districts, such as urban school districts.[19] The American Cancer Society recommends that school health coordinators have the following responsibilities, regardless of the coordinator's professional preparation or training:[17]

- Assessing the local need for and status of health education
- Articulating the importance of and gaining support for school health programs within the school and community
- Providing leadership for the school health program team to ensure a coordinated approach and for the community-represented school health council
- Planning effective school health instruction based on a K–12 sequential framework
- Identifying current school health–related funding streams and coordinating with the school health program council to maximize usage
- Planning for and providing access to school health professional preparation opportunities
- Assisting with the identification, evaluation, and selection of resources
- Providing assistance in designing and evaluating the different components of the school health program

School Health Services

School health services are those health "services provided for students to appraise, protect, and promote health."[20] Specifically, those services offered by schools include health appraisals (screenings and examinations), emergency care for injury and sudden illness, management of chronic disease, prevention and control of communicable disease, provisions for special needs students, health advising, and remediation of detected health problems within the limits of state laws through referral and follow-up by the school nurse and teachers (see Figure 6.4). Originally the intent of school health services was to supplement rather than to supplant the family's responsibility for meeting the health care needs of its children. However, due to the poorer health status of youth, the involvement of youth in high-risk behaviors (such as smoking, drinking, substance abuse, and unprotected sexual intercourse), and such barriers to health care as inadequate health insurance and lack of providers, there has been a broadening of the role of schools in providing health care.

> **school health services**
> health services provided by school health workers to appraise, protect, and promote the health of students

Because school attendance is required throughout the United States, schools represent our best opportunity to reach many of those children in need of proper health care. More than 95% of all youths aged 5 to 17 years are enrolled in schools.[21] "The school's ability to reach children and youth slipping through the cracks of the health care system and at highest risk for poor health and potentially health-threatening behaviors is unmatched."[22] The advantages of having school health services include:[23]

1. Equitability: School health services provide a point of entry into the health care system for all children in school.
2. Breadth of coverage: Many preventive services are provided that are not covered in a majority of health insurance policies.
3. Confidentiality.
4. User friendliness: The school is an environment with which students are familiar and in which they feel comfortable.
5. Convenience: Services are accessible to all students.

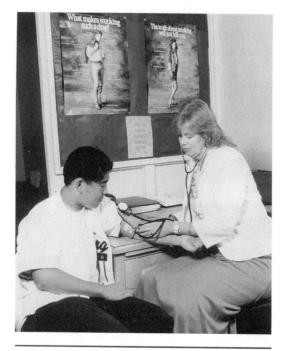

FIGURE 6.4

Health screenings are important components of school health services.

Each school district is unique, from the demographics of its students to the availability of its health resources. As such, three models have been developed that describe the delivery of school health services: (1) core health services, (2) core plus expanded school health services model, and (3) services through school-based or school-linked health centers.[23] The core health services model views the school district in the role of health screener. In this model, emphasis is placed on the detection of health problems and the referral to providers in the community for treatment. This is the model most commonly found in schools today.

The core plus expanded school health model builds upon the core health services model and extends it by providing additional services when students are unable to access community-based services or when the communities lack health care providers.[24] The most common services added for students include assistance with behavioral, mental health, and substance abuse treatment.[24]

The third model for offering school health services is through either school-based or school-linked health centers. Such centers are the most comprehensive means for offering school health services. Though the services offered by the centers differ by location, many operate like many primary care clinics. School-based health centers (SBHCs) have been defined as "a health center located in a school or on school grounds that provides, at a minimum, on-site primary and preventive health care, mental health counseling, health promotion, referral and follow-up services for young people enrolled."[25] While school-linked health centers (SLHC) have been defined as health centers "located beyond school property that serve one or more schools."[25] SLHCs usually have formal or informal agreements with schools and may serve more than just young people enrolled in school.[25] Both SBHCs and SLHCs employ a number of health care professionals on a full-time basis. The idea of school-based/linked clinics is gaining momentum throughout the country and will be discussed in greater detail later in this chapter.

Healthy School Environment

healthy school environment
the promotion, maintenance, and utilization of safe and wholesome surroundings in a school

The term *healthy school environment* designates the part of a coordinated school health program that provides for a safe—both physically and emotionally—learning environment (see Figure 6.5). If children are not placed in a safe environment, learning becomes difficult at best. The most recent definition of healthy environment was provided by the 1972–1973 Joint Committee on Health Education Terminology. They stated that providing a **healthy school environment** includes "the promotion, maintenance, and utilization of safe and wholesome surroundings, organization of day-by-day experiences and planned learning procedures to influence favorable emotional, physical and social health."[26]

By law, school districts are required to provide a safe school environment. However, the responsibility for maintaining this safe environment should rest with all who use it. Everyone, including those on the board of education, administrators, teachers, custodial staff, and students, must contribute to make a school a safer place through their daily actions. An unsafe school environment can exist only if those responsible for it and those who use it allow it to exist.

The Physical Environment

The physical environment of a school can be divided into two major categories. The first is the actual physical plant—the buildings and surrounding areas and all that come with them. The second is the behaviors of those using the buildings. The factors that must be considered when looking at the physical plant include (1) where the school is located, (2) the age of the buildings, (3) the traffic patterns in and around the school, (4) temperature control, (5) lighting, (6) acoustics, (7) water supply, (8) sanitation, (9) food service, (10) playgrounds, (11) school bus safety, and other items. Each school district should have an appropriate protocol for dealing with and maintaining these aspects of the physical environment.

The behavior of both the school personnel and students in the school environment also has an impact on the safety of the environment. Each year a significant number of students throughout the country are injured on their way to, at, or on their way home from school. Some of these injuries occur from an unsafe physical plant that is in need of repair, but many occur from inappropriate behavior. Unsafe behavior that is observed too frequently in schools includes acts of violence between students and lack of proper supervision by school employees. However, most do not worry about a safe environment until they are faced with a problem. Every school building in the United States could become a safer environment if greater attention were given to prevention than to a cure.

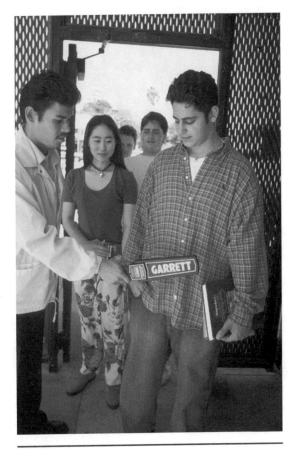

FIGURE 6.5
The school should be a safe and healthy place to learn.

The Psychosocial Environment

Although a safe physical environment is important, a safe psychosocial environment is equally important. This portion of the school environment "encompasses the attitudes, feelings, and values of students and staff."[27] Students who are fearful of responding to a teacher's question because the teacher might make fun of them if they answer incorrectly or students who are afraid to say hello to the school principal because he is never nice to anyone are not learning in a healthy psychosocial environment. For many, learning does not come easily, and anxiety-producing factors like these can only make it more difficult.

The ways in which school personnel and students treat each other can also add much to the teaching/learning process (see Figure 6.6). All individuals within the school should be treated with respect. People should be polite and courteous to each other. This does not mean that high academic standards should be abandoned and that everyone should agree with all that others do, but students and teachers should not be afraid to express themselves in a cooperative, respectful way. For example, think back to your middle school and high school days. Think about the teachers you liked best. Did you like them because they were great teachers and knew their subject well? Or, did you like them because of the way they treated and respected you? The psychosocial environment can have a significant impact on the school environment!

FIGURE 6.6

A healthy social environment, conducive to learning, is an important component of good school health.

School Health Education

school health education
the development, delivery, and evaluation of a planned curriculum, preschool through grade 12

School health education (e.g., classroom instruction)[28] has been defined as the "planned, sequential, K–12 curriculum that addresses the physical, mental, emotional and social dimensions of health. The curriculum is designed to motivate and assist students to maintain and improve their health, prevent disease, and reduce health-related risk behaviors."[20] If designed properly, school health education could be one of the most effective means to reduce serious health problems in the United States, including cardiovascular disease, cancer, motor vehicle crashes, homicide, and suicide.[29] Such a curriculum should include, but is not limited to, the following content areas:[30]

Community health

Environmental health

Family health

Growth and development/sexuality

Mental and emotional health

Injury prevention and safety

Nutrition

Personal health

Prevention and control of disease

Prevention of substance use and abuse

BOX 6.3	NATIONAL HEALTH EDUCATION STANDARDS

1. Students will comprehend concepts related to health promotion and disease prevention.
2. Students will demonstrate the ability to access valid health information and health-promoting products and services.
3. Students will demonstrate the ability to practice health-enhancing behaviors and reduce health risks.
4. Students will analyze the influence of culture, media, technology, and other factors on health.
5. Students will demonstrate the ability to use interpersonal communication skills to enhance health.
6. Students will demonstrate the ability to use goal-setting and decision-making skills to enhance health.
7. Students will demonstrate the ability to advocate for personal, family, and community health.

Source: Joint Committee on National Health Education Standards (1995). *National Health Education Standards.* American School Health Association, Association for the Advancement of Health Education, and the American Cancer Society.

Additionally, emphasis should be placed on addressing the Centers for Disease Control and Prevention's six priority health risk behaviors that contribute to the leading causes of death, disability, and social problems in America: tobacco use, unhealthy dietary patterns, inadequate physical activity, alcohol and other drug use, sexual behaviors that contribute to unintended pregnancy and sexually transmitted diseases, including HIV infections, and behaviors that contribute to unintentional injuries and violence.[31]

School health education includes all health education in the school. It includes health education that takes place in the classroom as well as any other activities designed to positively influence the health knowledge and skills of students, parents, and school staff. For example, health education can take place when the school nurse gives a vision screening test to a student or when coaches talk with their teams about the abuse of drugs.

For health education to be effective, it should be well conceived and carefully planned. The written plan for school health education is referred to as the health **curriculum.** The curriculum not only outlines the **scope** (what will be taught), and the **sequence** (when it will be taught), but also provides (1) learning objectives, (2) learning activities, (3) possible instructional resources, and (4) methods for assessment to determine the extent to which the objectives are met. If health instruction is to be effective, the health curriculum should include lessons of appropriate scope and sequence for all grades from kindergarten through the twelfth grade.

As with the coordinated school health program, results from CDC's School Health Policies and Program Study (SHPPS) show that good school health instruction is not widespread. To enhance the state of health instruction in schools, the Joint Committee of National Health Education Standards was developed in 1993 by five health organizations—the American Association for Health Education, the American School Health Association, the American Public Health Association, the American Cancer Society, and the Society of State Directors of Health, Physical Education, and Recreation. The Joint Committee developed a set of standards that "describe the knowledge and skills essential to the development of health literacy."[32] The standards were developed "to serve as a framework for organizing health knowledge and skills into curricula at the state and local levels,"[32] and were not intended to define a national curriculum or to be a federal mandate.

There are seven standards (see Box 6.3), and each standard has grade-level performance indicators set for grades 4, 8, and 11. "The standards evolved from the health education profession's current thinking about what constitutes grade-appropriate and challenging content and performance expectations for students."[32] Currently, over 75% of states mandating

curriculum
a written plan for instruction

scope
part of the curriculum that outlines what will be taught

sequence
part of the curriculum that states in what order the content will be taught

standards-based health education have used the National Health Education Standards as their basis for requirements and recommendations.[6]

Development of and Sources of Health Education Curricula

Each year, many school districts throughout the United States are faced with the task of developing a curriculum to guide health education. Such a task can be completed in one of several ways. First, a school district could obtain a prepackaged curriculum that has been developed by nationally recognized specialists. Some of these are prepared and sold by for-profit organizations and others are available free of charge from nonprofit agencies (i.e., voluntary health agencies). A second means would be to use the approved curriculum of either the state departments of education or health. A third method would be to adopt a new health textbook series and consider the series as a district's curricular guide. And fourth, some districts may even develop their own in-house curriculum. Each of these approaches has its strengths and weaknesses, and school districts have to decide which approach best suits their particular situation.

Determining what is and what is not a good curriculum can be a difficult process. Some very poor curricula, packaged in a "slick" way, can convince administrators that they have purchased a very fine product. Conversely, some educationally sound programs may not be well packaged. Fortunately, resources are available to help reduce the guesswork for those who must select curricula. A number of federal agencies have created processes for reviewing, approving, and rating health education programs that are effective. The CDC maintains a list of registries sponsored by federal agencies that include programs effective in reducing youth risk behaviors.[33] Most of these registries allow curriculum developers to nominate their curricula for review. The review process typically involves peer review by three or more professionals with expertise in the specific area. Following the review, programs receive a rating, such as "promising," "exemplary," "effective," or "model" programs. Model programs, according to the National Registry of Effective Programs and Practices, which facilitates the review processes for the Substance Abuse and Mental Health Services Administration (SAMHSA) and CDC, are well-implemented, well-evaluated programs whose developers have agreed to participate in SAMHSA dissemination efforts and provide training and technical assistance to practitioners who wish to adopt their programs.[34]

In addition to the curricula that appear on the Centers for Disease Control and Prevention's *Registries of Programs Effective in Reducing Youth Risk Behaviors,*[33] there are a number of other sources for obtaining health curricula. As a matter of fact, if we tried to create a list, it would consume many pages of this book and probably still would not be entirely inclusive. The following is a list of places where you may be able to find other health curricula. Some of them may be comprehensive (include a variety of topics and for every grade level, K–12), and others may be topic and/or grade-level specific. These other sources include:

1. The Centers for Disease Control and Prevention: Over the past several years the CDC has developed guidelines to assist schools and others in developing programs for healthy lifestyles. Examples include (a) Guidelines for Effective School Health Education to Prevent the Spread of AIDS,[35] (b) Guidelines for School Health Programs to Prevent Tobacco Use and Addiction,[36] (c) Guidelines for School Health Programs to Promote Lifelong Healthy Eating,[37] and (d) Guidelines for School and Community Health Programs to Promote Physical Activity Among Young People.[38] These and others are available from CDC, Division of Adolescent and School Health (DASH).[39]

2. State departments of education or health: A number of states have either recommended or required a particular curriculum. Some states do not have comprehensive curricula but require instruction in some of the more controversial health topics, such as substance use and abuse and sexuality education.

3. Health agencies and associations: Many of the voluntary health agencies (e.g., American Cancer Society, American Heart Association, and American Lung Association) and other health-related associations (e.g., National Dairy Council, American Health Foundation, and United Way) have developed curricula for grades K–12. Most of these are not comprehensive, but they are usually well done, supported by audiovisuals and handouts, and available either at very low or no cost.
4. Commercially produced curricula: These curricula have been developed by private corporations for schools.

Counseling, Psychological, and Social Services

Counseling, psychological, and social services are services provided to improve students' mental, emotional, and social health. These services can include individual and group assessments, interventions, and referrals. Professionals such as certified school counselors, psychologists, and social workers provide these services.[20]

Physical Education

Physical education is defined as a "planned, sequential K–12 curriculum that provides cognitive content and learning experiences in a variety of activity areas."[20] Emphasis is placed on physical fitness and skill development that lead to lifelong physical activity. Physical education should be taught by qualified teachers.[20]

School Nutrition Services

School nutrition services should provide access to a variety of nutritious and appealing meals that accommodate the health and nutrition needs of all students in a school district. Additionally, the school nutrition services program should offer students a learning laboratory for classroom nutrition and health education. The program should also serve as a resource for links with nutrition-related community services.[20]

Parent/Community Involvement for School Health

Parent/community involvement allows for an "integrated school, parent, and community approach for enhancing the health and well-being of students."[20] The school is an agency within a community that cannot function in isolation. Schools that actively engage parents and community resources in their school health councils, curriculum committees, and other health-related programming respond more effectively to the health-related needs of students.[20]

School-Site Health Promotion for Staff

School-site health promotion for staff includes "opportunities for school staff to improve their health status" through health-related assessments and activities.[20] These opportunities encourage staff to engage in healthy behaviors, resulting in improved health status, improved morale, positive health role modeling, reduced health insurance costs, and decreased absenteeism.[20]

ISSUES AND CONCERNS FACING THE SCHOOL HEALTH PROGRAM

Like most other community health programs, the school health program is not without its issues and concerns. "In the 1940's, the three leading school discipline problems were talking, chewing gum, and making noise."[40] Today, many of the problems are health related. In the remainder of this chapter, we will summarize a few of the challenges that still lie ahead of those who work in school health.

BOX 6.4

BARRIERS TO COMPREHENSIVE SCHOOL HEALTH EDUCATION

Although the importance of coordinated school health education is being recognized more and more, there are several barriers to its implementation. Butler surveyed the Council of Chief State School Officers to get their perception of the greatest barriers. She had the Council members rank-order perceived barriers, with (1) being the greatest barrier. Findings showed the barriers in the following order:

1. Lack of local administrative commitment
2. Lack of adequately prepared teachers
3. Lack of time in the school day/year
4. Lack of money/funds
5. Health education's lack of credibility as an academic subject
6. Lack of community/parental support and controversial topics

The top three barriers were seen as the most significant. Recommendations to address them included inviting administrators to workshops and conferences dealing with effective coordinated school health education, conducting quality in-service programs, and marketing to school administrators and professors of education.

Source: Adapted from Butler, S. C. (1993). "Chief State School Officers Rank Barriers to Implementing Comprehensive School Health Education." *Journal of School Health,* 63(3): 130–132. Taken from Bender, S. J., J. J. Neutens, S. Skonie-Hardin, and W. D. Sorochan (1997). *Teaching Health Science: Elementary and Middle School,* 4th ed. Boston: Jones and Bartlett Publishers, 32.

Coordinated School Health Program

"Schools offer the most systematic and efficient means available to improve the health of youth and enable young people to avoid health risks,"[41] yet, ironically, school health advocates have been unsuccessful in getting a coordinated school health program implemented in even a majority of the school districts in the country. We have already pointed out that healthy children are better learners and that a coordinated school health program can contribute to the health of children. More globally, a coordinated school health program "facilitates the attainment of the goal of schooling; an educated populace whose health permits continued productivity through the lifespan."[42]

While many Americans support the idea that everyone is entitled to good health, we have not supported through legislation the notion that everyone is entitled to a coordinated school health program. Obviously, getting legislation passed is a complicated process and is dependent on a number of different circumstances, including, but not limited to, economics, social action, and politics. This difficult task should not deter those who feel coordinated school health is vital (see Box 6.4). It is becoming clearer that many of the answers to current and future health problems lie with the resources found in the school—the one institution of society through which all of us must pass. The following are a few examples of the impact school health can have:

1. At the present time, the key to dealing with the AIDS problem is education.
2. The biggest stride in improving the health of the country will not come from new technology but from the health behavior in which we engage.
3. Many of the primary health care services needed by the children of this country are not available because of the barriers of the health care system.
4. "Every dollar invested in effective tobacco education saves society an estimated $18.80 in health care and other costs caused by smoking. Each dollar invested in alcohol and other drug prevention saves an estimated $5.69. And each education dollar spent to prevent too-early and unprotected sexual behaviors saves $5.10."[43]

The need for coordinated school health should be obvious to all. We have taken the liberty to rephrase a quote from a group of school health experts who say it best: Society should

FIGURE 6.7
There are still many controversial issues that surround health education in schools.

not be as concerned with what happens when we implement a coordinated school health program as about what is likely to happen if we do not.[44]

Dealing with Controversy in the Curriculum

The words *sexual intercourse, suicide, AIDS, substance use and abuse, sexually transmitted diseases, abortion, contraception,* and *death and dying* get attention. The very nature of the topics covered in a school health education curriculum today create controversy. Yet, controversy is not new to school health education; it has followed health education ever since it first attempted to deal with the many issues that face youth (see Figure 6.7).

Controversy is a part of health education for a number of reasons. Part of it deals with the pressure applied to schools by present-day conservative groups. These groups are interested in discouraging health instruction that includes values-clarification activities and open-ended decision-making processes.[45] Others believe that controversy exists due to the differences in family value systems and religious beliefs. Bensley and Harmon[46] have suggested that controversies fall into two major categories: issues that center around the values and beliefs of the content taught and issues that arise from improper implementation of the curriculum. The former category deals with questions such as (1) Do students really need to learn in school how to use a condom? (2) Doesn't talk of suicide lead some students to think that it might be the best alternative for them? (3) Aren't chiropractors just health quacks? and (4) Why do students need to know about funeral preplanning in high school? These are legitimate concerns, but they are also issues that today's adolescents face. Lack of awareness, knowledge, and skills are not excuses for undesirable health behavior. If the students do not get this information at school, where will they get it? Studies have shown that the institutions of church and family have taught little about the controversial topics included in health curricula.

Improper implementation of the curriculum is indeed a concern. Because health is not considered a "core" subject in most school districts, it has received little attention and support. In many school districts throughout the United States, the low priority given to health has meant that much of the health education is provided by individuals other than health education specialists. These people are not incapable of teaching health, but they have not been educated to do so. Therefore, the health curriculum is sometimes improperly implemented, and controversy arises.

School districts can help reduce controversy by (1) implementing age-appropriate curricula, (2) using acceptable teaching methods, (3) gaining parent/guardian approval of curricula and teaching methods, (4) developing a school policy that enables parents/guardians to review the curricula and to withdraw their children from lessons that go against family or religious beliefs, (5) implementing a school policy that provides for the handling of concern by parents/guardians,[43] and (6) making sure qualified and interested teachers teach health.

School-Based Health Centers (SBHCs) or School-Linked Health Centers (SLHCs)

Early in the chapter we mentioned that a number of school districts across the country are opening school-based or school-linked health centers to help meet the health needs of their students. Yet, the concept of offering comprehensive health care services through school-based or school-linked health centers is a relatively new one. In 1970, there was only one U.S. school that had a SBHC/SLHC.[47] By 1984, that number had jumped to 31, then to 150 in 1989.[48] In 2002, there were more than 1,350 SBHCs nationally.[49] Most (63%) of the SBHCs operating today are found in urban areas. Of these 1,350 SBHC, 39% are found in high schools, 18% in middle schools, and 23% in elementary schools. The other 20% are located in alternative, K–8, 6–12, or K–12 schools.[49]

Although there is no single model for SBHCs, "they share some common features:[50]

- They are located in schools.
- Parents sign written consents for their children to enroll in the health center.
- An advisory board of community representatives, parents, youth, and family organizations participate in planning and oversight of the health center.
- The health center works cooperatively with school nurses, coaches, counselors, classroom teachers, and school principals and their staff to assure that the health center is an integral part of the life of the school.
- Clinical services are the responsibility of a qualified health provider (hospital, health center, health department, group medical practice, etc.).
- A multidisciplinary team of nurse practitioners, clinical social workers, physicians, and other health professionals care for students.
- The health center provides a comprehensive range of services that specifically meets the serious health problems of young people in the community as well as provides general medical care.

As mentioned earlier in the chapter, there are a number of sound reasons why health centers should be based in schools—the primary reason being the ability to reach, in a cost-effective manner, a large segment of the population that is otherwise without primary health care. Yet, SBHCs have been the frequent targets of intense criticism at the local and national levels by political and religious groups.[51-53] Much of the controversy surrounding SBHCs has centered on three issues: (1) cultural wars, (2) funding, and (3) partisan politics.[54] The issue of cultural wars revolves around the views of conservatives versus liberals, and how and where people should receive their health care. While some people who support SBHCs would want their child treated as quickly and effectively as possible for a health problem, others who oppose the centers can see nothing but the "image of a condom on a cafeteria tray."[54] The key to working through the "cultural wars" problem is compromise. That is, each area of the country is different and what would be reasonable health services provided in a SBHC in one area would be unacceptable in another. Thus, advocates of the centers would say that the services provided by SBHCs are so badly needed that a single issue like reproductive health care should not keep a SBHC from existing.[54]

Since their inception, funding for SBHCs has always been an issue. They do not have the sophisticated computers to bill for services, and they are typically not open 24 hours a day to qualify, at least in the eyes of insurance companies, as primary care health centers.[52] Also, the SBHCs' means of operation really do not match well with the concept of managed care (see Chapter 14). Therefore, most of the funding for SBHCs comes from state appropriations (61%), maternal and child health block grants (19%), and Medicaid (19%). Only 1% comes from private insurance.[55]

Violence in Schools

Over the years, schools have been viewed as safe and nurturing environments.[56] But more recently, there have been a number of high-profile incidents of violence in schools (e.g., Paducah, KY; Pearl, MS; Moses Lake, WA; Springfield, OR; Littleton, CO; and San Diego, CA) that have made the general public more aware of the violence in schools. "Violence in schools is certainly not new; almost every adult remembers the school bully."[57] The difference between violence in the schools today and years past is the means by which disagreements are settled. "Today the possibility that a disagreement among students will be settled with some type of weapon rather than an old-fashioned fist fight has significantly increased."[58] (See Chapter 8 for data on students carrying weapons). Grunbaum and colleagues[59] have reported that 5.4% of U.S. high school students had missed at least one day of school in the preceding month because they felt unsafe either being at school or going to and from school; one of 11 students had been threatened or injured with a weapon on school property during the preceeding year; one of eight had been in a physical fight on school property; and approximately one in three had his or her property stolen or deliberately damaged on school grounds.

We know that males are involved in more violent acts than females.[59] We also know that certain racial and ethnic groups participate and are victims of violence at school more often than other students.[59] Yet, it is close to impossible to predict who will be next to commit a violent act in a school.

Like most other health problems, risk factors need to be identified and steps taken to reduce the risk of violent acts occurring in the schools. Many schools have taken steps to try to reduce the chances for violence, yet many more have stated that violence is not a problem at "our school." These are the schools that are most vulnerable to such a problem. Included in some of the actions taken by schools are (1) creating new educational opportunities that include the development of skills in conflict resolution, negotiation, and communication;[56] (2) using programs that increase self-esteem;[56] (3) developing programs that provide for less free time like extracurricular school activities, tutoring projects, and job development; (4) increasing security on school grounds with the use of hall and grounds monitors, off-duty police officers, and/or metal detectors; and (5) the development of new school rules and policies that outline acceptable school behavior.[58]

Violence is not a problem that will be going away soon. Many school personnel do not believe it is something that can happen in their schools. It can happen anywhere.[60] It is an issue that all schools need to face and something for which they need to plan to reduce the risks to school children and personnel.

CHAPTER SUMMARY

- The potential impact of a coordinated school health program on the health of children, their families, and the community is great, because the school is the one institution through which we all must pass.

- To date, the full potential of school health has not been reached, due to lack of support and interest.

- If implemented properly, coordinated school health can improve access to health services, educate students about pressing health issues, and provide a safe and healthy environment in which students can learn and grow.

- The foundations of the school health program include (1) a school administration that supports such an effort, (2) a well-organized school health council that is genuinely interested in providing a coordinated program for the students, and (3) written school health policies.

- The components of a coordinated school health program include (1) school health services, (2) a healthy school environment, (3) school health education, (4) counseling, psychological, and social services, (5) physical education, (6) school nutrition services, (7) parent/community involvement for school health, and (8) school-site health promotion for staff.

- The seven National Health Education Standards emphasize a skills-based curriculum focusing on the following: (1) core concepts, (2) accessing valid health information, products, and services, (3) practicing health-enhancing behaviors, (4) analyzing influences, (5) demonstrating interpersonal communication skills, (6) utilizing goal-setting and decision-making skills, and (7) advocating for personal, family, and community health.

- A number of registries of effective health education programs are maintained to assist health educators locate and assess available curricula.

- There are a number of issues that face school health advocates, including a lack of support for coordinated school health, dealing with controversy in the health curriculum, the implementation of school-based health centers, and violence in schools.

REVIEW QUESTIONS

1. What is meant by the term *coordinated school health program*?

2. What individuals (name by position) should be considered for inclusion on the school health council?

3. What foundations are needed to ensure a coordinated school health program? Why?

4. Why are written school health policies needed?

5. Who should approve written school health policies?

6. What are the eight components of a coordinated school health program as noted by Allensworth and Kolbe?

7. What are the differences among (a) core health services, (b) core plus expanded school health services, and (c) services through school-based or school-linked health centers?

8. Explain the importance of using a standards-based health curriculum.

9. How would a health educator go about locating credible health education curricula?

10. State four issues facing school health advocates and explain why they are issues.

ACTIVITIES

1. Make arrangements to observe an elementary classroom in your town for a half-day. While observing, keep a chart of all the activities that take place in the classroom that relate to a coordinated school health program. Select one activity from your list and write a one-page paper describing the activity, why it was health related, how the teacher handled it, and what could have been done differently to improve the situation.

2. Visit a voluntary health agency in your community and ask the employees to describe the organization's philosophy on health education and inquire if their health education materials are available for use in a school health program. Summarize your visit with a one-page reaction paper.

3. Make an appointment to interview either a school nurse or a school health coordinator. During your interview, ask the person to provide an overview of what his or her school offers in the way of a coordinated school health program. Ask specifically about the eight components of the school health program and the issues of controversy presented in this chapter. Summarize your visit with a two-page written paper.

4. Make arrangements to interview a school administrator or school board member in a district where a school-based or school-linked center exists. Ask the person to describe the process that the school district went through to start

SCENARIO: ANALYSIS AND RESPONSE

It was obvious that Ms. Graff had a very full day, which included several issues related to a coordinated school health program. Based upon what you read in this chapter and other knowledge you have about school health, respond to the following questions:

1. Identify five school health concerns with which Ms. Graff had to deal.

2. For each of the concerns you identified in Question 1, state how written policies may have helped or hindered Ms. Graff with her responsibilities.

3. How important do you feel is the role of the classroom teacher in making a coordinated school health program work? Why do you feel this way?

4. Say the school district in which Ms. Graff works was interested in opening up a school-based health center, but the superintendent needed more data to help "sell" the idea to the school board. Using a search engine on the Internet (e.g., Google, Excite, or Lycos), enter "school-based health centers." Could you recommend some Web sites to the superintendent that would be useful?

the center, what resistance the district met in doing so, and what the district would do differently if it had to implement it again or start another center.

COMMUNITY HEALTH ON THE WEB

The Internet contains a wealth of information about community and public health. Increase your knowledge of some of the topics presented in this chapter by accessing the Jones and Bartlett Publishers Web site at **health.jbpub.com/communityhealth/5e** and follow the links to complete the following Web activities.

- American School Health Association
- The Center for Health and Health Care in Schools
- Division of Adolescent and School Health

REFERENCES

1. U.S. Department of Health and Human Services, Public Health Service (1996). *Progress Review: Educational and Community-Based Programs*. Washington, DC: U.S. Government Printing Office.

2. Dryfoos, J. (2000). "The Mind-Body-Building Equation." *Educational Leadership,* 57(6): 14–17.

3. Joint Committee on Health Education and Promotion Terminology (2001). "Report of the 2000 Joint Committee on Health Education and Promotion Terminology." *American Journal of Health Education,* 32(2): 89–103.

4. Allensworth, D. D., and L. J. Kolbe (1987). "The Comprehensive School Health Program: Exploring an Expanded Concept." *Journal of School Health,* 57(10): 409–412.

5. U.S. Census Bureau (2002). School Enrollment—Social and Economic Characteristics of Students: October 2002. Available at http://www.census.gov/population/www/socdemo/school/cps2002.html.

6. Division of Adolescent and School Health, Centers for Disease Control and Prevention (2004). *School Health Policies and Programs Study*. Available at http://www.cdc.gov/healthyyouth/shpps/index.htm.

7. McGinnis, J. M., and C. DeGraw (1991). "Healthy Schools 2000: Creating Partnerships for the Decade." *Journal of School Health,* 61(7): 292–296.

8. American Cancer Society (1999). *Improving School Health: A Guide to School Health Councils*. Atlanta, GA: American Cancer Society.

9. Fetro, J. V. (1998). "Implementing Coordinated School Health Programs in Local Schools." In E. Marx, S. F. Wooley, and D. Northrop, eds., *Health Is Academic: A Guide to Coordinated School Health Programs.* New York: Teachers College Press, 15–42.

10. National Association of School Nurses (2002). "Issue Brief: Role of the School Nurse." Available at http://www.nasn.org/briefs/briefs.htm.

11. Cornacchia, H. J., L. K. Olsen, and J. M. Ozias (1996). *Health in Elementary Schools,* 9th ed. St. Louis, MO: Mosby, 47–48.

12. McGinnis, J. M. (1981). "Health Problems of Children and Youth: A Challenge for Schools." *Health Education Quarterly,* 8(1): 11–14.

13. American Association for Health Education (2002). *The School Nurse in Education: A Position Statement*. Available at http://www.aahperd.org/aahe/template.cfm?template=publications-position.html.

14. Bruess, C. E., and J. E. Gay (1978). *Implementing Comprehensive School Health.* New York: Macmillan.

15. Grebow, P. M., B. Z. Greene, J. Harvey, and C. J. Head (2000). "Shaping Health Policies." *Educational Leadership,* 57(6): 63–66.

16. McKenzie, J. F. (1983). "Written Policies: Developing a Solid Foundation for a Comprehensive School Health Program." *Future Focus: Ohio Journal of Health, Physical Education, Recreation, and Dance,* 4(3): 9–11.

17. American Cancer Society (1999). *Improving School Health: A Guide to the Role of the School Health Coordinator*. Atlanta, GA: American Cancer Society.

18. Maylath, N. S. (1991). "Employment of School Health Coordinators." *Journal of School Health,* 61(2): 98–100.

19. Winnail, S., S. Dorman, and B. Stevenson (2004). "Training Leaders for School Health Programs: The National School Coordinator Leadership Institute." *Journal of School Health,* 74(3): 79–84.

20. Division of Adolescent and School Health, Centers for Disease Control and Prevention (2004). *Coordinated School Health Programs: What Is Coordinated School Health?* Available at http://www.cdc.gov/healthyyouth/CSHP/index.htm.

21. U.S. Department of Health and Human Services. (2000). *Healthy People 2010: Understanding and Improving Health.* Washington, DC: U.S. Government Printing Office.

22. Schlitt, J. J. (June 1991). "Issue Brief—Bringing Health to School: Policy Implications for Southern States." Washington, DC: Southern Center on Adolescent Pregnancy Prevention and Southern Regional Project on Infant Mortality. Printed in *Journal of School Health, 62(2):* 60a–60h.

23. Klein, J. D., and L. S. Sadowski (1990). "Personal Health Services as a Component of Comprehensive Health Programs." *Journal of School Health,* 60(4): 164–169.

24. Duncan, P., and J. B. Igoe (1998). "School Health Services." In E. Marx, S. F. Wooley, and D. Northrop, eds., *Health Is Academic: A Guide to Coordinated School Health Programs.* New York: Teachers College Press, 169–194.

25. National Health and Education Consortium (1995). *Starting Young: School-Based Health Centers at the Elementary Level.* Washington, DC: Author.

26. Joint Committee on Health Education Terminology (1974). "New Definitions: Report of the 1972–73 Joint Committee on Health Education Terminology." *Journal of School Health,* 44(1): 33–37.

27. Henderson, A., and D. E. Rowe. (1998). A Healthy School Environment." In E. Marx, S. F. Wooley, and D. Northrop, eds., *Health Is Academic: A Guide to Coordinated School Health Programs.* New York: Teachers College Press, 96–115.

28. Grunbaum, J. A., L. Kann, B. I. Williams, S. A. Kinchen, J. L. Collins, E. R. Baumler, and L. J. Kolbe (2000). "Surveillance for Characteristics of Health Education among Secondary Schools—School Health Education Profiles, 1998." *MMWR,* 49(No. SS-8): 1–41.

29. Institute of Medicine (1997). *Schools and Health: Our Nation's Investment.* Washington, DC: National Academic Press.

30. Lohrmann, D. K., and S. F. Wooley (1998). "Comprehensive School Health Education." In E. Marx, S. F. Wooley, and D. Northrop, eds., *Health Is Academic: A Guide to Coordinated School Health Programs.* New York: Teachers College Press, 43–66.

31. Division of Adolescent and School Health, Centers for Disease Control and Prevention (2004). *Healthy Youth! An Investment in Our Nation's Future, 2004.* Available at http://www.cdc.gov/healthyyouth/about/healthyyouth.htm.

32. Joint Committee on National Health Education Standards (1995). *National Health Education Standards.* Atlanta, GA: American Cancer Society.

33. Division of Adolescent and School Health, Centers for Disease Control and Prevention (2004). *Healthy Youth! Registries of Programs Effective in Reducing Youth Risk Behaviors.* Available at http://www.cdc.gov/healthyyouth/healthtopics/registries.htm.

34. Center for Substance Abuse Prevention, Substance Abuse and Mental Health Services Administration, U.S. Department of Health and Human Services (2004). *SAMHSA Model Programs: Background Information.* Available at http://modelprograms.samhsa.gov/template.cfm?page=background.

35. Centers for Diseases Control and Prevention (1988). "Guidelines for Effective School Health Education to Prevent the Spread of AIDS." *MMWR,* 37(S-2): 1–14.

36. Centers for Diseases Control and Prevention (1994). "Guidelines for School Health Programs to Prevent Tobacco Use and Addiction." *MMWR,* 43(RR-2): 1–18.

37. Centers for Diseases Control and Prevention (1996). "Guidelines for School Health Programs to Promote Lifelong Healthy Eating." *MMWR,* 45(RR-9): 1–41.

38. Centers for Diseases Control and Prevention (1997). "Guidelines for School and Community Health Programs to Promote Physical Activity Among Young People." *MMWR,* 46(RR-6): 1–36.

39. Division of Adolescent and School Health, Centers for Disease Control and Prevention (2004). *Healthy Youth! Publications & Links.* Available at http://www.cdc.gov/healthyyouth/publications/index.htm.

40. U.S. Department of Health and Human Services, Office for Substance Abuse Prevention (1989). *Drug-Free Committees: Turning Awareness Into Action* (HHS pub. no. ADM 89-1562). Washington, DC: U.S. Government Printing Office.

41. No author (1991). "Healthy People 2000: National Health Promotion and Disease Prevention Objectives and Health Schools." *Journal of School Health,* 61(7): 298–299.

42. Association for the Advancement of Health Education (1991). "Position Statement: Comprehensive School Health." Reston, VA: Author.

43. Centers for Disease Control and Prevention (1997). "Is School Health Education Cost-Effective? An Exploratory Analysis of Selected Exemplary Components." Division of Adolescent and School Health. As stated in F. D. McKenzie, and J. B. Richmond (1998). "Linking Health and Learning: An Overview of Coordinated School Health Programs." In E. Marx, S. F. Wooley, and D. Northrop, eds., *Health Is Academic: A Guide to Coordinated School Health Programs.* New York: Teachers College Press, 1–14.

44. Gold, R. S., G. S. Parcel, H. J. Walberg, R. V. Luepker, B. Portnoy, and E. J. Stone (1991). "Summary and Conclusions of the THTM Evaluation: The Expert Work Group Perspective." *Journal of School Health,* 61(1): 39–42.

45. Cleary, M. J. (1991). "School Health Education and a National Curriculum: One Disconcerting Scenario." *Journal of School Health,* 61(8): 355–358.

46. Bensley, L. B., Jr., and E. O. Harmon (May/June 1992). "Addressing Controversy in Health Education." *Update,* 9–10.

47. Council on Scientific Affairs, American Medical Association (1990). "Providing Medical Services through School-Based Health Programs." *Journal of School Health,* 60(3): 87–91.

48. Lear, J. G., L. L. Montgomery, J. J. Schlitt, and K. D. Rickett (1996). "Key Issues Affecting School-Based Health Centers and Medicaid." *Journal of School Health,* 66(3): 83–88.

49. Center for Evaluation and Quality, National Assembly of School-Based Health Care (2002). *School-Based Health Centers: National Census School Year 2001–2002.* Available at http://www.nasbhc.org/EQ/National_2001Data.htm.

50. Making the Grade (2001). *School-Based Health Centers—Background.* Available at http://www.gwu.edu/~mtg/sbhcs/sbhc.htm.

51. Pacheco, M., W. Powell, C. Cole, N. Kalishman, R. Benon, and A. Kaufmann (1991). "School-Based Clinics: The Politics of Change." *Journal of School Health,* 61(2): 92–94.

52. Rienzo, B. A., and J. W. Button (1993). "The Politics of School-Based Clinics: A Community-Level Analysis." *Journal of School Health,* 63(6): 266–272.

53. The School-Based Adolescent Health Care Program (1993). *The Answer Is at School: Bringing Health Care to Our Students.* Washington, DC: Author.

54. Morone, J. A., E. H. Kilbreth, and K. M. Langwell (2001). "Back to School: A Health Care Strategy for Youth." *Health Affairs,* 20(1): 122–136.

55. Making the Grade (1999). *School-Based Health Centers—National Survey, 1997/1998 Report.* Washington, DC: Author.

56. Hill, S. C., and J. C. Drolet (1999). "School-Related Violence among High School Students in the United States, 1993–1995." *Journal of School Health,* 69(7): 264–272.

57. Prothrow-Smith, D., and S. Quanday (1996). "Communities, Schools, and Violence." In A. M. Hoffman, ed., *Schools, Violence, and Society.* Westport, CT: Praeger, 153–161.

58. Anspaugh, D. J., and G. Ezell (2001). *Teaching Today's Health,* 6th ed. Boston: Allyn and Bacon.

59. Grunbaum, J., L. Kann, S. Kinchen, J. Ross, J. Hawkins, R. Lowry, W. A. Harris, T. McManus, D. Chyen, and J. Collins (2004). "Youth Risk Behavior Surveillance—United States, 2003." *CDC Surveillance Summaries: MMWR,* 53(SS-02).

60. Ross, M. A. (16 March 2001). "Safety Workshop Stresses Preparation." *The Muncie Star Press.*

U N I T
T W O

THE NATION'S HEALTH

Chapter 7

Maternal, Infant, and Child Health

Chapter Objectives

After studying this chapter you will be able to:

1 Define *maternal, infant,* and *child health*.

2 Explain the importance of maternal, infant, and child health as indicators of a society's health.

3 Define *family planning* and explain why it is important.

4 Identify consequences of teenage pregnancies.

5 Define *legalized abortion* and discuss *Roe v. Wade* and the pro-life and pro-choice movements.

6 Define *maternal mortality rate*.

7 Define *prenatal care* and the influence this has on pregnancy outcome.

8 List the major factors that contribute to infant health and mortality.

9 Explain the differences among infant mortality, neonatal mortality, and post-neonatal mortality.

10 Identify the leading causes of childhood morbidity and mortality.

11 List the immunizations required in order for a two-year-old child to be considered fully immunized.

12 Explain how health insurance and health care services impact childhood health.

13 Identify important governmental programs developed to improve maternal and child health.

14 Briefly explain what WIC programs are and whom they serve.

15 Identify the major groups who are recognized as advocates for children.

SCENARIO

Joan is 18 years old and a recent high school graduate. She lives in a small town of about 2,700 people. Most of the town's residents rely on a larger city nearby for shopping, recreation, and health care. Joan had dated Dave the past two years, but there was never any talk of marriage. Just before graduation she learned that she was pregnant. At Thanksgiving, just as she was completing her seventh month of pregnancy, she went into premature labor. An ambulance rushed her to the emergency room of the hospital in the nearby city for what became a premature birth of her baby. While Joan was in recovery, doctors determined that her baby was not only premature, it also appeared to have other "developmental abnormalities." When asked whether she had received any prenatal care, Joan replied, "No, I couldn't afford it; besides, I didn't know where to go to get help."

INTRODUCTION

Creating a health profile of Americans requires a clear understanding of the health-related problems and opportunities of all Americans. In Chapter 3 we dicussed the role of descriptive epidemiology in understanding the health of populations. In describing the personal characteristics of a population, age is the first and perhaps the most important population characteristic to consider when describing the occurrence of disease, injury, and/or death in a population. Almost every health-related event or state has greater differences with age than in any other population characteristic. For this reason, community health professionals use age-specific rates when comparing the amount of disease between populations. When they analyze data by age, they use groups that are narrow enough to detect any age-related patterns, which may be present as a result of either the natural life cycle or behavioral patterns. Viewing age-group profiles in this manner enables community health workers to identify risk factors for specific age groups within the population and to develop and propose interventions aimed at reducing these risk factors. Health promotion and disease prevention programs successful at reducing exposure of specific age groups to such risk factors can improve the health status of the entire population.

In this chapter, we present a health profile of mothers, infants (those less than one year old), and children (ages 1–14 years). In the following two chapters, the health profiles will be presented of adolescents and young adults (15–24), adults (25–64), and older adults or seniors (65 and older). These same age subgroupings are used by the *Healthy People 2010* report and many other documents produced by the National Center for Health Statistics (NCHS) to describe and measure the health status of Americans.

**maternal, infant,
and child health**
the health of women
of childbearing age
and that of the child
through adolescence

Maternal, infant, and child health encompasses the health of women of childbearing age from pre-pregnancy, through pregnancy, labor, and delivery, and the postpartum period and the health of the child prior to birth through adolescence.[1] In this chapter, we define and discuss commonly used indicators for measuring maternal, infant, and child health; examine the risk factors associated with maternal, infant, and child morbidity and mortality; and review selected community programs aimed at improving the health of women of childbearing age, infants, and children in the United States.

Maternal, infant, and child health are important to a community for several reasons. First, maternal, infant, and child health statistics are regarded as important indicators of the effectiveness of the disease prevention and health promotion services in a community. It is known that unintended pregnancies, lack of prenatal care, poor maternal and child nutrition, maternal drug use, low immunization rates, poverty, limited education, and insufficient child

FIGURE 7.1
The health of a nation is often judged by the health of its youngest members.

care—combined with a lack of access to health care services in a community—are precursors to high rates of maternal, infant, and childhood morbidity and mortality. Second, we now know that many of the risk factors specified can be reduced or prevented with the early intervention of educational programs and preventive medical services for women, infants, and children. These early community efforts reduce the need for more costly medical or social assistance to these same members of society later in their lives and strengthen the well-being of our next generation.

It has been said that the health of a nation can best be judged by the health of its youngest members—the *infants*—those who have not yet reached one year of age (see Figure 7.1). During the past several decades the United States has made dramatic progress in reducing infant mortality (see Figure 7.2). Likewise, there has been a significant decrease in maternal mortality rates in the past couple of decades (see Figure 7.3). However, despite these declines in mortality rates, challenges remain. Possibly the most important concern is that infant and maternal mortality data for the United States are characterized by a continual and serious disparity between mortality rates for white and black infants. This disparity is not directly attributable to race, although certain diseases occur more often in certain races. Rather, the disparity can be traced to differences in the socioeconomic status between segments of the American population. For example, research indicates that low income and limited education correlate very highly with poor health status.[2] Second, the United States has higher infant and maternal mortality rates than other industrialized nations; it ranked 28th in infant mortality (see Figure 7.4) and 21st in maternal morality in 1998.[2] These differences

FIGURE 7.2

Infant mortality rates by race: United States, 1940–2001.

Note: Infant deaths are classified by race of decedent. For 1940–1990, live births are classified by race of parents, and for 1980–2001, by race of mother.

Source: National Center for Health Statistics (2003). *National Vital Statistics Report,* 52(11): 13.

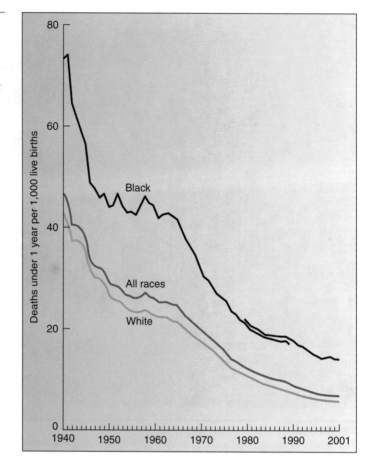

FIGURE 7.3

Age-adjusted maternal mortality by race and Hispanic origin, selected years 1970–1999.

Note: Rates are age adjusted to the 1970 distribution of live births by mother's age in the United States.

*Starting with 1999 data, changes have been made in the classification and coding of maternal deaths under ICD-10. The increase in the number of maternal deaths between 1998 and 1999 is due to changes associated with ICD-10.

†Data not available prior to 1990; excludes data from states lacking an Hispanic-origin item on their death and birth certificates.

Source: National Vital Statistics System.

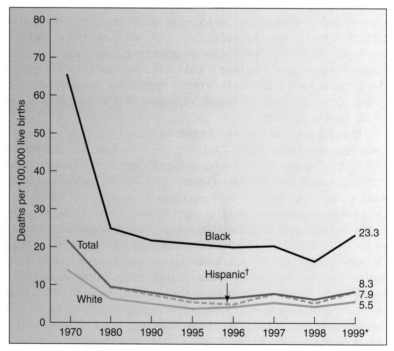

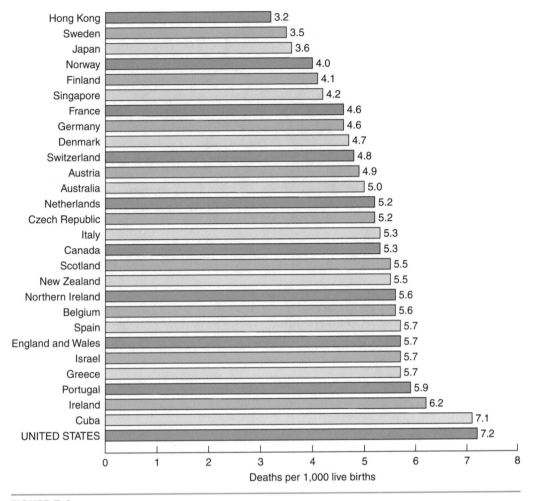

FIGURE 7.4

Comparison of national infant mortality rates: 1998.

Source: National Center for Health Statistics.

among industrialized nations mirror differences in the health status of women before and during pregnancy as well as the ease of access and quantity and quality of primary care for pregnant women and their infants.

Similar to the decline in infant and maternal mortality rates, the mortality rates of *children* (ages 1–14) have gone down significantly in the past couple of decades. The death rate declined by nearly one-half in 1- to 4-year-old children (see Figure 7.5) and by more than one-third in 5- to 14-year-old children from 1980 to 2000 (see Figure 7.6).[2]

Even with these improvements in child mortality rates, there is still much to be done to improve the health of American children. First, we must recognize that children today face other concerns that can significantly put them at risk for poor health. These concerns have been referred to as the "new morbidities" and include their family and social environments, behaviors, economic security, and education (see Box 7.1).[2] Second, we must be concerned about the difference in mortality rates between races. If the young are indeed the hope for the future, the United States must continue to work hard to ensure the health of each infant and child, regardless of race or socioeconomic status.

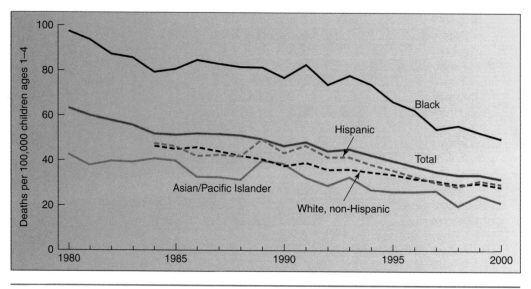

FIGURE 7.5

Death rates among children ages 1 to 4 by race and Hispanic origin, 1980–2000.

Note: Death rates for American Indians/Alaska Natives are included in the total but are not shown separately because the numbers of deaths were too small to calculate reliable rates.

Source: Centers for Disease Control and Prevention, National Center for Health Statistics, National Vital Statistics System.

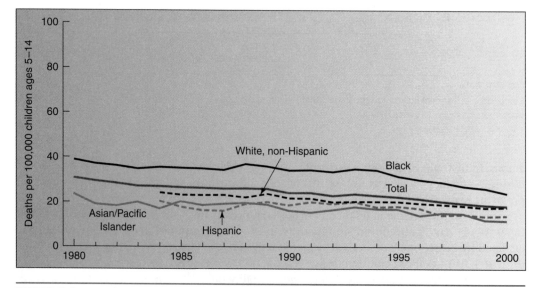

FIGURE 7.6

Death rates among children ages 5 to 14 by race and Hispanic origin, 1980–2000.

Note: Death rates for American Indians/Alaska Natives are included in the total but are not shown separately because the numbers of deaths were too small to calculate reliable rates.

Source: Centers for Disease Control and Prevention, National Center for Health Statistics, National Vital Statistics System.

BOX 7.1	KEY FACTS ABOUT AMERICAN CHILDREN

3 in 5	preschoolers have their mothers in the labor force.	1 in 7	never graduates from high school.
2 in 5	preschoolers eligible for Head Start do not participate.	1 in 8	has no health insurance.
		1 in 8	lives in a family receiving food stamps.
1 in 2	never complete a single year of college.	1 in 8	has a worker in their family but still is poor.
1 in 2	will live in a single-parent family at some point in childhood.	1 in 9	is born to a teenage mother.
1 in 3	is born to unmarried parents.	1 in 12	has a disability.
1 in 3	will be poor at some point in their childhood.	1 in 13	was born with low birth weight.
		1 in 13	will be arrested at least once before age 17.
1 in 3	is behind a year or more in school.	1 in 14	lives at less than half the poverty level.
1 in 4	lives with only one parent. Family living arrangements.	1 in 35	lives with grandparents (or other relative) but neither parent.
1 in 5	is born to a mother who did not graduate from high school.	1 in 28	is born to a mother who received late or no prenatal care.
1 in 5	was born poor.	1 in 60	sees their parents divorce in any year.
1 in 5	children under 3 is poor now.	1 in 83	will be in state or federal prison before age 20.
1 in 6	is poor now.		
1 in 6	is born to a mother who did not receive prenatal care in the first three months of pregnancy.	1 in 146	will die before their first birthday.
		1 in 1,339	will be killed by guns before age 20.
1 in 7	children eligible for federal child care assistance through the Child Care and Development Block Grant receives it.		

Source: Children's Defense Fund (2004). *The State of America's Children Yearbook 2004.* Reprinted with permission.

Whereas there are numerous factors that affect the health of both infant and child, many reflect or are related to the health status of the mother and her immediate environment. One of the first steps to ensure healthy children is to ensure that pregnant women have access to pre-natal care early in a pregnancy and that they receive proper care throughout it. There is nothing more dependent than a fetus in a mother's uterus relying on her to eat nutritiously and to avoid drugs or a newborn that is reliant upon an adult to survive and develop into a healthy child. Therefore, we will begin by looking at the health status of mothers and the family structure.

FAMILY AND REPRODUCTIVE HEALTH

The family is one of society's most treasured foundations. It represents a primary social group that influences and is influenced by other people and establishments. Moreover, families are the primary unit in which infants and children are nurtured and supported regarding their healthy development.[1] The Census Bureau defines a family as "a group of two people or more (one of whom is the householder) related by birth, marriage, or adoption and residing together."[3] This definition does not include a variety of cultural styles and optional family structures that exist in our society today. Friedman broadens the definition of family to include "two or more persons who are joined together by bonds of sharing and emotional closeness and who identify themselves as being part of the family."[4] These definitions not only provide a basis for delineating a family, but are important to consider because most people, at some point in their life, will consider becoming a parent.

From a community health perspective, a marriage, or having two parents, serves as an important family characteristic in relation to a child's well-being. Research indicates there are

FIGURE 7.7

Birth rate for teenagers aged 15 to 19 years and percentage of teenage births to unmarried teenagers: United States, 1950–2000.

Note: Data for 2000 are preliminary.

Source: Ventura, S. J., T. J. Mathew, and B. E. Hamilton (2001). "Births to Teenagers in the United States, 1940–2000." *National Vital Statistics Reports,* 49(10).

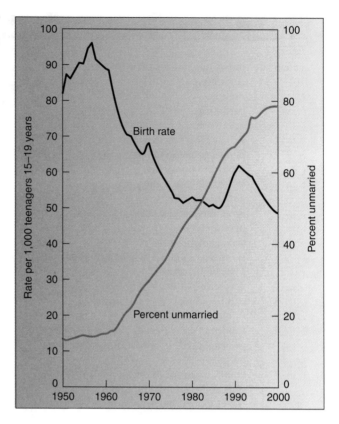

increased health risks for infants and children who are raised in single-parent families, including adverse birth outcomes, low birth weight, and infant mortality, and that these children are more likely to live in poverty than children of married mothers.[5,6] Significant increases in births to unmarried women in the last two decades among all age groups are among the many changes in American society that have affected family structure and placed the child at a social, financial, and health disadvantage (see Figure 7.7).[7] In fact, despite an overall decline in teen birth rates in the last decade, the proportion of births to unmarried teenage mothers continues to increase (see Figure 7.7).[8]

Teenage Births

Teenage childbearing represents a significant social and financial burden on both the family and the community. Teenagers who become pregnant and have a child are more likely than their peers who are not mothers to (1) drop out of school, (2) not get married or have a marriage end in divorce, (3) rely on public assistance, and (4) live in poverty.[9] Teenage pregnancy is tightly connected to single parenthood and poverty. Out-of-wedlock childbearing is currently the mobilizing force behind the growth in the number of single parents, and half of first out-of-wedlock births are to teens.[10] Finally, the majority of teenagers who become mothers are living in poverty at the time of the birth.[9]

Teenage pregnancies also result in serious health consequences for these women and their babies. Teenage mothers are much less likely than women over the age of 20 to receive early prenatal care and are more likely to smoke during pregnancy and have a preterm birth and low-birth-weight baby (see Figure 7.8).[8] As a consequence of these and other factors, babies born to teenagers are more likely to die during the first year of life and more likely to suffer certain serious health problems than a baby born to a mother in her twenties and

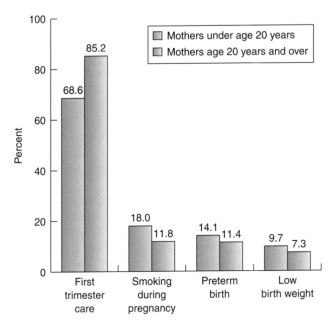

FIGURE 7.8

Selected characteristics for teenage mothers and mothers aged 20 years and older: United States, 1999.

Note: Smoking data exclude information for California and South Dakota.

Source: Ventura, S. J., T. J. Mathew, and B. E. Hamilton (2001). "Births to Teenagers in the United States, 1940–2000." *National Vital Statistics Reports,* 49(10).

thirties. A teenage mother is at greater risk than a woman over the age of 20 for pregnancy complications (such as premature labor, anemia, and high blood pressure).[8] Therefore, teenage pregnancies are a significant community health concern in the United States.

Each year, almost 900,000 teenage women become pregnant (35% of teenage girls get pregnant at least once before they reach age 20).[8] The majority of all teenage pregnancies are unintended, including 90% of unmarried teenage pregnancies. Out of teenage pregnancies, 55% end in birth, 31% end in abortions, and 14% end in miscarriages.[9] Due in large part to public health campaigns aimed at reducing teenage pregnancies, teen birth rates have declined steadily since the early 1990s, reversing the trend of the late 1980s (refer to Figure 7.7). Although the rates are declining, teenage birth rates in the United States are still twice that of any other industrialized nation.[11] Similarly, the number of abortions by teenagers is also decreasing. However, the teen abortion rate is still more than three times that of many other nations.

As stated in the introduction, the future of our Nation depends upon our children. The extent to which we actually believe this can be measured through the degree in which we plan, provide for, educate, and protect our children. Yet, every day in America, approximately 7,500 unintended pregnancies occur; 2,500 mothers younger than 20 years of age become pregnant, with less than one-quarter intending to get pregnant; 4,000 abortions are performed; 2,500 babies are born to mothers who are not high school graduates; 2,600 children are born into poverty; and 400 babies are born to mothers who received late or no prenatal care.[12] The need to plan a pregnancy and thereby place children first in families and in communities must be re-emphasized. Unwanted and unplanned childbearing have long been linked with adverse consequences for mothers, couples, and families, as well as to the children themselves.[13]

The choice to become a parent is a critical decision that affects the individual and the community. People who become parents acquire the major responsibility for another human being. They must provide an environment conducive to child development—one that protects and promotes health. However, the broader community also contributes to this growth and development.[13] This is best illustrated by an African proverb "it takes an entire village to educate and raise a child."[14] Therefore, the community must also make provisions for their care, nurture, and socialization.

Family Planning

Planning for the birth of a child can be one of life's splendid experiences. The first step is making a conscious decision on whether or not to become a parent. This determination will perhaps be one of the most important and consequential decisions couples will make during their lifetime. Parenthood requires enormous amounts of time, energy, and financial commitment, but most notably it requires the willingness to take full responsibility for a child's growth and development. In general, it is considered important that a pregnancy be planned to ensure the best health for the mother and fetus during the pregnancy. Unfortunately, nearly half of first births are to women who are either unmarried, teenagers, or without a high school degree.[15] Too many children are born into families that are not fully prepared to help them succeed.

Public health professionals measure the degree of control women or couples have related to pregnancy by determining the number of "wanted and unwanted births." Nearly half of all pregnancies in the United States are unintended.[16] In the United States, those at greatest risk for unwanted births are teenagers, unmarried women, women with three or more births, black women, and women at the lowest income level and educational attainment.[17] In addition, 48% of women (aged 15 to 44) have had at least one unplanned pregnancy in their lives, and 30% have had one or more abortions. Whether the unintended pregnancy ends in abortion or an unplanned birth, it comes at a significant cost both to the people involved and society.

The National Family Growth Study collects information to better understand unintended pregnancy. Using a 10-point scale, with 1 being "very unhappy to be pregnant" and 10 being "very happy to be pregnant," women were asked to report their feelings of pregnancy. The average mean rating was 9.2 for intended pregnancies and 2.9 for unintended pregnancies.[9] These indicators re-emphasize the importance of community health education programs regarding family planning.

Therefore, an important approach to reducing unwanted pregnancies and their adverse consequences is effective family planning by the community.[13] **Family planning** is defined as the process of determining the preferred number and spacing of children in one's family and choosing the appropriate means to achieve this preference. While many maternal, infant, and child morbidity and mortality outcomes cannot be completely prevented by effective family planning, the frequency of occurrence can be reduced. Thus, preconception education and good gynecological, maternal, and child health care are required for effective family planning.[13]

Community involvement in family planning and care programs has historically included both governmental and nongovernmental health organizations in the United States. See Box 7.2. The federal and state governments provide funding assistance through a myriad of family planning services, including Title X of the Public Health Service Act, Medicaid, state funds, the Maternal and Child Health Bureau, and Social Service block grants. Of these, Title X, or the Family Planning Act, is the only federal program dedicated solely to funding family planning and related reproductive health care services through the National Family Planning Program (PL 91-572).[18] **Title X** of the Public Health Service Act was signed into law by President Nixon in 1970 to provide family planning services and help to all who wanted them but could not afford them. For more than three decades, Title X has been this nation's major program to reduce unintended pregnancy by providing contraceptive and other reproductive health care services to low-income women. Currently, it provides funding support to approximately 75% of the 4,000-plus nationwide family planning clinics. Every year more than six million women receive health care services at family planning clinics funded by Title X.[19] Eighty percent of the women who are served report that this is the only source of family planning service they have. Those served are predominantly young and poor, and have never had a child.[19]

These family planning clinics are located in every state and in 85% of all counties. The administration of all Title X grants is through state health departments or regional agencies

family planning determining the preferred number and spacing of children and choosing the appropriate means to accomplish it

Title X a portion of the Public Health Service Act of 1970 that provides funds for family planning services for low-income people

---

BOX 7.2

TEN GREAT PUBLIC HEALTH ACHIEVEMENTS, 1900–1999: FAMILY PLANNING

Changes in Family Planning

In 1900, the average life span was 47 years, and 10% of infants died during their first year of life. The average woman had 3.5 children, and 6 to 9 women per 1,000 died in childbirth. Distribution of information regarding contraception and contraceptive devices was generally illegal under federal and state Comstock laws, which had been enacted in the late 1800s. In 1900, the most common methods of contraception included withdrawal before ejaculation, rhythm, contraceptive douches, and vaginal pessaries (diaphragms, for example).

Milestones in Family Planning, United States, 1900–1999

1914	Margaret Sanger arrested for distributing information regarding birth control
1916	First birth control clinic, Brooklyn, New York; closed after 10 days by the New York City Vice Squad
1917	Federal registration of birth certificates
1928	Timing of ovulation during the menstrual cycle established
1955	First national fertility survey
1960	First licensure of birth control pills
1960	Modern intrauterine device licensed
1965	*Griswold v. Connecticut;* Supreme Court legalizes contraception
1970	Title X created
1972	Medicaid funding for family planning services authorized
1972	*Roe v. Wade;* Supreme Court legalizes abortion
1973	First National Survey of Family Growth taken
1990	Norplant licensed
1992	Depo-Provera licensed
1993	Female condom licensed

Source: Available at http://www.cdc.gov/phtn/tenachievements/family2/fp2.htm.

---

that subcontract with local agencies and clinics. Currently, slightly more than half of the grants are administered by state and local health departments, one-fifth by Planned Parenthood affiliates, and the remaining one-fourth by regional or local family planning councils located in community organizations and hospitals.[19]

For clinics to receive funding under the Title X program, they must offer a broad range of acceptable family planning methods (oral contraceptives, condoms, sterilization, and abstinence); they must encourage family participation; they must give priority to low-income families, and they must not use abortion as a method of family planning.[18] In addition to family planning methods, clinics also provide a comprehensive group of other health services (see Figure 7.9).

In 1981, family planning clinics that received federal funds were required to provide counseling on all options open to a pregnant woman, including abortion, as outlined in Title X. However, these facilities were not allowed to perform abortions. In 1988, the "**gag rule**" regulations were enacted. These regulations barred physicians and nurses in clinics receiving federal funds from counseling clients about abortions. Family planning providers challenged this legislation on the grounds that it denied women their rights to information that was needed to make an informed decision. Many health care providers felt that the gag rule restricted their rights to counsel a client even when childbirth could be detrimental to her health.[18] Supporters of the gag rule regulation felt that Title X was created to help prevent unwanted pregnancy by providing education and contraception services and was not intended to provide services related to pregnancy options.

In 1992, congressional action loosened the gag rule and allowed for abortion options to be discussed between a client and her physician at Title X facilities. While this may appear to be a

gag rule regulations that barred physicians and nurses in clinics receiving federal funds from counseling clients about abortions

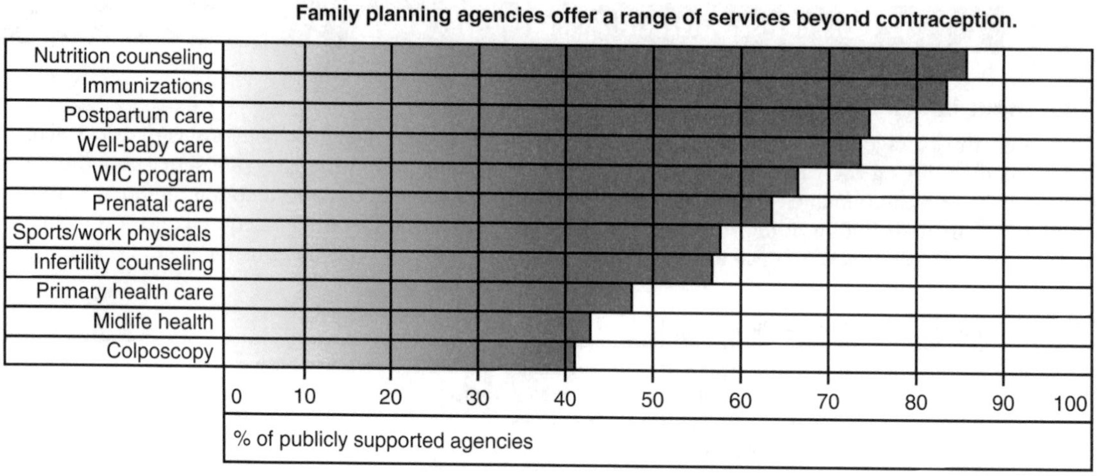

Family planning agencies offer a range of services beyond contraception.

Nutrition counseling										
Immunizations										
Postpartum care										
Well-baby care										
WIC program										
Prenatal care										
Sports/work physicals										
Infertility counseling										
Primary health care										
Midlife health										
Colposcopy										

0 10 20 30 40 50 60 70 80 90 100

% of publicly supported agencies

FIGURE 7.9

A significant proportion of women rely on family planning clinics for their reproductive health care.

Source: Allan Guttmacher Institute (2000). *Fulfilling the Promise: Public Policy and U.S. Family Planning Clinics.* New York: Author, 18. Reprinted with permission.

reasonable compromise, in reality most women who visit family planning clinics are served by a nurse or nurse-practitioner and never see a physician; therefore this change in the gag rule still did not permit the free exchange of information between clients and all professionals in the clinic. In 1993, a presidential memorandum reversing the gag rule regulations was signed. This change, which is still in effect today, enables Title X facilities to discuss abortion as an option to the pregnancy. The presidential memorandum also enables abortions to be performed on U.S. military bases in foreign countries, provided that private funds pay for the abortion.

Controversy regarding acceptable family planning methods is not new in our country. In the early 1900s, a maternity nurse by the name of Margaret Sanger delivered babies in the homes of poor, mostly immigrant women. She described her experiences by writing: "Tales were poured into my ears, a baby born dead, great relief, the death of an older child, sorrow but again relief of a sort, . . . the story told a thousand times of death and abortion and children going into institutions. I shuddered with horror as I listened to the details and studied the reasons in back of them—destitution with excessive childbearing. The waste of life seemed utterly senseless."[20]

The women Sanger cared for knew nothing of how to prevent pregnancy and because of the "Comstock Laws" they could get no information from their doctors. Sanger further explained her experiences by writing "I came to a sudden realization that my work as a nurse and my activities in social service were entirely palliative and consequently futile and useless to relieve the misery I saw all about me."[20] So, disheartened by her ability to care for them, she decided to try to prevent these unwanted conditions in the first place.

In 1914, Margaret Sanger, with the help of funds from numerous supporters worldwide, founded the National Birth Control League. The establishment of this organization is credited with starting the birth control movement in the United States. The purpose of this organization was to win greater public support for birth control by demonstrating the association between a woman's ability to limit her fertility and improve both her health and the health of children. In addition, Sanger also challenged the morality of the times by declaring that women had the right to experience sexual pleasure and that freeing them from the fear of pregnancy would assist women in achieving this. In 1942, the National Birth Control League joined with hundreds of family planning clinics nationwide and formed the Planned Parenthood Federation of America.

Today, Planned Parenthood Federation of America, Inc., has grown to be the largest voluntary reproductive health care organization in the world and is still dedicated to the principle that every woman has the fundamental right to choose when or whether to have children.[21] Currently, Planned Parenthood operates nearly 900 health centers, which are located in every state and the District of Columbia. This not-for-profit organization receives its funding from a variety of sources, including one-third from governmental grants, specifically from Title X grant funds.[21]

Evaluating the Success of Community Health Family Planning Programs

The establishment of local family planning clinics, many of which receive funding through Title X, has resulted in an improvement in maternal and child health indicators for the communities served.[19] Many people in need of family planning services are uninsured, and private health insurance usually does not provide coverage for contraceptive services. Title X funding enables for the support network of over 4,000 clinics that provide comprehensive family planning services to nearly 5 million women each year, 85% of whom are low income and a third of whom are adolescents. By providing access to contraceptive materials and instructions on how to use these materials effectively and counseling about reproductive health matters, community family planning clinics are able to show large reductions in unintended pregnancies, abortions, and births. Each year, publicly subsidized family planning services prevent approximately 1.3 million unintended pregnancies, which would have resulted in 632,000 abortions, 534,000 births, and 165,000 miscarriages.[19]

From an economic perspective, each public dollar spent by federal and state governments to provide family planning services saves $3 in Medicaid costs for pregnancy-related and newborn care.[22] The total annual savings is estimated at nearly $2 billion, which represents money currently being spent on welfare, medical, and nutritional services as required by law. One study compared the cost of contraception methods to the cost of unintended pregnancies if no contraception was used and found that the total savings to the health care system fall between $9,000 and $14,000 per woman over five years of contraceptive use.[23]

Furthermore, each year the U.S. government spends through various funded programs an estimated $40 billion on behalf of families in which the first birth occurred when the mother was a teenager.[24] The funded programs that support the teenage mother and her family include Aid to Families with Dependent Children (ADC), Medicaid, and food stamps. Estimates suggest that if teen pregnancies were delayed until the mother was in her twenties, the United States would save approximately $10 billion a year.[23]

Abortion

One of the most important outcomes of community family planning programs is preventing abortions. Abortion has been legal throughout the United States since 1973 when the Supreme Court ruled in the **Roe v. Wade** case that women, in consultation with their physician, have a constitutionally protected right to have an abortion in the early stages of pregnancy free from government interference.[25] Since the early 1970s, the CDC has been documenting the number and characteristics of women obtaining legal induced abortions to monitor unintended pregnancy and to assist with efforts to identify and reduce preventable causes of morbidity and mortality associated with abortions.[26] As a result of the *Roe v. Wade* decision, the number of women dying from illegal abortions has diminished sharply during the last three decades in the United States. However, doubters remain, largely among those whose main strategy for reducing abortion is to outlaw it. However, while it may seem paradoxical, the legal status of abortion appears to have relatively little connection to its overall pervasiveness.

Starting in 1973, the number, ratio, and rate of legal abortions in the United States increased steadily until 1979 and remained stable in the 1980s and early 1990s; it has declined in most years thereafter (see Figure 7.10). In 2000, 857,475 abortions were reported.[26] According to the CDC, the overwhelming majority of all abortions were performed on

Roe v. Wade
a 1973 Supreme Court decision that made it unconstitutional for state laws to prohibit abortions

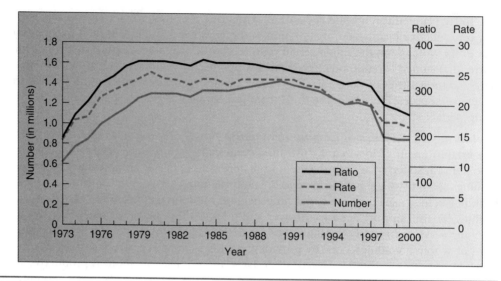

FIGURE 7.10

Number, ratio, and rate of legal abortions performed, by year: United States, 1973-2000.

Note: Ratio is calculated as number of abortions per 1,000 live births; rate is calculated as number of abortions per 1,000 women aged 15 to 44 years. For 1998-1999, data are from 48 reporting areas, and for 2000, from 49 reporting areas.

Source: Elam-Evans, L. D., L. T. Strauss, J. Herdon, et al. (2003). "Abortion Surveillance—United States, 2000." *MMWR,* 52(SS12): 1-25.

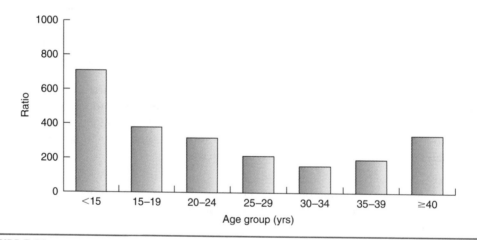

FIGURE 7.11

Abortion ratio, by age group of women who obtained a legal abortion in selected states: United States, 2000.

Note: Ratio is calculated as number of abortions per 1,000 live births. Data are from 46 states, the District of Columbia, and New York City.

Source: Elam-Evans, L. D., L. T. Strauss, J. Herdon, et al. (2003). "Abortion Surveillance—United States, 2000." *MMWR,* 52(SS12): 1-25.

unmarried mothers (81%), of whom 57% were white and more than half (52%) were under age 25 (see Figure 7.11).

The fate of legalized abortion itself is as unclear as the right of a client to discuss abortion options in federally funded clinics. The Hyde Amendment of 1976 made it illegal to use federal funds to perform an abortion except in cases where the woman's life was in danger. In 1992, the Supreme Court was asked to rule on the constitutionality of the landmark court decision of *Roe v. Wade.* The *Roe v. Wade* Supreme Court ruling made it unconstitutional for state laws

FIGURE 7.12
Political appointments and elections can be won or lost on the issue of abortion.

to prohibit abortions. In effect, this decision concluded that an unborn child is not a person and therefore has no rights under the law. The decision of whether to have an abortion or not was left up to the woman until she was 12 weeks pregnant. After the twelfth week, an abortion was permissible only when the health of the mother was in question. In 1989, the Supreme Court appeared to reverse this decision. It ruled that the individual states could place restrictions on a woman's right to obtain an abortion. Some states now have a 24-hour waiting period after counseling before permitting an abortion.

The issue of abortion has become a hotly debated topic. Political appointments can be won or lost depending upon a candidate's stance as "pro-life" or "pro-choice" on the abortion issue (see Figure 7.12).

Pro-life groups argue that performing an abortion is an act of murder. Generally, they believe that life begins at conception and that an embryo is a person. The pro-choice position is that women have a right to reproductive freedom. **Pro-choice** advocates feel that the government should not be allowed to force a woman to carry to term and give birth to an unwanted child. They support this argument by raising issues of child abuse and neglect against unwanted children. To counter this argument, pro-life advocates support adoption as an alternative. Clearly, there is no easy solution to the question of abortion. The question of when life begins can only be decided by each individual based upon his or her own values and beliefs.[21]

pro-life
a medical/ethical position that holds that performing an abortion is an act of murder

pro-choice
a medical/ethical position that holds that women have a right to reproductive freedom

MATERNAL HEALTH

Maternal health encompasses the health of women in the childbearing years, including those in the pre-pregnancy period, those who are pregnant, and those who are caring for young children (see Figure 7.13). The effect of pregnancy and childbirth on women is an

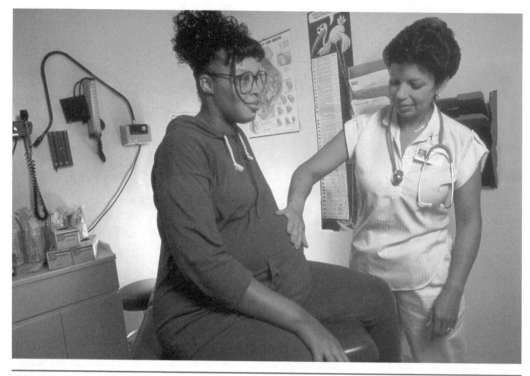

FIGURE 7.13
Maternal health encompasses the health of women in the childbearing years.

important indicator of their health. Pregnancy and delivery can lead to serious health problems. Maternal mortality rates are the most severe measure of ill health for pregnant women.

The Tenth Revision of the *International Classification of Diseases* (ICD 10) defines a *maternal death* (maternal mortality) as "the death of a women while pregnant or within 42 days of termination of pregnancy, irrespective of the duration and site of the pregnancy, from any cause related to or aggravated by the pregnancy or its management but not from accidental or incidental causes."[27] The *maternal mortality rate* is the number of mothers dying per 100,000 live births in a given year. The number of live births is used in the denominator because the total number of pregnant women is unknown.

Between 1970 and 1980, maternal mortality decreased from 21.5 deaths per 100,000 live births to 9.4 deaths per 100,000 live births, more than a 50% reduction (see Figure 7.3). However, since 1982 the risk of dying has remained relatively constant. This is disturbing because an estimated half of all maternal deaths could be prevented through improved health care, better quality of care, and changes in health and lifestyle habits.[28] The five leading causes of maternal deaths are hemorrhage, embolism, pregnancy-induced hypertension, sepsis/infection, and anesthesia complications.

Additionally, the gap between rates for black and white women remains, with black women being four times more likely than white women to die from pregnancy and its complications. Ensuring early initiation of prenatal care during maternity greatly contributes to reductions in perinatal illness, disability, and death for both the mother and the infant.[29] In addition, a number of underlying causes of high maternal morbidity and mortality rates include poverty, the sociocultural factor, and a limited education.

BOX 7.3

OPPORTUNITIES TO REDUCE MATERNAL AND INFANT MORTALITY

Prevention measures that reduce maternal and infant mortality and promote the health of all childbearing women and their newborns should start before conception and continue through the postpartum period. Some of these prevention measures include the following.

Before conception

- Screen women for health risks and pre-existing chronic conditions such as diabetes, hypertension, and sexually transmitted diseases.
- Counsel women about contraception and provide access to effective family planning services (to prevent unintended pregnancies and unnecessary abortions).
- Counsel women about the benefits of good nutrition; encourage women especially to consume adequate amounts of folic acid supplements (to prevent neural tube defects) and iron.
- Advise women to avoid alcohol, tobacco, and illicit drugs.
- Advise women about the value of regular physical exercise.

During pregnancy

- Provide women with early access to high-quality care throughout the phases of pregnancy, labor, and delivery. Such care includes risk-appropriate care, treatment for complications, and use of antenatal corticosteroids when appropriate.

- Monitor and, when appropriate, treat pre-existing chronic conditions.
- Screen for and, when appropriate, treat reproductive tract infections including bacterial vaginosis, group B streptococcus, and human immunodeficiency virus.
- Vaccinate women against influenza, if appropriate.
- Continue counseling against use of alcohol, tobacco, and illicit drugs.
- Continue counseling about nutrition and physical exercise.
- Educate women about the early signs of pregnancy-related problems.

During postpartum period

- Vaccinate newborns at age-appropriate times.
- Provide information about well-baby care and the benefits of breastfeeding.
- Warn parents about exposing infants to secondhand smoke.
- Counsel parents about placing infants to sleep on their backs.
- Educate parents about how to protect their infants from exposure to infectious diseases and harmful substances.

Source: Centers for Disease Control and Prevention. Available at http://www.cdc.gov/phtn/tenachievements/mothers1/mb1.htm.

Prenatal Health Care

High-quality **prenatal health care** is one of the fundamentals of a safe motherhood program and includes three major components—risk assessment, treatment for medical conditions or risk reduction, and education.[13,29] Prenatal health care should begin before pregnancy when a couple is considering having a child, and it should continue throughout pregnancy (see Box 7.3). The goals of prenatal care include providing the best care for the pregnant woman and the unborn child, as well as preparing the mother-to-be for the delivery of a healthy baby. During prenatal visits, tests are performed on both the mother and fetus to assess any potential risks, to treat any maternal or fetal complications, and to monitor the growth and development of the fetus. In addition, counseling and guidance are provided regarding the various aspects of pregnancy, including weight gain, exercise, nutrition, and overall health.

Prenatal care is crucial to maternal and infant health. Women who receive early and continuous prenatal health care have better pregnancy outcomes than women who do not. A pregnant woman who receives no prenatal care is three times as likely to give birth to a **low-birth-weight infant** (one that weighs less than 5.5 pounds or 2,500 grams) as one who receives the appropriate care, and she is four times as likely to have her baby die in infancy. Getting pregnant women into prenatal care early (during the first three months of pregnancy) is the main policy goal of most publicly funded programs designed to reduce the incidence of

prenatal health care
medical care provided to a pregnant woman from the time of conception until the birth process occurs

low-birth-weight infant
one that weighs less than 2,500 grams, or 5.5 pounds, at birth

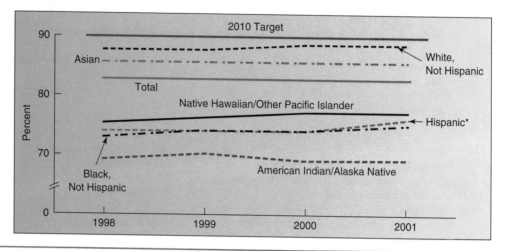

FIGURE 7.14

Early prenatal care (first trimester) by race and ethnicity, 1998–2001.

*Persons of Hispanic origin may be of any race.

Source: Centers for Disease Control and Prevention, National Center for Health Statistics, National Vital Statistics System.

low birth weight and infant mortality in the United States. The percentage of women receiving prenatal care during the first trimester was 83.4% in 2001, a slight increase from the 2000 rate of 83.2%, demonstrating a continuing upward trend toward the *Healthy People 2010* goal of 90%. However, racial and ethnic variations exist in receiving early prenatal care. Non-Hispanic black, Hispanic, and American Indian/Alaska Native women were 2.7 to 3.7 times more likely to begin care late or to receive no prenatal care than non-Hispanic white women in 2001 (see Figure 7.14). Black, Native American, Latino, poorly educated teenage women, and those most likely to be poor and without health insurance are significantly less likely to receive early and comprehensive prenatal care.[29] Another important factor found to affect early prenatal care was whether or not the woman wanted the pregnancy. Women who were pregnant and did not want their babies were less likely to participate in prenatal care programs.[28]

INFANT HEALTH

An infant's health depends upon many factors, which include the mother's health and her health behavior prior to and during pregnancy, her level of prenatal care, the quality of her delivery, and the infant's environment after birth. The infant's environment includes not only the home and family environment, but also the availability of essential medical services such as a postnatal physical examination by a *neonatologist* (a medical doctor who specializes in the care of newborn children up to two months of age), regular visits to a physician, and the appropriate immunizations. The infant's health also depends on proper nutrition and other nurturing care in the home environment. Shortcomings in these areas can result in illness, developmental problems, and even the death of the child.

Infant Mortality

Infant death is an important measure of a nation's health because it is associated with a variety of factors, such as maternal health, quality of access to medical care, socioeconomic conditions, and public health practices.[13] An *infant death* (infant mortality) is the death of a child under one year of age (see Figure 7.15). The *infant mortality rate* is expressed as the number of deaths of children under one year of age per 1,000 live births.

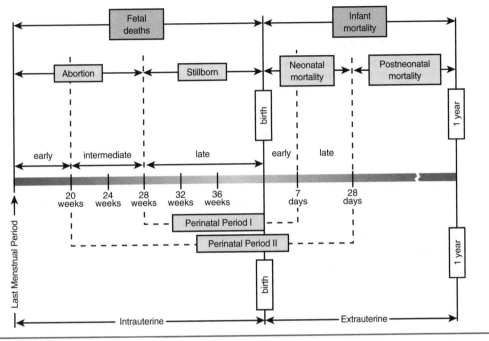

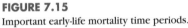

FIGURE 7.15
Important early-life mortality time periods.

Since 2000, the infant mortality rate in the United States has ranged between 6.8 and 7.0 deaths per 1,000 live births, which is substantially below the 1940 rate of 47.0 deaths per 1,000 live births (see Figure 7.2).[30] Decreases in the infant mortality rate during this period have been attributed to improved disease surveillance, advanced clinical care, improved access to health care, better nutrition, and increased educational levels.[13]

Infant deaths, or infant mortality, can be further divided into neonatal mortality and post-neonatal mortality (see Figure 7.15). *Neonatal mortality* is deaths that occur during the first 28 days after birth. Approximately two-thirds of all infant deaths take place during this period. The most common causes of neonatal death are disorders related to short gestation (premature births) and low birth weight, and congenital birth defects. These causes currently account for approximately one-half of all neonatal deaths. *Postneonatal mortality* is deaths that occur between 28 days and 365 days after birth. The most common causes of post-neonatal deaths are sudden infant death syndrome and congenital birth defects.

Improving Infant Health

Due in part to medical research and public health and social services supported by both public and private organizations, infant mortality has declined considerably during the past couple of decades. However, there are many opportunities for decreasing infant deaths and improving infant health even further through reducing risk factors associated with these conditions.

Premature Births

Premature (or preterm) babies are born prior to 37 weeks' gestation. The average length of gestation is 40 weeks, and normal is considered 38 to 42 weeks. The number of babies born prematurely in the United States has been rising steadily since 1981, and in 2001 reached 11.9%, representing one in eight babies being born prematurely.[31] Disorders related to short gestation and low birth weight are the leading causes of neonatal death in the United States. Since premature babies usually have less developed organs than full-term babies, they are more likely to face serious multiple health problems following delivery. Premature babies often require neonatal intensive care, which utilizes specialized medical personnel and equipment. In 2000, hospital charges for prematurity-related infant hospital stays averaged $58,000 per baby, compared with $4,300 for a typical newborn stay.[32]

Approximately half of all premature births have no known cause. Known major risk factors associated with preterm labor and birth include a woman's past history of preterm delivery, multiple fetuses, late or no prenatal care, cigarette smoking, drinking alcohol, using illegal drugs, exposure to domestic violence, lack of social support, low income, diabetes, anemia, high blood pressure, obesity, and women younger than 17 or older than 35.[31]

Therefore, although a number of causes of premature birth may have eluded researchers and are currently beyond our control, prenatal care and lifestyle changes can help women reduce their risk of having a premature delivery. Consequently, there is a lot that community health programs can do to assist a woman in reducing her risk of having a premature baby—specifically, educating parents about premature labor and what can be done to prevent it and expanding access to health care coverage so that more women can get prenatal care.

Low Birth Weight

Today, it is widely accepted that low birth weight (LBW) is the single most important factor in neonatal death, as well as being a significant predictor of postneonatal mortality and infant and later childhood morbidity. Most infants weigh 3,400 grams (7 pounds) at birth. LBW infants are those that weigh 2,500 grams, or about 5.5 pounds. LBW infants are 40 times more likely to die in their first year of life than normal-weight babies. LBW babies often require extensive medical attention early in life and subsequently may suffer from a variety of physical, emotional, and intellectual problems. LBW babies have a higher incidence of cerebral palsy, deafness, blindness, epilepsy, chronic lung disease, learning disabilities, and attention deficit disorder.[33]

The percentage of U.S. infants born at LBW has remained relatively stable (between 7.0% and 8.0%) in the last two decades (see Figure 7.16). LBW must continually be aggressively targeted, especially among various racial/ethnic groups, because significant differences exist among these groups (see Chapter 10).

The two factors that are generally recognized to govern infant birth weight are the duration of gestation (premature births) and intrauterine growth rate. Approximately two-thirds of LBW infants are born premature. Therefore, reduction in premature births holds the most potential for overall reduction in LBW. Research on the causes of intrauterine growth retardation (IRG) leading to LBW babies finds that maternal cigarette smoking during pregnancy is by far the most important risk factor. Other maternal characteristics that are risk factors connected with IRG include maternal LBW, prior LBW history, low pre-pregnancy weight, drinking alcohol, multiple births, and low pregnancy weight gain.[13] Therefore, all pregnant women should (1) get early, regular prenatal care; (2) eat a balanced diet, including adequate amounts of folic acid; (3) gain enough weight; and (4) avoid smoking and drinking alcohol.[34]

Cigarette Smoking

Research has shown that maternal cigarette smoking during pregnancy is the leading modifiable cause of LBW in the United States, therefore making it an ideal target for intervention. Researchers estimate that smoking during pregnancy is linked to 20% to 30% of LBW infants and 10% of infant deaths.[35] The incidence of LBW infants among mothers who smoke is more than twice that of nonsmokers. The good news is that the percentage of births to women who smoked during pregnancy has been dropping, from 19.5% in 1989 to 11.4% in 2002 (see Figure 7.17). This would seem to indicate that the United States is definitely progressing in the right direction when it comes to reaching its goal of 99% reduction for 2010.

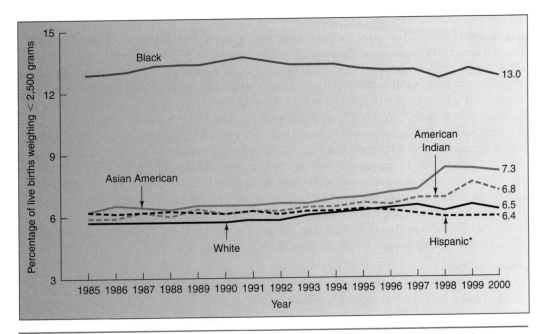

FIGURE 7.16

Percentage of infants born at low birth weight by race, 1985–2000.

*Persons of Hispanic origin may be of any race.

Note: 1985–1988 data are based on race of child; 1989–2000 data are based on race of mother.

Source: National Center for Health Statistics.

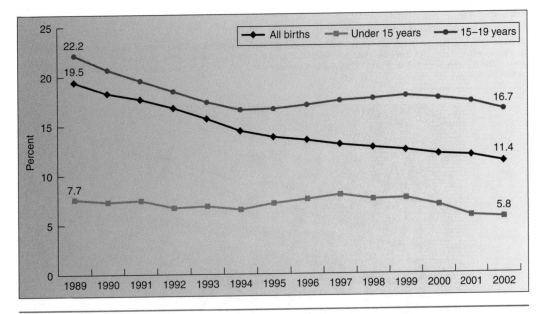

FIGURE 7.17

Percentage of total births to women who smoked during pregnancy, by age of mother, 1989–2002.

Sources: Data for 1970–1999: Eberhardt, M. S., D. D. Ingram, D. M. Makuc, et al. (2001). *Urban and Rural Health Chartbook: Health, United States, 2001.* Hyattsville, MD: National Center for Health Statistics. Data for 2000–2001: National Center for Health Statistics (2003). *Health, United States 2003 with Chartbook on Trends in the Health of Americans.* Hyattsville, MD: Author. Data for 2002: Martin, J. A., P. E. Hamilton, P. D. Sutton, et al. (2003). "Births: Final Data for 2002." *National Vital Statistics Reports,* 52(10).

fetal alcohol syndrome (FAS) a group of abnormalities that may include growth retardation, abnormal appearance of face and head, and deficits of central nervous system function, including mental retardation, in babies born to mothers who have consumed heavy amounts of alcohol during their pregnancies

Alcohol and Other Drugs

Heavy maternal alcohol consumption can lead to a condition known as **fetal alcohol syndrome (FAS),** a group of abnormalities that may include growth retardation, abnormal appearance of face and head, and deficits of central nervous system function, including mental retardation. A safe level of alcohol consumption during pregnancy has not been determined, but adverse effects are associated with heavy consumption during the first few months of pregnancy.[35] In general, no alcohol during pregnancy is strongly recommended.

Other drug use can also result in a number of deleterious effects on the developing fetus, including impaired fetal growth, that can lead to congenital defects. Crack cocaine use during pregnancy can result in genital and urinary tract malformations in the baby. Marijuana use has also been associated with an increased risk of birth defects. A study showed that infants born to women using marijuana and/or cocaine were significantly smaller than infants of nonusers. Marijuana's effect of increasing maternal heart rate, blood pressure, and carbon monoxide levels may be responsible for impairing the growth of the fetus. Maternal use of cocaine results in lower fetal oxygen levels by inducing uterine contractions.[35]

Breastfeeding

The American Academy of Pediatrics recommends that babies be breast-fed for the first year of life. Breast milk is the ideal food for babies, newborn through four to six months. Breastfeeding has many advantages for both baby and mother. Breast milk contains substances that help babies resist infections and other diseases. Breast-fed babies have fewer ear infections and colds, less diarrhea, and vomit less often. In addition, breastfeeding has been shown to improve maternal health by reducing postpartum bleeding, allowing for an earlier return to prepregnancy weight and reducing the risk of osteoporosis.[13]

Breastfeeding rates for women of all races have increased in the last decade. See Figure 7.18 and Box 7.4. Breastfeeding rates were highest among women 35 years and older,

---

FIGURE 7.18

In-hospital breastfeeding, by race/ethnicity, 1990–2001.

Sources: U.S. Department of Health and Human Services, Health Resources and Services Administration, Maternal and Child Health Bureau. *Women's Health USA 2003.* Rockville, Maryland: U.S. Department of Health and Human Services, 2003; and *Years 1991–1998: Breast feeding Trends 1998 (1999). Mother's Survey, Years 1999–2001: Unpublished data.* Ross Products Division. Abbott Laboratories.

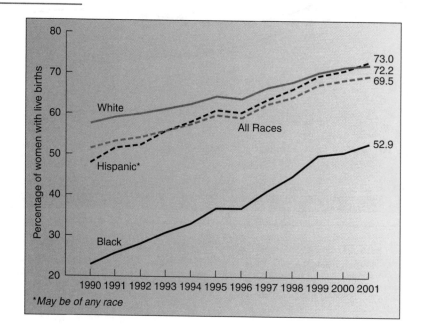

*May be of any race

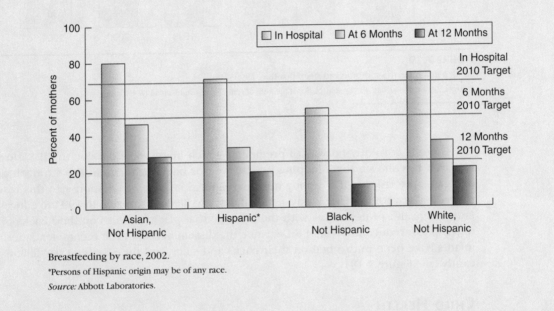

BOX 7.4	HEALTHY PEOPLE 2010: OBJECTIVES

16.19   Increase the proportion of mothers who breastfeed their babies.

Target and baseline:

Objective	Increase in Mothers Who Breastfeed	1998 Baseline	2002 Status	2010 Target
			Percent	
16.19a	In early postpartum period	64	70	75
16.19b	At 6 months	29	33	50
16.19c	At 1 year	16	20	25

Breastfeeding by race, 2002.

*Persons of Hispanic origin may be of any race.

Source: Abbott Laboratories.

For Further Thought

An important public health goal is to increase the number of mothers who breastfeed. Human milk is acknowledged by the American Academy of Pediatrics as the most complete form of nutrition for infants, with a broad realm of benefits for infants' growth and development. What types of programs would you recommend to educate new mothers and their partners and to educate health care providers?

those who are college educated, and women participating in the Women, Infants, and Children (WIC) dietary supplemental program. Women least likely to breastfeed were those younger than 20 years of age, those not employed, those with low income, and those who were black.[13] Two voluntary community groups, the La Leche League and the Nursing Mother's Council, are good sources for breastfeeding information, advice, and support.

Sudden Infant Death Syndrome
Sudden infant death syndrome (SIDS) strikes approximately 2,200 babies each year in the United States. SIDS is defined as the sudden unanticipated death of an infant in whom, after examination, there is no recognizable cause of death. Because most cases of SIDS occur when a baby is sleeping in a crib, SIDS has been referred to as *crib death*. SIDS is the third leading cause of infant death. Moreover, after the first month of life, it is the leading cause of infant death (postneonatal mortality), accounting for one-third of deaths during the period.[13,36]

sudden infant death syndrome (SIDS) sudden unanticipated death of an infant in whom, after examination, there is no recognized cause of death

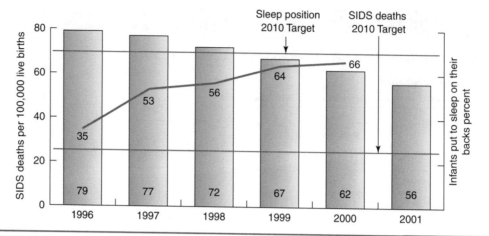

FIGURE 7.19

Sudden infant death syndrome and sleep position: 1996–2001.

Sources: National Vital Statistics System; National Institute of Child Health and Human Development.

There is currently no way of predicting which infants will die due to SIDS. However, research has shown that sleeping on the side or back rather than the stomach greatly decreases the risk of SIDS among healthy full-term infants.[37] In response to this research, the federal government initiated a national "Back to Sleep" campaign in 1994 to educate parents and health professionals with the message that placing babies on their backs or sides to sleep can reduce the risk of SIDS. Since the dissemination of the recommendation, more infants have been put to bed on their backs and sides, and the SIDS rate has fallen significantly (see Figure 7.19).

CHILD HEALTH

Good health during the childhood years (ages 1–14) is essential to each child's optimal development and America's future. America cannot hope for every child to become a productive member of society if children in this country are allowed to grow up with poverty or live in a violent environment, with mediocre child care, or with no health insurance. Failure to provide timely and remedial care leads to unnecessary illness, disability, and death—events that are associated with much greater costs than the timely care itself. The previous example of the cost of not providing prenatal care given earlier in this chapter presents a vivid example. For those who believe that access to basic care is a standard of justness and fairness in any socialized society, America lingers sadly behind many other nations in the health of her children (see Box 7.5).[38]

Childhood Mortality

Childhood mortality rates are the most severe measure of health in children. The death of a child is an enormous tragedy for family and friends, as well as a loss to the community. As mentioned in the introduction of this chapter, the mortality rates of children have generally declined over the past couple of decades (see Figures 7.5 and 7.6). Unintentional injuries are the leading cause of mortality in children (see Figure 7.20). In fact, unintentional injuries kill more children than all diseases combined. The overwhelming majority of unintentional injury deaths in children are due to motor vehicle crashes. Moreover, the majority of children were not wearing a seatbelt or other restraint.[39] All 50 states have primary child restraint laws. They

BOX
7.5

WHERE AMERICA STANDS

Among industrialized nations, the United States ranks:

1st in military technology
1st in military exports
1st in Gross Domestic Product
1st in the number of millionaires and billionaires
1st in health technology
1st in defense expenditures
12th in living standards among our poorest one-fifth of children
13th in the gap between rich and poor children
14th in efforts to lift children out of poverty
16th in low-birth-weight rates
18th in the percent of children in poverty
23rd in infant mortality
Last in protecting our children against gun violence

According to the Centers for Disease Control and Prevention, U.S. children under age 15 are

9 times more likely to die in firearm accident
11 times more likely to commit suicide with a gun

12 times more likely to die from gunfire
16 times more likely to be murdered with a gun than children in 25 other industrialized countries combined.

Of all the members of the United Nations, the United States of America and Somalia (which has no legally constituted government) are the only two nations that have failed to ratify the U.N. convention on the Rights of the Child.

Black infant mortality rates in our nation's capital exceed those in 50 nations including Bahamas, Barbados, Cuba, Dominica, and Oman.

In UNICEF's 2004 *State of the World's Children,* the U.S. ranked lower on maternal mortality than 32 other countries (140 of 172) including Ghana, Lithuania, Croatia, and Syria. We lagged behind 33 other nations (160 of 193) on infant mortality rank.

Source: Children's Defense Fund (2004). *The State of America's Children Yearbook 2004.* Reprinted with permission.

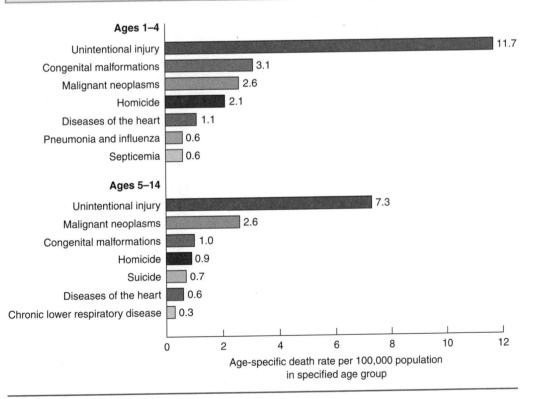

FIGURE 7.20

Leading causes of death in children aged 1 to 14: preliminary data for 2000.

Source: National Center for Health Statistics.

FIGURE 7.21

Unintentional injuries are the leading cause of childhood morbidity and mortality.

allow law enforcement officers to stop a driver if a child is not restrained according to the state law. However, the provisions of these laws vary from state to state.

Childhood Morbidity

Although childhood for many children represents a time of relatively good overall health, it is a time when far too many suffer from acute illness, chronic disease, and disabilities. Morbidity statistics on children are more difficult to calculate because they consist of a variety of perspectives. These include unintentional injuries, child maltreatment, and infectious diseases.

Unintentional Injuries

The United States needs to do a better job of protecting its children from unintentional injuries. Even though unintentional injuries are the leading cause of death among children, deaths are a rare event. However, injury-related morbidity is much more prevalent among children (see Figure 7.21). For each childhood death by injury, there are approximately 34 hospitalizations and 1,000 emergency department visits.[40] Every year about one-fourth of all children sustain an injury severe enough to require medical attention, missed school, and bed rest. Moreover, more than 100,000 children are permanently disabled annually.[40]

In addition to the physical and emotional effects on the children and their families, these injuries have enormous financial effects. It is estimated that the annual economic cost of unintentional injury among children aged 14 and under is approximately $180 billion.[39] Estimates are that 90% of the more than 4,000 unintentional injuries suffered by children each day in a manner seriously enough to require medical treatment could be prevented. (Unintentional injuries are discussed in more detail in Chapter 17.)

Child Maltreatment

Child maltreatment is another source of injury to children. Child maltreatment includes physical abuse, neglect (physical, educational, emotional, and/or medical), sexual abuse, emotional abuse (psychological/verbal abuse and/or mental injury), and other types of maltreatment such as abandonment, exploitation, and/or threats to harm the child. The causes of child maltreatment are not well understood. Child abuse or neglect is often associated with physical injuries and delayed physical growth. However child abuse and neglect is also associated with psychological problems such as aggression and depression. The rate of children maltreated annually has remained between 12 and 15 per 1,000 children over the past decade (see Table 7.1).[41]

The oldest federal agency for children, the Children's Bureau (CB) located in the Administration for Children and Families, has worked to lead the public in taking a more informed and active part in child abuse prevention. The CB has been instrumental in defining the scope of the problem of child maltreatment and in promoting community responsibility for child protection. The CB believes that parents have a right to raise their children as long as they are willing to protect them. When parents cannot meet their children's needs and keep them from harm, the community has a responsibility to act on behalf of the child. If one suspects a child is being abused or neglected, it is important to call the proper authorities. Any action into the family life should be guided by federal and state laws. According to the

Table 7.1

Percentage of Children Who Are Victims of Child Maltreatment, and Distribution by Gender, Age, Race, and Hispanic Origin, and Type of Maltreatment

	1990	1991	1992	1993	1994	1995	1996	1997	1998	1999	2000	2001
Number of victims*	860,577	911,690	994,655	1,026,331	1,032,000	1,005,511	1,011,973	956,711	904,000	829,000	881,000	903,000
Rate per 1,000	13.4	14.0	15.1	15.3	15.2	14.7	14.7	13.8	12.9	11.8	12.2	12.4
Gender (as % of all victims)												
Male	44	45	45	41	41	40	39	40	48	48	48	48
Female	50	52	51	47	46	45	43	44	52	52	52	52
Age of victim (as % of all victims)												
1 year and younger	13	14	13	12	12	11	11	11	14	14	15	16
2–5 years old	24	25	25	23	23	23	22	21	25	24	24	24
6–9 years old	22	23	23	21	20	21	21	21	25	25	24	24
10–13 years old	19	20	19	18	17	17	16	17	20	20	20	21
14–17 years old	14	15	15	14	13	13	13	12	15	15	15	15
18 and older	1	1	1	1	1	1	1	0	1	1	0	0
Race and hispanic origin of victim† (as % of all victims)												
White	53	56	53	51	48	47	50	49	56	54	51	50
Black	25	27	27	25	25	24	22	22	25	26	25	25
Hispanic	10	10	10	9	9	9	9	9	13	14	14	15
American Indian/Alaskan Native	1	1	1	1	1	1	2	2	2	2	2	2
Asian/Pacific Islander	1	1	1	1	1	1	1	1	1	1	1	1
Multiple race	–	–	–	–	–	–	–	–	–	–	–	1
Unknown	1	2	2	1	1	2	3	3	2	11	7	6
Type of maltreatment (as % of all victims)												
Neglect	49	46	50	49	52	52	52	55	54	56	60	57
Physical abuse	27	26	23	24	24	24	24	24	23	21	19	19
Sexual abuse	17	16	14	14	14	13	12	12	12	11	10	10
Psychological or emotional abuse	7	6	5	5	5	4	6	6	6	8	8	7
Medical neglect	0	2	3	2	2	3	3	2	2	2	3	2
Other and unknown	10	13	21	17	16	17	19	12	26	28	17	20

*Indicated is a type of investigation disposition that concludes the allegation of maltreatment or risk of maltreatment was supported or founded by State law or State policy and is the highest level of finding by a State Agency. Indicated or reason to suspect is an investigation that cannot be substantiated, but there is a reason to suspect that the child may have been maltreated or was at risk of maltreatment. This is applicable only to states that distinguish between substantiated and indicated dispositions. All percentages reported here are based on reporting states, no estimates were made unless otherwise noted.

†Estimates for whites and blacks include Hispanics of those races. Persons of Hispanic origin may be of any race.

Sources: Rate per 1,000 for 1990–1999 and number of victims for 1994, 1998, 1999, and 2000: U.S. Department of Health and Human Services, Administration on Children, Youth, and Families. *Child Maltreatment 1999.* Population estimates for 1999: Population Estimates Program, Population Division, U.S. Census Bureau. Internet release date: April 11, 2000; All other estimates for 1990–1999 except rate per 1,000: Trends in the Well-Being of America's Children and Youth 2001. Table HC 2.10 U.S. Department of Health and Human Services. Office of the Assistant Secretary for Planning and Evaluation; Data for 2000: U.S. Department of Health and Human Services, Administration on Children, Youth and Families, Child Maltreatment 2000 (Washington, DC: U.S. Government Printing Office, 2002); Data for 2001: U.S. Department of Health and Human Services, Administration on Children, Youth and Families, *Child Maltreatment 2001* (Washington, DC: U.S. Government Printing Office, 2003); Population estimates for 2000 and 2001 from original analysis by Child Trends of Bridged Race 2000 and 2001 Population Estimates for Calculating Vital Rates, National Center for Health Statistics, Centers for Disease Control and Prevention, 2003. http://www.cdc.gov/nchs/about/major/dvs/popbridge/popbridge.htm.

CB, the community's responsibility for child protection is based on the following:[42]

- Communities should develop and implement programs to strengthen families and prevent the likelihood of child abuse and neglect.

- Child maltreatment is a community problem; no single agency or individual has the necessary knowledge, skills, resources, or societal mandate to provide the assistance to abused and neglected children and their families.

- Intervention must be sensitive to culture, values, religion, and other differences.

- Professionals must recognize that most parents do not intend to harm their children. Rather, abuse and neglect may be the result of a combination of psychological, social, situational, and societal factors.

- Service providers should recognize that many maltreating adults have the capacity to change their abusive/neglectful behavior, when given sufficient help and resources to do so.

- To help families protect their children and meet their basic needs, the community's response should be nonpunitive, noncritical, and conducted in the least intrusive manner possible.

- Growing up in their own family is optimal for children, as long as the children's safety can be assured.

- When parents cannot or will not meet their child's needs, removal from the home may be necessary. All efforts to develop a permanent plan for a child should be made as quickly as possible.[42]

See Chapter 17 for more detailed information on child abuse and neglect.

Infectious Diseases

In the past, infectious diseases were the leading health concern among children, but increased public health action has resulted in a substantial reduction in both morbidity and mortality rates. Infectious disease control resulted from improvements in sanitation and hygiene and the implementation of universal vaccination programs. Because many vaccine-preventable diseases are more common and more deadly among infants and children, the Centers for Disease Control and Prevention (CDC) recommends vaccinating children against most vaccine-preventable diseases early in life. The July to December 2004 recommended immunization schedule is shown in Figure 7.22.

The CDC's immunization schedule for very young children recommends four doses of the diphtheria, tetanus, and pertussis (DTP) vaccine, three or more doses of polio vaccine, one or more doses of measles-mumps-rubella (MMR) vaccine, three or more doses of *Haemophilus influenzae* type b (Hib) vaccine, the hepatitis B vaccine, and the varicella (chickenpox) vaccine. The combined immunization series is referred to as the 4:3:1:3 series. Immunization rates are considered an important indicator of the adequacy of health care for children and of the level of protection a community values related to preventable infectious diseases. The proportion of children aged 19 months to 35 months receiving the recommended combined series has increased from 69% in 1996 to 78% in 2002 (see Figure 7.23).

All children should be immunized at regular health care visits, beginning at birth and continuing to age six.[43] By immunizing, the community safeguards its children against the potentially devastating effects of vaccine-preventable diseases. No child should ever have to endure the effects of these diseases simply because he or she was not vaccinated on time.

Although progress in improving immunization rates has been substantial, about 1 million children in the United States under two years of age have not been fully vaccinated with the most critical vaccines. In addition, the National Immunization Survey data showed considerable variation between states and urban areas, indicating that children are not equally well protected in all parts of the United States. This large number of unvaccinated children has been

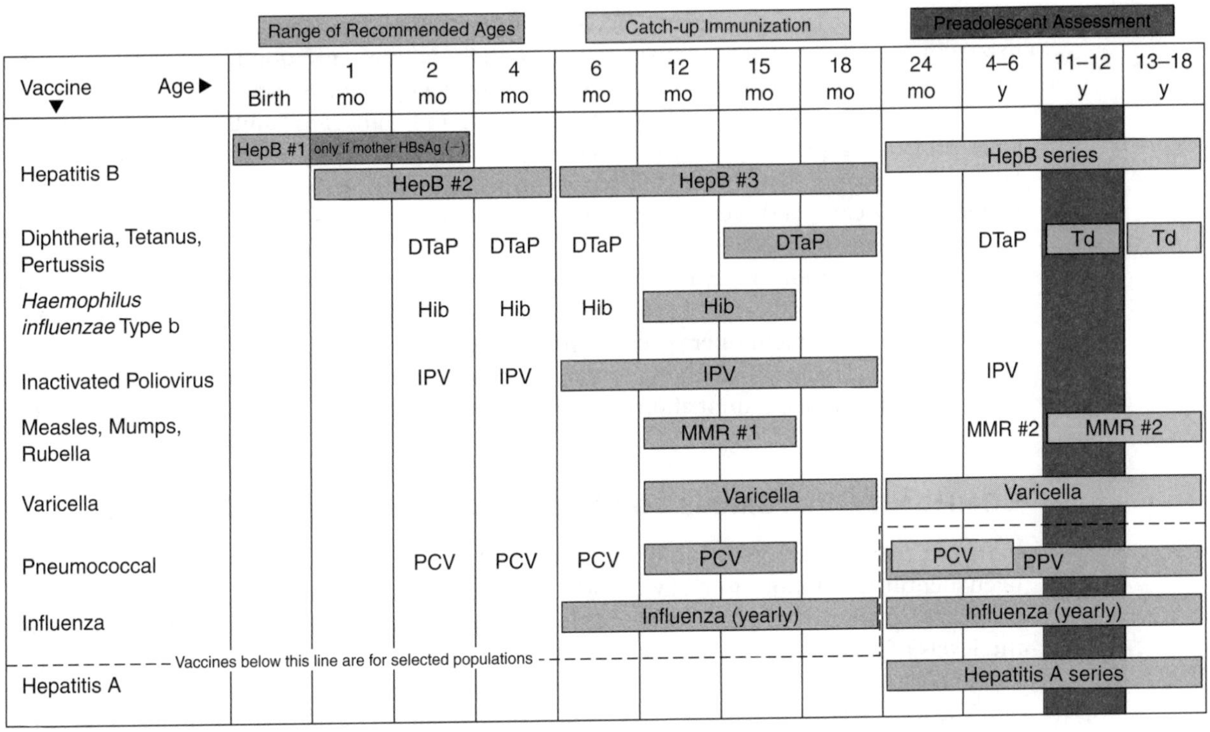

Range of Recommended Ages
Catch-up Immunization
Preadolescent Assessment
Vaccine ▼
Age ▶
Birth
1 mo
2 mo
4 mo
6 mo
12 mo
15 mo
18 mo
24 mo
4–6 y
11–12 y
13–18 y
Hepatitis B
HepB #1
only if mother HBsAg (−)
HepB #2
HepB #3
HepB series
Diphtheria, Tetanus, Pertussis
DTaP
DTaP
DTaP
DTaP
DTaP
Td
Td
Haemophilus influenzae Type b
Hib
Hib
Hib
Hib
Inactivated Poliovirus
IPV
IPV
IPV
IPV
Measles, Mumps, Rubella
MMR #1
MMR #2
MMR #2
Varicella
Varicella
Varicella
Pneumococcal
PCV
PCV
PCV
PCV
PCV
PPV
Influenza
Influenza (yearly)
Influenza (yearly)
Vaccines below this line are for selected populations
Hepatitis A
Hepatitis A series

FIGURE 7.22
Recommended childhood and adolescent immunization schedule: United States, July to December 2004.
Source: Centers for Disease Control and Prevention, National Immunization Program (2004).

Percentage
100
80
60
40
20
0
69
74
76
76
79
78
76
77
78
1994
1995
1996
1997
1998
1999
2000
2001
2002

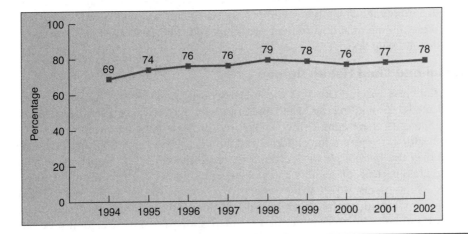

FIGURE 7.23
Percentage of children aged 19 to 35 months receiving the combined series vaccination (4:3:1:3), 1994–2002.
Sources: Data for 1994: Eberhardt, M. S., D. D. Ingram, D. M. Makuc, et al. (2001). *Urban and Rural Health Chartbook: Health, United States, 2001.* Hyattsville, MD: National Center for Health Statistics. Data for 1995–2001: National Center for Health Statistics (2003). *Health, United States 2003 with Chartbook on Trends in the Health of Americans.* Hyattsville, MD: Author. Data for 2002: National Immunization Program (2003). *Immunization Coverage in the U.S.* Results from National Immunization Survey, Centers for Disease Control and Prevention.

attributed to cost, lack of access to medical care, uneducated parents, and confusion on when to vaccinate children. The U.S. government's Childhood Immunization Initiative includes five strategies: (1) improving immunization services for needy families, especially in public health clinics; (2) reducing vaccine costs for lower-income and uninsured families, especially for vaccines provided in private physicians' offices; (3) building community networks to reach out to families and ensure that young children are vaccinated as needed; (4) improving systems for monitoring diseases and vaccinations; and (5) improving vaccines and vaccine use.[43]

More stringent measures by the medical community are needed to ensure that all children are immunized. Opportunities to vaccinate are frequently missed by health care practitioners in primary care settings that do not routinely inquire about the immunization status of the child. Parents and health practitioners need to work together to ensure that youth are protected from communicable diseases. Timely immunization of children must be accepted as a national obligation because America cannot afford the waste that results from unnecessary illness, disability, and death.[43]

COMMUNITY PROGRAMS FOR WOMEN, INFANTS, AND CHILDREN

In the preceding pages, many problems associated with maternal, infant, and child health have been identified. Solutions to many of these problems have been proposed, and in many cases programs are already in place. Some of these programs are aimed at preventing or reducing the levels of maternal and infant morbidity and mortality, while others are aimed at the prevention or reduction of childhood morbidity and mortality.

The federal government has over 35 health programs in 16 different agencies to serve the needs of our Nation's children. The majority of these programs are well respected and help meet the needs of many children. However, others are **categorical programs,** meaning they are only available to people who can be categorized into a specific group based on disease, age, family means, geography, financial need, or other variables. This means that too many children "fall through the cracks" and are not served. Some children require services from multiple programs, which complicates the eligibility determination of each child. At times, this can lead to an inefficient system of child health care. Nonetheless, federal programs have contributed to a monumental improvement in maternal, infant, and child health. We discuss some of the more consequential government programs and their past successes and future objectives in the following text.

categorical programs programs available only to people who can be categorized into a group based on specific variables

Maternal and Child Health Bureau

In 1935, Congress enacted Title V of the Social Security Act. Title V is the only federal legislation dedicated to promoting the health and improving the health of our Nation's mothers and children. Since its enactment, Title V–sponsored projects have been incorporated into the ongoing health care system for children and families. Although Title V has been frequently modified over the last couple of decades, the fundamental goal has remained constant: continued progress in the health, safety, and well-being of mothers and children. The most notable landmark achievements of Title V are projects that have produced "guidelines for child health supervision from infancy through adolescence; influenced the nature of nutrition care during pregnancy and lactation; recommended standards for prenatal care; identified successful strategies for the prevention of childhood injuries; and developed health safety standards for out-of-home child care facilities."[44]

In 1990, the Maternal and Child Health Bureau (MCHB) was established as part of the Health Resources and Services Administration in the Department of Health and Human Services to administer Title V funding. This means the MCHB is charged with the responsibility for promoting and improving the health of our Nation's mothers and children. MCHB's mission "is to provide national leadership with key stakeholders, to improve the physical and mental health, safety and well-being of the maternal and child health (MCH) population which includes all the nation's women, infants, children, adolescents, and their families, including fathers and children with special health care needs."[45] To fulfill its mission, the MCHB has set five broad goals for 2003 to 2007: (1) provide national leadership for maternal and child health, (2) promote an environment that supports maternal and child health, (3) eliminate health barriers and disparities, (4) improve the health infrastructure and systems of care, and (5) assure quality of care.[45]

The MCHB plans on accomplishing its goals through the administration of four core public health services: (1) infrastructure-building services, (2) population-based services, (3) enabling services, and (4) direct health care (gap-filling) services. MCHB uses the construct of a pyramid to provide a useful framework for understanding programmatic directions and resource allocation by the bureau and its partners (see Figure 7.24). MCHB continues to strive for a "society that recognizes and fully supports the important role that public health

FIGURE 7.24

MCH pyramid of health services. The conceptual framework for the services of Title V Maternal and Child Health is envisioned as a pyramid with four tiers of services and levels of funding that provide comprehensive services for mothers and children.

Source: U.S. Department of Health and Human Services (2003). *Maternal and Child Health Bureau Strategic Plan: FY 2003–2007.* Washington, DC: Health Resources and Service Administration, Maternal and Child Health Bureau.

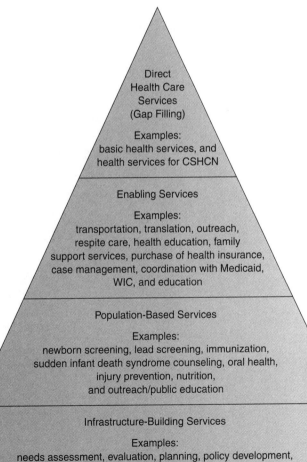

plays in promoting the health of the MCH population, including building, strengthening and assuring MCH health services and infrastructure at all levels."[45]

Women, Infants, and Children Program

WIC
a special supplemental food program for women, infants, and children, sponsored by the USDA

The Women, Infants, and Children (WIC) program is a clinic-based program designed to provide a variety of nutritional and health-related goods and services to pregnant, postpartum, and breastfeeding women, infants, and children under the age of five. The WIC program began as a pilot in 1972 and received permanent federal funding in 1974, in response to growing evidence linking nutritional inadequacies to mental and physical health defects. Congress intended that WIC, unlike other food programs, would serve as "an adjunct to good health care, during critical times of growth and development, to prevent the occurrence of health problems."[46]

The U.S. Department of Agriculture (USDA) administers WIC. The USDA administers grants to the states, where the WIC programs are most often offered through local health departments or state health and welfare agencies (see Figure 7.25). Pregnant or postpartum women, infants, and children up to age five are eligible if they meet the following three criteria: (1) reside in the state in which they are applying, (2) meet income requirements (applicant must have a household income below 185% of the federal poverty guideline), (3) determined to be at "nutritional risk" by a health care professional.[47]

Since WIC's inception as a national nutrition program, it has grown dramatically. In 1974, the average number of monthly WIC participants was 88,000; in 2003 that number was more than 7.5 million women and children (see Figure 7.26).[47] This constitutes half of all infants in America and one-quarter of children between one and five years of age.

FIGURE 7.25
The WIC program has proven to be extremely effective in improving the health of women, infants, and children in America.

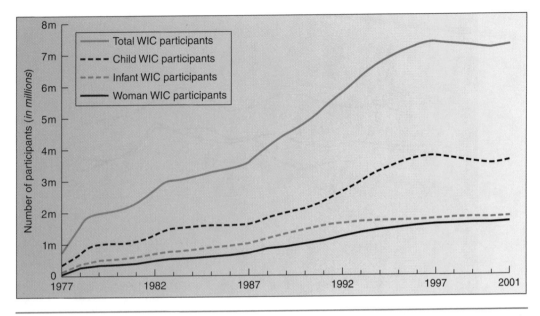

FIGURE 7.26

Trends in WIC program participation, 1977–2001.

Source: National Health Policy Forum, Maternal and Child Health Policy Research Center, based on information from the USDA Web site. Used with permission.

The WIC program has proved to be one of the most effective ways to improve the health of mothers, infants, and young children. Research indicates that participation in the WIC program during pregnancy provides women with a number of positive outcomes, some of which include birth to babies with higher birth weights and fewer fetal and infant deaths. The WIC program is also cost effective. USDA research has shown that for every dollar spent on WIC, the taxpayer saves $4 in future expenditures on Medicaid.[47] For this reason, the WIC program continues to possess strong bipartisan support in Congress.

Providing Health Insurance for Women, Infants, and Children

All children deserve to start life on the right track and to have access to comprehensive health services that provide preventive care when they are well and treatment when they are ill or injured. Health insurance provides access to critical preventive medical services as well as acute medical care in the case of illness or injury (see Chapter 14). When compared with children who are privately insured or have governmental insurance, children without health insurance are much more likely to have necessary care delayed or receive no care for health problems, putting them at greater risk for hospitalization.[48] Therefore, providing health insurance to low-income children is a critical health care safety net.

The government has two principal programs aimed at providing health care coverage to low-income children: the Medicaid program and the State Children's Health Insurance Program (SCHIP). Medicaid, created in 1965, provides medical assistance for certain low-income individuals and families, mostly women and children (see Chapter 14). Children represent slightly more than half of all Medicaid beneficiaries, yet account for only 17% of program spending. A major reason that Medicaid is working well for American children is the multiphase program for preventive health called the Early and Periodic Screening, Diagnostic, and Treatment (EPSDT) for individuals under the age of 21. The Medicaid EPSDT provisions entitle poor children to a comprehensive package of preventive health care and medically necessary diagnosis and treatment.

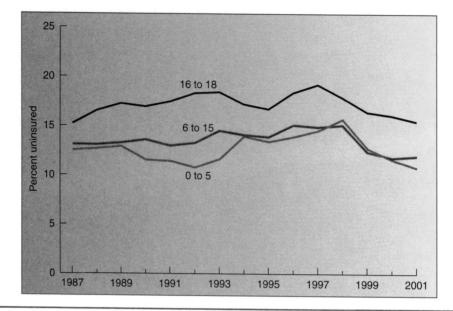

FIGURE 7.27

Uninsured children by age, 1987–2001.

Source: U.S. Census Bureau, *Current Population Survey,* 1988 to 2002 annual social and economic supplements.

Although the Medicaid program is a critical health care program for low-income children, being poor does not automatically qualify a child for Medicaid. Medicaid eligibility is determined by each state based on various age and income requirements. As a result, Medicaid coverage varies across the states and leaves a significant number of poor children uninsured. To broaden coverage to low-income children, Congress created SCHIP under provisions in the Balanced Budget Act of 1997 (see Chapter 14). The program targets uninsured children under 19 with family incomes below 200% of poverty who are not eligible for Medicaid or covered by private insurance. As a result of increased enrollment in Medicaid and SCHIP, the number of uninsured children has dropped since 1997 (see Figure 7.27). However, despite these programs, approximately 12% of youth under the age of 19 were uninsured in 2001. Children aged 16 to 18 are the most likely to be without health insurance, compared with children aged 6 to 15 and children under age 6. Advocates have encouraged state and community decision makers to continue the expansion of these programs to cover as many uninsured children as possible.

Providing Child Care

Experiences during the first years of childhood significantly influence the health of a child. Research shows that early investments in the nurturing of children provides major advantages for families and society later. While parents should accept the primary responsibility for raising their children, the government also can assist families who need help making important investments. Two important investments to the health and welfare of America's children are parenting during the first months of life and the accompanying need for secure relationships with a small number of adults in safe settings as they develop during the first few years of life.

To support new parents, the **Family and Medical Leave Act** (FMLA) was signed into law in 1993. The FMLA grants 12 weeks of unpaid job-protected leave to men or women after the birth of a child, an adoption, or in the event of illness in the immediate family.[49] This legislation has provided employed parents with the time to nurture their children and develop their parenting skills. However, the FMLA only affects businesses with 50 or more employees. Those employees covered by the law include those who have worked 1,250 hours for an employer over a 12-month period (an average of 25 hours per week). This excludes about 40% of American employees who work in small businesses that do not fall under the law's guidelines. Also, employers covered by the FMLA can exempt key salaried employees who are among their highest paid 10%, if they are needed to prevent "substantial and grievous" economic harm to the employer. Some experts feel the law divides the people by class, helping those who can afford the three months without pay, and bypassing those who cannot. Experts have recommended a six- to twelve-month family care leave program with partial pay for at least three months. America is the only industrialized nation that has not enacted a paid infant-care leave.

Today more families are in need of child care than ever before. Estimates are that as many as 13 million children under the age of six are in child care every day. The need for increased use of professional child care has come about as women increasingly are working outside the home and as more children grow up in single-parent households. However, for many families, especially those with low and moderate incomes, high-quality, affordable child care is simply not available. According to a recent study, much of the care we offer children is inadequate, yet a full day of child care costs an average of $4,000 to $10,000 annually per child.[12] These costs are beyond the reach of many working parents, half of whom earn $35,000 or less a year. The lack of high-quality child care prevents children from entering school ready to learn, hinders their success in school, and limits the ability of their parents to be productive workers. Furthermore, after-school care is crucial because juvenile crime peaks between the hours of 3 P.M. and 7 P.M., and school-age children may be at greater risk of engaging in activities that lead to problems like violence and teen pregnancy.

In 1988, Congress passed the Family Support Act, which provided funding for child care assistance to welfare parents who are employed or participating in an approved training program. Unfortunately, states must match federal funds for this program, which makes meeting the needs of eligible participants difficult for poor states.

In 1990, Congress passed the Child Care and Development Block Grant (CCDBG), which provides child care subsidies for low-income children and funding to improve the quality of child care services. The "At Risk" Child Care Program, also passed in 1990, provides additional funding to support child care assistance to low-income families at risk of going on welfare. With the initiation of the "At Risk" Child Care Program and the CCDBG, states were able to provide additional assistance to many more low-income families. However, according to state-reported statistics, of the 15 million children eligible for federal support, only 12% are receiving federal help due to limited federal funding.[50] This means that only one of ten children who are eligible for child care assistance under federal law receive any help. Not one state is currently serving all eligible families. This means that too many parents are unable to obtain necessary child care assistance.

Other Advocates for Children

There are numerous groups that advocate for children's health and welfare. Among them are the Children's Defense Fund, UNICEF, and the American Academy of Pediatrics.

Children's Defense Fund (CDF)

Since 1973, the Children's Defense Fund (CDF) has been working to create a nation in which the network of family, community, private sector, and government supports for children is so

> **Family and Medical Leave Act** federal law that provides up to a 12-week unpaid leave to men and women after the birth of a child, an adoption, or an event of illness in the immediate family

tightly intertwined that no child can slip through the cracks. The CDF is a private, nonprofit organization headquartered in Washington, DC, and it is dedicated to providing a voice for the children of America. It has never accepted government funds and supports its programs through donations from foundations, corporate grants, and individuals. The CDF focuses on the needs of poor, minority, and handicapped children and their families. The aim of the CDF is to educate the nation about the needs of children and to encourage preventive investment in children before they get sick or suffer. It provides information and technical assistance to state and local child advocates.

United Nations Children's Fund (UNICEF)

Founded in 1946, the United Nations Children's Fund (UNICEF) is the only organization of the United Nations assigned exclusively to children. This organization works with other United Nations' members, governments, and nongovernmental organizations to improve child conditions through community-based services in primary health care, basic education, and safe water and sanitation in over 140 developing countries. UNICEF gathers data on the health of children throughout the world. UNICEF has assisted in mass vaccinations and been involved in other international health efforts to protect children.

American Academy of Pediatrics (AAP)

The American Academy of Pediatrics (AAP) was founded in 1930 by 35 pediatricians who felt the need for an independent pediatric forum to address children's needs. When the Academy was established, the idea that children have special developmental and health needs was a new one. Preventive health practices now associated with child care, including immunizations and regular health exams, were only just beginning to change the custom of treating children as "miniature adults." The Academy is committed to the attainment of optimal physical, mental, and social health and well-being for all infants, children, adolescents, and young adults. The activities and efforts of the AAP include research, advocacy for children and youth, and public and professional education.

An example of a program that the AAP coordinates is the Healthy Child Care America Campaign. This program is sponsored by the Maternal and Child Health Bureau and the Administration on Children, Youth, and Families. The campaign is based on the principle that families, child care providers, and health care providers working collaboratively can promote the healthy development of young children. The specific goals of the Healthy Child Care America Campaign are to provide:

Safe, healthy child care environments for all children

Up-to-date and easily accessible immunizations for children in child care

Access to quality health, dental, and developmental screening and comprehensive follow-up for children in child care

Health and mental health consultation, support, and education for all families, children, and child care providers

Health, nutrition, and safety education for children in child care, their families, and child care providers

Since the Healthy Child Care America campaign was launched in 1995, many communities around the country have been promoting collaborative partnerships between health and child care professionals to ensure that children receive the best and the highest-quality care possible. By expanding and creating partnerships between families, child care providers, and government, the best care for millions of children continues to occur.

CHAPTER SUMMARY

- Maternal, infant, and child health are important indicators of a community's overall health. Maternal health encompasses the health of women of childbearing age from pre-pregnancy, through pregnancy, labor and delivery, and in the postpartum period. Infant and child health affect those individuals through 14 years of age.

- Families are the primary unit in which infants and children are nurtured and supported regarding healthy development. Significant increases in births to unmarried women in the last two decades, especially among teenagers, are among the many changes in American society that have affected family structure and the economic security of children. Teenage childbearing represents a significant social and financial burden on both the family and the community.

- The establishment of local Family Planning Clinics with Title X funding has resulted in an improvement in maternal and child health indicators for the communities served.

- High-quality prenatal care is one of the fundamentals of a safe motherhood program. Ensuring early initiation of prenatal care during pregnancy greatly contributes to reductions in perinatal illness, disability, and death for the mother and the infant.

REVIEW QUESTIONS

1. What has been the trend in infant mortality rates in the United States in the last 50 years? What is the current rate? How does this rate compare with that of other industrial countries?

2. What has been the trend in maternal mortality rates in the United States in the last 50 years? What factors have influenced this trend?

3. Why is prenatal care so important for mothers and infants? What types of services are included?

4. What are the consequences of teen pregnancy to the mother? To the infant? To the community?

5. What is included in family planning? Why is family planning important?

6. Discuss the pro-life and pro-choice positions on the abortion issue.

7. Why was the *Roe v. Wade* court decision so important?

8. What are the leading causes of death in children ages 1 to 4 and ages 5 to 14 years?

9. Why are childhood immunizations so important?

10. What is the WIC program?

11. Why is health insurance important for women, infants, and children?

12. Name three groups that are advocates for the health of children and what they have done to show their support.

ACTIVITIES

Write a two-page paper summarizing the results and/or information you gain from one of the following activities.

1. Survey 10 classmates and friends and ask them what leads to teen pregnancy. What prompts adolescents to risk pregnancy when they have adequate knowledge of contraception? Ask if they know anyone who became pregnant as an adolescent. Are the reasons given the same as your own? Divide your list into categories of personal beliefs, barriers to action, and social pressure. For example, a comment that might fit under beliefs is "they don't think they can get pregnant the first time"; under barriers, "they are too embarrassed to buy contraception"; and under social pressure, "all the messages in society promoting sex." Which of the three categories had the most responses? Does this surprise you? What implications does this have for programs trying to reduce the incidence of teen pregnancy?

2. Call your local health department and ask for information about the local WIC program. Ask permission to visit and talk to a representative about the program and clientele.

3. Visit, call, or get on the Web site of your state health department and obtain information concerning the number of childhood communicable diseases reported in your state. What are your state laws concerning immunization of children? Does your state provide immunizations free of charge? What qualifications must a person meet to receive free immunizations?

4. Call a local obstetrician's office and ask if he or she accepts Medicaid reimbursement. What is the normal fee for prenatal care and delivery? If he or she does not take Medicaid, ask the obstetrician to whom he or she would refer a pregnant woman with no private insurance.

5. Create a record of your own (or a family member's) immunizations. Find out when and where you were immunized for each of the immunizations listed in Figure 7.22. Are there any immunizations that are still needed? When are you scheduled to get your next tetanus/toxoid immunization?

SCENARIO: ANALYSIS AND RESPONSE

- Good health during the childhood years (ages 1–14) is essential for each child's optimal development and America's future. America cannot hope for every child to become a productive member of society if children in this country are allowed to grow up with poor or mediocre child care, have no health insurance, live in poverty, or live in a violent environment.

- The federal government has over 35 health programs within 16 different agencies helping states to serve the needs of our Nation's children. The majority of these programs are well respected and help meet the needs of many children.

We have learned that a lack of prenatal care increases the risk of premature delivery and possible health problems for the infant.

1. If Joan had received prenatal care, how could it have helped in the normal development of the infant? How could the doctor have counseled Joan?

2. How could Joan have found out about opportunities for affordable prenatal care?

3. The cost of treating Joan's infant could run into the hundreds of thousands of dollars, and there is no guarantee that the child will survive. Do you think it would be more cost effective to ensure prenatal care to all women or to continue under the system that is in place now? How would you suggest the United States approach this problem?

4. What programs mentioned in this chapter could have helped Joan?

5. Visit the Web site of the USDA (www.usda.gov) and read about WIC. After reading about WIC, do you think this is something that could help Joan with the raising of her child? Why or why not?

COMMUNITY HEALTH ON THE WEB

The Internet contains a wealth of information about community and public health. Increase your knowledge of some of the topics presented in this chapter by accessing the Jones and Bartlett Publishers Web site at **health.jbpub.com/communityhealth/5e** and follow the links to complete the following Web activities.

- Maternal and Child Health Bureau
- Women, Infants, and Children Program
- Insure Kids Now!

REFERENCES

1. Pillitteri, A. (2003). *Maternal and Child Health Nursing: Care of the Childbearing and Childrearing Family,* 4th ed. Philadelphia: J. B. Lippincott Company.

2. U.S. Department of Health and Human Services (2003). *Child Health—USA 2002* (Annual report, Maternal and Child Health Bureau). Washington, DC: U.S. Government Printing Office.

3. U.S. Census Bureau, Population Division, Fertility and Family Statistics Branch (2004). *Current Population Survey, Definitions and Explanations.* Available at http://www.census.gov/population/www/cps/cpsdef.html.

4. Friedman, M. (2003). *Family Nursing: Research, Theory and Practice,* 5th ed. Stamford, CT: Appleton & Lange.

5. McLanahan, S. (1995). "The Consequences of Nonmarital Childbearing for Women, Children, and Society." In National Center for Health Statistics, *Report to Congress on Out-of Wedlock Childbearing.* Hyattsville, MD: National Center for Health Statistics.

6. Ventura, S. J. (1995). "Births to Unmarried Mothers: United States, 1980-92." *Vital and Health Statistics,* 53 (Series 21). Hyattsville, MD: National Center for Health Statistics.

7. National Center for Health Statistics (2003). "Births: Final Data for 2002." *National Vital Statistics Reports,* 52(10): 1-24.

8. Ventura, S. J., T. J. Mathew, and B. E. Hamilton (2001). "Births to Teenagers in the United States, 1940-2000." *National Vital Statistics Reports,* 49(10).

9. Abma, J., A. Chandra, W. Mosher, W. Peterson, and L. Piccinino (1997). "Fertility, Family Planning and Women's Health: New Data from the 1995 National Survey of Family Growth." *Vital Health Statistics,* 23(19).

10. Sawhill, I. V. (1998). "Teen Pregnancy Prevention: Welfare Reform's Missing Component." *Brookings Policy Brief,* 38: 1-8.

11. Singh, S., and J. E. Darroch (2000). "Adolescent Pregnancy and Childbearing: Levels and Trends in Developed Countries." *Family Planning Perspectives,* 32(1): 14-23.

12. Children's Defense Fund (2002). *The State of America's Children 2002.* Washington, DC: Author.

13. U.S. Department of Health and Human Services (2000). *Healthy People 2010* (Conference Edition, in Two Volumes). Washington, DC: Author.

14. Jackson, S. (1993). "Opening Session Comments: Laying the Groundwork for Working Together for the Future." *Journal of School Health,* 63(1): 11.

15. National Campaign to Prevent Teen Pregnancy (1997). "Whatever Happened to Childhood? The Problem of Teen Pregnancy in the United States." Washington, DC: Author.

16. National Center for Health Statistics (1997). *Healthy People 2000 Review.* Hyattsville, MD: Public Health Service.

17. Henshaw, S. (1998). "Unintended Pregnancy in the United States." *Family Planning Perspectives,* 30(1): 24–29.

18. Congressional Digest (1991). "Title X Pregnancy Counseling Act." 70(8,9): 195–224.

19. Allan Guttmacher Institute (2000). *Fulfilling the Promise: Public Policy and U.S. Family Planning Clinics.* New York: Author.

20. Hyde, J., and J. DeLamater (1997). *Understanding Human Sexuality,* 6th ed. Boston: McGraw-Hill.

21. Planned Parenthood Federation of America (2004). *2002–03 Annual Report.* New York: Author.

22. Forrest, J., and R. Samara (1996). "Impact of Publicly Funded Contraceptive Services on Unintended Pregnancies and Implications for Medicaid Expenditures." *Family Planning Perspectives,* 28: 52–59.

23. Trussel, J. (1995). "The Economic Value of Contraception: A Comparison of 15 Methods." *American Journal of Public Health,* 85: 494–503.

24. Flinn, S. K., and D. Hauser (1998). *Teenage Pregnancy: The Case for Prevention. An Analysis of Recent Trends and Federal Expenditures Associated with Teenage Pregnancy.* Washington, DC: Advocates for Youth.

25. "Court Reaffirms Roe but Upholds Restrictions" (1992). *Family Planning Perspectives,* 24: 174–185.

26. Elam-Evans, L. D., L. T. Strauss, J. Herdon, W. Y. Parker, S. V. Bowens, S. Zane, and C. Berg (2003). "Abortion Surveillance—United States, 2000." *MMWR,* 52(SS12): 1–25.

27. World Health Organization (1992). *International Statistical Classification of Diseases and Related Health Problems, Tenth Revision.* Geneva: World Health Organization.

28. Pagnini, D. L., and N. E. Reichman (2000). "Psychosocial Factors and the Timing of Prenatal Care among Women in New Jersey's Healthstart Program." *Family Planning Perspectives,* 32(2): 56–64.

29. Centers for Disease Control and Prevention (2000). "Entry into Prenatal Care—United States, 1989–1997." *MMWR,* 49(18): 393–398.

30. National Center for Health Statistics (2003). "Deaths: Final Data for 2001." *National Vital Statistics Reports,* 52(3): 1–35.

31. March of Dimes (2004). "Premature Birth Rate in U.S. Reaches Historic High." Available at http://www.marchofdimes.com/prematurity/10651_10763.asp.

32. March of Dimes (2004). "Premature Births Soar in U.S., Now No. 1 Obstetric Problem." Available at http://www.marchofdimes.com/prematurity/5510_5810asp.

33. Paneth, S. N. (1995). "The Problem of Low Birth Weight." *The Future of Children,* 5(1): 35–56.

34. Chomitz, O. R., L. W. Cheung, and E. Lieberman (1995). "The Role of Lifestyle in Preventing Low Birthweight." *Future Children,* 5(1): 162–175.

35. Centers for Disease Control and Prevention (1998). "Trends in Infant Mortality Attributable to Birth Defects—United States, 1980–1995. *MMWR,* 47(37): 773–778.

36. Arias, E., R. Anderson, H. C. Kung, S. L. Murphy, and K. D. Kochanek (2003). "Deaths: Final Data for 2001." *National Vital Statistics Reports,* 51(3): 1–56.

37. Willinger, M., H. J. Hoffman, K. T. Wu, J. R. Hou, R. C. Kessler, S. L. Ward, T. G. Keens, and M. J. Corwin (1998). "Factors Associated with the Transition to Non-prone Sleep Positions of Infants in the United States. The National Infant Sleep Position Study." *Journal of the American Medical Association,* 280: 329–335.

38. Children's Defense Fund (2001). *The State of America's Children Yearbook 2001.* Washington, DC: Author.

39. National Highway Traffic Safety Administration (2001). *Traffic Safety Facts 2000: Children.* Washington, DC: U.S. Department of Transportation.

40. National Center for Injury Prevention and Control (1999). "Childhood Injury Fact Sheet." Available at http://www.cdc.gov/ncipc/factsheets/childh.htm.

41. U.S. Department of Health and Human Services, Administration on Children, Youth and Families (2003). *Child Maltreatment 2001.* Washington, DC: U.S. Government Printing Office.

42. U.S. Department of Health and Human Services, Administration for Children and Families (2004). "Community Responsibility for Child Protection." Available at http://nccanch.acf.hhs.gov/pubs/otherpubs/commresp.cfm.

43. Centers for Disease Control and Prevention (2000). *Immunization 2000. A History of Achievement, a Future of Promise.* Atlanta, GA: Author.

44. U.S. Department of Health and Human Services, Health Resources and Services Administration (2000). *Understanding Title V of the Social Security Act.* Rockville, MD: Author.

45. U.S. Department of Health and Human Services, Health Resources and Services Administration (2003). *Maternal and Child Health Bureau Strategic Plan: FY 2003–2007.* Available at http://mchb.hrsa.gov/about/stratplan03-07.htm.

46. Special Supplemental Nutrition Program for Women, Infants, and Children (7CFR246) (1 January, 2002). Available at http://frwebgate.access.gpo.gov/cgi-bin/multidb.cgi.

47. United States Department of Agriculture, Food and Nutrition Service (2004). *About WIC.* Available at http://www.fns.usda.gov/wic/.

48. U.S. Department of Agriculture (1993). *Code of Federal Regulations* 7 (parts 210–299). Washington, DC: U.S. Government Printing Office.

49. Ruhm, C. J. (1997). "The Family and Medical Leave Act." *The Journal of Economic Perspectives.* 3: 10–14.

50. U.S. Department of Health and Human Services (2000). "National Study of Child Care for Low-Income Families, State, and Community Substudy." ABS Associates. Available at http://acf.dhhs.gov/news/ccstudy.htm.

Adolescents, Young Adults, and Adults

Chapter Objectives

After studying this chapter, you will be able to:

1 Explain why it is important for community health workers to be aware of the different health concerns of the various age groups in the United States.

2 Define by age the groups of *adolescents and young adults* and *adults*.

3 Briefly describe key demographic characteristics of adolescents and young adults.

4 Explain what the Youth Risk Behavior Surveillance System (YRBSS) and the Behavioral Risk Factor Surveillance System (BRFSS) are and what type of data they generate.

5 Provide a brief behavioral risk profile for adolescents, college students, and adults.

6 Outline the health profiles for the various age groups—adolescents and young adults, and adults—listing the major causes of mortality, morbidity, and risk factors for each group.

7 Give examples of community health strategies for improving the health status of adolescents and young adults, and adults.

SCENARIO

Annie and Latasha are about half-way through their sophomore year at Garber University. Though they came from very different environments—Annie came from a small rural community with a population of about 1,500 and Latasha grew up in large metropolitan area—they have become good friends. This year, as chance would have it, they have similar class schedules and have ended up in the dining hall each morning at about the same time for breakfast.

One morning, while reading the school newspaper over breakfast, Annie came across an article that described an automobile crash involving some university students. Four university students riding in one car collided with a second car driven by a local middle-aged businessman. Annie asked Latasha if she knew any of the students. Latasha asked who they were, and Annie read their names. Latasha did not know them.

Annie said it looked like the students were in big trouble because they had all been drinking alcohol, and no one was 21 years old. When the police tested the driver, her blood alcohol concentration was 0.14%. So not only was she being charged with underage drinking, but also with driving while intoxicated. Luckily, none of the students was injured, but the local businessman was in serious condition in the hospital. The newspaper article indicated that the students were wearing their safety belts, but the businessman was not. Annie told Latasha that she only knew of one similar incident like this back home. She added, "Why would anyone drink and drive?" Latasha replied, "Don't worry about this Annie. It's no big deal. It happens all the time in the city; in fact it is so common this type of news seldom makes the papers."

INTRODUCTION

In this chapter, we will present a profile of the health of Americans in two different groups—adolescents and young adults (15 to 24 years of age) and adults (25 to 64 years of age). Just like the age groups of Americans presented in Chapter 7, each of these groups has its own sets of health risks and problems. Viewing these age group profiles enables public health workers to detect the sources of diseases, injury, and death for specific target populations and to propose programs to reduce those sources. Effective programs aimed at specific population age groups can reduce the risk factors that contribute to disease, injury, and death for the entire population. We hope that you, the student, will become knowledgeable about the specific health problems of each age group and also become mindful of the subpopulations within these groups that are at special risk.

The years of life between the ages of 15 and 64 are some of the most productive, if not the most productive, of people's lives. Consider all that takes place during these years. Most people complete their formal education, meet and commit to their life-long partners, become parents and raise a family, find and develop their vocation, become owners (or at least mortgage holders) of property, earn their greatest amount of wealth, actively engage in the development of their community, travel more than during any other time in their lives, become aunts or uncles and grandparents, become valued employees, serve as role models and mentors, and plan and save for retirement. It is also a time when they enjoy some of the best health of their lives as well as shape their health (through their lifestyle and health behavior) for their later years.

ADOLESCENTS AND YOUNG ADULTS

Adolescents and young adults are considered to be those people who fall into the 15- to 24-year-old range. The individuals in this age group are considered very important by our society because they represent the future of our nation. If the United States is going to maintain its

adolescents and young adults
those people who fall into the 15- to 24-year-old range

standard of living and pre-eminent position among the countries of the world that it enjoys today, it will depend in large part on these young people.[1]

This period of development of adolescence and young adulthood, often combined when reporting data about young people, can be further split into two subgroups. "Adolescence is generally regarded as the period of life from puberty to maturity."[2] It is not an easy stage of life for most because it is a period of transition from childhood to adulthood. It "is a time when children psychologically move from areas of relative comfort and emotional security to places and situations that are far more complex and often much more challenging."[3] In addition to the psychological changes, this population of teenagers is also experiencing "hormonal changes, physical maturation, and frequently, opportunities to engage in risk behaviors."[2]

Young adults also face many physical, emotional, and educational changes. For example, young adults complete their physical growth and maturity, leave home, marry and start families, attend post-secondary education, enlist in the military, or begin careers. Couple the demands of these personal changes with the demands of a fast-paced, ever-changing society and it is easy to see why this stage in life is considered one of the most difficult.[1]

The combined period of adolescence and young adulthood is a critical one healthwise. It is during this period in one's life that many health-related beliefs, attitudes, and behaviors are adopted and consolidated.[2,4,5] During this stage of life, young people have increased freedom and access to health-compromising substances and experiences—such as alcohol, tobacco, other drugs, and sexual risk-taking—as well as opportunities for health-enhancing experiences like regularly scheduled exercise and healthful diets.[2,4,5] It is also during this stage that certain lifestyle decisions are made that will have long-term influences on health in later years of life.

Demography

There are several demographic variables that impact the health of this age group, but the three variables that are most important to community health are the number of young people, their living arrangements, and their employment status.

Number of Adolescents and Young Adults

The number of adolescents and young adults peaked in 1979 when the baby boomers swelled their ranks to about 21% of the total population. Since 1979, the proportion of 14- to 24-year-olds has declined. Thus, in 2000 they made up just under 14% of the population, roughly the same proportion they made up in 1960.[6,7]

As we look to the future, the proportion of adolescents and young adults in the general population will continue to increase, and at the same time the racial and ethnic make-up will become increasingly more diverse (see Figure 8.1). In 2000, approximately 66% of the adolescents were white. It is estimated that in 2050, this percentage will decrease to 44%.[2]

Living Arrangements

The percentage of children under the age of 18 living in a single-parent family has been on the rise ever since 1965. In fact, the percentage increased sharply in the 1970s and continued to rise slowly through the 1990s. The sharp rise in the 1970s can be attributed to the great increase in the divorce rate.[1] In 2002, over one-fourth (27.8%)[8] of all children lived in single-parent families, versus approximately one-tenth (11%) in 1970.[7] Additionally, more black children (62%) lived in a single-parent home than white children (27%) or Hispanic children (35%).[7]

Family household statistics on single-parent families are only a "snapshot" of children's living status during a single year. Unfortunately, many children are affected over their lifetimes by growing up in single-parent families. Though the psychological and emotional consequences of single-parent families is not clear, the economic consequences are indeed. Children living in single-parent families are more likely to experience severe economic disadvantages.[1] These economic disadvantages adversely impact health.

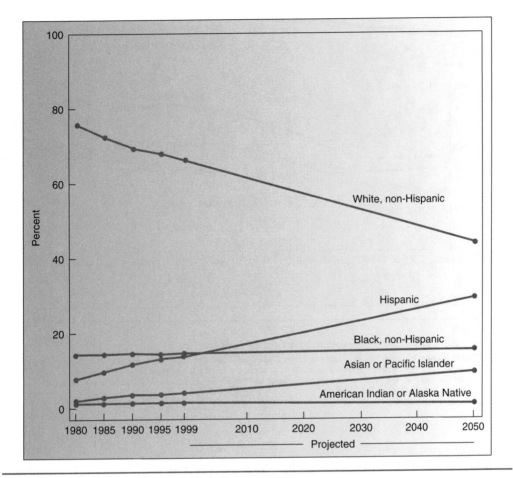

FIGURE 8.1

Race and Hispanic origin of adolescents 10–19 years of age: United States, 1980–2050.

Source: U.S. Department of Commerce, Bureau of the Census, Population Estimates and Projections. In MacKay, A. P., L. A. Fingerhut, and C. R. Duran (2000). *Health, United States, 2000 with Adolescent Health Chartbook.* Hyattsville, MD: National Center for Health Statistics, 27.

Employment Status

Since the years of 1960 and the early 1980s, when there were significant increases in the participation of young women in the labor force, the proportion of all adolescents and young adults in the labor force has remained relatively constant (see Figure 8.2). However, when the unemployment rates of this age group are separated by race and ethnicity, great differences appear. Regardless of sex, black adolescents and young adults are more likely to be unemployed than whites or Hispanics. White adolescents and young adults have the lowest proportion of unemployment.[9] These proportions, like so many others already discussed, are disproportionate by race/ethnicity. These figures are important to community health because most health insurance, and thus access to health care, is connected to employment status.

A Health Profile

With regard to the health profile of this age group, three major areas stand out—mortality, morbidity from specific infectious diseases, and health behavior and lifestyle choices.

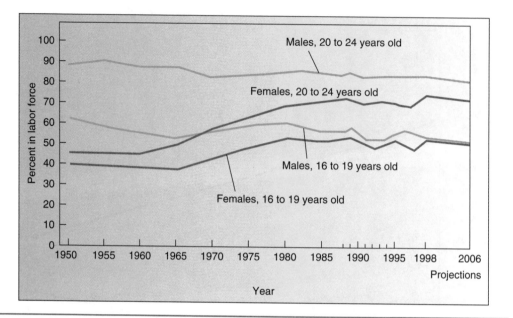

FIGURE 8.2

Labor force participation rate of young adults by sex and age, 1950–2006.

Source: U.S. Department of Labor, Bureau of Labor Statistics, *Employment and Earnings* (January issues); *Handbook of Labor Statistics,* Bulletin 2217. U.S. Department of Commerce, Bureau of the Census, *Statistical Abstract of the United States, 1956, 1987, and 1999;* and *Current Population Reports,* Series P-50, nos. 31 and 72; and unpublished data. Council of Economic Advisers, *Economic Report of the President,* 1987.

Mortality

While, on average, Americans are living longer than ever before, adolescents and young adults suffer their share of life-threatening problems.[1] As it has been with most other age groups, the death rate for adolescents and young adults has significantly declined. Between 1950 and 2000, the death rate of adolescents and young adults has declined by 38%, from 128.1 to 80 per 100,000.[10] This decline in death rates for adolescents and young adults, like that for children, can be attributed to advances in medicine and injury and disease prevention.[1,10]

Regardless of race or ethnicity, men have higher mortality rates than women.[10] Mortality rates for men and women were highest among black Americans and American Indians/Alaska Natives. The lowest mortality rates of both men and women belong to Asian/Pacific Islanders.[10]

Much of the physical threat to adolescents and young adults stems from their behavior rather than from disease.[1] For young people overall, approximately three-fourths of all mortality can be attributed to four causes—motor vehicle crashes (39%), other unintentional injuries (11%), homicide (16%), and suicide (12%).[10] Mortality from unintentional injuries in this age group declined during the last half-century of the twentieth century. Even so, unintentional injury deaths remain the leading cause of death in adolescents and young adults, accounting for almost half of all deaths in this age group (see Figure 8.3).

About three-fourths of deaths from unintentional injuries result from motor vehicle crashes, and in more than half of all the fatal crashes, alcohol was a contributing factor.[1] Unlike other mortality data in this age group, white males have a higher rate of death in motor vehicles than black males. The mortality rates for women of both races are lower than those for males of either race. Overall, the rate of motor vehicle deaths for 15- to 24-year-olds is lower now than it was in 1950.[2]

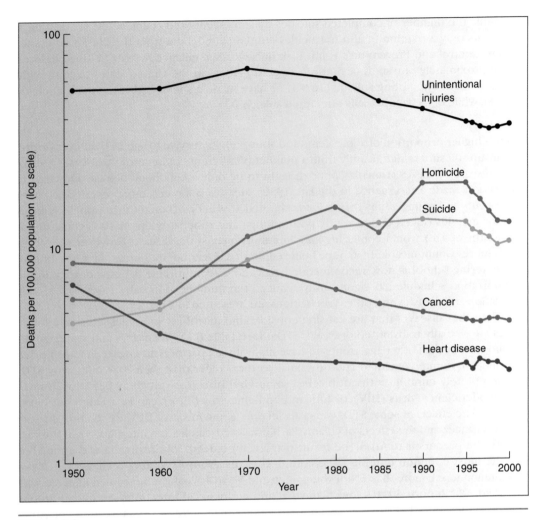

FIGURE 8.3

Death rates for leading causes of death for ages 15 to 24, 1950–2000.

Source: Freid, V. M., K. Prager, A. P. MacKay, and H. Xia (2003). *Health, United States, 2003, with Chartbook on Trends in Health of Americans.* Hyattsville, MD: National Center for Health Statistics, 50.

The most alarming mortality trend in this age group is the growing number of homicides and suicides. During the period from 1950 to 1998, homicide and suicides rates increased between 200% and 300%.[2] Homicide is the second leading cause of death in the 15- to 24-year age group, and it is the leading cause of death among black Americans.[11] It is not race, per se, that is a risk factor for violent death, but rather socioeconomic status and environment. Differences in homicide rates between races are significantly reduced when socioeconomic factors are taken into account. However, alcohol and drugs are involved in about 60% of all homicides and legal interventions.[12]

Suicide is the third leading cause of death in adolescents and young adults, and it is the second leading cause of death of white males in this age group. The rate among black males is about three-fourths that of whites males.[10] The suicide rate in females is significantly lower than that for males, although young women attempt suicide approximately twice as often as young men.[13]

While the number of completed suicides by adolescents and young adults is alarming, it represents only a fraction of all the suicides contemplated. Data from the 2003 Centers for Disease Control and Prevention's Youth Risk Behavior Surveillance System (YRBSS) indicate that approximately one-sixth of ninth to twelfth graders in the United States have thought seriously about attempting suicide (16.9%) or have made a specific plan to attempt suicide (16.5%), while 8.5% have actually attempted suicide.[13]

Morbidity

While a higher proportion of adolescents and young adults survive to age 24 than ever before, this group still suffers significantly from a number of different communicable diseases. One of these diseases, measles (rubeola), once thought to be only a childhood disease and close to eradication, made a resurgence in the late 1980s. Measles is a much more severe disease for adolescents and young adults than it is for children. It was first thought that a single vaccination for measles (taken concurrently with mumps and rubella, as the MMR vaccination, at 15 months of age) would confer life-long immunity against the disease. However, measles is much more communicable than once believed, so that a second immunization at the time of first entering school is now recommended. As can be seen in Table 8.1, this change in the immunization schedule has significantly reduced the number of measles cases. The recommendations for measles and other vaccinations are presented in Chapter 7.

The other diseases that are causing considerable morbidity in adolescents and young adults are sexually transmitted diseases (STDs) (see Table 8.1). "Teenagers and young adults are more likely than other age groups to have multiple sex partners, to engage in unprotected sex, and, for young women, to choose sexual partners older than them."[14] While many STDs are completely curable with antibiotics, some viral infections, such as hepatitis, human immunodeficiency virus (HIV), or human papillomavirus (HPV), can be treated but never cured.[15] "The effects of some STDs can last a lifetime; some forms of HPV are the precursor to cervical cancer, and the effects of chlamydia, if untreated, can lead to infertility. As in the case of HIV, the precursor to AIDS, the result may even be death."[15] Chlamydia and gonorrhea are the most common curable STDs among this age group.[14] Among teenagers, it is not uncommon to see more than 5% of young men and 5% to 10% of young women infected with chlamydia.[16] "Reported rates for chlamydial and gonococcal infections are higher among female adolescents 15–19 years of age than among male adolescents and adults of either gender."[2] In addition, it is estimated that up to half of all new HIV infections occurring in the

---

Table 8.1

Number of Reported Cases (and Incidence Rates) of Selected Communicable Diseases Among 15- to 24-Year-Olds, 1981 to 2002

Disease and Age	1981#	1990#	2002
AIDS	—	1,715	1,982[†]
Chlamydia	—	—	605,263 (3,093.4)
Gonorrhea*	617,994	384,490	208,774 (1069.4)
Measles	594	5,646	42[‡]
Polio	2	—	—
Syphilis*	12,965	16,408	1,193 (6.1)
Tuberculosis	2,198	1,867	1,499

Note: # = rates not available. — = data not collected. * = civilian cases only. [†] = 13- to 24-year-olds. [‡] = total cases for all ages in 2003. Incidence rates per 100,000 population.

Source: U.S. Department of Health and Human Services, Public Health Service, Centers for Disease Control. *Morbidity and Mortality Weekly Report: Annual Summaries,* various years; *HIV/AIDS Supplemental Report, 1998–2002,* and *Reported Tuberculosis in the United States, 2002.*

United States are found in people under the age of 25.[17] Overall, an estimated 4 million new cases of STDs are reported annually in the United States among adolescents.[18]

Health Behaviors and Lifestyle Choices of High School Students

While many behavioral patterns begin during the childhood years (ages 1–14), others begin in adolescence and young adulthood. During this period of experimentation, young people are susceptible to developing deleterious behaviors such as the abuse of alcohol and/or tobacco and other drugs, fighting, and weapon carrying.

In 1990, the Centers for Disease Control and Prevention (CDC) initiated the Youth Risk Behavior Surveillance System (YRBSS) to better track selected health behaviors among young people (see Chapter 3 for more information on the YRBSS). This system currently has three complementary components—national school-based surveys, state and local-based surveys, and a national household-based survey. In the spring of 1991, CDC conducted for the first time the national school-based Youth Risk Behavior Survey. This survey continues to be conducted biennially during odd-numbered years among national probability samples of ninth-through twelfth-grade students from private and public schools. Results of the 2003 survey are included in the following sections. In 1990, CDC began offering to each state and to selected local education departments the YRBSS questionnaire and fiscal and technical assistance to conduct the Youth Risk Behavior Survey. During 2003, 32 state and 20 local surveys were conducted.[13] The third component of YRBSS, national household-based surveys, was initiated when the Census Bureau incorporated a Youth Risk Behavior Supplement in the 1992 National Health Interview Survey (NHIS).[19]

In the short period of time the YRBSS has been in operation, it has proved to be very helpful at both the state and local levels. A number of states and local communities have put into place programs and policies to reduce risk behavior in youth. For example, "the Dallas Independent School District used YRBSS data to develop the District's strategic plan, Vision 2003, which identifies student well-being as one of the seven critical areas for improvement."[13] Continued support of YRBSS will help monitor and ensure the success of many public health and school health programs.[13]

Behaviors That Contribute to Unintentional Injuries

Four different behaviors of high school students that relate to unintentional injuries are monitored as part of the YRBSS. They include seat belt use, bicycle helmet use, riding with a driver who has been drinking alcohol, and driving after drinking alcohol. Since 1991, the numbers of students engaging in these risk behaviors have declined. Yet in 2003, almost one-third (30.2%) of students nationwide had ridden with a driver who had been drinking alcohol in the 30 days preceding the survey, and 12.1% had driven a vehicle after drinking alcohol in the previous 30 days.[13]

Behaviors That Contribute to Violence

Behaviors that contribute to violence-related injuries of high school students include carrying a weapon (e.g., gun, knife, or club), engaging in a physical fight, engaging in dating violence, having been forced to have sexual intercourse, engaging in school-related violence, suicide ideation, and suicide attempts. Nationwide about one-sixth (17.1%) of high school students reported having carried a weapon during the 30 days prior to the survey, and one-third (33.0%) of all high school students reported having been in a fight in the past 12 months. It is no wonder that many school districts around the country are taking steps to reduce violent behavior in school. Males are more likely than females to get in a fight or carry a weapon. However, females were more likely than males to have been forced to have sexual intercourse, and to report sadness, suicide ideation, and suicide attempts.[13] (See Chapter 17 for more on violence.)

FIGURE 8.4
More than a million teens begin smoking each year.

Tobacco Use

The use of tobacco products represents one of the most widespread, high-risk health behaviors for this group. In 2003, approximately one-fifth of high school students (21.9%) nationwide were current smokers—that is, smoked on at least one day in the past 30 days—which is a significant decrease from 1997, when 36.4% of students were current smokers. Similarly, a significant decrease has been seen among current frequent smokers—those who had smoked on 20 or more days in the past 30 days (2003, 9.7%; 1999, 16.8%). Overall, white students (24.9%) were significantly more likely to report current cigarette use than black (15.1%) and Hispanic (18.4%) students, as well as more frequent use of cigarettes (11.8%, 5.5%, and 5.5%, respectively).[13] The vast majority of people (approximately 90%) who become dependent upon nicotine develop that dependency between the ages of 15 and 24, and most before they reach the age of 18.[20]

More than one million teens begin smoking each year; three-fourths of these have parents who smoke. The most alarming trend is that smokers, especially females, are beginning at younger ages than in the past (see Figure 8.4).[21]

In addition to cigarette smoking, the use of **smokeless tobacco** or *spit tobacco* (snuff and chewing tobacco) and cigars are also a threat to the health of teenagers. In 2003, the overall prevalence of current smokeless tobacco use was 6.7% in high school students, which is a significant decrease from 1995 (11.4%). The prevalence was higher in males (11.0%) than females (2.2%), and higher in whites (7.6%) than Hispanics (4.7%) or blacks (3.0%). White males reported the highest rates of smokeless tobacco use (13.2%). Although the number of students using cigars has significantly decreased since 1997 (22%), approximately one-sixth

smokeless tobacco
snuff and chewing tobacco

(14.8%) of students reported current cigar use, which is more than double the number of smokeless tobacco users.[13]

Because use of tobacco that begins during adolescence can lead to a lifetime of nicotine dependence and a variety of negative health consequences, the federal government has exerted considerable effort to keep tobacco out of the hands of adolescents. Many believed, and data from the YRBSS verified, that most adolescents have had easy access to tobacco products. During his term of office, President Clinton was proactive in trying to restrict the distribution of tobacco to youth. One piece of legislation that was approved during President Clinton's term included a requirement that retailers must verify the age of persons who purchase cigarettes or smokeless tobacco products.[20] That guideline stated that anyone who appears to be 27 years of age or younger must be "carded" by retailers.

The most sweeping changes related to the sale of cigarettes came in 1998 when 46 state attorneys general agreed to a settlement with tobacco companies. (Florida, Minnesota, Mississippi, and Texas were not included in the settlement because they had already settled individually with the tobacco companies.) The settlement called for the companies to make payments of $206 billion to the states over 25 years beginning in 2000 and to finance antismoking programs in exchange for the states dropping their health care lawsuits for smokers who were treated with Medicaid funds. In addition to paying the states, the tobacco companies agreed to spend $1.7 billion to study youth smoking and to finance antismoking advertising and accept restrictions on marketing practices that appeal to children, such as the use of cartoon characters (e.g., Joe Camel).

Alcohol and Other Drugs

While, for some, the first use of alcohol or other drugs begins during the childhood years, for most experimentation with these substances occurs between the ages of 15 and 24 years. YRBSS data from 2003 indicate that 44.9% of all high school students reported drinking during the previous month. Further, the data indicate that 28.3% have experienced episodic heavy drinking, and 22.4% have used marijuana at least once in the preceding month.[13]

Although one-fifth of all high school students have used marijuana during the preceding month, alcohol use and abuse continue to be major problems for adolescents, particularly among high school dropouts. As was reported earlier in this chapter, alcohol contributes significantly to motor vehicle crashes and violence in this age group.

In addition to the use of marijuana, high school students also are reporting the use of other illicit drugs. The 2003 YRBSS data indicated that during the previous 30 days, 4.1% had used a form of cocaine and 3.9% used an inhalant, while during their lifetime 11.1% had used ecstasy, 3.3% had used heroin, 7.6% had used methamphetamines, 6.1% had used steroids without a doctor's prescription, and 3.2% had injected an illegal drug.[13] (Chapter 12 presents a more detailed examination of the problems of alcohol and other drug misuse and abuse.)

Sexual Behaviors That Contribute to Unintended Pregnancy and Sexually Transmitted Diseases (STDs)

Since the early 1980s, adolescents in the United States have experienced high rates of unintended pregnancies and STDs, including HIV infection.[22] YRBSS data from 2003 show that almost half (46.7%) of all high school students have engaged in sexual intercourse sometime in their lifetime. The prevalence of sexual intercourse ranged between 27.9% for ninth-grade girls to 60.7% for high school senior boys. Furthermore, it was much more likely for black (67.3%) and Hispanic (51.4%) students to have engaged in sexual intercourse than for whites (41.8%).[13] Table 8.2 shows the trends of selected sexual risk behaviors for high school students since 1990.

As you learned in Chapter 7, each year almost a million girls in the United States between the ages of 15 and 19 become pregnant;[23] 84% of these pregnancies are unintended. The teenage pregnancy rate in the United States is twice as high as in England, France, and Canada,

Table 8.2

Percentage of High School Students Who Reported Selected Sexual Risk Behaviors, by Year—Youth Risk Behavior Survey, United States, 1991, 1995, 1999, and 2003

Behavior	1991	1995	1999	2003
Ever had sexual intercourse	54.1	53.1	49.9	46.7
Ever had sexual intercourse with four or more partners	18.7	17.8	16.2	14.4
Had sexual intercourse during the three months preceding the survey	37.5	37.9	36.3	34.3
Used alcohol or drugs before last sexual intercourse	21.6	24.8	24.8	25.4
Used or partner used birth control pills at last sexual intercourse	20.8	17.4	16.2	17.0
Used or partner used condom at last sexual intercourse	46.2	54.4	58.0	63.0

Source: Centers for Disease Control and Prevention (2004). "National Youth Risk Behavior Survey: 1991–2003—Trends in the Prevalence of Sexual Behaviors." Available at http://www.cdc.gov/yrbss.

and it is nine times higher than the rate in the Netherlands and Japan.[24] In addition to the health risks associated with teenage pregnancies for both mother and child, there are educational, economic, and psychosocial risks as well. Teenage mothers are less likely to get or stay married, less likely to complete high school or college, and more likely to require public assistance and to live in poverty than their peers who are not mothers.[18]

Physical Activity

Lack of physical activity by young people has increasingly become a concern. In 2003, one-third (33.4%) of students had not participated in sufficient vigorous physical activity (activities that made them sweat and breathe hard for 20 minutes or more on three or more of the seven days preceding the survey) and had not participated in sufficient moderate physical activity (activities that did not make them sweat or breathe hard for 30 minutes or more on five or more of the seven days preceding the survey) during the seven days preceding the survey. Females (40.1%) were more likely than males (26.9%) to not engage in sufficient physical activity. The prevalence of lack of participation in a sufficient amount of physical activity was highest among black students. Nationally, 11.5% of students had not participated in either vigorous or moderate physical activity during the seven days preceding the survey.[13]

Overweight and Weight Control

Much like the concern for insufficient physical activity, the concern regarding students becoming overweight has received significant attention recently (see Figure 8.5). In 2003, approximately one-sixth of students were at risk for becoming overweight (15.4%) or were overweight (13.5%), while 29.6% described themselves as slightly or very overweight. Almost one-half of students were trying to lose weight (43.8%). Eating less food, fewer calories, or foods low in fat (42.2%) and exercising (57.1%) were commonly documented behaviors for losing weight or avoiding weight gain. The prevalence for engaging in weight loss behaviors and avoiding weight gain behaviors was higher among females (56.2% and 65.7%, respectively) than males (28.9% and 49.0%). Nationally, 13.3% of students had gone without eating for 24 hours or more to lose weight or to keep from gaining weight during the 30 days preceding the survey.[13]

Health Behaviors and Lifestyle Choices of College Students

In 1995, the national college-based survey—the National College Health Risk Behavior Survey (NCHRBS)—was added to the YRBSS process. Prior to that time, the prevalence of health risk behaviors of college students nationwide had not been well characterized.[25] However, the survey did not become a regular component of the YRBSS, and has not been conducted since.

Two currently available data sources regarding the health behaviors of college students are the National College Health Assessment (NCHA)[26] and Monitoring the Future.[27] The NCHA, first implemented in Spring 2000, is a national, nonprofit research effort organized by

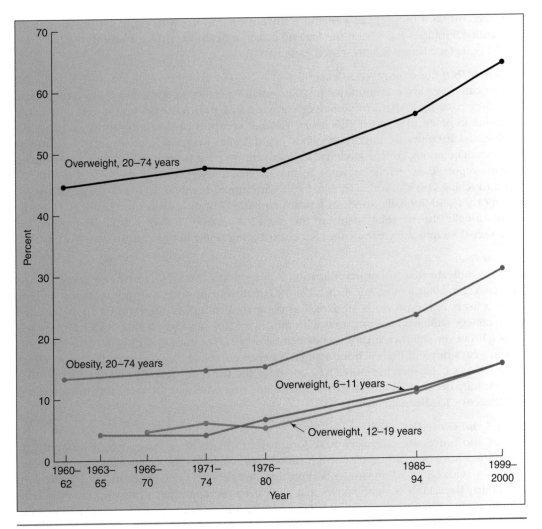

FIGURE 8.5

Overweight and obesity rates by age, 1960–2000.

Note: Overweight for adults is defined as a body mass index (BMI) greater than or equal to 25, and obesity as a BMI greater than or equal to 30. Obesity is a subset of the percentage with overweight.

Source: Freid, V. M., K. Prager, A. P. MacKay, and H. Xia (2003). *Health, United States, 2003, with Chartbook on Trends in Health of Americans.* Hyattsville, MD: National Center for Health Statistics, 38.

the American College Health Association.[26] Monitoring the Future is conducted at the University of Michigan's Institute for Social Research and, since its inception in 1975, has been funded by the National Institute on Drug Abuse. Monitoring the Future examines drug behaviors and related attitudes of a broad participant age range: eighth, tenth, and twelfth graders to adults through age 40.[27] The NCHA examines a wide range of health behaviors, whereas Monitoring the Future specifically looks at drug use. These data sources, among others, can be helpful to those responsible for delivering health promotion education and services to many of the 15.5 million students enrolled in the nation's 3,600+ colleges and universities.[28]

Behaviors That Contribute to Unintentional Injuries

Motor vehicle crashes, operating motor vehicles after consuming alcohol, riding with a driver who has consumed alcohol, swimming or boating while using alcohol, and not wearing seat belts are common incidences causing unintentional injuries to college-age students.[25] Unintentional injuries have been the leading cause of death for young adults throughout the past 50 years (see Figure 8.3 presented earlier).[10]

Behaviors That Contribute to Violence

College campuses are communities just like small towns or neighborhoods in large cities. Thus, they have their share of violence. Knowing this, most colleges and universities have programs in place to address this issue. Though weapon carrying, fighting, and suicide ideation and attempts are important public health issues, sexual assault seems to be particularly prevalent among college students. Collectively, approximately one-fifth of female college students reported experiencing some form of sexual abuse/assault in the last 12 months—sexual touching (11.5%), verbal threats (3.5%), attempted penetration (4.0%), or sexual penetration (1.9%). Additionally, 16.9% of females and 10.6% of males reported being involved in an emotionally abusive relationship in the last 12 months.[26] Though not all the reasons for these sexual assaults are clear, alcohol is a contributing factor in many of these episodes.

Tobacco Use

Statistics indicate that the more education a person has, the less likely he or she is to use tobacco. Yet in 2002, almost one-fourth (26.7%) of all college students reported being current tobacco users in the previous 30 days,[27] as compared to 25% of the total U.S. population.[29] When college students are compared with other young adults one to four years beyond high school, however, significant differences can be seen. Over one-third (37.6%) of others one to four years beyond high school reported being current tobacco users in the previous 30 days.[27] As can be seen in Figures 8.6a and 8.6b, the use of tobacco by college students had been steadily declining until the early 1990s. Since that time, and for some unknown reason, its prevalence has been inconsistent.[27]

Alcohol and Other Drug Use

College and university campuses have long been thought of as places where alcohol and other drugs have been abused. Table 8.3 shows that alcohol is the drug of choice on college campuses, with 68.9% of the students reporting that they had consumed alcohol in the previous thirty days. Table 8.3 also shows that illicit drug use continues to rise, but it is still considerably lower than it was in 1980.[27] Figures 8.7a and 8.7b present the 20-year trends for alcohol use on college campuses. It can be seen in these figures that use is lower than 20 years ago and has stayed fairly steady for the past eight years.[27]

Although alcohol abuse prevention programs have been implemented on many college campuses, more effective policies and programs are needed to address the issue. BACCHUS (Boost Alcohol Consciousness Concerning the Health of University Students) and GAMMA (Greeks Advocating for Mature Management of Alcohol) are two national collegiate peer-education networks that, combined, have chapters on more than 750 campuses and an active student membership exceeding 24,000. These organizations provide training and support for peer-facilitated prevention activities, usually related to alcohol and other drug use and sexual responsibility.[25]

Sexual Behaviors That Contribute to Unintended Pregnancy and Sexually Transmitted Diseases (STDs)

Like adolescents, many college students put themselves at risk for unintended pregnancies and infections with STDs through the practice of unprotected sexual activity. Approximately 60% of all gonorrhea cases and three-fourths of all chlamydia cases occur among persons under 25 years of age (see Box 8.1).[30] Only approximately one-quarter (26%) of college students always or mostly used a condom when having intercourse in the 30 days prior to being surveyed, and 19% relied on the withdrawal method or no method for pregnancy prevention.[26]

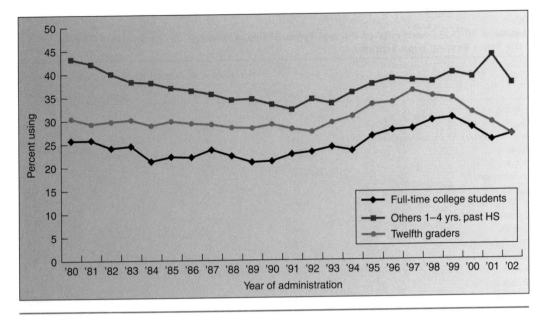

FIGURE 8.6a

Cigarettes: Trends in 30-day prevalence among college students versus others one to four years beyond high school.

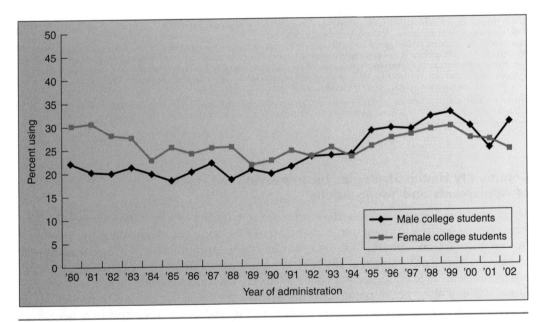

FIGURE 8.6b

Cigarettes: Trends in 30-day prevalence among male and female college students.

Source: Johnston, L. D., P. M. O'Malley, and J. G. Bachman (2003). *Monitoring the Future National Survey Results on Drug Use, 1975–2002. Vol. II: College Students and Adults Ages 19–40.* Bethesda, MD: National Institute on Drug Abuse.

Table 8.3

Trends in 30-Day Prevalence of Various Types of Drugs among College Students One to Four Years Beyond High School

		Percentage Who Used in Past 30 Days		
	1980	**1990**	**2000**	**2002**
Approx. wtd. N =	1040	1400	1350	1260
Any illicit drug[a]	38.4	15.2	21.5	21.5
Any illicit drug other than marijuana[a]	20.7	4.4	6.9	7.8
Marijuana	34.0	14.0	20.0	19.7
Inhalants[b,c]	1.5	1.0	0.9	0.7
Hallucinogens[c]	2.7	1.4	1.4	1.2
LSD	1.4	1.1	0.9	0.2
MDMA (Ecstasy)[d]	NA	0.6	2.5	0.7
Cocaine	6.9	1.2	1.4	1.6
Heroine	0.3	0.0	0.2	0.0
Other narcotics[e]	1.8	0.5	1.7	1.6
Amphetamines, adj.[e,f]	NA	1.4	2.9	3.0
Barbiturates[e]	0.9	0.2	1.1	1.7
Tranquilizers[e]	2.0	0.5	2.0	3.0
Alcohol[g]	81.8	74.5	67.4	68.9
Cigarettes	25.8	21.5	28.2	26.7

Notes: NA indicates data not available.

[a]"Any illicit drug" includes use of marijuana, hallucinogens, cocaine, or heroine, or other narcotics, amphetamines, sedatives (barbiturates), methaqualone (until 1990), or tranquilizers not under a doctor's orders.

[b]This drug was asked about in four of the five questionnaire forms in 1980–1989 and in three of the six forms in 2000–2001. Total N in 2002 (for college students) is 630.

[c]Unadjusted for known underreporting of certain drugs.

[d]This drug was asked about in two of the five questionnaire forms in 1989, in two of the six questionnaire forms in 1990–2001, and in three of the six questionnaire forms in 2002. Total N in 2002 (for college students) is 630.

[e]Only drug use that was not under a doctor's orders is included here.

[f]Based on the data from the revised question, which attempts to exclude inappropriate reporting of nonprescription amphetamines.

[g]In 1993 and 1994, the question text was changed slightly in three of the six questionnaire forms to indicate that a "drink" meant "more than just a few sips." Because this revision resulted in rather little change in reported prevalence in the surveys in high school graduates, the data for all forms combined are used in order to provide the most reliable estimate of change. After 1994, the new question text was used in all six of the questionnaire forms.

Source: Johnston, L. D., P. M. O'Malley, and J. G. Bachman (2003). *Monitoring the Future National Survey Results on Drug Use, 1975–2002. Vol. II: College Students and Adults Ages 19–40.* Bethesda, MD: National Institute on Drug Abuse.

Community Health Strategies for Improving the Health of Adolescents and Young Adults

There are no easy, simple, or immediate solutions to reducing or eliminating the health problems of adolescents and young adults. As noted in Chapter 1, community health is impacted by four major factors—physical factors, community organizing, individual behavior, and social and cultural factors. Of these four, the two that need special attention when dealing with the health problems of adolescents and young adults are social and cultural factors and community organizing. Many health problems originate from the social and cultural environments in which people have been raised and live, and the culture and social norms that have been with us in some cases for many years. Take, for example, the use of alcohol. It is safe to say that the biggest health problem facing adolescents and young adults in the United States today is the use of alcohol. Alcohol contributes to all the leading causes of mortality and morbidity in these age groups. If the norm of a community is to turn its back on adolescents consuming alcohol or young adults (of legal age) abusing alcohol, efforts need to be made to change the culture. However, in most communities, culture and social norms do not change quickly. Efforts to turn these health problems around will need to be community-wide in nature and

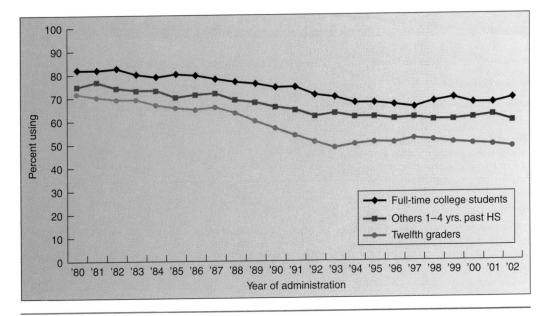

FIGURE 8.7a

Alcohol: Trends in 30-day prevalence among college students versus others one to four years beyond high school.

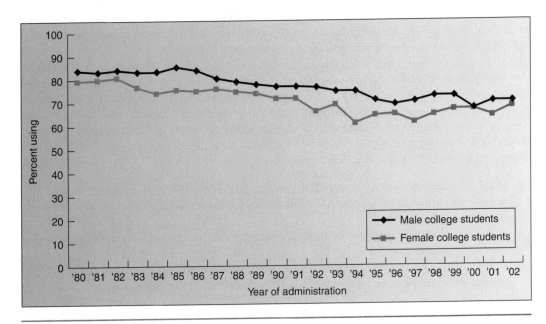

FIGURE 8.7b

Alcohol: Trends in 30-day prevalence among male and female college students.

Source: Johnston, L. D., P. M. O'Malley, and J. G. Bachman (2003). *Monitoring the Future National Survey Results on Drug Use, 1975–2002. Vol. II: College Students and Adults Ages 19–40.* Bethesda, MD: National Institute on Drug Abuse.

sustained over a long period of time. By "community-wide," we mean the involvement of all the stakeholders in a community, not just those who are associated with health-related professions—in other words, a community organizing effort is needed. By "sustained over a long period," we mean institutionalizing the change in the culture.

BOX
8.1

HEALTHY PEOPLE 2010: OBJECTIVES

25-1. Reduce the proportion of adolescents and young adults with *Chlamydia trachomatis* infections.

Target, 2000 status, and baseline:

Objective	Reduction in *Chlamydia trachomatis* infections	1997 Baseline	2002 Status	2010 Target
			Percent	
25-1a.	Females aged 15–24 years attending family planning clinics	5.0	6.0	3.0
25-1b.	Females aged 15–24 years attending STD clinics	12.2	13.5	3.0
25-1c.	Males aged 15–24 years attending STD clinics	15.7	17.5	3.0

For Further Thought

If you were given the responsibility of lowering the incidence of chlamydia in the United States, what community health activities would you recommend?

Source: Centers for Disease Control and Prevention (2003). *Sexually Transmitted Disease Surveillance, 2002.* Atlanta, GA: Author.

To change the culture as it relates to adolescents' use of alcohol, research has shown that alcohol prevention efforts need to be a part of a comprehensive school health education effort and should include components outside the classroom. Thus, prevention programs need to include components that focus on changing norms, interaction among peers, social skills training, and developmental and cultural appropriateness.[31-33]

Many colleges and universities are trying to change the culture on campus as it relates to the use of alcohol. In fact, some schools have signed up for national programs to change campus culture to reduce drinking. Some schools are increasing the number of Friday classes to try to reduce the amount of Thursday-night partying. Others have banned alcohol from campus and toughened penalties for those caught drinking, while still others have restricted tailgating and stadium sales.[34] And almost all schools have developed alcohol education programs that include the following four principles:

1. Legal principle: According to state law you must be 21 years old to consume alcohol.
2. Abstinence principle: If you do not drink alcohol, do not start; it is okay to abstain; many students do abstain.
3. Social norming principle: Not as many of your peers drink alcohol as you think; every college student does not drink.
4. Harm reduction principle: If you do consume alcohol, do so in such a way that you reduce your risk of hazardous outcomes; learn harm reduction skills.

Finally, some colleges and universities feel that they have done such a good job of changing the alcohol culture on campus that they advertise such on their Web homepage.

ADULTS

The adult age group (those 25 to 64 years old) represents slightly more than half of the U.S. population. The size of this segment of the overall population is expected to remain stable over the next couple of decades, but in proportion to the rest of the population this segment will become smaller. Therefore, provisions to deal with the health concerns of this age group will need to be maintained.

A Health Profile

The health profile of this age of adults is characterized primarily by mortality from chronic diseases stemming from poor health behavior and poor lifestyle choices made during the earlier years of life.

Mortality

With life expectancy at birth between 70 and 80 years,[2] most Americans can expect to live beyond their 65th birthday. However, many do not. During the 1950s and 1960s, it was revealed that many of the leading causes of death in this age group resulted from preventable conditions associated with unhealthy behaviors and lifestyles. As such, many adults have quit smoking, and more Americans than ever before are exercising regularly and eating healthier diets. These lifestyle improvements along with successes in public health and advances in medicine have resulted in a significant decline in the death rate for adults in the last half of the twentieth century, a decline that is projected to continue in the twenty-first century.

In the past, leading causes of death for adults were reported only for the 25- to 64-year-old age group. More recently, the adult years have been subdivided into two groups: 25 to 44 years and 45 to 64 years, with some data being reported in 10-year age spans. In 2001, the death rate for all adults ages 25 to 34 years was 105.2 per 100,000, and for ages 35 to 44 years it was 203.6 per 100,000.[10] The leading causes of death for those in this age group in 2001 were unintentional injuries, malignant neoplasms (cancer), heart disease, suicide, HIV, and homicide. With the exception of HIV, the current leading causes of death were also at the top of the list in 1980.[10] When the mortality data for this age group are broken down by race and ethnicity, some differences appear. Five of the six leading causes of death for whites, blacks, and Hispanics are the same, but differ in rank order by race and ethnic group (see Table 8.4). For whites and Hispanics, suicide is among the six leading causes, whereas among blacks, the six leading causes include cerebrovascular disease (stroke) rather than suicide.[15]

In 2001, the death rate for 45- to 54-year-olds was 428.9 per 100,000, twice that of the 35-to-44 age group. The death rate for 55- to 64-year-olds was 964.6 per 100,000, two times greater than the 45-to-54 age group. The majority of these deaths were the result of noncommunicable health problems. They include cancer, heart disease, unintentional injuries, stroke, diabetes, and chronic lower respiratory disease, which includes emphysema, asthma, and bronchitis. Like with the 25- to 44-year-olds, there are racial and ethnic disparities. Though cancer and heart disease are the first and second causes of death for all three groups presented in Table 8.5, chronic lower respiratory disease appears in the list of the six leading causes for whites, HIV appears in the list for blacks, and liver disease and cirrhosis appears in the Hispanic list.

Cancer

Since 1983, the Number 1 cause of death in the adult age group has been cancer (malignant neoplasms). (For a review of malignant neoplasms, see Chapter 4.) Age-adjusted cancer death

Table 8.4
Death Rates, Adults, Ages 25–44 (Rate per 100,000 Population)

Non-Hispanic White (139.4)	Non-Hispanic Black (303.7)	Hispanic (130.2)
Unintentional injuries (31.6)	Heart disease (43.5)	Unintentional injuries (33.4)
Cancer (25.3)	HIV (43.3)	Cancer (16.8)
Heart disease (18.3)	Unintentional injury (40.1)	Homicide (13.1)
Suicide (17.0)	Cancer (38.0)	HIV (12.1)
HIV (4.8)	Homicide (36.2)	Heart disease (10.3)
Homicide (4.7)	Stroke (10.2)	Suicide (7.8)

Source: Murphy, S. L. (2000). "Deaths: Final Data for 1998." *National Vital Statistics Reports,* 48(11): 1–105.

Table 8.5
Death Rates, Adults, Ages 45–64 (Rate per 100,000 Population)

Non-Hispanic Whites (623.1)	Non-Hispanic Blacks (1,184.4)	Hispanics (483.8)
Cancer (230.0)	Cancer (345.3)	Cancer (136.7)
Heart disease (164.4)	Heart disease (327.3)	Heart disease (110.6)
Unintentional injuries (29.8)	Stroke (68.9)	Liver disease and cirrhosis (31.8)
Chronic lower respiratory disease (24.3)	Diabetes (54.4)	Unintentional injuries (31.7)
Stroke (21.3)	Unintentional injuries (49.8)	Diabetes (28.6)
Diabetes (18.2)	HIV (37.8)	Stroke (26.5)

Source: Murphy, S. L. (2000). "Deaths: Final Data for 1998." *National Vital Statistics Reports,* 48(11): 1–105.

rates have remained relatively steady since 1950 (193.9 per 100,000 in 1950 compared to 196.0 per 100,000 in 2001). However, the crude death rates have jumped from 139.8 per 100,000 to 194.4 per 100,000 during that same time, reflecting an aging American population.[10]

Three types of cancers account for these large numbers—lung, colorectal, and breast. The leading cause of cancer deaths and the most preventable type of cancer for both men and women is lung cancer. This trend is expected to continue as large numbers of smokers continue to age. Of all lung cancer deaths, 87% can be attributed to smoking.[29] The second leading cause of death due to cancer is colorectal cancer. Risk factors for this type of cancer include personal or family history, smoking, physical inactivity, alcohol consumption, a low intake of fruits and vegetables, and diets high in fat or low in fiber[35] (such as those available from many fast-food restaurants).

Breast cancer is the other cancer of much concern. Until it was surpassed by lung cancer in the mid-1980s, it was the leading cause of cancer deaths in women. Although it is less deadly than lung cancer, the number of cases of breast cancer is more than twice that of lung cancer in women.[35] Because of increased community awareness and the availability of diagnostic screening for breast cancer, survival rates are much higher than for lung cancer. However, breast cancer rates could be reduced even further if a higher percentage of women over 39 years of age complied with the screening recommendations.[18]

To help people understand the prevalence of cancer in their community, the American Cancer Society has created a table that can be used to estimate the number of cancer statistics locally. This information is presented in Table 8.6.

Cardiovascular Diseases

Some of the greatest changes in cause-specific mortality rates in adults are those for the cardiovascular diseases. Age-adjusted mortality rates from diseases of the heart dropped from 586.8 per 100,000 in 1950 to 247.8 per 100,000 in 2001, while deaths from strokes dropped from 180.7 per 100,000 to 57.9 per 100,000 during the same period of time.[10] These figures represent drops of about 58% and 68%, respectively. These changes are due primarily to the public health efforts that have encouraged people to stop smoking, increase their physical activity, and eat more nutritionally. The reduction or postponement of deaths from heart disease has resulted in cancer becoming the leading cause of deaths in adults 25 to 64 years of age.

Health Behaviors and Lifestyle Choices

Many of the risk factors associated with the leading causes of morbidity and mortality in American adults are associated with health behavior and lifestyle choices. Adults have a unique opportunity to take personal action to substantially decrease their risk of ill health, and in recent years, many have taken such action. Today, more than ever before, adults are watching what they eat, wearing their seat belts, controlling their blood pressure, and exercising with regularity. The prevalence of smoking among adults has declined, as has the

Table 8.6
How to Estimate Cancer Statistics Locally, 2004

To obtain the estimated number of . . .	Multiply community population by:				
	All Sites	Female Breast*	Colon or Rectum	Lung	Prostate*
New cancer cases	0.0048	0.0015	0.0005	0.0006	0.0016
Cancer deaths	0.0020	0.0003	0.0002	0.0006	0.0002
People who will eventually develop cancer	0.4111	0.1351	0.0567	0.0664	0.1728
People who will eventually die of cancer	0.2054	0.0303	0.0217	0.0531	0.0305

*For female breast cancer multiply by female population, and for prostate cancer multiply by male population.

Note: These calculations provide only a rough approximation of the number of people in a specific community who may develop or die of cancer. These estimates should be used with caution because they do not reflect the age or racial characteristics of the population, access to detection and treatment, or exposure to risk factors. State cancer registries count the number of cancers that occur in localities throughout the state. The American Cancer Society recommends using data from these registries, when it is available, to more accurately estimate local cancer statistics.

Source: Cancer Facts and Figures—2004. American Cancer Society (2004). Used with permission of the American Cancer Society, Inc. All rights reserved.

incidence of drinking and driving. While these are encouraging signs, there is still much more that can be done.

As with the other age groups discussed in this chapter, the National Center for Heath Statistics (NCHS) collects self-reported behavior risk data on adults. These data are collected via the Behavioral Risk Factor Surveillance System (BRFSS). (See Chapter 3 for a discussion about the BRFSS.) One limitation of the data from this system is that it is collected, and is usually reported, on all adults over 18 years of age; the data are not broken down by the specific age groups (18–24, 25–44, and 45–64) discussed in this chapter. More detailed information about the health behaviors and lifestyle choices of adults in the United States is presented next.

Risk Factors for Chronic Disease
The best single behavioral change Americans can make to reduce morbidity and mortality is to stop smoking. Smoking is responsible for 30% of deaths in the United States.[36] It is an important risk factor for cancer, heart disease, and stroke. In 2001, over one-fifth (22.7%) of those who were aged 18 years and older smoked.[10] This amounts to about 47 million Americans.[29] The proportion of Americans who smoke has dropped considerably since 1965, when 40% of all Americans smoked. While more men than women (24% versus 22%) smoke,[10] the gap between the genders is decreasing. In general, smoking rates are higher among American Indians and Alaska Natives, people with fewer years of education, and those with lower incomes.[18]

Three other interrelated risk factors that contribute to disease and death in this age group are lack of exercise, failure to maintain an appropriate body weight, and alcohol consumption. Though American adults are exercising more than ever before, few are exercising on a regular basis. The American Heart Association has stated that "24 percent of Americans age 18 or older are not active at all. Fifty-four percent of adults get some exercise, but they don't do it regularly or intensely enough to protect their hearts. Only 22 percent of American adults get enough leisure time exercise to achieve cardiovascular fitness."[37] It was once thought that **intensity** had to be high in order for cardiovascular benefits from exercise to accrue. But now it is believed that even light-to-moderate physical activity can have significant health benefits if done regularly and long-term. Such activities include walking, gardening, housework, and dancing.

intensity
cardiovascular workload measured by heart rate

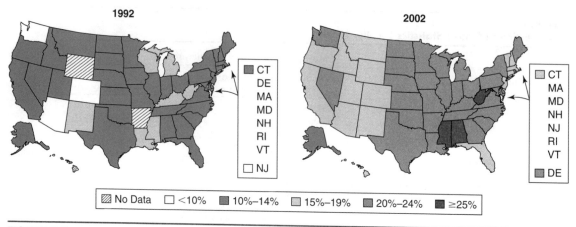

FIGURE 8.8

Obesity trends among U.S. adults.

Note: Obesity is defined as a BMI > 30, or about 30 pounds overweight for a five-foot, four-inch person.

Source: CDC, Behavioral Risk Factor Surveillance System.

---

body mass index (BMI)
the ratio of weight (in kilograms) to height (in meters, squared)

Being overweight increases one's chances of a number of health problems, including heart disease, some cancers, hypertension, elevated blood cholesterol, diabetes, stroke, gallbladder disease, and osteoarthritis. In 2002, according to the BRFSS, 37% of adults were overweight, and 22.1% were obese as defined by **body mass index (BMI).**[44] Obesity in America is truly an epidemic, with obesity rates increasing by more than 60% in the last 10 years (see Figure 8.8).[38] The trend of weight-gain increases with age. The key to maintaining an appropriate weight throughout life is a combination of diet and exercise; total reliance on either factor alone makes it a difficult process.[39]

As with other age groups, alcohol consumption often places adults at greater health risk. Approximately 70% of adult Americans consume alcohol. While most do so in moderation, a relatively small percentage develop serious problems with their alcohol use. In 2002, 16.1% of adults reported binge drinking (i.e., consumption of five or more alcoholic beverages on at least one occasion in the previous month).[38] Men are about three times more likely to report binge drinking than women.[38] It is estimated that the 5% who consume the greatest amount of alcohol consume about 36% of all the alcohol consumed in America.[40] These people are at greatest risk for developing a dependence upon alcohol and for developing such alcohol-related health problems as cirrhosis, alcoholism, and alcohol psychosis.

One does not have to become dependent on alcohol to have a drinking problem. Alcohol contributes to society's problems in a great many other ways. As noted in other chapters of this text, alcohol increases the rates of homicide, suicide, family violence, and unintentional injuries such as those from motor vehicle crashes, boating incidents, and falls. The use of alcohol by pregnant women can cause fetal alcohol syndrome, the leading cause of birth defects in children. Clearly, alcohol consumption adversely affects the health and well-being of Americans.

Risk Factors for Personal Injury

Like individuals in the other age groups, adults also put themselves at risk for personal injury by the way they behave. Two such areas of concerns are both related to the operation of motor vehicles—the use of seat belts and the operation of a motor vehicle after drinking alcohol. The percentage of adults who reported that they always wore a seat belt while driving or riding in a car was 76.6%.[38] When asked via the BRFSS in 1999, the median percentage of adults who reported operating a motor vehicle at least once in the previous month after having drunk perhaps too much alcohol was 2.5%.[41] The data on both of these behaviors are interesting because both behaviors are regulated by public health laws. This suggests that a society can only be controlled by regulations to the extent that it wants to be.

Awareness and Screening of Certain Medical Conditions
There are a number of regular, non-invasive or minimally invasive health screenings that are recommended for adults to participate in, such as screenings for hypertension, diabetes, high blood cholesterol, and cancer.

There is no "ideal" blood pressure. Instead, the acceptable blood pressure falls within a range considered healthy. **Hypertension** exists when systolic pressure is equal to or greater than 140 mm of mercury (Hg) and/or diastolic pressure is equal to or greater than 90 mm Hg for extended periods of time. Statistics show that hypertension is found in about 25% of adults in the United States and overall afflicts about 50 million Americans, making it the most prevalent risk factor for cardiovascular disease in the United States.[37] Fortunately, once detected hypertension is

FIGURE 8.9
Hypertension is a highly modifiable risk factor.

a risk factor that is highly modifiable (see Figure 8.9). The most desirable means of controlling hypertension is through a combination of diet modification, appropriate physical exercise, and weight management. In cases in which these measures prove ineffective, hypertension can usually still be controlled with medication. Unfortunately, a great many Americans with hypertension are unaware of their problem. The keys to reducing morbidity and mortality resulting from hypertension are mass screenings that result in early detection of previously unidentified cases and their appropriate treatment.

hypertension
systolic pressure equal to or greater than 140 mm of mercury (Hg) and/or diastolic pressure equal to or greater than 90 mm Hg for extended periods of time

Diabetes results from failure of the pancreas to make a sufficient amount of insulin. Without insulin, food cannot be properly used by the body. Diabetes cannot be cured, but it can be controlled through a combination of diet, exercise, and insulin injections. It has already been reported earlier in the chapter that with the exception of 15- to 24-year-olds, diabetes is one of the leading causes of death for all adults. The death rates are highest in American Indians/Alaska Natives and black Americans.[10] However, many deaths resulting from diabetes could be postponed if diabetes was detected and treated appropriately. Approximately 17 million Americans have diabetes, with almost 800,000 new cases diagnosed each year. The percentage of adults with diagnosed diabetes has increased 61% over the past 10 years (see Figure 8.10). Furthermore, one in three persons with diabetes is unaware that he or she has the disease.[38]

Cholesterol is a soft, fat-like substance that is necessary to build cell membranes. However, elevated cholesterol levels in blood can put people at greater risk for heart disease and stroke. The higher the cholesterol level, the greater the risk.[15] Cholesterol is produced by the liver in sufficient quantities to meet the needs of the body. A person's cholesterol level is also affected by his or her age, heredity, and diet. There is nothing we can do about heredity and age, but diet is something we can modify.

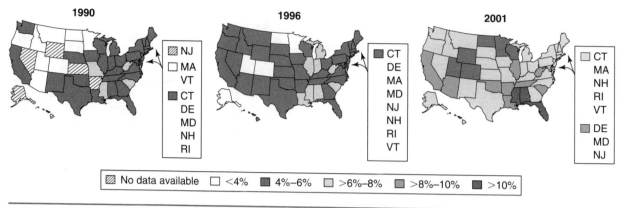

FIGURE 8.10

The percentage of adults with diagnosed diabetes increased 61% from 1990 to 2001. These figures include women with a history of gestational diabetes.

Source: Centers for Disease Control and Prevention, Behavioral Risk Factor Surveillance System.

Dietary factors are associated with five of the ten leading causes of death in this age group. Many dietary components are involved in the diet-health relationship, but chief among them is the disproportionate consumption of foods high in fat, often at the expense of foods high in complex carbohydrates and dietary fiber. Total dietary fat (saturated and unsaturated) accounts for too many total calories consumed in the United States. A diet that contains no more than 30% fat is recommended.[42] Currently, the largest source of fat in diets comes from cheeses and oils. Diets high in fat and cholesterol are part of the reason why an estimated 50% of American adults have blood cholesterol levels of 200 mg/dL (milligrams per deciliter) and higher, and why about 20% have levels of 240 mg/dL or above.[43] Based on several studies, blood cholesterol levels less than 200 mg/dL in middle-aged adults seem to indicate a relatively low risk of coronary heart disease. In contrast, people with a blood cholesterol level of 240 mg/dL have twice the risk of having a coronary heart attack as people who have a cholesterol level of 200 mg/dL.[43] **Hypercholesterolemia** is the term used for high levels of cholesterol in the blood. Like diabetes, the key to controlling hypercholesterolemia is screening and treatment.

> **hypercholesterol-emia**
> high levels of cholesterol in the blood

The other prevalent medical condition in this age group that should be screened for on a regular basis is cancer. As noted earlier, malignant neoplasms are the leading cause of death in 45- to 64-year-olds. The American Cancer Society recommends a number of screenings for various age groups (see Table 8.7). However, many more adults in the United States could be getting screened. The earlier that cancer is detected, the greater the chance for successful treatment.

Community Health Strategies for Improving the Health of Adults

As noted in the previous pages, adults in the United States are faced with a number of health issues. Even so, for most individuals the years between 25 and 64 are some of the healthiest of their lifetime. A key for keeping these people healthy is to re-emphasize the importance of individual responsibility for health. That is, individuals must engage in behaviors that are health-enhancing. From a community health perspective, this means that community health workers must continue to offer primary, secondary, and tertiary prevention programs that are

Table 8.7
Summary of American Cancer Society Recommendations for the Early Detection of Cancer in Asymptomatic People

Cancer-related checkup	For individuals undergoing periodic health examinations, a cancer-related checkup should include health counseling, and depending on a person's age, might include examinations for cancers of the thyroid, oral cavity, skin, lymph nodes, testes, and ovaries, as well as for some nonmalignant diseases.
Breast	Women 40 and older should have an annual mammogram, an annual clinical breast exam (CBE) performed by a health care professional, and should perform monthly breast self-examination (BSE). The CBE should be conducted close to and preferably before the scheduled mammogram. Women ages 20–39 should have a clinical breast exam performed by a health care professional every three years and should perform monthly BSEs.
Colon and rectum	Beginning at age 50, men and women at average risk should follow one of these examination schedules: 1. A fecal occult blood test (FOBT) every year, or 2. Flexible sigmoidoscopy every five years,* or 3. FOBT every year and flexible sigmoidoscopy every five years,* **(of these three options, the American Cancer Society prefers Option 3, annual FOBT and flexible sigmoidoscopy every five years)** or 4. Double-contrast barium enema every 5 years,* or 5. Colonoscopy every 10 years.*
Prostate	Beginning at age 50, the prostate-specific antigen (PSA) test and the digital rectal exam should be offered annually to men who have a life expectancy of at least ten years. Men at high risk (black American men and men who have a first-degree relative who was diagnosed with prostate cancer at a younger age) should begin testing at age 45. Patients should be given information about the benefits and test limitations so they can make an informed decision.
Uterus	Cervix: All women who are or have been sexually active or who are 18 and older should have an annual Pap test and pelvic examination. After three or more consecutive satisfactory examinations with normal findings, the Pap test may be performed less frequently. Discuss the matter with your physician. Endometrium: The American Cancer Society recommends that all women should be informed about the risks and symptoms of endometrial cancer, and strongly encouraged to report any unexpected bleeding or spotting to their physicians. Annual screening for endometrial cancer with endometrial biopsy beginning at age 35 should be offered to women with or at risk for hereditary nonpolyposis colon cancer (HNPCC).

*A digital rectal exam should be done at the same time as sigmoidoscopy, colonoscopy, or double-contrast barium enema. People who are at increased or high risk for colorectal cancer should talk with a doctor about a different testing schedule.

Source: Cancer Facts & Figures—2004. American Cancer Society (2004). Used with permission of the American Cancer Society, Inc. All rights reserved.

aimed at the needs of this age group. For example, primary prevention programs could include exercise and nutrition programs that help reduce the risks of cancer and cardiovascular disease. Secondary prevention programs that emphasize self or clinical screenings to identify and control disease processes in their early stages, such as mammography, self-testicular exams, and cholesterol screenings, would also be appropriate for this age group. In addition, tertiary prevention programs such as medication compliance to prevent disability by restoring individuals to their optimal level of functioning after the onset of disease or injury could also be useful.

CHAPTER SUMMARY

- Adolescence and young adulthood (15 to 24 years old) and adulthood (25 to 64 years old) are the most productive periods of people's lives. While most people enjoy good health during these years, there is substantial room for improvement.

- The overall health status of these age groups could be improved by reducing the prevalence of high-risk behaviors (e.g., cigarette smoking, excessive alcohol consumption, and physical inactivity) and by increasing participation in health screenings and institutionalizing preventive health care in our society.

- Seventy percent of adolescent and young adult mortality can be attributed to motor vehicle crashes, other unintentional injuries, homicide and legal intervention, and suicide.

- Adolescents and young adults remain at considerable risk for STD morbidity.

- College students put themselves at considerable risk through unprotected sexual activity, and the use of alcohol, tobacco, and other drugs.

- Mortality rates for older adults (45 to 64 years old) have declined slightly in recent years, but cancer is still the overall leading cause of death, followed by cardiovascular disease.

- Reductions in deaths from cardiovascular diseases in adults have been substantial, but health problems resulting from unhealthy behaviors—like smoking and drinking—can be reduced further if adults are willing to modify their behavior.

- No matter how the health of adolescents and young adults and adults in the United States is broken down and described, it can be summarized by saying that the health of Americans in these age groups has come a long way in the past 50 years, but there is still room for improvement.

REVIEW QUESTIONS

1. Why it is important for community health workers to be aware of the significant health problems of the various age groups in the United States?

2. What ages are included in the following two age groups: adolescents and young adults, and adults? What are the ages of the two subgroups of adults?

3. Why are the number of adolescents and young adults, living arrangements, and employment status such key demographic characteristics of young people in regard to community health? Briefly summarize the data available on these characteristics.

4. What are the leading causes of death for adolescents and young adults, and adults?

5. What are the Youth Risk Behavior Surveillance System (YRBSS) and the Behavioral Risk Factor Surveillance System (BRFSS), and what type of data do they generate?

6. What are the behaviors that put each of these cohorts—adolescents, college students, and adults—at greatest risk?

7. How would you summarize the health profile of the two cohorts (adolescents and young adults, and adults) presented in this chapter?

ACTIVITIES

1. Obtain a copy of the most recent results of the Youth Risk Behavior Surveillance System (YRBSS) and the Behavioral Risk Factor Surveillance System (BRFSS) for your state. Review the data presented and then prepare a two-page summary on the "Health Behavior Profile of the Adolescents and Young Adults and Adults" of your state.

2. Using the information presented in Table 8.6 and the most recent census data for your community, calculate its estimated cancer statistics.

3. Interview a small group (about ten) of adults (aged 45 to 64) about their present health status. Ask them questions about their health behavior and health problems. Then, summarize the data you collect in writing and compare it to the information in this chapter on this age group. How are the data similar? How do they differ?

4. Pick either adolescents and young adults or adults and write a two-page paper that presents ideas on how the health profile of that age group can be improved in your state.

COMMUNITY HEALTH ON THE WEB

The Internet contains a wealth of information about community and public health. Increase your knowledge of some of the topics presented in this chapter by accessing the Jones and Bartlett Publishers Web site at **health.jbpub.com/communityhealth/5e** and follow the links to complete the following Web activities.

- Youth Risk Behavior Surveillance System

- Vital Statistics

- Adult Health Division

REFERENCES

1. Snyder, T., and L. Shafer (1996). *Youth Indicators, 1996* (NCES 96-027). Washington, DC: U.S. Department of Education, National Center for Education Statistics.

2. MacKay, A. P., L. A. Fingerhut, and C. R. Duran (2000). *Health, United States, 2000 with Adolescent Health Chartbook*. Hyattsville, MD: National Center for Health Statistics.

SCENARIO: ANALYSIS AND RESPONSE

1. What primary prevention measures would have been helpful for the four university students? What primary prevention measures would have helped the businessman?

2. Why do you think that adolescents and young adults and adults engage in high-risk behaviors like those presented in the scenario? If you were a community health worker in this community, what kind of programs would you recommend to lower the health risks of these individuals?

3. Comment on the attitudes of Annie and Latasha toward drunk driving and the automobile crash. Do you agree with one or the other? Why or why not?

4. Do colleges and universities have an obligation to develop prevention programs to keep students out

of situations like the one described in the scenario? Why or why not?

5. Say you were friends with Annie. She got so concerned with the problem of alcohol abuse on campus that she wanted to take action. She thought that maybe she should look into starting a chapter of Boost Alcohol Consciousness Concerning the Health of University Students (BACCHUS). She wanted to see what was on the Web about BACCHUS, but because of a busy afternoon of classes she knew she wouldn't have time to check it, so she asked you if you would do it for her. Go to the Web and use a search engine (e.g., Google, Excite, or Lycos) and enter "BACCHUS." What did you find that might be of help to Annie?

3. American Medical Association (2000). *Talking to Your Teenagers 11-14: Discussion Guide*. Chicago, IL: Author.

4. Seffrin, J. R. (1990). "The Comprehensive School Health Curriculum: Closing the Gap between State-of-the-Art and State-of-the-Practice." *Journal of School Health*, 60(4): 151-156.

5. Valois, R. F., W. G. Thatcher, J. W. Drane, and B. M. Reininger (1997). "Comparison of Selected Health Risk Behaviors between Adolescents in Public and Private High Schools in South Carolina." *Journal of School Health*, 67(10): 434-440.

6. Hobbs, F., and N. Stoops (2002). *Demographic Trends in the 20th Century* (Census 2000 Special Reports, Series CENSR-4). Washington, DC: U.S. Government Printing Office.

7. U.S. Bureau of Census (1999). *Statistical Abstract of the United States, 1999*, 119th ed. Washington, DC: Author.

8. U.S. Census Bureau (2004). *USA Statistics in Brief—Population and Vital Statistics*. Available at http://www.census.gov/statab/www.

9. Bureau of Labor Statistics (2004). *Labor Force Statistics from the Current Population Survey*. Available at http://www.bls.gov/cps/home.htm.

10. Freid, V. M., K. Prager, A. P. MacKay, and H. Xia (2003). *Health, United States, 2003 with Chartbook on Trends in the Health of Americans*. Hyattsville, MD: National Center for Health Statistics.

11. Murphy, S. L. (2000). "Deaths: Final Data for 1998." *National Vital Statistics Reports*, 48(11): 1-105.

12. U.S. Department of Health and Human Services (1991). *Healthy Children 2000: National Health Promotion and Disease Prevention Objectives Related to Mothers, Infants, Children, Adolescents, and Youth* (HHS pub. no. HRSA-M-CH-91-2). Washington, DC: U.S. Government Printing Office.

13. Grunbaum, J., L. Kann, S. Kinchen, J. Ross, J. Hawkins, R. Lowry, W. Harris, T. McManus, D. Chyen, and J. Collins (2004). "Youth Risk Behavior Surveillance—United States, 2003." *MMWR*, 53(SS-2): 1-100.

14. Centers for Disease Control and Prevention (2001). *Tracking the Hidden Epidemics: Trends in STDs in the United States 2000*. Available at http://www.cdc.gov/nchstp/dstd/Stats_Trends/Trends2000.pdf.

15. Centers for Disease Control and Prevention (2001). *CDC Fact Book 2000/2001*. Available at http://www.cdc.gov/maso/factbook/main.htm.

16. Mertz, K. J., G. M. McQuillan, W. C. Levine, et al. (1998). "A Pilot Study of the Prevalence of Chlamydial Infection in a National Household Survey." *Sexually Transmitted Diseases*, May, 225-228.

17. The Henry J. Kaiser Family Foundation (2000). *National Survey of Teens on HIV/AIDS*. Menlo Park, CA: Author.

18. U.S. Department of Health and Human Services (2000). *Healthy People 2010: Understanding and Improving Health*. Washington, DC: U.S. Government Printing Office.

19. Kolbe, L. J., L. Kann, and J. L. Collins (1993). "Overview of the Youth Risk Behavior Surveillance System." *Public Health Reports*, 108(1): 2-10.

20. Centers for Disease Control and Prevention (1996). "Tobacco Use and Usual Source of Cigarettes among High School Students—United States—1995." *MMWR*, 45(20): 413-418.

21. U.S. Department of Health and Human Services (1990). *Prevention '89/'90: Federal Programs and Progress*. Washington, DC: U.S. Government Printing Office.

22. Centers for Disease Control and Prevention (1996). "Trends in Sexual Risk Behavior among High School Students—United States—1990, 1991, and 1993." *MMWR*, 44(7): 124-125, 131-132.

23. Ventura, S. J., S. C. Curtin, and T. J. Mathew (2000). "Variations in Teenage Birth Rates, 1991-98: National and State Trends." *National Vital Statistics Reports*, 48(6): 1-16.

24. The Alan Guttmacher Institute (1994). *Sex and America's Teenagers*. New York: Author.

25. Centers for Disease Control and Prevention (1997). "Youth Risk Behavior Surveillance: National College Health Risk Behavior Survey—United States, 1995." *MMWR*, 46(SS-6): 1-56.

26. American College Health Association (2004). National College Health Assessment Web Summary. Available at http://www.acha.org/projects_programs/assessment.cfm.

27. Johnston, L. D., P. M. O'Malley, and J. G. Bachman (2003). *Monitoring the Future National Survey Results on Drug Use, 1975-2002. Vol. II: College Students and Adults Ages 19-40*. Bethesda, MD: National Institute on Drug Abuse.

28. U.S. Bureau of the Census (1999). "School Enrollment—Social and Economic Characteristics of Students (Update)." *Current Population Reports*, P20-521. Washington, DC: U.S. Government Printing Office, 1.

29. American Cancer Society (2001). *Cancer Facts and Figures—2001*. Atlanta, GA: Author.

30. Centers for Disease Control and Prevention (2003). *Sexually Transmitted Disease Surveillance, 2002*. Atlanta, GA: Author.

31. Lachter, R. B., K. A. Komro, S. Veblen-Mortenson, C. L. Perry, and C. L. Williams (1999). "High School Students' Efforts to Reduce Alcohol Use in their Communities: Project Northland's Youth Development Component." *Journal of Health Education,* 30(6): 330–342.

32. Drug Strategies (1997). *Making the Grade: A Guide to School Drug Prevention Programs*. Washington, DC: Author.

33. Dusenbury, L., and M. Falco (1995). "Eleven Components of Effective Drug Abuse Prevention Curricula." *Journal of School Health,* 65: 420–425.

34. McGinn, D. (2000). "Scouting a Dry Campus." *Newsweek* (November 27): 83–84.

35. American Cancer Society (2003). *Cancer Facts and Figures—2003*. Atlanta, GA: Author.

36. Mokdad, A. H., J. S. Marks, D. F. Stroup, and J. L. Gerberding (2004). "Actual Causes of Death in the United States, 2000." *Journal of the American Medical Association,* 291(10): 1238–1245.

37. American Heart Association (2001). *Physical Activity and Cardiovascular Health: Fact Sheet*. Available at http://www.americanheart.org/Health/Lifestyle/Physical_Activity/PAfact.html.

38. Centers for Disease Control and Prevention (2004). *Behavioral Risk Factor Surveillance System*. Available at http://www.cdc.gov/brfss/index.htm.

39. U.S. Department of Health and Human Services (1991). *Healthy People 2000: National Health Promotion and Disease Prevention Objectives,* (HHS pub. no. PHS-91-50212). Washington, DC: U.S. Government Printing Office.

40. Manning, W. G., L. Blumberg, and L. H. Moulton (1995). "The Demand for Alcohol: The Differential Response to Price." *Journal of Health Economics,* 14(2):123–145.

41. Centers for Disease Control and Prevention (2001). *Prevalence Data*. Available at http://www2.cdc.gov/nccdphp/brfss/index.asp.

42. American Heart Association (2001). *Dietary Guidelines for Healthy American Adults*. Available at http://www.americanheart.org/Heart_and_Stroke_A_Z_Guide/dietg.html.

43. American Heart Association (2001). *Am I at Risk?* Dallas, TX: Author.

44. Centers for Disease Control and Prevention (2004). *BMI: Body Mass Index*. Available at http://www.cdc.gov/nccdphp/dnpa/bmi/.

Elders

Chapter Objectives

After studying this chapter you will be able to:

1 Identify the signs of an aging population.
2 Define the following groups—*old, young old, old old,* and *oldest old.*
3 Define the terms *aged, aging, elders, gerontology,* and *geriatrics.*
4 Refute several commonly held myths about the senior population.
5 Explain the meaning of an age pyramid.
6 List the factors that affect the size and age of a population.
7 Define fertility and mortality rates and explain how they impact life expectancy.
8 Explain the difference between support and labor-force ratios.
9 Describe the typical elder with regard to marital status, living arrangements, racial and ethnic background, economic status, and geographic location.
10 Explain how four health behaviors can improve the quality of later life.
11 Briefly outline elder abuse and neglect in the United States.
12 Identify the six instrumental needs of elders.
13 Briefly summarize the Older Americans Act of 1965.
14 List the services provided for elders in most communities.
15 Explain the difference between respite care and adult day care.
16 Identify the four different levels of tasks with which elderly need assistance.

SCENARIO

Carl and Sarah have been retired for about five years. Carl retired in good health after 35 years as an insurance agent, and Sarah stopped working outside the home after their children were grown and had families of their own. Upon retirement, they sold their home and paid cash for a condominium that had about half the square footage of their home. This relocation forced them to pare down their belongings to fit into their new and smaller surroundings. As a consequence, though, they felt less tied down to possessions and felt more freedom to do the traveling they had anticipated for several years. Although they now live on a fixed income, the profit from their home has allowed them to live out the retirement they had dreamed about, that is, having the financial resources to sign up for elderhostel programs in other cities, and to visit or host their children and grandchildren over the holidays.

All is not completely rosy for Carl and Sarah, however. Though they enjoy their lives very much, they are faced with an increasing number of health problems. They have accepted this challenge and have begun to do brisk walking on a near daily basis, and Sarah has signed up for a yoga program. Carl is considering joining a Tai Chi program offered at the senior center. They have also suffered the loss of good friends, several of whom have died, and their best friends and neighbors recently moved to be closer to their kids. Carl and Sarah are going to attend an orientation session at the local elementary school to help students read, in hopes of adding more meaning and purpose to their lives and to dwell less on their losses.

They look to the future with a mix of optimism and anxiety. The optimism is based on their consistent ability to meet the challenges of aging, even those losses that are very discouraging in the beginning. The anxiety is based on the unknown: What if their property taxes increase beyond what they can afford? What if their medication costs continue to rise, and the newly passed Medicare prescription legislation turns out to be not as helpful as advertised? Many questions arise, with no definite answers. But Carl and Sarah feel up to the challenge of aging into the future, and take satisfaction in looking back at lives well lived.

INTRODUCTION

The American population is growing older. The number of elders in America and their proportion of the total population increased dramatically during the twentieth century. In 1950, there were 12 million (8% of the population) people aged 65 years, and by 2000, that number had increased to 35 million (13% of the population).[1] For the first time in U.S. history, a significant number of Americans will achieve elder status and, in doing so, live long enough to assume some responsibilities for the care of their aging parents.[2] We need only to look around us to see the change that is taking place (see Figure 9.1). The number of gray heads in restaurants, malls, and movie theaters is increasing. Senior centers, retirement villages, assisted living facilities, and nursing homes are being built in record numbers. And today, more than ever before, many people belong to multigenerational families, where there are opportunities to develop long-lasting relationships with parents, grandparents, and even great-grandparents.[2] There are now families in which members of three successive generations receive monthly Social Security checks. Now in the twenty-first century, the economic, social, and health issues associated with the growing proportion of people over the age of 65 in America have become major political concerns. In this chapter, we will define terminology, describe the demographics, and discuss the special needs of and community service for the aging.

FIGURE 9.1
The number of elders in the United States is on the rise, and they are more energetic than previous cohorts.

Definitions

How old is old? The ageless baseball pitcher Satchel Paige once said, "How old would you be if you didn't know how old you was [sic]?" While his English might be found wanting, Paige's point is important (see Figure 9.2). A person's age might depend upon who measures it and how they define it. For example, while demographers might define old according to chronological years, clinicians might define it by stages of physiological development, and psychologists by developmental stages. Children might see their 35-year-old teacher as old, while the 35-year-old teacher might regard her 61-year-old principal as old. Age is and always will be a relative concept.

In the United States and other developed countries, people are considered old once they reach the age of 65. But because there are a number of people who are very active and healthy at age 65 and will live a number of productive years after 65, researchers have subdivided old into the *young old* (65–74), the *old old* (75 and over), and the *oldest old* (85 and over). Interestingly enough, it is this latter group, the oldest old, that makes up the fastest growing segment of the elder population.

Also for the purposes of our discussion in this chapter, we will use terms that are associated with aging as they have been defined in *Age Words: A Glossary on Health and Aging*.[3]

FIGURE 9.2
Some would say you are only as old as you think you are. (Satchel Paige remained active in professional baseball long after reaching the age at which others retired.)

aged   The state of being old. A person may be defined as aged on the basis of having reached a specific age; for example, 65 is often used for social or legislative policies, while 75 is used for physiological evaluations.

aging   The changes that occur normally in plants and animals as they grow older. Some age changes begin at birth and continue until death; other changes begin at maturity and end at death.

gerontology   The study of aging from the broadest perspective. Gerontologists examine not only the chemical and biological aspects of aging, but also psychosocial, economic, and historical conditions. Elie Merchmkoff, of the Pasteur Institute in Paris, first used the term in 1903 to describe the biological study of senescence (aging).

geriatrics   The branch of medicine that deals with the structural changes, physiology, diseases, and hygiene of old age.

Many terms have been used to describe individuals who are 65 years of age and older, including seniors, "senior citizens, golden agers, retired persons, mature adults, elderly, aged, and old people. There is no clear preference among older people for any of these terms."[4] As Ferrini and Ferrini have stated, "many gerontologists have chosen to adopt the term 'elder' to describe those 65 and older. This term is an attempt to redefine aging in a more positive way that connotes wisdom, respect, leadership, and accumulated knowledge."[4] We agree with Ferrini and Ferrini and the other gerontologists and will use the term **elders** to designate those who have reached their 65th birthday.

elders
those 65 years of age and older

Myths Surrounding Aging

Like other forms of prejudice and discrimination, **ageism** is the result of ignorance, misconceptions, and half-truths about aging and the elderly. Because most people do not interact with older people on a daily basis, it is easy to create a stereotypical image of elders based upon the atypical actions of a few.

ageism
prejudice and discrimination against the aged

When you think of older people, who comes to mind? Do you immediately think of a lonely man with a disheveled appearance sitting on a park bench or an older person lying in bed in a nursing home making incomprehensible noises? Or, do you think of Clint Eastwood and Sean Connery (each past 65) in an action-packed, high-suspense thriller?

Ferrini and Ferrini and Dychtwald and Flower have identified a number of commonly held myths about elders.[4,5] They are presented here to remind all that elders are not run-down, worn-out members of our society, but are for the most part independent, capable, and valuable resources for our communities. Do not forget that several U.S. presidents have been eligible for Social Security and Medicare while in office. Here are the myths and the reasons why they are only myths:

1. Myth: "After age 65 life goes steadily downhill."
   Truth: Any chronological age that defines old age is arbitrary. Nonetheless, many gerontologists are substituting age 85 for age 65 as the new chronological definition of old age.
2. Myth: "Old people are all alike."
   Truth: There are more differences among elders than any other segment of the U.S. population.
3. Myth: "Old people are lonely and ignored by their families."
   Truth: Elders are the least likely to be lonely of any age group; and those who live alone are likely to be in close contact, either in person, e-mail, or by telephone, with close friends and/or their family.
4. Myth: "Old age used to be better."

Truth: It is only in the last half of the twentieth century that a large portion of the U.S. population lived to be 65 years old. If people did live to be old, they were not treated any better than they are today.

5. Myth: "Old people are senile."
   Truth: Senility is the result of disease and only affects about 5% of elders living in noninstitutional settings.

6. Myth: "Old people have the good life."
   Truth: Though elders do gain certain advantages when they retire and when their children leave home, they still face a number of concerns, such as loss of loved ones, loss of health, and loss of value in society.

7. Myth: "Most old people are sickly."
   Truth: Most older people do have at least one chronic health problem, but the majority of elders live active lifestyles.

8. Myth: "Old people no longer have any sexual interest or ability."
   Truth: Sexual interest does not diminish with age, but there is an alteration in sexual response. Nonetheless, many elders in reasonably good health have active and satisfying sex lives.

9. Myth: "Most old people end up in nursing homes."
   Truth: Only approximately 4% of those above the age of 65 live in nursing homes, homes for the aged, or other group quarters. Only 1% of those aged 65 to 74 reside in such a place, though the percentage jumps to 19% for the oldest old (those 85 and older). However, this number is still well below half.

10. Myth: "Older people are unproductive."
    Truth: Older adults are more likely to be retired, but they are very likely to be productively engaged at home and in the community.

Though a number of issues and concerns facing elders are presented later in this chapter, the majority of elders in the United States today are active and well (see Figure 9.3). In all parts of the country, many elders are still working. Many of the retired elders are (1) attending **elderhostel** programs, (2) remaining politically active (AARP, formerly called the American Association of Retired Persons, is one of the most active lobbying groups in the United States), and (3) volunteering countless hours as tutors at schools, workers for hospices and hospitals, advocates and companions for the mentally ill, intake personnel at crisis centers, members of community agency boards, and churches, to name a few. Elders are an important part of society and play active roles in making communities work.

DEMOGRAPHY OF AGING

Demography is "the study of a population (an aggregate of individuals) and those variables bringing about change in that population."[3] The demography of aging is typically defined as a study of those who are 65 years and over and of the variables that bring about change in their lives. In the following paragraphs, we review some of the demographic features of the elder population, including size, growth rate, and the factors that contribute to this growth. We also discuss other demographic characteristics of this population, such as living arrangements, racial and ethnic composition, geographic distribution, economic status, and housing.

elderhostel
education programs specifically for elders, held on college campuses

demography
the study of a population and those variables bringing about change in that population

FIGURE 9.3

This 81-year-old long-jumper is one of many elders who remain active well after retirement age.

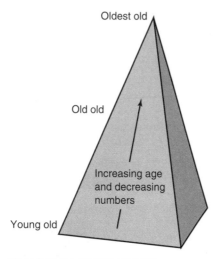

FIGURE 9.4
Theoretical age pyramid.

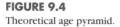
median age
the age at which half
of the population is
older and half is
younger

Size and Growth of the Elder Population

The aging of any population can be graphically illustrated with a theoretical age pyramid[6] (see Figure 9.4). The base of this pyramid represents the youngest and largest segment of the population. The sloping sides indicate higher mortality rates and limited life expectancy. Until the mid-1950s, the population pyramid for the United States was not so very different from the traditional age pyramid (see Figure 9.5).

Since the mid-1950s, however, the shape of America's population pyramid has changed. As noted earlier in the chapter, both the number of elders and the proportion of the total population made up of elders grew significantly during the twentieth century. At the beginning of the twentieth century, only one in 25 Americans was over the age of 65 years. In 2000, that number had increased to almost one in about 7.5.[7] Demographers' projections suggest that populations will continue to age, not only in this country, but in most other countries as well. In 2011, the *baby boom* generation will begin to turn 65, and by 2030, it is projected that 71 million people (one in five) will be age 65 or older.[8] The population aged 85 and older is currently the fastest growing segment of the older population. It will double in size by 2025 and increase fivefold by 2050.[9] During this same time, it is expected that the percentage of people aged 18 and younger will remain about the same, around 26%.[7] These changes will alter the shape of the population pyramid and make it more like the shape of a population rectangle (see Figure 9.6).

As one might guess, the projected growth of the elder population is expected to raise the **median age** of the U.S. population. In 1995, the median age was 34.3 years. In 2000, it was 35.7 (the highest ever recorded). It should peak in 2035 at 38.7 and then decrease to 38.1 by 2050.[9]

Factors That Affect Population Size and Age

There are three factors that affect the size and age of a population: its fertility rates, its mortality rates, and its gain or loss from migration of individuals into or out of that population.[2]

FIGURE 9.5

Population by age and sex: United States, 1955 (in millions).

Source: U.S. Bureau of the Census (1965). "Estimates of the Population of the United States by Single Years of Age, Color, and Sex: 1900 to 1959." *Current Population Reports,* series P-25, no. 311. Washington, DC: U.S. Government Printing Office, 2–5.

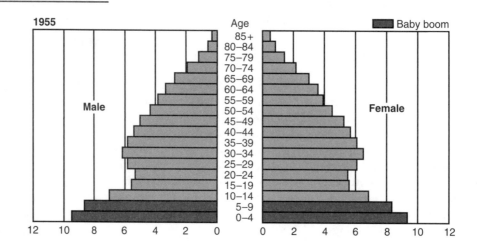

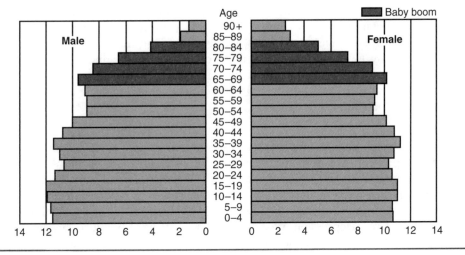

FIGURE 9.6

Projected population by age and sex, 2030 (in millions).

Source: Day, J. C., U.S. Bureau of the Census (1993). "Population Projections of the United States by Age, Sex, Race, and Hispanic Origin: 1993 to 2050." *Current Population Reports,* series P25-1104. Washington, DC: U.S. Government Printing Office (middle series projections), 2-7.

Though one might assume that all populations will age with time, that is not necessarily true. In fact, a population could get younger with time.[2] If fertility rates and mortality rates are both high, life expectancy would be low, and the age of a population could grow younger. However, this has not been the case in the United States.

Fertility Rates

The *fertility rate* is an expression of the number of births per 1,000 women of childbearing age (15–44) in the population during a specific time period. Fertility rates in the United States were at their highest at the beginning of the twentieth century. Those rates dipped during the Depression years but rebounded after World War II. The period of consistently high fertility rates immediately following World War II has become known as the "baby boom years," hence the name *baby boomers* for those born from 1946 through 1964. During those years, 76 million babies were born. As the baby boomers continue to age, a "human tidal wave" (bulge) will continue to move up the U.S. age pyramid. American society has tried to adjust to the size and needs of the baby boom generation throughout the stages of the life cycle. Just as this generation had a dramatic impact on expanding obstetrics and pediatrics, creating split shifts for students in public schools, and disrupting government policy toward the Vietnam War, the baby boom cohorts will also place tremendous strain on programs and services (e.g., Social Security and Medicare) required of an elderly population. A window of opportunity now exists for planners and policy makers to prepare for the aging of the baby boom generation.[10]

Mortality Rates

The *mortality or death rate* (usually expressed in deaths per 100,000 population) also has an impact on the aging population. The annual crude mortality rate in the United States in 1900 was 1,720 per 100,000. That figure dropped by half to 854 in 2000.[1] The decrease in the annual mortality rate achieved over the first 75 years of the twentieth century was the result of triumphs in medical science and public health practice.[2]

Another demographic variable that interacts with the mortality rate is life expectancy. While the mortality rate in the United States has been fairly constant for 20+ years, life expectancy has continued to increase. During the twentieth century, there was an overall jump in life expectancy at birth from 47.3 years in 1900 to 76.9 years in 2000. The life expectancy of men and black Americans has always trailed those for women and white Americans, respectively. While the increase in life expectancy in the first half of the twentieth century could be attributed to the decrease in infant and early childhood deaths, the increase in life expectancy since 1970 can be traced to the postponement of death among the middle-aged and elder population.[1]

Migration

net migration
the population gain or loss resulting from migration

The movement of people from one country to another, *migration,* has also contributed to the aging of the population. **Net migration** is the population gain or loss from the movement of migrants in (immigration) and out (emigration) of a country. Historically, in the United States, net migration has resulted in population gain; more people immigrate than emigrate. The greatest immigration in the United States occurred between the end of the Civil War and the beginning of the Great Depression. Most of the immigrants were between the ages of 18 and 35 years—of childbearing age. As these immigrants had children, the population of the United States remained young. However, the decline in immigration following the Depression led to the aging of the American populace as the early immigrants grew old and were not replaced by younger immigrants.[2,11]

Fortunately, however, the United States continued to absorb young immigrants during the closing decades of the twentieth century. As a consequence, the dependency ratio of workers to older adults in the United States is declining more slowly than in many other developed countries. The future, however, is not so bright. We turn to this topic next.

Support and Labor-Force Ratios

support ratio
a ratio that compares the number of individuals whom society considers economically unproductive to the number it considers economically productive

Other demographic signs of an aging population are changes in support and labor-force ratios. The **support ratio** is a comparison between those individuals whom society considers economically unproductive (the nonworking or dependent population) and those it considers economically productive (the working population). Traditionally, the productive and nonproductive populations have been defined by age; the productive population includes those who are 15 to 59 years old, 18 to 64, or 20 to 64. The unproductive population includes both youth (0–14, 0–17, or 0–19 years old) and the elderly (60+ or 65+ years). When the support ratio includes both youth and the elderly, it is referred to as a **total support ratio.** When only the youth are compared to the productive group, the term used is **youth support ratio;** when only the elderly are compared, it is called **elderly support ratio.**[2]

total support ratio
the support ratio that includes both youth and elderly

youth support ratio
the support ratio that includes only youth

Changes in support ratios "provide an indirect broad indication of periods when we can expect the particular age distribution of the country to affect the need for distinct types of social services, housing, and consumer products."[10] Thus, communities can refer to support ratio data as a guide for making the best social policy decisions and as a way to allocate resources. For example, leaders in a community with a relatively high youth support ratio compared to the elderly support ratio may want to concentrate community resources on programs like education for the young, health promotion programs for children, special programs for working parents, and other youth-associated concerns. Communities with high elderly support ratios might increase programs for elders.

elderly support ratio
the support ratio that includes only elderly

The total support ratio (SR) (calculated by adding the number of youth and elderly, divided by the number of persons 20 to 64 years, times 100) in the United States in 1990 was close to its lowest point (SR = 70.5) in the twentieth century, and it is projected to stay at about that same level until about 2010. The total support ratio will begin to climb in 2010 and will peak around the year 2035 at about 90 as the baby boomers reach their elder years. At its peak, the total support ratio will include a youth support ratio of about 50 and an elderly

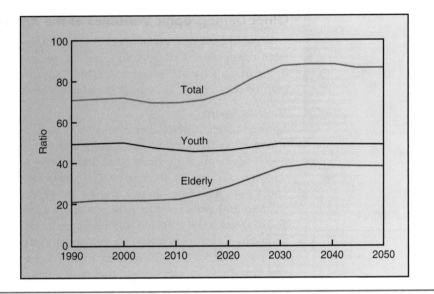

FIGURE 9.7

Total, youth, and elderly support ratios, 1990 to 2050.

Source: U.S. Bureau of the Census, 1990 from 1990 Census of Population and Housing, CPH-L-74, "Modified and Actual Age, Sex, Race, and Hispanic Origin Data;" 2050 from "Population Projections of the United States, by Age, Sex, Race, and Hispanic Origin: 1993 to 2050." *Current Population Reports,* series P25-1104. Washington, DC: U.S. Government Printing Office (middle series projections), 1993.

support ratio of 40 (see Figure 9.7). It is this big change (from 1990 to 2035) in the elderly support ratio that will guide future social policy.

Such an increase in the elderly support ratio provides an interesting political scenario because the costs to support youth and the elderly are not the same.[12] Parents pay directly for most of the expenditures to support their children, with the primary exception being public education, which is paid for by taxes. In contrast, much of the support for elders comes from tax-supported programs such as Social Security, Medicare, and Medicaid. In order to meet the impending burden of the elderly, taxes will most certainly need to be raised. Therefore, the two questions for the future are, Will the productive population be willing to pay increased taxes to support elders? or, Will services to the elderly be drastically reduced?

While support ratio data clearly show one trend, they are merely an estimate and should not be the only accepted estimate. Actually, the support ratios presented in Figure 9.7 are based on the assumption that everyone of productive age supports all members of the non-productive age group. Obviously, this is not the case. Many of those in the productive age group (for instance homemakers, the unemployed, and the disabled) do not participate in the paid labor force. Conversely, many teenagers and elders do. Thus, dependency ratios, in some situations, could provide misleading figures for decision makers.

Schulz and colleagues believe that labor-force support ratios also need to be considered.[12] **Labor-force support ratios** differ from support ratios in that they are based on the number of people who are actually working and those who are not, independent of their ages. When labor-force participation rates are used to calculate the labor-force support ratios, it is projected that the burden of support for the labor force in the future will be somewhat lighter than that projected through support ratios. Nonetheless, under either method of calculation, the ratio of dependents to workers will be lower in the future than it is today.

labor-force support ratio
a ratio of the total number of those individuals who are not working to the number of those who are

FIGURE 9.8

Elder women are three times more likely to be widowed than elder men.

Other Demographic Variables of the Aging

Other demographic variables that impact the community health programs of older Americans include marital status, living arrangements, racial and ethnic composition, geographic distribution, economic status, and housing.

Marital Status

Approximately three-fourths of elder men are married, whereas less than half of elder women are married. In addition, elder women are three times more likely as men to be widowed.[8] There are three primary reasons for these differences. First, men have shorter average life expectancies than women and thus tend to precede their wives in death. Second, men tend to marry women who are younger than themselves. Finally, men who lose a spouse through death or divorce are more likely to remarry than women in the same situation. These statistics reveal that most elderly men have a spouse for assistance, especially when health fails, while most women do not.[10] However, "in many ways, the current generation of elderly women are pacesetters as they defy stereotypes of aging. Many have dealt with the shortage of men by developing new interests and friendships. For elderly women (and men) with protective social networks, living alone does not necessarily mean being lonely"[10] (see Figure 9.8).

The number of divorced elderly continues to rise. As the baby boomers move into their older years, the number of divorced elders will grow two- to threefold. These divorced elders represent a new type of need group—those who lack the retirement benefits, insurance, and net worth assets associated with being married.

Living Arrangements

"Like marital status, the living arrangements of America's older population are important because they are closely linked to income, health status, and the availability of caregivers. Older persons who live alone are more likely to be in poverty than older persons who live with their spouses."[8] Two-thirds of non-institutionalized elders live with someone else (spouse, relative, or other non-relatives), while the remainder live alone.[13] Of those living alone, women are much more likely (almost 4 to 1) to be living alone. The proportion of those living alone is projected to remain about the same, but the numbers are expected to increase dramatically over the next 20 years.[10] Reasons for these increased numbers revolve around the aging of the baby boomers and the improved economic status of the elderly, coupled with their strong desire to live as independently as possible.

assisted-living facility
a special combination of housing, personalized supportive services and health care designed to meet the needs—both scheduled and unscheduled—of those who need help with activities of daily living

Only a small percentage of the elderly population in the United States resides in nursing homes. In 2001, about 1.5 million of those aged 65 years and over were in nursing homes, representing 4% of the elder population.[1] This percentage is down from previous years due in part to the increase in **assisted-living facilities,** which have provided an alternative to long-term care in a nursing home.[8] Of those who do live in nursing homes, older women at all ages have higher usage rates than men. Approximately three-fourths of nursing home residents are women, and over half of all nursing home residents are over 85 years old. As one might expect, the proportion of elders living in a nursing home increases with age.[8]

Racial and Ethnic Composition

As the elder population grows larger, it will also grow more diverse, reflecting the demographic changes in the U.S. population as a whole.[8] In 2000, the elder population in the United States was predominately white. Of the total elder population in 2000, it was estimated

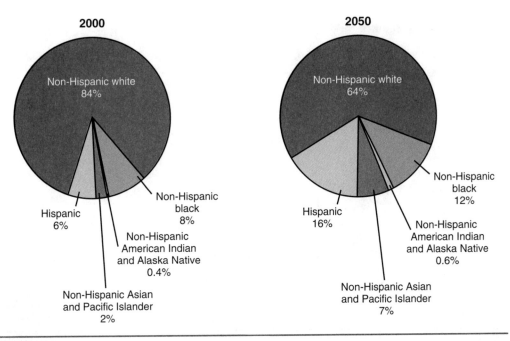

2000

Non-Hispanic white
84%

Hispanic
6%

Non-Hispanic
black
8%

Non-Hispanic
American Indian
and Alaska Native
0.4%

Non-Hispanic Asian
and Pacific Islander
2%

2050

Non-Hispanic white
64%

Hispanic
16%

Non-Hispanic
black
12%

Non-Hispanic
American Indian
and Alaska Native
0.6%

Non-Hispanic Asian
and Pacific Islander
7%

FIGURE 9.9

Projected distribution of the population age 65 and older, by race and Hispanic origin, 2000 and 2050.

Note: Data are middle-series projections of the population. Hispanics may be of any race.

Reference population: These data refer to the resident population.

Source: U.S. Census Bureau (2000). *Population Projections of the United States by Age, Sex, Race, Hispanic Origin, and Nativity: 1999 to 2100.* Available at http://www.census.gov/population/www/projections/natproj.html.

that about 84% were white, 8% were black, 6% were of Hispanic origin, 2% were Asian/Pacific Islanders, and less than 1% were American Indian and Alaska Native.[8] By 2050, the elder white population is expected to decline to 64%, while Americans of Hispanic origin will increase to 16%, black Americans will increase to 12%, Asian/Pacific Islanders will increase to 7%, and American Indians and Alaska Natives will stay at less than 1% but will still grow by a rate of 50% (see Figure 9.9).[8] The growth in minority groups will be the result of continued immigration and the higher fertility rates in non-whites over the past 50 years.[14]

Geographic Distribution

In 2000, it was estimated that about one-third of America's elders lived in Southern states (see Figure 9.10), and just over half lived in the following nine states: California, Florida, Illinois, Michigan, New Jersey, New York, Ohio, Pennsylvania, and Texas. Each of these states had over 1 million elders. By 2015, Georgia, North Carolina, Virginia, and Washington are expected to join this group. California had the greatest number, with 3.3 million, while Florida had the greatest proportion, with 18% (2.7 million people). Other states in which the population includes 15% or more of elders are Iowa, North Dakota, Pennsylvania, and West Virginia.[8] Some states, including many in the Midwest, have a small total number of elders, but the elders make up a large percentage of their total population.

The populations of some states (such as Florida) "age" because of the inward migration of elders; others (like the Farm Belt states) "age" because their young people leave. Still other states "age" because of low fertility or some combination of factors.[10]

From an ethnic and racial standpoint, the regional concentrations of the elderly are similar to the concentrations of the total population of each group.[10]

FIGURE 9.10
Many elders choose to spend their retirement years in states with warm weather.

Economic Status

The overall economic position of elders has improved significantly since the 1970s.[13] In 1970 about 25% of the elderly lived in poverty, whereas in 2001 the figure had dropped to approximately 10%.[1] Today, in fact, a smaller percentage of the elderly are impoverished than among those under age 65.[15]

When the sources of income of elders is examined, it is found that 39% of elder income comes from Social Security, almost equal percentages come from asset income (16%), pensions (18%), and earnings (24%), and a small percentage (3%) comes from other miscellaneous sources.[16] Because only one-fourth of elder income comes from work earnings, they are economically more vulnerable to circumstances beyond their control, such as the loss of a spouse; deteriorating health and self-sufficiency; changes in Social Security, Medicare, and Medicaid legislation; and inflation.[14]

Housing

In general, most older Americans live in adequate, affordable housing.[8,17] Almost 75% live in single family homes, another 20% lives in multi-unit structures (mostly apartments), and approximately 6% live in mobile homes (mostly in rural areas).[17] However, millions of elderly continue to live in housing that costs too much, is in substandard condition, or fails to accommodate their physical capabilities or assistance needs.[17] Characteristics of the homes of elders versus those of younger people are that elders have (1) older homes, (2) homes of lower value, (3) homes in greater need of repair, (4) homes less likely to have central heating and air conditioning, and (5) homes less likely to have telephones.[14,18]

For most elders, housing represents an asset because they have no mortgage or rental payments, or they can sell their home for a profit. But for others with low incomes, housing becomes a heavy burden. Approximately 30% (7.4 million) of all elderly households pay more for housing than they can afford.[17] The cost of utilities, real estate taxes, insurance, repair, and maintenance have forced many to sell their property or live in a less-desirable residence.

HEALTHY PEOPLE 2010: OBJECTIVES

1-9. Reduce the hospitalization rates for three ambulatory-care-sensitive conditions—pediatric asthma, uncontrolled diabetes, and immunization-preventable pneumonia and influenza.

Target and baseline:

Objective	Reduction in Hospitalizations for Ambulatory-Care-Sensitive Conditions	1996 Baseline	2001 Status	2010 Target
		Admissions per 10,000 Population		
1-9a.	Pediatric asthma—persons under age 18 years	23.0	21.4	17.3
1-9b.	Uncontrolled diabetes—persons aged 18–64 years	7.2	7.7	5.4
1-9c.	Immunization-preventable pneumonia and influenza—persons aged 65 years and older	10.6	11.2	8.0

For Further Thought

If you were given the responsibility for increasing the number of elders who are immunized against preventable pneumonia and influenza, what community health activities would you recommend to get elders to the immunizations?

A HEALTH PROFILE OF ELDERS

The health status among elders has improved over the years, both in terms of living longer and remaining functional. The percentage of chronically disabled older persons—those with impairments for three months or longer that impede daily activities—has been slowly falling. However, we do know that the most consistent risk factor of illness and death across the total population is age, and that in general, the health status of elders is not as good as their younger counterparts. In this section of the chapter, we will examine some of the health concerns of aging, including mortality, morbidity, and health behaviors and lifestyle choices.

Mortality

In 2000, the top five causes of death for elders, in order of number of deaths, were heart disease, cancer, stroke, chronic lower respiratory disease (CLRD), and pneumonia and influenza (see Box 9.1). The top three causes of death were responsible for almost seven of every ten deaths. Over the past 50 years, the overall age-adjusted mortality rate for elders has continued to fall. The primary reason for this has been the declining death rates for heart disease and stroke. Despite such drops, heart disease remains the leading cause of death in this age group, and it is responsible for about one-third of the deaths.[1] Unlike the death rates for heart disease and stroke, the cancer death rate has stayed about the same in recent years. The biggest jump in death rates for elders has occurred with diabetes and CLRD.

Morbidity

"The quality of life in later years may be diminished if illness, chronic conditions, or injuries limit the ability of one to care for oneself without assistance. Older persons maintain their independence and eliminate costly caregiving services by, among other things, shopping on their own, cooking their meals, bathing and dressing themselves, and walking and climbing stairs without assistance."[13] Among non-institutionalized persons age 70 and over, almost a

BOX
9.2

HEALTHY PEOPLE 2010: OBJECTIVES

2-9.   Reduce the proportion of adults with osteoporosis.

Target: 8 percent

Baseline: 10 percent of adults aged 50 years and older had osteoporosis as measured by low total femur bone mineral density (BMD) in 1988–1994 (age adjusted to the year 2000 standard population).

Status: No measurement since baseline.

For Further Thought

Have you seen any health care facilities in your community that have been advertising that they do bone density testing? How is bone density measured? What are some community health activities that could be carried out in a community to reduce the proportion of adults with osteoporosis?

third had difficulty performing and one-fourth were unable to perform at least one of nine physical activities (walking a quarter mile; walking up ten steps without resting; standing or being on one's feet for about two hours; sitting for about two hours; stooping, crouching, or kneeling; reaching up over head; reaching out as if to shake someone's hand; using fingers to grasp or handle; lifting or carrying something as heavy as ten pounds). Activity limitations increase with age, and women are more likely than men to have physical limitations.[13] The causes of this reduced activity can be classified into two types—chronic conditions and impairments.

Chronic Conditions

Chronic conditions are systemic health problems that persist longer than three months, such as hypertension, arthritis, heart disease, diabetes, and emphysema. "While not all chronic conditions are life threatening, they are a substantial burden on the health and economic status of individuals, their families, and the nation as a whole."[13] The actual number of chronic conditions increases with age; therefore, limitations from activities become increasingly prevalent with age. In 2001, about 35% of elders reported a limitation of activity due to chronic conditions.[1] Furthermore, many chronic conditions can result in impairments, such as the loss of sight from diabetes. Chronic conditions of elders vary by gender and race. More men experience life-threatening acute illnesses (e.g., heart disease and hypertension-induced stroke), while more women experience physically limiting chronic illness (e.g., osteoporosis and arthritis).

Impairments

Impairments are deficits in the functioning of one's sense organs or limitations in one's mobility or range of motion. Like chronic conditions, impairments are far more prevalent in older elders. The four primary impairments are hearing impairments, orthopedic impairments (see Box 9.2), cataracts, and other visual impairments. Another impairment of great concern is memory impairment. "Memory skills are important to general cognitive functioning, and declining scores on tests of memory are indicators of general cognitive loss for older adults. Low cognitive functioning (i.e., memory impairment) is a major risk factor for entering a nursing home."[8]

Like rates for chronic conditions, rates for impairments differ by gender and race. But unlike chronic conditions, impairments are affected by two other variables—previous income level and previous occupational exposure. The smaller the income and the more occupational exposure to health hazards, the greater the number of impairments.

Health Behaviors and Lifestyle Choices

There is no question that health behavior and social factors play significant roles in helping elders maintain health in later life. Some elders believe that they are too old to gain any benefit from changing their health behaviors. This, of course, is not true; it is never too late to make a change for the better.

In interviews, elders generally report more favorable health behaviors than their younger counterparts. They are less likely to (1) consume large amounts of alcohol, (2) smoke cigarettes, and (3) be overweight or obese. However, it should be noted that many of those who abused alcoholic beverages, smoked cigarettes, and were overweight or obese died before 65 and thus were unavailable for interview.

Even though in general elders report better health behaviors than their younger counterparts, there is still room for improvement. The health behaviors that can impact the health of elders the most are healthy eating, exercise, and immunizations. Healthy eating plays a major role in preventing or delaying the onset of chronic diseases. The dietary quality habits of elders are better than their younger counterparts, but they still have room for improvement.

The 1996 Surgeon General's Report on Physical Activity and Health reported that inactivity increased with age. While a substantial majority of adults at all age levels did not achieve the recommended level of physical activity, the number of sedentary persons—those who engage in *no* discretionary physical activity at all—increased with age. By age 75 about one in three men and one in two women engage in the dangerous practice of inactivity.

The good news is that walking briskly (about twice as fast as a normal pace) for at least 30 minutes a day most days of the week is almost as beneficial for reducing the death rate as jogging up to 40 miles a week.[19] One study reported that walking four hours per week decreased the risk of future hospitalization for cardiovascular disease.[20] Another study reported that brisk walking three hours a week reduced the incidence of coronary events between 30% and 40%.[21]

Though aerobic conditioning has been considered the exercise of choice for improved cardiorespiratory function, other forms of exercise have proved beneficial as well. Tai chi[22] and resistance exercise,[23,24] for example, provide cardiorespiratory benefits. Resistance exercise, in fact, appears to reduce blood pressure level[25] and cholesterol level,[26,27] outcomes previously obtained primarily through aerobic exercise interventions.

Most people do not think of elders when they hear the word *immunizations*. "But for adults, especially those 65 and older, getting immunized against certain diseases is important and can prevent thousands of deaths each year."[28] As noted earlier in the chapter, influenza and pneumonia are the fifth leading cause of death in elders. Vaccinations against these diseases are recommended for elders, especially those who are at increased risk for complications from influenza and pneumonia. Influenza vaccinations are given annually, while pneumococcal vaccinations are usually given once in a lifetime, with possible revaccination with severe comorbidity after five years.[8]

Due in large measure to the onset of Medicare reimbursement, the pneumococcal vaccination rate increased dramatically, from 10% in 1989 to 55% in 1999.[29] Nonetheless, almost half of elders remained unvaccinated, and there was considerable racial disparity. In 1999, 57% of whites received pneumonia vaccination, compared with 36% of blacks and 35% of Hispanics.[30]

Thanks once again to Medicare reimbursement, the influenza vaccination rate also increased dramatically, from 20% in 1989 to 68% in 1999.[29] While this improvement is dramatic and gratifying to public health officials, almost a third of elders are still not getting an annual flu shot. And among older blacks, the influenza vaccination rate was 21% lower than among older whites.[31]

Elder Abuse and Neglect

Reports of elder abuse and neglect have increased greatly in recent years. In a 10-year period between the mid-1980s and the mid-1990s, reports of elder abuse in the United States increased by more than 150%.[32] Perhaps a substantial part of the increase in these numbers was due to all 50 states having passed some form of elder abuse prevention laws. Though the laws and definitions of terms vary from state to state, all states have set up reporting systems. Prior to the reporting systems, many incidences of abuse were never recorded. "Generally, adult protective service (APS) agencies receive and investigate reports of suspected elder abuse."[32] According to the first-ever National Elder Abuse Incidence Study, released in 1998, an estimated total of 551,000 elderly persons over the age 60 had experienced abuse (physical, emotional/psychological), neglect, or self-neglect in a domestic setting during the year of the study.[33] This study also revealed the following:

- Female elders are abused at a higher rate than men.
- Elders 80 years and older are abused or neglected at two to three times the rate of their proportion of the elderly population.
- In almost 90% of all elder abuse and neglect incidents where a perpetrator is identified, the perpetrator is a family member, and two-thirds of the perpetrators are adult children or spouses.
- Victims of self-neglect are usually depressed, confused, or extremely frail.

Elder abuse and neglect are special problems for elders because they are (1) frail, (2) unable to defend themselves, (3) vulnerable to telemarketing scams and mail-order swindles, and (4) the most common victims of theft of their benefit checks. But on a positive note, elder abuse is a problem that has responded well to community health programming.

INSTRUMENTAL NEEDS OF ELDERS

Atchley lists six instrumental needs that determine lifestyles for people of all ages.[34] These are income, housing, personal care, health care, transportation, and community facilities and services. However, the aging process can alter these needs in unpredictable ways. While those elders in the young old group (65–74) usually do not experience appreciable changes in their lifestyles relative to these six needs, elders in the old old group (75–84) and the oldest old group (85 and older) eventually do. The rest of this chapter will explore these six needs, discuss their implications for elders, and describe community services for elders.

Income

Though the need for income continues throughout one's life, achieving elder status often reduces the income needs. Perhaps the major reduction occurs with one's retirement. Retirees do not need to purchase job-related items such as special clothing or tools, pay union dues, or join professional associations. Expenses are further reduced because retirees no longer commute every day, buy as many meals away from home, or spend money on business travel. Reaching elder status also usually means that children are grown and no longer dependent, and, as noted earlier, the home mortgage has often been retired. Taxes are usually lower because income is lower. In addition, many community services are offered at reduced prices for elders.

However, aging usually means increased expenses for health care and for home maintenance and repairs that aging homeowners can no longer do themselves. In spite of these increased costs, the overall need for income seems to decrease slightly for people after retirement.

As noted earlier in this chapter, there are five sources of income for elders: Social Security, pensions (e.g., government employee pensions, private pensions, or annuities), earnings from jobs, income from assets (e.g., savings accounts, stocks, bonds, real estate, etc.), and other miscellaneous sources (e.g., public assistance for the poor elders). Social Security benefits account for about two-fifths of income for elders; and asset income, pensions, and personal earnings each provide about one-fifth of total income. During 2001, approximately 91% of elders received some income from Social Security, 20% received all their income from Social Security, 33% depended on Social Security for almost all (90% or more) of their income, and it was the major source (at least 50% of total income) for 65% of the beneficiaries. Yet, Social Security payments are modest. In 2004, the average monthly Social Security payment to retired individuals was $843.[35] This amounts to an average of about $10,000 per year. The elders who rely most heavily on Social Security income are the poorest.

In recent years, the income of elders has improved significantly. When income and other assets of elders are combined, the economic status of elders and those under 65 is not that far apart. However, the fact remains that 10% of the elder population lives in poverty. Certain subgroups of elders have higher rates. Nonmarried women and minorities have the highest poverty rates, ranging from 18% to 22%. Married persons have the lowest poverty rates at 4%.[35]

Housing

Housing, a basic necessity for all, is a central concern for elders in terms of needs and costs. It is an important source of continuity for elders. A home is more than just a place to live. It is a symbol of independence; a place for family gatherings; a source of pleasant memories; and a link to friends, the neighborhood, and the community.[34]

When housing for the elderly is examined, four major needs are discussed. They include appropriateness, accessibility, adequacy, and affordability.[17] These needs are not independent of each other; in fact, they are closely intertwined. Elders may live in affordable housing, but the housing may not be appropriate for their special needs. Or, certain housing may be accessible to the elderly, but it may not be affordable to elders, or there may not be an adequate number available to meet demand.

Housing requirements may change more rapidly than housing consumption during the course of retirement years as a result of changes in household composition, decreasing mobility, and/or increasing morbidity.[18] Thus, the single biggest change in the housing needs of elders is the need for special modifications due to physical disabilities. Such modifications can be very simple—such as handrails for support in bathrooms—or more complex—such as chair lifts for stairs. Sometimes there is need for live-in help, while at other times disabilities may force seniors to leave their homes and seek specialized housing.

The decision to remove elders from their long-term residences is not easily made. Because of the psychological and social value of the home, changing an elder's place of residence has negative effects for both the elder and the family members who help make the arrangements for the move. Recognizing the importance of a home and independence, families often feel tremendous conflict and guilt in deciding to move an elder relative. If the elder does not adjust to the new situation, the guilt continues. Sometimes family members continue to question their decision even after the elder dies. Though moving an elder is very difficult, it is usually best for all involved. For example, moving a frail person from a two-story to a one-story home makes good sense, and moving an elder from a very large home to a smaller home or an apartment is logical.[2]

One of the biggest fears associated with relocating an elder is the move to group housing, especially a nursing home. The stereotype that many people have about group housing is not very positive, and most know it can be very expensive: $35,000 to $60,000 per year for a total care nursing home. However, just like any other consumer product, good group homes are available. There is some evidence that not-for-profit homes—which constitute about one-third of the nation's 17,000 nursing homes—may be more concerned about quality of care and less concerned about keeping costs down and profits up.[36]

Perhaps the ideal model for long-term care facilities, however, is the Eden Alternative, founded by William Thomas, M.D., in 1991. The basic premise of the Eden Alternative is that nursing homes should treat residents as people who need attentive care in a homelike setting. To accomplish this goal, nursing homes need to contain pets, plants, children, and other amenities that make life worth living.[37] A few hundred nursing homes around the country have incorporated the Eden Alternative into their facilities.

To ease the stress and anxiety of relocating an elder, Borup has noted the following:[38]

1. Relocation stress is usually temporary.
2. Those unwilling to move are most likely to experience stress.
3. Making the new environment predictable to the elder can help to reduce stress.
4. Keeping those being moved and their families informed can help to reduce stress.

The relocation of elders is not always traumatic or done against their will. Many elders are finding housing in communities that have been planned as **retirement communities.** Though these communities are available in all areas of the country, they are most popular in areas with temperate climates (see Figure 9.11). Some of the communities are built as private associations, while others are developed as special areas within larger, already established communities. Legally, the private associations are able to adopt by-laws that put restrictions on the residents, such as a minimum age to move into the area, no children under a certain age living in the residence, and no pets. Retirement communities usually offer a variety of housing alternatives ranging from home or condominium ownership to apartment living. Because these communities are developed to meet the needs of elders, special accommodations are usually made for socializing, recreation, shopping, transportation, and selected educational programs.

In recent years, there have been a number of new housing options for elders. Two of these include **continuing-care retirement communities** (CCRCs) and assisted living residences. CCRCs guarantee the residents a lifelong residence and health care. They work in the following way: The retirees either purchase or term lease (sometimes lifelong) a living unit on a campus-like setting. The living unit could be a single-family dwelling, an apartment, or a room, as in a nursing home. In addition to the living units, the campus usually includes a health clinic and often has either a nursing home or health care center. These other facilities are available to the residents for an additional fee. Residents of the CCRCs can live as independently as they wish but have available to them a variety of services, including housekeeping, meals, transportation, organized recreational and social activities, health care, and security. Many living units are equipped with emergency call buttons.

CCRCs are a housing alternative for well-to-do seniors. Unfortunately, CCRCs are beyond the reach of many elders; the

retirement communities residential communities that have been specifically developed for those in their retirement years

continuing-care retirement communities (CCRCs) planned communities for seniors which guarantee a lifelong residence and health care

FIGURE 9.11
The number of planned retirement communities in the United States continues to increase.

purchase or lifelong lease is more than $100,000, and the fee for many of the services is extra. Obviously, seniors who enter into contractual agreements for CCRCs should read their contracts carefully before signing them.

An assisted living residence is a more recent housing option than CCRCs, but it includes many of the same concepts. It is a model of residential care that blends many of the characteristics of the nursing home and community-based long-term care. The Assisted Living Federation of America has defined an assisted living "residence as a special combination of housing, personalized supportive services and health care designed to meet the needs—both scheduled and unscheduled—of those who need help with activities of daily living."[39] Such facilities may include a high-rise apartment complex, a converted Victorian home, or a renovated school.[39] "Residences may be freestanding or housed with other residential options, such as independent living or nursing care. They may be operated by non-profit or for-profit companies."[39] Most of these facilities offer a variety of services, including the following:[39]

- Three meals a day served in a common dining area
- Housekeeping services
- Transportation
- Assistance with eating, bathing, dressing, toileting, and walking
- Access to health and medical services
- 24-hour security and staff availability
- Emergency call systems for each resident unit
- Health promotion and exercise programs
- Medication management
- Personal laundry services
- Social and recreational activities

Costs for assisted living vary according to facility and parts of the country, but daily basic fees typically "range from approximately $15 to $200—generally less than the cost of home health services and nursing home care."[39]

It has been estimated that there are about 20,000 assisted-living facilities nationwide.[39] In a recent national study, about a fourth of the residents of these facilities received assistance with three or more activities of daily living, such as bathing, dressing, and mobility, and about one-third had moderate to severe cognitive impairment.[40]

Of all the housing problems that confront seniors, the availability of affordable housing is the biggest. Unfortunately, those seniors who are most in need of such housing are often frail and disabled, have low incomes, and live in rural areas. Until recently, many of the needs of this group of elders went unmet. However, during the Clinton presidency, funding was provided for the *Housing Security Plan for Older Americans* administered in the Office of Housing and Urban Development (HUD).[17] This plan embodied three overarching goals:

- "Help seniors remain in their homes and connected to their families and communities.
- Expand affordable housing opportunities for lower income seniors.
- Improve the range and coordination of affordable housing and supportive service combinations available to seniors."[17]

To reach these goals, HUD was working with older homeowners to help them convert the equity in their homes into funds for needed health and safety home improvements, including home rehabilitation loans through HUD's reverse mortgage program. HUD was also providing more money to help build more affordable rental housing for low-income elderly, in addition to helping finance the conversion of some existing housing units to assisted living residencies.[17] With each subsequent administration, however, presidential politics may (and usually does) change funding levels for programs like this.

Personal Care

While most elders are able to care for themselves, there is a significant minority of elders who require personal assistance for an optimal or even adequate existence. The size of this minority increases as the elders attain old old (75–84) and oldest old (85+) status.

Several authors have identified four different levels of tasks with which seniors may need assistance:[2,10,41,42]

1. Instrumental tasks—such as housekeeping, transportation, maintenance on the automobile or yard, and assistance with business affairs
2. Expressive tasks—including emotional support, socializing and inclusion in social gatherings, and trying to prevent feelings of loneliness and isolation
3. Cognitive tasks—assistance that involves scheduling appointments, monitoring health conditions, reminding elders of the need to take medications, and in general acting as a backup memory
4. Tasks of daily living—such as eating, bathing, dressing, toileting, walking, getting in and out of bed or a chair, and getting outside

Note that this last group of tasks, in addition to being a part of this listing, has special significance. These items have been used to develop a scale, called **Activities of Daily Living (ADLs),** to measure **functional limitations.** Functional limitation refers to the difficulty in performing personal care and home management tasks. However, ADLs do not cover all aspects of disability and are not sufficient by themselves to estimate the need for long-term care. As previously noted, some elders have cognitive impairments that are not measured by ADLs. An additional, commonly used measure called **Instrumental Activities of Daily Living (IADLs)** measures more complex tasks such as handling personal finances, preparing meals, shopping, doing housework, traveling, using the telephone, and taking medications.[13]

When elders begin to need help with one or more of these tasks, it is usually a spouse, adult children, or other family members who first provide the help, thus assuming the role of informal caregivers. An **informal caregiver** has been defined as one who provides unpaid care or assistance to one who has some physical, mental, emotional, or financial need that limits his or her independence.[2,42,43] It has been estimated that there are more than 7 million informal caregivers in the United States.[44] An informal caregiver can be either a care-provider or care-manager.[45] The **care-provider** helps identify the needs of the individual and personally performs the caregiving service. Obviously, this can only be done if the person in need and the caregiver live in close proximity to each other. The **care-manager** also helps to identify needs, but due to living some distance away or for other reasons, does not provide the service. The care-manager makes arrangements for someone else (volunteer or paid) to provide the services.

With the aging of the population, it is now highly probable that many, if not most, adults can expect to have some responsibility as caregivers for their parents (see Figure 9.12). Their role may be as care-provider, care-manager, or in making the decision to relocate their parents by bringing them into their home, moving them to a smaller home or apartment, or moving them into a group home. This is a relatively new task because many of the elders of today did not have to care for their parents. Life expectancy was much shorter, and most did not live long enough to be cared for by their adult children.

Activities of Daily Living (ADLs)
eating, toileting, dressing, bathing, walking, getting in and out of a bed or chair, and getting outside

functional limitations
difficulty in performing personal care and home management tasks

Instrumental Activities of Daily Living (IADLs)
more complex tasks such as handling personal finances, preparing meals, shopping, doing housework, traveling, using the telephone, and taking medications

informal caregiver
one who provides unpaid assistance to one who has some physical, mental, emotional, or financial need limiting his or her independence

care-provider
one who helps identify the health care needs of an individual and also personally performs the caregiving service

FIGURE 9.12
Adult children are gaining greater responsibility as caregivers.

Caregivers for elders face a number of problems, including decreased personal freedom, lack of privacy, constant demands on their time and energy, resentment that siblings do not share in the caregiving, and an increased financial burden. Many experience feelings of guilt for asking a spouse to help with the care of an in-law, or in knowing that the end of caregiving responsibilities usually means either the elder person's death or placement in a group home. Caregivers often experience a change in lifestyle, especially associated with time for leisure and recreation.[2,41,45,46] Caregiving can also lead to a negative impact on health.[15]

And yet even this onerous task of caregiving has its intimate qualities. One study of older caregivers reported that more than 70% of caregivers had positive feelings toward at least one aspect of caregiving for an older adult.[47] Some of the positive aspects included companionship, fulfillment, enjoyment, and the satisfaction of meeting an obligation. In addition, caregivers are typically not isolated in their role. One study reported that 88% of caregivers had social support from others who helped them with their caregiving responsibilities.[48]

The need for personal care for elders is projected to increase in the coming years. The primary responsibility for providing and financing this care will fall on the family. Due to the financial burden, more families will begin purchasing long-term health care insurance policies. These policies are very expensive if purchased after age 75 but do provide elders with sufficient income protection against the depletion of assets.[34] However, the high premium and co-payment costs of long-term care insurance policies mean that most Americans cannot afford them unless they are willing to purchase them when they are quite young and the costs are considerably more modest. In actuality, though, most policies are bought by people later on in life, when the risk of needing long-term care is great. Not surprisingly, therefore, it is estimated that 50% of long-term care insurance policies lapse due to high premiums.[49]

care-manager
one who helps identify the health care needs of an individual but does not actually provide the health care services

To assist caregivers, federal legislation was passed called the Older Americans Act Amendments of 2000 (Public Law 106-501). This law established the National Family Caregiver Support Program (NFCSP), which has been administered by the Administration on Aging (AoA) of the U.S. Department of Health and Human Services. It was modeled in large part after successful state long-term care programs in California, New Jersey, Wisconsin, Pennsylvania, and others, and after listening to the needs expressed by hundreds of family caregivers in discussions held across the country. The program calls for all states, working in partnership with area agencies on aging and local community-service providers, to have the following five basic services for family caregivers:

- Information to caregivers about available services
- Assistance to caregivers in gaining access to services
- Individual counseling, organization of support groups, and caregiver training to assist them in making decisions and solving problems relating to their caregiving roles
- Respite care to enable caregivers to be temporarily relieved from their caregiving responsibilities
- Supplemental services, on a limited basis, to complement the care provided by caregivers

Health Care

Health care is a major issue for all segments of our society, particularly for elders. While significant progress has been made in extending life expectancy, a longer life does not necessarily mean a healthier life. Health problems naturally increase with age. With these problems comes a need for increased health care services.

Elders are the heaviest users of health care services. Twenty-five percent of elders have 10 or more visits a year to a physician, compared with 13% for all people in the United States.[50] They are also hospitalized more often and for longer stays. Although persons 65 years of age and older only represented 13% of the total population in 2001, they accounted for 37% of the roughly 33 million patient discharges from non-federal short-stay hospitals,[50] and they spend over three times as much per person on prescription drugs as those under 65 years of age.[1] In addition, elders have higher usage rates for professional dental care, vision aids, and medical equipment and supplies than people under age 65. Usage of health care services increases with age, and much of the money spent on health care is spent in the last year of life.

While private sources, such as employer-paid insurance, are the major sources of health care payment for people under age 65, public funds are used to pay for the majority of the health care expenses for elders. Medicare, which was enacted in 1965 and became effective July 1, 1966, provides almost universal health insurance coverage for elders. Medicare coverage, however, is biased toward hospital care, while chronic care health needs such as eyeglasses (see Figure 9.13), hearing aids, and most long-term services are not covered.

In 2001, the Medicare program had 40 million enrollees and expenditures of almost $245 billion.[1] With the increasing cost of health care and the aging population, these numbers will only grow. Of those elders covered in 2001, about 10% were covered by Medicare only, while the other 90% were covered by both Medicare and a private insurance to supplement their Medicare coverage.[1] This private insurance is referred to as *Medigap*, because it helps to fill the gaps in health care cost that Medicare leaves. In addition, Medicaid, a federal-state program that was also approved in 1965, helps to cover the health care costs of poor elders, primarily for nursing home care (continuing care), home health care, and prescription drugs. In 2001,

FIGURE 9.13
Medicare provides almost universal health insurance for elders.

about 6% of the elders were covered by both Medicare and Medicaid.[1] (See Chapter 14 for a complete discussion of Medicare, Medicaid, and Medigap.)

All indications are that the health care costs for elders will continue to escalate because of the aging population and rising health care costs. Future legislators will be forced to choose from among the following alternatives: (1) raising taxes to pay for the care, (2) reallocating tax dollars from other programs to pay for care, (3) cutting back on coverage presently offered, (4) offering care to only those who truly cannot afford it otherwise (also known as *means testing*), or (5) completely revamping the present system under which the care is funded.

In the meantime, the importance of instilling in Americans the value of preventing the onset of chronic diseases through healthy living cannot be overstated. While it is not possible to prevent all chronic health problems, encouraging healthy behaviors is a step in the right direction.

Transportation

The National Institute on Aging estimates that 600,000 people aged 70 and older give up their driving each year. On average, elders live about 10 years after they stop driving.[51] There is little guidance, however, not only on when to stop driving, but also on how to compensate for no longer having personal control over one's transportation.

Transportation is of prime importance to elders because it enables them to remain independent. "Housing, medical, financial and social services are useful only to the extent that transportation can make them accessible to those in need."[52] The two factors that have the greatest effect on the transportation needs of elders are income and health status. Some elders who have always driven their own automobiles eventually find that they are no longer able to do so. The ever-increasing costs of purchasing and maintaining an automobile sometimes become prohibitive on a fixed income. Also, with age comes physical problems that restrict one's ability to operate an automobile safely. In addition, those with extreme disabilities may find that they will need a modified automobile (to accommodate their disability) or specialized transportation (e.g., a vehicle that can accommodate a wheelchair) in order to be transported.

With regard to transportation needs, elders can be categorized into three different groups: (1) those who can use the present forms of transportation, whether it be their own vehicle or public transportation, (2) those who could use public transportation if the barriers of cost and access (no service available) were removed, and (3) those who need special services beyond what is available through public transportation.[34]

The unavailability of transportation services has stimulated a number of private and public organizations that serve elders (e.g., churches, community services, and local area agencies on aging) to provide these services. Some communities even subsidize the cost of public transportation by offering reduced rates for elders. While these services have been helpful to elders, mobility is still more difficult for elders than for other adults. Try to imagine what it would be like if you had to depend constantly on someone else for all your transportation needs.

The ideal solution to the transportation needs of elders, according to Atchley, would include four components: (1) fare reductions or discounts for all public transportation, including that for interstate travel, (2) subsidies to ensure adequate scheduling and routing of present public transportation, (3) subsidized taxi fares for the disabled and infirm, and (4) funds for senior centers to purchase and equip vehicles to transport seniors properly, especially in rural areas.[34]

Community Facilities and Services

As has been mentioned previously, one of the most common occurrences of the aging process is loss of independence. Even some of the most basic activities of adults become major tasks for elders because of low income, ill health, and lack of transportation. Because of the limitations of elders and the barriers they must face, they have special needs in regard to community facilities and services. If these needs are met, the lifestyles of elders are greatly enhanced. If not, they are confronted with anything from a slight inconvenience to a very poor quality of life.

Older Americans Act of 1965 federal legislation to improve the lives of elders

With a view toward improving the lives of elders, Congress enacted the **Older Americans Act of 1965** and has amended it several times. Among the programs created by key amendments are the national nutrition program for elders, the State and Area Agencies on Aging, and other programs (e.g., the caregiver program discussed earlier) to increase the services and protect the rights of elders.

Though the initial act was important, the services and facilities available to elders were greatly improved after the passage of the 1973 amendments, which established the State Departments on Aging and Area Agencies on Aging. These systems inform, guide, and link older persons to available, appropriate, and acceptable services in order to meet their needs. The amendments were written to provide the state and area agencies with the flexibility to develop plans that allow for local variations. In 2001, there were 57 State Units on Aging and 655 Area Agencies on Aging within the United States.[53]

With each part of the country—and for that matter each community—having its own peculiarities, the services available to elders can vary greatly from one community to another. Even the names of the local agencies (few of which are called Area Agency on Aging) can vary a great deal, and it may require a phone call to the National Association of Area Agencies on Aging (202-296-8130) to locate your local Area Agency on Aging.

It is important to keep in mind, however, that the growth in our nation's elder population, combined with this population's financial ability to pay for service, has created an entrepreneurial atmosphere surrounding adult care services. In some larger communities, or in those communities with a large number of elder residents, the range of services can be astonishing.[2] In the following text, we provide brief descriptions of facilities and services available in many communities.

FIGURE 9.14

Congregate meals programs are not only valuable because of the enhanced nutrition but also because of the social interaction.

Meal Service

The 1972 amendments to the Older Americans Act outlined a national nutrition program for elders and provided funds for communities to establish meal services. Today's meal services are provided through home-delivered meal and congregate meal programs. The concept of the home-delivered meal programs (often known as **Meals on Wheels**) is the regular delivery of meals—usually once a day, five to seven days per week—to elders in their homes. These meals are prepared in a central location, sometimes in a hospital, school, or senior center, and are delivered by community volunteers.

Congregate meal programs are provided for individuals who can travel to a central site, often within senior centers or publicly funded housing units. Usually, it is the noon meal that is provided. Generally, these meals are funded by federal and state monies and make use of commodity food services.[2] In recent years, congregate meal programs seem to be gaining favor over home-delivered meal programs because they also provide social interaction (see Figure 9.14) and the opportunity to tie in with other social services.[34] However, there will always be a segment of the population requiring home-delivered meals because of their homebound status.

Both types of meal programs are strictly regulated by federal and state guidelines to ensure that the meals meet standard nutritional requirements. The cost of the meals varies by site and client income level. Elders may pay full price, pay a portion of the cost, or just make a voluntary contribution.

Meals on Wheels a community-supported nutrition program in which prepared meals are delivered to elders in their homes, usually by volunteers

congregate meal programs community-sponsored nutrition programs that provide meals at a central site, such as a senior center

Homemaker Service

For a number of elders, periodic homemaker services can be the critical factor enabling them to remain in their own homes. For these elders, physical impairment restricts their ability to carry out normal housekeeping activities such as house cleaning, laundry, and meal preparation. The availability of these services allows many elders to live semi-independently and delays their moving in with relatives or into group housing.

Chore and Home Maintenance Service

Chore and home maintenance service includes such services as yard work, cleaning gutters and windows, installing screens and storm windows, making minor plumbing and electrical repairs, maintaining furnaces and air conditioners, and helping to adapt a home to any impairments seniors might have. This adaptation may include provisions for wheelchairs and installing ramps or special railings to assist elders to move from one area to another.

Visitor Service

visitor services
one individual taking time to visit with another who is unable to leave his or her residence

Social interaction and social contacts are an important need for every human being, regardless of age. **Visitor services** amount to one individual taking time to visit with another person who is **homebound**, or unable to leave his or her residence. This service is usually done on a voluntary basis, many times with elders doing the visiting, and serves both the homebound and those who are institutionalized. It is not uncommon for church or social organizations to conduct a visitor program for homebound members.

homebound
a person unable to leave home for normal activities

Adult Day Care Service

adult day care programs
daytime care provided to elders who are unable to be left alone

Adult day care programs provide care during the daytime hours for elders who are unable to be left alone. These services are modeled after child day care services. Most programs offer meals, snacks, and social activities for the clients. Some either provide or make arrangements for the clients to receive therapy, counseling, health education, or other health services. Other day care programs are designed for elders with special needs, such as Alzheimer clients, the blind, or veterans. Adult day care programs allow families to continue with daytime activities while still providing the primary care for a family member.

Respite Care Service

respite care
planned short-term care, usually for the purpose of relieving a full-time informal caregiver

Respite care is planned, short-term care. Such care allows families who provide primary care for an elder family member to leave their elder in a supervised care setting for anywhere from a day to a few weeks. Respite services provide full care, including sleeping quarters, meals, bathing facilities, social activities, and the monitoring of medications.[2] This is the service most frequently requested by informal caregivers. (See the section on personal care earlier in chapter.) Such a program allows primary caregivers to take a vacation, visit other relatives, or to be otherwise relieved from their constant caregiving responsibilities.

Home Health Care Service

home health care services
health care services provided in the patient's place of residence

Home health care "is an important alternative to traditional institutional care. Services such as medical treatment, physical therapy, and homemaker services often allow patients to be cared for at lower cost than a nursing home or hospital and in familiar surroundings of their home."[13] These programs, run by official health agencies like the local health department, hospitals, or private companies, provide a full range of services, including preventive, primary, rehabilitative, and therapeutic services, in the client's home. The care is often provided by nurses, home health aides, and personal care workers (licensed health care workers). About half of all home health care expenditures are paid for by Medicare,[13] with a significant portion of the other half being paid for by families out of pocket. Other means of paying for this care could include long-term care insurance policies, Medicaid, or reimbursement by Medigap.

Senior Centers

The enactment of the Older Americans Act of 1965 provided funds to develop multipurpose senior centers, facilities where elders can congregate for fellowship, meals, education, and recreation. More recently, a number of communities have built senior centers with local tax dollars. Senior centers are widespread in the United States and are the most common community facility aimed at serving seniors.[34] However, they are found much less commonly in rural areas.

In addition to the traditional services (meals, fellowship, and recreation) offered at senior centers, some communities use the centers to serve as a central location for offering a variety of other senior services, including legal assistance, income counseling, income tax return assistance, program referrals, employment services, and other appropriate services and information.

Other Services

There are many other services available to seniors in some communities. Usually, larger communities and those with more seniors provide a greater variety of services. The types of services provided in any one community are limited only by the creativity of those providing the service. Conner even reports that in some communities, "service packages" are being offered.[2] Such packages allow seniors to pick several services they need and to pay for them as if they were a single service.

CHAPTER SUMMARY

- The median age of the U.S. population is at an all-time high and will continue to increase through the first third of this century.

- There are many myths about the elderly population.

- The increasing median age is impacted by decreasing fertility rates, declining mortality rates, and the decline in immigration.

- We are now at a point in history when a significant portion of Americans will assume some responsibility for the care of their aging parents.

- One of the most common occurrences of the aging process is the loss of independence.

- An aging population presents the community with several concerns, which means legislators and taxpayers will be faced with decisions about how best to afford the costs (Social Security, government employee pensions, Medicare, etc.) of an ever-increasing elderly support ratio.

- Communities will also need to deal with the special needs of income, housing, personal care, health care, transportation, and community facilities and services for elders.

- All projections indicate that the incomes of seniors will remain lower than those of the general population, that the need for affordable and accessible housing will increase, that there will be increased needs for personal services and care, that health care needs and costs will increase, and that the demand for barrier-free transportation will increase for elders.

- The growth in our nation's elder population, combined with this population's financial ability to pay for service, has created an entrepreneurial atmosphere surrounding adult care services.

REVIEW QUESTIONS

1. What are some signs, visible to the average person, that the U.S. population is aging?

2. What years of life are defined by each of the following groups—old, young old, old old, and oldest old?

3. What is meant by the terms *aged, aging, elder, gerontology,* and *geriatrics*?

4. Why is it that there is a myth that old people are sickly?

5. What are demographers? What do they do?

6. Why does a pyramid represent the age characteristics of the U.S. population of the 1950s?

7. What are the three factors that affect the size and age of a population?

8. How have life expectancy figures changed over the years in the United States? What were the major reasons for the change in the first half of the twentieth century? The second half?

9. Why are support and labor-force ratios so important?

10. How are support and labor-force ratios calculated?

11. Are all elders the same in regard to demographic variables? If not, how do they differ?

12. How do the income needs of people change in retirement?

13. Why do adults feel so guilty when they have to relocate their aged parents?

14. What is the difference between a care-provider and a care-manager?

15. What are some of the major problems caregivers face?

16. Why are continuing-care retirement communities so attractive to elders?

17. What is an assisted living residence?

SCENARIO: ANALYSIS AND RESPONSE

1. Based upon what you read in this chapter, how would you predict that Carl and Sarah's lives might progress over the next 20 years? Consider the six instrumental needs presented in the chapter.

2. What could Carl and Sarah have done when they were working to better plan for their retirement?

3. If you had to give Carl and Sarah two pieces of health care advice, what would they be?

18. What is the difference between Activities of Daily Living (ADLs) and Instrumental Activities of Daily (IADLs)?

19. What are the most frequently occurring health problems of elders?

20. From what financial sources do elders normally pay for health care?

21. What does the term *Medigap* mean?

22. How do income and health status impact the transportation needs of elders?

23. What is the ideal solution for the transportation needs of elders?

24. What are State Departments on Aging and Area Agencies on Aging?

25. Why is a visitor service so important for homebound and institutionalized persons?

26. What is the difference between adult day care and respite care?

ACTIVITIES

1. Make arrangements with a local long-term care facility to visit one of their residents. Make at least three one-hour visits to a resident over a six-week period of time. Upon completion of the visits, write a paper that answers the following questions:

   What were your feelings when you first walked into the facility?

   What were your feelings when you first met the resident?

   What did you learn about the elderly that you did not know before?

   What did you learn about yourself because of this experience?

   Did your feeling about the resident change during the course of your visits? If so, how?

   If you had to live in a long-term care facility, how would you be able to adjust to it? What would be most difficult for you in your adjustment? What character traits do you have that would help you adjust?

2. Interview a retired person over the age of 65. In your interview, include the following questions. Write a two-page paper about this interview.

   What are your greatest needs as an elder?

   What are your greatest fears connected with aging?

   What are your greatest joys at this stage in your life?

   If you could have done anything differently when you were younger to impact your life now, what would it have been?

   Have you had any problems getting health care with Medicare? If so, what were they? Do you have a Medigap policy? If so, has your Medigap policy been worth the cost?

   In what ways are you able to contribute to your community?

3. Spend a half-day at a local senior center. Then, write a paper that (a) summarizes your experience, (b) identifies your reaction (personal feelings) to the experience, and (c) shares what you have learned from the experience.

4. Review a newspaper obituary column for 14 consecutive days. Using the information provided in the obituaries: (a) demographically describe those who died, (b) keep track of what community services are noted, and (c) consider what generalizations can be made from the group as a whole.

COMMUNITY HEALTH ON THE WEB

The Internet contains a wealth of information about community and public health. Increase your knowledge of some of the topics presented in this chapter by accessing the Jones and Bartlett Publishers Web site at **health.jbpub.com/communityhealth/5e** and follow the links to complete the following Web activities.

- American Association of Retired Persons
- Administration on Aging
- National Institute on Aging

REFERENCES

1. Freid, V. M., K. Prager, A. P. MacKay, and H. Xia (2003). *Health, United States, 2003, with Chartbook on Trends in Health of Americans.* Hyattsville, MD: National Center for Health Statistics.

2. Conner, K. A. (1992). *Aging America: Issues Facing an Aging Society.* Englewood Cliffs, NJ: Prentice Hall.

3. U.S. Department of Health and Human Services (1986). *Age Words: A Glossary on Health and Aging* (NIH pub. no. 86-1849). Washington, DC: U.S. Government Printing Office.

4. Ferrini, A. F., and R. L. Ferrini (2000). *Health in the Later Years,* 3rd ed. Boston: McGraw-Hill Higher Education.

5. Dychtwald, K., and J. Flower (1989). *Age Wave: The Challenges and Opportunities of an Aging America.* Los Angeles: Jeremy P. Tarcher.

6. Thomlinson, R. (1976). *Population Dynamics: Causes and Consequences of World Demographic Change.* New York: Random House.

7. Centers for Disease Control and Prevention (2001). *CDC Fact Book 2000/2001.* Available at http://www.cdc.gov/maso/factbook/main.htm.

8. Federal Interagency Forum on Aging-Related Statistics (2001). *Older Americans 2000: Key Indicators of Well-Being.* Available at http://www.agingstats.gov/chartbook2000/default.htm.

9. Day, J. C. (1996). *Population Projections of the United States by Age, Sex, Race, and Hispanic Origin: 1995 to 2050* (Current Population Reports P25-1130). Washington, DC: U.S. Bureau of the Census.

10. U.S. Bureau of the Census (1996). *65+ in the United States* (Current Population Reports P23-190). Washington, DC: U.S. Government Printing Office.

11. Rosenwaike, I. (1985). *The Extreme Aged in America: A Portrait of an Expanding Population.* London: Greenwood Press.

12. Schulz, J. H., A. Borowski, and W. H. Crown (1991). *Economics of Population Aging: The "Graying" of Australia, Japan, and the United States.* New York: Auburn House.

13. Kramarow, E. H., H. Lentzner, R. Rooks, J. Weeks, and S. Saydah (1999). *Health and Aging Chartbook: Health United States, 1999* (HHS pub. no. PHS-99-123-1). Hyattsville, MD: National Center for Health Statistics.

14. U.S. Department of Health and Human Services (1991). *Aging America: Trends and Projections* (HHS pub. no. FCOA-91-28001). Washington, DC: U.S. Government Printing Office.

15. Hooyman, N., and H. Kiyak (2002). *Social Gerontology: A Multidisciplinary Perspective.* Boston: Allyn and Bacon.

16. Social Security Administration (2003). *Fast Facts & Figures about Social Security.* Available at http://www.ssa.gov/policy/docs/chartbooks/fast_facts/2003/ff2003.pdf.

17. U.S. Department of Housing and Urban Development, Office of Policy Development and Research (1999). *Housing Our Elders.* Washington, DC: Author.

18. Naifeh, M. L. (1993). *Housing of the Elderly: 1991* (Current Housing Reports Series H123/93-1). Washington, DC: U.S. Government Printing Office.

19. Blair, S., et al. (2001). "Physical Fitness and All-Cause Mortality: A Prospective Study of Healthy Men and Women." *Journal of the American Medical Association,* 262: 2395-2401.

20. LaCroix, A., et al. (1996). "Does Walking Decrease the Risk of Cardiovascular Disease Hospitalization and Death in Older Adults?" *Journal of the American Geriatrics Society,* 44: 113-120.

21. Manson, J., et al. (1999). "A Prospective Study of Walking as Compared with Vigorous Exercise in the Prevention of Coronary Heart Disease in Women." *New England Journal of Medicine,* 341: 650-658.

22. Lan, C., et al. (1999). "The Effect of Tai Chi on Cardiorespiratory Function in Patients with Coronary Artery Bypass Surgery." *Medical Science Sports Exercise,* 31: 634-638.

23. Tanassescu, M., et al. (2002). "Exercise Type and Intensity in Relation to Coronary Heart Disease in Men." *Journal of the American Medical Association,* 288: 1994-2000.

24. Vincent, K., et al. (2002). "Resistance Exercise and Physical Performance in Adults Aged 60 to 83." *Journal of the American Geriatrics Society,* 50: 1100-1107.

25. Kelley, G., and K. Kelley (2000). "Progressive Resistance Exercise and Resting Blood Pressure: A Meta-analysis of Randomized Controlled Trials." *Hypertension,* 35: 838-843.

26. Kraus, W., et al. (2002). "Effects of the Amount and Intensity of Exercise on Plasma Lipoproteins." *New England Journal of Medicine,* 347: 1483-1492.

27. Prabhakaran, B., et al. (1999). "Effect of 14 Weeks of Resistance Training on Lipid Profile and Body Fat Percentage in Premenopausal Women." *British Journal of Sports Medicine,* 33: 190-195.

28. Brooks, J. (May 2000). "Immunizations: Not Just for the Young." *Closing the Gap,* 10-12.

29. Haber, D. (2003). *Health Promotion and Aging: Practical Applications for Health Professionals,* 3rd ed. New York: Springer Publishing.

30. Mieczkowski, T., and S. Wilson. (2002). "Adult Pneumococcal Vaccination: A Review of Physician and Patient Barriers." *Vaccine,* 20: 1383-1392.

31. Schneider, E., et al. (2001). "Racial Disparity in Influenza Vaccination." *Journal of the American Medical Association,* 286: 1455-1460.

32. Administration on Aging (2001). "Elder Abuse Prevention." Available at http://www.aoa.gov/Factsheets/abuse.htm.

33. Administration on Aging (2001). *The National Elder Abuse Incidence Study.* Available at http://www.aoa.gov/abuse/report/Cexecsum.htm.

34. Atchley, R. C. (1994). *Social Forces and Aging: An Introduction to Social Gerontology,* 7th ed. Belmont, CA: Wadsworth.

35. Social Security Administration (2004). *Monthly Statistical Snapshot.* Available at http://www.ssa.gov/policy/docs/quickfacts/stat_snapshot/index.html.

36. Harrington, C., et al. (2001). "Does Investor Ownership of Nursing Homes Compromise the Quality of Care?" *American Journal of Public Health,* 91: 1452-1455.

37. Thomas, W. (1995). *The Eden Alternative.* Acton, MA: VanderWyk & Burnham.

38. Borup, J. H. (1981). "Relocation: Attitudes, Information Network and Problems Encountered." *The Gerontologist,* 21: 501-511.

39. The Assisted Living Federation of America (2004). *What Is Assisted Living?* Available at http://www.alfa.org/public/articles/details.cfm?id=126.

40. Hawes, C., M. Rose, and O. S. Phillips (1999). *A National Study of Assisted Living for the Frail Elderly. Executive Summary: Results of a National Survey of Facilities.* Available at http://aspe.os.dhhs.gov/daltcp/reports/facreses.htm.

41. Brody, E. M., and C. B. Schooner (1986). "Patterns of Parent-Care When Adult Daughters Work and When They Do Not." *The Gerontologist,* 26: 372-381.

42. U.S. House of Representatives, Select Committee on Aging (October 1987). *Long-Term Care and Personal Impoverishment: Seven in Ten Elderly Living Alone Are at Risk.* Washington, DC: U.S. Government Printing Office.

43. Horowitz, A. (1985). "Sons and Daughters as Caregivers to Older Parents: Differences in Role Performance and Consequences." *The Gerontologist,* 25: 612-617.

44. Oxendine, J. (May 2000). "Who Is Helping the Care Givers?" *Closing the Gap,* 4.

45. Archbold, P. G. (1983). "Impact of Parent-Caring on Women." *Family Relations,* 32: 39–45.

46. Kleban, M. H., E. M. Brody, C. B. Schoonover, and C. Hoffman (1989). "Family Help to the Elderly: Perceptions of Sons-in-Law Regarding Parent Care." *Journal of Marriage and the Family,* 51: 303–312.

47. Cohen, C., et al. (2002). "Positive Aspects of Caregiving: Rounding Out the Caregiver Support System." *The Gerontologist,* 35: 489–497.

48. Penrod, et al. (1995). "Who Cares? The Size, Scope, and Composition of the Care Giver Support System." *The Gerontologist,* 35: 489–497.

49. Weiner, J., and L. Illston (1996). "Financing and Organization of Health Care." In R. Binstock and L. George, eds., *Handbook of Aging and the Social Sciences,* 4th ed. San Diego: Academic Press.

50. U.S. Bureau of the Census (2003). *Statistical Abstract of the United States, 2003,* 123rd ed. Washington, DC: Author.

51. Foley, D., et al. (2002). "Driving Life Expectancy of Persons Aged 70 Years and Older in the United States." *American Journal of Public Health,* 92: 1284–1289.

52. Administration on Aging (2001). *Transportation and the Elderly.* Available at http://www.aoa.gov/may98/transportation.html.

53. Administration on Aging (2001). "Older Americans Act Information and Assistance Systems and Services." Available at http://www.aoa.gov/may2001/factsheets/oaa%Dianda%Dsystems.html.

Chapter 10

Community Health and Minorities

Chapter Objectives

After studying this chapter, you should be able to:

1 Explain the concept of diversity as it describes the American people.

2 Explain the impact of a more diverse population in the United States as it relates to community health efforts.

3 Explain the importance of the 1985 landmark report, *The Secretary's Task Force Report on Black and Minority Health.*

4 List the racial and ethnic categories currently used by the U.S. government in statistical activities and program administration reporting.

5 List some limitations related to collecting racial and ethnic health data.

6 Identify some of the sociodemographic and socio-economic characteristics of minority groups in the United States.

7 List some of the beliefs and values of minority groups in the United States.

8 List and describe the six priority areas of the *Race and Health Initiative.*

9 Define *socioeconomic gradient* and provide an example as it relates to minority health.

10 Define *cultural sensitivity* and *cultural and linguistic competence* and the importance of each related to minority community health.

11 Identify the three kinds of power associated with empowerment and explain the importance of each related to minority community health.

SCENARIO

Tom just returned from a cross-country business trip that took him from New York City to Miami, to San Antonio, to Los Angeles, and back to his Midwest hometown, Middletown, U.S.A. When his curious teenage children asked him to tell them about the people who live in the "big cities," he began by saying, "There seem to be more minorities and foreigners in the cities than before. I heard at least five or six different languages spoken. Signs in the hotels and in the storefronts are written in at least two, and sometimes three or four languages.

"Another thing that always amazes me is the number of ethnic restaurants. Here, we have just one Mexican, one Italian, and one Chinese restaurant, but in New York City and other big cities there are hundreds of restaurants serving foods from other cultures. I get the feeling that the United States is more culturally diverse than at anytime in its past, even when it was considered the 'melting pot' for the world's populations."

INTRODUCTION

The strength and greatness of America lies in the diversity of its people. Over the centuries, wave after wave of immigrants have come to America to start new lives. They have brought with them many of their traditions and cultures. However, it is recognized that even as America rapidly becomes the world's first truly multiracial democracy, race relations remains an issue that too often divides the Nation and keeps the American dream from becoming a reality for all Americans. In 1997, former President Bill Clinton announced "One America in the 21st Century: The President's Initiative on Race."[1] This initiative was a critical element in an effort to prepare the country to live as one America in the twenty-first century and was based on opportunity for all, responsibility for all, and one community for all Americans. The goal of Clinton's "Initiative on Race" was to strengthen our shared foundation as Americans so we can all live in an atmosphere of trust and understanding. Every American must invest in creating "One America," so that as a nation, people can effectively act together to fulfill the promise of the American dream in the twenty-first century. As we progress through the twenty-first century, we must continue to recognize that the strength and greatness of America lies in the diversity or "differences" of its people (see Figure 10.1). The failure to understand and appreciate these "differences" can have serious implications not only with race relations, but also when it comes to improving the health of diverse communities.

majority
those with characteristics that are found in over 50% of a population

minority groups
subgroups of the population that consist of less than 50% of the population

minority health
refers to the morbidity and mortality of American Indians/Alaska Natives, Americans of Hispanic origin, Asians and Pacific Islanders, and black Americans in the United States

Today in the United States, the **majority** of Americans (69.1%) are referred to as "white, non-Latino." The remaining 30.9% of the U.S. population are members of what is traditionally viewed as racial or ethnic **minorities** (see Figure 10.2). Accordingly, **minority health** refers to the morbidity and mortality of American Indians/Alaska Natives, Asian Americans and Pacific Islanders, black Americans, and Hispanics in the United States. Current projections suggest that the U.S. population will become increasingly diverse. By 2050, nearly one-half of the U.S. population will be composed of racial minorities (see Figure 10.3). Thus, by the middle of this century, the number of persons considered as members of a minority group will have nearly doubled.[2] The impact of a more diverse population in the United States in relation to community health efforts connected with minorities will be important based on what we learned about our past. "The health status of the nation as a whole has improved significantly during the twentieth century. Advances in medical technology, lifestyle improvements, and environmental protections have all led to health gains. Yet these changes have not produced equal benefit in some racial and ethnic populations. This is the continuing challenge to public health professionals and the standard we must keep in mind when measuring our progress: what is the health status of the least empowered among us?"[3] As the racial and ethnic

FIGURE 10.1
The strength and greatness of America lies in the diversity of its people.

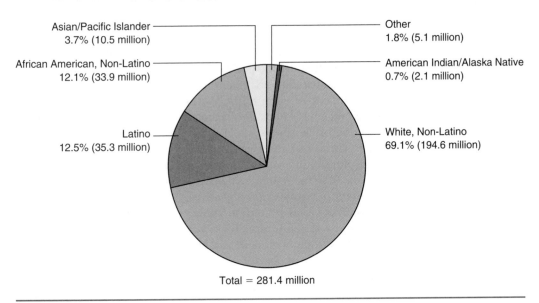

Asian/Pacific Islander
3.7% (10.5 million)

Other
1.8% (5.1 million)

African American, Non-Latino
12.1% (33.9 million)

American Indian/Alaska Native
0.7% (2.1 million)

Latino
12.5% (35.3 million)

White, Non-Latino
69.1% (194.6 million)

Total = 281.4 million

FIGURE 10.2
Percent distribution of U.S. population by race/ethnicity, 2000.

Note: Data do not include residents of Puerto Rico, Guam, the U.S. Virgin Islands, or the Northern Marina Islands. Non-Latino individuals who reported "Some other race" or "Two or more races" are included in the "Other" category. For the purposes of this chart, Asians and Native Hawaiians or Other Pacific Islanders are combined into one category.

Source: U.S. Census Bureau, Census 2000 redistricting data.

minority groups currently experiencing poorer health status grow in proportion to the total U.S. population, the future health of all Americans will be influenced by the success in improving the health of these groups. It is the nature of health disparities among the least empowered (primarily minorities) that is the main focus of this chapter.

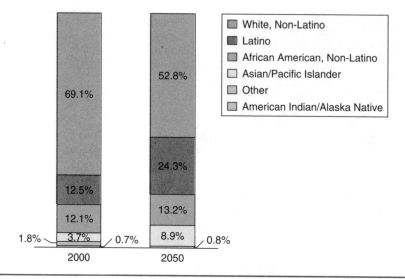

FIGURE 10.3

Percent distribution of U.S. population by race/ethnicity, 2000 and 2050.

Note: Data do not include residents of Puerto Rico, Guam, the U.S. Virgin Islands, or the Northern Marina Islands. 2050 data do not include estimates for the "Other" category, which includes non-Latino individuals who reported "Some other race" or "Two or more races."

Source: U.S. Census Bureau, Census 2000 redistricting data and Population Projections Program, Population Division.

A landmark 1985 report, *The Secretary's Task Force Report on Black and Minority Health,* first documented the health status disparities of minority groups in the United States.[4] This report provided substantial data documenting that minority populations, compared to the Nation as a whole, experience higher rates of morbidity and mortality. Specifically, the report identified six causes of death that accounted for more than 80% of the excess mortality observed among black Americans, Hispanics, Asian Americans and Pacific Islanders, and Native Americans. These six causes were infant mortality, cancer, cardiovascular disease and stroke, diabetes, homicide and accidents, and chemical dependency. *The Secretary's Task Force Report on Black and Minority Health* contributed significantly to the development of a number of *Healthy People 2000* objectives.[5] Work toward these objectives via the community health initiatives concentrated on minority populations produced some measurable decreases in age-adjusted death rates for seven specific causes of death (see Table 10.1). In an attempt to further document racial and ethnic changes over time in important Health Status Indicators (HSI), index of disparity measures are provided in Table 10.2 for 1990 and 1998. The index of disparity measure summarizes differences among racial and ethnic minority groups' rates to the total group. "This statistic provides a basis for comparing the degree of difference in race and ethnic specific rates in 1990 with the disparity in race/ethnic rates in 1998."[6] As shown in Table 10.2, there was a decline in 12 of the 17 HSIs. However, in some instances the disparities remained the same or in some cases widened, as evidenced by an increase in 5 of the 17 HSIs.

In 1998, then-President Clinton declared that the United States would continue to commit to a national goal of eliminating racial and ethnic health disparities by the year 2010.[7] Following this announcement, the *Initiative to Eliminate Racial and Ethnic Disparities in Health,* or the *Race and Health Initiative,* was launched. The purpose of this national effort was to enhance efforts in (1) preventing disease, (2) promoting health, and (3) delivering care to racial and ethnic minority communities. One of the primary aims of this initiative consists

Table 10.1
Age-Adjusted Death Rates for Selected Causes of Death by Race and Hispanic Origin, 1990 and 1998, and Percent Change from 1990 to 1998: United States

	Total	Non-Hispanic White	Non-Hispanic Black	Hispanic	American Indian or Alaska Native	Asian or Pacific Islander	Ratio Highest/ Lowest[2]
Total deaths							
1990[1]	518.0	483.7	785.2	395.2	441.7	295.5	2.7
1998	471.7	452.7	710.7	342.8	458.1	264.6	2.7
Percent change, 1990–98	−8.9	−6.4	−9.5	−13.3	3.7	−10.5	
Heart disease							
1990[1]	151.3	145.3	211.8	101.5	106.0	78.0	2.7
1998	126.6	123.6	188.0	84.2	97.1	67.4	2.8
Percent change, 1990–98	−16.3	−14.9	−11.2	−17.0	−8.4	−13.6	
Stroke							
1990[1]	27.5	25.1	47.8	20.7	19.1	24.7	2.5
1998	25.1	23.3	42.5	19.0	19.6	22.7	2.2
Percent change, 1990–98	−9.0	−7.2	−11.1	−8.2	2.6	−8.1	
Lung cancer							
1990[1]	39.8	39.8	50.9	15.7	19.6	17.6	3.2
1998	37.0	38.3	46.0	13.6	25.1	17.2	3.4
Percent change, 1990–98	−7.0	−3.8	−9.6	−13.4	28.1	−2.3	
Female breast cancer							
1990[1]	23.0	23.0	27.3	14.0	9.9	9.9	2.8
1998	18.8	18.7	26.1	12.1	10.3	9.8	2.7
Percent change, 1990–98	−18.3	−18.7	−4.4	−13.6	4.0	−1.0	
Motor vehicle crash							
1990[1]	18.4	18.1	18.3	19.2	33.0	12.5	2.6
1998	15.6	15.7	17.2	14.9	31.8	8.6	3.7
Percent change, 1990–98	−15.2	−13.3	−6.0	−22.4	−3.6	−31.2	
Suicide							
1990[1]	11.5	12.5	7.0	7.2	12.4	6.0	2.1
1998	10.4	11.8	6.1	6.0	13.4	5.9	2.3
Percent change, 1990–98	−9.6	−5.6	−12.9	−16.7	8.1	−1.7	
Homicide							
1990[1]	10.2	4.1	39.6	17.5	11.1	5.2	9.7
1998	7.3	3.2	26.1	9.9	9.9	3.7	8.2
Percent change, 1990–98	−28.4	−22.0	−34.1	−43.4	−10.8	−28.8	

[1]Age-adjusted death rates for 1990 were calculated based on population estimates for July 1, 1990. Rates published elsewhere for 1990 are based on the enumerated population on April 1, 1990, for the year in which the decennial census was taken. Rates for noncensus years are based on July 1 (midyear) populations. In order to measure changes over time, rates based on the July 1 populations are used.
[2]Ratio of the highest race/ethnic-specific rate to the lowest race/ethnic-specific rate for each year.

Source: Keppel, K. G., J. N. Pearcy, and D. K. Wagener (January 2002). *Trends in Racial and Ethnic-Specific Rates for the Health Status Indicators: United States 1990–1998* (Healthy People Statistical Notes no. 23). Hyattsville, MD: National Center for Health Statistics.

of consultation and collaboration among federal agencies; state, local, and tribal governments; and community professionals to research and address issues of education, income, environment, and other socioeconomic factors that affect health outcomes. Accordingly, the *Race and Health Initiative* is a paramount part of *Healthy People 2010*'s broad health goal to "eliminate health disparities among Americans."[8] This initiative will be addressed in more detail after a brief discussion on how racial and ethnic populations are classified.

Table 10.2
Index of Disparity among Five Racial/Ethnic Groups for the Health Status Indicators:
United States, 1990, 1998, and Percent Change

	Index of Disparity		Percent Change 1990–98	
	1990	1998	Decrease	Increase
Infant mortality rates	38.9	36.4	−6.4	
Low birth weight (percent)	28.4	23.0	−19.0**	
No prenatal care in first trimester (percent)	46.9	43.5	−7.2**	
Live birth rates for women aged 15–17 years	65.4	67.7		3.5**
Total death rates	27.9	25.8	−7.5**	
Heart disease death rates	31.1	30.9	−0.6**	
Stroke death rates	29.6	26.4	−10.8**	
Lung cancer death rates	39.0	35.4	−9.2**	
Female breast cancer death rates	34.3	33.6	−2.0	
Motor vehicle crash death rates	23.6	32.8		39.0**
Suicide death rates	28.2	33.8		19.9**
Homicide death rates	95.5	86.8	−9.1**	
Work-related injury death rates (1993–98)[1]	6.3	22.1		250.8[a]
Tuberculosis case rates	160.4	170.3		6.2[a]
Primary and secondary syphilis case rates	175.3	153.1	−12.7[a]	
Children under age 18 years in poverty (percent)[2]	64.7	56.2	−13.1	
Percentage with poor air quality (1992–1998)	31.1	29.5	−5.1[a]	

**The difference in the index of disparity is statistically significant at the 0.05 level.
[a]The statistical significance of the difference in the index of disparity was not tested. Methods for assessing the reliability of the underlying rates are not available.
[1]The index of disparity for work-related injury deaths is not strictly comparable with the index of disparity for the other indicators because the data are available for the following groups: white, black, Hispanic, American Indian, Aleut and Eskimo, and Asian or Pacific Islanders. Persons of Hispanic origin may be of any race.
[2]The index of disparity for the percentage of children in poverty is not strictly comparable with the index of disparity for the other indicators because the data are available for the following groups: white non-Hispanic, black, Hispanic, and Asian or Pacific Islander.

Source: Keppel, K. G., J. N. Pearcy, and D. K. Wagener (January 2002). *Trends in Racial and Ethnic-Specific Rates for the Health Status Indicators: United States 1990–1998* (Healthy People Statistical Notes no. 23). Hyattsville, MD: National Center for Health Statistics.

RACIAL AND ETHNIC CLASSIFICATIONS

It is standard practice for the federal government to describe participants and populations in terms of "race" or "ethnicity." The racial and ethnic categories are used in statistical activities and program administration reporting, including the monitoring and enforcement of civil rights. In the 1980s, the regulations used for the statistical classification of racial and ethnic groups by federal agencies were based on the 1978 publication by the Office of Management and Budget (OMB) of Directive 15 titled "Race and Ethnic Standards for Federal Statistics and Administrative Reporting."[9] This directive presented brief rules for classifying persons into four racial categories (American Indian or Alaskan Native, Asian or Pacific Islander, black, and white) and two ethnic categories (of Hispanic origin or not of Hispanic origin) (see Appendix 2). It required the categorization of blacks and whites into one of the two ethnic categories. Directive 15 was not intended to be scientific or anthropological in nature, but rather a way to **operationalize** race and ethnicity. The operational definitions detailed in Directive 15 provided the standards by which federal government agencies collected and classified racial and ethnic data in the 1980s and 1990s.

In the early 1990s, this classification system came under increasing criticism from those who asserted that the minimum categories set forth in Directive 15 did not reflect the increasing diversity of our Nation's population. In response to those criticisms, OMB committed to a comprehensive review process in the mid-1990s in collaboration with the Interagency Committee for the Review of the Racial and Ethnic Standards that would enhance the accuracy of the demographic information collected by the federal government. In 1997,

operationalize
(operational
definition) provide
working definitions

revised standards were issued.[10] These revised standards were used in the year 2000 decennial census. (See Appendix 3 for a listing of the operational definitions that were used by the Bureau of Census to collect the 2000 decennial census.) One of the first federal programs to support and adopt the revised standards was the Department of Health and Human Services (HHS). In October 1997, the Secretary of the HHS issued a policy supporting the inclusion of the new revised federal standards for racial and ethnic data for employment in the HHS data systems and consequently in developing and measuring *Healthy People 2010* objectives.

The 1997 classification standards expanded race from four to five categories by separating the "Asian or Pacific Islander" category into two categories—"Asian" and "Native Hawaiian or Other Pacific Islander." Additionally, the term "Hispanic" was changed to "Hispanic or Latino" and "Negro" can be used in addition to "Black or African American." Finally, the reporting of more than one race for multiracial persons was strongly encouraged, along with specifying that the Hispanic origin question should precede the race question. The Census 2000 form best illustrates these changes (see Figure 10.4). There are 15 check box response

FIGURE 10.4
U.S. Census 2000 form questions for race and ethnicity.

→ **NOTE: Please answer BOTH questions 7 and 8.**

7. **Is Person 1 Spanish/Hispanic/Latino?** *Mark* ☒ *the "No" box if* ***not*** *Spanish/Hispanic/Latino.*

- ☐ **No**, not Spanish/Hispanic/Latino
- ☐ Yes, Mexican, Mexican Am., Chicano
- ☐ Yes, other Spanish/Hispanic/Latino—*Print group.*
- ☐ Yes, Puerto Rican
- ☐ Yes, Cuban

8. **What is Person 1's race?** ***Mark*** ☒ ***one or more races*** *to indicate what this person considers himself/herself to be.*

- ☐ White
- ☐ Black, African Am., or Negro
- ☐ American Indian or Alaska Native—*Print name of enrolled or principal tribe.*

- ☐ Asian Indian
- ☐ Chinese
- ☐ Filipino
- ☐ Other Asian—*Print race.*
- ☐ Japanese
- ☐ Korean
- ☐ Vietnamese
- ☐ Native Hawaiian
- ☐ Guamanian or Chamorro
- ☐ Samoan
- ☐ Other Pacific Islander—*Print race.*

- ☐ Some other race—*Print race.*

→ **If more people live here, continue with Person 2.**

categories and three write-in areas on the Census 2000 questionnaire for indicating race and ethnicity. The Hispanic origin question (Question 7) is asked before the race question (Question 8), and "Asian and Pacific Islander" has been divided into two categories—"Asian" and "Native Hawaiian and Other Pacific Islander." There are six designated Asian and three specified Pacific Islander categories, as well as "Other Asian" and "Other Pacific Islander." Finally, the category "some other race," which was intended to gain responses such as Mulatto, Creole, and Mestizo, has a write-in area.

It is important to consider a couple of aspects related to the collecting of data on race and ethnicity. First, the categories of race are more of a social category than a biological one.[11] Although race historically has been viewed as a biological construct, it is now known to be more accurately characterized as a social category that has changed over time and varies across societies and cultures.[11,12] As you will read later in this chapter, numerous studies have shown that racial disparities in health generally do not mirror biologically determined differences in these groups.[13] Second, self-reported data regarding race and ethnicity may be unreliable because individuals of varied cultures and heritage and multiple races can have difficulty classifying their racial or ethnic identity on standardized forms. Third, many non-federal health data systems do not collect self-reported race or ethnicity data, or in some cases, it may be uncertain who recorded the race and ethnicity data. For example, in a medical care setting the information may be entered by clerical staff or hospital personnel. This can make analyzing health information concerning the health status of minorities a challenging task.

Health Data Sources and Their Limitations

The reporting of accurate and complete race and ethnicity data provides essential information to target and evaluate public health inventions aimed at minority populations.[14] However, because of the diversity in America's population, community health professionals and researchers have long recognized many crucial issues in the way that racial and ethnic variables are assessed in the collection, analysis, and dissemination of health information.[15] In the same manner, the HHS is aware of the serious gaps in its own information systems and databases regarding racial and ethnic data. For example, in a recent longitudinal study completed by the CDCs National Electronic Telecommunications System for Surveillance, it was found that data regarding a patient's race and ethnicity was received in only one-half of the cases of selected notifiable diseases.[14] In comparison, data on age and sex was reported between 95% to 99% of the time during that same period. According to the authors of the study, race and ethnicity may not be reported by health care providers for at least four reasons:[14]

1. Providers may not know what the federal standards for data collection are about race and ethnicity on their patients for surveillance purposes.
2. If a health care provider forgets or is reluctant to ask a patient's racial/ethnic background, this information may not be recorded.
3. Patients may choose not to provide information about their race and ethnicity.
4. Clinical laboratory staff may not report race and ethnicity data because they do not have access to that information.

In addition to incomplete data collection, there are many cases of *bias analysis*. Bias analysis occurs when two separate data reporting systems are used to obtain rates by race and Hispanic origin. An illustration of analysis bias that is currently happening is the misreporting of race and Hispanic origin in the numerator of deaths on death certificates combined with the underreporting in the denominator of the population subgroups.[16] As a consequence of the combined effect of numerator and denominator biases, it has been estimated that death rates for the white population are overestimated by about 1% and by 5% for the black

American population. At the same time, death rates are underestimated for the American Indian or Alaska Native population by nearly 21%, by 11% for Asian or Pacific Islanders, and by 2% for Hispanics.[16]

Collecting appropriate racial and ethnic data is a significant challenge facing public health. The HHS has developed a long-term strategy for improving the collection and use of racial and ethnic data throughout the department and its agencies and, more specifically, for the *Race and Health Initiative.*[17] The diversified aspects of this plan will require time and resources by the department and its agencies. One national health objective for 2010, which the HHS is overseeing, is the upgrading of data collection on race and ethnicity in public health surveys that use the self-reported race of the respondent. In addition, the HHS is working with health data systems that do not collect self-reported race or ethnicity on individuals, to do so. Increasing both the reliability and amount of data will assist in monitoring and assessing the outcomes related to meeting the proposed goal of eliminating racial and ethnic health disparities in *Healthy People 2010.* A standard data table will be used to display the baseline status of each subpopulation group by race and ethnicity (*American Indian* or *Alaska Native, Asian American, Pacific Islander, Black* or *African American, White, Hispanic* or *Latino,* or *Not Hispanic* or *Latino*) for each objective listed in *Healthy People 2010.*[8] Data will be presented for all minorities, whether or not a disparity exists when compared to the total population. It is believed that this approach will better identify missing data on racial and ethnic minorities and encourage further attempts by the appropriate agencies or community advocate groups to collect this information. For example, 157 (36%) of the 434 population-based *Healthy People 2010* objectives and subobjectives did not have data available for Hispanics in 2000.

Recognizing some of the limitations and gaps in collecting racial/ethnic data is important. Knowing that in some cases data are not available or the available data are not as precise as we would like, we present the best information about the community health issues faced by the primary minority groups. However, as you continue to read this chapter please be reminded of the limitations of the data on racial and ethnic minority groups. Finally, please note that throughout the remainder of the chapter we use the terms *Americans of Hispanic origin, Asian Americans, Pacific Islanders, black Americans, Native Americans,* and *white Americans,* unless there is a direct quotation or extrapolation from data or documents that use other terminology (e.g., *American Indians* in lieu of *Native Americans*).

Next, in order to gain a better understanding of minority groups in the United States, we will briefly review several sociodemographic and socioeconomic characteristics along with broad general health beliefs for each group. These characteristics will eventually be used to discuss why health disparities exist in minority groups later in the chapter. Furthermore, all cultural and ethnic groups hold concepts related to health and illness and associated practices for maintaining well-being or providing treatment when it is indicated. However, caution is needed to avoid stereotyping. There is a considerable amount of heterogeneity within these groups, and therefore making summary statements of cultural beliefs is difficult and can be questionable. The world's 210 nations are well represented in the United States, and these diverse cultures are continually being integrated and intermixed. Additionally, members of a cultural or ethnic group who are younger or more **acculturated** into mainstream America society may not adhere to popular and folk health beliefs.

acculturated
cultural modification of an individual or group by adapting to or borrowing traits from another culture

BLACK AMERICANS

In 2000, black Americans numbered 33.9 million and constituted 12.1% of the population, making them the second largest minority group in the Nation (see Figure 10.2).[18] Even though black Americans live in all regions of the United States, more than one-half live in the

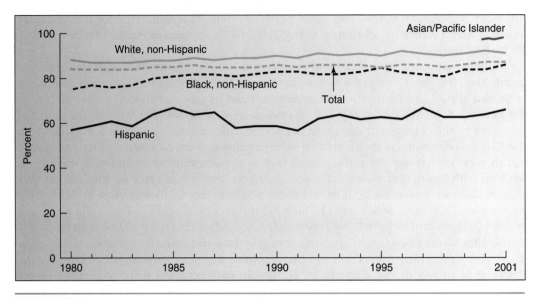

FIGURE 10.5

Percentage of adults aged 18 to 24 who have completed high school, by race and Hispanic origin, 1980 to 2001.

Note: Percentages are based only on those not currently enrolled in high school or below. Prior to 1992, this indicator was measured as completing four or more years of high school rather than the actual attainment of a high school diploma or equivalent.

Source: U.S. Census Bureau (2001). *October Current Population Survey.* Tabulated by the U.S. Department of Education, National Center for Education Statistics.

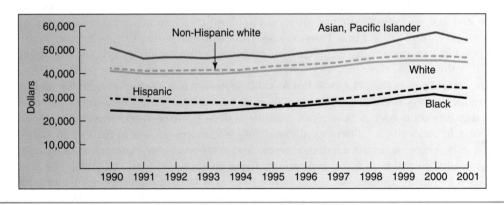

FIGURE 10.6

Median income of households by race and Hispanic origin, in constant 2001 dollars: 1990 to 2001.

Note: People of Hispanic origin may be of any race.

Source: U.S. Census Bureau (2002). *Statistical Abstract of the United States: 2003.* Washington, DC: U.S. Government Printing Office.

Southern regions of the United States. As mentioned earlier, disparities in health statistics among minorities can be traced to differences in education and income. A high school education is considered an essential basic training requirement to enter the labor force (see Figure 10.5). Black Americans have slightly lower high school graduation rates than white Americans.[19] Linked with education is earning power. The median income for black Americans has consistently ranked below all racial and ethnic groups (see Figure 10.6).[20] The poverty rate for black Americans fell to a record low in 2000, with less than one in four (22.0%) living in poverty (see Figure 10.7).[21] However, this record low was still three times higher than the poverty rate for white Americans.

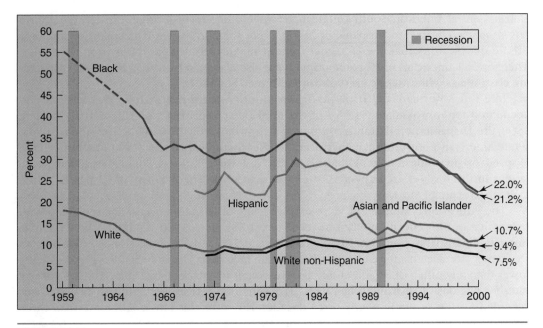

FIGURE 10.7

Poverty rates by race and Hispanic origin, 1959 to 2000.

Note: Rates are based on November 2001 weighting corrections. The data points represent the midpoints of the respective years. The latest recession began in July 1990 and ended in March 1991. Data for blacks are not available from 1960 to 1965. Data for the other race and Hispanic-origin groups are shown from the first year available. Hispanics may be of any race.

Source: U.S. Census Bureau (2002). *Current Population Survey, 1960–2001.* Washington, DC: U.S. Government Printing Office.

When discussing black American culture, it is important to mention the effect of slavery. Many cultural traits of black Americans can be traced back to the period when slavery was practiced in the United States. Owners of slaves provided health care to their slaves for several reasons. "One was that slaves not be allowed to malinger; another concern was for the owner's property; a third concern was preventing disease from spreading; and the fourth was an actual concern for the health of the slaves."[22] These concerns plus the law that forbade slaves from providing health care to each other with the threat of death, led to an underground system of health care by mostly untrained providers.

After the Civil War, poverty, discrimination, and poor living conditions led to a high prevalence of disease, disability, and death among black Americans.[23] Racial discrimination limited this group's access to adequate health care through the middle of the twentieth century, much as it did education and voting rights. This discrimination continues to have an impact on the health status of black Americans today. Many black Americans still find it difficult to gain access to health care because of discrimination. Lacking access to more formalized American health care, first by slavery and then by segregation and discrimination, many black Americans implemented traditional healing methods.[24] These traditional methods include curing illnesses with roots, herbs, barks, and teas by an individual knowledgeable about their use. Many black Americans continue to use traditional healing methods today because they are acceptable, available, and affordable.

AMERICANS OF HISPANIC ORIGIN

As we begin our discussion of Americans of Hispanic origin, readers are reminded that Hispanic origin is an ethnicity classification, not a race. The term *Hispanic* was introduced by the OMB in 1977, creating an ethnic category that included persons of Mexican, Puerto Rican,

Cuban, Central American, South American, or some other Spanish origin.[9] In 1997, the term *Hispanic* was changed to "Hispanic or Latino."[10] For the purposes of data collection, the only ethnic distinctions that the U.S. government makes are "Hispanic" or "non-Hispanic." Therefore, all Americans of Hispanic origin were also classified by a race. Nearly all Hispanics are classified as white Americans (96%) in the United States.

In 2000, Americans of Hispanic origin numbered approximately 35.3 million and accounted for approximately 12.5% of the total U.S. population (see Figure 10.2).[18] Since 1990, the Hispanic population has grown by approximately 30%, while the non-Hispanic white American population has increased 3%. Nearly three-quarters (74%) of Americans of Hispanic origin reside in either California, Texas, New York, Florida, or Illinois.[2] Hispanic populations in these states are expected to continue to grow. The majority of Hispanics in the United States are of Mexican origin.[25]

The educational attainment level of Americans of Hispanic origin has remained well below that of the general population (see Figure 10.5). Since 1980, the high school completion rate for Hispanic youth has fluctuated between 57% and 67%.[19] Economic status follows the same pattern as that for education. The median income of Hispanic families is consistently lower than any other racial and ethnic group, except for blacks (see Figure 10.6).[20] Poverty rates for persons of Hispanic origin were 21.2% in 2000, reflecting the lowest poverty rates recorded for this group in nearly three decades. However, this rate is still more than three times the rate for white Americans (see Figure 10.7).[21]

Traditional health beliefs of Mexican-Americans and other Latin cultures include the "Role of God."[26] Good health is seen as a matter of fortune or reward from God for good behavior. Maintaining harmony and balance with God is linked to the concept of good health, and warding off evil influences is important to maintain this balance. *Curanderismo* (a healer) is the most common form in Mexican-American folk medicine.[26] A curandera's or healer's ability includes a varied repertoire of religious belief systems (mainly Catholicism), herbal knowledge, witchcraft, and scientific medicine.

ASIAN AMERICANS AND PACIFIC ISLANDERS

As we begin our discussion of Asian Americans and Pacific Islanders, it is important to remind readers about the 1997 "Revisions to the Standards for the Classification of Federal Data on Race and Ethnicity." The most distinct change was separating Asian Americans and Pacific Islanders (see Figure 10.4 and Appendix 3).

In June 1999, former President Clinton signed Executive Order 13125 to improve the quality of life of Asian Americans and Pacific Islanders through increased participation in federal programs where they may be underserved (e.g., health, human services, education, housing, labor, transportation, and economic and community development).[27] One important goal of the order is collecting separate data on each group. Asian and Pacific Islanders are really two distinct groups, and combining the data tended to conceal substantial socioeconomic and health differences among these groups. However, even by 2001, most federal agencies were still not collecting separate data on these two groups, citing methodological and funding constraints.[27] Accordingly, the following data on Asian Americans and Pacific Islanders is presented in aggregate, unless otherwise noted.

According to the 2000 Census, Asian/Pacific Islander Americans (APIAs) comprised 3.7% (10.5 million) of the U.S. population (see Figure 10.2). Of the nearly 12 million APIAs, approximately 95% were Asian Americans and 5% were Pacific Islanders.[18] APIAs remain the fastest growing racial/ethnic population in the United States, increasing 95% from 1980 to 1990 and another 43% from 1990 to 2000.[27] If this growth continues at the present rate, it is projected that these minority groups will comprise 8.9% (see Figure 10.3) of the total projected U.S. population in the year 2050. When education, income, and poverty data are reported in aggregate for APIAs, they appear well off (see Figures 10.5 to 10.7). The high school completion rates of 18- through 24-year-olds and the median incomes were the highest compared to all other racial and ethnic groups.[19,20] In addition, the poverty rate was at an all-time low for these groups.[21] Unfortunately, these aggregated data mask the large variation within the APIA population.[28] According to Yoon and Chien,[29] the education and income of APIAs form a *bipolar distribution* (skewed toward each extreme with few in the middle). To better understand this concept, consider the following: Among people 25 years and older, APIAs are more likely than whites (42% vs. 28%) to have earned a college degree; however, they are also more likely than white Americans (8% vs. 5%) to have less than a ninth-grade education.[30] Additionally, 33% of APIA families had incomes of $75,000 or more compared to 29% of white families, while at the same time more APIA families had incomes under $25,000 than whites (21% vs. 19%). This deceptive view, formed by examining aggregate data only, has led to the myth that APIAs are a "model community," when in fact they suffer from as many disparities as other racial and ethnic minority groups.[29]

As mentioned previously, Asian Americans and Pacific Islanders are two discrete groups. Therefore, we now proceed with a brief overview of each. The term *Asian American* refers to people of Asian descent who are American citizens. Immigration is an integral part of Asian American community growth, as many are seeking better economic and employment opportunities and/or are reuniting with family members. They or their ancestors came from more than 20 different Asian countries, including Cambodia, China, India, Japan, Korea, Malaysia, Pakistan, the Philippine Islands, Thailand, and Vietnam.[30] Among these groups, the Chinese and Filipinos are the two largest subgroups. Even among those who have come from the same country, immigration to America may have occurred at different times, and thus there are generational differences. For example, some families may have immigrated well over a hundred years ago as laborers, while those coming today carry with them professional degrees.[31] These differences contribute to a substantial diversity in socioeconomic status among these groups, thus creating the myth discussed earlier that Asian Americans are a "model group."

Although variations among Asian Americans is the norm, many share similarities based on their religious background and the belief of equilibrium or balance.[32] The concept of balance is related to health, and imbalance is related to disease. This balance or imbalance is highly related to diet, which influences people's daily activities of living within their environment. Therefore, to achieve health and avoid illness, people must adjust to the environment in a holistic manner.

The term *Pacific Islander* (PI) includes peoples of Hawaii, Guam, Samoa, or other Pacific Islands and their descendants.[30] The Native Hawaiian population forms the majority of PIs. In contrast to Asian Americans, there is no large-scale immigration of PIs into the continental United States. Because Hawaii is the state in which the majority of PIs live, this will be our main focus. Similar to other minority groups, there are many health disparities among PIs.[33] Two key health issues for Native Hawaiians include health care allocation and the question of reimbursement for medical care.

Nearly 90% of Hawaii's land mass is federally designed as rural. Approximately 20% of Native Hawaiians live in rural Hawaii. However, the majority of the state's health care resources are fixed in the capitol city of Honolulu. As a result of this imbalance of health care resource allocation, there is an inadequate number of health care professionals on the neighboring islands.[34] Additionally, transportation issues between the islands make it more difficult to access health care in Honolulu. Even public transportation on the separate islands is unreliable, so local access to medical care is challenging. The second medical care issue deals with the Native Hawaiian health belief, which suggests that the healer cannot be reimbursed directly for his or her therapeutic work. According to Blaisell,[35] such healer skill is not a question of learning but rather a question of righteousness. Therefore, it is not considered appropriate to be paid for doing what is right.

NATIVE AMERICANS AND ALASKA NATIVES

Native Americans, the original inhabitants of America, numbered nearly 2.1 million in 2000, or 0.7% of the population (see Figure 10.2).[18] It has been estimated that prior to the arrival of European explorers, 12 million Native Americans lived and flourished throughout what is now the United States. Exposure to diseases and ecological changes introduced by explorers and colonists decimated the Native American population. While many of the descendants were assimilated by intermarriages or successfully adapted to the new culture, as a group, the Native Americans became economically and socially disadvantaged, and this status is reflected in their relatively poor health status.[36] Data on socioeconomic indicators for all 500+ tribes and villages nationwide remain vague. For example, recent annual population surveys did not include Native Americans since the sample size was not large enough for the data to be accurate. However, the 1997–1999 average poverty rate for Native Americans was 25.9%, which is the highest among all racial and ethnic groups (see Figure 10.7).[21] Similarly, the median income ($20,000) (see Figure 10.6) and high school completion rates (65.3%) (see Figure 10.5) were the lowest among all racial and ethnic groups.[37]

Native Americans comprise many different American Indian tribal groups and Alaskan villages. Each of these tribes/villages has distinct customs, language, and beliefs. The majority, however, share the same cultural values that have been identified by Edwards and Egbert-Edwards:[38]

- Appreciation of individuality with emphasis upon an individual's right to freedom, autonomy, and respect
- Group consensus in tribal/village decision making
- Respect for all living things
- Appreciation, respect, and reverence for the land
- Feelings of hospitality toward friends, family, clanspeople, tribesmen, and respectful visitors
- An expectation that tribal/village members will bring honor and respect to their families, clans, and tribes. Bringing shame or dishonor to self or tribe is negatively reinforced
- A belief in a supreme being and life after death. Indian religion is the dominant influence for traditional Indian people

Central to Native American culture is that the people "strive for a close integration within the family, clan and tribe and live in harmony with their environment. This occurs simultaneously on physical, mental, and spiritual levels; thus, individual wellness is considered as harmony and balance among mind, body, spirit and the environment."[38] This concept is not congruent with the medical model approach or public health approach that is generally accepted by the majority of Americans. As a result, in many Native American communities there is conflict between the medical/public health approach and the approaches used by Native American healers (see Table 10.3).[38] Providing appropriate health care for Native Americans usually involves resolving conflicts between the two approaches in such a way that they complement each other.

U.S. Government, Native Americans, and the Provision of Health Care

Though classified by definition and for statistical purposes as a minority group, Native Americans are unlike any other subgroup in the United States. Some (but not all) tribes are sovereign nations, based in part upon their treaties with the U.S. government. Tribal sovereignty, which is

Table 10.3
A Comparison of Indian Medicine and Modern Medicine

Indian Medicine	Modern Medicine
Behavior-oriented	Complaint-oriented
Whole-specific	Organ-specific
Imbalance	Caused
Visionary diagnosis	Technical diagnosis
Wellness-oriented	Illness-oriented

Source: Garrett, J.T. (1990). "Indian Health: Values, Beliefs, and Practices." In M. S. Harper, ed., *Minority Aging: Essential Curricula Content for Selected Health and Allied Health Professionals* (HHS pub. no. HRS-P-DV90-4). Washington, DC: U.S. Government Printing Office.

perhaps the most important Native American issue, creates a distinct and special relationship between various tribes and the U.S. government. This sovereignty came about when the tribes transferred virtually all the land in the United States to the federal government in return for the provision of certain services. The U.S. government agreed to manage the land, water, agriculture, and mineral and timber resources, and to provide education and health services to tribe members. Each of these services is owed to them, and if they become indignant when people suggest they are getting them free, it is a rightful indignation.[39]

Provisions of education for Native Americans date back to the Civilization Act of 1819, while provisions for health services began in 1832.[36] The first medical efforts were carried out by Army physicians who vaccinated Native Americans against smallpox and applied sanitary procedures to curb other communicable diseases among tribes living in the vicinity of military posts. The health services provided for Native Americans after the signing of the early treaties were limited. It was common for the U.S. government, through the treaties, to impose time limits of 5 to 20 years on the provisions of health care.[40]

The original government agency overseeing the welfare of Native Americans was the Bureau of Indian Affairs (BIA). When this Bureau was transferred from the War Department to the Department of the Interior in 1849, physician services were extended to Native Americans. Over the next 70+ years, health care services were continually improved, with the first Native American hospital built in 1882. However, comprehensive health services were still lacking. It was not until 1921, when the Snyder Act created the BIA Health Division, that more emphasis was given to providing health services to Native Americans. In 1954 with the passage of Public Law 83-568, known as the Transfer Act, the responsibility of health care for Native Americans was transferred from the Department of Interior's BIA to the Public Health Service (PHS). It was at this time that the Indian Health Service (IHS) was created. With this Act, the health needs of Native Americans were finally met in a comprehensive way.

In keeping with the concept of tribal sovereignty, the Indian Self-Determination and Education Assistance Act (PL 93-63) of 1975 authorized the IHS to involve tribes in the administration and operation of all or certain programs under a special contract. It authorized the IHS to provide grants to tribes, on request, for planning, development, and operation of health programs.[36] Today, a number of programs are managed and operated under contract by individual tribes.[37]

Indian Health Service (IHS)

The IHS, an agency within the HHS, is responsible for providing federal health services to Native Americans and Alaska Natives.[37] This agency is organized into 12 areas throughout the United States (see Figure 10.8) and operates hospitals, clinics and health stations, and a variety

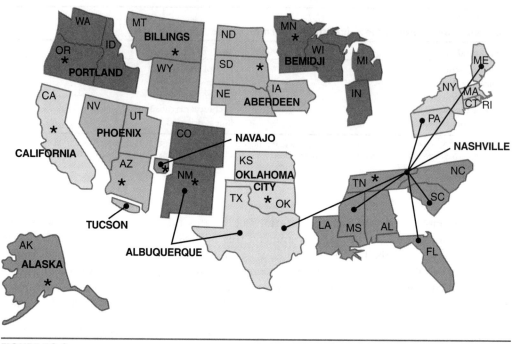

FIGURE 10.8

Indian Health Service (IHS) structure.

*Area office

Note: Texas is administered by Nashville, Oklahoma City, and Albuquerque.

Source: U.S. Department of Health and Human Services (2000). "Regional Differences in Indian Health 1998–99." Indian Health Services, Program Statistics Team, 31. Available at http://www.ihs.gov/publicinfo/publications/trends98/region98.asp.

of other programs. The goal of the IHS is to raise the health status of American Indians and Alaska Natives to the highest possible level. To attain this goal, the IHS

1. Assists Indian tribes in developing their health programs through activities such as health management training, technical assistance, and human resource development
2. Facilitates and assists Indian tribes in coordinating health resources available through federal, state, and local programs, in operating comprehensive health care services and in health program evaluation
3. Provides comprehensive health care services, including hospital and ambulatory medical care, preventive and rehabilitative services, and development of community sanitation facilities
4. Serves as the principal federal advocate for Indians in the health field to ensure comprehensive health services for American Indian and Alaska Native people[37]

> **refugee**
> a person who flees one area or country to seek shelter or protection from danger in another

REFUGEES: THE NEW IMMIGRANTS

> **immigrant**
> individuals who migrate from one country to another for the purpose of seeking permanent residence

In this section we introduce several new terms that describe people who have arrived in the United States relatively recently. Because of their status as new arrivals, these people sometimes share similar health problems. The first term, **refugees,** means people who flee one area, usually their home country, to seek shelter or protection from danger. Refugees arriving in the United States may be seeking political asylum, refuge from war, or escape from famine or other environmental disaster. The second term, **immigrants,** describes individuals who migrate here from another country for the purpose of seeking permanent residence and hopefully a better life. **Aliens** are people born in and owing allegiance to a country other than the one in which they live. Thus, aliens are not citizens and are only allowed to stay in a foreign country for a specified period of time defined by law or policy. Many aliens, including college students, although in the United States legally, are not permitted to work. Sometimes, however, they violate this provision and find employment illegally. Lastly, **illegal aliens** are those who enter this country without any permission whatsoever. Most of these illegal aliens have entered from Mexico simply by crossing the Rio Grande river at night.

Although all refugees who enter this country can be classified into one of the existing racial/ethnic categories used by our government, as a single group they present many special concerns not seen in minorities who are born and raised in the United States. Most of the refugees currently entering the United States arrive from *developing countries,* countries with meager economic resources. These refugees usually settle in urban areas, even though they may have a rural orientation. Many refugees are poor, have low levels of formal education, and have few marketable work skills. Many arrive with serious health problems, including undernourishment or starvation, physical and emotional injuries from hostile action or confinement in refugee camps, poor health care, and overcrowdedness.[41] A majority of the refugees are young, many of the women are of childbearing age, and most come from Latin American and Southeast Asian countries.

The arrival of such refugees places additional strains on both public and private health and social services. Some of the problems that have surfaced include the following:

- Lack of jobs to fit the skills of the refugees
- New competition for the lower socioeconomic groups in the United States for work and housing
- Strain on the budgets of the public education systems to meet the needs of the non-English-speaking refugee children
- Further burden on the human, health, and mental health services provided mostly by minority communities
- Cultural barriers to using the U.S. health care system, including lack of financial resources, cultural ignorance of health care providers, lack of bilingual health care workers, distrust and unfamiliarity with Western medicine, poor understanding of the etiology of certain diseases, difficulties of accessing services, and ignorance of available services

This immigration has resulted in growing backlash movements against refugees in some areas of the country. Examples include the "only English" movement and the Immigration Reform and Control Act of 1986 that requires employers to prove the identity and work authorization for every prospective employee—the logic of which is based on the perception of work as a privilege associated with citizenship and, by extension, with legal residence.[41]

The difficulties facing refugees in the United States, including finding employment and obtaining access to education and appropriate human, health, and mental health services, represent significant barriers to the social integration of refugees into American society. Like most of the other minority groups in the United States, refugees may become a part of those disadvantaged in this country. There is, however, one bright note to the increase of refugees in this country—the enrichment of the U.S. culture. Until 1970, the United States was primarily composed of only black and white Americans. In the last 30+ years, this country has been significantly enriched by the cultures of those coming from other countries, and as noted earlier, the minority groups are the fastest growing segments of the U.S. population.[42]

alien
a person born in and owing allegiance to a country other than the one in which he/she lives

illegal alien
an individual who entered this country without permission

RACE AND HEALTH INITIATIVE

As mentioned previously, in 1998, former President Clinton committed the Nation to an ambitious goal by the year 2010: Eliminate health disparities among racial and ethnic minority populations in six areas of health while maintaining the progress on overall health of the American people.[7] The *Race and Health Initiative*'s six priority areas include (1) infant mortality, (2) cancer screening and management, (3) cardiovascular disease, (4) diabetes, (5) HIV/AIDS, and (6) adult and child immunization.

The *Race and Health Initiative* reaffirms the government's extensive focus on minority health issues by emphasizing key areas that are representative of the larger minority health picture.[7] The six health issues account for a substantial burden of disease that is highly modifiable if appropriate interventions are applied. In addition, enough current data exists in each major area to be able to measure improvement and progress. Thus, the *Race and Health Initiative* is intertwined with *Healthy People 2010* and the goals of the Nation for the next decade.[8]

It is important to note that *Healthy People 2010* will continue to pursue other areas of concern related to minority health that are not directly covered under these six major areas. Similarly, we acknowledge that disparities exist in many other areas of minority health; however, this chapter will present data on the six health areas identified in the *Race and Health Initiative*. We will begin by providing data documenting the disparities that exist in each of the categories, as well as data related to major risk factors that contribute to each of the conditions. As you continue to read, it is important not to stereotype any group, for it is known that each health concern cuts across all racial and ethnic groups.

Infant Mortality

As noted in Chapter 7, infant mortality is defined as the death of an infant before his or her first birthday. The infant mortality rate correlates highly to the general health and well-being of the Nation. The United States made significant improvement in the twentieth century regarding infant health. However, while the vast majority of infants born in America today are healthy at birth, many are not. As a result, many industrialized nations report infant mortality rates that are better than those of the United States (see Figure 7.4). Additionally, infant mortality data within the United States is characterized by a long-standing and serious disparity among racial and ethnic minorities (see Figure 10.9). Infant death rates among black Americans, American Indians and Alaska Natives, and Americans of Hispanics origin have all been above the national average of approximately seven deaths per 1,000 live births in the 1990s. The greatest disparity exists for black Americans, whose infant death rate is more than two times that of white American infants.

There are many reasons associated with higher infant mortality rates among black Americans. Two of the more important explanations include lack of prenatal care and giving birth to low-birth-weight (LBW) babies. Prenatal care is crucial to maternal and infant health (see Chapter 7). Women who receive early and continuous prenatal health care have better pregnancy outcomes than woman who do not. Black American, Native American, and Hispanic women are less likely to receive early and comprehensive prenatal care (see Figure 7.14).[43] In the same manner, black Americans and Native Americans are more likely to give birth to LBW babies (see Figure 10.10).

Cancer Screening and Management

Annually there are approximately 1.2 million new cases of invasive cancer diagnosed in the United States.[44] Nearly half of those who develop cancer will die from it. Cancer is the second leading cause of death in the United States, accounting for more than 500,000 deaths annually

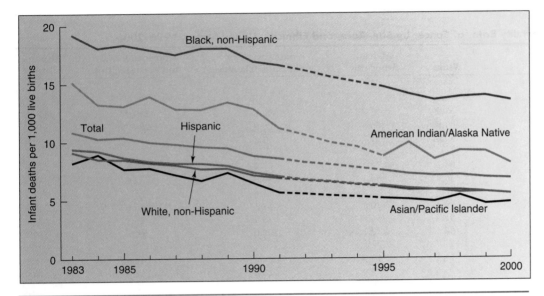

FIGURE 10.9

Infant mortality rates by race and Hispanic origin: selected years, 1983 to 2000.

Note: Data are available for 1983–1991 and 1995–2000. Infant deaths are deaths before a child's first birthday.

Source: Centers for Disease Control and Prevention, National Center for Health Statistics, National Linked File of Live Births and Infant Deaths.

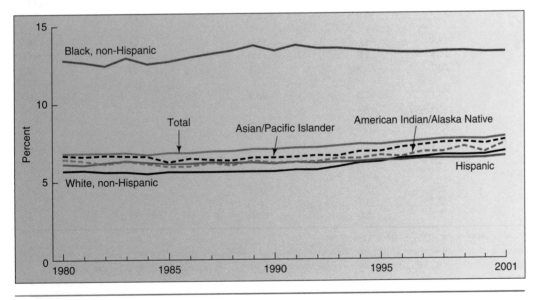

FIGURE 10.10

Percentage of infants born of low birth weight, by mother's race and Hispanic origin, 1980 to 2001.

Source: Centers for Disease Control and Prevention, National Center for Health Statistics, National Vital Statistics System.

(see Chapter 4 and Chapter 8).[44] From 1996 to 2000, cancer incidence rates per 100,000 population were 696.8 among black Americans, 555.9 among white Americans, 419.3 among Hispanics, 392.0 among Asian/Pacific Islanders, and 259.0 among American Indians (see Table 10.4). During this same period of time, cancer death rates per 100,000 population were 356.2 among black

Table 10.4
Incidence and Mortality Rates of Cancer by Site, Race, and Ethnicity: United States, 1996–2000

	White	African American	Asian American and Pacific Islander	American Indian and Alaska Native	Hispanic/ Latino*
Incidence					
All sites					
Males	555.9	696.8	392.0	259.0	419.3
Females	431.8	406.3	306.9	229.2	312.2
Breast (female)	140.8	121.7	97.2	58.0	89.8
Colon & rectum					
Males	64.1	72.4	57.2	37.5	49.8
Females	46.2	56.2	38.8	32.6	32.9
Lung & bronchus					
Males	79.4	120.4	62.1	45.6	46.1
Females	51.9	54.8	28.4	23.4	24.4
Prostate	164.3	272.1	100.0	53.6	137.2
Stomach					
Males	11.2	19.9	23.0	14.4	18.1
Females	5.1	9.9	12.8	8.3	10.0
Liver & intrahepatic bile duct					
Males	7.3	11.0	21.1	6.1	13.8
Females	2.8	3.9	7.7	5.5	5.6
Uterine cervix	9.2	12.4	10.2	6.9	16.8
Mortality					
All sites					
Males	249.5	356.2	154.8	172.3	176.7
Females	166.9	198.6	102.0	115.8	112.4
Breast (female)	27.2	35.9	12.5	14.9	17.9
Colon & rectum					
Males	25.3	34.6	15.8	18.5	18.4
Females	17.5	24.6	11.0	12.1	11.4
Total	20.7	28.5	13.1	14.7	14.3
Lung & bronchus					
Males	78.1	107.0	40.9	52.9	40.7
Females	41.5	40.0	19.1	26.2	15.1
Prostate	30.2	73.0	13.9	21.9	24.1
Stomach					
Males	6.1	14.0	12.5	7.0	9.9
Females	2.9	6.5	7.4	4.2	5.3
Liver & intrahepatic bile duct					
Males	6.0	9.3	16.1	7.6	10.5
Females	2.7	3.7	6.7	4.3	5.0
Uterine cervix	2.7	5.9	2.9	2.9	3.7

Note: Rates are per 100,000, age-adjusted to the 2000 U.S. standard population.

*Hispanic/Latinos are not mutually exclusive from whites, African Americans, Asian Americans and Pacific Islanders, and American Indians and Alaska Natives.

Source: Ries, L. A. G., M. P. Eisner, C. L. Kosary, et al., eds. (2003). *SEER Cancer Statistics Review, 1975–2000.* Bethesda, MD: National Cancer Institute.

Americans, 249.5 among white Americans, 176.7 among Hispanics, 154.8 among Asian/Pacific Islanders, and 172.3.0 among American Indians (see Table 10.4). A number of these disparities in cancer incidence and death rates among minorities are attributed to lifestyle factors, late diagnosis, and access to health care.[45]

The good news is that cancer is preventable. Primary cancer prevention refers to preventing the occurrence of cancer. The American Cancer Society estimates that approximately 60% of all cancers in the United States could be prevented through lifestyle behavior changes (i.e., avoiding smoking, avoiding excessive sun exposure, and eating nutritiously).[44] Smoking is

Table 10.5
Stage at Diagnosis of Colorectal, Breast, Prostate, and Cervical Cancer, by Race and Ethnicity, 1996–2000

	Localized		Regional		Distant	
	Rate	**%**	**Rate**	**%**	**Rate**	**%**
Colorectal						
White	21.4	42	19.7	39	9.6	19
African American	22.4	39	21.0	36	14.2	25
Hispanic/Latino	14.6	39	14.4	39	7.9	22
American Indian and Alaska Native	11.8	35	13.2	40	8.5	25
Asian American and Pacific Islander	18.9	42	17.9	40	7.7	18
Breast (female)						
White	90.2	66	39.8	29	7.5	5
African American	65.6	55	40.6	36	10.6	9
Hispanic/Latino	50.7	57	29.2	35	6.2	7
American Indian and Alaska Native	32.4	56	19.9	36	4.8	8
Asian American and Pacific Islander	63.1	65	28.2	30	4.3	5
Prostate*						
White	145.2	95			8.2	5
African American	225.9	93			20.0	7
Hispanic/Latino	112.1	93			9.7	7
American Indian and Alaska Native	42.6	88			7.2	12
Asian American and Pacific Islander	84.9	92			8.0	8
Uterine cervix						
White	5.0	58	2.9	33	0.8	9
African American	5.5	51	4.4	39	1.2	10
Hispanic/Latino	8.1	57	5.8	34	1.6	9
American Indian and Alaska Native	3.3	57	2.5	36	0.5	7
Asian American and Pacific Islander	5.0	54	3.8	38	0.9	8

Note: Rates are per 100,000, age-adjusted to the 2000 U.S. population. Hispanics/Latinos are not mutually exclusive from whites, African Americans, Asian Americans and Pacific Islanders, and American Indians and Alaska Natives.

*The rate and percent for localized stage represents local and regional stages combined.

Source: Ries, L.A.G., M.P. Eisner, C.L. Kosary, et al., eds. (2003). *SEER Cancer Statistics Review, 1975–2000.* Bethesda, MD: National Cancer Institute.

the most preventable cause of lung cancer death in our society. The death rate for lung cancer is 25% higher in black Americans than white Americans (see Table 10.4). Paralleling this death rate is the fact that black Americans have a higher incidence of smoking than white Americans.

Secondary cancer prevention refers to early detection of cancer through screening tests. The earlier a cancer is detected, the greater the chances one will survive. The disparity in lower survival rates among black Americans is reflected in Table 10.5, which shows that black Americans are less likely to have their cancers detected in a localized stage. One particular cancer of significant interest related to the *Race and Health Initiative* is breast cancer. Breast cancer is the second leading cause of cancer death among women. Most deaths from breast cancer are unnecessary. Breast cancer survival rates are significantly increased if the cancer is detected early through monthly self-examination and/or periodic mammograms (breast x-rays). Despite the importance of mammography, it is underutilized as an early detection procedure by many minority women (see Box 10.1). The goal of *Healthy People 2010* is to have a percentage of at least 70% of women from all racial or ethnic groups aged 40 and older that have received a mammogram within the preceding two years.[8]

Cardiovascular Diseases

Cardiovascular disease (CVD), primarily in the form of coronary heart disease and stroke, kills more Americans annually than any other disease. In fact, CVD claims more lives each year than the next five leading causes of death combined. Death rates from coronary heart disease and

BOX
10.1

HEALTHY PEOPLE 2010: OBJECTIVE

3.13 Increase the proportion of women aged 40 years and older who have received a mammogram within the preceding two years.

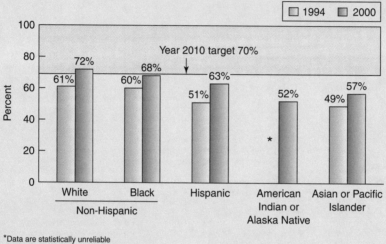

Mammogram in the last two years among women 40 years of age and older
(age-adjusted to the year 2000 standard population)

*Data are statistically unreliable
Source: COC, NOHS, National Health Interview Survey.

For Further Thought

Research indicates that mortality due to breast cancer can be reduced through the use of mammography. Data for 2000 show that substantial progress has been made in increasing the percentage of women receiving mammograms. However, despite the improvement shown by all race and ethnicity groups, minority groups are still well below whites. What type of program could be implemented to further increase the percentage of minority women who participate in mammograms?

stroke vary widely among racial and ethnic groups (see Figures 10.11 and 10.12). Black Americans suffer disproportionately higher rates of death from coronary heart disease and stroke than other racial and ethnic groups.

One of the major modifiable risk factors for coronary artery disease and stroke is hypertension.

One in five Americans aged six and older suffers from hypertension. The prevalence of hypertension varies noticeably according to race/ethnicity, with the highest prevalence among black Americans (see Figure 10.13).[46] In addition, black Americans tend to develop hypertension earlier in life than whites. The reasons for this are unknown. In fact, the cause of 90% to 95% of the cases of hypertension in all races and ethnic groups is unknown. Therefore, secondary prevention or screening for hypertension is essential. Hypertension is easily detected and normally controllable. However, because hypertension presents no symptoms, approximately one-third of people with high blood pressure do not know they have it.

Diabetes

Approximately 6% of the population (nearly 18 million people) have diabetes—a condition in which the body does not produce or properly use insulin. The prevalence of diabetes has

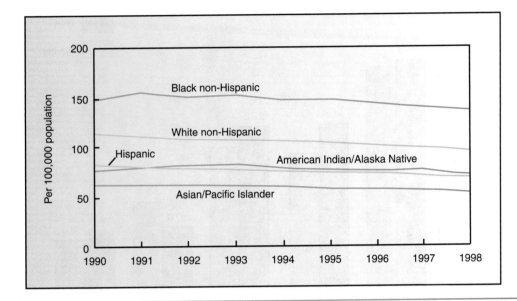

FIGURE 10.11

Coronary heart disease death rates (age adjusted to the year 2000 standard population).*

*Age adjustment to the year 2000 standard population will begin in 1999.

Source: CDC, NCHS, National Vital Statistics System.

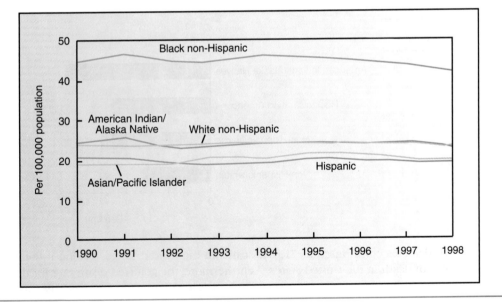

FIGURE 10.12

Stroke death rates (age adjusted to the year 2000 stand population).*

*Age adjustment to the year 2000 standard population will begin in 1999.

Source: CDC, NCHS, National Vital Statistics System.

risen in recent years, and this trend is projected to continue. Furthermore, the prevalence of diabetes in people aged 20 years or older is varied in minority groups. Hispanics are 1.9 times more likely, black Americans 2.0 times more likely, and American Indians 2.6 times more likely to have diabetes than whites of similar age (see Figure 10.14).

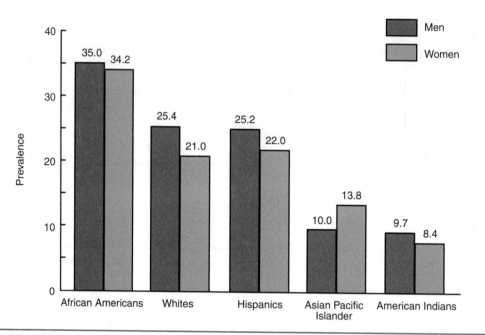

FIGURE 10.13

Prevalence of hypertension among adults aged 20 and older by race/ethnicity and gender in the United States.

Source: U.S. Department of Health and Human Services, Joint National Committee on Prevention, Detection, Evaluation, and Treatment of High Blood Pressure (1997). *The Sixth Report of the Joint National Committee on Prevention, Evaluation, and Treatment of High Blood Pressure* (NIH publication no. 98-4080). Bethesda, MD: Author.

FIGURE 10.14

Age-adjusted total prevalence of diabetes in people aged 20 years or older, by race/ethnicity: United States, 2002.

Source: 1999–2001 National Health Interview Survey and 1999–2000 National Health and Nutrition Examination Survey estimates projected to the year 2002.

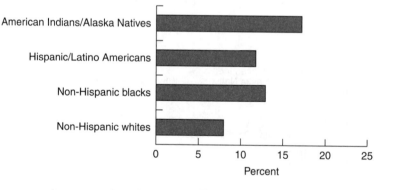

In 2001, diabetes contributed to 71,372 deaths in the United States, making it the sixth leading cause of death in the United States.[47] Furthermore, the adjusted death rate for deaths related to diabetes has increased by approximately 40% in the last two decades. This increase in age-adjusted death rates occurred in all racial and ethnic groups. However, diabetes death rates do vary considerably among racial and ethnic groups. Compared to white non-Hispanics, diabetes death rates were nearly two and a half times higher among black Americans and American Indians, and nearly two times higher among Americans of Hispanic origin.[47]

In addition to causing death, other serious complications from diabetes include heart disease, stroke, blindness, and kidney disease. In fact, diabetes is the leading cause of new cases of blindness in people aged 20 to 74, and the leading cause of end-stage renal disease (ESRD), accounting for nearly half of all new cases. In 2001, a total of 142,963 people with ESRD due to diabetes were living on chronic dialysis or with a kidney transplant.[48] Between

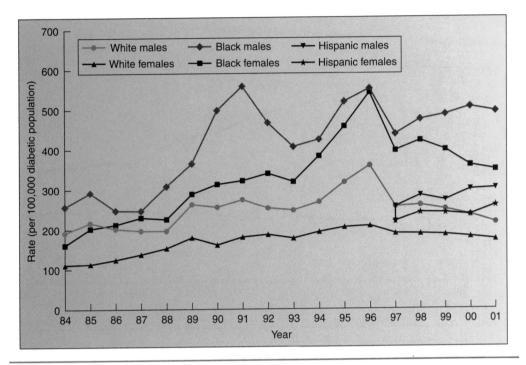

FIGURE 10.15

Age-adjusted incidence of end-stage renal disease related to diabetes per 100,000 diabetic population, by race, ethnicity, and sex: United States, 1984 to 2001.

Source: Centers for Disease Control and Prevention, Diabetes Program. "Data and Trends: End-Stage Renal Disease." Available at http://www.cdc.gov/diabetes/statistics/esrd/Fig5.htm.

1984 and 2001, ESRD attributable to diabetes was greatest among black men and women and lowest among white women (see Figure 10.15). Inpatient hospitalization care is one of the most expensive venues for diabetes care. Hospital admissions for long-term care of diabetes are highest among black Americans and Hispanics.

HIV Infection/AIDS

AIDS stands for acquired immune deficiency syndrome, a disorder first documented in the United States in 1981, through which the body's immune system is impaired to varying degrees. As of December 31, 2002, a total of 886,575 AIDS cases among adults and adolescents and 9,300 cases among children under 13 have been reported to the CDC.[49] An estimated 501,669 people of all ages have died from the opportunistic diseases stemming from AIDS during the same period. The cause of AIDS is a virus known as human immunodeficiency virus, or HIV. It is estimated that nearly 1 million people in the United States are currently living with HIV. An HIV infection is a chronic condition that progressively damages the body's immune system, making an otherwise healthy person less able to resist a variety of infections and disorders. Presently, there is no known cure for HIV infection or AIDS and no vaccine to prevent it. Additionally, no major cure breakthroughs are expected for years to come.

AIDS has had a disproportionate impact on racial and ethnic minority groups in the United States since the disease was first recognized in 1981. Through December 31, 2002, well over half of all identified cases since 1981 were reported among racial and ethnic groups.[49] In fact, the proportional distribution of AIDS cases among racial and ethnic groups has shifted since the beginning of the epidemic. The proportion of cases has increased among

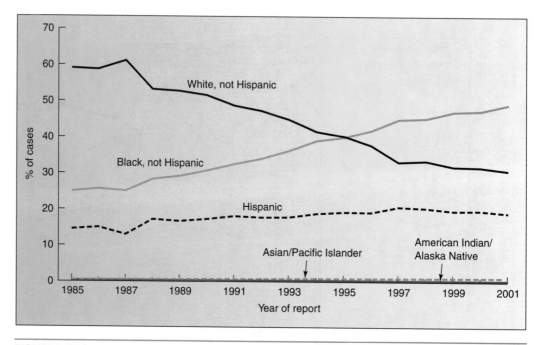

FIGURE 10.16

Proportion of AIDS cases, by race/ethnicity and year of report, 1985 to 2001, United States.

Source: Centers for Disease Control and Prevention.

black Americans and Hispanics and decreased among whites (see Figure 10.16). In 2001, black Americans and Americans of Hispanic origin represented about one-quarter of the country's population, but more than one-half of the new AIDS cases reported in the United States (see Figure 10.17). Consistent with the AIDS case rates is the higher AIDS death rates for black Americans and Americans of Hispanic origin.

Part of the reason for the disproportionate numbers of HIV and AIDS cases in black Americans and Americans of Hispanic origin has been attributed to a higher prevalence of unsafe or risky health behaviors (e.g., unprotected sexual intercourse and intravenous drug use), existing co-conditions (e.g., genital ulcer disease), and the lack of access to health care that would provide early diagnosis and treatment. A prevailing barrier to HIV/AIDS prevention may be that this condition is not being viewed as among the highest priorities in some minority communities when compared with other life survival problems.[50] With no cure for HIV/AIDS in sight, better health education to reduce and eliminate unsafe behaviors and increased access to medical resources for existing cases are essential to prevention.

Child and Adult Immunization Rates

As a result of widespread immunization practices, many infectious diseases that were once common have been significantly reduced. Childhood immunization rates provide one measure of the extent to which children are protected from dangerous vaccine-preventable illnesses.[51] The proportion of children aged 19 to 35 months receiving the recommended combined vaccine series increased from 69% to 79% between 1994 and 1998 (see Figure 7.23). Since that time, the rate has fluctuated mildly and was 78% in 2002. The combined immunization series rate measures the extent to which children have received four key vaccinations. However, disparities exist in child immunization rates among minorities (see Figure 10.18). Black American children were least likely to receive the combined vaccination

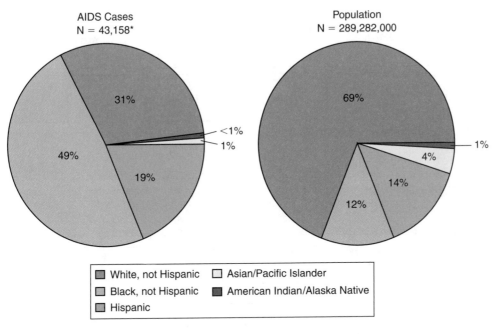

*Includes 57 persons with unknown race/ethnicity

FIGURE 10.17

AIDS cases reported in 2001 and estimated 2001 population, by race/ethnicity, United States.

Source: Centers for Disease Control and Prevention.

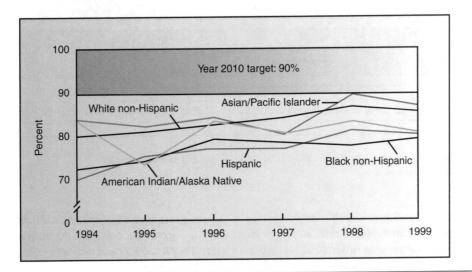

FIGURE 10.18

Vaccination coverage with four or more diphtheria-tetanus-pertussis doses (DTP/DT).*

*Rates are for children aged 19–35 months who have received four or more doses of the DTP/DT vaccine (diphtheria, tetanus, pertussis).

Source: CDC, NIP, and NCHS, National Immunization Survey.

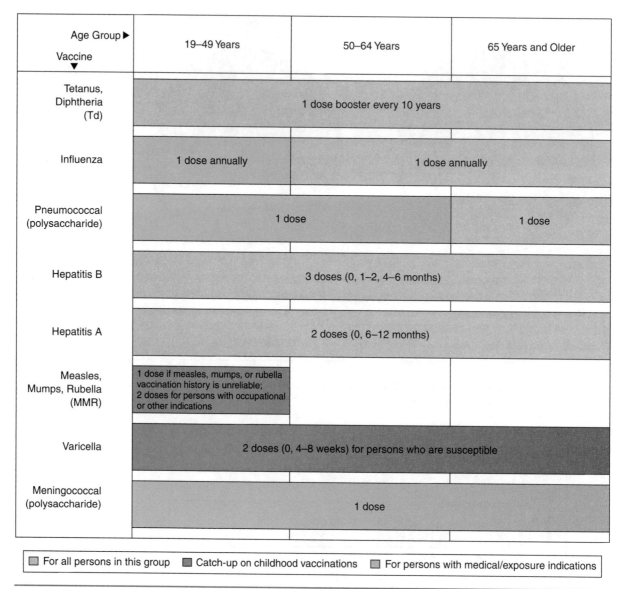

Age Group ► Vaccine ▼	19–49 Years	50–64 Years	65 Years and Older
Tetanus, Diphtheria (Td)	1 dose booster every 10 years		
Influenza	1 dose annually	1 dose annually	
Pneumococcal (polysaccharide)	1 dose		1 dose
Hepatitis B	3 doses (0, 1–2, 4–6 months)		
Hepatitis A	2 doses (0, 6–12 months)		
Measles, Mumps, Rubella (MMR)	1 dose if measles, mumps, or rubella vaccination history is unreliable; 2 doses for persons with occupational or other indications		
Varicella	2 doses (0, 4–8 weeks) for persons who are susceptible		
Meningococcal (polysaccharide)	1 dose		

☐ For all persons in this group ☐ Catch-up on childhood vaccinations ☐ For persons with medical/exposure indications

FIGURE 10.19

Recommended adult immunization schedule, United States, 2003-2004, by age group and medical condition.

Source: Centers for Disease Control and Prevention.

series. The good news is that rates among minority groups in the last decade have been increasing at a more rapid rate, and thus narrowing the gap. This rise in child immunization rates must continue in order to achieve the *Healthy People 2010* target of 90% coverage for all recommended childhood immunizations in all populations.[8]

Immunization does not end with childhood. It is important for adults, especially those 65 years and older, to become immunized against certain infectious diseases that can cause illness, disability, or death. Figure 10.19 shows the 2003-2004 adult immunization schedule recommended by the CDC's National Immunization Program. Two important adult immunizations included on the schedule, as well as among the infectious disease objectives stated in *Healthy People 2010,* are immunizations for influenza and pneumoccocal diseases.[8] The goal

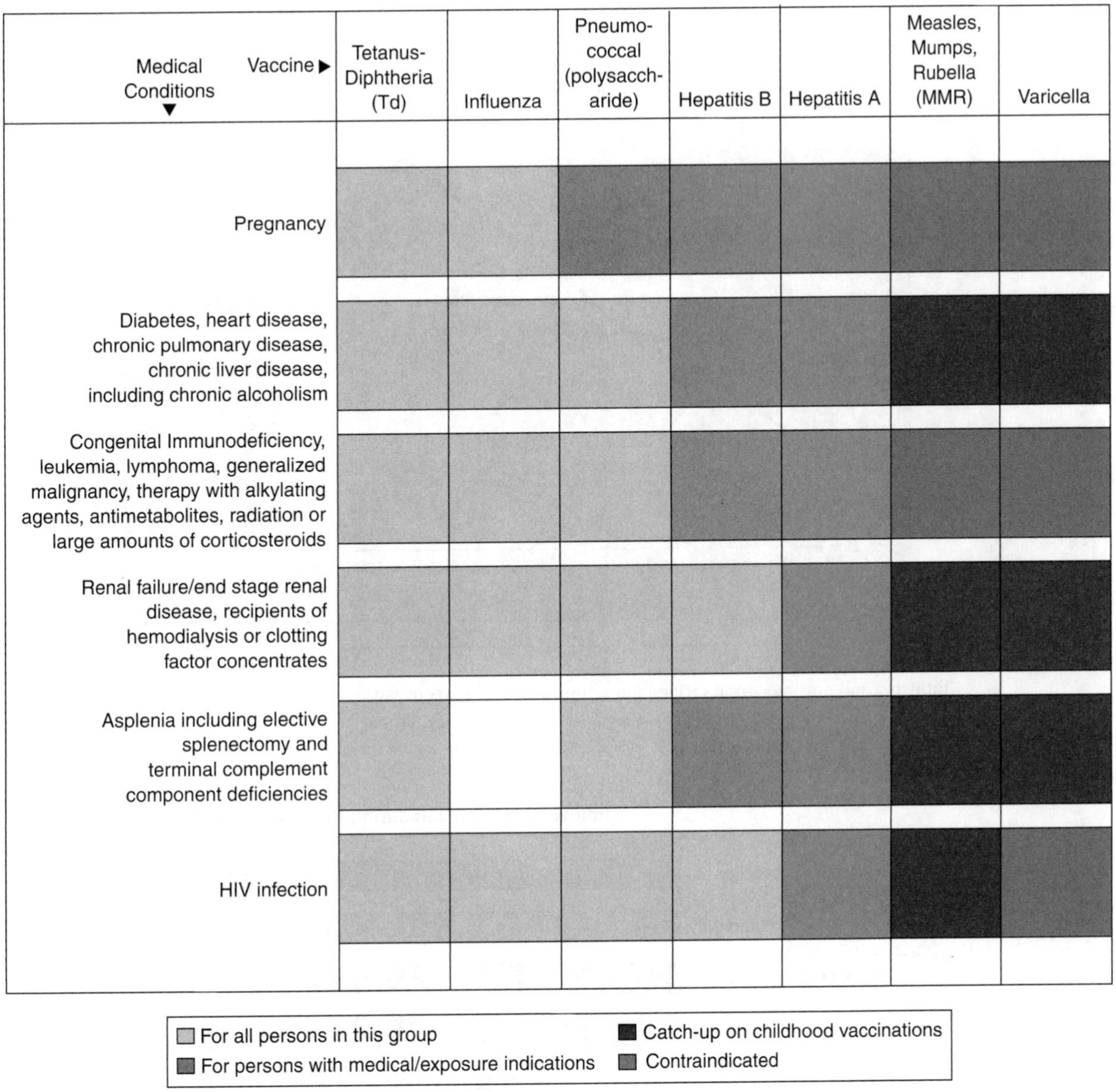

Medical Conditions ▼ Vaccine ▶	Tetanus-Diphtheria (Td)	Influenza	Pneumo-coccal (polysacch-aride)	Hepatitis B	Hepatitis A	Measles, Mumps, Rubella (MMR)	Varicella
Pregnancy							
Diabetes, heart disease, chronic pulmonary disease, chronic liver disease, including chronic alcoholism							
Congenital Immunodeficiency, leukemia, lymphoma, generalized malignancy, therapy with alkylating agents, antimetabolites, radiation or large amounts of corticosteroids							
Renal failure/end stage renal disease, recipients of hemodialysis or clotting factor concentrates							
Asplenia including elective splenectomy and terminal complement component deficiencies							
HIV infection							

☐ For all persons in this group   ■ Catch-up on childhood vaccinations
■ For persons with medical/exposure indications   ■ Contraindicated

FIGURE 10.19
Continued

is to increase the number of noninstitutionalized adults 65 and over who are immunized annually against influenza and who have ever received an immunization against pneumoccocal disease to 90% (see Figure 10.20). Increased immunization rates of influenza and pneumoccocal diseases would significantly lower the number of infectious deaths caused in elders. Annually an estimated 40,000 adults over 65 die from influenza and pneumoccocal infections, making it the fifth leading cause of death among the elder population.[47] Immunization rates among minorities for influenza and pneumococcal infections are substantially lower than for white Americans (see Figure 10.21).[52] Therefore, even though these two immunization rates among all adults have shown a significant increase in the 1990s, in order to reach the goal of 90% by 2010, increased efforts must be focused on minority populations.[8]

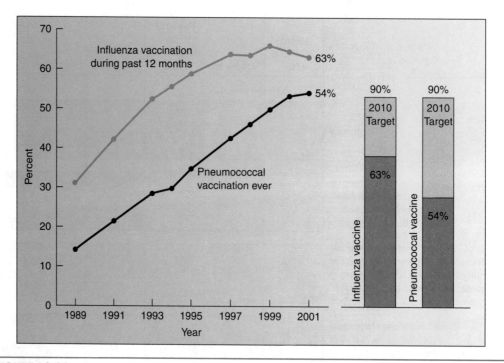

FIGURE 10.20

Influenza and pneumococcal vaccination among adults 65 years of age and over: United States, 1989 to 2001.

Note: Data are for the civilian noninstitutionalized population and are age adjusted.

Source: Centers for Disease Control and Prevention, National Center for Health Statistics, National Health Interview Survey.

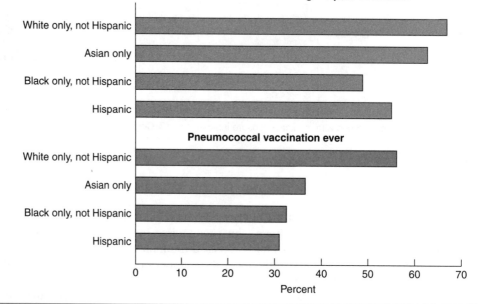

FIGURE 10.21

Influenza and pneumococcal vaccination among adults 65 years of age and over, by race and Hispanic origin: United States, 1999 to 2001.

Source: Fried, V. M., K. Prager, A. P. MacKay, and H. Xia (2003). *Chartbook on Trends in the Health of Americans: Health, United States, 2003.* Hyattsville, MD: National Center for Health Statistics.

SOCIOECONOMIC STATUS AND RACIAL AND ETHNIC DISPARITIES IN HEALTH

Preceding our discussion of the *Race and Health Initiative*, we acknowledged that disparities exist in many other areas of minority health. However, we limited our focus to the six health areas identified in the initiative. In like manner, there are many factors that contribute to these disparities. These include economics, education, and behavioral factors—such as lifestyle and health practices—as well as cultural, legal, and political factors (see Figure 10.22). We will focus our discussion on **socioeconomic status** (SES), which has been considered the most influential single contributor to premature morbidity and mortality by many public health researchers.[53] However, it is important to emphasize that the association between SES and race and ethnicity is complicated and cannot fully explain all disparities in health status. Furthermore, many of these factors are not always direct in nature—they are what are referred to as *indirect causal associations* or *intermediary factors*. For example, poverty by itself may not cause disease and death; however, by precluding adequate nutrition, preventive medical care, and housing, it leads to increased morbidity and premature mortality.

As we stated earlier, the categories of race are more of a social category than a biological one. Racial disparities in health generally do not reflect biologically determined differences.[53]

socioeconomic status
relating to a combination of social and economic factors

FIGURE 10.22

A framework for understanding the relationship between race and health.

Source: Williams, D. R. (1993). "Race in the Health of America: Problems, Issues and Directions," *MMWR,* 42(RR-10): 9.

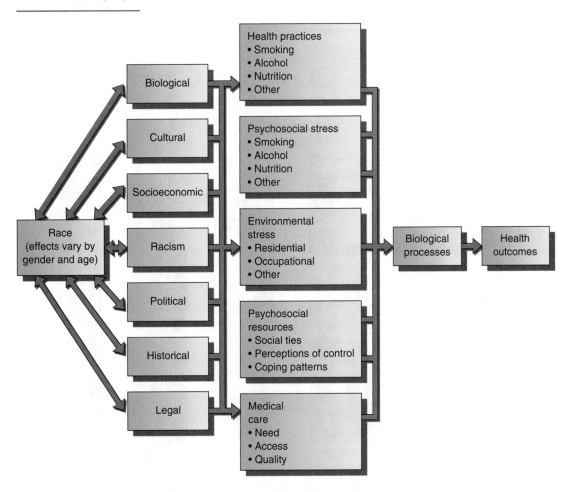

In fact, biological differences between racial groups are small compared with biological differences within groups.[54] More than 90% of the differences in genetic makeup occur within racial and ethnic groups rather than between the groups. Such disparities in health status among minority groups are much better understood in terms of the groups' living circumstances.[55] A group's living circumstances may be referred to as its socioeconomic status (SES). Common SES factors studied include level of education, level of income, and poverty.

Public health research has long studied SES factors and their relationship to health. These studies have shown that better health is associated with more years of education and having more income, a more prestigious job, and living in superior neighborhoods. Similarly, elevated levels of morbidity, disability, and mortality are associated with less education lower income, poverty, unemployment, and poor housing. An extensive amount of research documents that SES factors play a significant role in the association of race and ethnicity with health.[8] Furthermore, research in the last couple of decades indicates that the relationship between SES and health occurs at every socioeconomic level and for a broad range of SES indicators.[56] This relationship between SES and health can be described as a gradient. For example, research has documented that the more family income increases above the poverty threshold, the more health improves, and that the greater the gap in income, the greater the gap in health.

FIGURE 10.23

Prenatal care use in the first trimester among mothers 20 years of age and over by mother's education, race, and Hispanic origin in the United States, 1996.

Source: Pamuk, E., D. Makuc, K. Heck, C. Reuben, and K. Lochner (1998). *Socioeconomic Status and Health Chartbook, Health, United States, 1998* (HHS pub. no. PHS 98-1232). Hyattsville, MD: National Center for Health Statistics.

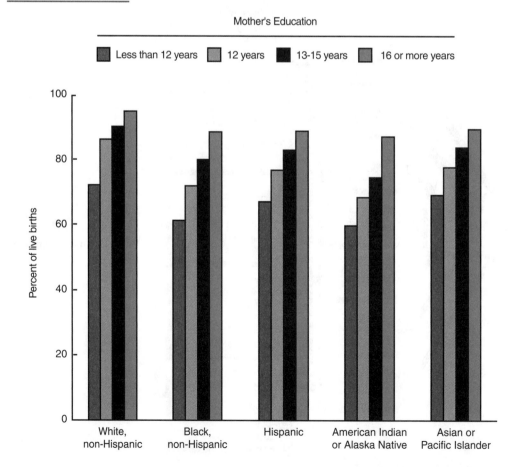

This gradient effect between SES and health has important implications that are related to the gap between the privileged and non-privileged, or the "haves and have-nots." In the United States, many inequalities still exist between all racial and ethnic groups related to level of education, income, and poverty (see Figures 10.5, 10.6, and 10.7). Minority groups often occupy the lowest socioeconomic rankings in the United States. These low rankings become a significant community health concern when one recognizes that progress toward the *Healthy People 2000* objectives was found to be greatest among higher SES groups and least among the lower SES groups.[5] Next, we will concentrate on the overlap between race, ethnicity, and SES by illustrating a few examples of health disparities across various levels of education and income within racial and ethnic groups.

Level of education is an important indicator related to health status because it appears to lead to better health indirectly—presumably because it increases knowledge about health and the beliefs that develop and assert health-promoting behaviors to maintain health and participate in prevention activities.[8] Two important health indices related to reducing infant morbidity and mortality include prenatal care for pregnant women and avoiding cigarette smoking if pregnant (see Chapter 7). As shown in Figures 10.23 and 10.24, level of education

FIGURE 10.24

Cigarette smoking during pregnancy among mothers 20 years of age and over by mother's education, race, and Hispanic origin in the United States, 1996.

Source: Pamuk, E., D. Makuc, K. Heck, C. Reuben, and K. Lochner (1998). *Socioeconomic Status and Health Chartbook, Health, United States, 1998* (HHS pub. no. PHS 98-1232). Hyattsville, MD: National Center for Health Statistics.

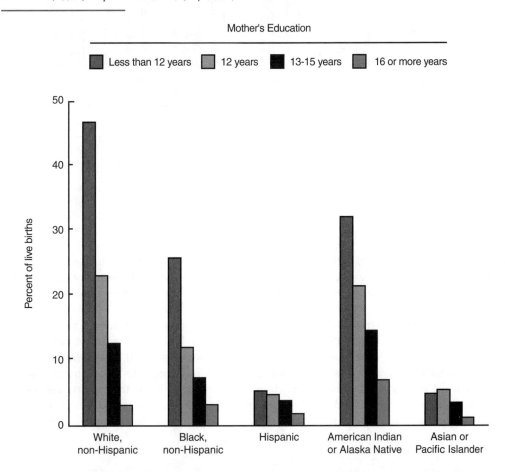

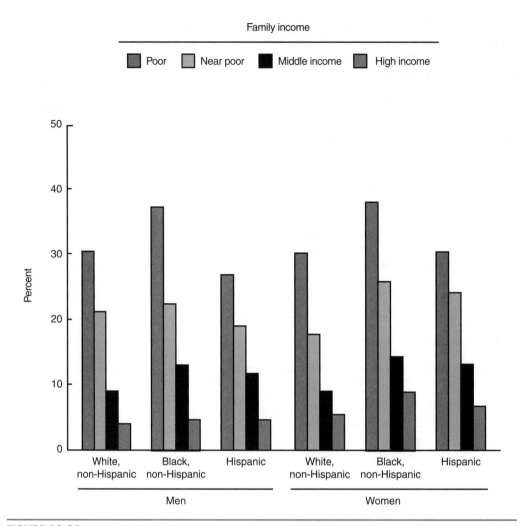

FIGURE 10.25

Fair or poor health among adults 18 years of age and over by family income, race, and Hispanic origin in the United States, 1995.

Source: Pamuk, E., D. Makuc, K. Heck, C. Reuben, and K. Lochner (1998). *Socioeconomic Status and Health Chartbook, Health, United States, 1998* (HHS pub. no. PHS 98-1232). Hyattsville, Maryland: National Center for Health Statistics.

is a strong indicator of use of early prenatal care and cigarette smoking during pregnancy. The more educated mothers are, the more likely they are to receive prenatal care in every race and ethnic group. Likewise, the more educated a woman was, the less likely she was to smoke during pregnancy.[57]

A number of studies have demonstrated that self-assessed health can be a valid and reliable index of a person's overall health.[58] Respondents are asked to assess their general health by selecting "excellent," "very good," "good," "fair," or "poor." Figure 10.25 demonstrates that there is a strong SES gradient among white Americans, non-Hispanic black Americans, and Americans of Hispanic origin. The poorer people are, the more likely they are to assess their health status as poor. Similarly, the poorer people are, the less likely they are to have health insurance coverage (see Figure 10.26) and the less likely they are to have physician contact (see Figure 10.27).

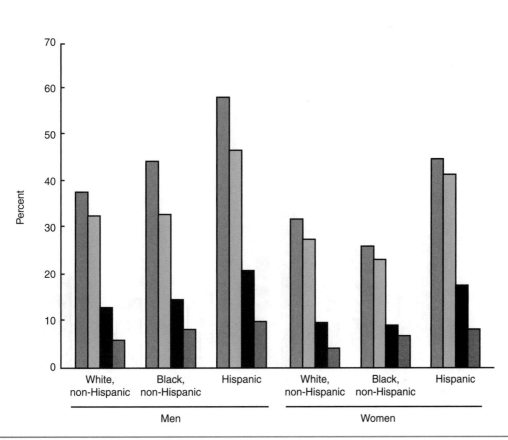

FIGURE 10.26

No health insurance coverage among persons 18 to 64 years of age by family income, race, and Hispanic origin in the United States, average annual 1994–1995.

Source: Pamuk, E., D. Makuc, K. Heck, C. Reuben, and K. Lochner (1998). *Socioeconomic Status and Health Chartbook, Health, United States, 1998* (HHS pub. no. PHS 98-1232). Hyattsville, Maryland: National Center for Health Statistics.

These examples of SES disadvantage contribute to a better understanding of racial and ethnic health disparities and provide direction toward possible intervention strategies that may help narrow the differences. Ultimately, closing the gaps between racial and ethnic minority health disparities will require altering socioeconomic conditions.[59]

EQUITY IN MINORITY HEALTH

One of the primary aims of the *Race and Health Initiative* consists of consultation and collaboration among federal agencies; state, local, and tribal governments; and community professionals to research and address issues of education, income, environment, and other socioeconomic factors that affect health outcomes. We know that many health problems faced by minorities are attributable not to race or ethnic origin, but to social or economic conditions or disenfranchisement. These health problems are inseparable from a variety of

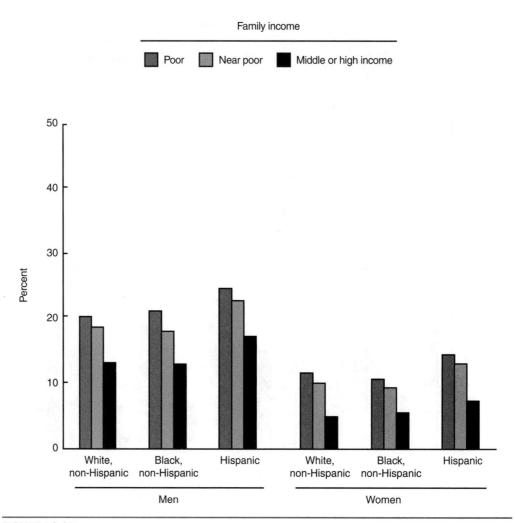

FIGURE 10.27

No physician contact within the past year among adults 18 to 64 years of age by family income, race, and Hispanic origin in the United States, average annual 1994–1995.

Source: Pamuk, E., D. Makuc, K. Heck, C. Reuben, and K. Lochner (1998). *Socioeconomic Status and Health Chartbook, Health, United States, 1998* (HHS pub. no. PHS 98-1232). Hyattsville, Maryland: National Center for Health Statistics.

other social problems, making simple solutions unlikely. We also know that multiple resources will be required to resolve these social and economic problems, and that solutions to these problems for one group may not work for another. Americans of Hispanic origin, Asian Americans, Pacific Islanders, black Americans, and Native Americans each have unique cultural traditions that must be respected if the solutions are to be successful. In other words, we must operationally integrate an understanding of the culture of the target population; solutions must be *culturally sensitive.* In a more general sense, significant strides in the improvement of health in minority groups can be achieved if community health professionals become more culturally competent and are able to empower local communities.

Cultural Competence

In this chapter's introduction, we stated that the strength and greatness of America lies in the diversity of its people and their cultures. However, cultural differences can and do present major obstacles to implementing effective community health programs and services. The demographic shifts in minority populations and the resulting diversity in health providers treating more patients has increased interest among health professionals to increase culturally appropriate services that lead to improved outcomes, efficiency, and satisfaction for their clients.[60] This increased interest is not only being found among health care providers, but also among patients, policy makers, educators, and accreditation and credentialing agencies. In March 2001, the HHS and the Office of Minority Health published standards for culturally and linguistically appropriate services (CLAS) in health care (see Box 10.2).[60] These criteria are the first comprehensive and nationally recognized standards of cultural and linguistic competence in health care service delivery that have been developed. In the past, national organizations and federal agencies independently developed their own standards and policies. The result was a wide spectrum of ideas about what constitutes culturally appropriate health services. The CLAS report went further and defined **cultural and linguistic competence** as

> A set of congruent behaviors, attitudes, and policies that come together in a system, agency, or among professionals that enables effective work in cross cultural situations. *Culture* refers to integrated patterns of human behavior that include language, thoughts, communications, actions, customs, beliefs, values, and institutions of racial, ethnic, religious or social groups. *Competence* implies having the capacity to function effectively as an individual and an organization within the context of the cultural beliefs, behaviors, and needs presented by consumers and their communities.[60]

cultural and linguistic competence a set of congruent behaviors, attitudes, and policies that come together in a system, agency, or among professionals that enables effective work in cross-cultural situations

Based on this definition, culture is a vital factor in both how community health professionals deliver services and how community members respond to community health programs and preventive interventions. In a society as culturally diverse as the United States, community health educators need to be able to communicate with different communities and understand how culture influences health behaviors.[61] It is important that community health promotion/disease prevention programs be understandable and acceptable within the cultural framework of the population to be reached. Lee has published the following list of 10 principles related to cultural competency that are considered important for community health practitioners to understand when planning and implementing health promotion/disease prevention programs:[62]

1. Having a self understanding of race, ethnicity, and power
2. Understanding the historical factors that impact the health of minority populations, such as racism and immigration patterns
3. Understanding the particular psycho-social stressors relevant to minority participants (such as socioeconomic status and migration)
4. Understanding the cultural differences within minority groups
5. Understanding the minority client within a family life cycle and in an intergenerational conceptual framework
6. Understanding the differences between the "culturally acceptable" behaviors of psycho-pathological characteristics of different minority groups.
7. Understanding the indigenous healing practices and the role of religion in the treatment of minority patients
8. Understanding the cultural beliefs of health and help seeking patterns of minority individuals
9. Understanding the health service resources for minority patients
10. Understanding the public health policies and its impact on minorities and communities

For community health educators whose role it is to educate groups and communities of diverse cultural backgrounds, cultural competence is critical (see Appendix 4). Additionally, successful community health intervention and educational activities should be firmly

BOX
10.2

NATIONAL STANDARDS FOR CULTURALLY AND LINGUISTICALLY APPROPRIATE SERVICES IN HEALTH CARE

1. Health care organizations should ensure that patients/consumers receive from all staff members effective, understandable, and respectful care that is provided in a manner compatible with their cultural health beliefs and practices and preferred language.

2. Health care organizations should implement strategies to recruit, retain, and promote at all levels of the organization a diverse staff and leadership that are representative of the demographic characteristics of the service area.

3. Health care organizations should ensure that staff at all levels and across all disciplines receive ongoing education and training in culturally and linguistically appropriate service delivery.

4. Health care organizations must offer and provide language assistance services, including bilingual staff and interpreter services, at no cost to each patient/consumer with limited English proficiency at all points of contact, in a timely manner during all hours of operation.

5. Health care organizations must provide to patients/consumers in their preferred language both verbal offers and written notices informing them of their right to receive language assistance services.

6. Health care organizations must assure the competence of language assistance provided to limited English proficient patients/consumers by interpreters and bilingual staff. Family and friends should not be used to provide interpretation services (except on request by the patient/consumer).

7. Health care organizations must make available easily understood patient-related materials and post signage in the languages of the commonly encountered groups and/or groups represented in the service area.

8. Health care organizations should develop, implement, and promote a written strategic plan that outlines clear goals, policies, operational plans, and management accountability/oversight mechanisms to provide culturally and linguistically appropriate services.

9. Health care organizations should conduct initial and ongoing organizational self-assessments of CLAS-related activities and are encouraged to integrate cultural and linguistic competence-related measures into their internal audits, performance improvement programs, patient satisfaction assessments, and outcomes-based evaluations.

10. Health care organizations should ensure that data on the individual patient's/consumer's race, ethnicity, and spoken and written language are collected in health records, integrated into the organization's management information systems, and periodically updated.

11. Health care organizations should maintain a current demographic, cultural, and epidemiologial profile of the community as well as a needs assessment to accurately plan for and implement services that respond to the cultural and linguistic characteristics of the service area.

12. Health care organizations should develop participatory, collaborative partnerships with communities and utilize a variety of formal and informal mechanisms to facilitate community and patient/consumer involvement in designing and implementing CLAS-related activities.

13. Health care organizations should ensure that conflict and grievance resolution processes are culturally and linguistically sensitive and capable of identifying, preventing, and resolving cross-cultural conflicts or complaints by patients/consumers.

14. Health care organizations are encouraged to regularly make available to the public information about their progress and successful innovations in implementing the CLAS standards and to provide public notice in their communities about the availability of this information.

Note: The standards are organized by three themes.
  1. Culturally competent care (Standards 1–3)
  2. Language access services (Standards 4–7)
  3. Organizational supports for cultural competence (Standards 8–14)

Source: U.S. Department of Health and Human Services, Office of Minority Health (2001). *National Standards for Culturally and Linguistically Appropriate Services in Health Care: Final Report.* Washington, DC: Author.

grounded in an understanding and appreciation of the cultural characteristics of the target group. *Healthy People 2010* is firmly devoted to the principle that "every person in every community across the Nation deserves equal access to comprehensive, culturally competent, community-based health care systems that are committed to serving the needs of the individual and promoting community health."[8]

Empowering the Self and the Community

Another principle steeply etched in *Healthy People 2010* with respect to achieving equity is the ideal that the "greatest opportunities for reducing health disparities are in *empowering* individuals to make informed health care decisions and in promoting community-wide safety, education, and access to health care."[8] One reason why minority groups lack the resources to eliminate community health problems is their lack of empowerment. To *empower* means to give power or authority; to enable or permit. With reference to our discussion, it means to enable people to work to solve their community health problems. Simply put, to acquire better health and health care services, a community must be empowered to do so.

Friedman identified three kinds of power associated with empowerment—social, political, and psychological.[63] An increase in social power brings with it access to "bases" of production such as information, knowledge and skills, participation in social organizations, and financial resources. Increased productivity enables for greater influence on markets, which in turn can influence change.

A social power-base is needed to gain political power. Political power is more than just being able to vote; it is also the power of voice and of collective action. In a democracy, seldom does a single voice effect change; it is the collective voice that can make things happen. The early labor movement in this country that led to the establishment of unions is a good example.

Psychological power is best described as an individual sense of potency demonstrated in self-confident behavior. It is often the result of successful action in the social and political domains. With the investiture of all three types of power, empowerment can take place. Empowerment replaces hopelessness with a sense of being in control and a sense that one can make a difference. Once people are empowered, the power then needs to be transferred to the communities. When communities are empowered, they can cause change and solve problems. See Chapter 5 for a discussion of community organization as a means of empowering a community.

The process of empowerment may seem abstract because of the theoretical concepts that are involved, but it is not. Follow the process in this example. A group of people, a community, lacks access to the appropriate health care. For this group to be empowered, they must build a foundation with social power. To do this, the group must gain access to the bases of production. They must acquire information about available health care programs and obtain the knowledge and skills to access care. Some in the group need to become members of social organizations that are concerned with health care (such as health departments or voluntary agencies), and the group has to obtain the necessary financial resources to enable them to be noticed in the marketplace as a consumer group. To gain such social power, it is imperative that the group be literate and have the appropriate education. Many groups never gain social power because they do not possess the education to access the bases of production.

When the group has attained social power, a subgroup is able to work toward political power. The subgroup can be heard in the marketplace with its vote and voice. Members of this subgroup can organize to present a united front for collective action. Minority groups have the potential to have a loud voice if united. Once united, they are in a position to influence decision makers at various governmental levels. In the specific case in which the goal is greater access to health care, this could mean getting the local health department to expand the types and numbers of available clinics.

Increased political power can lead to psychological power. Such power would give this particular group the confidence that the expansion of health department clinics is just the first of many achievements. Therefore, through this same process, other community improvements also can be made.

Chapter Summary

- One of the great strengths of the United States has been, and remains, the diversity of its people.

- The federal government has recently categorized the U.S. population into five racial groups (American Indian or Alaska Native, Asian, black or African American, Native Hawaiian or Other Pacific Islander, and white) and two ethnic groups (Hispanic or Latino and non-Hispanic or Latino).

- The reporting of accurate and complete race and ethnicity data provides essential information to target and evaluate public health inventions aimed at minority populations.

- All cultural and ethnic groups hold concepts related to health and illness and associated practices for maintaining well-being or providing treatment when it is indicated.

- The *Race and Health Initiative* includes six priority areas: (1) infant mortality, (2) cancer screening and management (3) cardiovascular disease, (4) diabetes, (5) HIV/AIDS, and (6) adult and child immunization. These key areas are representative of the larger minority health picture and account for a substantial burden of disease that is highly modifiable if the appropriate interventions are applied.

- Socioeconomic status (SES) has been considered the most influential single contributor to premature morbidity and mortality by many public health researchers. Research in the last couple of decades indicates that the relationship between SES and health occurs at every socioeconomic level and for a broad range of SES indicators. This relationship between SES and health can be described as a gradient.

- Significant strides in the improvement of health in minority groups can be achieved if community health professionals become more culturally sensitive and competent.

- Minority groups must be empowered to solve their own problems through the processes of social, political, and psychological empowerment.

Review Questions

1. Why is it said that the United States was built on diversity?

2. What is the Office of Management and Budget's Directive 15?

3. Why is it important for community health workers to be aware of the significant health disparities among various minority groups in the United States?

4. What were the significant findings of the 1985 landmark report, *The Secretary's Task Force Report on Black and Minority Health?*

5. List and explain the six priorities areas in the *Race and Health Initiative.*

6. What role does socioeconomic status play in health disparities among racial and ethnic minority groups?

7. Why is it important for community health professionals and workers to be culturally sensitive and competent?

8. List each of the three kinds of power associated with empowerment. What is the importance of each in empowering individuals and communities?

Activities

1. Using the most recent Census report (available in your library or on the Web), create a demographic profile of the state and county in which you live. Locate the following information—population; racial/ethnic composition; percentage of people represented by the different age groups, gender breakdown, and marital status; and percentage of people living in poverty.

2. Make an appointment with an employee of the health department in your hometown. Find out the differences in health status between the racial/ethnic groups in the community by obtaining the race/ethnicity-specific morbidity and mortality data. Discuss these differences with the health department employee, then summarize your findings in a one-page paper.

3. In a two- to three-page paper, present the proposal you would recommend to the President of the United States for closing the health status gap between the races and ethnic groups.

4. Identify a specific racial/ethnic minority group and select a health problem. Study the topic and present in a three-page paper the present status of the problem, the future outlook for the problem, and what could be done to reduce or eliminate the problem.

5. Write a two-page position paper on "Why racial/ethnic minority groups have a lower health status than the majority white Americans."

Community Health on the Web

The Internet contains a wealth of information about community and public health. Increase your knowledge of some of the topics presented in this chapter by accessing the Jones and Bartlett Publishers Web site at **health.jbpub.com/communityhealth/5e** and follow the links to complete the following Web activities.

- Office of Minority Health
- Eliminating Racial and Ethnic Disparities in Health
- Indian Health Service

SCENARIO: ANALYSIS AND RESPONSE

1. Do you agree with Tom when he says the United States is more culturally diverse than at any time in the past? Why or why not? Do you see this as a strength or weakness for the country?

2. What signs are there in your community that the United States is becoming more internationalized and that minority groups are growing?

3. What strengths do you see as a result of an increasingly diverse population in the United States? What weaknesses?

4. Do you agree with the major health priorities as outlined in the *Race and Health Initiative* regarding the community you live in? Why or why not?

REFERENCES

1. The White House (1999). *One America Initiative*. Available at http://www.whitehouse.gov/Initiatives/OneAmerica/america.html.

2. U.S. Bureau of the Census, Population Division (2000). *Projections of the Resident Population by Race, Hispanic Origin, and Nativity*. Washington, DC: Author.

3. Centers for Disease Control and Prevention (1997). *Minority Health Is the Health of the Nation*. Washington, DC: U.S. Government Printing Office.

4. U.S. Department of Health and Human Services (1988). *Report of the Secretary's Task Force on Black and Minority Health*. Washington, DC: Author.

5. U.S. Department of Health and Human Services (1990). *Healthy People 2000: National Health Promotion Disease Prevention Objectives* (HHS pub. no. PHS 90-50212). Washington, DC: U.S. Government Printing Office.

6. Keppel, K. G., J. N. Pearcy, and D. K. Wagener (2002). *Trends in Racial and Ethnic-Specific Rates for the Health Status Indicators: United States 1990-1998* (Healthy People Statistical Notes no. 23). Hyattsville, MD: National Center for Health Statistics.

7. U.S. Department of Health and Human Services (2000). *Race and Health Initiative*. Available at http://raceandhealth.hhs.gov/.

8. U.S. Department of Health and Human Services (2000). *Healthy People 2010: Understanding and Improving Health,* 2nd ed. Washington, DC: U.S. Government Printing Office.

9. Office of Management and Budget (1978). "Directive 15: Race and Ethnic Standards for Federal Statistics and Administrative Reporting." In U.S. Department of Commerce, Office of Federal Statistical Policy and Standards, *Statistical Policy Handbook*. Washington, DC: Author, 37-38.

10. Office of Management and Budget (30 October 1997). "Revisions to the Standards for the Classification of Federal Data on Race and Ethnicity." *Federal Register*.

11. Nelson, H., and R. Jurmain (1998). *Introduction to Physical Anthropology,* 4th ed. St. Paul, MN: West Publishing.

12. Williams, D. R., R. Lavizzo-Mourey, and R. C. Warren (1994). "The Concept of Race and Health Status in America." *Public Health Reports,* 109: 26-41.

13. Senior, P. A., and R. Bhopa (1994). "Ethnicity as a Variable in Epidemiological Research." *British Medical Journal,* 309: 327-330.

14. Centers for Disease Control and Prevention (1999). "Reporting Race and Ethnicity Data—National Electronic Telecommunications System for Surveillance, 1994-1997." *MMWR,* 48(15): 305-312.

15. Centers for Disease Control and Prevention (1993). "Use of Race and Ethnicity in Public Health Surveillance: Summary of the CDC/ATSDR Workshop." *MMWR,* 42(10): 1-17.

16. Rosenberg, H. M., J. D. Maurer, and P. D. Sorlie (1999). "Quality of Death Rates by Race and Hispanic Origin: A Summary of Current Research." *Vital Statistics Reports,* 2(128).

17. U.S. Department of Health and Human Services (1999). *Improving the Collection and Use of Racial and Ethnic Data in HHS*. Available at http://aspe.os.dhhs.gov/datacncl/racerpt.

18. U.S. Census Bureau, Population Division (2001). *National Population Projections: Total Population by Race, Hispanic Origin, and Nativity*. Available at http://www.census.gov/population/www/projections/natsum-T5.html.

19. Federal Interagency Forum on Child and Family Statistics (2003). *America's Children: Key National Indicators of Well-Being*. Washington, DC: U.S. Government Printing Office.

20. U.S. Census Bureau (2002). *Statistical Abstract of the United States: 2003*. Washington, DC: U.S. Government Printing Office.

21. U.S. Census Bureau (2002). *Current Population Survey, 1960-2001*. Washington, DC: U.S. Government Printing Office.

22. U.S. Department of Health and Human Services (1993). "Advance Report of Final Mortality Statistics, 1990." *Monthly Vital Statistics Report,* 41(9): 42.

23. Satcher, D., and D. J. Thomas (1990). "Dimensions of Minority Aging: Implications for Curriculum Development for Selected Health Professions." In M. S. Harper, ed., *Minority Aging: Essential Curricular Content for Selected Health and Allied Health Professions* (HHS pub. no. HRS-P-DV 90-4). Washington, DC: U.S. Government Printing Office, 23-32.

24. Airhihenbuwa, C. O., and I. E. Harrison (1993). "Traditional Medicine in Africa: Past, Present and Future." In P. Conrad and E. Gallagher, eds., *Healing and Health Care in Developing Countries*. Philadelphia: Temple University Press.

25. National Association of Hispanic Publications (2000). *Hispanics-Latinos: Diverse People in a Multicultural Society*. Washington, DC: Author.

26. Fishman, B., L. Bobo, K. Kosub, and R. Womeodu (1993). "Cultural Issues in Serving Minority Populations: Emphasis on Mexican Americans and African Americans." *American Journal of the Medical Sciences,* 306: 160-166.

27. President's Advisory Committee on Asian Americans and Pacific Islanders (2001). *A People Looking Forward: Action for Access and Partnerships in the 21st Century*. Available at http://www.aapi/gov/intreport.htm.

28. Mayeno, L., and S. M. Hirota (1994). "Access to Health Care." In N. W. S. Zane, D. T. Takeuchi, and K. N. J. Young, eds., *Confronting Critical Health Issues of Asian and Pacific Islander Americans*. Thousand Oaks, CA: Sage Publications.

29. Yoon, E., and E. Chien (1996). "Asian American and Pacific Islander Health: A Paradigm for Minority Health." *Journal of the American Medical Association,* 275: 736-737.

30. Humes, K., and J. McKinnon (2000). "The Asian and Pacific Islander Population in the United States." In U.S. Census Bureau, *Current Population Reports* (Series P20-529). Washington, DC: U.S. Government Printing Office.

31. Kitano, H. H. L. (1990). "Values, Beliefs, and Practices of Asian-American Elderly: Implications for Geriatric Education." In M. S. Harper, ed., *Minority Aging: Essential Curricular Content for Selected Health and Allied Health Professions* (HHS pub. no. HRS-P-DV 90-4). Washington, DC: U.S. Government Printing Office, 341–348.

32. Frye, B. A. (1995). "Use of Cultural Themes in Promoting Health among Southeast Asian Refugees." *American Journal of Health Promotion*, 9: 269–280.

33. Aiu, P. (June/July 2000). "Comparing Native Hawaiians' Health to the Nation." *Closing the Gap*, 8–9.

34. Jiang, S. (June/July 200). "Correcting the Visions of Paradise." *Closing the Gap*, 4.

35. Blaisdell, R. K. (1989). "Historical and Cultural Aspects of Native Hawaiian Health." In E. Wegner, ed., *Social Process in Hawaii*. Honolulu: University of Hawaii Press, 32.

36. Garrett, J. T. (1990). "Indian Health: Values, Beliefs and Practices." In M. S. Harper, ed., *Minority Aging: Essential Curricular Content for Selected Health and Allied Health Professions* (HHS pub. no. HRS-P-DV 90-4). Washington, DC: U.S. Government Printing Office, 179–191.

37. U.S. Department of Health and Human Services (2000). "Regional Differences in Indian Health, 1998–99." Available at http://www.hhs.gov/publicinfo/publications/trends98/region98asp.

38. Edwards, E. D., and M. Egbert-Edwards (1990). "Family Care and Native American Elderly." In M. S. Harper, ed., *Minority Aging: Essential Curricular Content for Selected Health and Allied Health Professions* (HHS pub. no. HRS-P-DV 90-4). Washington, DC: U.S. Government Printing Office, 145–163.

39. Rhoades, E. R. (1990). "Profile of American Indians and Alaska Natives." In M. S. Harper, ed., *Minority Aging: Essential Curricular Content for Selected Health and Allied Health Professions* (HHS pub. no. HRS-P-DV 90-4). Washington, DC: U.S. Government Printing Office, 45–62.

40. U.S. Department of Health and Human Services (1992). *Comprehensive Health Care Program for American Indians and Alaska Natives*. Washington, DC: U.S. Government Printing Office.

41. Uba, L. (1992). "Cultural Barriers to Health Care for Southeast Asian Refugees." *Public Health Reports*, 107(5): 544–548.

42. Sotomayor, M. (1990). "The New Immigrants: The Undocumented and Refugees." In M. S. Harper, ed., *Minority Aging: Essential Curricular Content for Selected Health and Allied Health Professions* (HHS pub. no. HRS-P-DV 90-4). Washington, DC: U.S. Government Printing Office, 627–637.

43. Lewitt, E. M., et al. (1995). "The Direct Cost of Low Birth Weight." *The Future of Children*, 5(1): 35–56.

44. American Cancer Society (2004). "Cancer Statistics 2003." *CA: A Cancer Journal for Clinicians*, 54(1): 15–37.

45. Freeman, H. P. (2004). "Poverty, Culture, and Social Injustice: Determinants of Cancer Disparities." *CA: A Cancer Journal for Clinicians*, 54(2): 72–77.

46. U.S. Department of Health and Human Services (2003). *Seventh Report of the Joint National Committee on Prevention, Evaluation, and Treatment of High Blood Pressure* (NIH pub. no. 03-5233). Bethesda, MD: National Institutes of Health.

47. National Center for Health Statistics (2003). "Deaths: Final Data for 2001." *National Vital Statistics Reports*, 52(3): 1–35.

48. American Diabetes Association (2003). "Diabetes Facts and Figures." Available at http://www.diabetes.org/ada/facts.asp.

49. Centers for Disease Control and Prevention (2003). *HIV/AIDS Surveillance Report*, 14: 1–37.

50. U.S. Department of Health and Human Services (1995). *Progress Report for Black Americans*. Washington, DC: U.S. Government Printing Office.

51. Fried, V. M., K. Prager, A. P. MacKay, and H. Xia (2003). *Chartbook on Trends in the Health of Americans: Health, United States, 2003*. Hyattsville, MD: National Center for Health Statistics.

52. Centers for Disease Control and Prevention (2003). "Racial/Ethnic Disparities in Influenza and Pneumococcal Vaccination Levels among Persons Aged 65 Years and Older, United States, 1989–2001." *MMWR*, 52(40): 598–962.

53. Senior, P. A., and R. Bhopa (1994). "Ethnicity as a Variable in Epidemiological Research." *British Medical Journal*, 309: 327–300.

54. Shiver, M. D. (1997). "Ethnic Variation as a Key to the Biology of Human Disease." *Annals of Internal Medicine*, 127: 401–403.

55. Navarro, V. (1990). "Race or Class Versus Race and Class: Mortality Differentials in the United States." *Lancet*, 336: 1238–1240.

56. Adler, N., and J. Ostrove (2000). "Socioeconomic Status and Health: What We Know and What We Don't." *Annals of the New York Academy of Sciences*, 896: 3–15.

57. Pamuk, E., D. Makuc, K. Heck, C. Reuben, and K. Lochner (1998). *Socioeconomic Status and Health Chartbook: Health, United States, 1998* (HHS pub. no. PHS 98-1232). Hyattsville, MD: National Center for Health Statistics.

58. Idler, E. L., and S. V. Kasl (1995). "Self-Ratings of Health: Do They Also Predict Change in Functional Ability?" *Journal of Gerontology*, 50B(6): S344–S353.

59. Pappas, G. (1994). "Elucidating the Relationships between Race, Socioeconomic Status, and Health." *American Journal of Public Health*, 84(6): 892–893.

60. Office of Minority Health (2000). "Assuring Cultural Competence in Health Care: Recommendations for National Standards and an Outcomes-Focused Research Agenda." Available at http://www.omhrc.gov/inetpub/wwwroot/clas/indexfinal.htm.

61. Loustaunau, M. (2000). "Becoming Culturally Sensitive: Preparing for Service as a Health Educator in a Multicultural World." In S. Smith, ed., *Community Health Perspectives*. Madison, WI: Coursewise Publishing, 33–37.

62. Lee, E. (2000). *Working with Asian Americans*. New York: Guilford Press.

63. Friedmann, J. (1992). *Empowerment: The Politics of Alternative Development*. Cambridge, MA: Blackwell.

Community Mental Health

Chapter Objectives

After studying this chapter, you will be able to:

1 Define *mental health* and *mental disorders.*

2 Explain what is meant by the *DSM-IV-R.*

3 Identify the major causes of mental disorders.

4 Explain why mental health is one of the major
community health problems in the United States.

5 Define *stress* and explain its relationship to
physical and mental health.

6 Briefly trace the history of mental health care
in America, highlighting the major changes both
before and after World War II.

7 Define the term *deinstitutionalization* and list
and discuss the propelling forces that brought it
about.

8 Describe the movement toward community mental
health centers.

9 Explain what is meant by *Community Support
Program* and list some of the services provided by
successful programs.

10 Identify the major mental and physical problems of
the homeless.

11 Define *primary, secondary,* and *tertiary prevention* as they relate to mental health care services
and give an example of each.

12 List and briefly describe the three basic approaches
to treatment for mental disorders.

13 Define *self-help groups,* give examples, and explain
how they are helpful to their members.

14 Explain the purpose of the Substance Abuse and
Mental Health Services Administration.

15 Define what is meant by *behavioral health care
services.*

16 Define *evidenced-based practices* in behavioral
health interventions.

17 Explain what is at issue when the phrase *parity* in
health care services is used in reference to health
care services for those with mental illness.

SCENARIO

In recent months, Angelina, 17, had been crying often. She spent much of the time alone. She had lost interest in her friends, in school, and even in her church. Her mother told her, "Angelina, get a hold of yourself." But Angelina felt listless and tired lately and had been spending more time sleeping. "There is nothing to get out of bed for," she said. Her mother then called her a spoiled brat, but nonetheless insisted that she have a check-up with their doctor who now worked for a managed care organization. Angelina answered all of the doctor's questions as truthfully as she could, but, perhaps because she was shy, she did not express all of her thoughts and feelings. The doctor prescribed vitamins and suggested that it might just be a stage she was going through.

Angelina's mother was a trim person who was very active in the community. Angelina's older brother and sister had been good students and were often praised by their parents and teachers. Angelina, although an average student, felt rejected by everyone she knew. Recently, when Angelina was awake, she was often eating. She had gained 15 pounds in the last few months, a fact that had not escaped the notice of her mother. "Angelina, you better watch your weight. No one likes a fatty." Angelina ran to her room crying and locked her door.

One night, Angelina felt particularly despondent and worthless. She sat on her bed. Sometimes she felt better after a nap, but lately those feelings were minimal and short-lived. She wondered if her life or anything else really mattered. Her mother just didn't understand her. As if in a trance, Angelina opened her door and walked down the hall to the bathroom where she opened the medicine cabinet. Slowly she read some of the labels— Tylenol, Robitussin-DM, Benadryl, and Phenobarbital. Slowly she reached for the bottle of Phenobarbital. They had been prescribed for her mother last year for insomnia. She opened the bottle and counted the capsules. Quickly she filled a cup with water and swallowed the entire contents of the bottle. She walked back to her bedroom and lay down on her bed.

The next thing that Angelina remembered was hearing voices. They were talking about her. "She'll be all right now. You can take her home when she wakes up, but you should keep an eye on her tonight," the man's voice was saying. "It is a good thing you called when you did."

"I called as soon as I discovered the empty bottle in the bathroom. Why would she do such a thing?" she heard her mother ask.

"She must have had some reason," said the man. "She needs counseling."

INTRODUCTION

Mental illness is one of the major health issues facing every community. It is the leading cause of disability in the United States, Canada, and Western Europe (see Figure 11.1).[1] Approximately 22% to 23% of American adults (about 44 million people) have diagnosable mental disorders during a given year. Another 6% have addictive disorders, and another 3% have both mental and addictive disorders. Thus, about 28% to 30% of the adult population have either a mental or addictive disorder.[2] About 5 million adults in the United States have serious mental illness (SMI), illness that interferes with some aspect of social functioning.[2,3] Only between one-fourth to one-third of those diagnosed with a mental disorder receive treatment.[2] Some of these people require only minimal counseling, followed by regular attendance of supportive self-help group meetings to remain in recovery, while others suffer repeated episodes of disabling mental illness. These individuals have conditions for which they require more frequent medical treatment and more significant community support. Finally, there are the most severely disturbed individuals, who require repeated hospitalization.

College students and youth also experience a variety of mental and addictive disorders. A study of client problems seen by a university counseling center revealed that, in addition to the occurrence of typical problems such as relationship problems and development issues, more severe problems such as anxiety, depression, suicidal ideation, sexual assault, and personality disorders were often diagnosed. During the 13-year period of the study, depression

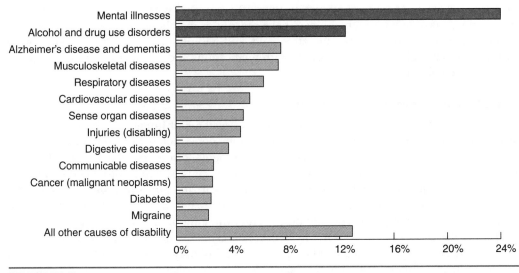

FIGURE 11.1

Causes of disability for all ages combined: United States, Canada, and Western Europe, 2000.

Note: Measures of disability are based on the number of years of "healthy" life lost with less than full health (i.e., YLD: years lost due to disability) for each incidence of disease, illness, or condition.

Source: President's New Freedom Commission on Mental Health (2003). *Achieving the Promise: Transforming Mental Health Care in America.* Rockville, MD: Author, 20.

had doubled and the number of suicidal students had tripled.[4] Approximately four million children and adolescents suffer from a major mental illness that results in significant impairment at home, at school, and with peers.[2] While 1 in 10 youths has an impairing mental illness, only 1 in 5 receives mental health services in a given year.[5]

Because the needs of the mentally ill are many and diverse, the services required to meet these needs are likewise diverse and, as we will explain, include not only therapeutic services but social services, too. Because many mental disorders are chronic in nature, significant community resources are required to meet the continuing demands for care.

Definitions

Mental health is the "state of successful performance of mental function, resulting in productive activities, fulfilling relationships with other people, and the ability to adapt to change and to cope with adversity."[2] Characteristics of people with good mental health include possessing a good self-image, feeling right about other people, and being able to meet the demands of everyday life.

Good mental health can be expressed as emotional maturity. In this regard, adults who have good mental health are able to:

1. Function under adversity
2. Change or adapt to changes around them
3. Maintain control over their tension and anxiety
4. Find more satisfaction in giving than receiving
5. Show consideration for others
6. Curb hate and guilt
7. Love others

"**Mental illness** is a term that refers collectively to all diagnosable mental disorders. **Mental disorders** are health conditions that are characterized by alterations in thinking,

mental health
emotional and social well-being, including one's psychological resources for dealing with day-to-day problems of life

mental illness
a collective term for all diagnosable mental disorders

mental disorders
health conditions characterized by alterations in thinking, mood, or behavior (or some combination thereof) associated with distress and/or impaired functioning

mood, or behavior (or some combination thereof) associated with distress and/or impaired functioning."[2] People with mental illness have organic or metabolic (biochemical) disorders that prevent them from functioning effectively and happily in society. Many people with mental illness can be treated successfully with medications and are thus able to live successfully in our communities.

Classification of Mental Disorders

It is important to keep in mind that classification systems of human origin are imperfect attempts to arrange natural phenomena into carefully constructed, but sometimes arbitrary, categories. Such is the case with the classification of mental disorders, which are for the most part based on descriptions of behavioral signs and symptoms. The most often cited reference for the classification of mental disorders is the *Diagnostic and Statistical Manual of Mental Disorders,* 4th edition, revised (*DSM-IV-R*).[6] The *DSM-IV-R,* published by the American Psychiatric Association, represents the best current thinking on the diagnosis and classification of mental disorders but does not in all cases describe the causes of these disorders.

One criterion for classifying mental disorders is age of onset. The onset of some disorders occurs in infancy, others in adulthood. Examples of mental disorders that are first evident at an early age include developmental disorders (such as mental retardation), behavioral disruptive disorders (such as attention-deficit hyperactivity), and gender-identity disorders of childhood. Disorders of adolescence and adulthood include psychoactive substance abuse disorder, schizophrenia, and mood disorders. Each of these disorders can be mild, moderate, or severe, and each may result in mild to severe impairments of social functioning. Disorders classified in the *DSM-IV-R* are listed in Table 11.1.

Origins and Causes of Mental Disorders

The origins of mental disorders, while not always fully understood, can usually be attributed to either hereditary or environmental factors or to a combination of both. When such is not the case, disorders may be referred to as *idiopathic* (of unknown origin).

There are several causes of mental disorders, including mental deficiency at birth, physical (or physiological) impairment, and psychological causes. Mental deficiency at birth can

affective disorder a mental disorder characterized by a disturbance of mood, either depression or elation (mania); examples: bipolar disorder, major depression

Table 11.1
Diagnostic Categories of Mental Disorders

Category	Example
Disorders usually first evident in infancy, childhood, or adolescence	Mental retardation; attention-deficit hyperactivity disorder
Organic mental disorders	Alzheimer's disease; dementia associated with alcoholism or chronic drug use
Psychoactive substance use disorders	Alcohol, nicotine, cocaine, or other drug dependence
Schizophrenia	Paranoid schizophrenia
Delusional (paranoid) disorder	Persecutory delusional (paranoid) disorder
Miscellaneous psychotic disorders	Brief reactive psychosis
Mood disorders	Major depression; bipolar disorder
Anxiety disorders	Panic disorder; obsessive compulsive disorder; post-traumatic stress disorder
Somatoform disorders	Conversion disorder; hypochondriasis
Dissociative disorders	Multiple personality disorder
Sexual disorders	Paraphilias (exhibitionism, fetishisms); sexual dysfunctions
Sleep disorders	Insomnia disorder; dream anxiety disorder
Impulse control disorders	Kleptomania; pathological gambling
Adjustment disorders	Anxious mood; withdrawal
Personality disorders	Avoidant; dependent; obsessive

BOX 11.1	CRITERIA FOR MAJOR DEPRESSIVE EPISODE

A. Five (or more) of the following symptoms have been present during the same two-week period and represent a change from previous functioning. At least one of the symptoms is either (1) depressed mood or (2) loss of interest or pleasure.

Note: Do not include symptoms that are clearly due to a general medical condition, or mood-incongruent delusions or hallucinations.

(1) Depressed mood most of the day, nearly every day, as indicated by either subjective report (e.g., feels sad or empty) or observation made by others (e.g., appears tearful). Note: In children and adolescents, can be irritable mood

(2) Markedly diminished interest or pleasure in all, or almost all, activities most of the day, nearly every day (as indicated by either subjective account or observation made by others)

(3) Significant weight loss when not dieting or weight gain (e.g., a change of more than 5% of body weight in a month), or decrease or increase in appetite nearly every day. Note: In children, consider failure to make expected weight gains

(4) Insomnia or hypersomnia nearly every day

(5) Psychomotor agitation or retardation nearly every day (observable by others, not merely subjective feelings of restlessness or being slowed down)

(6) Fatigue or loss of energy nearly every day

(7) Feelings of worthlessness or excessive or inappropriate guilt (which may be delusional) nearly every day (not merely self-reproach or guilt about being sick)

(8) Diminished ability to think or concentrate, or indecisiveness, nearly every day (either by subjective account or as observed by others)

(9) Recurrent thoughts of death (not just fear of dying), recurrent suicidal ideation without a specific plan, or a suicide attempt or a specific plan for committing suicide

B. The symptoms do not meet criteria for a Mixed Episode.

C. The symptoms cause clinically significant distress or impairment in social, occupational, or other important areas of functioning.

D. The symptoms are not due to the direct physiological effects of a substance (e.g., a drug of abuse, a medication) or a general medical condition (e.g., hypothyroidism).

E. The symptoms are not better accounted for by bereavement, that is, after the loss of a loved one, the symptoms persist for longer than two months or are characterized by marked functional impairment, morbid preoccupation with worthlessness, suicidal ideation, psychotic symptoms, or psychomotor retardation.

Source: Adapted from American Psychiatric Association (2000). *Diagnostic and Statistical Manual of Mental Disorders,* 4th ed., rev. Washington, DC: American Psychiatric Association.

---

be inherited (genetic causes), have an idiopathic (unknown) origin, or be the result of maternal exposure to physical, chemical, or biological agents. Two-thirds of mental retardation cases are traceable to environmental factors such as poor prenatal care, poor maternal nutrition, or maternal exposure to alcohol, tobacco, or other drugs; as such, they are preventable. For example, Fetal Alcohol Syndrome, a condition that includes mental deficiency, is the result of maternal (and fetal) exposure to excessive amounts of alcohol during gestation. One study revealed that an estimated 757,000 women used alcohol during their pregnancies, while 820,000 used cigarettes and 221,000 used at least one illicit drug.[7]

Inherited causes of mental disorders can be present at birth or appear later in life. For example, an imbalance in the levels of neurotransmitters in the brain could appear during adolescence or young adulthood. Abnormal neurotransmitter levels, which often have a genetic origin, can result in such **affective (mood) disorders** as **bipolar disorder** and **major depression** (see Box 11.1).

Mental disorders can also occur from postnatal exposure to physical, chemical, and biological agents. Brain function impairment can be caused by trauma, such as a car crash or bullet wound, or by disease, such as syphilis, cancer, or stroke. Mental impairment can also be caused by such environmental factors as chronic nutritional deficiency or by lead poisoning.

bipolar disorder
an affective disorder characterized by distinct periods of elevated mood alternating with periods of depression

major depression
an affective disorder characterized by a dysphoric mood, usually depression, or loss of interest or pleasure in almost all usual activities or pastimes

FIGURE 11.2
A dysfunctional family environment can increase one's risk for mental illness.

Psychological sources of mental disorders include dysfunctional family environments. Children reared in abusive, neglectful, or violent family environments can develop mental disorders (see Figure 11.2). The prevalence of child abuse and neglect has reached epidemic proportions in America. Each year there are nearly 1 million confirmed victims of maltreatment in the United States, according to the Children's Defense Fund.[8]

It is estimated that 1 in 5 youths has some sort of diagnosable disorder. Furthermore, the prevalence of serious emotional disturbance in youth (9 to 17 years old) ranges from 5% to 13%. Thus, a minimum of 1 in 20 to a maximum 1 in 7.7 youths suffers from emotional disturbances that include functional impairment[2,3] (see Figure 11.3).

The negative influences of unhealthy neighborhoods, deviant peer groups (such as gangs), and challenging economic conditions or growing up in dysfunctional families may further increase the risk that these young people will develop mental disorders. Broken families add to the burden on our Nation's mental health services, leading children's advocates to question the priorities of federal programs that provide more money to the states for foster care than for programs designed to strengthen families. The U.S. Department of Health and Human Services estimates that there were 581,000 children in foster care in 1999.[8]

MENTAL ILLNESS IN AMERICA

Health and social statistics clearly indicate that mental illness constitutes one of our Nation's most pervasive public health problems. For many healthy Americans, exposure to stressful lifestyles represents an increased risk of mental illness.

Statistical Indicators of Mental Illness

Center for Mental Health Services (CMHS)
the federal agency, housed within the Department of Health and Human Services' Substance Abuse and Mental Services Administration, that is the Nation's leading mental health services agency

The **Center for Mental Health Services (CMHS)** in the Substance Abuse and Mental Health Services Administration estimates that 4.8 million American adults had a severe and persistent mental illness (SPMI) during the 1990 calendar year and 5.6 million adults had a serious mental illness (SMI) during that same period.[2] It has been estimated that 15.4% of the U.S. population 18 years of age and older have had at least one incident that would meet the criteria of a mental health or substance abuse disorder within the past 30 days.[2] About 35% of the population aged 15 to 54 have had a mental disorder in their lifetime. Of these, 39% also had substance abuse/dependence. Among those with a mental disorder in the past year, 21% also had abuse/substance dependence (see Figure 11.4).[9] Frequently, these mental disorders are chronic in nature; approximately half of those admitted to mental institutions have had previous admissions. On any given day, 3.4 million Americans are in specialty mental health treatment, and another 944,000 are in substance abuse treatment.[9]

Social Indicators of Mental Illness

The social statistics that reflect the depth and breadth of the mental illness problem in our society are staggering. There are approximately 30,000 suicides each year in the United States. In 2001, the Number 2 and Number 3 leading causes of death in youth aged 15 to 24 were homicide (including legal intervention) and suicide, respectively (see Chapter 8).[10] One of the objectives of *Healthy People 2010* aimed at improving the mental health status of

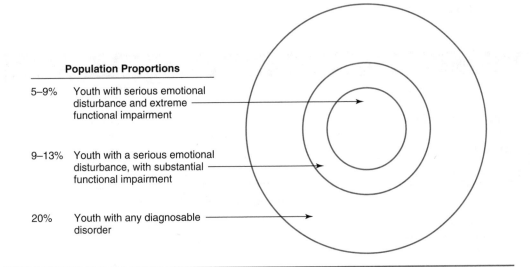

Population Proportions

5–9%   Youth with serious emotional
        disturbance and extreme
        functional impairment

9–13% Youth with a serious emotional
        disturbance, with substantial
        functional impairment

20%   Youth with any diagnosable
        disorder

FIGURE 11.3

Prevalence of serious emotional disturbance in 9- to 17-year-olds.

Source: Center for Mental Health Services (1996). *Mental Health, United States, 1996.* Mandersheid, R.W., and M.A. Sonnenschein, eds. (HHS pub. no. SMA 96-3098). Washington, DC: U.S. Government Printing Office, 83.

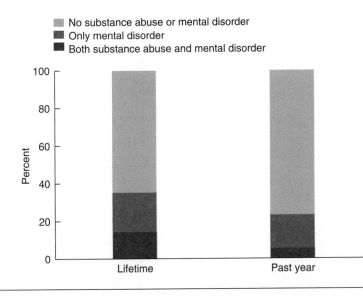

Percent of the population with a mental disorder
with and without substance abuse/dependence, ages 15 to 54, 1991

	Percent of population		Percent of persons with mental disorder	
	Lifetime	Past year	Lifetime	Past year
Any mental disorder	**35.1%**	**22.9%**	–	–
Only mental disorder	21.4	18.2	61%	79%
Both substance abuse and mental disorder	13.7	4.7	39	21

FIGURE 11.4

Percentage of the population with a mental disorder with or without substance abuse/dependence, ages 15 to 54, 1991.

Source: Rouse, B.A., ed. (1995). *Substance Abuse and Mental Health Statistics Sourcebook* (HHS pub. no. SMA 95-3064). Washington, DC: U.S. Government Printing Office, 39.

BOX
11.2

HEALTHY PEOPLE 2010: OBJECTIVES

18-1.   Reduce the suicide rate.

Target: 5.0 suicides per 100,000 population.

Baseline: 11.3 suicides per 100,000 population occurred in 1998 (age-adjusted to the year 2000 standard population).

Target setting method: Better than best.

Total Population, 1998	Suicides
	Rate per 100,000
TOTAL	11.3
Race and ethnicity	
American Indian or Alaska Native	12.6
Asian or Pacific Islander	6.6
Asian	DNC
Native Hawaiian and other Pacific Islander	DNC
Black or African American	5.8
White	12.2
Hispanic or Latino	6.3
Not Hispanic or Latino	11.8
Black or African American	6.0
White	12.8
Gender	
Female	4.3
Male	19.2
Education level (aged 25 to 64 years)	
Less than high school	17.9
High school graduate	19.2
At least some college	10.0
Age (not age adjusted)	
10 to 14 years	1.6
15 to 19 years	8.9
20 to 24 years	13.6

DNA = Data have not been analyzed. DNC = Data are not collected. DSU = Data are statistically unreliable.

Note: Age is adjusted to the year 2000 standard population.

Source: National Vital Statistics System (NVSS), CDC, NCHS.

For Further Thought

Think about the relationship between alcohol and other drug use and depression. If the rates of binge drinking and illicit drug use by teenagers were to decline during this decade, how would it affect the suicide rate?

(continued)

Americans is to reduce the suicide rate (see Box 11.2). Perhaps another social indicator of mental illness in America is the proportion of failed marriages. One in five marriages is disrupted in 5 years; one in three in 10 years.[11]

The prevalence of alcohol, tobacco, and other drug abuse in this country is yet another social indicator of the mental illness problem. For example, 40% of the college-aged young adults and 29% of high school seniors interviewed had drunk at least five or more drinks in a row in the past two weeks.[12,13] The percentage of twelfth graders reporting the use of any illegal drug in the past 30 days increased to 25% in 2002.[12] These figures, which will be discussed in more detail in Chapter 12, are further evidence that many of our youth lack the necessary psychological resources for coping with life's problems.

BOX 11.2	HEALTHY PEOPLE 2010: OBJECTIVES (CONTINUED)

18-2. Reduce the suicide attempts by adolescents.

Target: 12-month average of 1%.

Baseline: 12-month average of 2.6% adolescents in Grades 9 through 12 attempted suicide in 1999.

Target setting method: Better than best.

Students in Grades 9 through 12, 1999	Suicide Attempts
	Percent
TOTAL	2.6
Race and ethnicity	
American Indian or Alaska Native	DSU
Asian or Pacific Islander	DSU
Asian	DSU
Native Hawaiian and other Pacific Islander	DSU
Black or African American	3.1
White	2.2
Hispanic or Latino	3.0
Not Hispanic or Latino	2.6
Black or African American	2.9
White	1.9
Gender	
Female	3.1
Male	2.1
Parents' education level	
Less than high school	DNC
High school graduate	DNC
At least some college	DNC
Sexual orientation	DNC

DNA = Data have not been analyzed. DNC = Data are not collected. DSU = Data are statistically unreliable.

Source: Youth Risk Behavior Surveillance System (YRBSS), CDC, NCCDPHP.

Stress: A Contemporary Mental Health Problem

Stress can be defined as one's psychological and physiological response to stressors—stimuli in the physical and social environment that produce feelings of tension and strain. Stress, as a contributor to mental health problems, is likely to remain important as life becomes increasingly complex. Even Americans who believe they have good mental health carry out their everyday activities under considerable stress. Stressors can be subtle—such as having to wait in line, getting stuck in traffic, or having to keep an appointment—or they can be major life events such as getting married or divorced or losing a loved one. Coping with a physical health problem such as hypertension, obesity, or other disease can increase stress and raise one's risk of developing a mental disorder. While some exposure to stressors is good, perhaps even essential to a satisfying life, chronic exposure to stressors that exceed one's coping resources—biological, psychological, and social—can undermine one's health. Holmes and Rahe actually classified and ranked various stressors and found a relationship between these stressors and physical health.[14]

The process through which exposure to stressors results in health deficits has been described by Selye[15] and Sarafino.[16] According to Selye's model, which he called the **General Adaptation Syndrome (GAS),** confrontation with a stressor results in a three-stage physiological response: (1) an alarm reaction stage, (2) a stage of resistance, and finally (3) a stage of exhaustion (see Figure 11.5). In the alarm reaction stage, the body prepares to strongly resist the

General Adaptation Syndrome (GAS) the complex physiological responses resulting from exposure to stressors

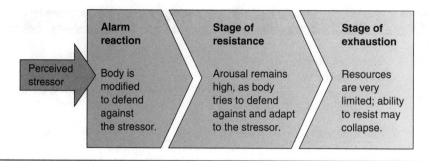

FIGURE 11.5
General Adaptation Syndrome.

Source: Sarafino, E. P. (1990). *Healthy Psychology: Biopsychosocial Interactions.* New York: John Wiley & Sons, 84. Reprinted with permission.

fight or flight reaction
an alarm reaction that prepares one physiologically for sudden action

diseases of adaptation
diseases that result from chronic exposure to excess levels of stressors, which produce a General Adaptation Syndrome response

stressor. Various hormonal changes in the body increase the individual's heart rate, respiration, and blood pressure. This is the **fight or flight reaction,** a response that the body cannot maintain for very long. Continued presence of the stressor produces a stage of resistance. In this stage, the body tries to adapt to the stressor. The level of physiological arousal declines somewhat but still remains above normal. During the stage of resistance, the body begins to replenish the hormones released in the alarm reaction stage, but the body's ability to resist new stressors is impaired. As a result, the person is increasingly vulnerable to certain health problems that are referred to as **diseases of adaptation.** Such diseases include ulcers, high blood pressure, coronary heart disease, asthma, and other diseases related to impaired immune function.[16]

The third stage of Selye's GAS is the stage of exhaustion. Prolonged physiological arousal produced by continual or repeated stress can deplete energy stores until one's physical ability to resist is very limited. During this stage, physiological damage, physical diseases, mental health problems, and even death can occur.

Evidence suggests that stress can affect health either directly by way of physiologic changes in the body or indirectly through a change in a person's behavior. The clearest connection between stress and disease is demonstrated by the release of hormones by the endocrine system during the alarm reaction stage of the GAS. During this stage, both the cardiovascular and immune systems of the body are affected. Hormones produce fast or erratic beating of the heart, which can be fatal. The same hormones have been associated with increases in levels of blood lipids. High blood lipids cause a buildup of plaque on the blood vessel walls and greatly increase the likelihood of hypertension, stroke, and heart attack.[17,18] The release of certain hormones also impairs the functioning of the immune system.[19,20] These hormones reduce the activity of T-cells and natural killer (NT) cells, making it more difficult for the immune system to fight cancer and other diseases.[21] Table 11.2 provides a list of psychophysiological disorders that have been found to be associated with stress.

The indirect effects of stress on health occur when those who experience high levels of stress respond with unhealthy behaviors. For example, it has been shown that individuals under more stress drink more alcohol and smoke more cigarettes than those under less stress.[22,23] Use of these substances has been associated with higher risks for heart disease and cancer, as well as injury and death from unintentional injuries.

The relationship between stress and mental illness is complicated. The effects of severe stress, such as that experienced under military combat conditions and by children who are sexually and physically abused, have been well documented. It stands to reason that even exposure to less intense stressors would likewise result in stress and impact one's health adversely.

Table 11.2
Psychophysiological Disorders Associated with Stress

Allergies (asthma, tissue inflammation, rheumatoid arthritis)	Gastrointestinal problems (colitis, stomach pain, ulcers)
Cancer	
Cardiovascular conditions	Headaches (muscle-contraction and migraine)
Coronary artery disease	Infectious diseases (colds and influenza)
Depression	Hypertension
Dysmenorrhea (painful menstruation)	Irritable bowel syndrome
Exhaustion	Skin disorders (eczema, hives, psoriasis)

HISTORY OF MENTAL HEALTH CARE IN AMERICA

Before discussing our Nation's current response to mental illness, we present a brief history of past efforts to confront this issue. The collective response to mental illness in America has been a cyclic phenomenon, marked by enthusiastic reform movements followed by periods of national ambivalence toward those suffering from mental disorders. The following reform movements we discuss began when an existing system for caring for those with mental illness became intolerable for society and ended when their economic burden became unbearable.

Mental Health Care before World War II

In Colonial America, when communities were sparsely populated, people experiencing mental illness were cared for by their families or private caretakers. Those "distracted" persons or "lunatics," as they were called, who were not cared for by their families usually became the responsibility of the local community. In the eighteenth century as the size and complexity of communities grew, institutionalization of the insane first appeared. This often took place in undifferentiated poorhouses or almshouses where, along with those who had mental retardation, those with physical disabilities, the homeless, and the otherwise deviant were also housed.[24]

As America's population grew in the late eighteenth and early nineteenth centuries, so did the number of people who were unable to live independently. Gradually, as the situation in the poorhouses and almshouses worsened, efforts were made to separate people by their type of disability. One of the first efforts was that of Dr. Thomas Bond, who had been to England and visited the famous Bedlam Hospital in which those with mental illness were housed. In 1751 he built Pennsylvania Hospital, a public hospital for indigents with mental illness in Philadelphia.[25] Pennsylvania Hospital was the first institution in America specifically designed to care for those with mental illness. Conditions in the hospital were harsh (see Figure 11.6), and treatments, which consisted of "blood letting, blistering, emetics, and warm and cold baths," were unpleasant.[26]

The Moral Treatment Era

While care for indigents with mental illness during most of the eighteenth century was gruesome, there were those who, at the end of the century, started a different movement. One of these was Philippe Pinel of France, who developed what he called *traitement moral,* or in English, "moral treatment." This treatment was based upon the assumption that environmental changes could affect an individual's mind and thus alter behavior.[24] In America, William Tuke, an English Quaker, put **moral treatment** into practice beginning in 1792 at York Retreat. This treatment was based on his belief that the causes of mental illnesses were moral deterioration, exemplified by "infidelity, overwork, envy, gluttony, drinking, sexual excesses, and the like."[26] In a peaceful rural setting, people with mental illness were removed from the everyday life stressors of their home environments and given "asylum" in a quiet country environment. They received a regimen of rest, light food, exercise, fresh air,

moral treatment
treatment for mental illness based on belief that mental illness was caused by moral decay

FIGURE 11.6

Treatment for mental illness in the eighteenth and nineteenth centuries was often inhumane and unsuccessful.

and amusements. A caring and respectful staff cared for them. It was believed that the environment of the asylum would result in the spontaneous recovery of patients who had come to their state through immoral behavior. While actual recovery rates are debatable, this approach, at the time, was deemed successful and became widely accepted as the ideal form of treatment for relatively well-to-do persons with mental illness in small, relatively homogeneous, New England Protestant communities of that era.[27]

The apparent successes of the moral treatment approach in the private sector led to attempts to adapt this model of mental health care to the public sector. However, by the 1840s, because of massive immigration and rapid urbanization, there was such a heterogeneous mass of people with mental illnesses that the capacity of the public asylums was soon overcrowded. The majority of those who were mentally and socially unfit again ended up in the urban almshouses, which were chronically underfunded and overpopulated. This was the state of affairs when Dorothea Lynde Dix undertook her campaign to close down county-run almshouses and establish state-run hospitals.

Dorothea Dix (1802–1897) (see Figure 11.7) was a Sunday-school teacher from Cambridge, Massachusetts, who worked tirelessly for 45 years advocating decent care for indigents with mental illness. It was her belief that it was the responsibility of the state to care for those with mental illness. She publicized the deplorable conditions in the public almshouses, and over a period of seven years (1847–1854), she lobbied Congress for a bill granting the proceeds of a federal land sale for the building of public mental hospitals. Others, who felt that mental illness was a medical problem that could be made to yield before the advance of medical science, eventually joined in her cause. Congress finally passed the bill she

FIGURE 11.7
Dorothea Dix helped to establish public mental hospitals in many states.

FIGURE 11.8
The state mental hospital was at one time viewed as the appropriate public response to the needs of those with mental illness.

supported. President Franklin Pierce, however, vetoed it, citing his conviction that the treatment of those with mental illness was the province of the individual states, not the federal government. Following a brief rest, Dix resumed her lobbying, this time on a state-by-state basis. Her efforts were in most cases successful, and all in all, Dix was personally involved in the founding of 32 public mental hospitals.[28]

The State Hospitals

The institutional movement during this period was a general one that included the building of institutions for prisoners, orphans, and wayward youth, as well as for those with mental illness. There was widespread fear that the waves of immigrants included too many poor and insane people and that the social order in America was at risk. Also, a popular misinterpretation of Darwin's theories about evolution, called "social Darwinism," in which only those adapted to society's demands could be expected to survive, was used to justify the removal of misfits and mad persons to state-run institutions where they could receive custodial care.[27] The state mental institutions were supposed to provide an environment in which medical care would be provided by professional staff, trained to work with each patient individually (see Figure 11.8). Initially, the upper limit of patients was set at 250 so that treatment could occur within the bonds of close personal relationships between caregiving staff members and patients, as prescribed in the methods of the moral treatment.

Unfortunately, even as new state hospitals continued to be built, the deterioration of those already in existence had begun. The chronic nature of mental illness was a large part of the problem. It became increasingly apparent that long-term or even lifetime stays were the norms for many patients.[28] "Maximum capacities" were quickly reached, exceeded, and repeatedly revised upward. The ability to provide personalized care was lost, as was the promise of significant medical treatment. Staff members were unable to reward patients for efforts at self-control, and physical restraints became more practical, especially in large wards.[25] As funding for these institutions became increasingly susceptible to state budget cuts, the level of care also diminished until all that remained was custodial care. The institutions at that point had become little more than places to "warehouse" people with mental illness. It became increasingly difficult to find dedicated staff to work at the unrewarding jobs in these institutions, and the turnover rate was high. Administration became more of a bureaucracy, and treatment and cure became almost nonexistent.

The Mental Hygiene Movement

The next movement in mental health care in the United States was the **mental hygiene movement,** which occurred during the first decades of the twentieth century, a period known as the Progressive Era. The leaders of this movement believed that mental illness could be prevented if it was identified and treated early. They proposed addressing the problem of mental illness at the community level. They did not concern themselves so much with the problems of the state hospitals, and they did not offer any solution to the problems existing in these institutions.

One of the prominent figures in the reform movement was *Adolf Meyer* (1866–1950), a psychiatrist who felt that psychiatrists should provide acute care for patients with mental illness in new psychopathic hospitals, after which the same patients would be remitted to community-based aftercare. The psychopathic hospitals would receive, diagnose, treat, and release patients, or in certain cases, remand them over to the state hospitals. Some of the receiving hospitals that were established during this period, such as Bellevue in New York and Boston Psychopathic Hospital, remain in operation today.[25]

Another name associated with the mental hygiene movement is that of *Clifford W. Beers* (1876–1943). Clifford Beers (see Figure 11.9) was a graduate of Yale University who suffered from a bipolar mood disorder that resulted in repeated hospitalizations throughout his life.[29] His book, *A Mind That Found Itself,* published in 1908, described his illness and experiences in mental hospitals. He was able to enlist the support of others in his cause to improve conditions and to promote research on the prevention and treatment of mental illness. He founded the National Committee on Mental Hygiene, which in 1950 became the National Association of Mental Health and in 1979 changed its name to the **National Mental Health Association (NMHA).** While Meyer and Beers contributed to mental health education in many ways, the mental hygiene movement did little to advance institutional reform of state mental facilities.

During the first part of the twentieth century, conditions in the state mental hospitals continued to deteriorate. This period was also characterized by the struggle of psychiatry for acceptance as a legitimate form of medical practice. By associating itself with the popular and progressive prevention movement, rather than with the practice of housing the chronically ill in state institutions, psychiatry was able to gain stature. Public interest in mental hygiene also increased during this period, especially when it was reported that 20% of those discharged from the army in 1912 were found to have mental illness and that the mental illness rate of those discharged in 1916 was three times the national rate.[25]

In 1934 John Maurice Grimes, M.D., headed a study panel for the American Medical Association charged with surveying state mental

---

mental hygiene movement
a movement based on the belief that mental illness can be cured if identified and treated early

---

National Mental Health Association (NMHA)
a voluntary health agency, with state and local affiliates, that sponsors education and prevention programs

---

FIGURE 11.9

Clifford Beers, whose book described his treatment in mental hospitals, founded the National Committee on Mental Hygiene and led the fight for those with mental illness.

institutions. Grimes's report provided suggestions for reducing the populations in these institutions and for developing community aftercare clinics staffed by social workers.[30] Unfortunately, Grimes's suggestions were not acted upon, and conditions continued to deteriorate for another 25 years.

By 1940 the population in state mental institutions had grown to nearly one half million, many of whom were elderly and senile. Budget cuts continued, and caseloads per worker in the institutions became so large that only subsistence care was possible.

At about this time two new treatments began to gain prominence in psychiatric medicine—electroconvulsive shock therapy and the lobotomy. **Electroconvulsive shock therapy (ECT)** evolved from several earlier types of shock therapy, including fever shock therapy, insulin shock therapy, and chemical shock therapy. Shock therapy was practiced after it was observed that mental patients experienced improvements in their conditions after suffering convulsions and that there were very few people who suffered from both schizophrenia and epilepsy. In ECT, electric current is used to produce convulsions in the patient. The practice was introduced into the United States in 1939 and grew in popularity until the 1960s, when it became apparent that in too many cases ECT was being used to control mental patients for the convenience of hospital staff, rather than to help the patient recover from illness.[31]

The **lobotomy,** the surgical severance of nerve fibers of the brain by incision, was introduced at about the same time. First developed and used in dogs in Germany in 1890 and a couple of years later on schizophrenic patients in Switzerland, the procedure was popularized by a Portuguese neuropsychiatrist, Dr. Antônio Egas Moniz. In the United States the procedure was popularized by Dr. Walter Freeman, who invented the so-called ice-pick lobotomy. Between 1939 and 1951, the procedure was carried out on more than 18,000 patients in the United States[32] (Figure 11.10). The popularity of the lobotomy procedure was undoubtedly prolonged when, in 1949, Dr. Moniz was awarded the Nobel Prize for Medicine and Physiology. However, by 1950 voices of opposition to the procedure began to gather strength. It was shown that following the surgery, only one-third of patients demonstrated improvement, while another one-third became worse off. Also, the surgery was not reversible. The appearance of new antipsychotic and antidepressive drugs in the 1950s made the widespread use of ECT and lobotomies unnecessary.[31,32]

When World War II began, more than 1 million of the 15 million men who underwent military examinations were rejected for mental health reasons; about half of these were because of mental retardation and half because of mental illness.[25] The military's need for psychiatrists meant that even fewer trained professionals were available to manage state mental institutions.

One result of the war was that new crisis intervention methods were developed, and the image of psychiatry improved. After the war, practicing psychiatrists were discharged from military service armed with new techniques and prepared to attack the problem of mental disorders in American civilians.

Mental Health Care after World War II

Following World War II, the Nation's attention was again directed toward the serious problems existing in the state mental institutions. A growing sense of urgency to respond to this problem was now joined by new feelings of optimism and a "can do" spirit that sprung from America's achievements in the war. There was a belief that any social problem could be solved with enough dedication and hard work.

In the postwar 1940s, a number of alliances formed to urge greater federal involvement in mental health care. One of these groups was the National Mental Health Foundation (NMHF), founded by a group of conscientious objectors (COs), people who objected to serving in the military on religious grounds. In place of military duty, many COs had spent their war years working in these mental institutions. Through the NMHF, the COs publicized the deterioration

electroconvulsive therapy (ECT) method of treatment for mental disorders involving the administration of electric current to induce a coma or convulsions

lobotomy surgical severance of nerve fibers of the brain by incision

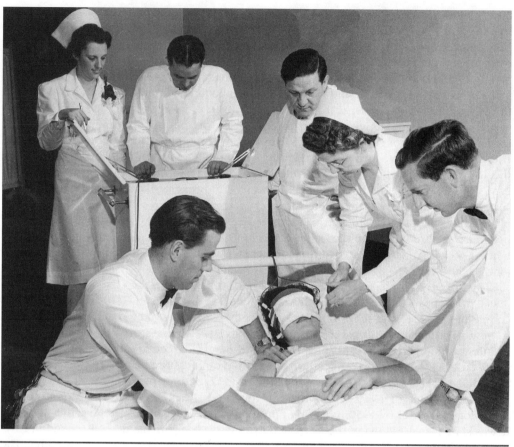

FIGURE 11.10

A team of doctors and nurses prepares to demonstrate the procedures involved in electroconvulsive therapy (shock treatment), 1942.

National Institute of Mental Health (NIMH)
the Nation's leading mental health research agency, housed in the National Institutes of Health

of the state mental hospitals and lobbied for improvements. Other interest groups included influential private citizens and mental health professionals themselves. The mood of the country, together with testimony before Congress by both military and civilian experts, soon resulted in the passage of the *National Mental Health Act of 1946,* which established the **National Institute of Mental Health (NIMH).** Modeled after the National Cancer Institute, established in 1937, NIMH came under the umbrella of the National Institutes of Health. The purposes of NIMH were (1) to foster and aid research related to the cause, diagnosis, and treatment of neuropsychiatric disorders; (2) to provide training and award fellowships and grants for work in mental health; and (3) to aid the states in the prevention, diagnosis, and treatment of neuropsychiatric disorders.[28] For the third responsibility, that of providing aid to states, a precedent had been set earlier with the federal venereal disease and tuberculosis control programs.

The NIMH enjoyed a great deal of support, not only from the public but also from some very influential private citizens, highly placed members of the psychiatric profession, and influential Congressmen. Funding for NIMH, which had begun at $7.5 million in 1947, grew to $18 million by 1953 and to $315 million by 1967.[33]

Meanwhile, in the early 1950s, public distress about the conditions in state mental hospitals continued to grow, fed not only by the NMHF movement but also by published articles and books, like *The Shame of the States,* by Albert Deutsch, and *The Snake Pit,* by Mary Jane Ward.[25] In 1950 a council of state governments came together to discuss the problem of mental health care costs. One of their conclusions was that, although there was an undeniable need for greater revenues, there was an even greater need for fewer patients. They suggested more support for research into the etiology and treatment of those with mental illness so that they could be discharged.[26] The seeds of the next movements in mental health care—deinstitutionalization, the community mental health centers movement, and the community support movement—were now sown.

Deinstitutionalization

The term **deinstitutionalization,** first suggested by Grimes in 1934, has been used to describe the discharging of thousands of patients from state-owned mental hospitals and the resettling and maintaining of these discharged persons in less restrictive community settings. The magnitude of the process can be documented with the following statistics. In 1955 there were 558,922 resident patients in state and county mental institutions.[34] By 1970 the number had dropped to 337,619, by 1980 to 150,000, and by 1990 to between 110,000 and 120,000.[34,35] Deinstitutionalization, which began in the 1950s and continued through the 1980s, was not a preplanned policy. Rather, it occurred as a result of social and economic forces that had built up for more than half a century.

> **deinstitutionalization**
> the process of discharging, on a large scale, patients from state mental hospitals to less restrictive community settings

Deinstitutionalization was propelled by four forces: (1) economics, (2) idealism, (3) legal considerations, and (4) the development and marketing of antipsychotic drugs.[26] Economically, there was not only a push, there was also a pull. The push was the states' need to reduce expenditures for mental hospitals so that more could be spent on the other three major state budgetary items—education, roads, and welfare. Meanwhile, a pulling economic force began to germinate with the prospect of profits from providing outpatient and inpatient services to those with mental illness. This prospect became brighter with changes in federal legislation (Medicare and Medicaid) permitting these services to be paid for by federal funds.

Examples of such legislation were the Social Security Amendments of 1962, known as *Aid to the Permanently and Totally Disabled (APTD)*.[26] Other federal legislation in the 1960s affected the direction of community mental health care services. A 1960 amendment to the old-age assistance program and regulatory changes permitting welfare payments to discharged psychiatric patients were two important actions. However, the major changes came about as a result of the 1965 amendments to the Social Security Act of 1935, known as Medicare and Medicaid, that took effect in 1966. Medicare provided hospital and physician services for the aged; Medicaid provided grants to the states for medical assistance to indigent persons. A remarkable feature of these amendments was the inclusion of psychiatric benefits.[34] With the passage of the social legislation of the Kennedy and Johnson presidencies, patient populations in state and county hospitals decreased even faster.[34]

Another force propelling deinstitutionalization was idealism. Idealists felt that everything possible should be done to keep people out of mental hospitals and that perhaps it would be best if these institutions were shut down altogether.[28] They believed that life inside the state mental hospitals was destructive to human values, that therapies actually made patients' conditions worse, that patients held in these institutions were isolated and hard to visit, and that those who were discharged were often worse off than when they entered. Books, like Ken Kesey's *One Flew over the Cuckoo's Nest* (1962), and movies, like *Diary of a Mad Housewife* (1970), which depicted the unsavory conditions in state mental hospitals, helped to mold public opinion against public mental institutions.[34]

In the early 1960s questions began to be raised about the legality of keeping people locked up, especially if no real effort was being made to treat them. The American Bar Association published a study in 1961 of the laws relating to this issue. One of the points raised in its review was that mental patients, even when institutionalized, had certain rights, including the right to treatment. That same year, Congressional hearings were held on the commitment procedures operating in Washington, DC. These hearings focused on broad issues, including the constitutional rights of patients. The fundamental issue discussed was "whether society, which is unable or unwilling to provide treatment, has the right to deprive a patient of his liberty on the sole grounds that he is in need of care."[34]

Over the ensuing decade, there was a subtle change in how the courts viewed civil commitment. There was more concern for the rights of individuals with mental illness—who were viewed as needing the courts' protection from inappropriate involuntary commitment—and less concern for society's right to be protected from these individuals.[26] Eventually, the test for involuntary civil commitment became one of whether these individuals could be considered dangerous to themselves or others.

While economics, idealism, and legal considerations all helped to launch deinstitutionalization, another force expedited it—new antipsychotic drugs. The most widely used drug was **chlorpromazine**, introduced as **Thorazine** by Smith, Kline, and French in 1954. Chlorpromazine was termed **neuroleptic** because it appeared to reduce nervous activity. When used in the institutional setting, the purpose of Thorazine and the other phenothiazines introduced later was to make patients more amenable to other forms of therapy. The drug did produce a remarkably calming effect in psychotic patients, and as a result, patients became more cooperative and hospital psychopathic wards became much quieter. So unusual were the effects of chlorpromazine that the drug in many cases became the *only* form of treatment provided. In these situations, a "**chemical straitjacket**" was said to have been substituted for a physical one.

Prior to its appearance on the U.S. market as an antipsychotic, chlorpromazine had been tested as a cure for several other conditions. Thus, at the time of its introduction, only three research studies on its use for treating mental disorders had been published. These studies were not of the quality that would be required under today's more rigorous Food and Drug Administration guidelines. In the haste to put this drug into use, some of its acute and chronic side effects were overlooked. Acute side effects (such as blurred vision, weight gain, and constipation) can cause compliance failures resulting in relapses or in attempts to self-medicate with other drugs, including drugs of abuse. Long-term use of chlorpromazine can result in deleterious consequences for the central nervous system. The most grave of these chronic side effects is **tardive dyskinesia**—the irreversible, involuntary, and abnormal movements of the tongue, mouth, arms, and legs.[25] In spite of these deleterious effects, Thorazine and the other phenothiazines are still used extensively to treat psychotic patients.

Community Mental Health Centers

In 1961 the report of the Joint Commission on Mental Illness and Health (JCMIH) was released. The JCMIH, established in the 1950s, was made up of representatives of both the American Medical Association and the American Psychiatric Association along with members of several volunteer citizen groups. Among the JCMIH's recommendations was that acute mental illness be treated in community-based settings. Treatment in these settings was viewed as a form of secondary prevention, in which the development of more serious mental breakdowns would be prevented. There would still be a need for the hospitals to provide tertiary prevention when secondary prevention failed and to treat those with chronic mental illness. The goals of the voluntary citizen members—namely, the establishment of primary prevention programs in community mental health—were not prominent in the JCMIH report.[28]

President John Kennedy read the Commission's report, and in February 1963, he addressed the issue of mental health care in a speech to Congress.[23] The **Mental Retardation Facilities and Community Mental Health Centers (CMHC) Act** was passed later that year and was signed on October 31, 1963. Funding for the legislation was not completed until 1965, and it did not go into effect until 1966.

In funding the CMHC Act, the federal government did exactly what President Franklin Pierce refused to do in 1854. It made the federal government responsible, at least in part, for mental health care services in all the states. Even more remarkable was that the funding for this program bypassed the traditional federal to state, state to local funding route by providing money directly to the localities themselves. In bypassing the state governments, the act created a situation in which the states had no ownership in the program or in the CMHCs. Furthermore, the act included a declining federal funding scheme but provided no incentive to states to gradually take over the financing of these centers. This situation was eventually addressed in President Carter's Mental Health Systems Act of 1980. However, before President Carter's act could take effect, President Reagan's Omnibus Budget Reconciliation Act of 1981 repealed it. The Omnibus Budget Reconciliation Act restored the traditional federal-state relationship in funding, at reduced levels, through block grants to states.[27]

The original goal of the CMHC Act was to provide one fully staffed, full-time **community mental health center** in each of 1,499 designated catchment areas containing a population of between 50,000 and 200,000. These catchment areas were constituted to cover essentially 100% of the geographic territory in the United States. By 1989, about 650 to 700 of these centers had been built with federal support; others arose independently without federal support. It is difficult to determine just how many of the original centers remain in existence today, because with a few exceptions, federal oversight of these centers ended long ago. However, there are approximately 1,150 community mental health centers that currently meet the requirements for Medicare reimbursement by providing four core services: (1) outpatient services to the elderly, children, and the severely mentally ill; (2) 24-hour-a-day emergency care; (3) day treatment or other partial hospitalization services; and (4) screenings to determine whether to admit patients to state mental facilities.[36] Community mental health centers should be accessible to the community's citizens and coordinate their activities with those of other community agencies to provide a continuity of care for those in the community with mental illness (Figure 11.11).

community mental health center (CMHC) a fully staffed center originally funded by the federal government that provides comprehensive mental health services to local populations

FIGURE 11.11
Between 1966 and 1989, 750 community mental health centers were established.

While the CMHCs did provide mental health care services to residents in the communities in which they were built, they did not live up to their original expectations of serving those deinstitutionalized persons with chronic mental illness. The latter arrived in communities that in most cases could not provide the type of comprehensive social service network they needed. The necessary funding and services for this were simply not there.

Meanwhile, many older patients with chronic mental illness were never truly deinstitutionalized. Instead they were "**transinstitutionalized**" to nursing homes, where the cost of their care was now paid for with federal, rather than state funds, and where the cost of the care turned out to be higher. Many younger patients were also transinstitutionalized when they ended up in jails for minor offenses. This problem has continued to the present day. A 1999 Department of Justice report states that "16% or an estimated 283,800 inmates reported either a mental condition or an overnight stay in a mental hospital, and were identified as mentally ill."[37] Still other patients were actually reinstitutionalized after being repeatedly admitted to psychiatric wards of community hospitals.[26]

In the 1980s, which came to be known as the "Me Decade," federal spending for many health and social programs was reduced. For deinstitutionalized people with chronic mental illness, the cuts in social and welfare programming were more destructive than those in health programming. Many people who had been just managing to get by in their communities were no longer able to do so. Without other adequate social support services, many of these people became part of the growing homeless population.

It has been pointed out that concurrent demographic phenomena contributed to the growing numbers of those in need of mental health care in the 1970s and 1980s.[38] It was during the late 1970s, as many of the baby boomers were reaching young adulthood, that the number of cases of schizophrenia had reached its peak. Compounding this problem was the increasing prevalence of alcohol and cocaine abuse in the 1980s. Also, the fastest-growing age group of the population was seniors, who are at the greatest risk for developing dementia and other age-related mental disorders.

Despite all of the problems that have been attributed to deinstitutionalization, there have been some positive outcomes. One is that a majority of released mental patients surveyed have stated a preference for life in the community over life in an institution. Also, in some communities, halfway houses and support services were forthcoming once the need for these became clear. Finally, the quality of inpatient stays has improved and their duration has been shortened.

The Community Support Movement

The response of NIMH to the criticism that the CMHCs were not meeting the need of deinstitutionalized people with chronic mental illness was the **Community Support Program (CSP)** of 1977. This program offered grants to communities to develop needed social support systems to assist people with chronic mental illness. A goal of Community Support Services is to promote "recovery" in people with serious and persistent mental disorders. The ideal CSP includes crisis care services, psychosocial rehabilitation services, supportive living and working arrangements, medical and mental health care, and case management.[24,39]

CSPs have been considered a novel approach because for the first time they recognize that the problems of those with chronic mental illness are—first and foremost—social welfare problems. CSPs arose with the recognition of the fact that many of those with serious mental illness also suffer from deficits in the resources necessary for successful independent living—namely, income, housing, food, medical care, transportation, vocational training, and opportunities for recreation.[40] Thus, CSPs offer an array of services, including housing support,[41] employment support,[42] and education support,[43] all which taken together can be considered *psychosocial rehabilitation*.[40] In summary, the focus of CSPs is on services, not on facilities as was true of the CMHC movement. Between 1986 and 1994, the use of CSPs by people with severe persistent mental disorders more than doubled.

One of the best-known and successful models of psychosocial rehabilitation is the Madison (Wisconsin) Model also called Assertiveness Community Training (ACT). Support services provided by ACT staff include "domestic skills, medication, finances, housing and advocacy with other providers."[40] Studies have shown that ACT reduces both hospital use and costs. As the Madison Model becomes disseminated into more communities and tested, its role in comprehensive community health care will become clearer.[40]

Mental Health Care in America Today

Perhaps the most disappointing observation that can be made about community mental health today is that America still has no national mental health program. Although progress in providing appropriate care and support for people with mental illness has been made in some communities, the availability of such care and services is by no means universal. Significant challenges must be met before the goal of universally accessible, supportive services for all people with mental illness can be achieved. One such challenge is how to provide these services to homeless people with serious mental illness and/or co-occurring substance use disorders. Another challenge is how to provide access to treatment for those with mental disorders under our current system of managed health care.

Serious Mental Illness in People Who Are Homeless

Deinstitutionalization was a double-edged sword. While it meant the possibility of better lives for many of those with mental illness who were now able to live in communities where support services were available, it also presented many American communities with the difficult challenge of providing appropriate treatment and supportive services to homeless people with serious mental illness and/or co-occurring substance use disorders.

More than 637,000 people are homeless during any given week in America, and 2.1 million adults experience homelessness over the course of a year.[44] It is estimated that 80% of these homeless individuals are temporarily homeless, 10% are episodically homeless, and 10% are chronically homeless (see Figure 11.12). Racial and ethnic minorities, including blacks and American Indians, are overrepresented among the homeless. Black non-Hispanics make up 40% of the homeless population but only 11% of the general population, while American Indians make up 8% of the homeless population compared with 1% of the general population. Another group that is overrepresented includes individuals who belong to sexual orientation minority groups: 42% of homeless youth were lesbian, gay, bisexual, or transgendered. Substance use disorders are higher in these groups as well.[44]

"Though only about five percent of people with serious mental illnesses are homeless at any given point in time, as many as two-thirds of all people with serious mental illnesses have experienced homelessness or have been at risk of homelessness at some point in their lives."[44]

Mental Health Problems among People Who Are Homeless

Various studies have assessed the prevalence of mental health and substance abuse problems in the homeless population. Because of variations in designs and samples, the prevalence of mental health problems ranges from 2% to 90%, alcohol problems from 4% to 86%, and other drug problems from 1% to 70%. As previously mentioned, about one-third of adult homeless people have mental problems.[45] Severe and disabling disorders such as schizophrenia, dementia, mental retardation, antisocial personality disorder, and multiple coexisting disorders were higher in homeless persons than in persons included in a household population. However, conditions such as anxiety disorders, major affective disorders, and substance abuse disorders were more common in domiciled population.[45] In one study, homeless people were 38 times more likely to have schizophrenia, 22 times more likely to have antisocial personality disorder, and 5 times more likely to be cognitively impaired than those who were not homeless.

FIGURE 11.12

As many as two-thirds of all people with serious mental illness have experienced homelessness or been at risk for homelessness at some point in their lives.

Approximately one-fifth of the homeless are women. While most homeless women do not suffer from serious mental illness, the prevalence rate of mental illness in homeless women is higher than that in the general female population. Many homeless women with mental illness do not receive the necessary care.[46]

Mental deficits were also detected in homeless children, who were more likely to experience developmental delays, emotional problems, and abuse than those who are not homeless. Rates of psychiatric morbidity were much higher for both children and adolescents. While figures vary, one sample of New York City homeless youth found 70% to 90% of the subjects suffering from mental problems.[45]

Substance Use Disorders in People Who Are Homeless

About half of all adults who are homeless have substance use disorders, and many have co-occurring mental illness as well. The problem of co-occurring disorders (serious mental illness and disordered substance use) as they relate to homelessness has been recognized by the U.S. Department of Health and Human Services, which in 2003 pledged $1.6 billion over the next five years to reduce drug use, build treatment capacity, and increase access to services that promote recovery from substance use among the homeless.[44] This federal effort, described in *Blueprint for Change: Ending Chronic Homelessness for Persons with Serious Mental Illnesses and/or Co-occurring Substance Use Disorders,* is meant to work hand-in-hand with state and community comprehensive plans to end homelessness.

These plans are expected to do the following: increase affordable housing opportunities, provide improved housing and service coordination, and establish better partnerships with mainstream systems and providers.[44] The new federal initiative has as its goal the establishment of a "comprehensive integrated system of care" arrived at through strategic planning with communities to streamline existing funding, secure additional resources, and leverage new funds. This system of care will incorporate a comprehensive set of essential services that are based on evidenced-based and promising practices. One of the program's core values recognizes that "people who are homeless are people first" and "the fact that they have illnesses that significantly disrupt their lives doesn't diminish their rights, their responsibilities, or their dreams."[44] Time will tell if this new federal initiative can live up to its promise to end chronic homelessness for those with serious mental illnesses and/or co-occurring substance use disorders.

Physical Health Problems among People Who Are Homeless

While the physical health problems of those homeless, including those homeless who have mental illness, parallel those of the general population, a number of environmental factors influence the health status of this group in a particularly severe way. For example, this group is more exposed to extremes in temperature, moisture, burns, crowding, assaults, and vehicular accidents. These physical problems are worsened by the anxiety about where to find the next meal and safe shelter and, sometimes, by the effects of chronic alcohol or drug abuse.[47]

Among the clinical conditions that occur at a significantly higher rate in the homeless are communicable diseases, injuries, and nutritional deficiencies. Living in crowded shelters or single room occupancy (SRO) hotels is conducive to the transmission of respiratory and skin diseases. Homeless children are twice as likely to have upper respiratory or ear infections and are four times as likely to have gastrointestinal infections. Skin infections are the second most common acute physical disorder, and homeless children are much more likely to have lice or scabies.[48]

The incidence of tuberculosis (TB) is also higher in the homeless. One study found that in a large New York shelter 42.8% of the men had a positive TB skin test and 6% had active TB.[49] There was an increased association between the probability of a positive test and the length of time spent in the shelter. Those living in the shelter who were also intravenous drug users were three times as likely to have active TB. TB infections also are correlated with HIV infections among shelter inhabitants. It is unusual for a TB-positive individual living in a shelter to test negative for HIV.

Trauma, resulting from both intentional and unintentional causes, occurs at a rate two to three times higher among the homeless than among domiciled persons. A life on the streets is not a safe life, particularly for women, children, and the elderly, who are perceived as weak and thus often become victims of assaults. But males, in at least some studies, were found to have the highest trauma rates and the most severe injuries, including stab wounds, fractures, head trauma, gunshot wounds, burns, and injuries from suicide attempts.[50]

Meeting the Needs of Those with Mental Illness: Prevention and Treatment

Meeting the needs of people with mental illness represents a significant challenge for many communities as they strive to provide effective and economical prevention and treatment services to this segment of the population.

Prevention

The basic concepts of prevention in community health were presented in Chapter 4. The concepts of primary, secondary, and tertiary prevention can be applied to community mental health. Application of prevention strategies is considered much more cost effective than treatment.[51]

Primary prevention in community mental health has as its goal forestalling the onset of mental illness. Two examples are training in cognitive problem solving to prevent failure in school and social support groups for the newly widowed to prevent depression. Effective primary prevention reduces the incidence (rate of new cases) of mental illness in the community.

Secondary prevention, while not reducing the incidence of mental illness, can reduce its prevalence by shortening the duration of episodes, through case finding and prompt intervention. Employee assistance programs, juvenile delinquency diversion programs, and crisis intervention programs are all examples of secondary prevention of mental illness.

Tertiary prevention, treatment, and rehabilitation do not actually reduce the prevalence of mental illness in the community. Instead they ameliorate the illness and prevent further problems for the individual and the community. Supported living programs previously discussed in "The Community Support Movement" section are examples of tertiary prevention.[51]

Preventive Services

Communities today are challenged with a difficult task in providing mental health care services for their members. These services need to be comprehensive, including primary, secondary, and tertiary prevention services.

The task of providing primary prevention services falls mainly on the private voluntary agencies, such as the National Mental Health Association and its state and local affiliates. These agencies provide educational speakers, videos, books, and pamphlets about mental health, mental illness, and services. They also may offer workshops on stress management, self-esteem development, and coping-skills development. Some sponsor support groups for parents of children who are emotionally disabled or suffer from some other behavioral disorder. These agencies also act as referral agencies for those in crisis.

The needs of those in the community who require mental health care (secondary prevention) are met by an assortment of providers, including treatment providers in private clinics, community mental health centers, hospital emergency rooms, and social service providers in Social Security, welfare, veterans, and housing offices. For securing the necessary services, this hodgepodge of federal, state, and local offices and social programs is overwhelming even to someone in good mental health.

While some would say that community mental health services are improving by and large, significant problems still remain. For example, a significant gap persists in the availability and quality of care for insured and uninsured patients. Continued federal and state budget constraints suggest that this gap will continue to widen.

Treatment Approaches

Treatment goals for mental disorders are (1) to reduce symptoms, (2) to improve personal and social functioning, (3) to develop and strengthen coping skills, and (4) to promote behaviors that make a person's life better. The two basic approaches to treating mental disorders are *psychotherapy* and *psychopharmacology*.[2]

Psychotherapy

Psychotherapy or psychosocial therapy involves treatment through verbal communication. Three common types are used—supportive, psychodynamic, and cognitive-behavioral therapy. The first two types involve face-to-face discussions with therapists who are trained to listen, interpret, define, and resolve the troubling personal problems of the patient (see Figure 11.13). There are numerous approaches to psychotherapy, including interpersonal, couple, group, and family approaches. Psychodynamic psychotherapy examines current problems as they relate to earlier experiences, even from childhood, while cognitive psychotherapy focuses on faulty or distorted thinking patterns. Psychotherapy is most likely to be successful in less severe cases of emotional distress or when used in conjunction with

psychotherapy
a treatment that involves verbal communication between the patient and a trained clinician

FIGURE 11.13
Psychotherapy is usually only one of the services needed by persons who are suffering from mental illness.

BOX **11.3**	**HEALTHY PEOPLE 2010: OBJECTIVES**

18-9.   Increase the proportion of adults with mental disorders who receive treatment.

Target and baseline:

Objective	Increase in Adults with Mental Disorders Receiving Treatment	1997 Baseline (unless noted)	2010 Target
		Percent	
18-9a.	Adults aged 18 to 54 years with serious mental illness	47 (1991)	55
18-9b.	Adults aged 18 years and older with recognized depression	23	50
18-9c.	Adults aged 18 years and older with schizophrenia	60 (1984)	75
18-9d.	Adults aged 18 years and older with generalized anxiety disorder	38	50

For Further Thought

Less than one in four adults with recognized depression receives treatment. What reasons can you think of that contribute to this statistic?

---

other approaches (such as psychopharmacologic therapy). **Cognitive-behavioral therapy** is a type of therapy that involves the use of learning theory in which a patient learns adaptive skills through rewards and satisfaction. Cognitive-behavioral therapy usually involves the cooperation of persons important to the patient, such as other family members. Included in behavioral therapy are biofeedback, stress management, and relaxation training. This type of therapy can also be used together with medication.

Psychopharmacology

Psychopharmacological therapy involves treatment with medications. This treatment is based upon the recognition that mental illnesses are medical illnesses just like hypothyroidism or diabetes and as such are treatable with drugs. Since the introduction of chlorpromazine in 1954, a number of useful medications for the treatment of mental disorders have been developed. Conditions for which medications exist are schizophrenia, bipolar disorder, major depression, anxiety, panic disorder, and obsessive-compulsive disorder.

Another form of biomedical therapy is electroconvulsive treatment (ECT), formerly known as shock therapy. In ECT, which was discussed earlier in this chapter, alternating electric current passes through the brain to produce unconsciousness and a convulsive seizure. This form of treatment is sometimes used for major depression, selected cases of schizophrenia, or overwhelming suicide ideation, especially when the need for treatment is seen as urgent. Contemporary ECT methods employ low doses of electric shock to the brain. General anesthetics are provided to reduce the unpleasant side effects.

One of the objectives of *Healthy People 2010* is to increase the proportion of adults with mental disorders who are receiving treatment (see Box 11.3). Unfortunately, the same force that is driving most of the other types of health care decisions, namely cost, also drives decisions about treatment for mental disorders. Thus, treatment goals are becoming more and more outcome based. An "effective outcome" is defined in terms that "balance employers' needs and interests with those of patients: alleviating a patient's symptoms of distress (to reduce overall medical expenditures), improving functioning (to boost job productivity), and enhancing employees' sense of well-being (to promote positive attitudes, job satisfaction and high morale)."[52]

Self-Help Support Groups

Another approach or adjunct to successful treatment is **self-help support groups,** groups of concerned members of the community who are united by a shared interest, concern, or

cognitive-behavioral therapy treatment based on learning theory in which a patient learns adaptive skills through rewards and satisfaction

psychopharmacological therapy treatment for mental illness that involves medications

self-help support groups groups of concerned members of the community who are united by a shared interest, concern, or deficit not shared by other members of the community (Alcoholics Anonymous, for example)

BOX 11.4	NATIONAL ALLIANCE FOR THE MENTALLY ILL

The National Alliance for the Mentally Ill (NAMI) "is a nonprofit, grassroots, self-help, support and advocacy organization of consumers, families and friends of people with severe mental illnesses." NAMI was founded in 1979 and works to "achieve equitable services and treatment for more than 15 million Americans living with severe mental illnesses and their families." Today NAMI has more than 1,000 local affiliates and state organizations in the United States.

According to its mission statement, "NAMI is dedicated to the eradication of mental illnesses and to the improvement of the quality of life of all whose lives are affected by these diseases." NAMI believes that:

- Mental illnesses are biologically based brain disorders that cannot be overcome through "will power."
- Mental illnesses are not the result of personal weakness, lack of character, or poor upbringing.

- Mental illnesses are treatable. The best treatments for serious mental illnesses today are highly effective.
- Most people with serious mental illness need medication to help control symptoms, but also rely on supportive counseling, self-help groups, assistance with housing, vocational rehabilitation, income assistance, and other community services in order to achieve their highest level of recovery.
- Early identification and treatment is of vital importance.
- The stigma attached to those with mental disorders erodes confidence that mental disorders are real, treatable health conditions. It is time to remove this stigma.

More information about NAMI is available at their Web site: www.NAMI.org.

National Alliance for the Mentally Ill (NAMI) a national self-help group that supports the belief that major mental disorders are brain diseases that are of genetic origin and biological in nature and are diagnosable and treatable with medications

deficit not shared by other members of the community. The shared characteristic is often stigmatizing or isolating and viewed as something not normal by the rest of the members of the community.[51] Self-help support groups usually operate without professional leadership; instead, leadership responsibilities are often shared by members of the group. The roles of help-giver and help-receiver are entirely interchangeable. These groups serve to replace the community that was "lost" through stigmatization or isolation. Self-help support groups also reduce vulnerability and supply feedback and guidance to their members. They also provide their members with a philosophy and an outlook on their affliction.[53] Examples of self-help groups are the **National Alliance for the Mentally Ill (NAMI),** Recovery, Inc., and Alcoholics Anonymous (AA). For more information on NAMI, see Box 11.4.

Federal Initiatives for Mental Health Care

Until recently, the federal government's leadership in community mental health has been spotty. While federal funds have been made available for research, surveillance, and goal setting for mental health, there has been less support for prevention, early intervention, and treatment for those with mental illness. The "decade of the brain" culminated in 1999 when the U.S. Department of Health and Human Services issued *Mental Health: A Report of the Surgeon General.* This comprehensive report attempted to put mental health and mental illness "front and center" among America's public health problems. It was more than just a status report, although it provided many useful statistics. It was an excellent compilation of mental health care services, service needs, and barriers to receiving these services. According to the foreword, "The report lays down a challenge to the Nation—to our communities, our health and social service agencies, our policy makers, employers, and citizens—to take action."[2]

In 2002 President George W. Bush created the New Freedom Commission on Mental Health. The commission's report, *Achieving the Promise: Transforming Mental Health Care in America,* is available at the commission's Web site, www.mentalhealthcommission.gov/. The commission recognizes that mental illnesses are the leading cause of disability in the United States, Canada, and Western Europe and that they carry a high financial cost—$79 billion in the United States alone. Further, the report notes the problems of fragmentation and gaps in care for children, adults, and older adults with serious mental illness and the "lack of national priority for mental health and suicide prevention."[1]

As its title indicates, the commission's report calls for a transformed mental health care system; it establishes six goals, with recommendations for achieving each goal. The commission envisions a mental health system in which (1) Americans understand that mental health is essential to overall health, (2) mental health care is consumer and family driven, (3) disparities in mental health services are eliminated, (4) early mental health screening, assessment, and referral to services are common practices, (5) excellent mental health care is delivered and research is accelerated, and (6) technology is used to access mental health care and information. Although the commission did not propose any new programs or agencies to assist the Nation in achieving these broad goals, it did cite a number of successful "model" programs as examples that could be followed by other communities. The report does a good job of identifying the burden of mental illness and the challenges America faces in transforming the systems involved in intervention, prevention, and treatment of mental disorders. Likewise, the commission's vision of a "transformed system" is praiseworthy. However, the report stops short of describing a road map or scheme for the transformation, and certainly doesn't recommend the expenditure of any federal funds to achieve the stated goals.

The federal agencies with primary responsibilities for mental health issues in the Department of Health and Human Services (HHS) are the National Institute of Mental Health (NIMH), one of the National Institutes of Health, and the **Substance Abuse and Mental Health Services Administration (SAMHSA).** The mission of NIMH is "to reduce the burden of mental illness and behavioral disorders through research on mind, brain and behavior."[54]

Within SAMHSA are three centers: the Center for Substance Abuse Treatment (CSAT), the Center for Substance Abuse Prevention (CSAP), and the Center for Mental Health Services (CMHS), mentioned earlier. The mission of the CMHS is to "improve the availability and accessibility of high quality community-based services for people with or at risk for mental illness and their families."[55]

Community Mental Health and Managed Care

Currently, all eyes in the mental health care field are watching the dramatic effects that managed care organizations (MCOs) are producing in community mental health care. One effect has been to reduce the cost of mental health services.[2] This reduction is achieved by removing overutilization, such as unnecessary hospitalization. For MCOs, the cost of providing care is of prime importance, and in each case cost must be justified by an outcome that is effective. The risk of cost containment is that it can result in undertreatment.

The term created by the managed care industry that applies to mental health and substance abuse care services is **behavioral health care services.**[56] Under managed care programs, medical services are provided only when a condition is serious enough that care is considered "medically necessary." Whether this requirement has been met may be difficult to determine in cases when a patient with mental illness presents with a "behavioral health" condition. Some MCOs issue separate contracts to specialized vendors known as **managed behavioral health care organizations (MBHOs).**

Furthermore, in treating "behavioral health" problems, there is rarely a consensus among the stakeholders as to what constitutes a good outcome. One important trend in behavioral health care today is the application of **evidence-based practices.** That is, only those interventions for which there is evidence of effectiveness are to be used. In an effort to document the effectiveness of interventions for substance abuse and mental health disorders, the Office of Managed Care in the Center for Mental Health Services has published a report describing cost-effective behavioral health interventions.[57] The report recommends six services for consideration by MCOs or MBHOs. These are prenatal and infancy home visits, smoking cessation education and counseling, targeted short-term mental health therapy, self-care education for

Substance Abuse and Mental Health Services Administration (SAMHSA) the parent agency within the Department of Health and Human Services that contains the Center for Mental Health Services

behavioral health care services the managed care term for mental health and substance abuse/dependence care services

managed behavioral health care organizations (MBHOs) managed care providers who specialize in providing mental health care services

evidence-based practices ways of delivering services to people using scientific evidence that shows that the services actually work

parity
the concept of equality in health care coverage for people with mental illness and those with other medical illnesses or injuries

adults, presurgical educational intervention for adults, and brief counseling and advice to reduce alcohol use. It remains to be seen whether MCOs and MBHOs will embrace this report and provide these recommended services.

Another issue in mental health care coverage is parity. **Parity** refers to the effort to treat mental health care financing on the same basis as financing for general health care services. Proponents for parity suggest it is simply a matter of fairness. In the past, care for mental illnesses has often not been provided or has been reimbursed at a lower level than that for other medical conditions. In 1996 the Mental Health Parity Act was passed. This act was implemented in 1998 but fell short of requiring complete parity between medical coverage and mental health care coverage.[2]

It is difficult to determine whether the Nation, states, and local communities will respond to the needs of those with mental illness in the future. It will depend on economics, on the degree to which taxpayers have been personally touched by mental illness, or on the degree to which they are willing to tolerate the spectacle of homeless people with mental illness in their communities and in their jails and prisons. A key task facing communities is to find ways to unite formal services and informal supports to promote recovery by people who are coping with mental disorders.

CHAPTER SUMMARY

- Mental illness constitutes a major community health concern because of its chronicity, prevalence, and the demands it places on community resources.

- Americans are afflicted with a variety of mental disorders, caused by genetic factors, environmental factors, or a combination of both. These disorders, which can range from mild to severe, are often chronic and may limit the ability of those afflicted to live independently.

- Stress, resulting from social and environmental forces, can have a detrimental influence on both physical and mental health.

- Over the years, society's response to the needs of those with mental illness has been characterized by long periods of apathy, interrupted by enthusiastic movements for new and enlightened approaches to care.

- Deinstitutionalization, in which thousands of mental patients housed in state and county hospitals were discharged and returned to their communities, was the most prominent movement of the twentieth century. The origins of many of the current problems in community mental health care, such as homeless people with mental illness, can be traced to this movement.

- Community support programs for those living in our communities with mental illness, such as the Madison Model, show promise that with community support, these individuals can achieve the level of recovery necessary for them to be successfully integrated into local communities.

- The basic concepts of prevention in community health (primary, secondary, and tertiary prevention) can be applied to the prevention and treatment of mental disorders.

- Among the most common treatment approaches are psychotherapy, including cognitive-behavioral therapy, and psychopharmacology, which is based on the use of medications.

- While there is no national program to provide treatment for those with mental illness, there have been several federal initiatives aimed at improving prevention and treatment.

- *Healthy People 2010* objectives include reducing the suicide rate among Americans and increasing the proportion of those with mental disorders who receive treatment.

- Important issues face those concerned with providing services for those with mental disorders. One is finding ways to provide a variety of preventive, intervention, and treatment services to a heterogeneous group of clients, such as the homeless, in a climate of cost containment under managed care. Another is finding a way to achieve parity in coverage and cost of service reimbursement between mental health care services and services for other types of medical conditions.

REVIEW QUESTIONS

1. What is meant by the term *mental health?*
2. What are the characteristics of a mentally healthy person?
3. What is a mental disorder?
4. Name and give examples of the different causes of mental disorders.

SCENARIO: ANALYSIS AND RESPONSE

1. Why did Angelina's managed care organization not provide her with any help when she went for a check-up?
2. Had Angelina's family had their own family physician how might the care she received have been different?
3. How might services for those with mental disorders actually be better under managed care?
4. How might services for those with mental disorders be worse under managed care?
5. What secondary prevention measures would have been helpful for Angelina?
6. What was it about Angelina's home environment that may have contributed to this crisis?
7. If you were a member of the National Alliance for the Mentally Ill (NAMI), how would you answer question 6? (*Hint:* See Box 11.4.)
8. What can be done to protect those with mental disorders from suffering the same experiences as those experienced by Angelina's family?

---

5. What evidence is there that mental illness is one of our most pervasive public health problems in the United States?

6. What is stress? Give some examples of stressors.

7. How can stress cause physical illness?

8. What is the relationship between stress and mental health?

9. How were those with mental illness cared for in Colonial America?

10. What was included in Tuke's therapy known as "moral treatment"?

11. What role did Dorothea Dix play in the treatment of indigent people with mental illness?

12. How would you characterize the treatment of those with mental illness in state hospitals prior to World War II?

13. When did the mental hygiene movement occur in the United States? What was the focus of this movement?

14. Who founded the National Committee on Mental Hygiene, which later became the National Mental Health Association?

15. What piece of legislation resulted in the establishment of the National Institute of Mental Health, and what were the purposes of the Institute?

16. Define the word *deinstitutionalization.* When did it start in the United States? What caused it?

17. What is a "chemical straitjacket?"

18. Why was there a movement toward community mental health centers in the early 1960s?

19. What services are provided by community mental health centers?

20. Why is the Community Support Program considered a novel approach?

21. What types of support are provided by Community Support Programs?

22. Approximately what percentage of the homeless are living with mental illness? What physical health problems do these people face?

23. Describe primary, secondary, and tertiary prevention of mental illness and give an example of a service for each level of prevention.

24. What is involved in psychotherapy for mental illness? In cognitive-behavioral therapy? In psychopharmacological therapy?

25. What are self-help support groups? How do they increase treatment effectiveness?

26. What is the mission of the National Institute for Mental Health?

27. What is the mission of the Center for Mental Health Services?

28. What does the term *behavioral health* mean with regard to mental health care?

29. What are evidence-based practices with regard to the case for those with mental illness?

30. What are some issues surrounding managed care for the mentally ill?

31. What does *parity* mean with regard to health care services for the mentally ill?

ACTIVITIES

1. Make a list of all the stressors you have experienced in the last two weeks. Select two of the items on the list and answer the following questions about them:
   Did you realize the stressor was a stressor when you first confronted it? Explain.

What physiological responses did you notice that you had when confronted with the stressor?

Have you confronted the stressor before? Explain your answer.

What stress mediators (coping responses) do you have to deal with each of the stressors?

Do you feel you will some day fall victim to a disease of adaptation?

2. Using a local telephone book or one from your hometown, identify the organizations in the community that you believe would provide mental health services. Then create a list of the agencies/organizations. Divide the list into three sections based upon the type of service (primary, secondary, tertiary prevention) offered. If you are not sure what type of services are offered, call the agency/organization to find out. After you have completed your list, write a paragraph or two about what you feel to be the status of mental health care in your community.

3. Make an appointment with someone in the counseling and psychological service center on your campus for an orientation to the services offered by the center. Most mental health services range from stress management to test anxiety to individual counseling. Find out what your school has to offer and write a one-page summary of available services.

4. Call agencies or service groups in your community to find out what services are needed for the homeless. Also find out how serious the homeless situation is in the community and what plans there are to deal with the problem. Summarize your findings in a two-page paper. Agencies or services to call include the American Red Cross, the local police department, the Salvation Army, the local soup kitchen, a community mental health center, local hospitals, local homeless shelters, and other shelters.

5. Look through your local phone book or call the community information/crisis center to locate a mental health or substance abuse self-help support group. Call the group's number and find out what kinds of open meetings or public education activities they have.

COMMUNITY HEALTH ON THE WEB

The Internet contains a wealth of information about community mental health. Increase your knowledge of some of the topics presented in this chapter by accessing the Jones and Bartlett Publishers Web site at **health.jbpub.com/communityhealth/5e** and follow the links to complete the following Web activities.

- Center for Mental Health Services
- National Institute of Mental Health
- National Alliance for the Mentally Ill

REFERENCES

1. President's New Freedom Commission on Mental Health (2003). *Achieving the Promise: Transforming Mental Health Care in America.* Rockville, MD: Author.

2. U.S. Department of Health and Human Services (1999). *Mental Health: A Report of the Surgeon General.* Rockville, MD: Substance Abuse and Mental Health Services Administration.

3. Manderscheid, R. W., and M. A. Sonnenschein, eds. (1996). *Mental Health, United States, 1996* (HHS pub. no. SMA 96-3098). Washington, DC: U.S. Government Printing Office.

4. Benton, S. A., J. M. Robertson, W. C. Tseng, F. B. Newton, and S. L. Benton (2003). "Changes in Counseling Center Client Problems across 13 Years." *Professional Psychology: Research and Practice,* 34(1): 66-72.

5. Office of the Surgeon General, U.S. Department of Health and Human Services (3 January 2001). "Surgeon General Releases a National Action Agenda on Children's Mental Health." *HHS News.*

6. American Psychiatric Association (2000). *Diagnostic and Statistical Manual of Mental Disorders,* 4th ed., rev. Washington, DC: Author.

7. National Institute on Drug Abuse (1996). *National Pregnancy and Health Survey: Drug Use among Women Delivering Livebirths: 1992* (NIH pub. no. 96-3819). Rockville, MD: National Institutes of Health.

8. Children's Defense Fund (2003). *The State of Children in America's Union 2002.* Available at http://www.childrensdefense.org.

9. Rouse, B. A. (1995). *Substance Abuse and Mental Health Statistics Sourcebook* (HHS pub. no. SMA 95-3064). Washington, DC: U.S. Government Printing Office.

10. Arias, E., R. N. Anderson, K. Hsiang-Ching, S. L. Murphy, and K. D. Kochanek (2003). "Deaths: Final Data for 2001." *National Vital Statistics Reports,* 52(3): 1-116.

11. Bramlett, M. D., and M. D. Mosher (2002). "Cohabitation, Marriage, Divorce, and Remarriage in the United States." *Vital Health Statistics,* 23(22): 1-93.

12. Johnston, L. D., P. M. O'Malley, and J. G. Bachman (2003). *Monitoring the Future: National Survey Results on Drug Use 1975-2002. Vol. I: Secondary School Students* (NIH pub. no. 03-5375). Rockville, MD: National Institute on Drug Abuse.

13. Johnston, L. D., P. M. O'Malley, and J. G. Bachman (2003). *Monitoring the Future: National Survey Results on Drug Use 1975-2002. Vol. II: College Students and Adults Ages 19-40* (NIH pub. no. 03-5376). Rockville, MD: National Institute on Drug Abuse.

14. Holmes, T. H., and R. H. Rahe (1967). "The Social Readjustment Rating Scale." *Journal of Psychosomatic Research,* 11: 213-218.

15. Selye, H. (1946). "The General Adaptation Syndrome and Disease of Adaptation." *Journal of Clinical Endocrinology and Metabolism,* 6: 117-130.

16. Sarafino, E. P. (1990). *Health Psychology: Biopsychological Interactions.* New York: John Wiley & Sons.

17. McKinney, M. E., P. J. Jofshire, J. C. Buell, and R. S. Eliot (1984). "Hemodynamic and Biochemical Responses to Stress: The Necessary Link between Type A Behavior and Cardiovascular Disease." *Behavioral Medicine Update,* 64(4): 16-21.

18. Scheiderman, N. (1983). "Animal Behavior Models of Coronary Heart Disease." In D. S. Krantz, A. Baum, and J. E. Singer, eds., *Handbook of Psychology and Health,* vol. 3. Hillsdale, NJ: Erlbaum.

19. Jemmott, J. B., and S. E. Locke (1984). "Psychosocial Factors, Immunologic Mediation, and Human Susceptibility to Infectious Diseases. How Much Do We Know?" *Psychological Bulletin,* 95: 78-108.

20. Schleifer, S. J., B. Scott, M. Stein, and S. E. Keller (1986). "Behavioral and Developmental Aspects of Immunity." *Journal of the American Academy of Child Psychiatry,* 26: 751-763.

21. Wimbush, F. B., and M. L. Nelson (2000). "Stress, Psychosomatic Illness, and Health." In V. H. Rice, ed., *Handbook of Stress, Coping and Health: Implications for Nursing Research, Theory and Practice.* Thousand Oaks, CA: Sage Publications.

22. Baer, P. E., L. B. Garmezy, R. J. McLaughlin, A. D. Pokorny, and M. J. Wernick (1987). "Stress, Coping, Family Conflict, and Adolescent Alcohol Use." *Journal of Behavioral Medicine,* 10: 449-466.

23. Conway, T. L., R. R. Vickers, H. W. Ward, and R. H. Rahe (1981). "Occupational Stress and Variation in Cigarette, Coffee, and Alcohol Consumption." *Journal of Health and Social Behavior,* 22: 155-165.

24. Grob, G. N. (1994). *The Mad Among Us: A History of the Care of America's Mentally Ill.* New York: The Free Press.

25. Johnson, A. B. (1990). *Out of Bedlam: The Truth about Deinstitutionalization.* New York: BasicBooks, 306.

26. Gerhart, U. C. (1990). *Caring for the Chronic Mentally Ill.* Itasca, IL: F. E. Peacock, 5.

27. Mosher, L. R., and L. Burti (1989). *Community Mental Health.* New York: W. W. Norton.

28. Foley, H. A., and S. S. Sharfstein (1983). *Madness and Government.* Washington, DC: American Psychiatric Press.

29. Dain, N. (1980). *Clifford Beers: Advocate for the Insane.* Pittsburgh, PA: University of Pittsburgh Press.

30. Grimes, J. M. (1934). *Institutional Care of Mental Patients in the United States.* Chicago: J. M. Grimes. Reprint, New York: Arno, 1980, viii-xii.

31. Sabbatini, R. M. E. (1997). The history of shock therapy in psychiatry. *Brain and Mind Magazine-Electronic Magazine on Neuroscience.* Available at http://www.epub.org.br/cm/n04/ historia/shock_i.htm.

32. Sabbatini, R. M. E. (1997). The history of lobotomy. *Brain and Mind Magazine-Electronic Magazine on Neuroscience.* Available at http://www.epub.org.br/cm/n02/historia/psicocirg_i.htm.

33. Chu, F. D., and S. Trotter (1974). *The Madness Establishment: Ralph Nader's Study Group on the National Institute of Mental Health.* New York: Grossman Publishers, 232.

34. Grob, G. N. (1991). *From Asylum to Community.* Princeton, NJ: Princeton University Press.

35. Peele, R. (1991). "Can a Public Psychiatric Administrator Be Ethical?" In S. L. Keill, ed., *Administrative Issues in Public Mental Health.* San Francisco: Jossey-Bass, 41-50.

36. Centers for Medicare and Medicaid Services (2002). "Medicare Expands Crackdown on Waste, Fraud and Abuse in Community Mental Health Centers." Press release available at http://www.cms.hhs.gov/ media/press/release.asp?Counter=89.

37. U.S. Department of Justice, Bureau of Justice Statistics (July 1999). *Mental Health and Treatment of Inmates and Probationers* (NCJ pub. no. 174463). Available at http://www.ojp.usdoj.gov/bjs/.

38. Mechanic, D. (1991). "Recent Developments in Mental Health: Perspectives and Services." *Annual Review of Public Health,* 12: 1-15.

39. Goldman, H. H., and J. P. Morrissey (1985). "The Alchemy of Mental Health Policy: Homelessness and the Fourth Cycle of Reform." *American Journal of Public Health,* 75(7): 727-730.

40. Levine, M., P. A. Toro, and D. V. Perkins (1993). "Social and Community Interventions." *Annual Review of Psychology,* 44: 525-558.

41. Carling, P. J. (1993). "Housing and Supports for Persons with Mental Illness: Emerging Approaches to Research and Practice." *Hospital and Community Psychiatry,* 44(5): 439-449.

42. Bond, G. R., R. E. Drake, K. T. Mueser, and D. R. Becker (1997). "An Update on Supported Employment for People with Severe Mental Illness." *Psychiatric Services,* 48(3): 335-346.

43. Mowbray, C., T. D. Bybee, and W. Shriner (1996). "Characteristics of Participants in a Supported Education Program for Adults with Psychiatric Disabilities." *Psychiatric Services,* 47(12): 1371-1377.

44. U.S. Department of Health and Human Services, Substance Abuse and Mental Health Services Administration (2003). *Blueprint for Change: Ending Chronic Homelessness for Persons with Serious Mental Illnesses and/or Co-occurring Substance Use Disorders* (HHS pub. no. SMA-04-3870). Rockville, MD: Author.

45. Fischer, P. J., R. E. Drake, and W. R. Breakey (1992). "Mental Health Problems among Homeless Persons: A Review of Epidemiological Research from 1980 to 1990." In R. H. Lamb, L. L. Bachrach, and F. I. Kass, eds., *Treating the Homeless Mentally Ill: A Report of the Task Force on the Homeless Mentally Ill.* Washington, DC: American Psychiatric Association, 75-93.

46. Robertson, M. J., and M. A. Winkleby (1996). "Mental Health Problems of Homeless Women and Differences across Subgroups." *Annual Review of Public Health,* 17: 311-336.

47. Brickner, P. W. (1992). "Medical Concerns of Homeless Patients." In R. H. Lamb, L. L. Bachrach, and F. I. Kass, eds., *Treating the Homeless Mentally Ill: A Report of the Task Force on the Homeless Mentally Ill.* Washington, DC: American Psychiatric Association, 249-261.

48. Lee, M. A., K. Haught, I. Redlener, et al. (1990). "Health Care for Homeless Families." In W. Brickner, L. K. Scharer, B. A. Conanan, M. Savarese, and B. C. Scanlan, eds., *Under the Safety Net: The Health and Social Welfare of the Homeless in the United States.* New York: W. W. Norton, 119-138.

49. McAdam, J. M., P. W. Brickner, et al. (1990). "Tuberculosis in the Homeless: A National Perspective." In W. Brickner, L. K. Scharer, B. A. Conanan, M. Savarese, and B. C. Scanlan, eds., *Under the Safety Net: The Health and Social Welfare of the Homeless in the United States.* New York: W. W. Norton.

50. Scanlan, B. C., and P. W. Brickner (1990). "Clinical Concerns in the Care of Homeless Persons." In W. Brickner, L. K. Scharer, B. A. Conanan, M. Savarese, and B. C. Scanlan, eds., *Under the Safety Net: The Health and Social Welfare of the Homeless in the United States.* New York: W. W. Norton.

51. Levine, M., D. D. Perkins, and D. V. Perkins (2004). *Principles of Community Psychology: Perspectives and Applications,* 3rd ed. New York: Oxford University Press.

52. National Institute of Mental Health (1998). "Mental Illness in America: The National Institute of Mental Health Agenda." Available at http://www.nimh.gov/research/amer.htm.

53. Levine, M., D. D. Perkins, and D. V. Perkins (2004). *Principles of Community Psychology: Perspectives and Applications,* 3rd ed. New York: Oxford University Press.

54. "About the National Institute of Mental Health." Available at http://www.nimh.nih.gov/about/nimh.cfm.

55. "SAMHSA: Who We Are." Available at http://www.samhsa.gov/ about/content/0500whoweare.htm.

56. Edmunds, M., R. Frank, M. Hogan, D. McCarty, R. Robinson-Beale, and C. Weisner, eds. (1997). *Managing Managed Care: Quality Improvement in Behavioral Health.* Washington, DC: National Academy Press.

57. Dorfman, S. (2000). *Preventive Interventions under Managed Care: Mental Health and Substance Abuse Services* (HHS pub. no. SMA 00-3437). Rockville, MD: Substance Abuse and Mental Health Services.

Chapter 12

Alcohol, Tobacco, and Other Drugs: A Community Concern

Chapter Objectives

After studying this chapter, you will be able to:

1 Identify personal and community consequences of alcohol and other drug abuse.

2 Describe the trends of alcohol and other drug use by high school students.

3 Define *drug use, misuse,* and *abuse.*

4 Define *drug dependence.*

5 List and discuss the risk factors for the abuse of alcohol and other drugs.

6 Explain why alcohol is considered the Number 1 drug abuse problem in America.

7 Describe the health risks of cigarette smoking.

8 Define the terms *over-the-counter* and *prescription drugs* and explain the purposes of these drugs and how they are regulated.

9 Define the terms *controlled substances* and *illicit (illegal) drugs* and provide examples.

10 Characterize recent trends in the prevalence of drug use among American high school seniors.

11 List and explain four elements of drug abuse prevention and control.

12 Give an example of primary, secondary, and tertiary prevention activities in drug abuse prevention and control programs.

13 Summarize the federal government's drug abuse control efforts.

14 List and describe an effective community and an effective school drug abuse prevention program.

15 List the five facets of a typical workplace substance abuse prevention program.

16 Name some voluntary health agencies and self-help support groups involved in the prevention, control, and treatment of alcohol, tobacco, and other drug abuse.

SCENARIO

It was 10:30 P.M. on a Friday night and 28-year-old Glenda Bates had half an hour left on her shift as an emergency room nurse at Clinton County Hospital. Glenda disliked working weekend nights because more injuries were admitted to the ER during that time. Some were victims of car crashes or falls; others had been injured in fistfights, shootings, and stabbings. Many of the victims had been drinking alcohol before their injuries occurred, and some were quite drunk.

Glenda didn't like working late on Friday nights for another reason; it was "girls' night out" for her and her friends. Usually, she and her friends would go out for drinks and dancing about 8:30 or 9:00 P.M. Working the 3:00–11:00 P.M. shift meant Glenda would miss out on most of the fun.

At 11:00 P.M., Glenda quickly changed clothes and left the hospital. She hurried to her car, opened the door, and anxiously felt under the seat for the paper bag containing the half-pint bottle of gin that she had purchased on her way to work. She hurriedly gulped a couple of burning swallows and started her car. Glenda planned to arrive at the bar ready to party.

Although Glenda's drinking habits caused some of her friends to be concerned, they never told her how they felt. She drank quite a bit and usually was not ready to stop drinking when the rest of the group would decide to go home. Sometimes, a member of the group drove her home to be sure she got there safely.

By 11:30 P.M. when she arrived at the bar, she had drunk more than half of the bottle of gin. As she hurried into the bar she felt warm, even though the night air was cold. As she joined her friends, Glenda noticed that some of them were already yawning. One of them said something about having to take her son to a soccer game at 8:30 the next morning; another announced that she had to be at work by 7:00 A.M.

By 11:45 P.M., four of her friends had apologetically said good night and departed. Glenda was visibly upset by their "early" departure "just when the evening was getting started" and became loud and obnoxious. Now she and the last member of the group, Iris, were all that was left at the "party." They had a few more drinks.

About 12:15 A.M., two free drinks arrived at their table, followed by two young guys. Glenda doesn't remember much of what happened after that. There was more drinking and laughing, some dancing she thought . . . then an argument, first inside, then outside the bar. The police arrived to intervene . . . .

When she awoke in her bed the next day at noon, still in the clothes she had worn the night before, she discovered her ankle was swollen and very sore. She felt sick and a glance into her dresser mirror revealed a bruise around her left eye. Had she fallen? Who brought her home? She felt terrible, and she was due at work at 3 P.M. She decided to phone the hospital and tell them she was sick.

INTRODUCTION

The use, misuse, and abuse of mind-altering substances undoubtedly predates our recorded history. It is perhaps part of human nature to wish to experience strange and unusual feelings or changes in mood and perceptions. Early civilizations may have used drugs as a vehicle to communicate with spirits. Even today, drugs are used for this purpose in some cultures.

For many Americans, drug-taking is experimental or social, a temporary departure from a natural, nondrugged physical and mental state. For many others, it is a misguided attempt to self-medicate or to cope with personal problems such as depression, loneliness, guilt, or low self-esteem. For a small but significant segment of the population, drug-taking ceases to be a matter of conscious choice; these people have become chronic drug abusers or drug dependent. In most cultures, chronic alcohol or other drug abuse or dependence is regarded as destructive behavior, both to oneself and to the surrounding community. Community members whose lives center around drug acquisition and use usually provide little benefit to their communities and often detract from their communities.

Table 12.1
The Annual Cost in Lives and Dollars Attributable to Alcohol, Tobacco, and Illicit Drug Abuse in the United States

Type of Drug	Estimated Number of Deaths Each Year	Economic Cost to Society (in Billions)
Alcohol	100,000	$166
Tobacco	430,000	$138
Illicit Drugs	16,000	$110
TOTAL	546,000	$414

Source: Horgan, C., K. C. Skwara, and G. Strickler (2001). *Substance Abuse: The Nation's Number One Health Problem.* Princeton, NJ: Robert Wood Johnson Foundation.

Scope of the Current Drug Problem in the United States

It is difficult to argue with those who state that the abuse of alcohol, tobacco, and other drugs is the Nation's number one community health problem. According to a recent study, more deaths, illnesses, and disabilities can be attributed to substance abuse than from any other preventable health condition.[1] One-fourth of the 2 million deaths each year are due to alcohol, tobacco, or illicit drug use (see Table 12.1). Estimates of the economic cost of substance abuse in the United States vary in range between $246 billion and $414 billion per year.[2,3] These estimates include direct costs (such as health care expenditures, premature death, and impaired productivity), and indirect costs, which include the costs of crime and law enforcement, courts, jails, and social work. Of the $414 billion annual drug bill, the cost of alcohol abuse and alcoholism is estimated at $166 billion, drug abuse at $110 billion, and smoking at $138 billion (see Table 12.1). Clearly, the abuse of alcohol and other drugs is one of America's most expensive community health problems.

Those abusing alcohol and other drugs represent serious health threats to themselves, their families, and their communities. They are a threat to themselves and their families because they put themselves and their families at risk for physical, mental, and financial ruin. The habitual drug user may develop a psychological and/or **physical dependence** on the drug and thus experience great difficulty in discontinuing use, even in the face of deteriorating physical and mental health and erosion of financial resources. If the drug is an illegal one, its use constitutes criminal activity and may carry with it the added risks of arrest and incarceration.

Abusers of alcohol and other drugs represent a serious threat to the community because they have greater health care needs, suffer more injuries, and are less productive than those who do not. Community consequences range from loss of economic opportunity and productivity to social and economic destruction (see Table 12.2). Additionally, those who abuse drugs may perpetrate more violent acts that result in economic loss, injury, and death. The violence associated with the abuse of alcohol and other drugs is depicted in Figure 12.1.

According to the annual Monitoring the Future surveys on drug use among those in grades 8, 10, and 12, drug use declined steadily until 1992 and then rose again until 1996 or 1997, depending upon the grade. Overall illicit drug use began to decline gradually among eighth graders, while holding steady for older students, until 2002, when a general decline was noted.[4,5] The decline continued in 2003, but usage still remained above the 1992 levels.[6] For example, in 2003 the use of marijuana (in the past 30 days) was reported by 21.2% of high school seniors, compared with only 11.9% in 1992. Cocaine use (in the past 30 days) was reported by 2.1% of high school seniors in 2003, compared with 1.3% in 1992[4,5] (see Table 12.3). The popularity of one drug declined significantly in 2003—ecstasy (MDMA).[6] However, the use of other drugs, such as the synthetic narcotics Vicodin and OxyContin, remains alarmingly high.

physical dependence
a physiological state in which discontinued drug use results in clinical illness

Table 12.2
Personal and Community Consequences of Drug Abuse

Personal Consequences	Community Consequences
Absenteeism from school or work	Loss of productivity and revenue
Underachievement at school or work	Lower average SAT scores
Scholastic failure/interruption of education	Loss of economic opportunity
Loss of employment	Increase in public welfare load
Marital instability/family problems	Increase in number of broken homes
Risk of infectious diseases	Epidemics of sexually transmitted diseases
Risk of chronic or degenerative diseases	Unnecessary burden on health care system
Increased risk of accidents	Unnecessary deaths and economic losses
Financial problems	Defaults on mortgages, loans/bankruptcies
Criminal activity	Increased cost of insurance and security
Arrest and incarceration	Increased cost for police/courts/prisons
Risk of adulterated drugs	Increased burden on medical care system
Adverse drug reactions or "bad trips"	Greater need for emergency medical services
Drug-induced psychoses	Unnecessary drain on mental health services
Drug overdose	Unnecessary demand for medical services
Injury to fetus or newborn baby	Unnecessary use of expensive neonatal care
Loss of self-esteem	Increase in mental illness, underachievement
Suicide	Damaged and destroyed families
Death	

FIGURE 12.1

Violence associated with the use of alcohol and other drugs.

Source: National Clearinghouse for Alcohol and Drug Information (1995). *Making the Link* [Fact sheets]. Rockville, MD: Author.

When the words *drug abuse* are mentioned, most people think of illicit drugs, such as heroin, LSD, cocaine, and other illegal substances. While the abuse of illicit drugs is certainly a major problem in America, abuse of alcohol and tobacco products are, perhaps, more serious challenges to America's health. Tobacco use by high school seniors has increased since 1992, while alcohol use remained high during the same period (see Figure 12.2).

America has been trying to solve the problem of drug abuse for decades. Most adults who abuse drugs eventually "mature out" of the behavior, but there is a constant supply of potential drug users among America's children. This "generational forgetting" means that drug prevention education is never finished. Instead, drug prevention efforts must become a permanent part of our culture. That is, we must teach our children about the dangers of experimental drug use in the same way we teach them to look both ways before they cross the street.

Definitions

We begin a discussion of alcohol, tobacco, and other drugs as a community health problem by defining some terms. A **drug** is a substance, other than food or vitamins, that upon entering the body in small amounts alters one's physical, mental, or emotional state. **Psychoactive drugs**

drug
a substance other than food that when taken in small quantities alters one's physical, mental, or emotional state

psychoactive drugs
drugs that alter sensory perceptions, mood, thought processes, or behavior

Table 12.3
Percentage of High School Seniors Who Have Used Drugs

	Class of 1992			Class of 2000		
	Ever Used	Past Month	Daily Use	Ever Used	Past Month	Daily Use
Alcohol	87.5%	51.3%	3.4%	76.6%*	47.5%	3.2%
Cigarettes	61.8	27.8	17.2	53.7	24.4	15.8
Marijuana	32.6	11.9	1.9	46.1	21.2	6.0
Amphetamines	13.9	2.8	0.2	14.4	5.0	†
Inhalants	16.6	2.3	0.1	11.2	1.5	†
Cocaine	6.1	1.3	0.1	7.7	2.1	†
Tranquilizers	6.0	1.0	†	10.2	2.8	†
LSD	8.6	2.1	0.1	5.9	0.6	†
MDMA	—	—	—	8.3	1.3	†
Crack	2.6	0.6	0.1	3.6	0.9	†
PCP	2.4	0.6	0.1	2.5	0.6	†
Heroin	1.2	0.3	†	1.5	0.4	†

*More than just a few sips.
†Less than 0.05%.
— No data.

Sources: For 1992 data: Johnson, L. D., P. M. O'Malley, and J. G. Bachman (1993). *National Survey Results on Drug Use from the Monitoring the Future Study, 1975-1992. Vol. I: Secondary School Students* (NIH pub. no. 93-3597). Washington, DC: U.S. Government Printing Office. For 2003 data: Johnson, L. D., P. M. O'Malley, and J. G. Bachman (2003). *Monitoring the Future National Survey Results on Drug Use, 1975-2002. Vol. I: Secondary School Students* (NIH pub. no. 03-5375). Bethesda, MD: National Institute on Drug Abuse.

drug use
a non-evaluative term referring to drug-taking behavior in general; any drug-taking behavior

drug misuse
inappropriate use of prescription or nonprescription drugs

FIGURE 12.2
The prevalence of alcohol use among American high school seniors in the middle and late 1990s remained high, while cigarette smoking rose dramatically.

are drugs that alter sensory perceptions, mood, thought processes, or behavior.

In this chapter, the term **drug use** is a non-evaluative term referring to drug-taking behavior in general, regardless of whether the behavior is appropriate. **Drug misuse** refers primarily to the inappropriate use of legally purchased prescription or nonprescription drugs. For example, drug misuse occurs when one discontinues the use of a prescribed antibiotic before the entire prescribed dose is completed or when one takes four aspirin rather than two as specified on the label. **Drug abuse** can be defined in several ways depending upon the drug and the situation. Drug abuse occurs when one takes a prescription or nonprescription drug for a purpose other than that for which it is medically approved. For example, drug abuse occurs when one takes a prescription diet pill for its mood altering effects (stimulation). The abuse of legal drugs such as nicotine or alcohol is said to occur when one is aware that continued use is detrimental to one's health. Because illicit drugs have no approved medical uses, any illicit drug use is considered drug abuse. Likewise, the use of alcohol and nicotine by those under the legal age is considered drug abuse.

Drug (chemical) dependence occurs when a user feels that a particular drug is necessary for normal functioning. Dependence may be **psychological,** in which case the user experiences a strong emotional or psychological desire to continue use of the drug even though clinical signs of physical illness may not appear; or it can be physical, in which discontinuation of drug use results in clinical illness. Usually, both psychological and physical dependence are present at the same time, making the discontinuation of drug use very difficult. Such is frequently the case with cigarette smoking.

FACTORS THAT CONTRIBUTE TO ALCOHOL, TOBACCO, AND OTHER DRUG ABUSE

The factors that contribute to the abuse of alcohol, tobacco, and other drugs are many, and the decision to use drugs lies ultimately with the individual; it's a matter of choice. However, studies have determined that individuals are differentially at risk for engaging in drug-taking behavior.[7] Factors that increase the probability of drug use are called *risk factors;* those that lower the probability of drug use are called *protective factors.* People with a high number of risk factors are said to be vulnerable to drug abuse or dependence, while those who have few risk factors and more protective factors are said to be resistant to drug abuse.

Risk and protective factors can be either genetic (inherited) or environmental. Numerous studies have concluded that inherited traits can increase one's risk of developing dependence on alcohol, and it is logical to assume that susceptibility to other drugs might also be inherited. Environmental risk factors, such as one's home and family life, school and peer groups, and society and culture have also been identified.

Inherited Risk Factors

The vast majority of the data supporting the notion that the risk of drug dependence can be inherited comes from studies on alcoholism. Evidence for the heritability of risk for alcoholism is provided by numerous studies,[8,9,10] which have been reviewed by Tabakoff and Hoffman[11] in the *Seventh Special Report to the U.S. Congress on Alcohol and Health,* from the Secretary of Health and Human Services.[12] Studies of alcoholics' families have found that there are at least two types of inherited alcoholism,[9] now referred to as Type I (or milieu-limited), and Type II (or male-limited) alcoholism.[12] These observational studies of alcoholics' families are supported by research using genetic and biological markers in animal models. Some of these markers predispose an individual biochemically to increased susceptibility to developing alcohol-related problems, while others may actually be protective in nature. For example, genes, which code for enzymes that inhibit the normal metabolism of alcohol, could cause one to respond positively to the effects of alcohol and thus to drink more, or respond negatively to alcohol and thus drink less or not at all.[11] A recent study has provided evidence in support of the idea that genes also influence cigarette smoking.[13] The heritability of susceptibility to other drugs is still under investigation.

Environmental Risk Factors

There are a great many environmental factors, both psychological and social, that influence the use and abuse of alcohol and other drugs. Included are personal factors, such as the influences of home and family life, school and peer groups, and other components of the social and cultural environment.

Personal Factors

Personal factors include personality traits, such as impulsiveness, depressive mood, susceptibility to stress, or possibly personality disturbances. Some of these factors have been reviewed by Needle and colleagues.[14] While models that involve personal factors provide frameworks for research and theorizing about the etiology of alcohol and drug abuse, they have their limitations. It is difficult to determine the degree to which these factors are inherited or are simply the product of the family environment. For example, one's choice to use alcohol or drugs in response to a stressful situation (and the outcome of that decision) could be the result of either inherited characteristics, learned behavior, or a combination of these factors.

Home and Family Life

The importance of home and family life on alcohol and drug abuse has been the subject of numerous studies, some of which have been reviewed by Meller[15] and Needle and

drug abuse
use of a drug when it is detrimental to one's health or well-being

drug (chemical) dependence
a psychological and sometimes physical state characterized by a craving for a drug

psychological dependence
a psychological state characterized by an overwhelming desire to continue use of a drug

FIGURE 12.3

Influences of home and family life can affect one's decisions about alcohol, tobacco, and other drugs.

colleagues.[14] Research demonstrates that not all family-associated risk is genetic in origin. Family structure, family dynamics, quality of parenting, and family problems can all contribute to drug experimentation by children and adolescents (see Figure 12.3). Family turmoil (deaths and divorces) have been associated with the initiation of alcohol and other drug use.[14] In this sense, alcohol and drug use are a symptom of personal and/or family problems, not a cause.[16]

The development of interpersonal skills, such as communication skills, independent living skills, and learning to get along with others, is nurtured in the home. The failure of parents to provide an environment conducive to the development of these skills can result in the loss of self-esteem and increase in delinquency, nonconformity, and sociopathic behavior, all personal risk factors for alcohol and drug abuse.[12]

Finally, family attitudes toward alcohol and drug use influence adolescents' beliefs and expectations about the effects of drugs. These expectations have been shown to be important factors in adolescents' choices to initiate and continue alcohol use.[12] The age of first use of alcohol, tobacco, and illicit drugs is correlated to later development of alcohol and drug problems, especially if use begins before age 15.[17]

School and Peer Groups

Perceived and actual drug use by peers influences attitudes and choices by adolescents (see Figure 12.4). Some studies have shown that perceived support of drinking by peers is the single most important factor in an adolescent's choice to drink.[12] Peers can also influence expectations for a drug. Alcohol may be perceived as "a 'magic elixir' that can enhance social and physical pleasure, sexual performance and responsiveness, power and aggression and social competence."[12] It is interesting to note that these are precisely the mythical qualities about alcohol portrayed in advertisements for beer and other alcoholic beverages.

FIGURE 12.4
Peers can influence one's expectations of the effects of a drug.

Sociocultural Environment

The notion of environmental risk includes the effects of sociocultural and physical settings on drug-taking behavior. The study of the effects of the physical and social environment upon the individual is termed *social ecology*.[18] Environmental risk for drug-taking can stem from one's immediate neighborhood or from society at large. For example, living in the inner city—with its sordidness, physical decay, and threats to personal safety—could set into motion a variety of changes in values and behaviors, including some related to alcohol or drug use.

Opportunities for community interventions exist, though. For example, federal, state, and local drug-prevention education programs, law enforcement successes, and treatment availability can improve the social environment and reduce the prevalence of drug abuse. Also, increasing taxes on tobacco products and alcoholic beverages and the development of zoning ordinances that limit the number of bars and liquor stores in certain neighborhoods can be effective in reducing the alcohol, tobacco, and other drug problems in a community.

TYPES OF DRUGS ABUSED AND RESULTING PROBLEMS

Almost any psychoactive drug available is subject to abuse by at least some segment of the population. Classification systems of drugs of abuse are many, but none of them is perfect. Problems of classification arise because all drugs have multiple effects and because the legal status of a drug can depend upon its formulation and strength, and in some cases, upon the age of the user. In this chapter, our classification system includes legal drugs and illegal drugs. Legal (licit) drugs include alcohol, nicotine, and nonprescription and prescription drugs. Illegal (illicit) drugs can be classified further on the basis of physiological effects as stimulants, depressants, narcotics, hallucinogens, marijuana, and other drugs.

Legal Drugs

Legal drugs are drugs that can be legally bought and sold in the marketplace, including those that are closely regulated, like morphine; those that are lightly regulated, like alcohol and tobacco; and still others that are not regulated at all, like caffeine.

Alcohol

Alcohol is the Number 1 problem drug in America by almost any standard of measurement—the number of those who abuse it, the number of injuries and injury deaths it causes, the amount of money spent on it, and its social and economic costs to society through broken homes and lost wages. Alcohol is consumed in a variety of forms, including beer, wine, fortified wines and brandies, and distilled spirits. While many people view distilled spirits as the most dangerous form of alcohol, it is now recognized that the form of alcohol involved in most of the heavy-episodic drinking is beer. Much of this beer is drunk by high school and college students, and much of this drinking is **binge drinking** (consuming five or more drinks on a single occasion for males and four or more drinks for females).

Drinking by high school and college students continues to be very widespread despite the fact that it is illegal for virtually all high school students and for most college students to purchase these beverages. In 2003 76.6% of high school seniors reported having drunk alcohol (more than a few sips) at least once in their lifetime, with 70% in the past year, and 47.5% in the past 30 days. Thirty-one percent (nearly one in three high school seniors) reported having been drunk in the past 30 days.[5] Twenty-eight percent of high school seniors reported occasions of binge drinking at least once in the prior two-week period. College students reported an even higher prevalence of binge drinking; 40% stated that they had consumed five or more drinks in a row in the past two-week period.[5]

Most of those who experiment with alcohol begin their use in a social context and become light or moderate drinkers. Alcohol use is reinforcing in two ways: It lowers anxieties and produces a mild euphoria. For many people, alcohol use does not become a significant problem, but for about 10% of those who drink it does. Some of these people become **problem drinkers;** that is, they begin to experience social, legal, or financial problems because of their alcohol consumption. Still others lose control of their drinking and develop a dependence upon alcohol. Physical dependence on alcohol and the loss of control over one's drinking are two important characteristics of **alcoholism.** According to the *Journal of the American Medical Association:*

> *Alcoholism* is a primary, chronic disease with genetic, psychosocial, and environmental factors influencing its development and manifestations. The disease is often progressive and fatal. It is characterized by impaired control over drinking, preoccupation with the drug alcohol, use of alcohol despite adverse consequences, and distortions in thinking, most notably denial. Each of these symptoms may be continuous or periodic.[19]

The cost of alcohol abuse and alcoholism in the United States was estimated for 1995 to be $166.5 billion.[3] That is $633 for every man, woman, and child. To put it another way, it costs America $19 million every hour for alcohol-related problems. More than 60% of the cost is due to lost employment or reduced productivity, and 13% of the cost is due to medical and treatment costs. Health care costs for alcoholics are about twice those for nonalcoholics.[12]

Alcohol and other drugs are contributing factors to a variety of unintentional injuries and injury deaths. The risk of a motor vehicle crash increases progressively with alcohol consumption and **blood alcohol concentration (BAC)** (see Figure 12.5).

> Compared with drivers who have not consumed alcohol, the risk of a single-vehicle fatal crash for drivers with BAC's between 0.02 and 0.04 percent is estimated to be 1.4 times higher; for those with BAC's between 0.05 and 0.09 percent, 11.1 times higher; for drivers with BAC's between 0.10 and 0.14 percent, 48 times higher; and for those with BAC's at or above 0.15 percent, the risk is estimated to be 380 times higher.[20]

binge drinking consuming five or more drinks in a row for males and four or more drinks in a row for females

problem drinker one for whom alcohol consumption results in a medical, social, or other type of problem

alcoholism a disease characterized by impaired control over drinking, preoccupation with drinking, and continued use of alcohol despite adverse consequences

blood alcohol concentration the percentage of concentration of alcohol in the blood

FIGURE 12.5
The risk of a motor vehicle crash increases progressively with alcohol consumption.

Young drivers are particularly at risk because they are inexperienced drivers and inexperienced drinkers. This combination can be deadly. One study found that 23% of drivers 16 to 20 years old who were involved in fatal motor vehicle crashes, and for whom any alcohol consumption is illegal, had alcohol in their blood.[20]

Despite these grim figures, significant progress has been made in reducing the overall rate of alcohol-related vehicle deaths. In 1987, there were 9.8 deaths per 100,000 people; in 1998 the rate had declined to 5.9 deaths per 100,000 people. The *Healthy People 2010* objective has set a target of 4 deaths per 100,000. The 2010 target for alcohol and drug-related injuries from motor vehicle crashes is 65 (see Box 12.1). Past success and the promise of future achievement come through public policy changes—raising the minimum legal drinking age, strengthening and enforcing state license revocation laws, and lowering the BAC tolerance levels from 0.10% to 0.08% in some states—stricter law enforcement, and better education for those cited for driving while intoxicated.[21] In October 2000 President Clinton signed a bill that made 0.08% BAC the national standard. States that refused to impose the standard by 2004 would lose millions of dollars of federal highway construction money.[22] By the end of 2004, all 50 states, Puerto Rico, and the District of Columbia had adopted the 0.08% standard.

Alcohol has also been found to increase one's risk for other types of unintentional injuries, such as drowning, falls, fires, and burns. Associations between unintentional injuries and the abuse of other drugs is less well documented, but given a knowledge of the effects of such drugs, one can assume that they increase neither the user's alertness nor coordination.

Alcohol also contributes to intentional violence in the community. For example, 50% of spouse abuse, 49% of murders, 62% of assaults, 52% of rapes, 38% of child abuse cases, and 20% to 35% of suicides are traceable to alcohol consumption (see Figure 12.1).

BOX
12.1

BOX 12.1 HEALTHY PEOPLE 2010 OBJECTIVES: ADVERSE CONSEQUENCES OF SUBSTANCE USE AND ABUSE

26-1. Reduce deaths and injuries caused by alcohol-related motor vehicle crashes.

Target and baseline:

Objective	Reduction in Consequences of Motor Vehicle Crashes	1998 Baseline	2010 Target
		Per 100,000 population	
26-1a.	Alcohol-related deaths	5.9	4
26-1b.	Alcohol-related injuries	113	65

For Further Thought

The reduction of alcohol-related vehicle deaths is one of the greatest success stories of public health during the 1990s. The 1987 baseline was 9.8 deaths per 100,000 people, and the objective for the year 2000 was 8.5 deaths. By 1998, a level of 5.9 deaths per 100,000 was achieved, and the 2010 target has been set for just 4 deaths per 100,000. Similar success has not been achieved for drug-related deaths overall, or for drug abuse–related emergency department visits. What explanation can you offer for these differences?

Source: United States Department of Health and Human Services (November 2000). *Healthy People 2010: Understanding and Improving Health,* 2nd ed. Washington, DC: U.S. Government Printing Office.

Nicotine

Nicotine is the psychoactive and addictive drug present in tobacco products such as cigarettes, cigars, smokeless or "spit" tobacco (chewing tobacco and snuff), and pipe tobacco. For many years the enforcement of state laws prohibiting the sale of cigarettes and other tobacco products to minors was uneven. In other cases, cigarettes could easily be purchased by youth from vending machines. Thus, until recently many American youths have had ready access to tobacco products, and American tobacco companies made the most of this situation during the 1990s. With their seductive "Joe Camel" advertisements (now retired) and other similar youth-oriented marketing approaches, they made smoking highly attractive to today's youth. The **Synar Amendment** is a federal law that requires all states to adopt legislation that prohibits the sale and distribution of tobacco products to people under age 18. States that do not comply with this regulation lose federal dollars for alcohol, tobacco, and other drug prevention and treatment programs.[24]

Synar Amendment
a federal law that requires states to set the minimum legal age for purchasing tobacco products at 18 years and requires states to enforce this law

The 30-day prevalence of cigarette smoking among high school seniors, which had declined to 27.8% in 1992 and then rebounded to 36.5% by 1997, reached a new low of 24.4% in 2003. The prevalence of daily smoking among high school seniors also declined in 2003, to 15.8%.[5] While it is true that some of these students are light smokers (less than half a pack a day), studies show that many light smokers become heavy smokers (more than half a pack a day) as they become older. The prevalence of cigarette smoking in people aged 18 and older in 2001 was 22.8% (25.1% for males, 20.6% for females).[25]

The health consequences of tobacco use are familiar to all, even smokers (see Box 12.2). They include increased risks for heart disease, lung cancer, chronic obstructive lung disease, stroke, emphysema, and other conditions. Smoking accounted for an estimated 435,000 deaths per year in the United States in 2000.[26] Tobacco use causes an estimated 4 million deaths worldwide annually.[27] The economic costs of tobacco smoking were estimated to be $138 billion in the United States in 1995, of which 58% or $80 billion was attributed to health costs.[1] It has also been estimated that 43% of health costs were paid by government funds, including Medicaid and Medicare.[23] Clearly, tobacco use and nicotine addiction continue to be a burden on society.

BOX 12.2

TEN GREAT PUBLIC HEALTH ACHIEVEMENTS, 1900–1999: RECOGNITION OF TOBACCO USE AS A HEALTH HAZARD

Less Smoke, More Prevention

During the twentieth century, smoking has gone from being an accepted norm to being recognized as the Number 1 preventable cause of death and disability in the United States. Although substantial progress has been made and millions of lives have been saved, increased prevention efforts are needed to reduce the impact of tobacco use on public health.

> **SURGEON GENERAL'S WARNING:** Smoking Causes Lung Cancer, Heart Disease Emphysema, And May Complicate Pregnancy

Each year, smoking kills more people than all of the following health hazards combined:

- AIDS
- Alcohol abuse
- Drug abuse
- Motor vehicle crash injuries
- Murders
- Suicides

Per capita consumption of cigarettes has decreased from a high of more than 4,000 cigarettes/year in the early 1960s to a low of 2,261/year in 1998, the lowest level seen since the early 1940s. Some of the changes appear to be associated with notable smoking and health events.

- 1964 Surgeon General's report
- Doubling of federal cigarette taxes
- Master Settlement Agreement
- Banning of tobacco advertising in many venues

During this century, smoking prevalence among adults aged 18 years decreased from appoximately 40% in the mid-1960s to 25% in 1999, with the rate for men being approximately five percentage points higher than for women.

Source: Centers for Disease Control and Prevention. Available at http://www.cdc.gov/phtn/tenachievements/tobacco1/to1.htm.

Well-established research findings have demonstrated that one does not have to use tobacco products to be adversely affected. The 1986 Surgeon General's report on the effects of **environmental tobacco smoke (ETS)** or **secondhand smoke** indicated that adults and children who inhale the tobacco smoke of others (passive smoking) are also at increased risk for cardiac and respiratory illnesses.[28,29] These findings resulted in new smoking regulations in many indoor environments. Then in December 1992, the Environmental Protection Agency (EPA) released its report, *Respiratory Health Effects of Passive Smoking: Lung Cancer and Other Disorders.*[30] This report stated that ETS is a human class A carcinogen (the same class that contains asbestos) and that it is responsible for 3,000 lung cancer deaths annually among nonsmoking Americans. Further, it stated that ETS exposure is causally associated with as many as 150,000 to 300,000 cases of lower respiratory infections (such as bronchitis and pneumonia) in infants and young children up to 18 months of age. The EPA study also found that ETS aggravates asthma in children and is a risk factor for new cases of childhood asthma.

environmental tobacco smoke (ETS) (secondhand smoke) tobacco smoke in the ambient air

The use of smokeless (spit) tobacco also carries with it serious health risks, including addiction, periodontal disease, and oral cancer. Approximately 3.4% of 12- to 17-year-old males and 9.4% of 18- to 25-year-old males reported using smokeless tobacco within the past 30 days in 2002.[31] The subgroup of Americans who reported the highest rate of smokeless tobacco use was the American Indians/Alaskan Natives. In 2002, 8.5% of this population aged 12 or older reported using smokeless tobacco in the past 30 days.[31] This habit begins in high school, where in 2003, 5.4% of eighth-grade males, 9.9% of tenth-grade, males, and 12.2% of twelfth-grade males reported using smokeless tobacco in the past 30 days.[5]

Over-the-Counter Drugs

over-the-counter (OTC) drugs (nonprescription drugs)
drugs (except tobacco and alcohol) that can be legally purchased without a physician's prescription

Over-the-counter (OTC) drugs are those legal drugs, with the exception of tobacco and alcohol, that can be purchased without a physician's prescription. Included in this category are internal analgesics such as aspirin, acetaminophen (Tylenol), and ibuprofen (Advil); cough and cold remedies (Robitussin, Contac); emetics; laxatives; mouthwashes; vitamins; and many others.[32] Thousands of different OTC products are sold by pharmacies, supermarkets, convenience stores, and in vending machines. These products are manufactured and sold to those who self-diagnose and self-medicate their own illnesses.

Food and Drug Administration (FDA)
a federal agency in the Department of Health and Human Services charged with assuring the safety and efficacy of all prescription and nonprescription drugs

Over-the-counter drugs are carefully regulated by the **Food and Drug Administration (FDA),** an agency of the Department of Health and Human Services. The FDA assures the safety and effectiveness of these products when they are used according to their label directions. There is no person or agency that supervises the actual sale or use of these substances.

Naturally, some of these substances are misused and abused. Examples of misuse are not following the dosage directions or using the drugs after their expiration date. A specific example of OTC drug abuse is the taking of laxatives or emetics to lose weight or to avoid gaining weight. Other OTC drugs that are often abused are appetite suppressants (Dexatrim), stimulants (NoDoz), and nasal sprays (Neo-Synephrine).

Most OTC drugs provide only symptomatic relief and do not provide a cure. For example, cough and cold remedies relieve the discomfort that accompanies a cold but do not in any way rid a person of the cold virus that is causing these symptoms. Therefore, a real danger of OTC drug misuse and abuse is that symptoms that should be brought to the attention of a physician remain unreported. Another danger is that those who abuse these drugs may become dependent, thus unable to live normally without them. Lastly, abuse of OTC drugs may establish a pattern of dependency that predisposes the abuser to developing dependent relationships with prescription drugs or illicit drugs.

Prescription Drugs

Because all prescription drugs have serious side effects for some people, they can be purchased only with a physician's (or dentist's) written instructions (prescription). Like OTC drugs, prescription drugs are carefully regulated by the FDA. More than 4,000 prescription drugs are listed in each annual edition of the *Physician's Desk Reference.*[33] The written prescription connotes that the prescribed drugs are being taken by the patient under the prescribing physician's supervision. Each prescription includes the patient's name, the amount to be dispensed, and the dosage.

Nonetheless, prescription drugs are also subject to misuse and abuse. Types of misuse include those previously cited for the OTC drugs and also the giving of one person's prescription drug to another. Furthermore, certain prescription drugs such as stimulants (amphetamines), depressants (Valium), and pain relievers such as narcotics (morphine, codeine) have a higher potential for abuse than others. Because prescription drugs are usually stronger or more concentrated than OTC drugs, there is a greater risk of developing dependence or taking an overdose from these drugs. Those who develop dependence may try to obtain duplicate prescriptions from other physicians or steal the drugs from hospital dispensaries or pharmacies.

While the abuse of prescription drugs is a concern, levels of abuse are much lower for these drugs than for alcohol and tobacco. After marijuana, however, this group of illicit drugs is the most abused. Nearly 5% of people aged 12 and older took one of these addictive drugs without a prescription in 2002. Included in this group of substances are Darvocet, Darvon, Percocet, Percodan, Vicodin (hydrocodone), and OxyContin, among others. Among those aged

12 to 17, the prevalence of use in the past month (3.5%) and past year (7.9%) is higher among females than among males (3.0% and 7.2%, respectively).[31]

One serious consequence of the misuse of prescription drugs, in addition to becoming dependent, is the development of drug-resistant strains of pathogens. When patients fail to complete the entire antibiotic treatment (i.e., three days of a ten-day prescription), some of the bacteria survive and multiply, re-infecting the body with drug-resistant organisms. Thus, succeeding treatments are less effective. When this strain of the disease is transmitted to another, the antibiotic treatment fails. New drugs are then needed to treat these patients. As drug misuse continues to occur, bacteria become resistant to multiple drugs. Multidrug-resistant tuberculosis (MDR-TB) is an example. The prevalence of MDR-TB points both to the dangers of drug misuse and the necessity to continue to develop new antibiotics for the treatment of bacterial infections.

Another problem with prescription drug use has recently been exposed—that of adverse drug reactions. Researchers estimated that in 1994 there may have been as many as 106,000 deaths in the United States from adverse drug reactions.[34] If this is true, adverse drug reactions would be one of the top ten leading causes of death in the country.

Controlled Substances and Illicit (Illegal) Drugs

Controlled substances are those regulated by the **Controlled Substances Act of 1970 (CSA),** officially called the Comprehensive Drug Abuse Control Act of 1970. Many of the drugs discussed next belong to Schedule I under this Act because they have a high potential for abuse and have no accepted medical uses and, hence, no acceptable standards of safe use. These are considered **illicit (illegal) drugs.** They cannot be cultivated, manufactured, bought, sold, or used within the confines of the law. Well over 100 drugs are listed in this category, including heroin, methaqualone, marijuana (see Figure 12.6), LSD, psilocybin, mescaline, MDMA, and DMT.[35]

Other drugs, which do have medical uses, are placed in Schedules II to V of the Act, depending upon their potential for abuse and risk of causing dependence. Included in Schedule II is a variety of very powerful compounds that have specific medical uses but have a high risk for potential abuse. Included in this category are many opium derivatives, such as morphine, fentanyl, and methadone. Also included in Schedule II are the stimulants amphetamine and methamphetamine, certain depressants such as amobarbital, pentobarbital, secobarbital and phencylcidine, and several other drugs. Schedule III drugs have medical uses and exhibit a lower risk of potential abuse than Schedule II drugs. Included are less concentrated

controlled substances drugs regulated by the Comprehensive Drug Abuse Control Act of 1970, including all illegal drugs and prescription drugs that are subject to abuse and can produce dependence

Controlled Substances Act of 1970 (Comprehensive Drug Abuse Control Act of 1970) the central piece of federal drug legislation that regulates illegal drugs and legal drugs that have a high potential for abuse

illicit (illegal) drugs drugs that cannot be legally manufactured, distributed, or sold, and that usually lack recognized medicinal value. Drugs that have been placed under Schedule I of the Controlled Substances Act of 1970

FIGURE 12.6
Marijuana is the Nation's most popular illicit drug.

Drug Enforcement Administration (DEA)
the federal government's lead agency with the primary responsibility for enforcing the Nation's drug laws, including the Controlled Substances Act of 1970

forms of certain Schedule II drugs and also many of the anabolic steroids. Schedule IV drugs exhibit even less potential for abuse than Schedule III drugs. Included are many milder stimulants and depressants. Schedule V drugs are primarily very dilute concentrations of opium or opiates used in such medicines as cough syrups.[35]

The **Drug Enforcement Administration (DEA),** under the Department of Justice, has the primary responsibility of enforcing the provisions of the Controlled Substance Act. Once a drug is placed in Schedule I of the CSA, it becomes the primary responsibility of the DEA to interdict the "trafficking" (manufacturing, distribution, and sales) of the substance. The only sources of these drugs are illegal growers and manufacturers. Schedule II to V substances often reach the "street" illegally, either by illegal production (in clandestine labs) or by diversion of legally manufactured prescription drugs.

Marijuana

marijuana
dried plant parts of the hemp plant, *Cannabis sativa*

Marijuana is the most abused illicit drug in the United States. "Pot" and the related products, hashish and hash oil, are derived from the hemp plant, *Cannabis sativa*. The products are most commonly used by smoking but can also be ingested. While marijuana abuse has declined, it remains a concern for several reasons. First, it is illegal, and therefore brings the user into contact with those involved in illegal activities. Second, the act of smoking is detrimental to one's health. Third, marijuana smoking often occurs in conjunction with the drinking of alcohol or the use of other drugs. The effects of **polydrug use** (the use of more than one drug at a time) may be more serious than those of single-drug use. Lastly, as is true of all drugs, the adolescent who uses marijuana is delaying the accomplishment of developmental tasks such as attaining an adult self-identity, achieving independence, and developing the interpersonal skills necessary for successful independent living.

polydrug use
concurrent use of multiple drugs

In a 2002 survey, the percentage of high school seniors who reported having smoked marijuana at least once in their lives was 46.1%. Also, 21.2% reported having smoked marijuana in the past 30 days. As with many of the other drugs, the prevalence of marijuana use has waxed and waned over the past 30 years. The perceived risk of use is one of the factors that seems to contribute to the level of use. In 1992, when 76.5% of high school seniors felt there was great risk associated with regular marijuana use, the 30-day use prevalence was 11.9%; 10 years later, when 53.0% of seniors felt there was great risk associated with regular marijuana use, the 30-day use prevalence was 21.2%.[31] Another measurement of students' attitudes is disapproval rates. National anti-drug use campaigns directed at youth, aimed at increasing disapproval rates, may be working. Although still lower than their highest levels in the early 1990s, disapproval rates for trying marijuana once or twice edged upward in eighth, tenth, and twelfth graders in 2002.[5] One of the objectives of *Healthy People 2010* is to increase the proportion of adolescents who disapprove of trying marijuana or hashish once or twice (see Box 12.3).

The acute health effects of marijuana use include reduced concentration, slowed reaction time, impaired short-term memory, and impaired judgment. Naturally, these effects can have serious consequences for someone operating a motor vehicle or other machinery or can even result in a medical emergency. The increase in both marijuana use and its potency in the 1990s were reflected in an increase in the number of marijuana-related emergency room episodes, which rose from 15,706 in 1990 to 87,150 in 1999.[36] Marijuana use in combination with alcohol can be especially dangerous because the two drugs in combination may affect the brain differently.[37]

amotivational syndrome
a pattern of behavior characterized by apathy, loss of effectiveness, and a more passive, introverted personality

The chronic effects of smoking marijuana include damage to the respiratory system by the smoke itself and, for some, the development of a controverisal condition known as **amotivational syndrome.** Amotivational syndrome has been described as a chronic apathy toward maturation and the achievement of the developmental tasks listed previously (e.g., developing skills for independent living, setting and achieving goals, and developing an

BOX
12.3

HEALTHY PEOPLE 2010 OBJECTIVES: ADVERSE CONSEQUENCES OF SUBSTANCE USE AND ABUSE

Objective: An increase in adolescents who disapprove of trying marijuana or hashish once or twice

Target and baseline:

Objective	1998 Baseline	2010 Target
	Percent	
26-16d. Eighth graders	69	72
26-16e. Tenth graders	56	72
26-16f. Twelfth graders	52	72

Target setting method: Better than the best.

Source: Monitoring the Future Study, NIH, National Institute of Drug Abuse (NIDA).

For Further Thought

Attitudes and beliefs are often a key factor influencing drug-taking behavior among adolescents. Studies have shown that when there is high level of disapproval of marijuana use by adolescents, the prevalence of marijuana use declines. Conversely, an increase in marijuana use occurs when there is an apparent decline in those expressing strong disapproval of use. How strong are prevailing feelings of disapproval of marijuana use in your community? Do adolescents in your community feel that it is "OK" to try marijuana once or twice?

Source: United States Department of Health and Human Services (2000). *Healthy People 2010: Understanding and Improving Health,* 2nd ed. Washington, DC: U.S. Government Printing Office.

adult self-identity). There is also evidence now that long-term marijuana users experience physiological and psychological withdrawal symptoms. While these "unpleasant behavioral symptoms are less obvious than those for heroin or alcohol, they are significant and do perhaps contribute to continued drug use."[38] Finally, one of the chief concerns with marijuana is that those who smoke marijuana are more likely to use other, more addictive drugs. For example, 89% of those who use cocaine first used cigarettes, alcohol, and marijuana.[39]

Narcotics: Opium, Morphine, Heroin, and Others

Opium and its derivatives, morphine and heroin, come from the oriental poppy plant, *Papaver somniferum.* These **narcotics** numb the senses and reduce pain. As such, they have a high potential for abuse. The narcotic that is most widely abused is heroin, a derivative of morphine. In 2000, about 3.5 million (1.6%) of the 235 million noninstitutionalized people over the age of 12 reported the use of heroin in their lifetime, while 404,000 (0.2%) reported use in the past year.[31] This estimate is low because this survey undoubtedly missed a great many addicts who may be homeless and living in shelters. Use in the past year among high school seniors has increased significantly, from 0.6% in 1992 to 0.8% in 2002.[5]

> **narcotics**
> drugs derived from or chemically related to opium that reduce pain and induce stupor, such as morphine

Opium poppies do not grow in the continental United States. Heroin arrives in the United States from four geographic areas: Southwest Asia, Southeast Asia, Mexico, and South America. While Asia and Mexico have supplied heroin to U.S. markets for many years, South America has only recently become an important source of heroin. The U.S. DEA estimated that in 2001, 56% of the samples of heroin analyzed came from South America, 30% from Mexico, 7% from Southwest Asia, and 7% from Southeast Asia.[40]

Heroin is the Number 1 narcotic of abuse and is also the illicit drug responsible for more deaths than any other.[1] But, there are many other narcotics that are also abused. Some of these are obtained through diversion of compounds intended for legitimate medical use as pain relievers. Examples include natural narcotics such as morphine and codeine, synthetic narcotics such as Demerol and Darvon, and quasi-synthetic narcotics such as Dilaudid and Percodan. As mentioned earlier, these prescription narcotics are highly addictive and subject to abuse.

FIGURE 12.7
Club drugs, often sold at raves, represent a significant health risk to youth.

tolerance
physiological and enzygmatic adjustments that occur in response to the chronic presence of drugs, which are reflected in the need for ever-increasing doses

Narcotics produce euphoria, analgesia, and drowsiness. They reduce anxiety and pain without affecting motor activity the way alcohol and barbiturates do. If use continues, the body makes physiological adjustments to the presence of the drug. This **tolerance** means that larger and larger doses are required to achieve the same euphoria and numbing as the initial dose. While tolerance develops rapidly to the euphoric effects, the depressing effects on respiration may continue to increase with dose level, increasing the risk of a fatal overdose (see Figure 12.7). As the cost of the drug habit becomes higher, the abuser usually attempts to quit. This results in withdrawal symptoms because the body has become physically dependent upon the drug. Heroin addicts have a difficult time changing their lifestyle for several reasons. First there is the addiction itself, both physical and psychological. Often too, there are underlying psychosocial problems such as poor self-image, lack of job skills, and absence of supporting family and friends. Addicts usually mistrust official programs set up to help them. They are usually in poor health mentally and physically. Because the duration of action of heroin is only four to five hours, the addict is usually too concerned with finding the next dose or recovering from the previous one to be productive in the community.

The community is affected by more than just the loss of productivity. The addict must obtain money to purchase heroin, and the price of the habit can be very high—as much as $200 per day. The money is usually obtained illegally through burglaries, thefts, robberies, muggings, prostitution (male and female), and selling drugs. If a prostitute can make $50 dollars a "trick," he or she needs to "turn" at least four tricks a day just to maintain the habit. The result is not only a deteriorating community but also epidemics of sexually transmitted diseases, such as gonorrhea, syphilis, chlamydia, herpes, and AIDS. Because most heroin addicts inject the drug, there are also epidemics of bloodborne diseases, such as those caused by HIV and hepatitis viruses. In this way, drug abuse increases the burden on community health resources. Addicts who turn to dealing drugs to support their habit do even more damage, because they increase the availability of the drug and may introduce it to first-time users. There is an additional burden on the criminal justice system when these addicts are arrested, prosecuted, incarcerated, and rehabilitated.

Cocaine and Crack Cocaine

Cocaine is the psychoactive ingredient in the leaves of the coca plant, *Erythoxolyn coca*, which grows in the Andes Mountains of South America. Cocaine is a **stimulant;** that is, it increases the activity of the central nervous system. For centuries, natives of the Andes Mountains have chewed the leaves to improve stamina during work and long treks. In its more purified forms, as a salt (white powder) or dried paste (crack), cocaine is a powerful euphoriant/stimulant and very addictive.

Cocaine use among high school seniors peaked in 1985, when 6.7% reported use within the past 30 days. By 1992 this figure had dropped to only 1.3%, but by 1999 those reporting use in the past 30 days had doubled to 2.6%.[5] The 2002 30-day prevalence rate among high school seniors is 2.1%.[31] Estimates for 2002 indicate that as many as 2 million Americans have used cocaine or crack in the past 30 days.[31] Therefore, cocaine remains a serious drug problem in the United States.

Hallucinogens

Hallucinogens are drugs that produce illusions, hallucinations, and other changes in one's perceptions of the environment. These effects are due to the phenomenon known as **synesthesia,** a mixing of the senses. Hallucinogens include both naturally derived drugs like mescaline, from the peyote cactus, and psilocybin and psilocin, from the Psilocybe mushroom; and synthetic drugs, such as lysergic acid diethylamide (LSD). While physical dependence has not been demonstrated with the hallucinogens, tolerance does occur. Though overdose deaths are rare, "bad trips" (unpleasant experiences) do occur, and a few people have experienced permanent visual disturbances. Because there are no legal sources for these drugs, users are always at risk for taking fake, impure, or adulterated drugs.

Stimulants

As previously mentioned, stimulants are drugs that increase the activity level of the central nervous system. Examples include the amphetamines, such as amphetamine itself (bennies), dextroamphetamine (dexies), methamphetamine (meth), and dextromethamphetamine (ice); methylphenidate (Ritalin); and methcathinone (cat). These drugs cause the release of high levels of the neurotransmitter dopamine, which stimulates brain cells. Tolerance builds quickly, so abusers must escalate their doses rapidly. Chronic abusers can develop tremors and confusion, aggressiveness, and paranoia. The long-term effects include permanent brain damage and Parkinson's disease-like symptoms.[41]

Amphetamines are Schedule II prescription drugs that have been widely abused for many years. Increased regulatory efforts in the 1970s probably contributed to the rise in the cocaine trade in the 1980s. When cocaine abuse declined in the late 1980s, there was a resurgence of amphetamine abuse, primarily **methamphetamine,** also known as, "crystal," "crank," "speed," "go fast," or just "meth." At first, the clandestine labs that produced methamphetamine, and those abusing the substance, were concentrated primarily in the southwestern states. However, by 1995 production and abuse had spread to the Midwest, and by 1999 methamphetamine abuse had become the fastest growing drug threat in America.[42] In 2002, 5.0% of high school seniors reported abusing amphetamines and 1.7% reported abusing methamphetamine in the past 30 days.[5] In 2001, federal, state, and local law enforcement officials seized 8,290 methamphetamine labs. Since 1995, the most rapid growth in the number of "meth" labs seized has been in the Midwest, especially in Kansas, Missouri, Oklahoma, and Arkansas, but California has the most labs.[42]

cocaine
the psychoactive ingredient in the leaves of the coca plant, *Erythoxolyn coca*, which, when refined, is a powerful stimulant/euphoriant

stimulant
a drug that increases the activity of the central nervous system

hallucinogens
drugs that produce profound distortions of the senses

synesthesia
impairment of mind characterized by a sensation that senses are mixed

amphetamines
a group of synthetic drugs that act as stimulants

methamphetamine
the amphetamine most widely abused

Methylphenidate (Ritalin) is a Schedule II drug used to treat attention-deficit hyperactivity disorder. Though not produced in clandestine labs, the drug is often diverted from its intended use and abused by those for whom it was not prescribed.

Depressants

Barbiturates, benzodiazapines, methaqualone, and other **depressants** slow down the central nervous system. They are attractive to some people because, like alcohol, among the first effects of taking these drugs are the lowering of anxiety and the loss of inhibitions. These effects produce the feeling of a "high," even though these drugs depress the central nervous system. As one continues to use these drugs, tolerance develops, and the user experiences the need for greater and greater doses in order to feel the same effects that the previous dose provided. Strong physical dependence develops, so that abstinence results in severe clinical illness; thus, abusers of these substances must often rely on medical assistance during detoxification and recovery.

benzodiazapines
nonbarbiturate
depressant drugs

Club Drugs and Designer Drugs

"**Club drugs** is a term for a number of illicit drugs, primarily synthetic, that are most commonly encountered at nightclubs and 'raves.'"[43] These drugs include MDMA, ketamine, GHB, GBL, Rohypnol, LSD, PCP, methamphetamine, and others. Because these drugs are illegal, there is no guarantee of their safety or even their identity. Also, these drugs are often taken in combination with alcohol or other drugs. As a result, the number of emergency reports for many of these club drugs quadrupled between 1994 and 1998.[43] MDMA, also known as "ecstasy," is the most popular of the club drugs. Use of MDMA rose sharply among eighth, tenth, and twelfth graders through 2001 and then declined sharply. Eight percent of high school seniors surveyed in 2000 had taken MDMA at least once, 4.5% in the past year.[5,6] Long-term effects of MDMA are still under evaluation, but there is evidence that the drug causes brain damage.[43]

Rohypnol (flunitrazepan) is another club drug that is also known as a date-rape drug. This drug, which exhibits all of the characteristics of a depressant, is a legal prescription drug in more than 50 countries. In the United States, the drug is regarded as more dangerous, and thus less medically useful than other sedatives. Thus, it is an illegal (Schedule I) drug.

Designer drugs is a term coined in the 1980s to describe drugs synthesized by amateur chemists in secret laboratories. By constantly changing the design of their drugs, these chemists hoped to stay one step ahead of law enforcement. Examples of designer drugs included MDMA (3,4-methylenedioxy-methamphetamine), synthetic narcotics, and dissociative anesthetics like PCP (angel dust) and ketamine. Under the Controlled Substance Act of 1970, only those drugs that were listed as illegal were illegal, whereas similar, but slightly altered, drugs were not. The Controlled Substances Analogue Act of 1986 was enacted to reduce the flow of designer drugs into the market and make it easier to prosecute those involved in manufacturing and distributing these drugs. Designer and club drugs are still a problem.

Anabolic Drugs

Anabolic drugs are protein-building drugs. Included are the anabolic/androgenic steroids (AS), testosterone, and human growth hormone (HGH). These drugs have legitimate medical uses, such as the rebuilding of muscles after starvation or disease and the treatment of dwarfism. But they are sometimes abused by athletes and body builders as a shortcut to increasing muscle mass, strength, and endurance. Abuse of steroids is accompanied by numerous acute and chronic side effects for men, including acne, gynecomastia (the development of breasts), baldness, reduced fertility, and reduction in testicular size. Side effects for women are masculinizing: development of a male physique, increased body hair, failure to ovulate (menstrual irregularities), and a deepening of the voice. Long-term abuse of anabolic steroids can result in psychological dependence, making the discontinuation of use very difficult.[44]

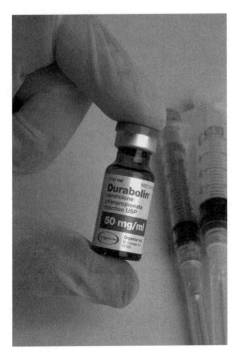

FIGURE 12.8
Abuse of anabolic drugs carries the risk of serious acute and chronic health problems.

In the late 1980s, it became apparent that increasing numbers of boys and young men of high school and college age were taking anabolic steroids as a shortcut to muscle building or to maturity (see Figure 12.8). Because of these trends in the abuse of anabolic steroids, these drugs were placed in Schedule III of the Controlled Substance Act in 1990. Abuse of steroids increased during the 1990s, but has leveled off recently.

Inhalants
Inhalants are a collection of psychoactive, breathable chemicals. They include paint solvents, motor fuels, cleaners, glues, aerosol sprays, cosmetics, and other types of vapor. Because of their easy availability and low cost, they are often the drug of choice for the young. The primary effect of most of the inhalants is depression. As with alcohol, the user may at first experience a reduction of anxieties and inhibitions, making the user feel high. Continued use may result in hallucinations and loss of consciousness. Many of these chemicals are extremely toxic to the kidneys, liver, and nervous system. The use of inhalants by youth results from boredom and perhaps peer pressure and represents a maladaptation to these conditions.

PREVENTION AND CONTROL OF DRUG ABUSE

The prevention and control of alcohol and other drug abuse require a knowledge of the causes of drug-taking behavior, sources of illicit drugs, drug laws, and treatment programs. Also required are community organizing skills, persistence, and cooperation among a vast array of concerned individuals and official and unofficial agencies.

From a community health standpoint, drug abuse tends to be a chronic condition. Thus, the activities of drug abuse and prevention agencies and organizations can be viewed as chronic disease-prevention activities. This approach, involving three different levels of prevention, was first discussed in Chapter 4 and is discussed next in relation to drug abuse prevention and control.

designer drugs
drugs synthesized illegally that are similar to, but structurally different from, known controlled substances

anabolic drugs
compounds, structurally similar to the male hormone testosterone, that increase protein synthesis and thus muscle building

inhalants
breathable substances that produce mind-altering effects

Levels of Prevention

Drug abuse prevention activities can be viewed as primary, secondary, or tertiary depending upon the point of intervention. *Primary prevention* programs are aimed at those who have never used drugs, and their goal is to prevent or forestall the initiation of drug use. Drug education programs that stress primary prevention of drug and alcohol use are most appropriate and successful for children at the elementary school age. In a broader sense, almost any activity that would reduce the likelihood of primary drug use could be considered primary prevention. For example, raising the price of alcohol, increasing cigarette taxes, arresting a neighborhood drug pusher, or destroying a cocaine crop in Bolivia could be considered primary prevention if it forestalled primary drug use in at least some individuals.

Secondary prevention programs are aimed at those who have begun alcohol or other drug use but who have not become chronic abusers and have not suffered significant physical or mental impairment from their drug or alcohol abuse. Alcohol and other drug abuse education programs that stress secondary prevention are often appropriate for people of high school or college age. They can be presented in educational, workplace, or community settings.

Tertiary prevention programs are designed to provide drug abuse treatment and after-care, including relapse prevention programs. As such, they are usually designed for adults. Tertiary programs for teenagers are far too uncommon. Tertiary prevention programs may receive clients who "turn themselves in" for treatment voluntarily, but more often than not their clients are referred by the courts.

Elements of Prevention

There are four basic elements that play a role in drug abuse prevention and control. These are (1) education, (2) treatment, (3) public policy, and (4) enforcement. The goals of education and treatment are the same: to reduce the demand for drugs. Likewise, setting effective public policy and law enforcement share the same goal: to reduce the supply and availability of drugs in the community.

drug abuse education providing information about drugs and the dangers of drug abuse, changing attitudes and beliefs about drugs, providing the skills necessary to abstain from drugs, and ultimately changing drug abuse behavior

Education

The purpose of **drug abuse education** is to limit the demand for drugs by providing information about drugs and the dangers of drug abuse, changing attitudes and beliefs about drugs, providing the skills necessary to abstain from drugs, and ultimately changing drug abuse behavior.[45] Education, principally a primary prevention activity, can be school-based or community-based. Examples of school-based drug abuse prevention programs are *Here's Looking at You, 2000* and *Project DARE (Drug Abuse Resistance Education)*. For these programs and other school-based programs to be successful, other community members such as parents, teachers, local business people, and others must visibly support the program. Examples of community-based programs are the American Cancer Society's *Great American Smokeout; Race Against Drugs (RAD),* a nationwide program that links drug abuse prevention with motor sports; and the *Reality Check Campaign,* a program to boost awareness of the harmful effects of marijuana smoking among youth.[45]

treatment (for drug abuse and dependence) care that removes the physical, emotional, and environmental conditions that have contributed to drug abuse and/or dependence

Treatment

The goal of **treatment** is to remove the physical, emotional, and environmental conditions that have contributed to drug dependency. Like education, treatment aims to reduce demand for drugs. It also aims to save money. It is estimated that for every $1 spent on treatment, $7 are saved in medical or crime-prevention costs.[46] Treatment for drug abuse occurs in a variety of settings and involves a variety of approaches. Treatment may be residential (inpatient) or nonresidential (outpatient). Under managed care, "behavioral health care" guidelines usually limit inpatient care to 28 days, after which the care may continue on an outpatient basis. In drug abuse treatment, what happens after the initial treatment phase is critical. **Aftercare,** the continuing care provided the recovering former drug abuser, often involves peer group or self-help support group meetings, such as those provided by Alcoholics Anonymous (AA) or Narcotics Anonymous (NA). Despite frequent relapses, treatment for drug dependence is viewed as an important component of a community's comprehensive drug abuse prevention and control strategy.

aftercare
the continuing care provided the recovering former drug abuser

Public Policy

Public policy embodies the guiding principles and courses of action pursued by governments to solve practical problems affecting society.[45] Examples include passing drunk-driving laws or zoning ordinances that limit the number of bars in a neighborhood and enacting ordinances that regulate the type and amount of advertising for such legal drugs as alcohol and tobacco. Public policy should guide the budget discussions that ultimately determine how much a community spends for education, treatment, and law enforcement. Further examples of public policy decisions are restrictions of smoking in public buildings, the setting of 0.08% blood alcohol concentration as the point at which driving becomes illegal, and zero tolerance laws for BACs for minors. Setting the level of state excise taxes on alcohol and tobacco is also a public policy decision.

public policy
the guiding principles and courses of action pursued by governments to solve practical problems affecting society

Law Enforcement

Law enforcement in drug abuse prevention and control is the application of federal, state, and local laws to arrest, jail, bring to trial, and sentence those who break drug laws or break laws because of drug use. The primary roles of law enforcement in a drug abuse prevention and control program are to (1) control drug use, (2) to control crime, especially crime related to drug use and drug trafficking—the buying, selling, manufacturing, or transporting of illegal drugs, (3) to prevent the establishment of crime organizations, and (4) to protect neighborhoods.[47] Law enforcement is concerned with limiting the supply of drugs in the community by interrupting the source, transit, and distribution of drugs. There are law enforcement agencies at all levels of government. The principle agencies are discussed next.

law enforcement
the application of federal, state, and local laws to arrest, jail, bring to trial, and sentence those who break drug laws or break laws because of drug use

Governmental Drug Prevention and Control Agencies and Programs

Governmental agencies involved in drug abuse prevention, control, and treatment include a multitude of federal, state, and local agencies. At each of these levels of government, there are numerous offices and programs aimed at reducing either the supply of, or the demand for, drugs.

Federal Agencies and Program

Our Nation's anti-drug efforts are headed up by the White House **Office of National Drug Control Policy (ONDCP),** which annually publishes a report detailing the Nation's drug control strategy and budget. The 2004 National Drug Control Strategy includes three priorities:[48]

1. Stopping drug use before it starts (prevention)
2. Healing America's drug users (treatment)
3. Disrupting the (drug) market (interdiction)

Office of National Drug Control Policy (ONDCP)
the headquarters of America's drug control effort, located in the executive branch of the U.S. government, headed by a director appointed by the President

The National Drug Control Strategy has set two- and four-year goals. The baselines for these goals are the Monitoring the Future survey for school-based data and the revised *2002 National Survey on Drug Use and Health* for adult data.

Two-Year Goals

- A 10% reduction in current use of illegal drugs by eighth, tenth, and twelfth graders.
- A 10% reduction in current use of illegal drugs by adults aged 18 and older.

Four-Year Goals

- A 25% reduction in current use of illegal drugs by eighth, tenth, and twelfth graders.
- A 25% reduction in current use of illegal drugs by adults aged 18 and older.

The National Drug Control Strategy budget request for the fiscal year (FY) 2005 was $12.65 billion.[49] Although this may seem like a lot of money, it is considerably less than the figure given in 2001, namely, $18.1 billion.[50] The department scheduled to received the largest portion of funds in FY 2005 is the Department of Health and Human Services (the National Institute on Drug Abuse and the Substance Abuse and Mental Health Services Administration). The Department of Justice (DOJ) is slated for the second-largest portion. DOJ agencies include the Bureau of Prisons, the Drug Enforcement Administration, the Interagency Crime and Drug Enforcement Agency, and the Office of Justice Programs. Two agencies that will receive significant funding belong in the Department of Homeland Security—the U.S. Coast Guard and Border and Transportation Security. The remainder of the funding is spread over the Departments of Defense, State, Education, and Veterans Affairs and the Office of National Drug Control Policy.[49]

Department of Health and Human Services

The Department of Health and Human Services (HHS) receives the largest portion of the federal drug budget, more than $3.66 billion in fiscal 2005. This money is spent on drug prevention education, treatment programs, and research into the causes and physiology of drug abuse. The preponderance of these funds is spent to reduce the demand for drugs. The approach of HHS to the drug problem is broad and includes research, treatment, and educational activities.

The misuse and abuse of tobacco, alcohol, and other drugs are addressed primarily as lifestyle problems, that is, as health promotion issues—like physical fitness and nutrition. As such, HHS recognizes that the problems of drug misuse and abuse are complex—involving inherited, environmental, social, and economic causes. Therefore, the solutions are also viewed as being complex. The typical approach involves the application of the three levels of prevention—primary, secondary, and tertiary. It also recognizes the importance of incorporating the three primary prevention strategies of education, regulation, and automatic protection. These are discussed in greater detail in Chapter 17.

The HHS has published health status, risk reduction, and service and protection objectives on the use of tobacco, alcohol, and other drugs in *Healthy People 2010* (see Boxes 12.1 and 12.2). These objectives set the direction and standards for success of all our national drug control efforts.

The lead agency within HHS is the **Substance Abuse and Mental Health Services Administration (SAMHSA).** Within SAMHSA, there are three centers: The Center for Substance Abuse Prevention (CSAP), the Center for Substance Abuse Treatment (CSAT), and the Center for Mental Health Services (CMHS). In addition to SAMHSA, there are two other important agencies that deal with the problems of alcohol and other drugs: The National Institute on Drug Abuse and the Food and Drug Administration (see Chapter 2 for more information on these agencies).

The **National Institute on Drug Abuse (NIDA)** is the largest institution in the world devoted to drug abuse research. At NIDA, research efforts are aimed at understanding the causes and consequences of drug abuse and at evaluating prevention and treatment programs. Within NIDA are several important divisions and centers, such as the Division of Clinical Research, the Division of Epidemiology and Prevention Research, the Division of Preclinical Research, the Division of Applied Research, the Medications Development Division, and the Addiction Research Center. These agencies conduct research and publish articles on the causes, prevention, and treatment of tobacco, alcohol, and other drug abuse.

Substance Abuse and Mental Health Services Administration (SAMHSA) the agency within the Department of Health and Human Services that provides leadership in drug abuse prevention and treatment. It houses the Center for Substance Abuse Prevention and the Center for Substance Abuse Treatment.

National Institute on Drug Abuse (NIDA) the federal government's lead agency for drug abuse research, one of the National Institutes of Health

Another important agency in HHS is the *Food and Drug Administration (FDA)*. As stated earlier, the FDA is charged with assuring the safety and efficacy of all prescription and non-prescription drugs. The FDA dictates which drugs reach the market, and how they must be labeled, packaged, and sold. The FDA is more concerned with drug misuse than abuse.

Department of Justice

The second-largest portion of federal spending for drug control, $2.75 billion in FY 2005, goes to the Department of Justice (DOJ).[49] The DOJ addresses the supply side of the drug trade most directly by identifying, arresting, and prosecuting those who break drug laws. It tries to protect the welfare of society by incarcerating the most serious offenders, deterring others from becoming involved in drug trade, and providing a clear picture to all of the cost of drug trade and abuse. Regarding the latter, the DOJ indirectly contributes to reducing the demand for drugs.

The DOJ's budget is large, because in addition to its enforcement responsibilities, the department maintains prisons and prisoners. The DOJ employs not only those who manage the penal system, but also many marshals, attorneys, and judges. The single largest portion of the DOJ's budget goes to the Bureau of Prisons. The DOJ also operates treatment, education, and rehabilitation programs in these prisons.

Within the DOJ are several important drug-fighting agencies. The lead agency in this respect is the Drug Enforcement Agency (DEA), which investigates and assists in the prosecution of drug traffickers and their accomplices in the United States and abroad and seizes the drugs as well as the assets on which they depend. The DEA employs more than 7,000 special agents and support personnel.

Three other important agencies in the DOJ that are involved in the prevention and control of drug abuse are the Federal Bureau of Investigation (FBI), the Office of Justice Programs (OJP), and the **Bureau of Alcohol, Tobacco, Firearms and Explosives (ATF).** The FBI investigates multinational organized-crime networks that control the illegal drug market. The OJP provides "federal leadership in developing the nation's capacity to prevent and control crime, improve the criminal and juvenile justice systems, increase knowledge about crime and related issues, and assist crime victims."[51] For example, the OJP forms partnerships with and provides funds for state and local programs to "control drug abuse and trafficking; reduce and prevent crime and rehabilitate neighborhoods."[51] The ATF was only recently transferred to the DOJ from the Department of the Treasury, where it had been administered since its inception. Part of ATF's mission is to prevent the diversion of taxes (loss of revenue) caused by trafficking in contraband tobacco and alcohol products and to bring those involved in this activity to justice.

> **Bureau of Alcohol, Tobacco, Firearms, and Explosives (ATF)** the federal agency in the Department of Justice that regulates alcohol and tobacco

Department of Homeland Security

Shortly following the terrorist attacks on the World Trade Center and the Pentagon on September 11, 2001, President George W. Bush authorized the establishment of the Department of Homeland Security (DHS). Subsequently, a number of federal agencies involved in drug control activities were transferred into this new department, which is scheduled to receive the third-largest portion of funding from the National Drug Control Budget ($2.52 billion).[49] Those agencies receiving funds are Immigration and Customs Enforcement, Customs and Border Protection, and the United States Coast Guard. In the current environment, in which protection from terrorist acts is DHS's primary concern, the prevention and control of drug trafficking seems somewhat less urgent by comparison. Nonetheless, it is part of the mission of these agencies. For example, Immigration and Customs Enforcement works to prevent the immigration to this country of criminals, including those involved in drug trafficking. Customs and Border Protection, made up of employees from the Department of Agriculture, the Immigration and Naturalization Service, the Border Patrol, and the U.S. Customs Service, works with the Immigration and Customs Enforcement to protect our borders from external threats, including illegal drugs (see Figure 12.9). The United States Coast Guard helps to interdict illegal drug trafficking in our coastal waters.

FIGURE 12.9
Customs agents assist in the arrest and prosecution of those involved in drug trafficking.

Other Federal Agencies
Other federal agencies involved in drug abuse prevention and control are the Departments of
State, Defense, Veterans' Affairs, and Education. The State Department, through various diplo-
matic efforts, including "drug summits," attempts to achieve a reduction in the production and
shipment of illicit drugs into this country. The Defense Department assists foreign allies to
control the cultivation of illegal drug crops and the production of illegal drugs. Funding slated
for the Department of Veterans' Affairs is aimed primarily at the treatment of drug-related
health problems of veterans.

The Department of Education (DE) launched a program to support drug-free schools and
communities in the late 1980s. The effort was aimed at encouraging schools to adopt clear "no
drug use" policies and to provide a message that both communities and schools do not con-
done or approve of alcohol or drug use by minors. A handbook titled *What Works: Schools
Without Drugs* was prepared and distributed to schools and communities.[52] The Department
of Education continues to be an important participant in the federal drug prevention effort,
although the amount of funding for the DE has declined annually since 2002. The National
Drug Control Budget for fiscal year 2005 calls for a $23 million increase in funding for drug
testing in schools.[48]

State and Local Agencies and Programs
While considerable economic resources can be brought to bear on the drug problem at the
federal level, it is becoming increasingly clear that to achieve success, the drug war in America
must be fought at the local level—in homes, neighborhoods, and schools. State support
usually comes in the form of law enforcement expertise in education, and mental health, the

coordination of local and regional programs, and sometimes funding initiatives. It is usually up to local citizens to put these state initiatives into action or to begin initiatives of their own.

State Agencies

State agencies that address drug abuse prevention and control issues include the offices of the governor, as well as state departments of health, education, mental health, justice, and law enforcement. Sometimes there is an umbrella agency that coordinates the activities of these various offices and departments; other times there is not. To review agencies involved in the prevention and control of drug abuse and drug dependence problems in your state, visit the Web site of the Office of National Drug Control Policy (www.whitehousedrugpolicy.gov/statelocal/index.html) and click on the State and Local button. This button should take you to a page that lists each of the states. By clicking on a state, you can view all the state agencies involved in drug abuse prevention and control. For example, the Minnesota page lists the governor's office, the state drug program coordinator, the state legislative contact, the attorney general, the corrections agency, the judicial agency, the statistical analysis center, the Uniform Crime Reports contact, the state's drug and alcohol agency, a prevention resource center, the Department of Children, Families and Learning (Safe and Drug Free Schools), the Department of Human Services (and the chemical dependency program division), and other agencies.

The role of these state-level agencies is evident from their titles. Some state agencies provide actual services; others provide statistics or other information. Still others provide expertise or serve as a conduit for federal funding aimed at local (city or county) governments.

The role of state government is to promote, protect, and maintain the health and welfare of its citizens. Thus, each state has its own laws regulating the sale of tobacco, alcohol, and prescription drugs. It is the states that issue licenses to doctors, dentists, pharmacists, liquor stores, and taverns. Each state also passes laws and sets the penalties for the manufacture, sale, and possession of illicit drugs such as marijuana. For example, in California, possession of 28.5 grams (one ounce) of marijuana or less is a misdemeanor but not an arrestable offense; it carries a $100 fine. Possession of more than 28.5 grams is also a misdemeanor, punishable by six months in jail and a $500 fine. In Utah, however, possession of less than one ounce of marijuana is a misdemeanor punishable by six months in jail and a $1,000 fine. Possession of more than one pound is a felony punishable by five years in jail and a $5,000 fine.[53]

In some cases, states have passed laws that conflict with federal laws. For example, some states have decriminalized marijuana cultivation and possession for medical use. In Hawaii, patients with a signed statement from their physician affirming that they suffer from a certain medical condition are protected under law. These patients must be on a state-run registry that issues identification cards. They are then permitted to cultivate up to seven marijuana plants (only three mature plants) and to be in possession of no more than one ounce of usable marijuana.[53] These people could still be arrested by the DEA and prosecuted under federal law.

Local Agencies

Agencies of local governments that are involved in drug abuse prevention and control include mayors' offices, police and sheriffs' departments, school corporations, health departments, family services offices, mental health services, prosecutors' offices, the juvenile justice system, judges and courts, drug task forces, and so on. In some communities, there is a community drug task force or coordinating council that includes both government officials and representatives of nongovernmental agencies. Such task forces or councils might include local religious leaders, representatives from local industry (both labor and management), health care providers, and members from local voluntary agencies. The task of these organizations is usually to prioritize problems faced by the community and decide on approaches to solving them. The goal is to develop a coordinated and effective effort to resolve the issue. Sometimes a solution might involve selecting an approach that has been used with success in another community or school system.

Nongovernmental Drug Prevention and Control Agencies and Programs

Many nongovernmental programs and agencies make valuable contributions to the prevention and control of drug abuse in America. Among these are community- and school-based programs, workplace programs, and voluntary agencies.

Community-Based Drug Education Programs

Community-based drug education can occur in a variety of settings, such as child care facilities, public housing, religious institutions, businesses, and health care facilities. Information about the abuse of alcohol, tobacco, and other drugs can be disseminated through television and radio programs, movies, newspapers, and magazines.

Community-based drug education programs are most likely to be successful when they include six key features:[54]

1. A comprehensive strategy
2. An indirect approach to drug abuse prevention
3. The goal of empowering youth
4. A participatory approach
5. A culturally sensitive orientation
6. Highly structured activities

Community-based drug education programs that address broader issues (e.g., coping and learning skills) are most effective, as are those embedded in other existing community activities (see Figure 12.10). Participation can be increased by planning drug education programs around sporting or cultural events. Culturally sensitive programs are crucial for reaching minorities in the community. Use of the appropriate language, reading level, and spokespersons can mean the difference between success or failure of a program.

FIGURE 12.10

Community efforts to get rid of drug dealers can be successful.

In the past 30 years a great many drug abuse prevention education programs have been conceived and tested. Some of these have been scientifically proven to be effective. The Center for Substance Abuse Prevention (CSAP), a branch of the Substance Abuse and Mental Health Services Administration (SAMHSA) in the U.S. Department of Health and Human Services, has developed a list of effective programs. The list is available online at the CSAP Web site.[55]

An example of a community-based program with a record of success is *Across Ages.*

> Across Ages is a school- and community-based drug prevention program for youth 9 to 13 years, that seeks to strengthen the bonds between adults and youth and provide opportunities for positive community involvement. The unique and highly effective feature of Across Ages is the pairing of older adult mentors (age 55 and above) with young adolescents, specifically youth making the transition to middle school. The program employs mentoring, community service, social competence training, and family activities to build youths' sense of personal responsibility for self and community.[55]

Across Ages has been able to demonstrate success in the following areas: decreased substance use, decrease in tobacco and alcohol use, increased problem-solving ability, increased school attendance, decreased suspensions from school, improved attitude toward adults, and improved attitude toward school and the future.[55] Many other successful community- and school-based drug abuse prevention programs are listed on the CSAP Web site.

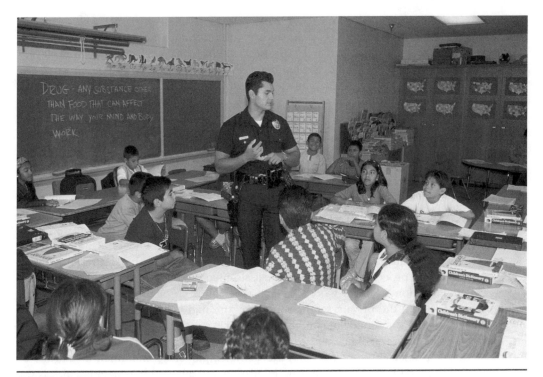

FIGURE 12.11
Drug Abuse Resistance Education (DARE) programs involve police in school drug education.

School-Based Drug Education Programs

Most health educators believe that a strong, comprehensive school health education program (see Chapter 6)—one that occupies a permanent and prominent place in the school curriculum—is the best defense against all health problems, including drug abuse. However, many schools lack these strong programs, and in their absence, substitute drug education programs developed specifically for school use.

One such program is the Drug Abuse Resistance Education (DARE) program, which began in Los Angeles. In the DARE program, local police enter the classroom to teach grade-school children about drugs (see Figure 12.11). While imparting some knowledge, the program's primary approach is to change attitudes and beliefs about drugs. It is also successful in improving children's images of the police themselves. Unfortunately, while very popular in many communities, DARE programs have been unable to demonstrate any real success in reducing actual drug use.[56]

An example of a program from the CSAP list that has been scientifically proven to be effective is Project ALERT. Project ALERT reduced students' initiation of marijuana use by 30%, decreased current marijuana use by 60%, reduced past-month cigarette use by 20% to 25%, decreased regular and heavy smoking by 33% to 55%, and substantially reduced students' pro-drug use attitudes and beliefs.[55]

Student assistance programs (SAPs) are school-based programs modeled after employee assistance programs in the workplace. They are aimed at identifying and intervening in cases of drug problems. **Peer counseling programs** are also present in some schools. In these programs, students talk about mutual problems and receive support and perhaps coping skills from peers who have been trained in this intervention activity and do not use drugs.

student assistance programs (SAPs) school-based drug education programs to assist students who have alcohol or other drug problems

peer counseling programs school-based programs in which students discuss alcohol and other drug-related problems with peers

Workplace-Based Drug Education Programs

In September 1986, concern about widespread drug use in the workplace led then President Ronald Reagan to sign Executive Order 12564, proclaiming a Drug Free Federal Workplace.[57] The rationale for the order signed in September 1986 was cited in the document itself: The desire and need for the well-being of employees, the loss of productivity caused by drug use, the illegal profits of organized crime, the illegality of the behavior itself, the undermining of public confidence, and the role of the federal government as the largest employer in the Nation to set a standard for other employers to follow in these matters. It had also become apparent to all that drug abuse is not just a personal health problem and a law enforcement problem, but that it also is a behavior that affects the safety and productivity of others, especially at work. Studies have shown that substance abusers (1) are less productive, (2) miss more work days, (3) are more likely to injure themselves, and (4) file more workers' compensation claims than their nonsubstance-abusing counterparts.

The Drug Free Federal Workplace order required federal employees to refrain from using illegal drugs, and it required agency heads to develop plans for achieving drug-free workplaces for employees in their agencies. The order further required the setting up of drug testing programs and procedures and employee assistance programs that would include provisions for rehabilitation.[57] Similar workplace substance abuse programs, which include drug testing, soon spread to the private sector, so that by the mid-1990s, such programs were in place in more than 80% of American companies.[58]

A typical workplace substance abuse prevention program has five facets.[59] The first is a formal written substance abuse policy that reflects the employer's commitment to a drug-free workplace. The second is an employee drug education and awareness program. Third is the supervisor training program. Fourth is the **employee assistance program (EAP)** to help those who need counseling and rehabilitation. The last component is a drug testing program. Large companies are more likely than small companies to have the major components of a drug-free workplace program.

employee assistance program (EAP) a workplace drug program designed to assist employees in recovering from their alcohol or other drug problems

While a substantial part of the problem can be attributed to alcohol consumption, illicit drug use remains a problem in many workplaces. While it is true that the prevalence of illegal drug abuse in the unemployed adult population is twice that of the employed adult population, 70% of all the illegal users are employed.[60] Fortunately, the prevalence of workplace drug use has declined significantly, in part because of the proliferation of workplace drug abuse and prevention programs that include drug testing. In 1987, the first year of workplace drug testing, 18.1% of all tests were positive;[61] by 1998, this figure had dropped below 5%, where it has remained[62] (see Figure 12.12).

Voluntary Health Agencies

Drug prevention and control programs are carried out at the local level with the cooperation and effort of many community members. Some of these programs are of local origin, while others have received national recognition and even endorsement. The people who actually deliver drug abuse prevention programs include teachers, community health educators, social workers, law enforcement officers, and volunteers.

The programs presented vary greatly in their message and approach. Some programs seek to educate or provide knowledge, others seek to change beliefs or attitudes about alcohol or other drug use, while still others seek to alter behavior by providing new behavior skills. Studies have shown that programs incorporating all these approaches are most successful.

A large number of voluntary health agencies have been founded to prevent or control the social and personal consequences of alcohol, tobacco, and other drug abuse. Among these are such agencies as Mothers Against Drunk Driving (MADD), Students Against Driving Drunk (SADD), Alcoholics Anonymous (AA), Narcotics Anonymous (NA), the American Cancer Society (ACS), and many others. Each of these organizations is active locally, statewide, and nationally.

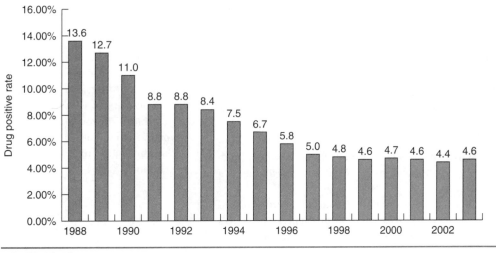

FIGURE 12.12

Drug positivity rates for combined U.S. workforce, 1988 through June 2003.

Source: Quest Diagnostics (2003). Drug Testing Index. Available at http://www.questdiagnostics.com/employersolutions/.

An important function of community leaders is to encourage parents, school officials, members of law enforcement, businesses, social groups, community health workers, and the media to work together in an effort to reduce the abuse of alcohol, tobacco, and other drugs. Every approach should be used, including seeking favorable legislation and judicial appointments, fairness in advertising, school and community education and treatment, and law enforcement. Only through citizen support and vigilance can there be a reduction in the threat that alcohol and other drugs pose to our community.

CHAPTER SUMMARY

- The abuse of alcohol, tobacco, and other drugs is a major community health problem in the United States.

- Alcohol, tobacco, and other drug abuse affects not only individuals but also communities, where it results in a substantial drain both socially and economically.

- Investigations into the causes of drug experimentation, drug abuse, and drug dependence indicate that both inherited and environmental factors contribute to the problem.

- Rates of tobacco, alcohol, and other drug use rose during the 1990s. After peaking in 1998, use of these drugs began to level off and decline.

- Chronic alcohol and tobacco use results in the loss of billions of dollars and thousands of lives in America each year.

- The misuse and abuse of prescription and nonprescription drugs remains a problem of concern.

- There are four principal elements of drug abuse prevention and control—education, treatment, public policy, and law enforcement.

- Prevention activities can be categorized as primary, secondary, and tertiary prevention.

- There are substantial federal, state, and local efforts to reduce the use, misuse, and abuse of drugs in the United States.

- Federal agencies involved include the Departments of Health and Human Services, Justice, Homeland Security, and many others.

- Efforts at the state level vary from state to state but usually include attempts to coordinate federal and local efforts.

- Drug testing in the workplace reveals a decline in illicit drug use in the workplace since testing began in 1987.

- Alcohol, tobacco, and other drug abuse continues to cause injuries and lost productivity in the American workplace.

SCENARIO: ANALYSIS AND RESPONSE

Please reread the scenario at the beginning of this chapter. How would you respond to the following questions?

1. How would spending a Saturday night in the emergency room of a large community hospital change your view of drinking?
2. Why hadn't Glenda's friends mentioned their concern about her drinking? What danger signs can you detect?
3. In what ways did Glenda put her own personal health at risk? What kinds of problems has Glenda's behavior caused for others in the community?
4. What do you think happened that Glenda can't recall?
5. Are any of your friends problem drinkers? Have you confronted them with your concern about them?
6. How much do you drink or use other drugs? Have you ever put another person in the community at risk through your drinking or other drug-taking behavior?

- A typical workplace substance abuse prevention program has five components: A written policy, a drug education program, a supervisor training program, an employee assistance program, and a drug testing program.
- A large number of voluntary health agencies are involved in drug abuse prevention and control activities.

REVIEW QUESTIONS

1. What are some personal consequences resulting from the abuse of alcohol and other drugs?
2. What are some community consequences resulting from the abuse of alcohol and other drugs?
3. What are the recent trends in drug use by high school seniors?
4. What do you feel is our most serious drug problem? Why?
5. Explain the differences among drug use, misuse, and abuse.
6. How are physical and psychological dependence different?
7. What are the two sources of risk factors that contribute to substance abuse?
8. Name the four categories of environmental risk factors that contribute to substance abuse and give an example of each.
9. What are the two major types of abused drugs? Give examples of each.
10. Why is alcohol considered the Number 1 problem drug in America?
11. In what forms do Americans consume nicotine, and in what groups of people do we see the heaviest users?
12. What agency regulates over-the-counter and prescription drugs? What two characteristics must a drug have to be approved for sale?
13. How can misuse of prescription drugs become a risk to your health?
14. What is the most commonly abused illicit drug? Why is this drug a concern?
15. What are controlled substances? Give some examples.
16. What are the side effects for both men and women that result from the use of anabolic drugs?
17. What are the four elements of drug prevention and control?
18. What are primary, secondary, and tertiary prevention strategies for the drug problem?
19. Describe the roles of each of the following federal departments in controlling drug abuse: Health and Human Services, Justice, and Homeland Security.
20. What role do state governments play in preventing and controlling drug abuse? Local governments?
21. What is Across Ages? What does it do? What is Project ALERT? What does it do?
22. How would you respond to the statement "Most drug abusers are unemployed"?
23. What are the names of four voluntary agencies and self-help groups involved in the prevention, control, and treatment of alcohol, tobacco, and other drug abuse?

ACTIVITIES

1. Schedule an appointment with the vice president of Student Affairs, the Dean of Students, or the alcohol and drug abuse prevention educator on your campus to find out more about drug (including alcohol) problems. Find out what the greatest concerns are and how the administration is trying to deal with the issues.

2. Make an appointment with the health educator or another employee in your local health department to find out more about the existing alcohol, tobacco, and other drug problems in the community. Collect the same information as noted in the first activity, except find information for the community, not the campus.

3. Find six articles that appeared in your local paper during the past two weeks that deal with drugs. Find two that related to problems at the national or international level, two at the state level, and two at the local level. Summarize each and present your reaction to these articles in a written paper.

4. Conduct a survey of at least 100 students on your campus. Try to get a random sample of people. Interview these people and find out what they think are the major drug problems on your campus and how they might be solved. Feel free to include other questions on your survey. Summarize the results in a two-page paper.

5. Attend a meeting of a community group that is involved in the prevention and control of drug abuse (e.g., local drug task force, AA, a smoking cessation group, MADD, or SADD). In a two-page paper, summarize the meeting and share your reaction to it.

COMMUNITY HEALTH ON THE WEB

The Internet contains a wealth of information about community and public health. Increase your knowledge of some of the topics presented in this chapter by accessing the Jones and Bartlett Publishers Web site at **health.jbpub.com/communityhealth/5e** and follow the links to complete the following Web activities.

- National Clearinghouse for Alcohol and Drug Information
- Mothers Against Drunk Driving
- Office on Smoking and Health

REFERENCES

1. Horgan, C., K. C. Skwara, and G. Strickler (2001). *Substance Abuse: The Nation's Number One Health Problem*. Princeton, NJ: Robert Wood Johnson Foundation.

2. Harwood, H., D. Fountain, and G. Livermore (1998). *The Economic Costs of Alcohol and Drug Abuse to Society, 1992* (NIH pub. no. 98-4327). Bethesda, MD: National Institute on Drug Abuse and National Institute on Alcohol Abuse and Alcoholism.

3. Horgan, C., K. C. Skwara, and G. Strickler (2001). *Substance Abuse: The Nation's Number One Health Problem*. Princeton, NJ: Robert Wood Johnson Foundation.

4. Johnston, L. D., P. M. O'Malley, and J. G. Bachman, J. G. (1993). *National Survey Results on Drug Use from the Monitoring the Future Study, 1975–1992. Vol. I: Secondary School Students* (NIH pub. no. 93-3597). Bethesda, MD: National Institute on Drug Abuse.

5. Johnston, L. D., P. M. O'Malley, and J. G. Bachman, J. G. (2003). *Monitoring the Future National Survey Results on Drug Use, 1975–2002. Vol. I: Secondary School Students* (NIH pub. no. 03-5375). Bethesda, MD: National Institute on Drug Abuse.

6. Johnston, L. D., P. M. O'Malley, and J. G. Bachman, J. G. (19 December 2003). "Ecstasy Use Falls for Second Year in a Row, Overall Teen Drug Use Drops." Ann Arbor: University of Michigan News and Information Services. Available at http://www.monitoringthefuture.org.

7. Glantz, M., and R. Pickens (1992). "Vulnerability to Drug Abuse: Introduction and Overview." In M. Glantz and R. Pickens, eds., *Vulnerability to Drug Abuse*. Washington, DC: American Psychological Association.

8. Cotton, N. S. (1979). "The Familial Incidence of Alcoholism: A Review." *Journal of Studies on Alcohol,* 40: 89–116.

9. Cloninger, C. R., M. Bohman, and S. Sigvardsson (1981). "Inheritance of Alcohol Abuse." *Archives of General Psychiatry,* 38: 861–868.

10. Schuckit, M. A., S. C. Risch, and E. O. Gold (1988). "Alcohol Consumption, ACTH Level, and Family History of Alcoholism." *American Journal of Psychiatry,* 145(11): 1391–1395.

11. Tabakoff, B., and P. L. Hoffman (1988). "Genetics and Biological Markers of Risk for Alcoholism." *Public Health Report,* 103(6): 690–698.

12. U.S. Department of Health and Human Services (1990). *Seventh Special Report to the U.S. Congress* (HHS pub. no. ADM-90-1656). Washington, DC: U.S. Government Printing Office.

13. Zickler, P. (2000). "Evidence Builds that Genes Influence Cigarette Smoking." *NIDA Notes,* 15(2): 1–2.

14. Needle, R., Y. Lavee, S. Su, et al. (1988). "Familial, Interpersonal, and Intrapersonal Correlates of Drug Use: A Longitudinal Comparison of Adolescents in Treatment, Drug-Using Adolescents Not in Treatment, and Non-Drug-Using Adolescents." *International Journal of Addictions,* 239(12): 1211–1240.

15. Meller, W. H., R. Rinehart, R. J. Cadoret, and E. Troughton (1988). "Specific Familial Transmission in Substance Abuse." *International Journal of Addictions,* 23(10): 1029–1039.

16. Shedler, J., and J. Block (1990). "Adolescent Drug Use and Psychological Health: A Longitudinal Inquiry." *American Psychologist,* 45(5): 612–630.

17. Horgan, C., K. C. Skwara, and G. Strickler 2001. *Substance Abuse: The Nation's Number One Health Problem*. Princeton, NJ: Robert Wood Johnson Foundation, 30.

18. Dembo, R., W. R. Blount, J. Schmeidler, and W. Burgos (1986). "Perceived Environmental Drug Use Risk and the Correlates of Early Drug Use or Nonuse Among Inner-City Youths: The Motivated Actor." *International Journal of Addictions,* 21(9–10): 977–1000.

19. Morse, R. M., and D. K. Flavin (1992). "The Definition of Alcoholism." *JAMA,* 268(8): 1012–1014.

20. National Institute on Alcohol Abuse and Alcoholism (January 1996). "Drinking and Driving." *Alcohol Alert,* 31(362): 1–4.

21. U.S. Department of Health and Human Services, Public Health Service (2000). *Healthy People 2010: Understanding and Improving Health*. Washington DC: U.S. Government Printing Office.

22. Hunt, T. (4 October, 2000). "Tough Standard Set for Drunken Driving." *USA Today,* 4A.

23. Insurance Institute for Highway Safety, Highway Loss Data Institute (2004). "DUI/DWI Laws as of March 2004." Available at http://www.hwysafety.org/safety_facts/state_laws/dui.htm.

24. Department of Health and Human Services (August 1993). "Substance Abuse Prevention and Treatment Block Grants: Sale or Distribution of Tobacco Products to Individuals Under 18 Years of Age: Proposed Rule." *Federal Register Part II,* 45: 96.

25. Freid, V. M., K. Prage, A. P. MacKay, and H. Xia (2003). *Chartbook on Trends in the Health of Americans. Health, United States, 2003.* Hyattsville, MD: National Center for Health Statistics.

26. Mokdad, A. H., J. S. Marks, D. F. Stoup, and J. L. Gerberding (2004). "Actual Causes of Death in the United States, 2000." *Journal of the American Medical Association,* 291(10): 1238–1245.

27. American Cancer Society (2003). *Cancer Facts and Figures— 2003.* Atlanta, GA: Author.

28. U.S. Department of Health and Human Services, Public Health Service, Centers for Disease Control (1986). *The Health Consequence of Involuntary Smoking. A Report of the Surgeon General* (HHS pub. no. CDC-87-8398). Washington, DC: U.S. Government Printing Office.

29. Byrd, J. C., R. S. Shapiro, and D. L. Schiedermayer (1989). "Passive Smoking: A Review of Medical and Legal Issues." *American Journal of Public Health,* 79(2): 209–215.

30. Environmental Protection Agency (1991). *Respiratory Health Effects of Passive Smoking: Lung Cancer and Other Disorders* (EPA/600/6-90/006F). Washington, DC: Indoor Air Quality Clearinghouse.

31. U.S. Department of Health and Human Services, Substance Abuse and Mental Health Services Administration (2003). *2002 National Survey on Drug Use and Health.* Available at http://www.samhsa.gov/ centers/clearinghouse/clearinghouses.html.

32. *Physicians' Desk Reference for Nonprescription Drugs and Dietary Supplements,* 24th ed. (2003). Montvale, NJ: Medical Economics.

33. *Physicians' Desk Reference,* 57th ed. (2003). Montvale, NJ: Medical Economics.

34. Lazarou, J., B. H. Pomeranz, and P. N. Corey (1998). "Incidence of Adverse Drug Reactions in Hospitalized Patients: A Meta-Analysis of Prospective Studies." *JAMA,* 279(15): 1200–1205.

35. Federal Register, Code fo Federal Regulations, Food and Drugs, Part 1308. *Schedules of Controlled Substances,* Rev. April 1, 1998. Washington, DC: Author.

36. Drug Enforcement Administration (2001). *Marijuana.* Available at www.dea.gov/concern/marijuana.htm.

37. Lucas, S., J. Mendelson, J. Henry, L. Amass, and A. Budson (1988). *Ethanol Effects on Marijuana-Induced Intoxication and Electroencephalographic Activity. Problems of Drug Dependence* (Research Monograph Series 90). Rockville, MD: National Institute of Drug Abuse, 62.

38. Zickler, P. (2000). "Evidence Accumulates That Long-Term Marijuana Users Experience Withdrawal." *NIDA Notes,* 15(1).

39. Center for Addiction and Substance Abuse at Columbia University (1994). *Cigarettes, Alcohol, Marijuana: Gateways to Illicit Drug Use.* New York: Author.

40. Department of Justice, National Drug Intelligence Center (2003). *National Drug Threat Assessment 2003.* Available at http://www.usdoj.gov/ndic/topics/ndtas.htm.

41. Leshner, A. I. (30 July, 1999). *The Drug Addiction Treatment Act of 1999. Testimony before the House Subcommittee on Health and Environment.* Available at http://165.112.78.61/Testimony/ 7-30-99Testimony.html.

42. Drug Enforcement Agency, Department of Justice (2000). *Methamphetamine.* Available at www.dea.gov/concern/meth.htm.

43. Drug Enforcement Administration, Intelligence Division (2000). *An Overview of Club Drugs* (DEA-20005). Washington, DC: Drug Enforcement Agency.

44. National Institute on Drug Abuse (2000). *Anabolic Steroid Abuse* (NIH pub. no. 00-3721). Bethesda, MD: National Institute on Drug Abuse.

45. Pinger, R. R., W. A. Payne, D. B. Hahn, and E. J. Hahn (1998). *Drugs: Issues for Today,* 3rd ed. Madison, WI: WCB McGraw-Hill.

46. Center for Substance Abuse Prevention, Substance Abuse and Mental Health Services Administration (1997). *A Look at Successful and Cost-Effective State Treatment Programs: Treatment Works Fact Sheet.* Rockville, MD: Author.

47. Bureau of Justice Statistics (1992). *Drugs, Crime and the Justice System 1992.* Washington, DC: U.S. Government Printing Office.

48. Office of National Drug Control Policy (March 2004). *2004 National Drug Control Strategy.* Available at http://www.whitehouse-drugpolicy.gov/publications/policy/ndcs04/index.html.

49. Office of National Drug Control Policy (February 2004). *National Drug Control Strategy FY 2005 Budget Summary.* Available at http://www.whitehousedrugpolicy.gov/publications/policy/ budgetsum04/index.html.

50. Office of National Drug Control Policy (February 2002). *2002 National Drug Control Strategy.* Washington, DC: U.S. Government Printing Office.

51. U.S. Department of Justice, Office of Justice Programs (2004). "About OJP." Available at http://www.ojp.usdoj.gov/about.htm.

52. U.S. Department of Education (1987). *What Works: Schools Without Drugs.* Washington, DC: U.S. Government Printing Office.

53. National Organization for the Reform of Marijuana Laws (2004). "State by State Laws." Available at http://www.norml.org.

54. Brown, M. E. (1993). "Successful Components of Community and School Prevention Programs." *National Prevention Evaluation Report: Research Collection,* 1(1): 4–5.

55. Center for Substance Abuse Prevention (2004). *SAMHSA Model Programs.* Available at http://modelprograms.samhsa.gov/.

56. Lynam, D. R., R. Milich, R. Zimmerman, S. P. Novak, T. K. Logan, C. Martin, C. Leukefeld, and R. Clayton (1999). "Project DARE: No Effects at 10-Year Follow-up." *Journal of Consulting and Clinical Psychology,* 67(4): 590–593.

57. *Drug-Free Federal Workplace* (Executive Order 12564) (17 September 1986). *Federal Register,* 51(180).

58. American Management Associates (1996). *1996 AMA Survey: Workplace Drug Testing and Drug Abuse Policy.* New York: Author.

59. U.S. Department of Labor (1991). *What Works: Workplaces Without Alcohol or Other Drugs* (pub. no. 282-148/54629). Washington, DC: U.S. Government Printing Office.

60. Substance Abuse and Mental Health Services Administration, Office of Applied Studies (1999). *Worker Drug Use and Workplace Policies and Programs: Results from the 1994 and 1997 NHSDA* (HHS pub. no. SMA 99-3352). Rockville, MD: Author.

61. SmithKline Beecham Clinical Laboratories (29 February 1996). "Drug Detection in the Workplace in 1995 Declines for the Eighth Straight Year [Press release]." Collegeville: PA: Author.

62. Quest Diagnostics (2003). "Drug Use Climbed in the U.S. Workforce in the First Half of 2003, Driven by Continued Use of Amphetamines, According to Quest Diagnostics' Drug Testing Index." Available at http://www.questdiagnostics.com/employersolutions/dit_10_2003/ dti_index.html.

UNIT
THREE

HEALTH CARE
DELIVERY

Chapter 13

Health Care System: Structure

Chapter Objectives

After studying this chapter, you will be able to:

1 Define the term *health care system*.

2 Trace the history of health care delivery in the United States from the mid-nineteenth century to the present.

3 Discuss and explain the concept of the spectrum of health care delivery.

4 Distinguish between the different kinds of health care, including population-based public health practice, medical practice, long-term practice, and end-of-life practice.

5 List and describe the different levels of medical practice.

6 List and characterize the various groups of health care providers.

7 Explain the differences among allopathic, osteopathic, and nonallopathic providers.

8 Define *complementary* and *alternative medicine*.

9 Explain why there is a need for health care providers.

10 Prepare a list of the different types of facilities in which health care is delivered.

11 Explain the differences among private, public, and voluntary hospitals.

12 Explain the concept behind ambulatory care facilities.

13 Briefly discuss the options for long-term care.

14 Explain what the Joint Commission on Accreditation of Healthcare Organizations (JCAHO) does.

SCENARIO

Marcus had had a busy summer. Not only was he working 45 hours a week in order to earn enough money to return to college in the fall, but he was a member of two different softball teams and played in the golf league sponsored by his summer employer. He really enjoyed sports. In fact, one of his softball teams was a traveling team that played a 60-game schedule, traveling as far as 100 miles away to play in some tournaments.

Marcus was an aggressive softball player who enjoyed good competition and was always willing to slide hard into second base to break up a double play. In fact, it was his excessive sliding into the different bases that led to his medical problem. Toward the end of the season, Marcus had realized that the scab on his leg really never got a chance to heal over the summer

because of his sliding, and now it was getting tender and a redness appeared around it. So he decided to go see his physician. After a quick look and a little probing, Dr. Duncan said "Marcus, you have a basic infection. Are you allergic to any antibiotics?" When Marcus said no, Dr. Duncan wrote a prescription and sent him on his way.

Two weeks passed. Marcus had taken all his medication, but his leg didn't look any better. He called Dr. Duncan for another appointment. At the second appointment, Dr. Duncan took another look at the leg and prescribed a second medication. Another two weeks passed and still no change. So at his third visit, Dr. Duncan stated, "I'm not sure what the problem is. I'd like to refer you to a specialist. I think you should see Dr. Kennedy, the dermatologist."

INTRODUCTION

providers
those individuals educated and trained to provide health care

The process by which health care is delivered in the United States is unlike the processes used in other countries of the world. Other developed countries have national health insurance run or organized by the government and paid for, in large part, by general taxes. Also, in these countries almost all citizens are entitled to receive health care services.[1] Health care in the United States is delivered by an array of **providers,** in a variety of settings, under the watchful eye of regulators, and paid for in a variety of ways. Because of this process, many question the notion that the United States has a health care delivery system. That is, "[a]lthough these various individuals and organizations are generally referred to collectively as 'the health care delivery system,' the phrase suggests order, integration, and accountability that do not exist. Communication, collaboration, or systems planning among these various entities is limited and is almost incidental to their operations."[2] Whether or not health care delivery in the United States should be called a "system," there is a process in place in which health care workers, located in a variety of facilities, provide services to deal with disease and injury for the purpose of promoting, maintaining, and restoring health to the citizens (see Figure 13.1). In this chapter, we will outline the history of health care delivery in the United States, examine the spectrum of health care delivery, and describe the various types of health care providers and the facilities in which health care is delivered.

A BRIEF HISTORY OF HEALTH CARE DELIVERY IN THE UNITED STATES

For as long as humankind has been concerned with disease, injury, and health, there has always been a category of health care in which people have tried to help or treat themselves. This category of care is referred to as *self-care* or *self-treatment.* For example, in most American homes, there are usually provisions to deal with minor emergencies, nursing care, and the relief of minor pains or ailments. This type of care continues today and includes actions taken with the goal of preventing problems before they occur. The following discussion of the history of health care in the United States does not include self-care, because it is assumed that most people would engage in some type of self-care prior to seeking professional help. Instead, we will

FIGURE 13.1
Do we really have a health care system?

review the development of professional care provided by those who have been formally educated in some aspect of health care.

Before 1850, health care occurred primarily in a physician-patient relationship, with most of the treatment taking place in the patient's home. This is not to say that physicians did not see patients in their offices, but it was more common for the physician to visit patients at their homes.

In the mid- to late-nineteenth century, formal health care gradually moved from the patient's home to the physician's office and into the hospital. The primary reason for this change was the building and staffing of many new hospitals. It was felt that patients could receive better care in a setting designed for patient care, staffed with trained people, and equipped with the latest medical supplies and instruments. In addition, physicians could treat more patients in a central location because of the reduced travel time.

It was also during the latter portion of the nineteenth century that the scientific method began to play a more important role in health care. Medical procedures backed by scientific findings began to replace "rational hunches," "good ideas," and "home remedies" as the standards for medical care. With the acceptance of the germ theory of disease and the identification of infectious disease agents, there was real hope for the control of communicable diseases, which were the leading health problems of that period.

At the beginning of the twentieth century, although communicable diseases were still the leading causes of death, mortality rates were beginning to decline. Although most of the decline can be attributed to improved public health measures, there also was change occurring in health care. New medical procedures such as X-ray therapy, specialized surgical procedures, and chemotherapy were developed, group medical practices were started, and new medical equipment and instruments (such as the electrocardiograph to measure heart function) were invented. The training of doctors and nurses also improved and became more specialized. By 1929 the

United States was spending about 3.9% of its gross domestic product (GDP) on health care, which means that 3.9% of all goods and services produced by the nation that year were associated with health care.

Even with some of these "new" advances in the practice of medicine, U.S. medicine was still limited pretty much to two parties—patients and physicians. "Diagnosis, treatment, and fees for services were considered confidential between patients and physicians. Medical practice was relatively simple and usually involved long-standing relationships with patients and, often, several generations of families. Physicians collected their own bills, set, and usually adjusted their charges to their estimates of patients' ability to pay. This was the intimate physician-patient relationship the professional held sacred."[3]

By 1940 noncommunicable diseases had replaced communicable diseases as the leading causes of death, and thus changed Americans' concern from communicable diseases to noncommunicable, chronic diseases. It was also a time when the country was facing another war. Huge technical strides were made in the 1940s and 1950s as medical developments that occurred during World War II found applications in civilian medicine. However, adequate health facilities to treat long-term diseases were lacking in many areas of the country. The **Hospital Survey and Construction Act of 1946,** better known as the **Hill-Burton Act** (after the authors of the legislation), provided substantial funds for hospital construction. The infusion of federal funds helped to remedy the serious hospital shortage caused by the lack of construction during the Depression and World War II. The Hill-Burton Act was primarily a federal-state partnership. State agencies were given grants to determine the need for hospitals and then were provided with seed money to begin construction of the facilities.[4] However, the major portion of construction dollars came from state and local sources.[5] Through the years, the Hill-Burton Act has been amended several times to help meet health care needs in the United States. Funds have been made available for additional construction, modernization, and replacement of other health care facilities and for comprehensive health planning.

With improved procedures, equipment, and facilities and the increase in noncommunicable diseases, the cost of health care began to rise. As the cost of health care rose, it became too expensive for some people. Concerns were expressed about who should receive health care and who should pay for it. The debate over whether health care is a basic right or a privilege in America began in earnest. By the end of the 1950s, there remained an overall shortage of quality health care in America. There was also a maldistribution of health care services—metropolitan areas were being better served than the less-developed rural areas.

In the 1960s, there was an increased interest in health insurance, and it became common practice for workers and their bargaining agents to negotiate for better health benefits (see Figure 13.2). Undoubtedly, some employers preferred to increase benefits rather than to raise wages. Few then could foresee the escalation in health care costs for Americans that would continue through the early 1990s. Thus, the **third-party payment system** for health care became solidified as the standard method of payment for health care costs in the United States. The third-party payment system gets its name from the fact that the insurer—either government or a private insurance company (third party)—reimburses (pays the bills) to the provider (second party) for the health care given to the patient (first party).[6] (A detailed explanation of the third-party payment system is presented in Chapter 14.) More recently, when some speak of the third-party payment system, they add a fourth party—the purchaser of the insurance, usually an employer.[7] It should be noted that the government and private insurers pay the medical bills with tax dollars and collected premiums, respectively—not with their own funds.

With the growth of the third-party system of paying for health care, the cost of health care rose even more rapidly than before because patients enjoyed increased access to care without out-of-pocket expenses. However, those without insurance found it increasingly difficult to afford care. When the Democrats regained the White House in the 1960s, they led a federal policy change to increase citizen access to health care, which culminated in 1965 with

Hospital Survey and Construction Act of 1946 (Hill-Burton Act) federal legislation that provided substantial funds for hospital construction

third-party payment system a health insurance term indicating that bills will be paid by the insurer and not the patient or the health care provider

FIGURE 13.2
Health benefits have become an important part of the total compensation package for workers.

the authorization of Medicare and Medicaid by Titles XVIII and XIX, respectively, of the Social Security Act. (These programs, which were enacted to help provide care for the elderly, the disabled, and the poor, are also discussed at length in Chapter 14.) Also in the 1960s, the federal government increased funding for medical research and technology to support transplants and life extension.

By the late 1960s and early 1970s, it had become apparent that the Hill-Burton Act had stimulated not only the growth of health care facilities, but also the demand for health care services. With this growth came a continuing rise in health care costs and a need for better planning in health care delivery.

Among the early attempts at planning were the 1964 amendments to the Hill-Burton Act. The amendments called for comprehensive planning on a regional level. Their purpose was to make more efficient use of federal funds by preventing the duplication of facilities. However, they depended on good faith efforts and could not be enforced. It soon became evident that more powerful legislation was needed to control costs and to coordinate and control rapid growth in health care facilities.

Another attempt was made to encourage better planning two years later. The Comprehensive Health Planning and Public Service Amendments of 1966 authorized funds for state- and area-wide Comprehensive Health Planning Agencies. These too failed because they had no "teeth." Then, in 1974, Public Law 93-641 was passed. This law, known as the National Health Planning and Resources Development Act of 1974, combined several pieces of previous legislation to put teeth into comprehensive planning efforts. There were high hopes and expectations that these pieces of legislation would provide reason and order to the development and modification of health care services.[8] This legislation led to the formation of Health Systems Agencies throughout the entire country. Their purpose was to cut costs by preventing the building of "unnecessary" facilities or the purchase of unnecessary equipment. While some money may have been saved, the Health Systems Agencies were viewed by some as yet another unnecessary government bureaucracy, and when the late President Reagan took office in 1980, he, along with Congress, eliminated this program.

Before leaving our health care discussion of the 1970s, it should be noted that another piece of legislation was passed that did not seem all that important at the time but would have a profound impact on the way health care was later delivered. This legislation was the Health Maintenance Organization (HMO) Act of 1973. This act "provided both loans and grants for the planning, development, and implementation of combined insurance and health care delivery organizations and required that a minimum prescribed array of services be included in the HMO arrangement."[3]

The 1980s brought many changes to the health care industry, the most notable of which was probably the deregulation of health care delivery. In 1981, with Ronald Reagan in the White House, it was announced that the administration would let the competitive market, not governmental regulation, shape health care delivery.[9] Open competition is a philosophy of allowing consumers to regulate delivery by making choices about where and from whom they receive their care. In theory, those who provide good care will get more patients and in turn be able to offer the care at a lower price.

There are some economists, however, who do not believe that the health care system behaves like a normal market. For example, it is not likely that an ill patient seeking medical care will shop for a less expensive physician. Physicians do not advertise the cost of their services. Also, it is the physician who tells the patient which hospital to go to and when to check in and out, due to the admitting privileges that physicians have. In addition, providers tend to offer more and more services to entice the market to "shop with us," which in effect drives up health care spending. For these reasons, the competitive market approach is of questionable value in lowering health care costs.

The 1980s also saw a proliferation of new medical technology (e.g., MRIs and ultrasound). Along with this new technology have come new health care issues such as medical ethics (e.g., prolonging life and ending life) and more elaborate health insurance programs (e.g., policies that cover specific diseases such as cancer and AIDS, home care, and rehabilitation).

Many of the concerns of the 1980s continued into the 1990s. The 1992 presidential campaign again brought attention to America's problems with health care delivery. Bill Clinton, then governor of Arkansas, based his election campaign strategy on being a new kind of Democrat—one who could take on the nation's domestic ills. He saw health care as one of those ills because the present system failed to cover all, and its spiraling costs threatened to bankrupt the government and cripple American industry.

Shortly after being elected president, Mr. Clinton appointed the first lady, Hillary Rodham Clinton, to head a committee to develop a plan to overcome the shortcomings of the health care system. By the fall of 1993, the committee had completed a plan that the president then presented to a joint session of Congress in front of a national television audience. This detailed plan, referred to informally as the president's Health Security Plan and formally as the **American Health Security Act of 1993,** was over 1,500 pages in length. The plan rested on six major points: (1) providing security (universal coverage), (2) controlling costs, (3) enhancing quality, (4) expanding access to traditionally undeserved areas, (5) reducing bureaucracy, especially paperwork, and (6) reducing fraud and abuse.[10] President Clinton's health care plan was much discussed in Congress in 1994; however, opposition kept it from ever reaching the

American Health Security Act of 1993
the comprehensive health care reform introduced by then President Clinton, but never enacted

managed care
health plans that integrate the financing and delivery of health care services to individuals who are covered by arrangements with selected providers who furnish comprehensive services to members; explicit criteria for the selection of health care providers; significant financial incentives for members to use providers and procedures that are associated with the plan; and formal programs for quality assurance and utilization review

floor for a vote before Congress adjourned. Although the plan was never approved, the pressures generated by the plan transformed the private health care system in the United States.

In the mid- to late-1990s, rapid changes occurred in the organization and financing of health care.[11] These changes can be summed up in two words—managed care. **Managed care** has many meanings but will be referred to here as health plans "that integrate the financing and delivery of health care services to covered individuals by means of arrangements with selected providers to furnish comprehensive services to members; explicit criteria for the selection of health care providers; significant financial incentives for members to use providers and procedures associated with the plan; and formal programs for quality assurance and utilization review."[12]

With the advent of managed care, the increase of health care costs slowed in the mid-1990s; in fact, the actual growth for several years was almost flat. Even so, both the percentage of the gross domestic product (GDP) and the dollars spent on health care continued to inch up. In 1996, for the first time in history, the total health care bill for the United States topped $1 trillion ($1,039 billion, 13.6% of the GDP).[13] In 2002, spending increased to $1,553 billion, which was 14.9% of the GDP (see Table 13.1 for comparisons to other countries in 2000).[14]

Table 13.1
Spending on Health Care in Selected Countries: 1960, 1980, and 2000

Country	Health Expenditures as a Percentage of GDP			Per Capita Health Expenditures* ($)		
	1960	1980	2000†	1960	1980	2000†
Australia	4.3	7.0	8.3	87	658	2,211
Austria	4.3	7.6	8.0	64	662	2,162
Belgium	—	6.4	8.7	—	577	2,269
Canada	5.4	7.1	9.1	109	710	2,535
Czech Republic	—	—	7.2	—	—	1,031
Denmark	—	9.1	8.3	—	819	2,420
Finland	3.9	6.4	6.6	54	509	1,664
France	—	—	9.5	—	—	2,349
Germany	4.8	8.8	10.6	90	824	2,748
Greece	—	6.6	8.3	—	348	1,399
Hungary	—	—	6.8	—	—	841
Iceland	3.3	6.1	8.9	50	576	2,608
Ireland	3.6	8.4	6.7	36	454	1,953
Italy	3.6	—	8.1	48	—	2,032
Japan	3.0	6.4	7.8	26	522	2,012
Korea	—	—	5.9	—	—	893
Luxembourg	—	5.9	—	—	605	—
Mexico	—	—	5.4	—	—	490
Netherlands	—	7.5	8.1	—	668	2,246
New Zealand	—	5.9	8.0	—	458	1,623
Norway	2.9	7.0	7.8	46	632	2,362
Poland	—	—	—	—	—	—
Portugal	—	5.6	8.2	—	265	1,441
Slovak Republic	—	—	5.9	—	—	690
Spain	1.5	5.4	7.7	14	328	1,556
Sweden	4.5	9.1	—	89	850	—
Switzerland	4.9	7.6	10.7	136	881	3,222
Turkey	—	3.3	—	—	75	—
United Kingdom	3.9	5.6	7.3	74	444	1,763
United States	5.1	8.8	13.3	143	1,067	4,672

GDP, gross domestic product. —, Data not available.
*Per capita health expenditures for each country have been adjusted to U.S. dollars using gross domestic product purchasing power parities for each year.
†Preliminary figures.

Source: Freid, V. M., K. Prager, A. P. MacKay, and H. Xia (2003). *Health, United States, 2003, with Chartbook on Trends in Health of Americans.* Hyattsville, MD: National Center for Health Statistics, 305.

Table 13.2
Consumer Price Index and Average Annual Percentage of Change for All Items and Selected Items: United States, Selected Years 1960–2002

[Data are based on reporting by samples of providers and other retail outlets.]

Year	All Items	Medical Care	Food	Apparel	Housing	Energy
1960	29.6	22.3	30.0	45.7	—	22.4
1970	38.8	34.0	39.2	59.2	36.4	25.5
1980	82.4	74.9	86.8	90.0	81.1	86.0
1990	130.7	162.8	132.4	124.1	128.5	102.1
2000	172.2	260.8	167.8	129.6	169.6	124.6
2002	179.9	285.6	176.2	124.0	180.3	121.7
Average Percent Change						
1960–1970	2.7	4.3	2.7	2.6	—	1.3
1970–1980	7.8	8.2	8.3	4.4	8.3	12.9
1980–1990	4.7	8.1	4.3	3.2	4.7	1.7
1990–2000	8.8	13.7	7.1	−0.2	8.9	17.8
2000–2002	4.4	9.3	5.0	−4.4	6.2	−2.1

—, Data not available.

Note: 1982–1984 = 100.

Sources: U.S. Department of Labor, Bureau of Labor Statistics, Consumer Price Index, various releases; and Freid, V. M., K. Prager, A. P. MacKay, and H. Xia (2003). *Health, United States, 2003, with Chartbook on Trends in Health of Americans.* Hyattsville, MD: National Center for Health Statistics.

Put another way, almost one-seventh of all the output of the United States in 2002 was spent on health care. Health care is the one segment of the U.S. economy that continues to grow consistently faster than the cost of inflation (see Table 13.2). Ever-newer technology, ever-increasing demands for the best care, growing medical liability, new diagnostic procedures, the lengthening of lifespans, the development of new drugs (e.g., Viagra), and newly identified diseases put great demands on the system.

By the mid- to late 1990s managed care had become the dominant form of health care financing and delivery, but it became apparent that support for it, with some exceptions, was not deep.[15] In addition, it was obvious that the slowdown in health care costs, which was attributed to managed care, would be just a one-time savings if other measures were not taken. President Clinton saw this as an opportunity to again seek health care reform.

This time then President Clinton treaded carefully, offering small but politically popular programs like health care coverage for uninsured children (see the discussion of SCHIP in Chapter 14) and a mandatory minimum hospital stay for childbirth to counter the so-called "drive-by deliveries" created by managed care.[16] So in 1996, through an Executive Order and with an amendment by way of a second Executive Order in 1997, President Clinton created the "Advisory Commission on Consumer Protection and Quality in the Health Care Industry."[17] Formally, "the Commission was charged to advise the President on changes occurring in the health care system and, where appropriate, to make recommendations on how best to promote and ensure consumer protection and health care quality."[17] Informally, this meant creating a "consumer bill of rights" and conducting a comprehensive review of the quality of health care in the nation.

In November 1997, the Commission delivered its interim report to the President entitled "A Consumer Bill of Rights and Responsibilities" (see Box 13.1). President Clinton endorsed the report and challenged insurance companies and managed care organizations to voluntarily adopt the Commission's "bill of rights." Only a handful did so, and President Clinton asked that Congress pass a federal law requiring health plans to adopt such protections.[18]

The final report of the Commission was delivered to President Clinton in March 1998. Included, in addition to the "Consumer Bill of Rights and Responsibilities," was a proposed

BOX 13.1 — CONSUMER BILL OF RIGHTS AND RESPONSIBILITIES

I. Information Disclosure

Consumers have the right to receive accurate, easily understood information and to require assistance in making informed health care decisions about their health care plans, professionals, and facilities.

II. Choice of Providers and Plans

Consumers have the right to a choice of health care providers that is sufficient to ensure access to appropriate high-quality health care.

III. Access to Emergency Services

Consumers have the right to emergency health care services when and where the need arises. Health plans should provide payment when the consumer presents to an emergency department with acute symptoms of sufficient severity— including severe pain—such that a "prudent lay person" could reasonably expect the absence of medical attention to result in placing that consumer's health in serious jeopardy, serious impairment to bodily functions, or serious dysfunction of any bodily organ or part.

IV. Participation in Treatment Decisions

Consumers have the right and responsibility to fully participate in all decisions related to their health care. Consumers who are unable to fully participate in treatment decisions have the right to be represented by parents, guardians, family members, or other conservators.

V. Respect and Nondiscrimination

A. Consumers have the right to considerate, respectful care from all members of the health care system at all times and under all circumstances. An environment of mutual respect is essential to maintain a quality health care system.

B. Consumers must not be discriminated against in the delivery of health care services consistent with the benefits covered in their policy or as required by law based on race, ethnicity, nationality, religion, sex, age, mental or physical disability, sexual orientation, genetic information, or source of payment.

C. Consumers who are eligible for coverage under the terms and conditions of a health plan or program or as required by law must not be discriminated against in marketing and enrollment practices based on race, ethnicity, nationality, religion, sex, age, mental or physical disability, sexual orientation, genetic information, or source of payment.

VI. Confidentiality of Health Information

Consumers have the right to communicate with health care providers in confidence and to have the confidentiality of their individually identifiable health care information protected. Consumers also have the right to review and copy their own medical records and request amendments to their records.

VII. Complaints and Appeals

All consumers have the right to a fair and efficient process for resolving differences with their health plans, health care providers, and the institutions that serve them, including a rigorous system of internal review and an independent system of external review.

VIII. Consumer Responsibilities

In a health care system that protects consumers' rights, it is reasonable to expect and encourage consumers to assume reasonable responsibilities. Greater individual involvement by consumers in their care increases the likelihood of achieving the best outcomes and helps support a quality improvement, cost-conscious environment.

Source: The President's Advisory Commission on Consumer Protection and Quality in the Health Care Industry (1998). *Quality First: Better Health Care for All Americans.* Washington, DC: U.S. Government Printing Office, A5–A12.

statement of purpose for the health care system, evidence of quality problems within health care, and more than 50 recommendations to advance health care in the United States. The Commission felt that the first step in improving health care in the United States was to create a statement of purpose that the President could articulate. The Commission proposed "The purpose of the health care system must be to continuously reduce the impact and burden of illness, injury, and disability and to improve the health and functioning of the people of the United States."[17] The quality problems identified by the Commission included (1) an unacceptably high rate of medical errors (e.g., medication errors), (2) the extensive overuse of some services (e.g., hysterectomies), (3) the underuse of other services (e.g., use of beta blockers in Medicare patients with myocardial infarctions), and (4) a wide variation in patterns of care across the country.[17,18] Few of the recommendations of the Commission were approved before President Clinton left office in 2001. However, in 2002 both the House and the Senate passed differing versions of the Patients' Bill of Rights,[3] but as of late 2004 Congress was still trying to work out a compromise bill. The major obstacle in reaching a compromise has been deciding whether or not patients should have the ability to sue their HMO for wrongful denials of medical care. At the time of the writing of this book, the U.S. Supreme Court was getting ready to make its ruling on the suing of HMOs. It should also be noted that while Congress has debated the issue, 40 states have already passed some version of the Patients' Bill of Rights.[3]

Today, both consumers and health care providers are in agreement that the American health care delivery system needs to be changed. Recent reports from the Institute on Medicine[2,19,20] claim that "health care today harms too frequently and routinely fails to deliver its potential benefits."[19] Further, the health care system suffers from lack of coordinated, comprehensive services, resulting in both the wasteful duplication of efforts and unaccountable gaps in care.[19] In its reports, the IOM outlines a number of recommendations for changing health care delivery in the United States. These recommendations, combined with the release of the World Health Organization's report "The World Health Report 2000—Health Systems: Improving Performance," in which the U.S. health system was ranked 37th out of 191 countries,[21] provide some direction for changing the current system.

Where is health care in the United States headed? "No one can predict accurately where the health care system will be in 5 years, let alone 10 or 20 years. Simple generalizations informed by past studies, even studies only a few years old, are limited in their ability to describe or explain current directions in health care."[11] However, a couple of things are certain. The U.S. health care system will continue to change and evolve; technology and the mapped human genome will play a bigger and bigger role in how health care is delivered; and the aging U.S. population, along with increasing health care costs, will mandate that change occur.

THE SPECTRUM OF HEALTH CARE DELIVERY

Because health care in the United States is delivered by an array of providers in a variety of settings, reference is sometimes made to the spectrum of health care delivery (see Table 13.3). The *spectrum of health care delivery* refers to the various types of care. Within this spectrum, four levels of practice have emerged: population-based public health practice, medical practice, long-term practice, and end-of-life practice.

Population-Based Public Health Practice

population-based public health practice incorporates interventions aimed at disease prevention and health promotion, specific protection, and a good share of case findings

Population-based public health practice incorporates interventions aimed at disease prevention and health promotion, specific protection, and a good share of case findings.[22,23] A primary component of population-based public health practice is education. If people are going to behave in a way that will promote their health and the health of their community, they first must know how to do so. Health education not only provides such information but also attempts to empower and motivate people to put this information to use by discontinuing unhealthy behaviors and adopting healthy ones. Though much of public health practice takes place in governmental health agencies, it also takes place in a variety of other settings (such as voluntary health agencies, social service agencies, schools, businesses and industry, and even in some traditional medical care settings).[22]

Medical Practice

Medical practice means "those services usually provided by or under the supervision of a physician or other traditional health care provider."[22] Such services are offered at several

Table 13.3
The Spectrum of Health Care Delivery

Level of practice	Description	Examples of Delivery Settings
Population-Based Public Health Practice	Practice aimed at disease prevention and health promotion that shapes a community's overall health; emphasizes education and prevention	Public, community, and school health programs; public health clinics
Medical Practice		
Primary care	Clinical preventive services, first-contact treatment services, and ongoing care for commonly encountered medical conditions; emphasizes early detection and routine care	Primary care provider offices; public clinics; managed care organizations; community mental health centers
Secondary care	Specialized attention and ongoing management for common and less frequently encountered medical conditions, including support services for people with special challenges due to chronic or long-term conditions	
Acute care	Short-term, intense medical care usually requiring hospitalization	Emergency rooms; inpatient surgical centers; hospitals
Subacute care	After acute care, need for more nursing intervention	Special subacute units in hospitals; urgent/emergent care centers; outpatient surgical centers; home health
Tertiary care	Subspecialty referral care requiring highly specialized personnel and facilities	Specialty hospitals (e.g., psychiatric, chronic disease) and general hospitals with highly specialized facilities
Long-Term Practice		
Restorative care	Intermediate follow-up care such as surgical postoperative care	Home health; progressive and extended care facilities; rehabilitation facilities; halfway houses; hospitals with transitional care units
Long-term care	Care for chronic conditions; personal care	Nursing homes; facilities for the mentally retarded or emotionally disturbed; geriatric day care centers
End-of-Life Practice	Care provided to those who have less than six months to live	Hospice services provided in a variety of settings

Sources: Cambridge Research Institute (1976). *Trends Affecting the U.S. Health Care System.* Washington, DC: U.S. Government Printing Office; U.S. Public Health Service (1994). *For a Healthy Nation: Return on Investments in Public Health.* Washington, DC: Author; Turnock, B. J. (2004). *Public Health: What It Is and How It Works,* 3rd ed. Sudbury, MA: Jones and Bartlett Publishers; Shi, L., and D. A. Singh (2004). *Delivering Health Care in America: A Systems Approach,* 3rd ed. Sudbury, MA: Jones and Bartlett Publishers.

different levels. You may remember that in Chapter 4 we used the terms *primary, secondary,* and *tertiary* as they related to levels of prevention. These terms have a similar meaning here, but they are now applied to health care delivery rather than prevention.

Primary Medical Care

Primary care is "front-line" or "first-contact" care. "The unique characteristic of primary care is the role it plays as a regular or usual source of care for patients and their families."[2] Formally,

BOX
13.2

HEALTHY PEOPLE 2010: OBJECTIVES

1-5 Increase the proportion of persons with a usual primary care provider.

Target: 85 percent

Baseline: 77 percent of the population had a usual primary care provider.

	1996 Baseline	1999 Status	2010 Target
		Percent	
TOTAL	77	78	85
Race and Ethnicity			
American Indian or Alaska Native	79	75	85
Asian or Pacific Islander	72	68	85
Asian	DNC	DNC	85
Native Hawaiian and other Pacific Islander	DNC	DNC	85
Black or African American	74	76	85
White	77	79	85
Hispanic or Latino	64	66	85
Not Hispanic or Latino	78	80	85
Black or African American	74	76	85
White	79	81	85
Gender			
Female	80	82	85
Male	73	74	85
Education Level (aged 18 years and older)			
Less than high school	69	71	85
High school graduate	74	74	85
At least some college	74	77	85
Geographic Location			
Within MSA	76	78	85
Outside MSA	78	80	85
Disability Status			
Persons with activity limitations	DNA	86	85
Persons without activity limitations	DNA	77	85

DNA = Data have not been analyzed. DNC = Data are not collected. DSU = Data are statistically unreliable. MSA = Metropolitan statistical area.

*Data for office hours, prescription medications, and treatments are displayed to further characterize the practices of primary care providers.

For Further Thought

Why is it important that the United States reach the objective previously noted by the year 2010?

---

primary care
the provision of integrated, accessible health care services by clinicians who are accountable for addressing a large majority of personal health care needs, developing a sustained partnership with patients, and practicing in the context of family and community

primary care has been defined as "the provision of integrated, accessible health care services by clinicians who are accountable for addressing a large majority of personal health care needs, developing a sustained partnership with patients, and practicing in the context of family and community."[11] Eighty percent of medical care is primary care.[22] Primary care includes routine medical care to treat common illnesses or to detect health problems in their early stages, and thus includes such things as semi-annual dental checkups; annual physical exams; health screenings for hypertension, high blood cholesterol, and breast or testicular cancer; and sore throat cultures. Primary care usually is provided in practitioners' offices, clinics, and other outpatient facilities by physicians, nurse practitioners, physician assistants, and an array of other individuals on the primary care team. Primary care is the most difficult for the poor and uninsured to obtain (see Box 13.2).

The World Health Organization has stated that primary health care rests on the following eight elements:[24]

- Education concerning prevailing health problems and the methods of preventing and controlling them.
- Promotion of food supply and proper nutrition.
- An adequate supply of safe water and basic sanitation.
- Maternal and child health care, including family planning.
- Immunization against the major infectious diseases.
- Prevention and control of locally endemic diseases.
- Appropriate treatment of common diseases and injuries.
- Provision of essential drugs.

In the United States, the supplies of food and clean water are taken for granted. But other elements, such as maternal and child health services, immunizations, and routine dental and medical care, are not available to large segments of our population—primarily for economic reasons.

Secondary Medical Care

Secondary medical care is specialized attention and ongoing management for common and less frequently encountered medical conditions, including support services for people with special challenges due to chronic or long-term conditions.[23] This type of care is usually provided by physicians, ideally upon referral from a primary care source.[22] Secondary medical care can be further divided into acute and subacute care. *Acute care* is "short-term, intense medical care for an illness or injury usually requiring hospitalization."[1] *Subacute care* provides specialty services for patients "who no longer need acute care but require more nursing intervention than nursing homes have traditionally provided,"[1] such as for the patient who is on a respirator.

Tertiary Medical Care

Tertiary medical care is even more highly specialized and technologically sophisticated medical and surgical care than secondary medical care.[22] It is "care for those with unusual or complex conditions (generally no more than a few percent of the need in any service category)."[22] This care is not usually performed in smaller hospitals; however, it is provided in specialty hospitals, academic health centers, or on specialized floors of general hospitals. Such facilities are equipped and staffed to provide advanced care for people with illnesses such as AIDS, cancer, and heart disease, and procedures such as gall bladder removal and heart bypass surgery.

Long-Term Practice

Long-term practice can be divided into two subcategories—restorative care and long-term care.

Restorative Care

Restorative care is the health care provided to patients after surgery or other successful treatment, during remission in cases of an oncogenic (cancerous) disease, or when the progression of an incurable disease has been arrested (see Figure 13.3). This level of care includes follow-up to secondary and tertiary care, rehabilitative care, therapy, and home care. Typical settings for this type of care include both inpatient and outpatient rehabilitation units, nursing homes, halfway houses, and private homes.

Long-Term Care

Long-term care includes the different kinds of help that people with chronic illnesses, disabilities, or other conditions that limit them physically or mentally need. In some situations

secondary medical care specialized attention and ongoing management for common and less frequently encountered medical conditions, including support services for people with special challenges due to chronic or long-term conditions

tertiary medical care specialized and technologically sophisticated medical and surgical care for those with unusual or complex conditions (generally no more than a few percent of the need in any service category)

restorative care care provided after successful treatment or when the progress of a incurable disease has been arrested

long-term care different kinds of help that people with chronic illnesses, disabilities, or other conditions that limit them physically or mentally need

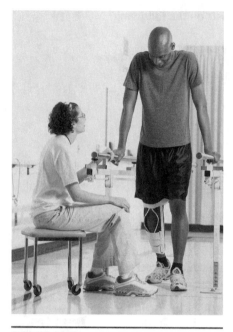

FIGURE 13.3
Restorative care can follow either secondary or tertiary care.

time-intensive skilled nursing care is needed, while some people just need help with basic daily tasks like bathing, dressing, and preparing meals. This type of care is provided in various settings such as nursing homes, facilities for the mentally and emotionally disturbed, and adult and senior day care centers, but often long-term care is used to help people live at home rather than in institutions.

End-of-Life Practice

The final level of practice in the health care delivery is end-of-life practice. **End-of-life practice** is usually thought of as those health care services provided to individuals shortly before death. The primary form of end-of-life practice is hospice care. **Hospice care** "is a program of palliative and support care services providing physical, psychological, social, and spiritual care for dying persons, their families, and other loved ones by a hospice program or agency."[14] The most common criterion for admission to hospice care is being terminally ill with a life expectancy of less than six months. The first hospice program in the United States was established in 1974.[25] In 2000, there were over 105,000 hospice patients in the United States; cancer is the most common diagnosis among these patients.[14] "Hospice services are available in home and inpatient settings."[14]

TYPES OF HEALTH CARE PROVIDERS

end-of-life practice
health care services provided to individuals shortly before death

hospice care
a program of palliative and support care services providing physical, psychological, social, and spiritual care for dying persons, their families, and other loved ones by a hospice worker

independent providers
health care professionals with the education and legal authority to treat any health problem

To offer comprehensive health care that includes services at each of the levels just mentioned, a great number of health care workers are needed. In 2002 the number of civilians employed in the health service industry was 12.6 million. These 12.6 million represented approximately one of every 11 (9.3%) employed civilians in the United States.[14]

Despite the large number of health care workers, the demand for more is expected to continue to grow. The primary reasons for this growth are the aging U.S. population (by the year 2030, it is estimated that 70 million [one in five] people will be 65 years old or older)[26] and the expectation of more demand for long-term health care. Due to the continuing geographic maldistribution of health care workers, the need will be greater in some settings than in others. The settings of greatest need will continue to be the rural and inner-city areas (see Box 13.3).

In 2002, almost half (42%) of all the health care workers were employed in hospitals, about 15% in nursing and personal facilities, 15% in physicians' offices and clinics, 6% in dentists' offices and clinics, and about 1% in chiropractors' offices and clinics.[14] The remaining 20% practice in a variety of settings, including official and unofficial health agencies, home health care, and other private practices. As changes have come to the way health care is offered, the proportions of health care workers by setting have also changed, with fewer persons working in hospitals (in 1970, 63% worked in hospitals), and more employed in nursing homes and ambulatory care settings (such as surgical and emergency centers).[14] This trend is expected to continue in the future, with special needs in the area of long-term care workers to meet the needs of the aging baby boom generation.

There are well over 200 different careers in the health care industry. To help simplify the discussion of the different types of health care workers, they have been categorized into five different groups—independent providers, limited care providers, nurses, allied health care professionals, and public health professionals.

HEALTHY PEOPLE 2010: OBJECTIVES

1-8.   In the health professions, allied and associated health profession fields and the nursing field, increase the proportion of all degrees awarded to members of underrepresented racial and ethnic groups.

Target and baseline:

Objective	Increase in Degrees Awarded to Underrepresented Populations	1996–97 Baseline (unless noted)	2002 Status	2010 Target
		Percent		
	Health professions, allied and associated health profession fields (For the baselines, health professions include medicine, dentistry, pharmacy, and public health.)			
1-8a.	American Indian or Alaska Native	0.6	0.7	1.0
1-8b.	Asian or Pacific Islander	16.2	20.4	4.0*
1-8c.	Black or African American	6.7	7.1	13.0
1-8d.	Hispanic or Latino	4.0	5.7	12.0
	Nursing			
1-8e.	American Indian or Alaska Native	0.7 (1995–96)	—	1.0
1-8f.	Asian or Pacific Islander	3.2 (1995–96)	—	4.0
1-8g.	Black or African American	6.9 (1995–96)	—	13.0
1-8h.	Hispanic or Latino	3.4 (1995–96)	—	12.0
	Medicine			
1-8i.	American Indian or Alaska Native	0.6	0.9	1.0
1-8j.	Asian or Pacific Islander	15.9	20.1	4.0*
1-8k.	Black or African American	7.3	7.0	13.0
1-8l.	Hispanic or Latino	4.6	6.2	12.0
	Dentistry			
1-8m.	American Indian or Alaska Native	0.5	0.5	1.0
1-8n.	Asian or Pacific Islander	19.5	25.1	4.0*
1-8o.	Black or African American	5.1	4.0	13.0
1-8p.	Hispanic or Latino	4.7	5.3	12.0
	Pharmacy			
1-8q.	American Indian or Alaska Native	0.4	0.6	1.0
1-8r.	Asian or Pacific Islander	17.5	21.5	4.0*
1-8s.	Black or African American	5.7	7.6	13.0
1-8t.	Hispanic or Latino	2.8	4.0	12.0

*The Asian or Pacific Islander group has exceeded its target, which represents the minimum target based on this group's estimated proportion of the population.

For Further Thought

Minority and disadvantaged Americans lag behind the general U.S. population on virtually all health status indicators. Furthermore, among the poor, minorities, and the uninsured, access to medical care has been deteriorating. What impact do you think meeting the just noted objectives will have on this community health problem? Please defend your response.

Independent Providers

Independent providers are those health care workers that have the specialized education and legal authority to treat any health problem or disease that an individual has. This group of workers can be further divided into allopathic, osteopathic, and nonallopathic providers.

Allopathic and Osteopathic Providers

Allopathic providers are those who use a system of medical practice in which specific remedies for illnesses, often in the form of drugs or medication, are used to produce effects

allopathic providers independent providers whose remedies for illnesses produce effects different from those of the disease different from those of diseases. The practitioners who fall into this category are those who are referred to as Doctors of Medicine (MDs). The usual method of practice for MDs includes the taking of a health history, a physical examination—perhaps with special attention to the area of the complaint—and the provision of specific treatment, such as antibiotics for a bacterial infection or a tetanus injection and sutures for a laceration.

Another group of physicians that provide services similar to those of MDs are **osteopathic providers**—Doctors of Osteopathic Medicine (DOs). At one time, MDs and DOs would not have been grouped together because of differences in their formal education, methods, and philosophy of care. While the educational requirements and methods of treatment used by MDs have remained essentially consistent over the years, those of DOs have not. The practice of osteopathy began in the later half of the nineteenth century. At that time, the education and training of osteopaths was aimed at a thorough understanding of the musculoskeletal system because, according to osteopathic theory, all health problems, including diseases, could be cured by manipulating this system. During that time, DOs were often referred to as "bone doctors" and were often called upon to set fractured bones. During the twentieth century, osteopathic medicine changed. It is now based on a philosophy of health care that emphasizes the interrelationships of the body's systems in the prevention, diagnosis, and treatment of illness, disease, and injury. The distinctive feature of osteopathic medicine is the recognition of the reciprocal interrelationship between the structure and function of the body. The actual work of DOs and MDs is very similar today. Both types of physicians use all available scientific modalities, including drugs and surgery, in providing care to their patients. Both can also serve as primary care physicians (about one-third of MDs and more than half of DOs are primary care physicians)[27] or as board-certified specialists. Their differences are most notably the DOs' greater tendency to use more manipulation in treating health problems and the DOs' perception of themselves as being more holistically oriented than MDs. Few if any patients today would be able to tell the difference between the care given by a DO and a MD.

The educational requirements for MD and DO degrees are very similar. Both educational programs generally accept students into their classes after they have completed a bachelor's degree. Medical education takes four years to complete. The first two years include course work in the sciences, while the final two years emphasize clinical experiences and rotations through the specialty areas of medicine. At the end of the second year of medical school and again at the end of the fourth year, medical students take the first two parts of their licensing examination. During the fourth year of medical school, the students apply for entrance into a medical residency program. It is during their residency program that the physicians receive the training to specialize in a particular field of medicine. The residency programs typically range in length from three (such as in family medicine) to five (such as in pathology) years. The first year of a residency is referred to the *internship year,* and the physicians are referred to as **interns** or first-year **residents.** During this year, the interns can only practice medicine under the guidance of a licensed physician. Upon successful completion of the internship year, the interns are then eligible to sit for the third part of the licensing examination. If they pass the exam, they are then entitled to practice medicine without the supervision of another licensed physician. At this point, almost all interns will complete the remaining years of residency (and are referred to generically as residents) in order to be eligible to sit for the board specialty examinations. Passing this examination will make them "board certified" in their specialty. A list of such medical care specialties and subspecialties is presented in Figure 13.4.

With so many specialties and subspecialties, some people are worried that not enough family medicine physicians will be trained. There are some data that support this claim. In 1949, 59% of active doctors of medicine (MDs and DOs) practiced as primary care physicians. This percentage dropped to 37% by 1970 and to approximately 33% by 1990. However, the

osteopathic providers independent health care providers whose remedies emphasize the interrelationships of the body's systems in prevention, diagnosis, and treatment

intern a first-year resident

resident a physician who is training in a specialty

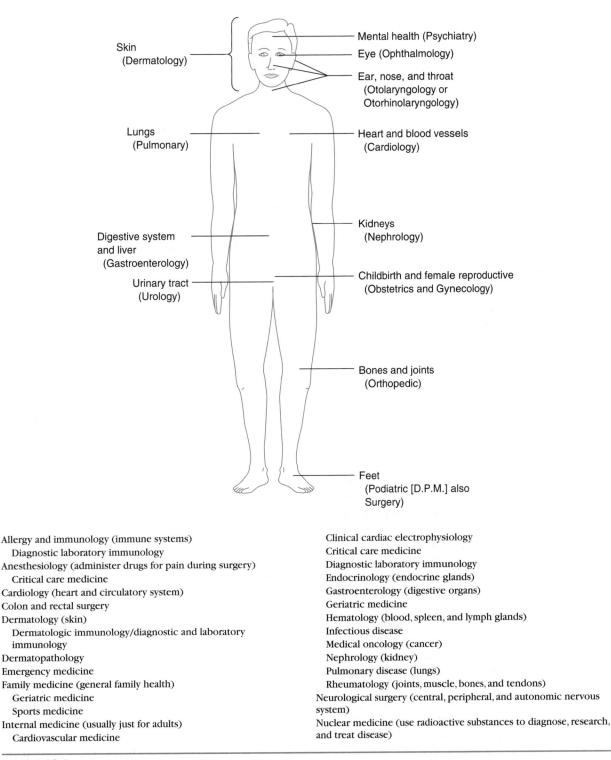

Skin
(Dermatology)

Mental health (Psychiatry)

Eye (Ophthalmology)

Ear, nose, and throat
(Otolaryngology or
Otorhinolaryngology)

Lungs
(Pulmonary)

Heart and blood vessels
(Cardiology)

Digestive system
and liver
(Gastroenterology)

Kidneys
(Nephrology)

Urinary tract
(Urology)

Childbirth and female reproductive
(Obstetrics and Gynecology)

Bones and joints
(Orthopedic)

Feet
(Podiatric [D.P.M.] also
Surgery)

Allergy and immunology (immune systems)
    Diagnostic laboratory immunology
Anesthesiology (administer drugs for pain during surgery)
    Critical care medicine
Cardiology (heart and circulatory system)
Colon and rectal surgery
Dermatology (skin)
    Dermatologic immunology/diagnostic and laboratory
    immunology
Dermatopathology
Emergency medicine
Family medicine (general family health)
    Geriatric medicine
    Sports medicine
Internal medicine (usually just for adults)
    Cardiovascular medicine

Clinical cardiac electrophysiology
Critical care medicine
Diagnostic laboratory immunology
Endocrinology (endocrine glands)
Gastroenterology (digestive organs)
Geriatric medicine
Hematology (blood, spleen, and lymph glands)
Infectious disease
Medical oncology (cancer)
Nephrology (kidney)
Pulmonary disease (lungs)
Rheumatology (joints, muscle, bones, and tendons)
Neurological surgery (central, peripheral, and autonomic nervous
system)
Nuclear medicine (use radioactive substances to diagnose, research,
and treat disease)

FIGURE 13.4
Listing of medical specialties and subspecialties.

Obstetrics and gynecology (female reproductive system, the fetus, and the newborn)
- Critical care
- Gynecologic oncology
- Maternal-fetal medicine
- Reproductive endocrinology

Ophthalmology (eye)
Orthopedic surgery (musculoskeletal problems)
Otolaryngology (ear and throat)
Otorhinolaryngology (ear, nose, and throat)
Pathology
- Blood banking/transfusion medicine
- Cytopathology (tumors)
- Dermatopathology
- Forensic pathology (cause of death)
- Hematology
- Immunopathology
- Medical microbiology
- Neuropathology
- Pediatric pathology
- Radioisotopic pathology

Pediatrics (children)
- Adolescent medicine (adolescents and young adults)
- Diagnostic laboratory immunology
- Neonatal–prenatal medicine (problems of the fetus and newborns)
- Pediatric cardiology
- Pediatric critical care workers
- Pediatric emergency medicine
- Pediatric endocrinology
- Pediatric gastroenterology
- Pediatric hematology-oncology
- Pediatric infectious disease
- Pediatric nephrology
- Pediatric rheumatology
- Pediatric sports medicine

Physical medicine and rehabilitation
- Sports medicine

Plastic and reconstructive surgery
- Hand surgery

Preventive medicine
- Public health and general preventive medicine
- Aerospace medicine
- Occupational medicine

Psychiatry and neurology
- Neurology
- Psychiatry

Radiology (radiation to diagnose and treat disease)
- Radiation oncology
- Diagnostic radiology
- Diagnostic radiology with special competence on nuclear radiology

Surgery
- General vascular surgery
- Hand surgery
- Pediatric surgery
- Surgical critical care
- Thoracic surgery (chest area)

Urology (genitals and urinary tract)

FIGURE 13.4
Continued

percentage has remained fairly stable since 1990. In 2001, the figure was 34.6%.[14] This stabilizing effect may in part be because of the managed care movement and its need for primary care practitioners and not specialists.

Nonallopathic Providers

nonallopathic providers independent providers who provide nontraditional forms of health care

Nonallopathic providers are identified by their nontraditional means of providing health care. Some have referred to much of the care provided by these providers as complementary/alternative medicine (CAM) or complementary/integrative medicine.[28] Included in this group of providers are chiropractors, acupuncturists (see Figure 13.5), naturopaths (those who use natural therapies), herbalists (those who use herbal brews for treating illness), and homeopaths (those who use small doses of herbs, minerals, and even poisons for therapy).

chiropractor a nonallopathic, independent health care provider who treats health problems by adjusting the spinal column

The best known and most often used nonallopathic providers in the United States are **chiropractors.** The underlying premise of the care provided by chiropractors is that all health problems are caused by misalignments of the vertebrae in the spinal column. The chiropractic (done by hand) approach to the treatment is (1) the identification of the misalignment through X-rays, and (2) the realignment of the bones through a series of treatments called "adjustments."

Chiropractors are educated in four-year chiropractic colleges. The Council on Chiropractic Education accredits colleges of chiropractic medicine in the United States. As with allopathic and osteopathic programs, students usually enter chiropractic programs after earning a bachelor's degree. Those who graduate from chiropractic colleges earn a Doctor of Chiropractic (DC) degree. Chiropractors are licensed in all 50 states and must pass either a state licensing examination or an examination given by the National Board of Chiropractic Examiners. Although the educational standards for chiropractors have improved over the years, many people still question their ability to help the ill and injured. However, it should be noted that the American Public Health Association recognizes chiropractors as a professional group, and many insurance companies and Medicare and Medicaid provide reimbursement for chiropractic care.

As noted earlier, much of the care provided by nonallopathic providers is often referred to as **complementary/alternative medicine (CAM).** CAM has been defined as the "diagnosis, treatment and/or prevention which complements mainstream medicine by contributing to a common whole, by satisfying a demand not met by orthodoxy or by diversifying the conceptual framework of medicine."[29] When used in addition to mainstream medical treatment, a therapy is most often identified as *complementary.* However, when a therapy is used instead of conventional treatment, it is labeled as *alternative.*[30] It has been reported that CAM is the fastest growing area in health care today.[28] Studies have estimated that between 30% and 62% of adults in the United States have reported using CAM.[31] The percentage varies greatly depending on what is considered CAM. The percentage is the highest when the definition of CAM therapy includes prayer specifically for health reasons. Compared to other countries, the United States is at the low end of using alternative forms of healing.[32] In 1997, the most recent data available, Americans paid $27 billion out of their own pockets for much of the CAM,[33] because many of the CAM therapies are not covered by health insurance. Yet, "insurers say that when traditional medicine is ineffective and an alternative form of therapy, such as acupuncture, for a condition like chronic pain costs less and satisfies the patient, they will pay for it."[3]

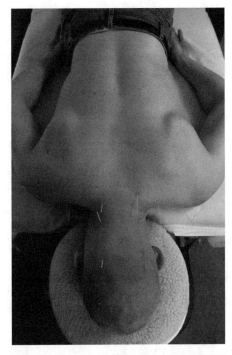

FIGURE 13.5
Many people seek out nontraditional means of health care, such as acupuncture.

The growth in the American public's interest in CAM therapies is evidenced by the emphasis placed on the research by the U.S. government. In 1992, the National Institutes of Health (NIH) created an Office of Alternative Medicine (OAM) with a budget of $2 million to investigate whether or not the CAM therapies actually work. In 1998, the NIH OAM "was elevated to the National Center for Complementary and Alternative Medicine (NCCAM) and its mandate expanded. Its funding also expanded, reaching $68.7 million in fiscal year 2000."[3]

There are literally hundreds of systems, approaches, and techniques that fall within the CAM rubric (see Box 13.4), but the NCCAM classifies them into five general categories.[34] They include:

- Alternative medical systems
- Mind/body interventions
- Biologically based therapies
- Manipulative and body-based methods
- Energy therapies

"Although alternative approaches use a wide range of techniques, most share a number of common features. These include:

1. A focus on disease prevention and health maintenance
2. A holistic approach in which the whole person-mind, emotions, and spirit are considered

complementary/ alternative medicine (CAM) diagnosis, treatment, and/or prevention which complements mainstream medicine by contributing to a common whole, by satisfying a demand not met by orthodoxy, or by diversifying the conceptual framework of medicine

BOX 13.4	COMPLEMENTARY/ALTERNATIVE MEDICINE APPROACHES

Alternative Medical Systems
 Acupuncture
 Ayurvedic Medicine (traditional medicine of India—means "Science of Life")
 Faith Healing
 Homeopathic Medicine
 Naturopathic Medicine
 Shamanism
 Traditional Oriental Medicine [includes several techniques and methods such as acupuncture, herbal medicine, oriental massage, and qi gong (a form of energy therapy)]
Mind-Body Interventions
 Bioenergetics
 Biofeedback
 Biorhythms
 Body-Oriented Psychotherapy
 Breathing Techniques
 Color Therapy
 Dance Therapy
 Growth Astrology
 Hypnosis
 Hypnotherapy
 Human Aura
 Martial Arts
 Music Therapy
 Past Life Therapy
 Relaxation Therapy
 Spiritual Healing
 Visualization
 Yoga
Biologically Based Therapy
 Bee Venom
 Colonics
 Copper
 Ginseng

Macrobiotics
Microdose Pharmacology
Natural Food Diets
Nutritional Therapy
Shark Cartilage
Veganism
Vegetarianism
Manipulative and Body-Based Methods
 Acupressure
 Alexander Technique
 Applied Kinesiology
 Belly Dancing
 Chiropractic Manipulation
 Massage
 Myotherapy
 Osteopathic Manipulation
 Polarity Therapy
 Reflexology
 Rolfing
 Shiatsu
 Trager Work
Energy Therapies
 Bioelectromagnetic-Based Therapies
 Qi Gong
 Reiki
 Therapeutic Touch

Sources: Levinson, D., and L. Gaccione (1997). *Health and Illness: A Cross-Cultural Encyclopedia.* Santa Barbara, CA: ABC-CLIO; Quander, L. (2001). "Complementary and Alternative Medicine Research on HIV/AIDS." *HIV Impact,* (Winter), 10; Sultz, H. A., and K. M. Young (2004). *Health Care USA: Understanding Its Organization and Delivery,* 4th ed. Sudbury, MA: Jones and Bartlett Publishers; National Center for Complementary and Alternative Medicine (2004). *What Is Complementary and Alternative Medicine (CAM)?* Available at http://nccam.nih.gov/health/whatiscam/.

3. The use of natural processes and materials in healing
4. A focus on the cause of the disease rather than symptoms
5. A consideration of lifestyle and emotional issues
6. A belief that the body has an innate ability to heal itself when it is brought into balance and harmony"[32]

Limited (or Restricted) Care Providers

limited (restricted) care providers health care providers who provide care for a specific part of the body

Much health care is provided by **limited (or restricted) care providers** who have advanced training, usually a doctoral degree, in a health care specialty. Their specialty enables them to provide care for a specific part of the body. This group of providers includes but is not limited to dentists (teeth and oral cavity), optometrists (eyes, specifically refractory errors), podiatrists (feet and ankles), audiologists (hearing), and psychologists (mind).

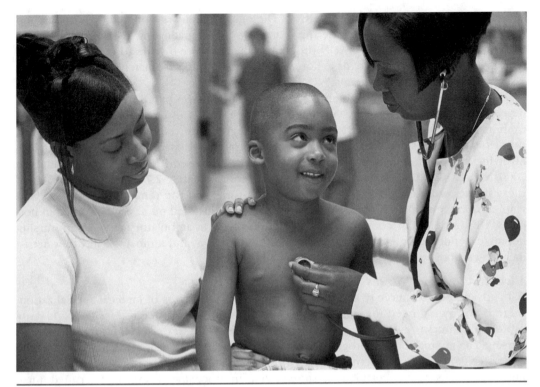

FIGURE 13.6
There is still a need for more nurses.

Nurses

We have categorized nurses into a group of their own because of their unique degree programs, the long-standing tradition of nursing as a profession, and their overall importance in the health care industry. It has been estimated that there are about 4 million individuals who work in the nursing profession. These include registered nurses, licensed practical nurses, and ancillary nursing personnel such as nurse's aids.[35] Nurses outnumber physicians, dentists, and every other single group of health care workers in the United States.[14] Even with such numbers, the need for nurses will continue. In 2000, it was reported that there was a 6% shortage of registered nurses that if not addressed in terms of supply and demand will grow to a 29% shortage by the year 2020.[36] This need is created by a combination of an aging U.S. population, the increasing average age of nurses, and the decreasing number of newly prepared nurses[36] (see Figure 13.6).

Training and Education of Nurses

Nurses can be divided into subcategories based on their level of education and type of preparation. The first are those who are prepared as licensed practical nurses. Once they complete their one to two years of education in a vocational, hospital, or associate degree program and pass a licensure examination, these nurses are referred to as **licensed practical nurses (LPNs)** or *licensed vocational nurses* (LVNs) in some states,[27] and are able to work under the supervision of physicians or registered nurses. They usually perform routine duties and provide nontechnical bedside nursing care. The present trend is to phase out LPN training programs, though some are wondering why because of the nurse shortage.

The second group of nurses includes those who have successfully completed a diploma program or an associate degree (ADN) and a state licensing (registration) examination. They

licensed practical nurse (LPN) those prepared in one- to two-year programs to provide nontechnical bedside nursing care under the supervision of physicians or registered nurses are referred to as **registered nurses (RNs).** Diploma programs are offered by hospitals and last about two to three years.[27] Of the approximately 71,500 graduating RNs in 2000, 4% were trained in diploma programs.[36] ADN programs take about two years to complete and are typically offered by community or junior colleges. In 2000, approximately 36% of graduating RNs were trained in ADN programs.[36]

The third group of nurses includes the baccalaureate-prepared nurses who hold the degree of Bachelor of Science in Nursing (BSN). These nurses also must pass a state licensing examination to become RNs. RNs holding BSN degrees are referred to as **professional nurses** and are considered to have been more thoroughly prepared for additional activities involving independent judgment. The total number of licensed RNs in the United States in 2000, regardless of their level of preparation, was approximately 2.7 million. Almost 59% of these nurses were employed full-time, 23% part-time, and the remaining 18% were not employed in the nursing profession. Of the employed registered nurses, 59% worked in hospitals, 18% in public or community health settings, 10% in ambulatory care, 7% in nursing homes/extended care facilities, 2% in nursing education, and almost 4% in other areas, including schools, prisons/jails, and insurance companies.[37]

Advanced Practice Nurses

With advances in technology and the development of new areas of medical specialization, there is a growing need for specialty-prepared advanced practice nurses (APNs). Many professional nurses continue their education and earn master's and doctoral degrees in nursing. The master's degree programs are aimed primarily at specialties such as nurse practitioners (NPs) (e.g., pediatric nurse practitioners and school nurse practitioners), clinical nurse specialists (CNSs), certified registered nurse anesthetists (CRNAs), and certified nurse midwives (CNMs). These APNs are qualified to conduct health assessments, diagnose and treat a range of common acute and chronic illnesses, and manage normal maternity care. Not only do they provide high-quality care in a cost-effective manner, but they are also considered primary care providers in chronically medically underserved inner-city and rural areas. Like other nurses, the demand for APNs is also expected to increase, especially as a greater portion of the population gains access to health care and more of the population becomes enrolled in managed care.[38] In 2000, the number of RNs prepared to practice in at least one advanced practice role was estimated to be 196,279, or 7.3% of the total RN population.[37] The largest portion of these advance practice nurses were nurse practitioners (see Figure 13.7).

The relatively few nurses who hold doctorate degrees in nursing are highly sought after as university faculty. Nurses with doctorates teach, conduct research, and otherwise prepare other nurses or hold administrative (leadership) positions in health care institutions.

Nonphysician Practitioners

Nonphysician practitioners (NPPs) (also known as nonphysician clinicians [NPCs] or physician extenders) constitute a relatively new classification of health care workers. This group is composed of those "clinical professionals who practice in many of the areas similar to those in which physicians practice, but do not have an MD or a DO degree."[1] NPPs are middle-level health workers with training and skills beyond those of RNs and less than those of physicians.[27] This group typically includes the just discussed nurse practitioners and certified midwives as well as physician assistants (PAs).[1] Because the former two were just presented as part of the section on advanced practice nurses, we will discuss only PAs here.

Physician assistant programs began in response to the shortage of primary care physicians. PAs' academic programs usually last two years and are offered in a variety of formats, including diploma and certificate programs, or as associate, bachelor's, or master's degrees. After completion of the program or degree, PAs must pass a national certifying examination. PAs always work under the direct supervision of a licensed physician (thus the name

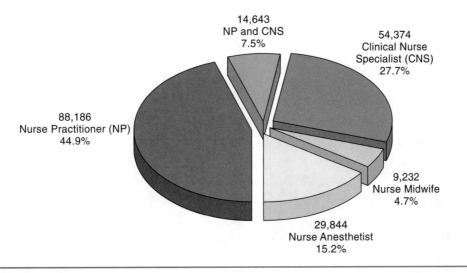

14,643
NP and CNS
7.5%

54,374
Clinical Nurse
Specialist (CNS)
27.7%

88,186
Nurse Practitioner (NP)
44.9%

9,232
Nurse Midwife
4.7%

29,844
Nurse Anesthetist
15.2%

FIGURE 13.7
Registered nurses prepared for advance practice, 2000.

Source: Health Resources and Services Administration, Bureau of Health Professions (2001). *The Registered Nurse Population, National Sample Survey of Registered Nurses—March 2000: Preliminary Findings.* Available at http://www.bhpr.Ursa.gov/.

physician extenders). They carry out many of the same duties that are thought of as the responsibilities of physicians, such as taking medical histories, examining patients, ordering and interpreting laboratory tests and X-rays, counseling patients, making preliminary diagnoses, treating minor injuries, and, in most states, prescribing medications.[27]

Allied Health Care Professionals

Allied health describes a large group of health-related professions that fulfill necessary roles in the health care delivery system. These **allied health care professionals** assist, facilitate, and complement the work of physicians, dentists, and other health care specialists. These health care workers provide a variety of services that are essential to patient care. Oftentimes they are responsible for highly technical services and procedures. Allied health care professionals can be categorized into several groups.[3] They include (1) laboratory technologists and technicians (e.g., medical technologists, emergency medical technicians, nuclear medicine technicians, operating room technicians, dental technicians and hygienists, and radiographers [X-ray technicians]); (2) therapeutic science practitioners (e.g., occupational, physical, radiation, and respiratory therapists and speech pathologists); (3) behavioral scientists (e.g., health educators, social workers, and rehabilitation counselors); and (4) support services (e.g., medical record keepers and medical secretaries). The educational backgrounds of allied health workers range from vocational training to master's degrees. Most of these professionals also must pass a state or national licensing examination before they can practice.

The demand for allied health care workers in all of the areas previously noted is expected to continue well into the twenty-first century. The primary reasons for this are the growth of the entire health care industry and the impending arrival of the baby boomers as senior citizens.

Public Health Professionals

A discussion about health care providers would be incomplete without the mention of a group of health workers who provide unique health care services to the community— **public health professionals.** Public health professionals support the delivery of health

allied health care professionals
health care workers who provide services that assist, facilitate, and complement the work of physicians and other health care specialists

public health professional
a health care worker who works in a public health organization

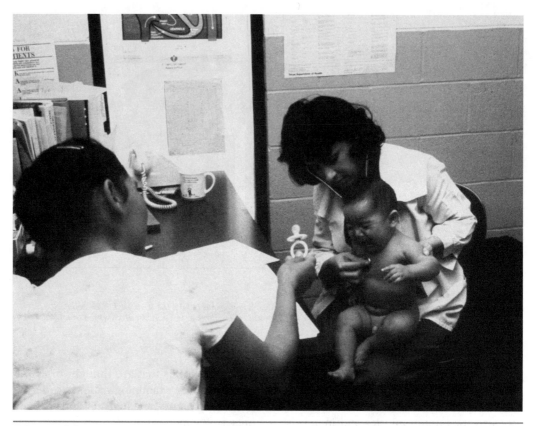

FIGURE 13.8
Public health workers make up a key component of the health care system.

care by such hands-on providers as public health physicians, dentists, nurses, and dieticians who work in public health clinics sponsored by federal, state, local, and voluntary health agencies (see Figure 13.8). Examples of public health professionals are environmental health workers, public health administrators, epidemiologists, health educators, public health nurses and physicians, biostatisticians, the Surgeon General, and the research scientists at the Centers for Disease Control and Prevention. Public health professionals often make possible the care that is practiced in immunization clinics, nutritional programs for women, infants, and children (WIC), dental health clinics, and sexually transmitted disease clinics. School nurses are also considered public health professionals. Public health services are usually financed by tax dollars and, while available to most taxpayers, serve primarily the economically disadvantaged.

HEALTH CARE FACILITIES AND THEIR ACCREDITATION

Health care is provided in a variety of settings in the United States. The major settings and the accreditation of these facilities are discussed in the sections that follow.

Health Care Facilities

Health care facilities are the physical settings in which health care is actually provided. They include practitioners' private offices, public and private clinics, hospitals, ambulatory care facilities, rehabilitation centers, and continuing care facilities. One other place that many people do not think of as a health care facility is a patient's home. Yet, for a variety of reasons, more and more health care is being provided in this setting.

Practitioner Offices

The setting for much of the preventive and primary care provided in America is the offices of health care practitioners. In 2000, there were over 800,000,000 patient visits to physician offices in the United States.[14] Practitioner offices are privately owned buildings such as physicians' and dentists' offices, where care is provided by the practitioner and his or her staff. Because it is very expensive to set up a private practice, it is increasingly common to see more than one practitioner sharing both an office and staff. These practices are often referred to as *group practices* to distinguish them from *solo (single practitioner) practices.*

Clinics

When two or more physicians practice as a group, the facility in which they provide medical services is called a *clinic*. Some clinics are small, with just a few providers, while others are very large with many providers, such as the Mayo Clinic in Rochester, Minnesota, or the Cleveland Clinic in Cleveland, Ohio. Some clinics provide care only for individuals with special health needs such as treatment of cancer or diabetes or assistance in family planning; others accept patients with a wide range of problems. A misconception held by many is that clinics are not much different from hospitals. One big difference is that clinics do not have inpatient beds, and hospitals do. Some clinics do have an administrative relationship with inpatient facilities so that if a person needs to be admitted to a hospital, it is a relatively simple process; other clinics may be free-standing, or independent of all other facilities.

Clinics funded by tax dollars are called *public health clinics.* Most of these are located in large urban areas or in rural areas that are underserved by the private sector.

> **private (proprietary) hospitals**
> for-profit hospitals

> **specialty hospital**
> a hospital that provides mainly one type of medicine, is for-profit, and is owned at least in part by the physicians who practice in it

Hospitals

Like clinics, hospitals vary in size, mission, and organizational structure. The major purpose of hospitals is to provide secondary and tertiary care.

Hospitals can be categorized in several different ways; one way is by hospital ownership (see Figure 13.9 and Table 13.4). A **private or proprietary hospital** is one that is owned as a business for the purpose of making a profit. "Most for-profit hospitals belong to one of the large hospital management companies that dominate the for-profit hospital network."[3] Recently, a new type of for-profit hospital has been popping up in the United States: the **specialty hospital.** These are hospitals that provide mainly one type of medicine—usually surgery, either cardiac or orthopedic; most are owned, at least in part, by the physicians who practice in them.[39] A lot of controversy surrounds these hospitals. Larger general hospitals, who are losing patients and revenue to the specialty hospitals, say that they are just a "grab for money" by the physicians who own them. Physicians say specialty hospitals allow them to practice medicine the way it should be practiced, without answering to a hospital administrator who is trying to cut corners to make a profit. Currently, specialty hospitals make up about 2% of all hospitals in the United States, with more being planned for construction in the near future.[39] Because of the controversy over these newest hospitals, in December 2003,

FIGURE 13.9
Hospitals are often categorized by ownership.

Table 13.4
Hospitals According to Ownership: United States, 2001

Type	Number
All hospitals	5,801
Federal	243
Non-Federal	5,558
Private or proprietary (for-profit)	754
Public (state or local)	1,156
Voluntary (nonprofit)	2,998

Source: Adapted from Freid, V. M., K. Prager, A. P. MacKay, and H. Xia (2003). *Health, United States, 2003, with Chartbook on Trends in Health of Americans.* Hyattsville, MD: National Center for Health Statistics.

public hospitals
hospitals that are supported and managed by governmental jurisdictions

voluntary hospitals
nonprofit hospitals administered by not-for-profit corporations or charitable community organizations

full-service hospitals
hospitals that offer services in all or most of the levels of care defined by the spectrum of health care delivery

limited-service hospitals
hospitals that offer only the specific services needed by the population served

ambulatory care facilities
free-standing health care facilities that provide a wide and rapidly expanding array of services

as part of the Medicare drug bill, an 18-month halt was placed on the construction of new hospitals while a study of their financial status could be conducted by a Medicare advisory panel.[39]

A second type is a **public hospital.** These hospitals are supported and managed by governmental jurisdictions and are usually found in larger cities. Public hospitals can be operated by agencies at all levels of government. Hospitals operated by the federal government include military hospitals (e.g., Walter Reed Army Hospital and the Bethesda Naval Hospital) and the many hospitals run by the Veterans Administration and Indian Health Service. There are also hospitals that are owned or partially financed by states and local governments. Examples include university hospitals, state mental hospitals, and local city and county hospitals.

Voluntary hospitals make up the third category of hospitals. These are nonprofit hospitals administered by not-for-profit corporations or religious, fraternal, and other charitable community organizations. These hospitals make up about one-half of all hospitals in the United States.[14] Examples of this latter group are the Southern Baptist hospitals, the many Shriners' hospitals, and many community hospitals. In recent years, voluntary hospitals have been expanding their scope of services and many now include wellness centers, stress centers, chemical dependency programs, and a variety of satellite centers.

A second way of classifying hospitals is by dividing them into teaching and nonteaching hospitals. Teaching hospitals have, as a part of their mission, the responsibility to prepare new health care providers. These hospitals are typically aligned with medical schools, universities, and medical residency programs.

A third means of categorizing hospitals is by the services offered. **Full-service hospitals,** or general hospitals, are those that offer care at all or most of the levels of care discussed earlier in the chapter. These are the most expensive hospitals to run and are usually found in metropolitan areas. **Limited-service hospitals** offer the specific services needed by the population served, such as emergency, maternity, general surgery, and so on, but they lack much of the sophisticated technology available at full-service hospitals. This type of hospital is more common in rural areas. Many limited-service hospitals were once full-service hospitals but have become limited-service hospitals because of the low volume of patients, a shortage of health care personnel, and financial distress.

Ambulatory Care Facilities

Care and procedures that once were performed only on an inpatient basis in a hospital are increasingly being performed in a variety of outpatient and ambulatory care settings.[25] **Ambulatory care facilities,** are free-standing facilities that provide a wide and rapidly expanding array of services. These facilities are designed for ambulatory patients without the hotel-like services traditionally available in hospitals (see Figure 13.10). "Ambulatory care facilities may be owned and operated by hospitals, hospital systems, or physician groups or by

FIGURE 13.10

Ambulatory care centers provide medical services efficiently without the overhead of a hospital or clinic.

independent, for-profit or not-for-profit, single entities or chains."[3] These alternative sites for care have developed because of technological advances that make their purchase, maintenance, and operation feasible and cost-effective; consumer demand for convenient, user-friendly environments; and profitability.[3] The types of ambulatory care facilities most often found in communities are primary care centers, urgent/emergent care centers, ambulatory surgery centers, and diagnostic imaging.

Primary care centers present another way to offer primary care in addition to the more traditional physician office mode. Though they may appear to be just another physician's office or group practice, many of these facilities are owned by hospitals and also include laboratory, radiology, and pharmacy services. "In hospital-operated facilities, staff physicians are commonly employees of the owner hospital, or, in the case of a teaching facility, physicians may be jointly compensated through a medical school—affiliated faculty practice group and the hospital."[3] In some parts of the country, depending on licensing procedures, it may be common to see nurse practitioners and physician assistants, under physician supervision, as the primary care practitioners in these facilities.[3]

Urgent/emergent care centers have been around in the United States since the early 1970s. They "fill gaps in the delivery system created by the rigidity of private physician appointment and unavailability during nonbusiness hours. The centers also can provide a much more convenient and user friendly alternative to a hospital emergency department during hours when private physicians are not available."[3] Urgent/emergent care centers often provide quicker service with less paperwork, particularly for those with cash or credit cards. These facilities (often not much larger than a fast-food restaurant) have sometimes been referred to as "Docs in a Box"! These facilities are not appropriate for all emergency cases. A majority of patients with life-threatening conditions are still taken to hospital emergency rooms, where top-of-the-line, advanced life support equipment and emergency physicians are on staff. Although emergency rooms are expensive for hospitals to maintain, they obviously perform a needed service.

Ambulatory (or outpatient) surgery centers do not perform major surgery, such as heart transplants, but perform same-day surgeries where a hospital stay following the surgery is not needed. It has been estimated that about half of all surgeries today are completed on an out-patient basis.[25] The factors that have promoted the increase in ambulatory surgical procedures as alternatives to inpatient surgery include the development of new, safe, and faster-acting general anesthetics, advances in surgical equipment and materials, development of noninvasive or minimally invasive surgical and nonsurgical procedures, and reduced coverage by insurance companies for hospital stays.

"Although clinicians still depend on long-established and relatively simple radiograph technology, they now have at their disposal several new and highly sophisticated computer-assisted imaging techniques that vastly expand their capability to visualize body structures and functions."[3] Because of these advances in medical technology, one of the newest forms of ambulatory care facility is diagnostic imaging facilities. The technologies that are often found in these facility is computed tomography (CT) and magnetic resonance imaging (MRI), which are used for viewing the body's anatomical structures in several planes. These technologies are ideal for ambulatory facilities because of their noninvasive nature and profitability.

The establishment of a new ambulatory care facility in a community is not always received with enthusiasm. In previously underserved communities, fast-growing communities, or communities with many temporary residents such as resort communities, they have been well received. However, in stable or shrinking communities where there is an adequate number of health providers, the arrival of a new free-standing acute-care facility is sometimes viewed as unfriendly competition. One result is that many voluntary (independent) hospitals have strengthened or built new outpatient service wings in response to this challenge.

Rehabilitation Centers

rehabilitation center
a facility in which restorative care is provided following injury, disease, or surgery

Rehabilitation centers are health care facilities in which patients work with health care providers to restore functions lost because of injury, disease, or surgery. These centers are sometimes part of a clinic or hospital but may also be stand-alone facilities. Rehabilitation centers may operate on both an ambulatory and an inpatient basis. Those providers who commonly work in a rehabilitation center include physical, occupational, and respiratory therapists as well as exercise physiologists.

Long-Term Care Options

Not too many years ago, when the topic of long-term care was mentioned, most people thought of nursing homes and state hospitals for the mentally ill and emotionally disabled. Today, however, the term *long-term care* includes not only the traditional institutional residential care, but also special units within these residential facilities (such as for Alzheimer patients), halfway houses, group homes, assisted living facilities, transitional (step-down) care in a hospital, day care facilities for patients of all ages with health problems that require special care, and personal home health care. Many of these options were discussed in Chapter 9 because elders are the biggest users of long-term care, but other users include those with disabilities or chronic conditions, and those with acute and subacute conditions who are unable to care for themselves.

home health care
care that is provided in the patient's residence for the purpose of promoting, maintaining, or restoring health

One area of long-term care that has received special attention in recent years is home health care. The demand for home health care has been driven by the restructuring of the health care delivery system, technological advances that enable people to be treated outside a hospital and to recover more quickly, and the cost containment pressures that have shortened hospital stays.[40] Home health care should not be confused with home care. Home care is a more inclusive term and "denotes a range of services provided in the home, including skilled nursing and therapies, personal care, and even social services, such as meals, and home modifications"[41] (see Chapter 9 for a discussion of personal care). **Home health care** involves providing health care via health personnel and medical equipment to individuals and families in their places of residence, for the purpose of promoting, maintaining, or restoring health or to maximize the level of independence while minimizing the effects of disability and illness, including terminal disease.[6] Home health care can be either long-term, to help a chronically ill patient avoid institutionalization, or it can be short-term to assist a patient following an acute illness and hospitalization until the patient is able to return to independent functioning.[3] Home health care can be provided either through a formal system of paid professional health care-givers (e.g., home health care agency), or through an informal system where the care is provided by family, friends, and neighbors[3] (see Chapter 9 for more on caregivers).

Though the need for professional health caregivers has increased and will continue to increase because of the aging population,[40] the total number of home health care patients dropped from about 2.5 million in 1996 to less than 1.4 million in 2000. The primary reason for this decline was the fact that Medicare was the biggest payer of home health care services, and the rules changed on how home health care agencies would be reimbursed. The Balanced Budget Act of 1997 mandated stricter limits on the use of home health services funded by Medicare and interim limits on Medicare payments until a prospective payment system (see Chapter 14 for a discussion of prospective payments) was implemented for Medicare home health care agencies in 2000.[14] These changes also led to some consolidations, mergers, and closures of home health care agencies as well as a decline in health care expenditures.[42]

Accreditation of Health Care Facilities

One way of determining the quality of a health care facility is to find out if it is accredited by a reputable group. **Accreditation** is the process by which an agency or organization evaluates and recognizes an institution as meeting certain predetermined standards.[43] The predominant organization responsible for accrediting health care facilities is the **Joint Commission on Accreditation of Healthcare Organizations** (JCAHO), often referred to as simply the Joint Commission. The Joint Commission is an independent, not-for-profit organization that accredits about 16,000 health care organizations in the United States and in many other countries. The health care facilities/organizations that can be accredited by the Joint Commission include ambulatory care organizations, assisted living facilities, behavioral health care organizations, critical access hospitals, clinical laboratories, health care networks, home care organizations, hospitals, long-term care facilities, and office-based surgery practices. To earn and maintain JCAHO accreditation, a facility or organization must undergo an on-site survey by a Joint Commission survey team at least every three years.[44] However, laboratories must be surveyed every two years. More information about the accreditation process and the standards used by the Joint Commission can be found at the JCAHO Web site, www.jcaho.org.

accreditation
the process by which an agency or organization evaluates and recognizes an institution as meeting certain predetermined standards

Joint Commission on Accreditation of Healthcare Organizations (JCAHO)
the predominant organization responsible for accrediting health care facilities

CHAPTER SUMMARY

- The concept of a health care system has been and continues to be questioned in the United States. Is it really a system or is treatment provided in an informal, cooperative manner?

- Health care in the United States has evolved from the modest services of the independent country doctor who often visited the sick in their homes to a highly complex trillion dollar industry.

- There are medical specialists and health care facilities for almost every type of illness and health problem.

- The spectrum of health care includes four domains of practice—population-based public health practice, medical practice, long-term practice, and end-of-life practice.

- Within the medical practice domain of health care are the following types of health care providers: independent providers (allopathic, osteopathic, and nonallopathic); limited (restricted) care providers; nurses; nonphysician practitioners; allied health care professionals; and public health professionals.

- Complementary and alternative medicine (CAM) is "diagnosis, treatment and/or prevention which complements mainstream medicine by contributing to a common whole, by satisfying a demand not met by orthodoxy or by diversifying the conceptual framework of medicine."[29]

SCENARIO: ANALYSIS AND RESPONSE

1. Have you ever experienced a situation similar to the one described in the scenario? If so, briefly describe it.

2. If we truly had a "health care system" in this country, how would this scenario be different?

3. If you were Marcus, how would you have handled this situation?

- Health care providers perform services in a variety of settings, including practitioners' offices, clinics, hospitals, ambulatory care facilities, rehabilitation centers, and long-term care facilities, including patients' places of residence.

- Ambulatory care facilities are free-standing facilities that provide a wide and rapidly expanding array of services.

- Long-term care options include traditional institutional residential care as well as special units within these residential facilities, halfway houses, group homes, assisted living facilities, transitional (step-down) care in a hospital, day care facilities for patients, and personal home health care.

- The predominant organization responsible for accrediting health care facilities is the Joint Commission on Accreditation of Healthcare Organizations (JCAHO).

REVIEW QUESTIONS

1. Why have some questioned whether or not the United States really has a health care system?

2. Describe some of the major changes that have taken place in health care delivery over the years.

3. What is meant by third-party payment?

4. Why has the cost of health care in the United States continued to grow faster than the cost of inflation?

5. What is meant by a spectrum of health care?

6. What are the domains of practice noted in the spectrum of health care?

7. Is there a demand for health care workers in the United States today? If so, why?

8. In what type of facility are most health care workers employed?

9. What is the difference between independent and limited (restricted) care providers?

10. What are the differences between allopathic and nonallopathic health care providers?

11. Define complementary and alternative medicine and give a few examples of each.

12. What kind of education do limited (restricted) care providers have?

13. What is the difference between LPNs and RNs?

14. What are advanced practice nurses (APNs)?

15. What are nonphysician practitioners?

16. What role do public health professionals play in health care delivery?

17. What are the advantages of ambulatory care facilities?

18. What is meant by a long-term care facility? Give two examples.

19. Why has the number of home health care patients dropped in recent years?

20. What is the Joint Commission on Accreditation of Healthcare Organizations (JCAHO)? What does the JCAHO do?

ACTIVITIES

1. Using Table 13.3 from this chapter, identify two different health care facilities in your community for each of the levels of care. Briefly describe each facility and determine whether each one is private, public, or voluntary.

2. Make an appointment to interview three health care workers in your community who have different types of jobs. Ask them what they like and dislike about their job, what kind of education they needed, whether they are happy with their work, and whether they would recommend that others seek this line of work. Summarize your findings in a written paper.

3. Obtain a copy of a local newspaper (the Sunday edition is best) and look through the "want ads" for health care worker jobs. In a one-page paper, briefly describe what you have found and summarize the status of health care position openings in your community.

4. Create a list of all the health care providers from whom your family has sought help in the past five years.

Group the individuals into the five provider groups outlined in the chapter. When appropriate, identify the providers' specialties and whether they were allopathic, osteopathic, or nonallopathic providers.

5. Make an appointment to interview an administrator in the local (city or county) health department. In the interview, find out what kind of people, by profession, work in the department. Also find out what type(s) of health care services and clinics are offered by the department. Summarize your findings in a two-page paper.

COMMUNITY HEALTH ON THE WEB

The Internet contains a wealth of information about community and public health. Increase your knowledge of some of the topics presented in this chapter by accessing the Jones and Bartlett Publishers Web site at **health.jbpub.com/communityhealth/5e** and follow the links to complete the following Web activities.

- Agency for Healthcare Research and Quality (AHRQ)
- Association of American Medical Colleges
- American Nursing Association

REFERENCES

1. Shi, L., and D. A. Singh (2004). *Delivering Health Care in America: A Systems Approach,* 3rd ed. Sudbury, MA: Jones and Bartlett Publishers.

2. Institute of Medicine (2003). *The Future of the Public's Health in the 21st Century.* Washington, DC: National Academy Press.

3. Sultz, H. A., and K. M. Young (2004). *Health Care USA: Understanding Its Organization and Delivery,* 4th ed. Sudbury, MA: Jones and Bartlett Publishers.

4. Cambridge Research Institute (1976). *Trends Affecting the U.S. Health Care System* (DHEW pub. no. HRA 75-14503). Washington, DC: U.S. Government Printing Office, 261.

5. U.S. Department of Health, Education and Welfare, Health Resources Administration (September 1974). "Fact Sheet: The Hill-Burton Program." Washington, DC: U.S. Government Printing Office.

6. Lokkeberg, A. R. (1988). "The Health Care System." In E. T. Anderson and J. M. McFarlane, eds., *Community as Client: Application of the Nursing Process.* Philadelphia: JB Lippincott, 3-14.

7. Centers for Disease Control and Prevention (1995). "Prevention and Managed Care: Opportunities for Managed Care Organizations, Purchasers of Health Care, and Public Health Agencies." *MMWR,* 44(RR-14): 1-12.

8. Koff, S. Z. (1987). *Health Systems Agencies: A Comprehensive Examination of Planning and Process.* New York: Human Services Press.

9. Stockman, D. A. (1981). "Premises for a Medical Marketplace: A Neoconservative's Vision of How to Transform the Health System." *Health Affairs,* 1(1): 5-18.

10. White House Domestic Policy Council (1993). *The President's Health Security Plan: The Clinton Blueprint.* New York: Times Books.

11. Donaldson, M., K. D. Yordy, K. N. Lohr, and N. A. Vanselow, eds. (1996). *Primary Care: America's Health in a New Era.* Washington, DC: National Academy Press.

12. U.S. Department of Health and Human Services (1996). *Assessing Roles, Responsibilities, and Activities in a Managed Care Environment: A Workbook for Local Health Officials* (AHCPR pub. no. 96-0057). Rockville, MD: Agency for Health Care Policy and Research.

13. MacKay, A. P., L. A. Fingerhut, and C. R. Duran (2000). *Health, United States, 2000, with Adolescent Health Chartbook.* Hyattsville, MD: National Center for Health Statistics.

14. Freid, V. M., K. Prager, A. P. MacKay, and H. Xia (2003). *Health, United States, 2003, with Chartbook on Trends in Health of Americans.* Hyattsville, MD: National Center for Health Statistics.

15. Zatkin, S. (1997). "A Health Plan's View of Government Regulation." *Health Affairs,* 16(6): 33-35.

16. Dickerson, J. F. (8 December 1997). "Dr. Clinton Scrubs Up." *Time,* 48.

17. President's Advisory Commission on Consumer Protection and Quality in the Health Care Industry (1998). *Quality First: Better Health Care for All Americans.* Washington, DC: U.S. Government Printing Office.

18. Findlay, S. (12 March 1998). "Panel Sizes Up Quality of Health Care." *USA Today,* 3A.

19. Institute of Medicine (2001). *Crossing the Quality Chasm: A New Health System for the 21st Century.* Washington, DC: National Academy Press.

20. Institute of Medicine (2000). *To Err Is Human: Building a Safer Health System.* Washington, DC: National Academy Press.

21. World Health Organization (2000). "World Health Organization Assesses the World's Health Systems." Available at http://www.who.int/whr/2000/en/press_release.htm.

22. Turnock, B. J. (2004). *Public Health: What It Is and How It Works,* 3rd ed. Sudbury, MA: Jones and Bartlett Publishers.

23. U.S. Public Health Service (1994). *For a Healthy Nation: Return on Investments in Public Health.* Washington, DC: U.S. Department of Health and Human Services.

24. Kekki, P. (2003). *Primary Health Care and the Millennium Development Goals: Issues for Discussion.* Available at http://www.who.int/chronic_conditions/primary_health_care/en/mdgs_final.pdf.

25. Bernstein, A. B., E. Hing, A. J. Moss, K. F. Allen, A. B. Siller, and R. B. Tiggle (2004). *Health Care in America: Trends in Utilization.* Hyattsville, MD: National Center for Health Statistics.

26. Federal Interagency Forum on Aging-Related Statistics (2001). *Older Americans 2000: Key Indicators of Well-Being.* Available at http://www.agingstats.gov/chartbook2000/default.htm.

27. Stanfield, P. S., and Y. H. Hui (2002). *Introduction to the Health Professions,* 4th ed. Sudbury, MA: Jones and Bartlett Publishers.

28. Udani, J. (1998). "Integrating Alternative Medicine into Practice." *Journal of the American Medical Association,* 280(18): 1620.

29. Ernst, E., D. M. Eisenberg, M. H. Pittler, et al. (2001). *The Desktop Guide to Complementary and Alternative Medicine.* Edinburgh, England: Mosby.

30. Quander, L. (Winter 2001). "Complementary and Alternative Medicine Research on HIV/AIDS." *HIV Impact,* 10.

31. Barnes, P. M., E. Powell-Griner, K. McFann, and R. L. Nahin (2004). "Complementary and Alternative Medicine Use Among Adults: United States 2002." *Vital and Health Statistics,* 343.

32. Levinson, D., and L. Gaccione (1997). *Health and Illnesses: A Cross-Cultural Encyclopedia.* Santa Barbara, CA: ABC-CLIO.

33. Fontanarosa, P. B., and G. D. Lundberg (1998). "Alternative Medicine Meets Science." *Journal of the American Medical Association,* 280(18): 1618-1619.

34. National Institutes of Health, Office of Alternative Medicine (2001). "Major Domains of Complementary and Alternative Medicine." Available at http://www.nccam.nih.gov/nccam/fop/classify/.

35. Bureau of Health Professions, Health Resources and Services Administration (2004). *Changing Demographics and the Implications*

for *Physicians, Nurses, and other Health Workers.* Available at http://bhpr.hrsa.gov/healthworkforce/reports/changedemo/default.htm.

36. Bureau of Health Professions, Health Resources and Services Administration (2002). *Projected Supply, Demand, and Shortages of Registered Nurses: 2000-2020.* Washington, DC: Author.

37. Health Resources and Services Administration, Bureau of Health Professions (2001). *The Registered Nurse Population, National Sample Survey of Registered Nurses—March 2000: Preliminary Findings.* Available at http://www.bhpr.hrsa.gov/.

38. Liken, L. H., M. E. Gather, and C. R. Frieze (1997). "The Registered Nurse Work Force: Infrastructure for Health Care Reform." In P. R. Lee and C. L. Ester, eds., *The Nation's Health,* 6th ed. Sudbury, MA: Jones and Bartlett Publishers, 240-245.

39. Carbonara, P., and J. Caplin (2004). "The Hospital Wars." *Money,* 33(2): 147-148, 151-152.

40. Ester, C. L. (2001). "The Uncertain Future of Home Care." In C. Barrington and C. L. Ester, eds., *Health Policy,* 3rd ed. Sudbury, MA: Jones and Bartlett Publishers, 102-113.

41. Coleman, B. (2000). *Assuring the Quality of Home Care: The Challenge of Involving the Consumer.* Washington, DC: American Association of Retired People.

42. Levit, K., C. Cowan, H. Lazenby, A. Sensenig, P. McDonnell, J. Stiller, A. Martin, and the Health Accounts Team (2001). "Health Spending in 1998: Signals of Change." In C. Harrington and C. L. Ester, eds., *Health Policy: Crisis and Reform in the U.S. Health Care Delivery System,* 3rd ed. Sudbury, MA: Jones and Bartlett Publishers, 254-262.

43. Timmreck, T. C. (1997). *Health Services Cyclopedic Dictionary,* 3rd ed. Sudbury, MA: Jones and Bartlett Publishers.

44. Joint Commission on Accreditation of Healthcare Organizations (2004). *Joint Commission Accreditation.* Available at http://www.jcaho.org/htba/index.htm.

Chapter 14

Health Care System: Function

Chapter Outline

Chapter Objectives

After studying this chapter you will be able to:

1 Identify the major concerns with the health care system in the United States.

2 Explain fee-for-service and prepaid health plans.

3 Briefly describe the purpose and concept of insurance.

4 Define the term *insurance policy*.

5 Briefly describe the State Children's Health Insurance Program (SCHIP).

6 Explain the insurance policy terms *deductible, co-insurance, co-payment, fixed indemnity, exclusion,* and *pre-existing condition*.

7 Explain what is meant when a company or business is said to be self-insured.

8 List the different types of medical care usually covered in a health insurance policy.

9 Briefly describe Medicare, Medicaid, and Medigap insurance.

10 Briefly explain long-term care health insurance.

11 Define *managed care*.

12 Define the terms *preferred provider organization* (PPO) and *exclusive provider organization* (EPO) and explain how these organizations function.

13 Briefly describe the two main organizational models of health maintenance organizations (HMOs).

14 Explain point-of-service, physician-hospital organizations, and Medicare Advantage.

15 Identify the advantages and disadvantages of managed care.

16 Identify the strengths and weaknesses of national health insurance, the Canadian health care system, and the Oregon Health Plan.

17 Briefly discuss health care reform in the United States.

SCENARIO

Greg, a young father, is awakened in the middle of the night by his 8-year-old son, Zack, who has all the typical signs and symptoms of influenza. Greg does not want to disturb his family physician at this time of night, but he does want Zack to receive appropriate medical care. Therefore, he decides to take Zack to the hospital emergency room for treatment. After examining the boy, Dr. Rainey, the attending physician, declares that Zack has the flu. Dr. Rainey then instructs Greg that Zack should drink plenty of clear fluids, take a nonaspirin analgesic for his fever, and get plenty of rest. Dr. Rainey concludes by indicating that the illness should pass in a couple of days. As Greg and Zack leave the hospital, they stop at the business desk to pay the bill. The billing clerk informs Greg that there is no charge. "You have zero deductible health insurance." The amount of the bill was for $743.00.

INTRODUCTION

In Chapter 13, we described the structure of the health care delivery system in the United States, including such concepts as the spectrum of health care delivery and levels of care. We also surveyed the various types of health care providers and the types of facilities in which health care is provided. In this chapter, we will build on that information by explaining how consumers obtain health care services, how these services are paid for, and by whom. We will also discuss three serious issues of concern with our health care delivery system—access, quality, and cost—and examine some current and potential solutions to these issues.

GAINING ACCESS TO AND PAYING FOR HEALTH CARE IN THE UNITED STATES

The quality of services offered by health care providers in the United States is perhaps the best offered anywhere in the world (see Figure 14.1). Unfortunately, the services are not accessible to all Americans because they cannot afford them. To further complicate this problem, the cost of health care service continues to rise. In a nutshell, the major problems with the health care system in the United States can be represented by the cost containment, access, and quality triangle noted by Kissick[1] (see Figure 14.2). In Kissick's equilateral triangle, the equal 60-degree angles represent equal priorities. That is, access is just as important as quality and cost containment and vice versa. However, an expansion of any one of the angles compromises one or both of the other two. For example, if we were interested in increasing the quality of our already good services, it would also increase the costs and decrease access. Or, some feel, if we increase access, costs will go up, and the quality will decrease. Or, if we concentrate on containing costs, both quality of care and access will decrease. With such dilemmas, the United States continues to struggle to find the right combination of policy and accountability to deal with these shortcomings.

Access to Health Care

Even with several different means of gaining access to health care services (see Figure 14.3), access has been and continues to be a major health policy issue in the United States. Health insurance coverage and the generosity of coverage are major determinants of access to health

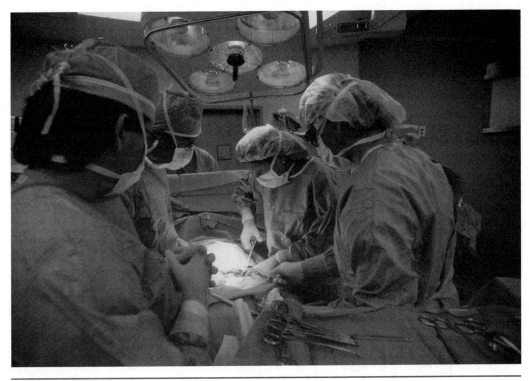

FIGURE 14.1
We have the finest health care in the world, but at what cost?

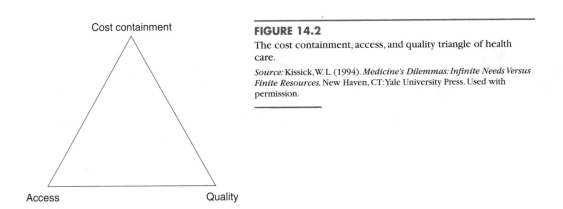

Cost containment

Access   Quality

FIGURE 14.2
The cost containment, access, and quality triangle of health care.

Source: Kissick, W. L. (1994). *Medicine's Dilemmas: Infinite Needs Versus Finite Resources.* New Haven, CT: Yale University Press. Used with permission.

care.[2,3] Although the majority of people (83%) in the United States do have health insurance, approximately 43 million Americans were uninsured throughout 2002. Another 12 million lacked health insurance coverage for shorter periods during that year[2] (see Box 14.1). The likelihood of being uninsured is greater for younger persons, those with less education, those with lower incomes, nonwhites, those who are not U.S. citizens, and males. It also increases based upon where one lives. Some states have fewer than 10% uninsured (e.g., Iowa, Massachusetts, Minnesota, Rhode Island, Wisconsin), whereas other states have 20% or more uninsured (Arizona, California, Florida, Louisiana, New Mexico, Oklahoma, and Texas).[3]

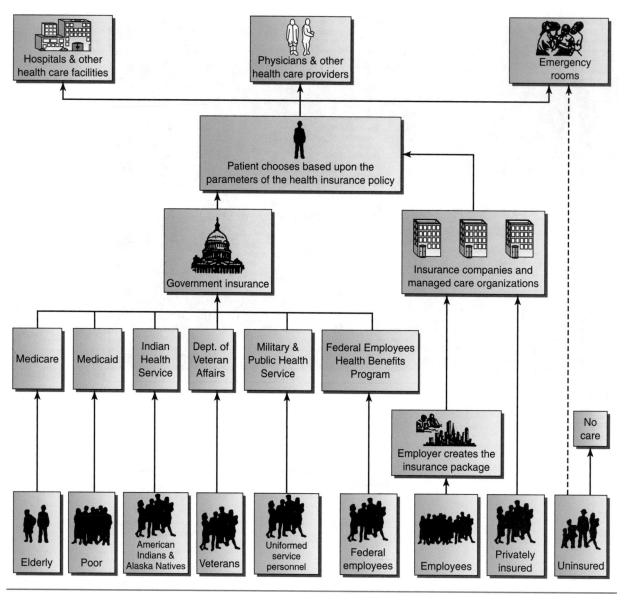

FIGURE 14.3
Means of gaining access to health care.

Interestingly enough, the uninsured do not lack emergency or urgent care because no one needing such care and willing to go to a hospital emergency room will be turned away. However, the uninsured usually do not have access to primary care (see Box 13.2 in Chapter 13), such as checkups, screenings for chronic illnesses, and prenatal care. Without adequate primary care, many patients eventually find themselves in need of more costly and often less effective medical treatment. The primary factors that limit access to this type of care are total lack of health insurance, inadequate insurance, and poverty. Those who are unable to receive primary medical care because they cannot afford it are referred to as "medically indigent."[4]

BOX
14.1

HEALTHY PEOPLE 2010: OBJECTIVES

1-1 Increase the proportion of persons with health insurance.

Target: 100 percent

Baseline: 83 percent of persons under age 65 years were covered by health insurance in 1997 (age-adjusted to the year 2000 standard population).

Persons Under 65 Years	1997 Baseline	2002 Status
	Percent	
TOTAL	83	83
Race and Ethnicity		
American Indian or Alaska Native	62	61
Asian or Pacific Islander	81	DNA
Asian	81	83
Native Hawaiian or other Pacific Islander	80	76
Black or African American	80	81
White	84	85
Hispanic or Latino	66	66
Cuban	79	79
Mexican American	61	63
Puerto Rican	81	81
Not Hispanic or Latino	85	86
Black or African American	80	81
White	86	87
Gender		
Female	84	85
Male	81	82
Family Income Level		
Poor	66	70
Near poor	69	70
Middle/high income	91	90
Geographic Location		
Within MSA	83	84
Outside MSA	80	81
Disability Status		
Persons with disabilities	83	85
Persons without disabilities	83	84
Sexual Orientation	DNC	DNC
Select Populations		
Age groups		
10–24 years	DNA	81
10–14 years	DNA	89
15–19 years	DNA	84
20–24 years	DNA	69

DNA = Data have not been analyzed. DNC = Data are not collected. MSA = Metropolitan statistical area.

Note: Age-adjusted to the year 2000 standard population.

Sources: National Health Interview Survey (NHIS), CDC, NCHS.

For Further Thought

In your opinion, what kinds of things will have to happen by the year 2010 for the previously noted objective to be met? Do you think this objective will be met? Why or why not?

The *medically indigent* in America include people and families with income above the poverty level who are thus ineligible for Medicaid, or government health insurance for the poor, but who are unable to afford health care or health insurance. "Eight out of ten uninsured persons are members of working families. In most of these cases, the worker holds a job that does not offer health insurance. In others, subsidized coverage may be offered, but the employee turns it down because of the cost or because they do not perceive the need for coverage."[2] Those who have a job but are unable to afford health insurance are referred to as the *working poor*. It has been estimated that there are 30 million working poor in the United States.[5] Others may be uninsured because "individual health policies are quite expensive and may be unavailable for those who have a preexisting health problem. Young adults often lose their eligibility under their parent's policy when they turn 19 or graduate from college. Spouses lose coverage under a family policy through separation, divorce, retirement, or upon the death of a policy holder."[2]

Even those who have adequate health insurance suffer. Most Americans pay three or four times for health care: "we pay once through taxes, a second time through insurance premiums and co-payments, a third time through supplemental insurance, and a fourth time through the cost of products we buy."[6]

Paying for Health Care

Health care in America has not only been labeled the best, but also the most expensive (see Table 13.1 in Chapter 13). Health care is the single largest expenditure in the country, surpassing defense, education, and housing. America spends more per capita annually on health care (approximately $5,440 in 2002) than any other nation.[7] Under the U.S. system, the actual cost of the service is usually not known until after the service has been provided, unless the consumer is bold enough to inquire ahead of time. Most are not.

Payments for the U.S. health care bill come from four sources. The first is the consumers themselves. In 2001 these direct or out-of-pocket payments represented approximately one-fifth (16.6%) of all payments. The remaining portion of health care payments, four-fifths, comes almost entirely from indirect, or third-party, payments. The first source of third-party payments is private insurance companies. Private insurance companies paid 35.4% of the health care bill in 2001. These payments were made from premiums paid to the insurance company by the employees and/or their employers. The second source of third-party payments is public or governmental insurance programs (i.e., Medicare, Medicaid, Veterans Administration, Indian Health Service, or military). These government programs are funded by a combination of taxes and premiums from those insured (as in the case of Part B Medicare coverage). In 2001, 43.4% of the health care bill was paid for by public or governmental insurance programs. And finally, a small percentage of health care bills are paid by other private funds. In 2001, it was 4.6%.[3]

fee-for-service a method of paying for health care in which after the service is rendered, a fee is paid

There are two broad divisions of arrangements for paying for and delivering health care—fee-for-service indemnity and prepaid health care. The most traditional system of health care financing is **fee-for-service.** At the beginning of the 1990s, this was the dominant format in the United States for most kinds of medical services, from routine preventive examinations to the most advanced hospital care. However, by the late 1990s and continuing today, prepaid health care became the primary way of paying for and delivering health care. Under the fee-for-service format, consumers select a provider, receive care (service) from the provider, and incur expenses (a fee) for the care. The provider is then reimbursed for covered services in part by the insurer (private insurance company or the government) and in part by the consumer, who is responsible for the balance unpaid by the insurer. With fee-for-service arrangements, there is no mechanism for integrating the care the consumer may receive from multiple providers.[8]

Under the fee-for-service format, consumers are obligated to pay their fee at the time the service is rendered. In the past, before health insurance was common, some physicians provided care when needed and worried about payment later. Others often accepted "in kind" payment, such as farm produce or other products or services, as payment in full for a medical service rendered. Today, in order for patients to receive care via fee-for-service, they are often required to demonstrate the ability to pay (to assume financial responsibility for the fee) before the service is rendered. A provider's receptionist may ask, "How do you plan to settle your bill?" In other cases, providers have signs placed around the waiting room that state, "Payment is expected when service is rendered, unless other arrangements have been made prior to the appointment."

Though prepaid health care has been available in the United States since the late 1920s, it was not until the 1970s that it achieved recognition as a mainstream approach to financing medical costs with the passage of the Health Maintenance Organization (HMO) Act of 1973. And it was not until the early to mid-1990s, with the advent of the managed care movement, that HMOs became the predominant form of health care coverage. Under **prepaid health care** arrangements, insurers make arrangements with health care providers to provide agreed-upon covered health care services to a given population of consumers for a (usually discounted) set price—the per-person premium fee—over a particular time period. This is also referred to as a *capitation system.* The consumers may pay additional fees (co-payments) for office visits and other services used. The insurer organizes the delivery of care by building an infrastructure of providers and implementing the systems to monitor and influence the cost and quality of care.

Of the two broad divisions of arrangements of paying for and delivering health care, prepaid health care arrangements have taken on the label of "managed care." However, both arrangements can include elements of managed care, and not all managed care plans use prepaid health care arrangements. Initially, many managed care plans focused on using their market power to obtain discounts from the providers. However, as they evolve, more organized arrangements are being developed where the providers are asked to assume some of the risk in the plan. Thus, providers are offered incentives for containing costs while maintaining patient satisfaction with the care received.[9]

> **prepaid health care**
> a method of paying for covered health care services on a per-person premium basis for a specific time period prior to the service being rendered (also referred to as capitation)

Third-Party Payment

The process for receiving a third-party payment usually begins when a health care provider or his or her staff requests information about the patient's health insurance plan. They normally request the name of the insuring company (e.g., Blue Cross/Blue Shield), the policy number, and a personal identification number (PIN). This information is usually provided to the insured on a wallet-sized card by the insurer. The provider may then ask the patient to sign an insurance claim form in two places (see Figure 14.4). The first signature indicates that the service has been provided and authorizes the provider to submit patient information with the claim for payment. The second signature instructs the insurance company to make the payment directly to the provider. Upon receiving and reviewing the completed and signed form, the insurance company then issues payments to the provider for services based upon the provisions of the insurance policy. Depending upon the level of reimbursement for the claim, the provider will either consider the bill paid in full or will request payment from the patient in the amount of the difference between the provider's full fee and the portion paid by the insurance company.

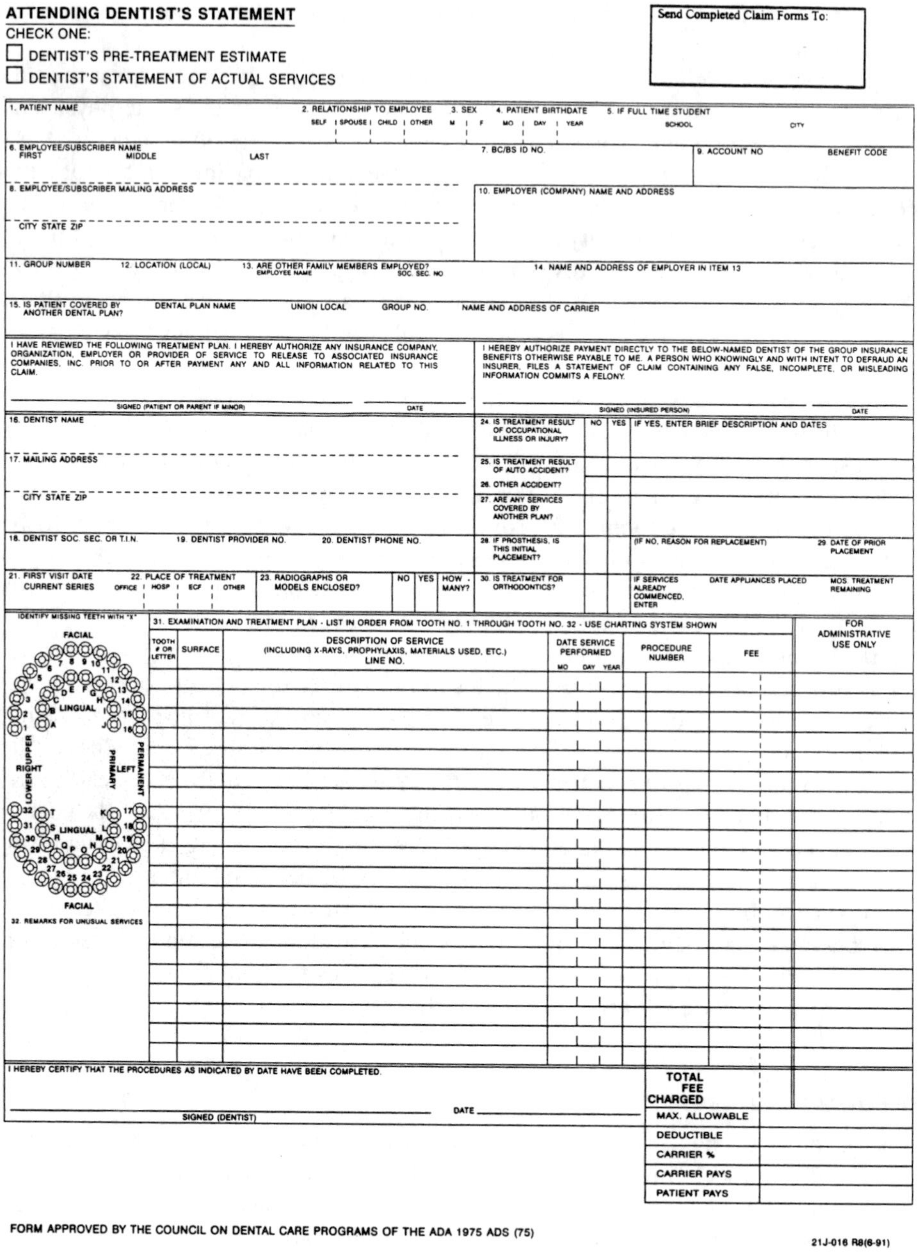

ATTENDING DENTIST'S STATEMENT
CHECK ONE:
☐ DENTIST'S PRE-TREATMENT ESTIMATE
☐ DENTIST'S STATEMENT OF ACTUAL SERVICES

Send Completed Claim Forms To:

1. PATIENT NAME	2. RELATIONSHIP TO EMPLOYEE	3. SEX	4. PATIENT BIRTHDATE	5. IF FULL TIME STUDENT
	SELF	SPOUSE	CHILD	OTHER	M	F	MO	DAY	YEAR	SCHOOL	CITY

6. EMPLOYEE/SUBSCRIBER NAME FIRST MIDDLE LAST	7. BC/BS ID NO.	9. ACCOUNT NO	BENEFIT CODE

8. EMPLOYEE/SUBSCRIBER MAILING ADDRESS

CITY STATE ZIP

10. EMPLOYER (COMPANY) NAME AND ADDRESS

11. GROUP NUMBER	12. LOCATION (LOCAL)	13. ARE OTHER FAMILY MEMBERS EMPLOYED? EMPLOYEE NAME SOC. SEC. NO	14. NAME AND ADDRESS OF EMPLOYER IN ITEM 13

15. IS PATIENT COVERED BY ANOTHER DENTAL PLAN? DENTAL PLAN NAME UNION LOCAL GROUP NO. NAME AND ADDRESS OF CARRIER

I HAVE REVIEWED THE FOLLOWING TREATMENT PLAN. I HEREBY AUTHORIZE ANY INSURANCE COMPANY, ORGANIZATION, EMPLOYER OR PROVIDER OF SERVICE TO RELEASE TO ASSOCIATED INSURANCE COMPANIES, INC. PRIOR TO OR AFTER PAYMENT ANY AND ALL INFORMATION RELATED TO THIS CLAIM.

I HEREBY AUTHORIZE PAYMENT DIRECTLY TO THE BELOW-NAMED DENTIST OF THE GROUP INSURANCE BENEFITS OTHERWISE PAYABLE TO ME. A PERSON WHO KNOWINGLY AND WITH INTENT TO DEFRAUD AN INSURER, FILES A STATEMENT OF CLAIM CONTAINING ANY FALSE, INCOMPLETE, OR MISLEADING INFORMATION COMMITS A FELONY.

SIGNED (PATIENT OR PARENT IF MINOR) DATE

SIGNED (INSURED PERSON) DATE

16. DENTIST NAME	24. IS TREATMENT RESULT OF OCCUPATIONAL ILLNESS OR INJURY?	NO	YES	IF YES, ENTER BRIEF DESCRIPTION AND DATES
17. MAILING ADDRESS	25. IS TREATMENT RESULT OF AUTO ACCIDENT?			
	26. OTHER ACCIDENT?			
CITY STATE ZIP	27. ARE ANY SERVICES COVERED BY ANOTHER PLAN?			

18. DENTIST SOC. SEC. OR T.I.N.	19. DENTIST PROVIDER NO.	20. DENTIST PHONE NO.	28. IF PROSTHESIS, IS THIS INITIAL PLACEMENT?	(IF NO, REASON FOR REPLACEMENT)	29. DATE OF PRIOR PLACEMENT

21. FIRST VISIT DATE CURRENT SERIES	22. PLACE OF TREATMENT OFFICE	HOSP	ECF	OTHER	23. RADIOGRAPHS OR MODELS ENCLOSED?	NO	YES	HOW MANY?	30. IS TREATMENT FOR ORTHODONTICS?	IF SERVICES ALREADY COMMENCED, ENTER	DATE APPLIANCES PLACED	MOS. TREATMENT REMAINING

IDENTIFY MISSING TEETH WITH "X"

FACIAL

LINGUAL

RIGHT PERMANENT LEFT

LOWER UPPER

PRIMARY

LINGUAL

FACIAL

32. REMARKS FOR UNUSUAL SERVICES

31. EXAMINATION AND TREATMENT PLAN - LIST IN ORDER FROM TOOTH NO. 1 THROUGH TOOTH NO. 32 - USE CHARTING SYSTEM SHOWN	FOR ADMINISTRATIVE USE ONLY

TOOTH # OR LETTER	SURFACE	DESCRIPTION OF SERVICE (INCLUDING X-RAYS, PROPHYLAXIS, MATERIALS USED, ETC.) LINE NO.	DATE SERVICE PERFORMED MO DAY YEAR	PROCEDURE NUMBER	FEE	

I HEREBY CERTIFY THAT THE PROCEDURES AS INDICATED BY DATE HAVE BEEN COMPLETED.

SIGNED (DENTIST) DATE

TOTAL FEE CHARGED	
MAX. ALLOWABLE	
DEDUCTIBLE	
CARRIER %	
CARRIER PAYS	
PATIENT PAYS	

FORM APPROVED BY THE COUNCIL ON DENTAL CARE PROGRAMS OF THE ADA 1975 ADS (75)

21J-016 R8(6-91)

FIGURE 14.4
Insurance claim form.

HEALTH INSURANCE

Health insurance, like all other types of insurance, is a risk- and cost-spreading process. That is, the cost of one person's injury or illness is shared by all in the group. Each person in the group has a different chance (or risk) of having a problem and thus needing health care. Some members of the group, for example, those who suffer from chronic and/or congenital health problems, will probably need more care while others in the group will need less. The concept of insurance has everyone in the group, no matter what their individual risk, helping to pay for the collective risk of the group. The risk of costly ill health is spread in a reasonably equitable fashion among all persons purchasing insurance, and everyone is protected from having to pay an insurmountable bill for a catastrophic injury or illness.

There are some exceptions to the "equitable fashion." If someone in the group knowingly engages in a behavior that increases his or her risk, such as smoking cigarettes or driving in a reckless manner, that person may have to pay more for the increased risk. In short, the greater the risk (or probability of using the insurance), the more the individual or group has to pay for insurance.

The concept of health insurance is not a new one in this country. Group health and life insurance are considered American inventions of the early twentieth century. In 1911 Montgomery Ward and Company sold health insurance policies based upon the principles still used today in the business. Currently, hundreds of companies in the United States sell health and life insurance policies.

Because of the expense of health care, those without health insurance find it difficult to pay for the care. If people do not have insurance, they are more likely to lack a usual source of primary medical care,[10] use less care, and often suffer adverse consequences due to delayed or postponed care.[11] As noted earlier in the chapter, 43 million Americans were without health insurance in 2002. One bright note for some of the uninsured came in 1997 when the 105th Congress enacted the **State Children's Health Insurance Program** (SCHIP; codified as Title XXI of the Social Security Act) as part of the Balanced Budget Act of 1997. SCHIP, which was authorized for 10 years (through 2008) at a cost of about $40 billion, was enacted to extend insurance to a significant portion of the estimated 11.3 million U.S. children without insurance (one in seven, and nearly one-quarter of all uninsured). For low-income and minority children, this proportion is even higher. The figure of 11.3 million was the highest one ever recorded by the Census Bureau, and roughly 3,000 children lose health insurance every day.[12] More than 92% of all uninsured children have working parents, and two-thirds have at least one parent that works full-time and year-round.[12] However, these parents either cannot afford family health care insurance through work, or they are included in those who cannot get family coverage through work at any price.

SCHIP is specifically targeted at low-income children who are ineligible for other insurance coverage, including Medicaid (see the discussion of Medicaid later in this chapter). "Uninsured children pay a heavy price: Study after study shows that they are more likely to report poor health, to see doctors less often (even when they are sick), to go without preventive care, and to turn to emergency rooms when they need treatment. The result is needless illness, learning problems, disabilities, and sometimes even death."[12]

SCHIP is a voluntary grant-in-aid program for states. That is, states can choose to participate or not. If they do, states can provide child health assistance by either expanding Medicaid or by creating a new health assistance program to aid children who are ineligible for Medicaid or are not covered by another form of "creditable coverage." States can also combine the two approaches by using some of their SCHIP funds to expand Medicaid and the rest to provide another form of child health assistance.[13]

At some point during 2002, approximately 5.3 million children were enrolled in SCHIP. This was an increase of 15% over the figures for 2001.[14] In addition, several states have sought and received approval (waivers) from the U.S. Department of Health and Human Services—the federal agency that administers the SCHIP program—to extend coverage to children not originally covered in the legislation, and to parents of children eligible under either SCHIP or Medicaid.[14] However, even with the SCHIP program, it is estimated that 8.3% of children under the age of 18 in the United States are still uninsured.[15]

The Health Insurance Policy

A *policy* is a written agreement between a private insurance company (or the government) and an individual or group of individuals to pay for certain health care costs during a certain

State Children's Health Insurance Program (SCHIP) a title insurance program under the Social Security Act that provides health insurance to uninsured children

time period in return for regular, periodic payments (a set amount of money) called *premiums.* The insurance company benefits in that it anticipates collecting more money in premiums than it has to pay out for services; hence, it anticipates a profit. The insured benefits by not being faced with medical bills he or she cannot pay, because the insurance company can and will pay them. The added benefit for those insured as a group is that group premiums are less expensive than premiums for individuals.

The expectations of both insurers and insured are not always met. An insurer occasionally has to pay out more than it collects in premiums. Alternatively, the insured often purchases insurance that is never used.

Although the language of health insurance policies can be confusing, everyone needs to understand several key terms. One of the most important is **deductible.** The deductible is the amount of expenses (money) that the beneficiary (insured) must incur (pay out of pocket) before the insurance company begins to pay for covered services. A common deductible level is $250 per individual policy holder, or a maximum of $1,000 per family. This means that the insured must pay the first $250/$1,000 of medical costs before the insurance company begins paying. The higher the deductible of a policy, the lower the premiums will be.

Usually, but not always, after the deductible has been met, most insurance companies pay a percentage of what they consider the "usual and customary" charge for covered services. The insurer generally pays 80% of the usual and customary costs, and the insured is responsible for paying the remaining 20%. This 20% is referred to as **co-insurance.** If the health care provider charges more than the usual and customary rates, the insured will have to pay both the co-insurance and the difference.[16] A form of co-insurance, often associated with managed care programs, is **co-payment.** A co-payment is a negotiated set amount a patient pays for certain services—for example, $10 for an office visit and $5 for a prescription. Some insurance policies may have both co-insurance and co-payments included. The greater the proportion of co-insurance paid by the insured, the lower the premiums.

A fourth key term, **fixed indemnity,** refers to the maximum amount an insurer will pay for a certain service. For example, a policy may state that the maximum amount of money paid for orthodontia is $2,000. Depending upon the language of a policy, the fixed indemnity benefit may or may not be subject to the provisions of the deductible or co-insurance clause. Costs above the fixed indemnity amount are the responsibility of the insured.

Another key term related to health insurance is **exclusion.** When an exclusion is written into a policy, it means that a specified health condition is excluded from coverage. That is, the policy does not pay for service to treat the condition. Common exclusions include a pregnancy that began before the health insurance policy went into effect or a chronic disease or condition such as diabetes or hypertension that has been classified as a pre-existing condition. A **pre-existing condition** is a medical condition that had been diagnosed or treated usually within the six months before the date the health insurance policy went into effect. Because of such exclusions, people who have a serious condition or disease are often unable to get health insurance coverage for the condition/disease or in general.[17] Some health insurance policies also exclude a condition/disease for a specified period of time, such as nine months for pregnancy or one year for all other exclusions.[17]

The rule that a pre-existing condition could be an exclusion "trapped" many people in jobs, because the employees were afraid of losing their health insurance for the condition if they changed employers. To deal with this issue, Congress passed the Health Insurance Portability and Accountability Act of 1996 (PL 104-102, known as HIPAA). This law was created, in part, to ensure that people will not have to wait for health insurance to go into effect when changing jobs. More specifically, a pre-existing condition will be covered without a waiting period when a person joins a new plan if the person has been insured for the previous 12 months. This means that if a person remains insured for 12 months or more, he or she will be able to go from one job to another, and the pre-existing condition will be covered—without

deductible
the amount of expenses that the beneficiary must incur before the insurance company begins to pay for covered services

co-insurance
the portion of the insurance company's approved amounts for covered services that a beneficiary is responsible for paying

co-payment
a negotiated set amount that a patient pays for certain services

fixed indemnity
the maximum amount an insurer will pay for a certain service

exclusion
a health condition written into the health insurance policy indicating what is not covered by the policy

pre-existing condition
a medical condition that had been diagnosed or treated usually within the six months before the date a health insurance policy goes into effect

Table 14.1
Types of Health Insurance Coverage

Dental	Dental procedures.
Disability (income protection)	Income when insured is unable to work because of a health problem.
Hospitalization	Inpatient hospital expenses including room, patient care, supplies, and medications.
Long-term care	An umbrella term for an array of supportive services to help people function in their daily lives. Services may include but are not limited to nursing care, home health care, personal care, rehabilitation, adult day care, case management, social services, assistive technology, and assisted living services. Services may be provided at home or in another place of residence like a nursing home.
Major medical	Large medical expenses usually not covered by regular medical or dental coverage.
Optical (vision)	Nonsurgical procedures to improve vision.
Regular medical	Nonsurgical service provided by health care providers. Often has set amounts (fixed indemnity for certain procedures).
Surgical	Surgeons' fees (for inpatient or outpatient surgery).

additional waiting periods—even if the person has a chronic illness. If a person has a pre-existing condition and it has not been covered the previous 12 months before joining a new plan, the longest that person will have to wait before being covered for that condition is 12 months.[16]

Types of Health Insurance Coverage

As has been noted in the previous discussions, there are a number of different types of services that health insurance policies cover. The more common types of coverage are hospitalization, surgical, regular medical, major medical, dental, and disability. Table 14.1 presents a short overview of each of these coverage types.

Though the types of health insurance coverage remain constant, several trends associated with health insurance plans and the products they offer are emerging. The trends that characterize health insurance plans today are (1) the plans are becoming more complex and are concentrated in a fewer number of companies, (2) there is an increase in the diversity of products, so consumers have many more options in the type of plan they select, (3) there is an increased focus on delivering care through a network of providers rather than independent providers, (4) there is a movement of shifting to financial structures and incentives between purchasers, health plans, and providers and away from the fee-for-service payment, and (5) more health insurance plans are developing clinical infrastructures to manage utilization and to improve the quality of care.[18] Such trends will make understanding health insurance plans more challenging for consumers. These trends will require a greater investment in education and information to help consumers understand how insurance products differ, how best to navigate managed care systems, and what differences exist in structure or performance across the plans.[18]

The Cost of Health Insurance

Over the years, the cost of health insurance has pretty much mirrored the cost of health care. From the early 1970s through the early 1990s, health care costs and the costs of health care insurance were growing in the neighborhood of 10% to 12% per year.[19] But as the cost of health care slowed in the early to mid-1990s, so did the cost of health insurance. This deceleration in premium growth paralleled the dramatic shift in the health insurance marketplace away from traditional fee-for-service indemnity insurance to managed care.[19] However, the managed care revolution created a one-time-only cost savings, and all the underlying cost drivers, such as an aging population, increased use of prescription drugs, and technology, have again increased costs. The burden of the cost of health insurance for those who are working falls primarily on the employer and, to a lesser extent, on the employee. Most Americans under 65 years of age receive their health insurance through their employer or the employer of their parent or spouse/partner. However, because of the increases in the cost of health insurance, most employers are shifting more of the cost onto their employees by (1) increasing the workers' share of the premium, (2) raising the deductibles that workers must pay, (3) increasing the co-payments for prescription drugs, and (4) increasing the number of items on the exclusion list.[20] A vivid example of the cost of health insurance comes from the automobile industry, where it has been estimated that workers' health insurance adds about $1,200 to the cost of every new car.[21]

In the end, the actual cost of a policy is determined by two major factors—the risk of those in the group and the amount of coverage provided. An increase in either risk or coverage will result in an increase in the cost of the policy.

Self-Insured Organizations

self-insured organization
one that pays the health care costs of its employees with the premiums collected from the employees and the contributions made by the employer

With the high cost of health care today, some employers "(or other group, such as a union or trade association)"[22] that provide health insurance for their employees are deciding to cut their costs by becoming self-insured. With such an arrangement, a **self-insured organization** pays the health care costs of its employees with the premiums collected from the employees and the contributions made by the employer instead of using a commercial carrier.[22] Self-insured organizations "normally use the services of an actuarial firm to set premium rates and a third-party administrator (TPA) to administer benefits, pay claims, and collect data on utilization. Many TPAs also are now providing case management services for potentially extraordinarily expensive cases to help coordinate care and control employee risk of catastrophic expenses."[22] There are several benefits to being self-insured. First, the organization gets to set most of the parameters of the policy—deductibles, co-insurance, fixed indemnities, and exclusions. If the organization wants to exclude some services and include others, it can. For example, if the organization has an older work force, it may wish to delete obstetrics from the policy but include a number of preventive health services. Second, the organization holds on to the cash reserves in the benefits account instead of sending them to a commercial carrier, and thus gets to accrue interest off of them. Third, the self-insured organizations have been exempt from the *Employee Retirement and Income Security Act of 1974* (ERISA), which mandates minimum benefits under state law.[22] And fourth, generally the administrative costs of self-insured organizations have been less than traditional commercial carriers and, in general, health insurance costs to these groups have risen at a slower rate.[22] For self-insurance to work, there must be a sizable group of employees over which to spread the risk. Larger organizations usually find it more useful than smaller ones. However, if a small workforce is comprised primarily of low-health-risk employees, say for example younger employees, self-insured programs make sense.

HEALTH INSURANCE PROVIDED BY THE GOVERNMENT

Medicare
a national health insurance program for people 65 years of age and older, certain younger disabled people, and people with permanent kidney failure

Although there are some in the United States who would like to see all health insurance provided by the government—a national health insurance plan—at the present time government health insurance plans are only available to select groups in the United States. The only government health insurance plans that exist today are Medicare and Medicaid, Veterans Administration benefits (see Figure 14.5), Indian Health Service, and health care benefits for the uniformed services (military and Public Health Service), federal employees (Federal

Employees Health Benefits Program), and prisoners. Our discussion here will be limited to Medicare and Medicaid. These programs were created in 1965 by amendments to the Social Security Act and were implemented for the first time in 1966.

Medicare

Medicare, which currently covers over 41 million people,[23] is a federal health insurance program for people 65 years of age or older, people of any age with permanent kidney failure, and certain disabled people under 65. It is administered by the Center for Medicare and Medicaid Services (CMS) of the U.S. Department of Health and Human Services (HHS). The Social Security Administration provides information about the program and handles enrollment. Medicare is considered a contributory program, in that employers and employees are required to contribute a percentage of each employee's wages/salaries through Social Security (FICA) tax to the Medicare fund. Medicare has two parts—hospital insurance (Part A) and medical insurance (Part B).

The Medicare hospital insurance (Part A) portion is mandatory and is provided for those eligible without further cost. Some elders who are not eligible for premium-free Part A because they or their spouses did not pay into Social Security at all or paid only a limited amount, may be able to purchase Part A coverage. In 2004, those premiums ranged

FIGURE 14.5
Insurance provided for veterans is one of several insurance plans paid for by the U.S. government.

from $189 to $343 per month, depending on how much a person had paid into Social Security.[23] While Medicare Part A has deductible ($876 in 2004) and co-insurance provisions, it helps pay for inpatient care in a hospital and in a skilled nursing facility after a hospital stay, hospice care, and some home health care.[23] Those who are enrolled in Part A of Medicare are automatically enrolled in Part B unless they decline. In 2004, the premium for Part B was $66.60 per month. Most Part A enrollees are also enrolled in Part B and have their premium deducted directly from their Social Security check.[23] Part B of Medicare helps cover physicians' services, outpatient hospital care, and selected other health care services and supplies that are not covered by Part A. Part B also has a deductible ($100 per year in 2004) and co-insurance (80/20 coverage). Both portions of Medicare are subject to yearly changes in coverage and administrative procedures (see Box 14.2). Finally, it should be noted that when health care providers take assignment (are willing to accept Medicare patients) on a Medicare claim, they agree to accept the Medicare-approved amount as payment in full. These providers are paid directly by the Medicare carrier, except for the deductible and co-insurance amounts, which are the patient's responsibility.

Medicare, like private health insurance programs, is affected by the high costs of health care and, therefore, the government is always looking for ways of cutting the costs of the programs. Several different procedures have been put into place. One procedure, added in 1983, that has helped to control the costs is the **prospective pricing system (PPS).** In the PPS, hospitals are paid predetermined amounts of money per procedure for services provided to Medicare patients. The predetermined amounts are based upon over 470 **diagnosis-related groups (DRGs)** rather than the actual cost of the care rendered. Each hospital stay by a Medicare patient is assigned a DRG. "The correct DRG for each patient is decided by considering the patient's major or principal diagnosis; any complications or other problems that might arise; any surgery performed during the hospital stay; and other factors."[24] The amount

prospective pricing system (PPS) one in which providers are paid predetermined amounts of money per procedure for services provided

diagnosis-related groups (DRGs) a procedure used to classify the health problems of all Medicare patients when they are admitted to a hospital

BOX
14.2   MEDICARE MODERNIZATION ACT OF 2003

Late in 2003 after much debate, Congress and President George W. Bush worked together to improve the benefits of Medicare by passing a bill called the Medicare Modernization Act of 2003 (MMA 2003). Since the new law was passed, there has been more debate on how beneficial the law really is and how much it will cost taxpayers. Here are the major features of the MMA 2003.

In 2004

- *Prescription drug discount cards:* Medicare-approved drug discount cards became available in 2004, at a cost of $30, to help elders save on prescription drugs. Medicare contracted with private pharmaceutical companies to offer the discount cards until a Medicare prescription drug benefit starts in 2006. A discount card with Medicare's seal of approval can save a person between 10% and 25% on prescription drugs.
- *$600 credit on discount card:* Medicare recipients may also qualify for a $600 credit on their discount card. There are several criteria for eligibility, but the primary criterion is income. The income levels change each year, but in 2004 to qualify, a single person could make no more than $12,569, and married couples could make no more than $16,862.
- *Medicare + Choice renamed Medicare Advantage:* Beginning in 2004, the options for Medicare coverage other than the original Medicare plan (sometimes called fee-for-service Medicare) got a name change, from Medicare + Choice (pronounced Medicare Plus Choice) to Medicare Advantage. In addition, the rules and payments in the Medicare Advantage plan were improved.

In 2005

Three new preventive benefits were added to Medicare:
1. A one-time initial wellness physical exam within six months of the day a person first enrolls in Medicare Part B
2. Screening blood tests for early detection of cardiovascular diseases
3. Diabetes screening tests for people at risk of getting diabetes

In 2006

- *Prescription drug benefits:* All Medicare recipients can enroll in plans that cover prescription drugs. The plans will vary, but in general (a) recipients will select a plan and pay a $35 per month premium, (b) there will be a $250 deductible, (c) Medicare will pay 75% of the prescription drug costs between $250 and $2,250, (d) recipients pay 100% of prescription drug costs between $2,250 and $3,600, (e) Medicare will pay 95% of the prescription drug costs after $3,600, and (f) premiums and deductibles will be waived for people with low incomes and limited assets.
- *Medicare Advantage will be expanded:* Regional preferred provider organizations (PPOs) will be added to the Medicare Advantage choices.

Sources: Center for Medicare and Medicaid (2004). *The Facts About Upcoming New Benefits in Medicare.* Baltimore, MD: Author; Center for Medicare and Medicaid (2004). *Introducing Medicare-Approved Drug Discount Cards.* Baltimore, MD: Author; and Center for Medicare and Medicaid (2004). *Guide to Choosing a Medicare-Approved Drug Discount Card.* Baltimore, MD: Author.

of money assigned to each DRG is not the same for each hospital. The figure is based on a formula that takes into account the type of service, the type of hospital, the location of the hospital, and the sex and age of the patient. Using this prospective pricing system, hospitals are encouraged to provide services at or below the DRG rate. If the hospital delivers the service below the DRG rate, the hospital can retain the difference. If it is delivered above the DRG rate, the hospital incurs the extra expenses. "However, when a Medicare patient's condition requires an unusually long hospital stay or exceptionally costly care, Medicare makes additional payment to the hospital."[24] Because of DRGs, some have felt that hospitals are quicker to discharge Medicare patients to keep their expenses down. This phenomenon has resulted in an increase in the need for skilled nursing care in homes, in adult day care facilities, and in nursing homes.

A second procedure that Medicare has instituted to help reduce costs is to offer other Medicare options (called Medicare Advantage, formerly known as Medicare + Choice) other than the original Medicare plan (referred to as a fee-for-service plan) discussed previously.

Medicare Advantage options are not available in all parts of the country. Current options include a *Medicare managed care plan* and/or a *Medicare private fee-for-service plan*. In Medicare-managed care plans, health care is provided by a health maintenance organization (HMO) (see the discussion of HMOs later in this chapter), while in the Medicare private fee-for-service plan, health care is covered by a private insurance company. These options are being well received in some parts of the country, while in other areas they have been tried without any success and have thus been eliminated. In some places where they have been successful, they have helped eliminate the need for many elders to purchase additional private insurance to supplement their Medicare coverage.

In recent years, much discussion has centered around whether there are sufficient funds in Medicare to pay for the health care costs of the 76 million baby boomers when they begin to become eligible in 2011. Most projections about the Medicare program indicate that there is enough money to begin to cover the baby boomers, but as they age Medicare will run out of money unless changes are made. The more difficult questions to answer now are:

When will Medicare run out of money, if no changes are made?

What changes should be made (e.g., decrease benefits, raise eligibility standards, reimburse health care providers less)?

Where should the money come from to build up the program (e.g., increase taxes, increase premiums)?

With the exception of the Medicare Modernization Act of 2003, there has been little agreement in Congress on what to do with Medicare. Both the Democratic and Republican parties agree changes need to be made, but they disagree on what and when changes should be made.

Medicaid

A second type of government health insurance is **Medicaid,** a health insurance program for the poor. Currently, approximately 43 million people are covered by Medicaid.[3] Eligibility for enrollment in Medicaid is determined by each state. Many Medicaid recipients are also enrolled in other types of public assistance programs (welfare). Unlike Medicare, there is no age requirement for Medicaid; eligibility requirements are strictly financial. Also, unlike Medicare, Medicaid is a noncontributory program jointly administered through federal and state governments. Both programs cover skilled nursing care but under different conditions.

Medicaid
a national health insurance program for the poor

For many states, the most costly item appearing in the annual state budget is the Medicaid program. Thus, like the federal government, state governments are always looking for ways to reshape their programs to become more efficient. As noted earlier in this chapter, several states have combined their Medicaid program with their State Children's Health Insurance Program (SCHIP) to provide better health care for the poor. In addition, the U.S. Department of Health and Human Services (HHS) has provided, on a competitive basis, some states with special grants to develop other plans for extending health care coverage to the uninsured.

Problems with Medicare and Medicaid

In theory, both the Medicare and Medicaid programs seem to be sound programs that help provide health care to two segments of the society who would otherwise find it difficult or impossible to obtain health insurance. In practice, there are two recurrent problems with these programs. One problem is that some physicians and hospitals do not accept Medicare and Medicaid patients because of the tedious and time-consuming paperwork, lengthy delays in reimbursement, and insufficient reimbursement. As a result, it is difficult if not impossible for many of those eligible for Medicare and Medicaid to receive health care. The second problem occurs when physicians and hospitals file Medicare and Medicaid paperwork for care or services not rendered or rendered incompletely. This is known as *Medicare/Medicaid fraud.*

Another drawback to these public insurance programs is the lack of coverage for catastrophic illness and long-term care, two situations that could quickly deplete the lifetime savings of an individual or family. People who wish to be protected in these situations must purchase their own catastrophic and long-term care insurance. The late President Ronald Reagan proposed that catastrophic illness insurance should be included with Medicare; in fact, Congress approved it in 1988 for implementation in 1990, but it was repealed in 1989 because the elderly objected to the increased cost.

SUPPLEMENTAL HEALTH INSURANCE

Medigap

Medigap
private health insurance that supplements Medicare benefits

As noted earlier, both portions of Medicare have deductibles and co-insurance stipulations. To help cover these out-of-pocket costs and some other services not covered by Medicare, people can purchase supplemental policies from private insurance companies. These policies have come to be known as **Medigap** policies because they cover the "gaps" not covered by Medicare. Federal law mandates national standardization of Medigap policies. Under these standards, insurance companies can offer no more than 10 standardized plans (see Box 14.3) that have been developed by the National Association of Insurance Commissioners. Each of these 10 plans is required to have a core set of benefits referred to as *basic benefits.* The plans vary from simple (basic benefits only) to more complex plans with additional benefits. The plans are identified by the letters A–J. By law, the letters and benefits of the individual plans cannot be changed by the insurance companies. However, they may add names or titles to the letter designations. While companies are not required to offer all the plans, they must make Plan A available if they sell any of the other nine plans. Three states—Minnesota, Massachusetts, and Wisconsin—have exceptions to the 10-plan setup because they had alternative Medigap standardization programs in effect before the federal legislation was enacted. Individuals should contact the state insurance office in these states if interested in these plans.

Two other variances to these Medigap rules should be noted. The first deals with those individuals enrolled in the Medicare Advantage program. Because Medicare Advantage is more comprehensive in coverage than the traditional Medicare program, Medigap policies are not needed. In fact, it is illegal for insurance companies to sell a Medigap policy if they know a person is enrolled in Medicare Advantage.[25] Another variance in Medigap policy deals with Medicare SELECT. *Medicare SELECT* is a type of Medigap policy that is available in some states. This type of policy still provides one of the standardized Medigap plans (A–J), but requires policy holders to use specific hospitals and, in some cases, doctors (except in emergencies) to receive full Medigap benefits.[25]

Other Supplemental Insurance

Medigap is a supplemental insurance program specifically designed for those on Medicare. However, a number of supplemental insurance policies exist for people regardless of their age. Included are specific-disease insurance, hospital indemnity insurance, and long-term care insurance. Specific-disease insurance, though not available in some states, provides benefits for only a single disease (such as cancer) or a group of specific diseases. Many policies are written as fixed-indemnity policies. Hospital indemnity coverage is insurance that pays a fixed amount for each day a person receives inpatient hospital services, and it pays up to a designated number of days. Long-term care insurance, which pays cash amounts for each day of covered nursing home or at-home care, is of great concern to many people, and it is presented next.

BOX
14.3

TEN STANDARD MEDICARE SUPPLEMENT (MEDIGAP) BENEFIT PLANS

Medigap policies (including Medicare SELECT) can only be sold in 10 standardized plans. This chart gives you a quick and easy look at all the Medigap plans and what benefits are in each plan.

Basic Benefits: Included in All Plans

- **Inpatient Hospital Care:** Covers the Part A *co-insurance* and the cost of 365 extra days of hospital

care during your lifetime after Medicare coverage ends.

- **Medical Costs:** Covers the Part B co-insurance (generally 20% of the *Medicare-approved payment amount*).
- **Blood:** Covers the first three pints of blood each year.

A	B	C	D	E	F*	G	H	I	J*
Basic Benefit	Basic Benefit	Basic Benefit	Basic Benefit	Basic Benefit	Basic Benefit	Basic Benefit	Basic Benefit	Basic Benefit	Basic Benefit
		Skilled Nursing Coinsurance	Skilled Nursing Coinsurance	Skilled Nursing Coinsurance	Skilled Nursing Coinsurance	Skilled Nursing Coinsurance	Skilled Nursing Coinsurance	Skilled Nursing Coinsurance	Skilled Nursing Coinsurance
	Part A Deductible	Part A Deductible	Part A Deductible	Part A Deductible	Part A Deductible	Part A Deductible	Part A Deductible	Part A Deductible	Part A Deductible
		Part B Deductible			Part B Deductible				Part B Deductible
					Part B Excess (100%)	Part B Excess (80%)		Part B Excess (100%)	Part B Excess (100%)
		Foreign Travel Emergency	Foreign Travel Emergency	Foreign Travel Emergency	Foreign Travel Emergency	Foreign Travel Emergency	Foreign Travel Emergency	Foreign Travel Emergency	Foreign Travel Emergency
			At-Home Recovery			At-Home Recovery		At-Home Recovery	At-Home Recovery
							Basic Drug Benefit ($1,250 Limit)	Extended Drug Benefit ($1,250 Limit)	Extended Drug Benefit ($3,000 Limit)
				Preventive Care**					Preventive Care**

*Plans F and J also have a high *deductible* option. Call your State Insurance Department for more information.

**Medigap policies cover some preventive care that is not covered by Medicare.

Note: This chart does not apply if you live in Massachusetts, Minnesota, or Wisconsin. Call your State Insurance Departments for more information on the policies that are offered in these states. You can also look on the Internet at www.medicare.gov and click on "Medigap Compare."

Source: U.S. Department of Health and Human Services, Centers for Medicare and Medicaid Services (2004). *2004 Choosing a Medigap Policy: A Guide for People with Medicare.* Baltimore, MD: Author.

Long-Term Care Insurance

With people living longer and the cost of health care on the rise, more and more individuals are considering the purchase of long-term care insurance. It has been estimated that more than 9 million people in the United States will receive some type of help with their daily activities—either at home or in assisted living facilities, board and care homes, adult foster care homes, nursing homes, and places that provide adult day care in 2005.[23] By 2020, 12 million older Americans will need long-term care.[23] Most will be cared for at home; family and friends are the sole caregivers for 70% of the elderly.[23] Yet, planning for long-term care requires people to think about possible future health care needs and how they will pay for it. Obviously, the cost of long-term care varies based on the level of care, the length of time the care is provided, and where the care is provided. The most costly long-term care is nursing home care. Recent figures show that the average cost of residing in a nursing home is about $4,000 per month,[3] and the average

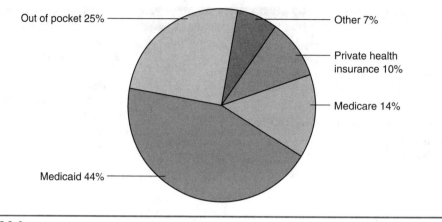

FIGURE 14.6

Who pays for long-term care services?

Source: Center for Medicare and Medicaid Services, Office of the Actuary, National Health Statistics Group (2004). "Personal Health Care Expenditures, 2001."

length of stay for a person is about 30 months.[26] About 10% of the people who enter a nursing home will stay there five years or more.[23] A study by the HHS says that people who reach age 65 will likely have a 40% chance of entering a nursing home.[23] The costs vary by parts of the country, but such costs for long-term care have many people worried about their financial future. This cost is something that can quickly deplete a lifetime of savings. In fact, the majority of Americans who have to pay for long-term care are impoverished within the first few years of making long-term health care payments. Those caring for a spouse find that they quickly exhaust both their spouse's resources and their own. Though much of long-term care is paid for by the government (see Figure 14.6), it is only after patients have exhausted many of their assets that Medicaid will begin to cover the costs.

Though long-term care is expensive, not everyone needs to buy long-term care insurance. Those who do not need it are those with low incomes and few assets who could be covered by Medicaid, and the very wealthy who are able to pay the cost of the care out of pocket. Those who are most likely to benefit from long-term care insurance are those in between the poor and wealthy, especially older women. About half of women over 65 will spend some time in a nursing home.[26] In addition, about 75% of nursing home residents are women and two-thirds of home care consumers are women.[7] However, there are several reasons why all people should consider purchasing long-term insurance. They include:

- To preserve financial assets
- To prevent the need for family members or friends to provide the care
- To enable people to stay independent in their homes longer
- To make it easier to get into the nursing home or assisted living home of their choice

As with life insurance, the earlier one purchases long-term care insurance the less expensive it is; however, it also may be purchased and never used. In 2004, the average annual cost of buying the same (fairly standard) long-term care policy for a resident of Indiana at different ages was about $395 at age 50, $1,340 at age 65, and $3,326 at age 75.[26]

MANAGED CARE

In 1993, when then President Bill Clinton took office, a comprehensive reform of the U.S. health care system seemed likely. After much debate, the comprehensive reform initiated by the government did not come to pass. Even so, the U.S. health care system did and continues to experience a great deal of change. The change, which has occurred with great speed and controversy, surfaced in the form of managed care.[27] Managed care plans include "a set of techniques used by or on behalf of purchasers of health care benefits to manage health care costs by influencing patient care decision making through case-by-case assessments of the appropriateness of care prior to its provision."[28] The transition to managed care in the United States was largely driven by a desire by employers, insurance companies, and the public to control soaring health care costs.[29] In fact, the goal of managed care is to control costs by controlling health care utilization.[30] Although the exact number of individuals enrolled in managed care programs is constantly changing, it has been estimated that at the end of 2004, almost 185 million Americans[31]—about two-thirds of the total population—belonged to some form of a managed health care plan. These numbers cover not only workers who received their health care coverage from employers, but also some individuals who were covered by Medicare and Medicaid.

Managed health care plans are offered by managed care organizations (MCOs). MCOs function like insurance companies by assuming all the risk. That is, MCOs take on the financial responsibility if the costs of the services exceed the revenue from the premiums. Approximately 17% to 20% of the premiums are used to manage the risk and to cover administrative expenses, while the remainder is spent on health care services.[30] These organizations have agreements with certain doctors, hospitals, and other health care providers to give a range of services to plan members at reduced cost. MCOs have been structured in a variety of ways and are similar to the other health care organizations we are familiar with (such as hospitals). Some are structured as nonprofit organizations, while others are for-profit and owned by a group of investors. "Regardless of their structure, their goals, however, are similar: to control costs through improved efficiency and coordination, to reduce unnecessary or inappropriate utilization, to increase access to preventive care, and to maintain or improve quality of care."[27]

The managed health care plans offered by these organizations also vary and are always evolving as managed care practices mature. The plans also differ, both in cost and ease of receiving needed services. Although no plan pays for all the costs associated with medical care, some plans cover more than others. Regardless of the type of managed health care plan offered, several basic concepts are involved: (1) Insurers negotiate a discounted provider fee in return for a certain volume of patients, (2) members are restricted to a selected group of providers, (3) there are significant financial incentives for members to use providers and procedures associated with the plan, and (4) the care provided is analyzed for type, amount, and quality by someone other than the patient and provider. This last concept is referred to as **utilization review** or **utilization management.**

utilization review or utilization management provided health care is analyzed by someone other than the patient and provider for its appropriateness

Types of Managed Care

As noted earlier, there are several different types of managed care arrangements, and because of the increasing cost of health care and the demands of consumers for better health care service these arrangements continue to be adapted and developed. "Until about 1988, the various types of MCOs were quite distinct. Since then, the differences between traditional forms of health insurance and managed care have narrowed considerably."[30] The following are the most commonly available arrangements.

Preferred Provider Organizations
The **preferred provider organization (PPO)** is a form of managed care closest to a fee-for-service plan. A PPO differs from the traditional fee-for-service plan in that the fee has been fixed (at a discounted rate) through a negotiation process between a health care provider (e.g., physicians, dentists, hospitals, etc.) and the PPO, and the provider agrees to accept this discounted rate as payment in full. It works in the following manner: A PPO approaches a provider, such as a group dental practice, and contracts with the dentists to provide dental

preferred provider organization (PPO) an organization that buys fixed-rate health services from providers and sells them to consumers services to all those covered by the PPO's insurance plan at a fixed (discount) rate. To the extent that the PPO succeeds in obtaining favorable prices, it can offer lower premiums, co-insurance, and co-payments, and hence can attract more patients to enroll in its insurance plan. In addition to the PPO doctors making referrals, plan members can refer themselves to other doctors, including ones outside the plan. However, if they do choose to go outside the plan, they will have to meet the deductible and pay higher co-insurance. In addition, they may have to pay the difference between what the provider charges and what the plan pays.[16] PPOs also control costs by requiring (1) preauthorization for hospital admissions (excluding emergencies), and (2) second opinions for major procedures such as surgery.[22] Advantages for the providers are that they (1) do not share in any financial risk as a condition of partici-pation,[22] (2) are reimbursed on a fee-for-service basis to which they are accustomed,[22] (3) are assured a certain volume of patients, and (4) are assured that the patients will pay promptly (via the PPO). PPOs are the most common form of managed care offered by employers.[32]

Exclusive Provider Organizations

exclusive provider organization (EPO)
like a PPO but with fewer providers and stronger financial incentives

Exclusive provider organizations (EPOs) are like PPOs except that they have stronger financial incentives for enrolled members to use the exclusive (only) provider. Stronger financial incentives usually mean no deductible, co-insurance, or co-payments. If the members were to go outside the plan to another provider, they would be responsible for a larger percentage of the bill. Typically, the number of providers (physicians, dentists, hospitals, etc.) is much smaller in an EPO, which strengthens the ability of the organization to receive a greater discount because the providers are guaranteed a larger share of patients. Because of such arrangements, a business or corporation is able to create a more stringent utilization and monitoring program with an EPO.

Health Maintenance Organizations

health maintenance organizations (HMOs)
groups that supply prepaid comprehensive health care with an emphasis on prevention

Health maintenance organizations (HMOs) are the oldest form of managed care and have grown in popularity since the early 1970s following the passage of the Health Maintenance Organization (HMO) Act of 1973. In 2002, just over 76 million people were enrolled in the 500 HMOs in the United States.[7] In an HMO, the insurance coverage and the delivery of medical care are combined into a single organization. The organization hires (through salaries or con-tracts) an individual doctor or groups of doctors to provide care and either builds its own hospital or contracts for the services of a hospital within the community. The organization then enrolls members, usually, but not always, through the workplace. Members (or their employers or the government [in the case of HMOs for Medicare and Medicaid]) make regular payments in advance on a fixed contract fee to the HMO. This contract may also include a deductible and co-payment when service is provided. In return, the HMO is contractually obligated to provide the members with a comprehensive range of outpatient and inpatient services that are spelled out in the contract for a specific time period.

mixed model HMO
a hybrid form of health maintenance organization

When members enroll in an HMO, they are given a list (network) of specific physicians/providers from which to select their primary care doctor (usually a family physician, internist, obstetrician-gynecologist, or pediatrician) and other health care providers. The primary care doctor (which some have referred to as the gatekeeper) serves as the member's regular doctor and coordinates the member's care, which means the member must contact his or her primary care doctor to be referred to a specialist. In many plans, care by a specialist is only paid for if the member is referred by the primary care doctor, thus the term *gatekeeper.* Also, if patients receive care outside the network, they must pay for all the costs, except in cases of emergency when physically not near a member of the network.

staff model HMO
a health maintenance organization that hires its own staff of health care providers

How do HMOs make a profit? An HMO's focus of care is different from that of a traditional fee-for-service provider. In an HMO, ill and injured patients become a "cost." An HMO does not make money on the ill but on keeping people healthy. The less the providers of an HMO see a patient, the lower the costs and the more profitable the organization. Therefore, most HMOs emphasize health promotion activities and primary and secondary care.

There are two main organizational models of HMOs—staff models and individual practice models—and each type has spawned several hybrids. These hybrids are referred to **mixed model HMOs** and made up almost 40% of the HMOs in 2002.[32]

Staff Model

In **staff model HMOs,** the health care providers are employed (usually salaried) by the HMO and practice in common facilities paid for by the HMO. Staff model HMOs employ providers in all common specialties to provide services to their members. Special contracts are established with subspecialties for infrequently needed services.[31] These providers are expected to follow the practice and procedures determined by the HMO.[8] With the exception of the special contracts, the providers work only for the HMO, and thus do not have their own private practices. In most instances, the HMO contracts with a hospital for inpatient services.[33] Nationwide, the number of staff model HMOs has been declining, and in 2002 they comprised the smallest segment (0.2%) of HMOs.[32]

Independent Practice Association Model

Under the **independent practice association (IPA) model,** community-based providers, individual practices, or group practices contract with an HMO to provide covered services for members according to the practices and procedures of the IPA model HMO. With this model, providers are free to contract with other HMOs and to maintain fee-for-service patients.[8] The IPA model is the most common form of HMO in the United States, comprising just over 40% of the HMOs.[32] Two variations of the IPA HMO are the group and network models. A **group model HMO** contracts with a multispecialty group practice instead of individual practitioners, whereas a **network model HMO** contracts with more than one medical group practice.[31] In 2002, the group model comprised about 10% and the network model comprised about 11% of all HMOs.[32]

Point-of-Service Option

One of the major objections to HMOs is that the patients cannot freely select their provider. They are restricted to those with whom the HMO has contracted. Some HMOs have solved this problem with the **point-of-service (POS) option,** which allows for a more liberal policy of enabling patients to select providers. With this option, members may choose a provider from within or outside the HMO network. Patients who obtain services outside the network generally must pay a higher deductible and co-insurance. POS plans are among the fastest growing type of managed care plans.

Physician-Hospital Organizations

In some parts of the country, there has been an emergence of a health care network characterized by a consolidation and integration of the management and delivery of services. One such arrangement is the **physician-hospital organization (PHO).** PHOs are agreements between physicians and hospitals to form units to negotiate with insurers as MCOs. In some PHOs, groups of physicians enter into agreements with hospitals in which both parties negotiate as a single MCO with insurance companies on behalf of all community providers. Other PHOs have been formed when a hospital buys the private or group practices of physicians. Under this arrangement, these physicians become employees of the hospital or hospital's system.

Medicare Advantage

As noted earlier, in some parts of the country Medicare recipients may have an HMO option available to them through the Medicare Advantage plan. In such plans, the Medicare recipient

independent practice association (IPA) model HMO community-based providers, individual practices, or group practices who contract with an HMO to provide covered services for members according to the practices and procedures of the IPA model HMO

group model HMO one that contracts with a multispecialty group practice

network model HMO one that contracts with more than one medical group practice

point-of-service (POS) option an option of an HMO plan that enables enrollees to be at least partially reimbursed for selecting a health care provider outside the plan

physician-hospital organization (PHO) various agreements between physicians and hospitals to form units to negotiate with insurers as MCOs

receives all Medicare-covered services from the HMO. In addition, the HMO may charge the beneficiary a premium (in addition to the Medicare Part B premium) to cover co-insurance and deductibles of Medicare and may include items and services not covered by Medicare. If this is the case, Medigap coverage cannot be purchased. In other cases, beneficiaries may receive other services not covered by Medicare at no charge or at a much lower cost than might be expected.

Medicaid and Managed Care

As has been noted throughout this chapter, managed care plans are also available for those covered by Medicaid. The rationale for offering such plans is to improve access to care by the establishment of contracted provider networks, as well as by promoting greater account-ability for quality and costs. Each state in the United States offers such a plan, and depending on the state requirements, enrollment may or may not be voluntary. If it is mandatory, then the state is required to offer a choice of managed care plans and make efforts to inform beneficiaries about their choices.[22]

Advantages and Disadvantages of Managed Care

Like all forms of health care delivery before it, managed care has its advantages and disadvantages. "The best features of managed care provide public benefits beyond those available in the fee-for-service system: comprehensive benefits, evidenced-based high-quality care, well-documented services provided through integrated delivery systems, and accountability for quality improvement."[34] However, many Americans are still worried about health care and the way it is delivered. A 2003 poll revealed that 54% of Americans were dissatisfied with the overall quality of their health care.[35] Another survey reported that (1) three in four Americans are worried about their health care coverage, (2) one in six had experienced delays in getting an appointment with a provider, (3) one in four cannot figure out his or her medical bills, and (4) one in five had trouble paying the bills. In addition, 50% of Americans were worried that doctors were basing their treatment decisions strictly on what the health plan covered,[21] three in five believed that managed care made it harder to be treated by a specialist,[36] and 55% of those in managed care plans worried that their health plan is concerned more about saving money than providing the best care.[37] Thus, the controversies in managed care seem to revolve around the way in which health care costs are being reduced.

Some have said that the term "managed care" is a misnomer; it should really be called "managed cost." Because Americans had become accustomed to a fee-for-service delivery system in which insurance companies paid almost every medical bill without question, they are now unsatisfied when MCOs question or refuse certain bills and medical procedures.[21] The forms of cost control that have caused the most concern include (1) authorizing only certain practitioners who are under contract to provide services to an enrolled population, (2) reviewing treatment decisions (i.e., utilization review), (3) closely monitoring high-cost cases (i.e., utilization management), (4) reducing the number of days of inpatient hospital stays (e.g., child birth), and (5) increasing the use of less expensive alternatives to hospitalization (e.g., outpatient surgery and home health care).[27]

As MCOs continue to grow and as Medicare and Medicaid enroll more individuals into managed care plans, the question of quality of care and the criteria and processes used to monitor and report it are being more closely examined.[22] The organization in the United States that is most influential in regard to the quality of managed care is the National Committee on Quality Assurance (NCQA). The NCQA is an independent, nonprofit organization whose mission is to improve health care quality everywhere. It evaluates health care in three different ways: (1) through accreditation (a rigorous on-site review of key clinical and administrative processes), (2) through the Health Plan Employer Data and Information Set (HEDIS—a tool used to measure performance in key areas like immunization and mammography screening rates), and (3) through the Consumer Assessment of Health Plans Study (CAHPS—a comprehensive member satisfaction survey).[38] Although participation in the accreditation and certification programs is voluntary, more than half the Nation's HMOs currently participate, and almost 90% of all health plans measure their performance using the HEDIS.[38] The data generated from these evaluations are available at NCQA's Web site. Many employers use the data as a way of selecting the best managed care program for their employees.

OTHER ARRANGEMENTS FOR DELIVERING HEALTH CARE

Because the majority of people in the United States receive their health care through a managed care plan or a fee-for-service plan, the majority of this chapter and Chapter 13 focused on those plans. However, there are other ways of delivering health care. A few of the more highly visible arrangements are discussed next.

National Health Insurance

National health insurance, or national health care, suggests a system in which the federal government assumes the responsibility for the health care costs of the entire population. In such a system, the costs are paid for with tax dollars. Presently among all the developed countries of the world, there is only one that does not have a national health care plan for its citizens: the United States.[38]

The national health care systems of the developed countries of the world fall into two basic models. The first is a national health service model with universal coverage and a general tax-financed government ownership of the facilities and doctors as public employees. Countries using this model include the United Kingdom, Spain, Italy, Greece, and Portugal. The second is a social insurance model that provides universal coverage under social security, financed by various ways including taxes or contributions paid by employers and employees. In Canada, contributions are made to a government entity. In France and Germany, contributions go to nonprofit funds with national negotiation on fees. Japan also has a compulsory system that relies heavily on employer-based coverage.

When one considers the level of satisfaction with health care, the better access to health care services, the lower health care costs, and the superior health status indicators in these other countries, one must ask why the United States has not adopted such a program. It is not because the United States has not considered such a plan. President Harry Truman presented a proposal to Congress on two different occasions, only to have it defeated twice.[39] Other unsuccessful attempts at national health care legislation were made during the Kennedy, Nixon, and Clinton administrations.

Though the push for national health insurance has not been successful, a few states have tried to move ahead and offer such a program for their citizens. One of the best examples is the state of Vermont. In 2000, Vermont reported that 93.5% of its residents have health insurance, including essentially all children.[40]

Canadian Health Care System

Because of the proximity of the United States to Canada and due to the similarities of the two countries and their cultures, we present the following information on the national health plan of Canada.

Canada has provided its legal residents with some form of health insurance coverage since 1957. Its current system, in place since 1984 (see Figure 14.7), is a predominantly publicly financed, privately delivered health care system that is best described as an interlocking set of 13 provincial and territorial health insurance plans. Known to the Canadians as

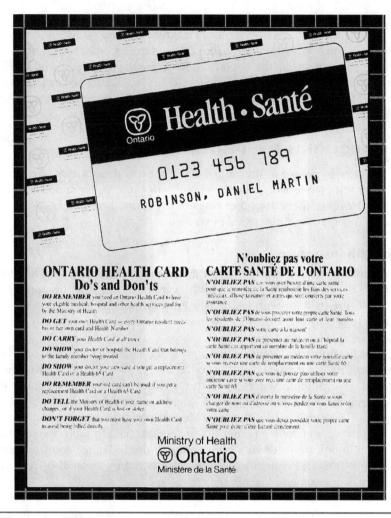

FIGURE 14.7
The United States health care system has often been compared to the Canadian health care system.

"Medicare," the system provides access to universal, comprehensive coverage for medically necessary hospital, inpatient, and outpatient physician services. Each provincial and territorial authority must ensure that all residents have access to care regardless of cost, that necessary hospital and physician services are available, that residents have continuous coverage as they travel from one province to another and abroad, and that the provincial programs are run as nonprofit organizations (see Box 14.4).[41]

Health care in Canada is financed through a combination of public funding coming from provincial, federal, and corporate taxes and private funds. With the collected tax dollars, the Canadian federal government provides block grants to the provinces and territories for the health and social programs; this is referred to as the Canada Health and Social Transfer. Some provinces and territories use ancillary funding methods to help support health care, including sales taxes, payroll levies, and lottery (also known as video gambling machines) proceeds, and two provinces (Alberta and British Columbia) utilize health care premiums to help cover costs. Thus, provinces can generate other revenue to help support health care, but they cannot impose user fees or extra billing without loss of federal support.[41]

| BOX 14.4 | THE PRINCIPLES OF THE CANADA HEALTH ACT |

The Canada Health Act (CHA) stipulates criteria and conditions related to insured health care services and extended health care services that the provinces and territories must meet in order to qualify for full federal transfer of payments under the Canada Health and Social Transfer (CHST). The principles of the CHA include the following:

Public administration: The administration and operation of the plans of provinces/territories must be carried out on a nonprofit basis by a public authority, which is responsible to the provincial/territorial government and subject to audits of their accounts and financial transactions.

Comprehensiveness: The plans of the provinces/territories must insure all medically necessary health services (hospital, physician, surgical-dental) and, where permitted, services rendered by other health care practitioners.

Universality: All insured residents in the province/territory must be entitled to public health insurance coverage on uniform terms and conditions. Provinces/territories usually require that residents register with the plans to establish entitlement.

Portability: Residents moving from one province/territory to another must continue to be covered for insured health services by the "home" province during a minimum waiting period, not to exceed three months, imposed by the new province/territory of residence. Residents temporarily absent from their home provinces/territories, or from the country, must also continue to be covered for insured health care services.

This principle does not entitle a resident to seek services in another province/territory or country, but is more intended to entitle one to receive necessary services in relation to an urgent or emergent need when absent on a temporary basis, such as on business or vacation. In some cases, coverage may be extended for elective (non-emergency) service in another province or territory, or out of the country. Prior approval may also be required.

Accessibility: Reasonable access by insured residents to medically necessary health services must be unimpeded by financial or other barriers, such as discrimination on the basis of age, health status, or financial circumstances. Reasonable access in terms of physical availability of medically necessary services has been interpreted under the CHA as access to insured services at the setting "where" the services are provided and "as" the services are available in that setting.

Sources: Health Canada (2002). *Canada's Health Care System at a Glance.* Available at http://www.hc-sc.gc.ca/english/media/releases/2002/health_act/glance.html; and Health Canada (2002). *Canada Health Act Overview.* Available at http://www.hc-sc.gc.ca/english/media/releases/2002/health_act/overview.htm.

As noted earlier, the Canadian health care system is not a national health service model of health care. It is a fee-for-service system whereby the government is the single third-party payer. Canadian residents get to select their physicians, who are independent physicians working for themselves—not the government. Providers must accept the provincial plan reimbursement as payment in full if the province is to receive the maximum federal support. In addition, there are no maximum limits on the amount of care provided as long as it is deemed medically necessary. Finally, Canada prohibits private health insurance except for items not covered under the provincial plan.[42]

Compared to the American health care system, the Canadian system has several major strengths. One is that "no Canadian is without health insurance. There is equity across income groups. The poor are treated as well as the rich."[43] Canadians regard health care as a basic right, and they value their health system highly. They identify strongly with their health system for several reasons. First, it exemplifies many of the shared values of their society. In addition to equity, it also exemplifies fairness, compassion, and respect for fundamental dignity of all.[41] Second, the administrative costs of the Canadian system are under control. The Canadian system is administered for about one-third the cost of the United States system.[44] Third, the Canadian system is less expensive to run overall. In 2000, the per capita expenditure on health care in Canada was $2,535 compared to $4,672 in the United States. These health care costs amount to 9.1% of the Canadian gross domestic product (GDP) versus 13.3%

in the United States.[3] The controls inherent in the single-payer (the government) approach to health care are recognized as a major contributor to Canada's recent cost containment success. Fourth, the Canadian system places emphasis on prevention and primary care. Though managed care has improved prevention and primary care in the United States for those with health insurance, it cannot match the prevention and primary care afforded through universal access to health care in Canada. One prime example of better prevention and primary care in Canada is the availability of prenatal care for all women (refer to Chapter 7). This is reflected in the lower infant mortality rate in Canada versus that of the United States.

Although the Canadian system sounds good, it is not without its disadvantages. The ever-increasing cost of health care, as in the United States, has also impacted the Canadian system. Therefore, the Canadian system has also been going through reform in an effort to become more efficient and cost-effective. Even with such change, the major complaint with the Canadian system remains the same: the long wait lists for procedures associated with the use of high-technology equipment and specialized physicians. The Canadian system does not limit care for life-threatening conditions but does have a tight supply for things such as scanners and magnetic resonance imaging (MRI) equipment. This tight supply has created waiting lists for certain types of care (procedures) in some provinces. Those critical of the Canadian system argue that the availability of innovative technologies conflicts with the quality-of-care concerns. Those Canadians who can afford it have gotten around this limitation by coming to the United States to get needed care.

Even with the many benefits of the Canadian system, the likelihood of a Canadian-type system in the United States is very small. The political and economic barriers are too great. Politically, there are too many people who benefit from not having such a program. Economically, it has been estimated that the implementation of a Canadian-type system in the United States would be prohibitive. In addition, due to the size of the United States, it would be difficult for the national government to be sensitive to regional and local differences and needs. As has been the case with the United States' Medicaid program, it is difficult to provide consistent and equitable administration of the program when the national government delegates authority to state or local agents.[4]

The Oregon Health Plan

Because of the slow pace at which the federal government undertook health care reform in the early 1990s, several states, including Florida, Hawaii, Minnesota, Oregon, and Vermont, passed major health care reform packages aimed at providing increased access to health insurance and basic health services to all or most of their residents. Of all of these reform movements, the one that attracted the most publicity was Oregon's health plan.

While the Canadian plan addresses access first and cost second, the Oregon plan addressed the problem of cost primarily, with the expected result of greater access. Oregon, like all other states, has a finite number of dollars to spend on health care and a significant number of people who lack access because, while they lack health insurance, they do not meet the eligibility for Medicaid, do not work for an employer who provides health insurance, or cannot afford it. Unlike other states, Oregon has attempted to come to grips with the question of whether to spend $250,000 dollars to try to save a prematurely born infant with little hope of a normal life or to spend the same amount to provide maternal and child health services for 400 families.

Beginning in 1989, several pieces of legislation were passed in the Oregon state legislature that set into motion a series of public and private health insurance reforms. Known as the Oregon Health Plan (OHP), these reforms had an initial goal of providing universal access to affordable, quality health care for all Oregonians. More specifically, the plan reformed Medicaid by extending eligibility to all residents with incomes under the federal poverty level, by

BOX 14.5	CATEGORIES OF SERVICES USED IN THE PRIORITIZATION PROCESS AND EXAMPLES OF CONDITION-TREATMENT (CT) PAIRS

Category	Description
"Essential" services	
1. Acute fatal	• Treatment prevents death with full recovery. Example: Appendectomy for appendicitis
2. Maternity care	• Maternity and most newborn care. Example: Obstetrical care for pregnancy
3. Acute fatal	• Treatment prevents death without full recovery. Example: Medical therapy for acute bacterial meningitis
4. Preventive care for children	• Example: Immunizations
5. Chronic fatal	• Treatment improves life span and quality of life. Example: Medical therapy for asthma
6. Reproductive services	• Excludes maternity/infertility services. Example: Contraceptive management
7. Comfort care	• Palliative therapy for conditions in which death is imminent. Example: Hospice care
8. Preventive dental care	• Adults and children Example: Cleaning and fluoride applications
9. Proven effective preventive care for adults	• Example: Mammograms
"Very important" services	
10. Acute nonfatal	• Treatment causes return to previous health state. Example: Medical therapy for vaginitis
11. Chronic nonfatal	• One-time treatment improves quality of life. Example: Hip replacement
12. Acute nonfatal	• Treatment without return to previous health state. Example: Arthroscopic repair of internal knee derangement
13. Chronic nonfatal	• Repetitive treatment improves quality of life. Example: Medical therapy for chronic sinusitis
Services that are "valuable to certain individuals"	
14. Acute nonfatal	• Treatment expedites recovery of self-limiting conditions. Example: Medical therapy for diaper rash
15. Infertility services	• Example: In-vitro fertilization
16. Less effective preventive care for adults	• Example: Screening of nonpregnant adults for diabetes
17. Fatal or nonfatal	• Treatment causes minimal or no improvement in quality of life. Example: Medical therapy for viral warts

Source: Oregon waiver application (August 1991). Congress of the United States, Office of Technology Assessment (May 1992). *Summary: Evaluation of the Oregon Medicaid Proposal* (pub. no. OTA-H-532). Washington, DC: U.S. Government Printing Office, 6.

providing options to small businesses (fewer than 25 employees) to offer health insurance to their employees, and by creating a high-risk insurance pool coordinated by state government. The cornerstone of the plan was the idea that benefit packages should be built on a list of health care services priorities. The initial list was comprised of 709 line items. Each line consisted of a health condition and its associated treatment. This list was created and prioritized by a state commission after 18 months of statewide hearings and community meetings featuring public input and expert testimony and a random-sample survey. The list was subdivided into 17 categories (priorities). Category 1 has the highest priority. Categories 1 to 9 are considered essential components, 10 to 13 very important, and 14 to 17 valuable to individuals but not certain to improve the health status of the population. It should be noted that the categories were not absolutely discrete. Some items conceptually belonged in one category but have special characteristics that led the commission to place them in another (see Box 14.5).

With the list in place, the state legislature then had to determine how many of the 709 services it could fund with the finite dollars available. They determined that there were enough state dollars available to fund items 1 through 587. Thus, items 588 to 709, or 121 services, would not be funded by state money.

Those who opposed this process did so primarily because they said it rationed health care: A person who needed a health service below item 587 on the list would not get it without being able to pay for it. Thus, the plan rationed care, as even the plan's developers will agree. However, the plan's proponents say that the previous system rationed care based on ability to pay; at least now it is rationed through a policy developed with input from those who help pay for and receive the care—the citizens of the state.

The reason the plan's development received so much publicity was that it needed federal approval. Because Medicaid is a jointly funded federal-state program, approval must be given by the federal Centers for Medicare and Medicaid Services to those states who in changing their program take away services once offered to Medicaid recipients. Obviously, some of the 121 services and procedures that were no longer offered were once available to those on Medicaid. Thus, the need for the waiver.

The waiver was not easily obtained. The state of Oregon applied for the waiver in 1991. This waiver was finally approved in 1993. By any measure, the OHP has been a success. The plan has made health coverage available to (1) almost everyone below the federal poverty level, (2) people who have been turned down or offered limited coverage by insurers because of health status, (3) employees of small businesses and their dependents, and (4) individuals ineligible for group coverage.

Yet even with the success, the Oregon officials still recognize there is work to be done. Some of the state's population remains uninsured, including a small number who are uninsured by choice—generally young, healthy, unmarried males. The state continues to look for ways to cover those people who are uninsured not by choice but because of circumstance. Also, because of the ever-changing technology and increasing cost of health care, the list of covered services needs to be revised periodically. As of April 2004, the list included 700 services, of which 549 were covered.[45]

Finally, when the initial development of the OHP began back in the late 1980s, fee-for-service was the predominant means of delivering care. As the plan evolved, so did managed care. The planners recognized the benefits of such changes and blended those into the plan. Today, most OHP Medicaid clients receive their care through prepaid health plans and a primary care practitioner who is a member of a plan. Others have a primary care case manager.

Health Care Reform in the United States

As has been pointed out throughout Chapters 13 and 14, the health care resources available in the United States are second to none. We have also identified some shortcomings associated with the delivery of health care in the United States, with the most obvious being the millions of people who are uninsured and thus unable to access an ongoing source of primary care. Some of the more current issues facing health care delivery in the United States include but are not limited to the following:

- The continuing cost of all areas of health care after a brief slowdown in the mid-1990s
- The continued health care disparities among minorities and low-income Americans
- The cost of prescription drugs and the fact that the same drugs are less expensive in Canada

- The high cost of malpractice insurance for health care providers, causing some to drop their specialties (e.g., obstetrics) or stop practicing altogether
- The number of medical errors that continue to occur
- The concerns over the privacy of medical information, especially with the use of computers
- The complexity of navigating the health care delivery system in general and managed care specifically
- The burden on the employer of providing health care insurance
- The ethical issues that arise with the use and availability of new knowledge (e.g., human genome) and technology (e.g., telemedicine)

With so many issues facing health care delivery, it is not a question of whether there will be health care reform but of when and in what form. At the heart of reform is access to care at an affordable price. In a series of recent reports, the Institute for Medicine (IOM) has put forth substantial and compelling evidence on the harmful effects of being uninsured.[46-51] The IOM has recommended five principles to assist policy makers as they consider health insurance reform.[51] The principles are supported by clinical, epidemiological, and economic research. The principles are as follows:

1. "Health care coverage should be *universal.*" That is, everyone in the United States should have health insurance. The IOM is not alone regarding this principle—support for a universal system is coming from others, too. The Democratic party, with its most vocal voice being Senator Edward Kennedy, has long pushed for such a program. And in 2003, 62% of Americans said that they preferred a universal system that would provide coverage to everyone under a government program, as opposed to the current employer-based program.[34] However, that support dropped significantly if the universal system would mean a limited choice of doctors or longer waits for nonemergency treatment.[35]
2. "Health care coverage should be *continuous.*" That is, there should never be gaps in coverage, such as when changing employers or when adult children are no longer covered on their parents' policy. Continuous care leads to improved health.
3. "Health care coverage should be *affordable to individuals and families.*" The primary reason given by those who are uninsured for being uninsured is the cost. In fact, six in ten people surveyed in a recent poll say they are worried about being able to afford health insurance in the future.[35]
4. "The health insurance strategy should be *affordable and sustainable for society.*" How much are people willing to spend on health care? It was reported earlier that the United States spends more per capita ($5,444 in 2002),[35] more total money ($1.553 trillion in 2002),[35] and more of its gross domestic product (14.9% in 2002)[35] on health care than any other country in the world. Is society willing to spend more?
5. "Health insurance should *enhance health and well-being* by promoting access to high-quality care that is effective, efficient, safe, timely, patient-centered, and equitable." In other words, the reform of health care should result in very good health care that is as free as possible from errors, without disparities among groups, and is responsive to the ones being served.

Finally, the IOM's Committee on the Consequences of Uninsurance "calls on the federal government to take action to achieve universal health insurance and to establish an explicit schedule to reach this goal by 2010."[51] Watching health care reform in the United States should be interesting!

Chapter Summary

- The major issues of concern with the health care system in the United States can be summed up by the cost containment, access, and quality triangle.

- Some of the barriers to access to health care in the United States are the lack of health insurance, inadequate insurance, and poverty.

- The two major means by which health care is delivered in the United States are fee-for-service and prepaid health plans.

- Most health care in the United States is paid for via third-party payment.

- State Children's Health Insurance Program (SCHIP) is for many children who were previously uninsured.

- Key health insurance terms include *deductible, co-insurance, co-payment, fixed indemnity, exclusion,* and *pre-existing condition.*

- The two largest government-administered health insurance programs in the United States are Medicare and Medicaid.

- Two major supplemental insurance programs in the United States are Medigap and long-term care insurance.

- A majority of Americans today are covered by some form of managed care.

- The more common forms of managed care include health maintenance organizations (HMOs), preferred provider organizations (PPOs), exclusive provider organizations (EPOs), point-of-service (POS) options, and physician-hospital organizations (PHOs).

- The United States is the only developed country in the world without national health insurance.

- Two alternative ways to provide health care are offered by Canada and the state of Oregon.

- Health care reform must take place in the United States.

Review Questions

1. What are three major problems facing the health care system in the United States?

2. Explain the terms *fee-for-service* and *prepaid health care.*

3. Upon what basic concept is insurance based?

4. What is a State Children's Health Insurance Program (SCHIP)?

5. Explain the following insurance policy provisions: (a) a $200 deductible, (b) 20/80 co-insurance, (c) a $4,500 fixed indemnity for a basic surgical procedure, (d) an exclusion of the pre-existing condition of lung cancer, and (e) a $10 co-payment.

6. What is the difference between Medicare and Medicaid? What relationship does Medigap insurance have to Medicare?

7. Briefly explain the differences among health maintenance organizations (HMOs), preferred provider organizations (PPOs), and exclusive provider organizations (EPOs).

8. Why might a company want to enter into an agreement with a preferred provider organization?

9. Distinguish between the following two main models of health maintenance organizations—staff (group) and independent practice association.

10. What are the point-of-service option and physician-hospital organizations? Medicare Advantage?

11. What are the advantages and disadvantages of managed care?

12. In what ways is the American health care system better than the Canadian system? In what ways is the Canadian system better than that of the United States?

13. Why was the Oregon Health Plan (OHP) considered to be so innovative?

14. Should the United States have universal health insurance?

Activities

1. Obtain a copy of the student health insurance policy available at your school. After reading the policy, summarize in writing what you have read. In your summary, indicate whether it is a fee-for-service or managed care plan, provide the premium costs, and list specifics about the deductible, co-insurance, co-payment, fixed indemnity, and any exclusions.

2. Contact the office in your community that handles the Medicaid insurance program. Find out who is qualified for coverage in your state and the process that one must go through to get registered for such coverage. Also, ask about whom to see if your state has a SCHIP, and if so who qualifies for it.

3. Visit an HMO in your area and find the answers to the following: (a) What type of HMO is it? (b) How does one enroll? (c) What does it cost? (d) What services are provided? and (e) Why should someone get his or her health care from an HMO instead of the more traditional private-practice physician?

4. Write a two-page position paper on one of the following topics: (a) The United States federal government should provide universal health insurance, (b) Health care is a right, or (c) Health care is a privilege.

SCENARIO: ANALYSIS AND RESPONSE

1. Reread the scenario. In your opinion, did Greg make the right decision in taking his son Zack to the emergency room? Why or why not?

2. What other actions could Greg have taken? What would you have done?

3. What impact do you think a zero deductible health insurance policy has on the health care system? What do you see as the advantages and disadvantages of such a policy? Explain your answer.

4. Do you think all people in the United States should have zero deductible health insurance? Why or why not?

5. How does managed care impact the type of behavior exhibited by Greg?

6. If we had national health insurance, how would this scenario differ?

7. Under the Oregon Health Plan (OHP), how would this scenario differ?

 ## COMMUNITY HEALTH ON THE WEB

The Internet contains a wealth of information about community and public health. Increase your knowledge of some of the topics presented in this chapter by accessing the Jones and Bartlett Publishers Web site at **health.jbpub.com/communityhealth/5e** and follow the links to complete the following Web activities.

- Medicare and Medicaid
- Canadian Health Care System
- AARP

REFERENCES

1. Kissick, W. L. (1994). *Medicine's Dilemmas: Infinite Needs Versus Finite Resources.* New Haven, CT: Yale University Press.

2. Institute of Medicine (2004). *Insuring America's Health: Principles and Recommendations.* Available at http://www.iom.edu/Object.File/Master/17/732/0.pdf.

3. Freid, V. M., K. Prager, A. P. MacKay, and H. Xia (2003). *Health, United States, 2003, with Chartbook on Trends in Health of Americans.* Hyattsville, MD: National Center for Health Statistics.

4. Butler, P. A. (1988). *Too Poor to Be Sick: Access to Medical Care for the Uninsured.* Washington, DC: American Public Health Association.

5. Institute of Medicine (2002). *Care Without Coverage: Too Little, Too Late.* Washington, DC: National Academies Press.

6. Clark, N. (2002). *A Letter from the Dean: Spring/Summer 2002.* Ann Arbor, MI: University of Michigan, School of Public Health.

7. U.S. Bureau of Census (2003). *Statistical Abstract of the U.S., 2003,* 123rd ed. Washington, DC: Author.

8. Centers for Disease Control and Prevention (1995). "Prevention and Managed Care: Opportunities for Managed Care Organizations, Purchasers of Health Care, and Public Health Agencies." *MMWR,* 44(RR-14): 1–12.

9. Donaldson, M., K. D. Yordy, K. N. Lohr, and N. A. Vanselow, eds. (1996). *Primary Care: America's Health in a New Era.* Washington, DC: National Academy Press.

10. U.S. Department of Health and Human Services (2000). *Healthy People 2010: Understanding and Improving Health,* 2 vols. Sudbury, MA: Jones and Bartlett Publishers.

11. Rowland, D., J. Feder, and P. Keenan (1998). "Uninsured in America: The Causes and Consequences." In S. H. Alterman, U. Reinhardt, and A. E. Shields, eds., *The Future U.S. Health Care System: Who Will Care for the Poor and Uninsured?* Chicago: Health Administration Press.

12. Dorn, S., M. Teitelbaum, and C. Cortez (1998). *An Advocate's Tool Kit for the State Children's Health Insurance Program.* Washington, DC: Children's Defense Fund.

13. Rosenbaum, S., K. Johnson, C. Sonosky, A. Markus, and C. DeGraw (1998). "The Children's Hour: The State Children's Health Insurance Program." *Health Affairs,* 17(1): 75–89.

14. U.S. Department of Health and Human Services (2003). "SCHIP Enrollment Numbers [Press release]." Washington, DC: Author.

15. Blumberg, S. J., L. Osborn, J. V. Luke, L. Olson, and M. R. Frankel (2004). *Estimating the Prevalence of Uninsured Children: An Evaluation of Data from the National Survey of Children with Special Health Care Needs, 2001.* Hyattsville, MD: National Center for Health Statistics.

16. Agency for Health Care Policy and Research (1997). *Choosing and Using a Health Plan* (AHCPR pub. no. 97-0071). Rockville, MD: Author.

17. Timmreck, T. C. (1997). *Health Services Cyclopedic Dictionary,* 3rd ed. Sudbury, MA: Jones and Bartlett Publishers.

18. The President's Advisory Commission on Consumer Protection and Quality in the Health Care Industry (1998). *Quality First: Better Health Care for All Americans.* Washington, DC: U.S. Government Printing Office.

19. Levit, K. R., H. C. Lazenby, B. R. Braden, and the National Health Accounts Team (1998). "National Health Spending Trends in 1996." *Health Affairs,* 17(1): 35–51.

20. Max, S. (2003). "Health Costs Skyrocket." Available at http://money.cnn.com/2003/09/09/pf/insurance/employerhealthplans/index.htm.

21. Brink, S. (9 March 1998). "HMOs Were the Right Rx." *U.S. News & World Report.*

22. Sultz, H. A., and K. M. Young (2004). *Health Care USA: Understanding Its Organization and Delivery,* 4th ed. Sudbury, MA: Jones and Bartlett Publishers.

23. Centers for Medicare and Medicaid Services (2004). *Medicare.* Available at http://www.medicare.gov.

24. U.S. Department of Health and Human Services (1989). *Your Hospital Stay Under Medicare's Prospective Payment System* (HHS pub. no. HCFA 02163). Washington, DC: U.S. Government Printing Office.

25. Centers for Medicare and Medicaid Services (2003). *Medicare Policies: The Basics.* Baltimore, MD: Author.

26. AARP (2004). *AARP Health Care Options*. Available at http://www. aarphealthcare.com/default.aspx.

27. Institute of Medicine (1997). *Managing Managed Care: Quality Improvement in Behavioral Health*. Washington, DC: National Academy Press.

28. Halverson, P. K., A. D. Kaluzny, C. P. McLaughlin, et al., eds. (1998). *Managed Care and Public Health*. Gaithersburg, MD: Aspen Publishers.

29. Brook, R. H., C. J. Kamberg, and E. A. McGlynn (1997). "Health System Reform in Quality." In P. R. Lee and C. L. Estes, eds., *The Nation's Health*, 5th ed. Sudbury, MA: Jones and Bartlett Publishers.

30. Shi, L., and D. A. Singh (2004). *Delivering Health Care in America: A Systems Approach*, 3rd ed. Sudbury, MA: Jones and Bartlett Publishers.

31. Managed Care On Line (2004). *Managed Care Fact Sheets*. Available at http://www.mcareol.com.

32. Kaiser Family Foundation (2004). *Trends and Indications in Changing Health Care Marketplace: 2004 Update*. Available at http://www.kff.org/insurance.

33. Wager, E. R. (1995). "Type of Managed Care Organizations." In P. R. Kongstvedt, ed., *Essentials of Managed Care*. Gaithersburg, MD: Aspen Publishers, 24–34.

34. Zatkin, S. (1997). "A Health Plan's View of Government Regulation." *Health Affairs*, 16(6): 33–35.

35. Associated Press (2003). "ABC News-Washington Post Poll: Public Supports Health Care for All." Available at http://www.commondreams. org?headlines03/1019-10.htm.

36. Jenkins, K. Jr (1 December 1997). "Health Care Politics: The Sequel." *U.S. News & World Report*.

37. Dickerson, J. R. (8 December 1997). "Dr. Clinton Scrubs Up." *Time*, 48.

38. National Committee for Quality Assurance (2004). *NCQA: Measuring the Quality of America's Health Care*. Available at http://www.ncqa.org.

39. Ginzberg, E. (1990). *The Medical Triangle: Physicians, Politicians, and the Public*. Cambridge, MA: Howard University Press.

40. Vermont Department of Health (2000). *Healthy Vermonters 2010*. Available at http://www.healthyvermonters.info/admin/pubs/hv2010/ pdf/hv2010.pdf.

41. Health Canada (2004). *Health Canada: Keeping You Informed*. Available at http://www.hc-sc.gc.ca/english/index.html.

42. U.S. General Accounting Office (1991). *Canadian Health Insurance: Lessons for the United States* (pub. no. GAO/HRD-91-90). Washington, DC: Author.

43. Holahan, J., M. Moon, W. P. Welch, and S. Zuckerman (1991). "An American Approach to Health System Reform." *Journal of the American Medical Association*, 265(19): 2537–2540.

44. Dingwall, D. C. (1997). *Building a Better Health System for Canadians*. Available at http://www.hc-sc.gc.ca/english/index.html.

45. Oregon Department of Human Services (2004). *Oregon Health Plan: An Overview*. Available at http://www.dhs.state.or.us/ healthplan/.

46. Institute of Medicine (2001). *Coverage Matters: Insurance and Health Care*. Washington, DC: National Academy Press.

47. Institute of Medicine (2002). *Care Without Coverage: Too Little, Too Late*. Washington, DC: National Academy Press.

48. Institute of Medicine (2002). *Health Insurance Is a Family Matter*. Washington, DC: National Academy Press.

49. Institute of Medicine (2003). *A Shared Destiny: Community Effects of Uninsurance*. Washington, DC: National Academy Press.

50. Institute of Medicine (2003). *Hidden Cost, Values Lost: Uninsurance in America*. Washington, DC: National Academy Press.

51. Institute of Medicine (2004). *Insuring America's Health: Principles and Recommendations*. Washington, DC: National Academy Press.

UNIT
FOUR

ENVIRONMENTAL HEALTH AND SAFETY

Chapter 15

Environmental Concerns: Wastes and Pollution

Chapter Outline

Chapter Objectives

After studying this chapter you will be able to:

1 Define the terms *environment, ecology,* and *biosphere*.

2 Explain how human activities affect the environment through the production of wastes and residues.

3 Name the primary sources of solid waste.

4 List and briefly explain the four approaches to solid waste management.

5 Define hazardous waste.

6 Explain the difference between sanitary and secured landfills.

7 Identify five approaches to hazardous waste management.

8 Explain what is meant by the term *Superfund*.

9 Explain the Pollutant Standard Index (PSI).

10 Briefly describe acid rain, ozone layer, global warming, and photochemical smog.

11 Identify the major indoor air pollutants.

12 Explain the difference in point source and nonpoint source pollution.

13 Identify the different types of water pollutants.

14 Briefly describe the purpose of wastewater treatment.

15 Identify and describe two important pieces of federal legislation that protect our Nation's water.

16 Name the primary sources of radiation.

17 Identify the pros and cons of nuclear power.

18 Explain the difference between sound and noise.

19 Identify approaches to reduce problems associated with noise pollution.

SCENARIO

Tom and Mary recently accepted jobs as teachers in the Blackford School Corporation. When they moved to the Blackford community, they purchased a modest home on five acres of land outside the city. They had only been living in their new home two months when they noticed that their water was beginning to taste "different." The source of their water was a well on their own property. A testing of the water by the local health department sanitarian revealed that their water was contaminated with lead and perhaps other chemicals. The sanitarian recommended that Tom and Mary drink bottled water until the well water could be tested further. After some investigation, county officials determined that Mary and Tom's 15-year-old home had been built close to a former landfill that had been closed about 20 years earlier. Tom and Mary were now faced with an expensive, unforeseen, and long-term problem, not to mention the devaluation of their property.

INTRODUCTION

As human beings, we are a part of the environment in which we live. Our lives and health are affected by the quality of our environment, and the way we live our lives influences the quality of that environment. In this chapter, we explain in detail and illustrate with examples the ways in which our interactions with the environment have direct consequences for the quality of our lives. While this chapter seeks to describe and define wastes and pollution, Chapter 16 examines more specifically the health consequences of these environmental hazards.

The **environment** is defined as all the external conditions, circumstances, and influences surrounding and affecting the growth and development of an organism or a community of organisms. In order to fully understand environmental concerns that threaten our health, we must understand how we interact with our environment. The study of how living things interact with each other and their environment is called **ecology,** and the zone of the earth where life is found is known as the **biosphere.**

environment
all the external conditions, circumstances, and influences surrounding and affecting the growth and development of an organism or community of organisms

ecology
the interrelationship between organisms and their environment

biosphere
the zone of the earth where life is found

natural hazards
conditions of nature that increase the probability of disease, injury, or death of humans

NATURAL ENVIRONMENTAL HAZARDS

While the purpose of this chapter is to point out environmental hazards associated with human activities, it is important to recognize the existence and influence of **natural hazards** in the environment that damage or destroy wildlife habitats, kill or harm humans, and damage property. These hazards may be physical, biological, chemical, psychological, or social in nature. Physical hazards are caused by forces either internal to the earth's surface or on the surface itself. Natural hazards resulting from internal forces include earthquakes and volcanoes. Those on the surface include winds, lightning, storms, floods, fires, and droughts.

Biological hazards for humans are, for the most part, limited to microbiological agents such as pathogenic bacteria, parasites and viruses, and their toxic biological products. Examples include malaria, plague, tuberculosis, and human immunodeficiency virus (HIV). Examples of biological toxins include the toxin produced by tetanus bacteria, poisons produced by certain mushrooms, and the poisoning of marine life by "red tides." Biological hazards and their resulting epidemics were the topic of Chapter 4 and will not be discussed here. Chemical hazards are nonbiological substances that are toxic enough to threaten human health.

Psychological hazards affect a person's outlook on life. Psychological hazards are just as real and damaging to health as physical hazards. Boredom, stress, fear, and depression represent psychological hazards that consume significant health care dollars. A workplace can be most unproductive if the workers are highly stressed, bored, or depressed. The fear of losing a job and other economic factors can also weigh heavily on members of a community. Acts of terrorism, such as the September 11, 2001, attacks on the World Trade Center and the Pentagon, are a psychological hazard because they increase the probability of mental health problems among the survivors.

Sociological hazards occur when societies interact in destructive ways or fail to interact in productive ways. Excessive population growth that results in overcrowding and war are sociological hazards. Many would say Adolph Hitler, the German dictator before and during World War II, was a sociological hazard, because he caused a great loss of human life.

RESIDUES AND WASTES FROM HUMAN ACTIVITIES

More than any other species on our planet, humans have the power to significantly alter the environment through individual and community activities. These activities include working, traveling, leisure-time activities, and simply living at home. Likewise, environmental conditions such as weather, climate, and topography affect human activities. As people participate in their daily activities, they continually produce **residues and wastes.** On any typical day, a person in the United States might generate the following types of residues and wastes:

residues and wastes
unwanted by-products of human activities

1. Human body wastes: urine and feces (wastewater)
2. Excess materials and foods: trash and garbage
3. Yard wastes: grass clippings and tree branches
4. Construction and manufacturing wastes: scrap wood and metal, contaminated water, solvents, excess heat, and noise
5. Agricultural wastes: animal dung, run-off from feedlot operations, crop residues, and animal carcasses
6. Transportation wastes: carbon monoxide, gaseous pollutants, and used motor oil
7. Energy production wastes: mining wastes, electrical power (combustion of coal) wastes, and nuclear power (radioactive) wastes
8. Defense wastes: weapons production (radioactive) wastes

A healthy environment, one relatively free of pollution, supports healthy communities (see Figure 15.1). Residues and wastes from human activities can adversely affect the environment by damaging wildlife habitats, undermining food production, contaminating sources of water, altering climate, and threatening human health.

Factors contributing to an ever-increasing number of environmental hazards are (1) urbanization, (2) industrialization, (3) human population growth, and (4) the production and use of disposable products and containers. **Urbanization,** the process in which people come together to live in cities, often results in people living in overcrowded conditions and inadequate space for the proper disposal of wastes, making waste management more difficult (see Figure 15.2). Concomitant industrialization, resulting in the generation of new types of wastes, has complicated the waste disposal problem because of the generation of hazardous waste.

urbanization
the process by which people come together to live in cities

Population growth has also contributed to the overall waste disposal problem, as has the reliance on disposable containers. Not only are there more people than there were 30 years ago, but the amount of refuse generated by each person in the twenty-first century is much greater than it was in the 1960s, when reusable containers began to be replaced by throw-away containers (see Table 15.1).

While it is unrealistic to expect communities to produce a pollution-free environment, it is possible to work toward minimizing the level of pollution. As the dominant species on this planet, our very survival depends upon our recognition of the deleterious effects our activities have on the rest of the biosphere and our taking responsibility (individually and collectively) for minimizing these effects. If the environment is to remain relatively stable, the

FIGURE 15.1
A healthy environment supports a healthy community.

FIGURE 15.2
Urbanization has led to overcrowding and pollution.

Table 15.1
Reusable versus Throwaway Consumer Goods

Reusable Goods	Throwaway Goods
Milk bottles	Cardboard cartons and plastic jugs
Returnable soft drink bottles	Aluminum cans and plastic bottles
Cloth diapers	Disposable diapers
Garbage cans	Trash bags
Lunch boxes	Paper bags
Cloth napkins	Paper napkins
Refillable pens	Disposable pens
Handkerchiefs	Facial tissues
Cloth towels or rags	Paper towels
Ceramic or plastic dishes	Paper plates

frequency and severity of environmental hazards stemming from human activities must be reduced.

TYPES OF WASTES AND POLLUTION

The types of wastes and pollution we discuss include solid wastes, hazardous wastes, air pollution, water pollution, radiation, and noise pollution. While some types of wastes may merely lower the aesthetic value of the environment, others constitute either an immediate or long-term threat to human health and well-being.

Solid Waste

Household trash, grass clippings, tree trimmings, manure, excess stone generated from mining, and steel scraps from automobile plants are all examples of **solid waste.** With only 4.6% of the world's population, the United States produces 33% of the world's solid waste.[1] This solid waste production has led to a major community problem—where to store it. Many communities have used up all available space to bury their solid waste and must look for a neighboring community willing to accept it (see Figure 15.3).

solid waste
solid refuse from households, agriculture, and businesses

Sources of Solid Waste
Most solid waste can be traced to four major sources: mining and gas and oil production; agriculture; industry; and municipalities (domestic sources) (see Figure 15.4). By far, mining and gas and oil production generate the greatest volume of solid waste, 75% of the total. Agricultural wastes, including crop residues, manure, and other vegetation trimmings, make up the next largest portion of solid waste (13%).[1]

The solid waste resulting from industrial production is quite varied and constitutes 9.5% of the total. Examples include paper, wood chips, and highly complex chemicals. Certain industrial waste products are especially hazardous because of their toxicity, corrosiveness, or flammability.

Household or municipal waste makes up just 2.5% of all solid waste generated each year. It includes wastes generated by individual households, businesses, and institutions located within municipalities. This waste is known as **municipal solid waste (MSW).** In 2001 we were generating MSW at a rate of 4.4 pounds per person per day, a significant increase from the 2.7 pounds of MSW generated per day in 1960 (see Figure 15.5).[2] While it makes up only 2.5% of the total volume, municipal solid waste receives considerable attention because it is visible, malodorous, and considered a threat to human health if not disposed of properly.

municipal solid waste (MSW)
waste generated by individual households, businesses, and institutions located within municipalities

FIGURE 15.3

Solid waste is becoming such a problem in some areas that it is shipped elsewhere.

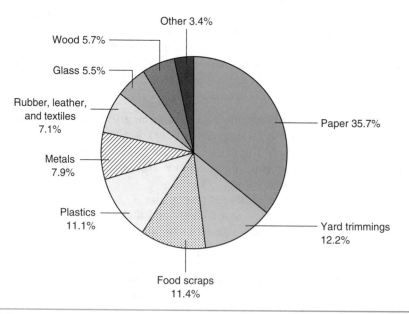

FIGURE 15.4

Types and percentages of municipal solid waste (before recycling). This pie chart depicts the percentage by which different materials contributed to the municipal solid waste stream in 2001.

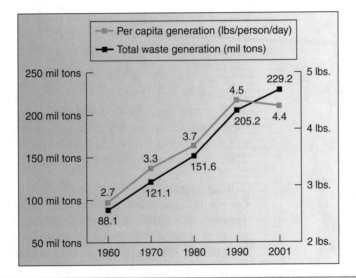

FIGURE 15.5

Trends in generation of municipal solid waste, 1960 to 2001. This line graph indicates the rate by which per capita generation of waste (in pounds per person per day) and total waste generation (in millions of tons) has increased from 1960 to 2001. In 1960, the per capita generation of waste was 2.7 pounds per person per day, and total waste generation was 88.1 million tons. In 1970, the per capita generation of waste was 3.3 pounds per person per day, and total waste generation was 121.1 million tons. In 1980, the per capita generation of waste was 3.7 pounds per person per day, and total waste generation was 151.6 million tons. In 1990, the per capita generation of waste was 4.5 pounds per person per day, and total waste generation was 205.2 million tons. In 2001, the per capita generation of waste was 4.4 pounds per person per day, and total waste generation was 229.2 million tons.

The heterogeneous makeup of MSW precludes efficient disposal. There are nine major categories—paper, yard waste, food scraps, rubber and textiles, wood, metal, glass, plastics, and other (see Figure 15.4).[2] Forty years ago, food wastes were the primary component in municipal solid waste, but garbage disposals in homes and the preprocessing of foods have reduced that greatly. Today, paper and paper products make up 35.7% of the total. Much of it is packaging. The last and smallest source of solid waste is utilities. The primary solid waste of utilities is cinders from the burning of coal.

Solid Waste Management

Strictly defined, **solid waste management** is the collection, transportation, and disposal of solid waste. A broader definition of solid waste management also includes source-reduction efforts that limit the production of solid waste in the first place. Though the preponderance of solid waste is created by agriculture and mining, the following discussion of solid waste management is aimed primarily at municipal and industrial wastes, which create greater environmental problems. The handling of municipal solid waste can be divided into two steps— collection and disposal.

solid waste management
the collection, transportation, and disposal of solid waste

Collection

Approximately 80% of the money spent on waste management is spent on the collection process. Faced with ever-increasing amounts of waste, greater efficiency is needed in collecting the wastes so that more money can be spent on environmentally sound disposal. Traditionally, crews of three people and a large truck have collected municipal wastes at the curb or alley. However, experience has shown that crew size, truck size, and special-feature trucks—like those that can be operated by a single person or those with different storage compartments for separating the trash—can improve efficiency and reduce cost (see Figure 15.6). Moreover, the

FIGURE 15.6
Household waste picked up at the curbside with a segregated-container recycling truck.

collecting and transporting of trash through pipelines hydraulically and/or pneumatically (the method used at Disney World) can make collection even more efficient and out of sight.

Disposal

To meet the need for better disposal of solid waste, communities have adopted a variety of approaches, including (1) sanitary landfills, (2) combustion (incineration), (3) recycling, and (4) source reduction.

Sanitary Landfills

Currently, most municipalities dispose of their wastes in **sanitary landfills,** sites judged suitable for inground disposal of solid waste. However, many of these municipal landfills are filling up, and the availability of land suitable for new landfill sites near cities is quickly disappearing. Disposal of municipal solid waste on unsuitable land can result in the contamination of groundwater (water found in the ground), which may be the community's only source of drinking water.

The passage of the **Resource Conservation and Recovery Act of 1976 (RCRA,** pronounced Rick-Rah) provided legislation that phased out open dumps and replaced them with sanitary landfills.[3] Only state-of-the-art landfills have been permitted to operate since 1997.[1] These are to be located at sites that can geographically and geologically support them—sites with natural clay soils. If clay soil cannot be found, a clay lining must be constructed to prevent **leachates,** liquids created when water mixes with wastes and removes soluble constituents from them by percolation, from reaching groundwater. Sanitary landfills are not to be located over sand or gravel deposits that would allow leachates to reach groundwater. In sanitary landfills, all refuse is spread and compacted in thin layers by bulldozers. At the end of each day, unlike an open dump, refuse is covered with a layer of soil. This process continues until the landfill is full, at which time a final layer of soil about two feet thick is placed on the top (see Figure 15.7). When this process is strictly followed, sanitary landfills provide little refuge for rodents and insects, and there is no reason why the area cannot be used for recreation.

Sanitary landfills are still not without problems. The production of leachates and contamination of groundwater can still occur if the clay seal breaks or if the landfill is located improperly. Contaminated groundwater has been detected at 86% of older landfills.[1] Some local governments have enacted legislation that requires sanitary landfills to be lined or double-lined with plastic liners. Another concern is the possibility of explosions and fires caused by the accumulation of dangerous amounts of methane gas created by the anaerobic decomposition of refuse. However, it should be noted that some communities have systems in place to harness the methane gas and use it as an energy source.

Today, about 56% of all municipal waste goes into landfills. However, the number of existing landfills in the United States declined from approximately 8,000 in 1988 to fewer than 1,858 in 2001.[2] There are even fewer today. This means that (1) it will be more costly to use existing landfills in the future because of supply and demand, (2) new sites for landfills will be needed, and (3) an alternative means of waste disposal must be developed.

sanitary landfills
waste disposal sites on land suited for this purpose and upon which waste is spread in thin layers, compacted, and covered with a fresh layer of clay or plastic foam each day

Resource Conservation and Recovery Act of 1976 (RCRA)
the federal law that sets forth guidelines for the proper handling and disposal of hazardous wastes

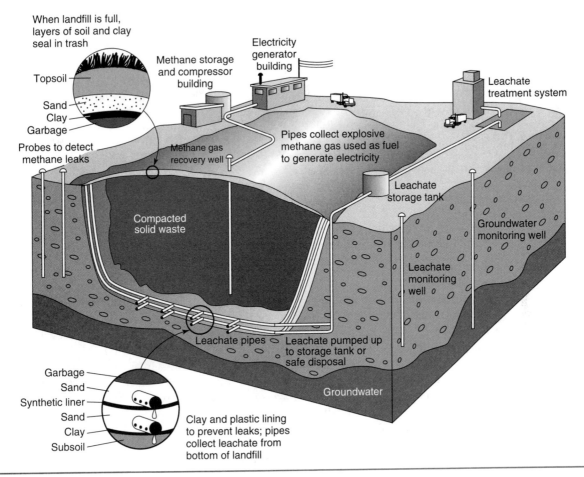

FIGURE 15.7

A state-of-the-art sanitary landfill.

Source: Miller, G.T. (2002). *Living in the Environment: Principles, Connections, and Solutions* (with InfoTrac), 12th ed. Pacific Grove, CA: Brooks/Cole, Thomson Learning. Reprinted with permission of Brooks/Cole, a division of Thomson Learning: www.thomsonrights.com.

Combustion (Incineration)

Combustion (incineration), or the burning of wastes, is the second major method of refuse disposal. The passage of the Clean Air Act of 1970 severely restricted the rights of individuals and municipalities to burn refuse because most could not comply with the strict emission standards. Today only about 15% of all municipal waste is combusted. In 2001, 97 of the nearly 200 municipal combustors were energy recovery plants.[2] That is, they are able to convert some of the heat generated from the incineration process into steam and electricity.

Incineration greatly reduces the weight and volume of solid waste. Generally, volume is reduced by as much as 90%, and weight is reduced by as much as 75%. While incineration might seem to be the ultimate solution to the solid waste disposal problem, it is not without its serious drawbacks. First of all, large commercial incinerators are expensive. Start-up costs can approach a quarter of a billion dollars. Some environmentalists feel that there are too many unanswered questions about incinerators to invest that type of money. One of their questions is about air quality. While most modern incinerators use filters to reduce harmful emissions, they do not eliminate them entirely. A second environmental concern has to do with the remaining ash. The ash may be toxic, particularly when plastics have been incinerated, which occurs with increasing frequency. A third concern is that at least 10% of the volume (25% of the weight) of the original

leachates
liquids created when water mixes with wastes and removes soluble constituents from them by percolation

combustion (incineration)
the burning of solid wastes

wastes remains to be dealt with. Most of this ash enters landfills, but because of its toxicity poses a threat to local groundwater. Also, it now appears that future restrictions on items placed in landfills may prohibit the disposal of this ash.

Recycling

recycling
the collection and reprocessing of a resource after use so it can be reused for the same or another purpose

Recycling is the collection and reprocessing of a resource so that it can be reused for the same or another purpose. This process conserves resources, energy, and sanitary landfill space. Although recycling makes good sense, only 28% to 30% of all MSW is recycled in this country. While this is twice the percentage of just 15 years ago, it is far below the recycling rate of Japan, which recycles approximately 50% of its MSW.[2-4] In an effort to encourage recycling, the federal government has set a goal of recycling 35% of MSW by 2005 and 38% by 2010 (see Box 15.1).[5] Several states have set higher standards for themselves.[3] In 2001, the United States recycled roughly 93.5% of auto batteries, 58.1% of steel cans, 56.5% of yard trimmings, 49.0% of aluminum cans, 45.4% of paper and paperboard, 35.6% of plastic soft drink containers, 21.2% of glass containers, and 38.6% of tires.[4]

composting
the natural, aerobic biodegradation of organic plant and animal matter to compost

One form of recycling, **composting,** can be done at home, since it doesn't require special knowledge or equipment. In composting, yard waste is recycled through a natural process of aerobic biodegradation during which microorganisms convert organic plant and animal matter into compost that can be used as a mulch or fertilizer. Composting can be done by individuals or on a community-wide basis. Because yard wastes make up a significant percentage (12.2%) of MSW going to municipal landfills, many municipalities now strongly encourage composting. As mentioned previously, Americans currently compost about 56.5% of yard trimmings.[4]

Source Reduction

source reduction
a waste management approach involving the reduction or elimination of the use of materials that produce an accumulation of solid waste

The ultimate approach to solid waste reduction is to limit its creation in the first place through **source reduction.** This can be achieved by avoiding the use of non-reusable products, such as paper towels and disposable diapers, and by reducing the amount of packaging associated with groceries and carryout foods such as hamburgers and pizzas.

Solid waste management has come a long way in the past 30 years. Today, most people know what is and what is not environmentally sound waste management, and the necessary technology to ensure appropriate disposal of waste is available. One question still remains: When will protecting the environment become a high enough priority for most Americans to act and insist upon wise waste management? Tips for more environmentally sound behaviors are plentiful (see Box 15.2).

Hazardous Waste

The RCRA of 1976, mentioned previously, was the first comprehensive law to address the collection and disposal of wastes. This law, and its 1984 amendments, provides for

---

BOX 15.2

TIPS FOR REDUCING SOLID WASTE

Reduce

1. Reduce the amount of unnecessary packaging.
2. Adopt practices that reduce waste toxicity.

Reuse

3. Consider reusable products.
4. Maintain and repair durable products.
5. Reuse bags, containers, and other items.
6. Borrow, rent, or share items used infrequently.
7. Sell or donate goods instead of throwing them out.

Recycle

8. Choose recyclable products and containers and recycle them.

9. Select products made from recycled materials.
10. Compost yard trimmings and some food scraps.

Respond

11. Educate others on source reduction and recycling practices. Make your preferences known to manufacturers, merchants, and community leaders.
12. Be creative—find new ways to reduce waste quantity and toxicity.

Source: U.S. Environmental Protection Agency (1998). *The Consumer's Handbook for Reducing Solid Waste.* Available at http://www.epa.gov/epaanswer/non-hw/reduce/catbook.the12/htm.

"cradle-to-grave" regulation of solid **hazardous wastes,** wastes that are dangerous to human health or the environment. According to this act:

> the term "hazardous waste" means a solid waste, or combination of solid wastes, which, because of its quantity, concentration, or physical, chemical, or infectious characteristics may (1) cause or significantly contribute to an increase in mortality or an increase in serious irreversible, or incapacitating reversible, illness; or (2) pose a substantial present or potential hazard to human health or the environment when improperly treated, stored, transported, or disposed of, or otherwise managed.

It is the responsibility of the **Environmental Protection Agency (EPA)** to implement the legislation created by the RCRA. There are now more than 400 substances that are considered hazardous wastes in the United States. The EPA list includes neither radioactive wastes, which are controlled by the Nuclear Regulatory Commission, nor biomedical wastes, which are regulated by the individual states.

Today, Americans are faced with the dual problem of appropriately disposing of new hazardous waste while working to correct the errors of mishandling of hazardous waste in the past. There are untold numbers of hazardous waste sites that are "polluted" from past actions—legal and illegal—that must be cleaned up. Meanwhile, the production of hazardous wastes continues at a record pace. The United States alone produces almost 300 million metric tons of hazardous industrial waste annually. That is more than 1 ton of waste for every person living in the country. This figure does not include any wastes that are discarded improperly or illegally.

Hazardous Waste Management

The office that has responsibility for overseeing the correct management of our hazardous waste is the EPA's Office of Solid Waste. A total of 214 million tons of hazardous waste was generated in the United States in 1995. Of this, 68% was managed in water treatment units. Deep well and underground injection accounted for 11% of the disposal. Less than 0.5% was accounted for by landfills, and 2% was managed by combustion (incineration). A majority of the remaining 17% underwent some other type of treatment.[6]

Secured Landfill

The least expensive and perhaps least environmentally sound means of disposing of hazardous waste is placing it in a **secured landfill.** Secured landfills must be (1) located above the 100-year flood plain and away from fault zones, (2) double-lined with clay or a synthetic

hazardous waste
a solid waste or combination of solid wastes that is dangerous to human health or the environment

Environmental Protection Agency (EPA)
the federal agency primarily responsible for setting, maintaining, and enforcing environmental standards

secured landfill
a double-lined landfill located above a flood plain and away from a fault zone, equipped with monitoring pipes for seepage, used primarily for hazardous waste

material, and (3) equipped with pipes that enable them to be monitored for any seepage. The owner must provide for area wells for the monitoring of groundwater, as well as monitor the surrounding **surface water** (water on the earth's surface).

There are several drawbacks to the use of secured landfills for the discarding of hazardous waste. Some authorities feel that even the best-built secured landfill will eventually leak because the clay liners will crack or the synthetic liners will break. Because of this concern, the legislation governing secured landfills continues to mount. There are now specific standards that stipulate which hazardous wastes can and cannot be placed in secured landfills without further processing (some wastes must undergo prior treatment before being placed in the landfill).

Deep Well Injection
Another means of disposing of liquid hazardous waste is deep well injection, a form of disposal developed by petroleum refineries. Deep well injection consists of pumping the hazardous waste, by way of lined wells, far below drinking water aquifers into layers of permeable rock that are surrounded by impermeable rock.

Incineration of Hazardous Waste
Appropriately controlled incineration is one of the most efficient means of managing hazardous waste; however, it is also one of the most expensive. This method of disposal consists of burning the wastes at very high temperatures. It requires the appropriate mixture of air and fuel to ensure complete combustion. Gaseous by-products are recombusted to minimize the release of hydrocarbons and other harmful gases. The benefits of this means of disposal are (1) conversion of toxic compounds to harmless ones, (2) reduction in the volume of waste, (3) destruction instead of isolation of waste, and (4) possible energy recovery during combustion.

Hazardous Waste Recycling and Neutralization
The best solution to hazardous waste disposal once it is created is recycling in a system in which a hazardous waste created by one process becomes the raw material for another. Examples include extracting toxic metals from waste, adding a base to an excessively acidic waste, and promoting the growth of microbes that feed on hazardous waste—a method that has been used successfully with oil spills.

Source Reduction
Source reduction represents the best solution to the problem of hazardous waste. Increased public concern and the high cost of disposal have led hazardous waste producers to invest in technological research to reduce the amount of waste produced. Unfortunately, this approach is limited because there are still few incentives for source reduction.

Hazardous Waste Cleanup
Managing present and future hazardous wastes is one issue; dealing with the inappropriate past disposal of hazardous wastes is another.

The primary participant in the cleanup of hazardous waste in America has been the federal government. In 1980 Congress passed the **Comprehensive Environmental Response, Compensation, and Liability Act (CERCLA)** in response to the public's demand to clean up leaking dump sites. This law, which has become known as *Superfund,* was created primarily to clean up abandoned hazardous waste sites. CERCLA:

1. Created a national priority list (NPL) of hazardous waste sites to be cleaned up
2. Stated that the government would make responsible parties pay for those cleanups whenever possible
3. Provided funds to support the identification and cleanup of the sites

---

surface water
water found on the earth's surface (for example, oceans, rivers, streams, ponds, and lakes)

Comprehensive Environmental Response, Compensation, and Liability Act (CERCLA)
the federal law (known as the Superfund) created to clean up abandoned hazardous waste sites

HEALTHY PEOPLE 2010: OBJECTIVE

BOX 15.3

8-12.   Minimize the risks to human health and the environment posed by hazardous sites.

Target: 98% of sites on the following lists:

8-12a.   National Priority List sites
8-12b.   Resource Conservation and Recovery Act facilities
8-12c.   Leaking underground storage facilities
8-12d.   Brownfield properties

Baseline: 1,200 National Priority List sites; 2,475 Resource Conservation and Recovery Act facilities; 370,000 leaking underground storage facilities; 1,500 brownfield properties in 1998.

For Further Thought

Do you feel it is the responsibility of the party who created a hazardous waste site to pay for the cleanup, even though at the time the site was created it was not illegal to dispose of the waste in such a manner? Why or why not?

The EPA was responsible for creating the NPL in cooperation with the individual states. These sites were placed on the list in order of priority based upon the threat to public health or the environment. Once on the NPL, sites were eligible for Superfund dollars. These dollars could be used for removing and destroying wastes and for the temporary or permanent relocation of residents impacted by the wastes, but not for compensation to victims for related health problems.

It is still unclear how many sites exist and what the final total cleanup costs will be. In 1999 the EPA listed 1,396 sites on its NPL because of their potential health threat.[3] Between 1981 and 2000, 750 sites were cleaned up and removed from the list.[7] There are various estimates on the number of sites. The Office of Technology Assessment and the Waste Management Research Institute have suggested that the Superfund list could reach 10,000 prority sites, with a cleanup cost of $1 trillion.[1] Other estimates are lower.

One source of hazardous waste is the estimated 370,000 leaking underground storage tanks.[7] These were primarily used to store gasoline, diesel fuel, and fuel oil at factories, gas stations, and homes. As these tanks corrode and deteriorate, they release toxic chemicals that find their way into the water supply. Just 1.5 cups of hazardous leaking chemical can contaminate more than one million gallons of groundwater.[3] Another problem is the more than 450,000 abandoned industrial plants and commercial worksites, most of which are contaminated. Examples include empty factories, abandoned junkyards, and old gas stations.[1] These so-called **brownfields** could be cleaned up, but the cost and legal struggle to do so are sometimes prohibitively expensive. One of the *Healthy People 2010* objectives addresses the cleanup of these hazardous waste sites. Its aim is to "Minimize the risks to human health and the environment posed by hazardous sites" (see Box 15.3).[7]

brownfields
abandoned gas stations, industrial plants, and commercial worksites, most of which are contaminated with hazardous chemicals

Air Pollution

Until a few hundred years ago, air pollution could be attributed almost entirely to natural causes—dust and sand storms, forest fires, volcanic eruptions, and the gases escaping from deep within the earth or given off by decaying organic matter. While these forms of air pollution still exist today, waste products created by a modern industrialized civilization constitute a greater threat to air quality and our health. About 160 million tons of pollutants are emitted into the atmosphere in the United States each year.[8]

Contaminants of Outdoor Air

Air pollution is the contamination of the air by substances in amounts great enough to interfere with the comfort, safety, or health of living organisms. These contaminants occur as gases,

air pollution
contamination of the air that interferes with the comfort, safety, and health of living organisms

Table 15.2
Criteria Pollutants

Pollutants (Designation)	Form(s)	Major Sources (in order of percentage of contribution)
Carbon monoxide (CO)	Gas	Transportation, industrial processes, other solid waste, stationary fuel combustion
Lead (Pb)	Metal or aerosol	Transportation, industrial processes, stationary fuel combustion, solid waste
Nitrogen dioxide (NO_2)	Gas	Stationary fuel combustion, transportation, industrial processes, solid waste
Ozone (O_3)	Gas	Transportation, industrial processes, solid waste, stationary fuel combustion
Particulate matter (total suspended particles—TSP)	Solid or liquid	Industrial processes, stationary fuel combustion, transportation, solid waste
Sulfur dioxide (SO_2)	Gas	Stationary fuel combustion, industrial processes, transportation, other wastes

liquids, or solids. The most prevalent sources of air pollution in the United States are (1) transportation, including privately owned motor vehicles; (2) electric power plants fueled by oil and coal; and (3) industry, primarily mills and refineries. In addition to these major sources, there are many smaller sources such as wood and coal burning stoves, fireplaces, and other incinerators.

The federal government has labeled the air pollutants of greatest concern in the United States as **criteria pollutants.** These are sulfur dioxide, carbon monoxide, nitrogen oxides, ozone, respirable particulate matter, and lead (see Table 15.2). The EPA has established national standards for allowable concentration levels of each of these six pollutants in the ambient (outdoor) air and closely monitors their levels. These standards are known as the **National Ambient Air Quality Standards (NAAQSs).**

Widespread concern about the possible ill effects of these criteria pollutants has led to efforts to reduce their concentrations in ambient air. Between 1983 and 2002, the United States substantially reduced the ambient air concentrations of five of the criteria pollutants, namely, lead by 94%, particulate matter by 13%, ozone by 22%, sulfur dioxide by 39%, and carbon monoxide by 41%. During this time period, nitrogen oxides increased by 21%.[8] Nonetheless, in 1999, approximately 146 million people in the United States live in counties with pollution levels above the NAAQSs.[8] Most of these people are exposed to unacceptable levels of ozone. The *Healthy People 2010* objective for the reduction of the levels of criteria pollutants in the ambient air requires that no U.S. residents be exposed to harmful levels of these pollutants (see Box 15.4).[7]

The Pollutant Standard Index

The deleterious effects of air pollution are many, including reduced visibility, weakened or ruined fabrics, defaced buildings and monuments, and injured or killed vegetation and aquatic life. Given these observations, there is naturally a concern about the effects of air pollution on human health.

Sensitivities to air pollutants vary with each individual. Variations are attributed to factors such as age and chronic diseases, including heart disease, lung diseases, and asthma. For those most susceptible individuals, it is important to be able to measure the quality of ambient air. Therefore, the EPA developed a **Pollutant Standard Index (PSI),** a scale that relates pollutant concentrations to health effects. Thus, with a single numeric figure, air-quality professionals can provide the public with an indication of the air quality—the higher the PSI, the poorer the air quality. The PSI and the major pollutants are often reported daily over television in conjunction with the weather report.

Special Concerns with Outdoor Air

Pollution of the outdoor air has resulted in a number of specific problems for the United States and the world. They include acid rain, global warming, destruction of the ozone layer, and photochemical smog. Acid rain and global warming currently have minimal effects on

criteria pollutants
the most pervasive air pollutants in the United States

National Ambient Air Quality Standards (NAAQSs)
standards created by the EPA for allowable concentration levels of outdoor air pollutants

Pollutant Standard Index (PSI)
a scale developed by the EPA that relates the air pollutant concentrations to health effects

acid rain
both wet and dry acidic deposits, which occur both within and downwind of areas that produce emissions containing sulfur dioxide and oxides of nitrogen

BOX
15.4

HEALTHY PEOPLE 2010: OBJECTIVE

8-1.   Reduce the proportion of persons exposed to air that does not meet the U.S. Environmental Protection Agency's health-based standards for harmful air pollutants.

Target and baseline:

Objective	Reduction in Air Pollutants	1997 Baseline	2010 Target
		Percent	
8-1a.	Ozone*	43	0
8-1b.	Particulate matter	12	0
8-1c.	Carbon monoxide	19	0
8-1d.	Nitrogen dioxide	5	0
8-1e.	Sulfur dioxide	2	0
8-1f.	Lead	< 1	0
		Number	
8-1g.	Total number of people	119,803,000	0

*The targets of zero percent for ozone and particulate matter are set for 2012 and 2018, respectively.

Note: For the purpose of this objective, EPA is counting persons living in nonattainment areas only. Data for population groups currently are not analyzed.

Target setting method: Consistent with the Clean Air Act (Public Law 101-549).

Source: Aerometric Information Retrieval System (AIRS), EPA, OAR. Office of Air and Radiation.

For Further Thought

Have you or any members of your family done anything during the past year to help reduce air pollution?

---

human health and are discussed below briefly. Destruction of the ozone layer and photochemical smog directly affect human health and are discussed in some detail.

Acid Rain

Acid deposition, often referred to as **acid rain** (also acid snow, acid dew, acid drizzle, acid fog, and acid sleet), may occur both within and downwind of areas that produce emissions that contain sulfur dioxide (SO_2) and oxides of nitrogen (NO_2 and NO_3). These emissions, which result from the burning of fossil fuels—oil, coal, and natural gas—react in the atmosphere and combine with water vapor to form sulfuric and nitric acids, which fall to the earth as acid rain. The primary problems associated with acid rain are the acidification of surface water, which results in the death of certain species of water life, damage to vegetation primarily at higher elevations, and erosion of monuments and buildings (see Figure 15.8). While acidic air pollutants can contribute to respiratory problems in humans, acid deposition itself is not considered a health hazard.

Global Warming

Global warming is the gradual increase in the earth's surface temperature. One of the conditions that seems to be contributing to global warming is the increase in levels of **greenhouse gases**—namely, carbon dioxide, **chlorofluorocarbons (CFCs)**, methane, and nitrous oxide—which are transparent to visible light but absorb infrared radiation. These gases permit the passage of sunlight to the earth's surface. However, when some of this energy is re-radiated as infrared radiation (heat), it is absorbed by the gases, causing air temperature to rise. Whether or not global warming is occurring at present is a matter of debate. Records show that the average global temperature has gradually increased 0.5–1.0°F since the late nineteenth century. Scientists do not agree on the significance of this increase. If global

global warming
the gradual increase in the earth's surface temperature

greenhouse gases
atmosphere gases, principally carbon dioxide, CFCs, methane, and nitrous oxide, that are transparent to visible light but absorb infrared radiation

chlorofluoro-carbons (CFCs)
a family of chemical agents used in industry for such items as propellants, refrigeration, solvent cleaning, and insulation

FIGURE 15.8

Acid rain defaces our art and our architecture and is hazardous to the environment.

warming is occurring and if it continues to occur, a number of serious complications can be expected. A few degrees increase in the earth's surface temperature would adversely affect our environment, including the quality of our air, our water, and our health. The George W. Bush administration, which has acknowledged that human activities are probably changing the climate, refused to pursue a policy to reduce emissions of carbon dioxide and other greenhouse gases and refused to force U.S. industries to report their carbon dioxide emissions.[1]

Destruction of the Ozone Layer

Although ground-level ozone (O_3) is considered a criteria pollutant, stratospheric ozone provides a great benefit to life on earth. This stratospheric **ozone layer** filters out 99% of the sun's harmful ultraviolet radiation (see Figure 15.9).[3] Without this protective filter, ultraviolet radiation would reach the earth's surface at dangerously high levels, causing increased rates of skin cancers and eye problems. Further, there would be an increase in the rate of mutations (genetic changes) and perhaps the disruption of the oceanic food chain.

The ozone layer is being depleted faster than originally believed. In fact, scientific evidence suggests that the rate of ozone depletion over the last decade is more than twice what was previously projected. Thinning of the ozone layer has been found over the polar regions and in the northern midlatitudes. Presently, a hole exists in the ozone layer in the Southern Hemisphere, and it is anticipated that one will

FIGURE 15.9

Regions of the atmosphere.

Source: Reprinted by permission of Waveland Press, Inc. from Nadakavukaren, A. (1990). *Man and Environment: A Health Perspective*, 3rd ed. Long Grove, IL: Waveland Press, Inc. All rights reserved.

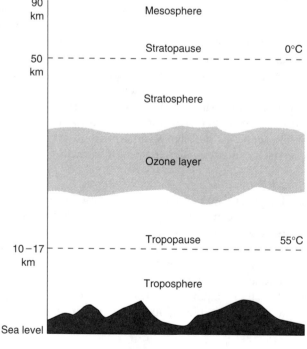

appear shortly in the Northern Hemisphere. Ozone levels over the Northern Hemisphere are 13% to 14% lower now than they were in the 1970s. The EPA estimates that 1% depletion of the ozone layer would lead to a 2% increase in ultraviolet radiation and that this, in turn, would lead to a 4% increase in the rate of skin cancer cases. Occurrences of cataracts (vision loss) are also expected to increase.[3]

The primary cause of the depletion of the ozone layer is the presence in the atmosphere of CFCs. CFCs are solely a product of the chemical industry; they do not occur naturally in the environment. CFCs are used for a wide range of purposes, including as propellants in aerosol cans, in the freon of air conditioners and refrigerators, and for blowing plastic foams. Because CFCs are implicated in both ozone depletion and global warming, considerable attention has been placed on controlling their production and release. In September 1987, in Montreal, Canada, diplomats from 31 countries agreed to freeze the consumption of CFCs at 1986 levels by 1990 and reduce production by 50% by the year 2000. The United States banned CFC production and sale in this country in 1996.

Photochemical Smog

Photochemical smog is created when other air pollutants, including nitrogen oxides, hydrocarbons, ozone, and peroxyacyl nitrates (PAN), react with oxygen and sunlight. The resulting photochemical smog, seen in the air as a brownish haze, is detrimental to human health and to the well-being of other living things.

The extent or quantity of photochemical smog, as well as other air pollutants, can be amplified by physical geography. For example, the cities of Denver, Los Angeles, Phoenix, and Salt Lake City have nearby mountains that restrict lateral air movement. This trapped air mass may also be subject to another phenomenon referred to as a **thermal inversion.** Normally, the air surrounding the earth's surface is heated by the sun and rises to mix with the cooler air above it. However, in cases of thermal inversion, a layer of warm air settles above the cooler air at the surface, preventing cooler air from rising. When the cooler air is trapped, it accumulates pollutants. If the thermal inversion continues, the pollutants can reach dangerously high levels (see Figure 15.10).[3]

Just as with other types of pollution, the best way to reduce photochemical smog is to reduce (or eliminate) emissions from the internal combustion engines of motor vehicles. Such a reduction can be achieved through more carpooling, better use of mass transit systems, and the development and use of electric and solar energy sources for motor vehicles.

Protection of Outdoor Air through Regulation

Steady deterioration of air quality in the 1950s and 1960s led to the Nation's first serious attempt to regulate air pollution, the **Clean Air Act (CAA)** of 1963.[3] The CAA provided the federal government with the authority to address interstate air pollution problems. The CAA was amended several times in the late 1960s, but much of the regulation was based upon voluntary compliance.

Public concern about air quality and other environmental issues continued to grow in the late 1960s and resulted in the largest one-day organized demonstration in U.S. history. This demonstration, held on April 22, 1970, marked the first national observance of **Earth Day.** Some experts have indicated that the first Earth Day gave rise to the modern environmental movement. The public outcry to preserve the environment convinced then President Richard Nixon to establish the EPA by executive order and led Congress to again amend the CAA in 1970. These two steps radically changed the course of pollution control.

The 1970 amendments to the CAA provided the first comprehensive approach to dealing with air pollution nationwide. Three significant components of these amendments were the development of the National Ambient Air Quality Standards (NAAQSs), tougher emission standards for automobiles, and *State Implementation Plans (SIPs)*. The SIPs required each state to submit to the EPA its plan for achieving and maintaining air-quality standards.

ozone layer
ozone gas (O_2) found in the stratosphere

photochemical smog
a secondary air pollutant created when primary and other secondary pollutants react with oxygen and sunlight

thermal inversion
a condition that occurs when warm air traps cooler air at the surface of the earth

Clean Air Act (CAA)
the federal law that provided the government with authority to address interstate air pollution

Earth Day
annual public observance for concerns about the environment

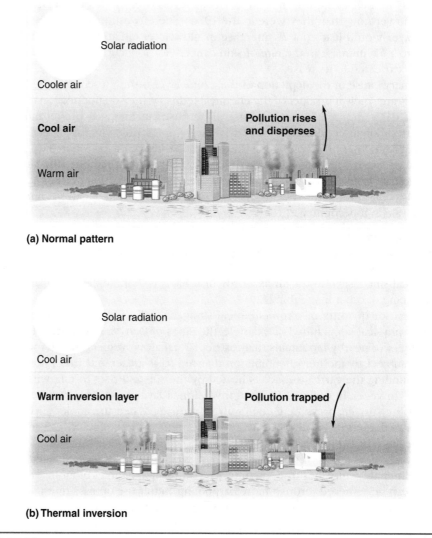

FIGURE 15.10

A thermal inversion.

Source: Chiras, D. D. (2002). *Environmental Science: Creating a Sustainable Future*, 6th ed. Sudbury, MA: Jones and Bartlett Publishers.

The CAA was amended again in 1977, empowering the EPA to regulate air quality. Specifically, the EPA was authorized to levy fines against those who violated the standards.[3] The CAA was amended again in 1990 to include (1) mandates to reduce urban smog, sulfur dioxide, and nitrogen oxides, (2) tighter controls on auto emissions, including a guarantee that auto emission controls will last 100,000 miles, (3) more efficient power plants, and (4) a total ban on the production of CFCs for use in the United States by the year 1996.[3]

Indoor Air

It was once believed that the comfortable confines of the indoors were protected from the ills of air pollution. However, it is now known that indoor air pollution can be a greater threat to human health than outdoor air pollution. Unlike outdoor air pollutants, which are regulated and can be dispersed by the wind, indoor air pollutants can be trapped and

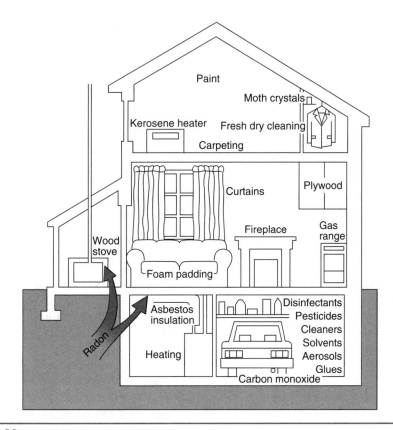

FIGURE 15.11

Air pollution sources in the home.

Source: U.S. Environmental Protection Agency (1991).

concentrated to dangerous levels. This buildup of undesirable gases and airborne particles inside a building is called **indoor air pollution.** Poor indoor air quality combined with the fact that Americans spend 80% to 90% of their time indoors presents a potentially significant health concern.[9]

Indoor Air Pollutants

Indoor air pollution can arise from a number of sources (see Figure 15.11). **Asbestos** is a naturally occurring mineral fiber that was commonly used as an insulation and fireproofing material. It was often used in older buildings to insulate pipes, walls, and ceilings; as a component of floor and ceiling tiles; and sprayed in structures for fireproofing. It is harmless if intact and left alone, but, when disturbed, the airborne fibers can cause serious health problems. **Biogenic pollutants** are airborne materials of biological origin such as living and non-living fungi and their toxins, bacteria, viruses, pollens, insect parts and wastes, and animal dander. They normally enter the human body by being inhaled. **Combustion by-products** include gases (e.g., CO, NO_2, and SO_2) and particulates (e.g., ash and soot). The major sources of these items are fireplaces, wood stoves, kerosene heaters, gas ranges and engines, candles, incense, secondhand tobacco smoke, and improperly maintained gas furnaces. Prolonged exposure to these substances can cause serious illness and possibly death.

Radon is a naturally occurring radioactive gas that cannot be seen, smelled, or tasted. Radon seeps into homes from surrounding soil, rocks, and water, and through openings (cracks, drains, sump pumps, etc.) in the foundation and floor. The only way to determine if a

indoor air pollution
the buildup of undesirable gases and particles in the air inside a building

asbestos
a naturally occurring mineral fiber that has been identified as a Class A carcinogen by the Environmental Protection Agency

biogenic pollutants
airborne biological organisms or their particles or gases or other toxic materials that can produce illness

combustion by-products
gases and particulates generated by burning

radon
a naturally occurring, colorless, odorless, radioactive gas formed during the radioactive decay of uranium-238

BOX
15.5

Healthy People 2010: Objectives

8-18. Increase the proportion of persons who live in homes tested for radon concentrations.

Target: 20%.

Baseline: 17% of the population lived in homes in 1998 that had been tested for radon (age adjusted to the year 2000 standard population).

Target setting method: Better than the best.

For Further Thought

Have you tested your house for radon? What was the reading?

Source: National Health Interview Survey (NHIS), CDC, NCHS.

---

secondhand smoke
environmental tobacco smoke (ETS)—tobacco smoke in the environment that can be inhaled by nonsmokers

mainstream smoke
tobacco smoke inhaled and exhaled by the smoker

sidestream tobacco smoke
tobacco smoke that comes off the end of burning tobacco products

passive smoking
the inhalation of environmental tobacco smoke by nonsmokers

carcinogens
agents, usually chemicals, that cause cancer

building has elevated levels of radon is to test for it. Homeowners can administer this inexpensive and easy test. Increasing the proportion of persons who live in homes that have been tested for radon is one of the *Healthy People 2010* objectives (see Box 15.5).

Environmental tobacco smoke (ETS), also known as **secondhand smoke,** includes both **mainstream smoke** (the smoke inhaled and exhaled by the smoker) and **sidestream smoke** (the smoke that comes off the end of a burning tobacco product). The inhalation of ETS by nonsmokers is referred to as **passive smoking.** There are hundreds of toxic agents and more than forty **carcinogens** (cancer-causing agents) in secondhand smoke. A few of these harmful agents are carbon monoxide (CO), nitrogen dioxide (NO_2), carbon dioxide (CO_2), hydrogen cyanide, formaldehyde, nicotine, and suspended particles.[10] The health effects of ETS will be discussed in Chapter 16.

Volatile organic compounds (VOCs) are compounds that exist as vapors over the normal range of air pressures and temperatures. In any one building, one might find hundreds of different VOCs. Sources of VOCs include construction materials (e.g., insulation and paint), structural components (e.g., vinyl tile and sheet rock), furnishings (e.g., drapes and upholstery fabric), cleansers and solvents (e.g., liquid detergent and furniture polish), personal care products (e.g., deodorant and eyeliner pencils), insecticides/pesticides, electrical equipment (e.g., computers and VCRs), and combustion of wood and kerosene.[11] **Formaldehyde,** a pungent water-soluble gas, is one of the most ubiquitous VOCs. It is a widely used chemical that can be found in hundreds of products. Exposure occurs when it evaporates from wood products such as plywood and particle board, in which it is a component of the glue that binds these products together. Formaldehyde can also be found in products such as grocery bags, wallpaper, carpet, insulation, wall paneling, and wallboard.[11]

Protection of Indoor Air

The energy crisis of the 1970s led to a conservation movement that included reducing the rate at which outside air was brought into buildings for ventilation. The accepted rate was reduced from 20 cubic feet per minute to 5 feet per minute as a cost savings and energy savings measure. These "tight buildings" soon became known as "sick buildings" as reports of illness traced to such buildings increased.[9] **Sick building syndrome** refers to a situation in which the air quality in a building produces nonspecific signs and symptoms of ill health in the building occupants. Electronic controls and more efficient filtration, heating, and cooling systems have enabled the ventilation rate of 20 cubic feet per minute to be reinstated.

Even though indoor air pollution may be more harmful to human health than outdoor air pollution, measures to monitor and correct indoor air pollution have been limited. The U.S. government has not yet established a framework for the development of indoor air policies as it has for outdoor air. It has, however, pursued voluntary industry standards. For example, there are safety codes for kerosene space heaters, an "action guideline" for radon, and smoking restrictions for commercial airlines. There also has been federal guidance on the handling of asbestos in schools and a prohibition on new uses of asbestos. In the absence of a federal indoor clean air act, some states and municipalities have developed their own. Most of these acts are aimed at restricting smoking in public places.

In the absence of any comprehensive policy, individuals are encouraged to take steps to reduce or eliminate sources of indoor air pollution and improve air quality. These may include:[12]

1. Selecting safer household products, such as "pump" dispensers instead of spray dispensers
2. Venting dryers outdoors instead of indoors to keep indoor humidity low and therefore discourage mold growth
3. Avoiding products containing formaldehyde
4. Having loose asbestos fibers removed, if found
5. Limiting or prohibiting indoor smoking
6. Maintaining heating, air conditioning, and ventilation systems in good working condition
7. Testing buildings for radon

Water and Its Pollution

Water is essential for life as we know it, but only a small fraction of the earth's water is available for our use. We acquire water for our needs from either surface water or groundwater. Unfortunately, much of this water has become polluted (see Figure 15.12).

Sources of Water

Water in streams, rivers, lakes, and reservoirs is called **surface water.** The water that sinks into the soil is referred to as *subsurface* or **groundwater.** Groundwater that is not absorbed by the roots of vegetation moves slowly downward until it reaches the underground reservoirs

volatile organic compounds (VOCs) compounds that exist as vapors over the normal range of air pressures and temperatures

formaldehyde (CH₂O) a water-soluble gas used in aqueous solutions in hundreds of consumer products

sick building syndrome a term to describe a situation in which the air quality in a building produces generalized signs and symptoms of ill health in the building's occupants

surface water precipitation that does not infiltrate the ground or return to the atmosphere by evaporation; the water in streams, rivers, and lakes

groundwater water located under the surface of the ground

FIGURE 15.12
Clean water is one of the community's most precious resources.

referred to as *aquifers*. **Aquifers** are porous, water-saturated layers of underground bedrock, sand, and gravel that can yield an economically significant amount of water.[1]

The earth's supply of freshwater available for our use is limited. The majority (over 97%) of the world's water supply is salt water found in the oceans. While it is possible to remove salt from this water by **desalinization,** it is a very expensive process. The remaining 3% is freshwater, 99% of which is found in ice sheets and glaciers at the poles. Only 0.003% of the earth's water is available for use by humans, and much of this is hard to reach and too costly to be of practical value.[3] Thus, the continual contamination of our groundwater through the improper disposal of solid and hazardous waste should be of paramount concern to everyone.

Surface and groundwater have very different characteristics. Surface water supports plant and animal life, including microorganisms, with the oxygen and nutrients that are contained in it. Conversely, groundwater is low in oxygen and contains few microorganisms. These microorganisms are filtered out as the water passes through the soil to the aquifers. The subsurface water is, however, higher in minerals such as iron, chloride, and salts because of its travel through the soil and rocks. Each of these characteristics is taken into account when preparing the water for human use.

Treatment of Water for Domestic Use

The greatest use of water is for agriculture (41%), utilities (38%), and industrial manufacturing (11%). Only 10% is used directly by the public.[1] Domestic water use in the United States includes water for drinking, cooking, washing dishes and laundry, bathing, flushing toilets, and outdoor use (such as watering lawns and gardens and washing cars). Most people are surprised to learn how much water we use in our homes. Americans use 75 to 80 gallons of water each day, just by flushing the toilet, showering, washing laundry, and other domestic uses.[13]

While many rural residents in the United States obtain their water from untreated private wells (groundwater), urban residents obtain their water from municipal water treatment plants. About two-thirds of the municipalities use surface water, while one-third use groundwater.

Virtually all surface water is polluted and needs to be treated before it can safely be consumed. The steps in surface water treatment vary from plant to plant, but the following four steps are almost always included:

1. *Coagulation and flocculation:* A chemical such as Alum (aluminum sulfate) is added to the water to cause suspended solids to attract one another and form larger particles (flakes, or floc).
2. *Sedimentation:* The water is permitted to stand so that the large particles (flakes) will settle out.
3. *Filtration:* The water is passed through filters (often carbon and sand filters) in order to remove any solids and dissolved chemicals remaining after sedimentation.
4. *Disinfection:* Chlorine is added to the water to kill viruses, bacteria, algae, and fungi. Disinfection is sometimes accompanied by fluoridation, which helps prevent dental decay.

The responsibility of municipal water treatment plants is to provide water that is chemically and bacteriologically safe for human consumption. It is also desirable that the water be aesthetically pleasing in regard to taste, odor, color, and clarity. Above all, the municipal water supply must be reliable. Reliability in regard to both quantity and quality has always been regarded as "nonnegotiable" in planning a treatment facility.

The treated water, now safe to drink, is pumped to community water storage tanks, many of which are familiar on the skylines of American towns. The water then must enter the distribution system through which it reaches homes. The integrity of this distribution system is not always reliable. There can be breaks in the pipes, sometimes in the vicinity of sewer lines that also may be leaking. Therefore, a residual level of chlorine to kill bacteria

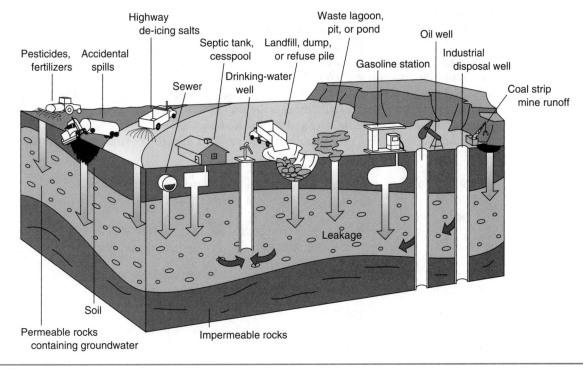

FIGURE 15.13
Sources of groundwater contamination.
Source: U.S. Environmental Protection Agency.

must remain in the water until it reaches the tap. This is insurance against contamination during distribution.

Sources of Water Pollution

Water pollution includes any physical or chemical change in water that can harm living organisms or make it unfit for other uses.[1] The sources of water pollution (see Figure 15.13) fall into two categories—point sources and nonpoint sources.[1] **Point source pollution** refers to a single identifiable source that discharges pollutants into the water, such as a pipe, ditch, or culvert. Examples of such pollutants might include release of pollutants from a factory or sewage treatment plant.

Nonpoint source pollution includes all pollution that occurs through the runoff, seepage, or falling of pollutants into the water. Examples include the runoff of chemicals from farm fields, seepage of leachates from landfills, and acid rain. Of these two sources of pollution, nonpoint source pollution is the greater problem because it is often difficult to track the actual source of pollution.

Types of Water Pollutants

As one might guess, the types and numbers of water pollutants are almost endless. The two types of pollutants of primary concern to community health are biological and toxic pollutants. These are briefly described below, but are discussed in more detail in Chapter 16.

Biological Pollutants

Biological pollutants include pathogens such as parasites, bacteria, viruses, and other undesirable living microorganisms. These pathogens enter the water mainly through human and other animal wastes.

water pollution
any physical or chemical change in water that can harm living organisms or make it unfit for other uses

point source pollution
pollution that can be traced to a single identifiable source

nonpoint source pollution
all pollution that occurs through the runoff, seepage, or falling of pollutants into the water

Nonbiological Pollutants

Nonbiological pollutants include inorganic chemicals such as lead, copper, and arsenic; organic chemicals; and radioactive pollutants. Among the organic chemicals are industrial solvents such as trichloroethylene (TCE), pesticides such as dichlorodiphenyltrichloroethane (DDT), and the insulating chemicals used in transformers and electrical capacitors, such as the polychlorinated biphenyls (PCBs). These toxic chemicals are also present in inks, paints, glues, waxes, and polishes. Finally, there is dioxin (TCDD), a substance that is a by-product of the incineration of paper products and chlorinated plastics.

Water quality in the United States has deteriorated in many communities. This deterioration can be attributed to four causes:[14]

1. Population growth—an increase in the number of people generating waste
2. Widespread and ever-increasing chemical manufacture and usage, particularly synthetic organic chemicals
3. Gross mismanagement and irresponsible disposal of hazardous wastes
4. Reckless land-use practices that result in runoff of pollutants into waterways

As the public's knowledge of the endangerment of water quality in the United States grows, so will the number of strategies and the public will to protect it.

Strategies to Ensure Safe Water

Strategies used to ensure safe water in America today include public policy, proper treatment of wastewater, and water conservation.

Policy

The *Federal Water Pollution Control Act Amendments* of 1972 and 1977 are now known as the **Clean Water Act (CWA).** Provisions of the CWA are aimed at (1) ensuring water quality in such a way as to make all rivers swimmable and fishable and (2) reducing the discharge of pollutants in U.S. waters to zero.

As with most other federal environmental legislation, the implementation of the CWA was given to the EPA, which in turn developed regulations to meet the goals of the act. A few of the more significant regulations include the limitation on industrial discharges of wastes, requirements for pollutant discharge permits, municipal sewage treatment plant discharge standards, and other water-quality standards. In 2001 it was estimated that 40% of the nation's waters did not meet the CWA standard for fishing, swimming, or other uses.[15]

The goals of the CWA have remained constant over the years, although there have been several amendments. Some amendments raised standards; others were necessary to keep up with new technology. A 2001 report by the EPA's inspector general called for the CWA to be strengthened, but there was opposition on the part of industry and agriculture.[1]

The George W. Bush administration has taken few steps to enforce provisions of the CWA and has actually taken steps to weaken it. On July 16, 2001, the EPA asked a federal court to delay a water cleanup rule issued under the Clinton administration. Furthermore, under President Bush, the EPA allowed mine wastes to be dumped into rivers, allowed factory farms to continue to pollute rivers with animal waste, and tried to weaken protection of our wetlands. The Bush administration reduced EPA's budget for fiscal year 2005 by $1.9 billion, including cuts for water and sewer funding and the EPA science budget.[15]

Other laws that have helped to ensure safe water are the **Safe Drinking Water Act (SDWA)** of 1974 and the *Safe Drinking Water Act Amendments (SDWAA)* of 1986 and 1996. These laws deal with public drinking water in a comprehensive manner by instructing the EPA to set maximum contaminant levels (MCLs) for specific pollutants in drinking water. It should be noted that the SDWA and the SDWAA cover only public drinking water and not water drawn from private wells. There are hundreds of different water contaminants; the EPA has promulgated a Drinking Water Contaminants Candidate List that includes biological and

Clean Water Act (CWA) the federal law aimed at ensuring that all rivers are swimmable and fishable and that limit the discharge of pollutants in U.S. waters to zero

Safe Drinking Water Act (SDWA) the federal law that regulates the safety of public drinking water

chemical contaminants or contaminant groups, which was revised in 1998 and again in 2003. The current revision includes 9 biological and 42 chemical contaminants; the list can be viewed at the EPA's Web site (www.epa.gov).[16]

Environmentalists and others would like to see the provisions of the SDWA strengthened and more vigorously enforced. But Congress is under pressure by water-polluting industries. Lobbyists for these industries, which include mining and timber industries, point to the high administrative and enforcement costs of this act and the cost burden it places on municipal and privately owned water supply systems as reasons not to strengthen the provisions. They also question the benefits of strengthening the act. How many cases of waterborne illness actually would be prevented by passage and enforcement of stricter regulations?

A case in point is the standard for the allowable level of arsenic in drinking water. Currently, that level is 50 ppb; that is, no more than 50 parts per billion of arsenic can be present in drinking water. This level is five times higher than the international standard set by the World Health Organization. In 1962, the U.S. Public Health Service proposed lowering the level to 10 ppb. Finally, in 1999, the EPA proposed 10 ppb as the new standard. But in 2001, President Bush withdrew implementation of the new EPA standard because it was deemed too expensive.[1]

Wastewater Treatment

Wastewater is the substance that remains after humans have used water for domestic or commercial purposes. Such water, also sometimes referred to as *liquid waste* or *sewage,* consists of about 99.9% water and 0.1% suspended and dissolved solids. Included in the solids are human feces, soap, paper, garbage grindings (food parts), and a variety of other items that are put into wastewater systems from homes, schools, commercial buildings, hotels/motels, hospitals, industrial plants, and others connected to the sanitary sewer system. Many municipalities also treat rain water, which has become contaminated by contact with surfaces such as roadways; this water is collected by a system of storm sewers.

> **wastewater**
> the aqueous mixture that remains after water has been used or contaminated by humans

The primary purpose of wastewater treatment is to improve the quality of wastewater to the point that it might be released into a body of water without seriously disrupting the aquatic environment, causing health problems in humans in the form of waterborne disease, or causing nuisance conditions. This is accomplished in two ways. One is by converting organic wastes to simple inorganic wastes so that they will not unduly enrich the waters receiving the treated wastewater. The second is by disinfecting the treated wastewater before releasing it back into the environment.

Municipal Wastewater Treatment

There are three stages of wastewater treatment—primary, secondary, and tertiary. Most municipalities and many large companies have wastewater treatment plants that incorporate at least primary and secondary treatment levels (see Figure 15.14).

Primary Treatment

Primary treatment of wastewater is a physical/mechanical process that results in the separation of liquids and solids. The wastewater is then placed in a holding tank or settling pond (lagoon). Here, heavier solid particles settle to the bottom, forming a layer referred to as **sludge.** Sludge is a gooey, semi-solid mixture that includes bacteria, viruses, organic matter, toxic metals, synthetic organic chemicals, and solids.[1] Above the sludge remains most of the water, including many bacteria and chemicals. On top of the water layer is a layer of oils and fats. The layers of sludge and fat then are removed, and the aquatic portion enters the secondary stage of treatment.

> **sludge**
> a semi-liquid mixture of solid waste that includes bacteria, viruses, organic matter, toxic metals, synthetic organic chemicals, and solid chemicals

Secondary Treatment

During secondary treatment, aerobic bacteria are added to the wastewater to break down the organic materials into inorganic carbon dioxide, water, and minerals. After secondary treatment, the water, which is about 90% clean, can be discharged into a waterway.

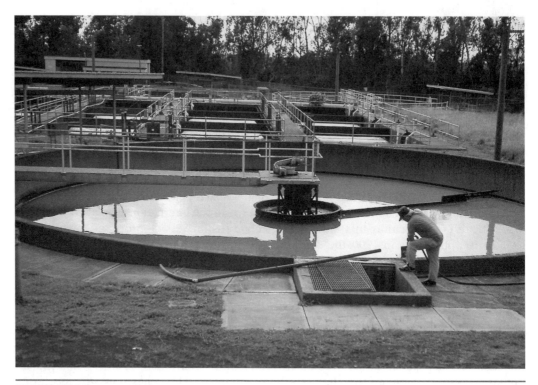

FIGURE 15.14
A wastewater treatment facility.

Tertiary Treatment (Advanced Sewage Treatment)
The third level of treatment usually involves sand and charcoal filters, or extended settling tanks that can remove 90% of the remaining dissolved pollutants left behind after the first two treatment levels. Most treatment facilities in the United States do not have capabilities to perform tertiary treatment of wastewater because it is not required by law, and the equipment to perform this treatment is very expensive.

Finally, whether wastewater is discharged after secondary or tertiary treatment, it is recommended that the wastewater be disinfected. The least expensive way of disinfecting is to chlorinate. About half of the wastewater treatment plants in the United States disinfect discharged water with chlorine. Some municipalities do not disinfect at all, while others have used more expensive methods such as ultraviolet light or ultrasound energy processes to do so.[1]

Septic Systems
Septic systems are the means by which those who live in unsewered areas dispose of sewage. Presently, approximately 25% of all Americans live in unsewered areas.[1]

A septic system consists of two major components—a **septic tank** and a buried sand filter or absorption field. The septic tank, which is a watertight concrete or fiberglass tank, is buried in the ground some distance from the house and is connected to it by a pipe. The system works in the following way. Sewage leaves the home via the toilets or drains and goes through the pipe to the septic tank. In the tank, the sewage is partially decomposed by bacteria under anaerobic conditions. The sludge settles to the bottom while the liquid portions of the waste are carried by a pipe to a series of perforated pipes that feed an **absorption field.** The tanks have to be cleaned out (pumped out) periodically to remove the sludge. Sewage disposal by septic tanks is perfectly safe if the system is (1) properly located in

septic tank
a watertight concrete or fiberglass tank that holds sewage; one of two main parts of a septic system

absorption field
the element of a septic system in which the liquid portion of waste is distributed

<table>
<tr><td>BOX
15.6</td><td colspan="2">**MORE EFFICIENT WATER USE**</td></tr>
</table>

What Individuals Can Do

More efficient water use begins with individuals in the home and workplace. Taking these and other steps and encouraging others to do so make good economic as well as environmental sense.

In the home

Install a toilet dam or plastic bottle in your toilet tank.
Install a water-efficient showerhead (2.5 gallons or less per minute).
When you buy a new toilet, purchase a low-flow model (1.6 gallons or less per flush).

Outdoors

Water in the morning or evening to minimize evaporation.
Install a drip-irrigation watering system for valuable plants.
Use drought-tolerant plants and grasses for landscaping, and reduce grass-covered areas.

At work or school

Adopt the same water-saving habits that are effective at home.
Ask about installing water-efficient equipment and reducing outdoor water use.
Encourage employers to explore the use of recycled "gray-water" or reclaimed wastewater.

What Communities Can Do

A water supplier or wastewater system operator (public or private) has cost-effective options to process and deliver water more efficiently. A community can do the same and can foster ways to use water wisely.

Not all of these steps are expensive. The best choices vary by region and by community; start by asking if these are appropriate where you live and work.

A water supplier or wastewater processor can

Identify who uses water, and reduce unaccounted-for water use.
Find and repair leaking pipes.
Consider a new pricing scheme that encourages conservation.
Reduce excess pressure in water lines.
Explore the reuse of treated wastewater for uses other than drinking water.
Charge hookup fees that encourage more efficient water use in new buildings.
Build water efficiency into future demand projections, facility planning, and drought planning.

A community can

Adopt plumbing and building codes that require water-efficient equipment and practices.
Adopt a water-efficient landscaping ordinance to reduce the water used for golf courses and commercial landscapes.
Refit older buildings with water-efficient equipment, starting with public buildings.
Reduce municipal water use for landscaping and other uses.
Conduct a public education campaign.
Require developers to build in water efficiency measures.

Source: Environmental Protection Agency (1990). *Preventing Pollution through Efficient Water Use* (pub. no. OPPE [pm-222]). Washington, DC: Author.

---

appropriate soil, (2) carefully constructed, and (3) properly maintained. Septic systems can contaminate groundwater if any of these conditions are not met; unfortunately, all too often, they are not.

Conservation

Americans waste water. It is estimated that simply changing to a high-efficiency shower head could save $200 to $250 a year for a family of four. Installation of these more efficient shower heads in 1,300 homes could save an estimated 31 million gallons of water a year.[3] That amount could be dramatically reduced if each of us took a few simple steps to conserve the water we use. Examples of domestic conservation include not letting the water run while brushing teeth, washing dishes, or washing a car. Also, shorter showers and water-saving showerheads conserve water. Box 15.6 gives you an opportunity to examine how you and your community might conserve water.

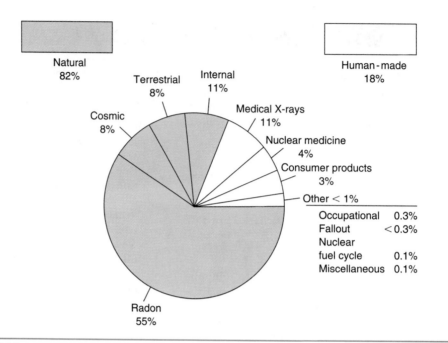

FIGURE 15.15
The percentage contribution of various radiation sources to the total average effective dose equivalent in the U.S. population.
Source: National Council on Radiation Protection and Measurements. NCRP Report no. 93. Reprinted with permission.

radiation
energy released when atoms are split or naturally decay from a less stable to a more stable form

Radiation

Radiation is the energy released when atoms are split or naturally decay from a less stable to a more stable form. When used appropriately, as in modern medicine, radiation provides many benefits. However, radiation can also pose a health risk, such as occurred in 1986 at the nuclear power plant in Chernobyl in the then Soviet Union.

cosmic radiation
radiation that comes from outer space and the sun

Sources of Radiation
We are exposed to low levels of radiation daily from both natural and human-made sources (see Figure 15.15).

Naturally Occurring Radiation
Naturally occurring radiation comes from three sources. That which comes to the earth from outer space and the sun is referred to as **cosmic radiation. Terrestrial radiation** comes from radioactive minerals that are within the earth—soil and rocks. Therefore, people who live near these substances (which include traces of uranium), or who live or work in buildings made of brick and stone that contain radioactive materials, have greater exposure. Radon gas is the biggest contributor to terrestrial radiation. The third source of naturally occurring radiation is **internal radiation**—that is, radiation internal to the human body. Exposure to such radiation occurs as a result of ingesting food or drugs and inhaling air that contains radioactive atoms.

terrestrial radiation
radiation that comes from radioactive minerals within the earth

internal radiation
radiation in the human body that occurs as a result of ingesting food and inhaling air containing radioactive particles

Individual behavior plays a definite role in the amount of exposure one has to radiation. For example, those who work or sunbathe outside, especially at higher elevations, increase their exposure to cosmic radiation. Similarly, miners and bricklayers are at greater risk for terrestrial exposure. Those who drink from contaminated wells may be at greater risk of exposure to internal radiation as well.

Human-Made Radiation

Sources of human-made radiation include the radiation used in medical and dental procedures such as X-rays, nuclear medicine diagnoses, and radiation therapy. Another source of
human-made radiation is nuclear power plants. Other sources include certain consumer products (such as smoke detectors), X-rays for security checks, tobacco, television and computer
screens, and nuclear weapons.

Do the benefits derived from the use of radiation outweigh the risks? Most would agree
that the use of radiation for medical purposes is justified. However, there is less agreement
about the cost/benefit question in the case of nuclear power plants, which currently provide
about 7% of our energy.[17]

There is a continually growing demand for energy in this country. The United States and
Canada make up only 5% of the world's population, but consume 25% of the available
energy.[17] America's access to oil is not unlimited, and much of our coal contains sulfur, which
contributes to acid deposition. There are advantages as well as dangers to nuclear energy. For
example, nuclear power plants do not produce carbon dioxide, and they reduce our reliance
on foreign oil reserves.

Currently, there are 103 nuclear power plants in 31 states. It has been more than twenty
years since there has been a serious nuclear accident in this country, and there is stirring
interest in maintaining these nuclear power plants and in building new ones. Many analysts
feel nuclear power is a technology whose time has passed. It is too centralized and too vulnerable to terrorist attacks. The George W. Bush administration argues that nuclear power is an
option we should keep open in case we need it. One concern with nuclear power is how to
dispose of high-level radioactive waste. This problem has yet to be resolved by the U.S.
Department of Energy.

Noise Pollution

Of all environmental pollution, the type that receives the least attention in this country is
noise pollution, or excessive or unwanted sound. However, noise pollution can contribute
to hearing loss, stress, and emotional problems; it can interrupt concentration and cause unintentional injuries.

noise pollution
excessive sound;
unwanted sound

What Is Noise and How Is It Measured?

Sound is heard when energy from vibrations, traveling through air, liquid, or solid media as pressure waves, is received by the ear. Unwanted, unpleasant sound is referred to as *noise.*[3]
However, what constitutes unwanted sound is a matter of subjective judgment. What is considered a reasonable amount of sound to teenagers often is noise to their parents. In this regard,
noise is measured by an annoyance factor. Yet, there are ways to scientifically measure and quantify noise (sound).

Amplitude refers to the sound volume; that is, its loudness or intensity. Amplitude is measured and expressed as **decibels (dB).** The decibel scale, which is logarithmic in nature, ranges
from 0 dB, the threshold of hearing, to 180 dB, the sound of a rocket engine.[3] Thus, a sound measured at 10 dB is 10 times louder than zero dB, and 20 dB is 100 times louder than zero dB.

amplitude
the loudness or
intensity of sound,
measured in decibels

Three standardized weightings—A, B, and C—are used. Currently, federal regulations
require the use of the A network when measuring sound in environmental and occupational
settings. Thus, the preferred notation using this network is dBA instead of dB. Most sound-
level meters are calculated using dBA. Table 15.3 lists some commonly encountered sounds
and their dBA levels.

decibels (dB)
a measure of sound
amplitude

Approaches to Noise Abatement

Because serious hearing problems can arise from noise pollution, communities need to take the
necessary steps to control unwanted sound. To date, the most common means of dealing with
noise pollution have been policy (legislation), educational programs, and environment changes.

Table 15.3
Commonly Encountered Sounds and Their Decibel (dBA) Levels

Sound Intensity Factor	Sound Level (dBA)	Sources	Effects		
			Perceived Loudness	Damage to Hearing	Community Reaction to Outdoor Noise
1,000,000,000,000,000,000	180	Rocket engine		Tramatic injury	
100,000,000,000,000,000	170				
10,000,000,000,000,000	160				
1,000,000,000,000,000	150	Jet plane at takeoff	Painful	Injurious range; irreversible damage	
100,000,000,000,000	140				
10,000,000,000,000	130	Maximum recorded rock music			
1,000,000,000,000	120	Thunderclap; textile loom; auto horn, 3.3 ft (1 m) away	Uncomfortably loud	Danger zone; progressive loss of hearing	
100,000,000,000	110	Riveter; jet flyover at 985 ft (300 m)			Vigorous action
10,000,000,000	100	Newpaper press			
1,000,000,000	90	Motorcycle, 26 ft (8 m) away; food blender	Very loud		
100,000,000	80	Diesel truck, 50 mph (80 km/hr), 50 ft (15 m) away; garbage disposal		Damage begins after long exposure	Threats
10,000,000	70	Vacuum cleaner			Widespread complaints
1,000,000	60	Ordinary conversation; air-conditioning unit, 20 ft (6 m) away	Moderately loud		Occasional complaints
100,000	50	Light traffic noise, 100 ft (30 m) away			
10,000	40	Average living room; bedroom	Quiet		No action
1,000	30	Library; soft whisper			
100	20	Broadcasting studio	Very quiet		
10	10	Rustling leaf			
1	0	Threshold of hearing	Barely audible		

Source: Jonathan Turk and Amos Turk (1987). *Physical Science with Environmental and Other Practices,* 3rd ed. Philadelphia: Saunders College Publishing. Reproduced by permission of the publisher.

Policy

The development of a federal policy for noise control has lagged behind that for other environmental problems—probably because by its very nature, noise is a local problem. However, in 1972, Congress passed the Noise Control Act (NCA). This act was aimed at regulating noise emissions from new consumer products. In 1978, Congress amended the NCA to include the Quiet Communities Act. This set of amendments authorized the EPA to assist local and state governments in developing noise reduction programs that would meet their specific needs. Through the amendments, federal dollars were provided to help local governments put their programs into action. Most people still view noise as a nuisance and not as a health problem. Until noise pollution becomes recognized as detrimental to health, it will continue to be overlooked and underfunded.

Educational Programs

Another approach to noise control is education. The goal in this approach is to alter the behavior of those generating the noise, thereby reducing noise at the source. So far, little measurable progress has been achieved through noise education programs, and no model noise education program has been widely accepted.

Environmental Changes

Noise abatement can be achieved through environmental modification. This modification can be made at the source of the noise, to the path it travels, or to the exposed parties. An example of reducing noise at its source is the common practice of placing a computer printer in a padded compartment. An example of altering the path on which noise travels can be seen in the large dirt mound placed at the beginning of the airport runway to absorb the jet engine sound from surrounding areas. Ways to protect against damaging effects of noise pollution include wearing ear protection in the form of earplugs or headsets, as is often practiced in manufacturing facilities.

CHAPTER SUMMARY

- The environment consists of all the external conditions, circumstances, and influences surrounding and affecting the growth and development of an organism or community of organisms.

- There are both natural and human-made hazards that threaten habitats, climates, and ultimately the health of both individuals and their communities.

- Residues and wastes from human activities have been increasing rapidly because of urbanization, industrialization, population growth, and reliance on disposable products and containers (especially in the United States).

- Types of wastes and pollution include solid wastes, hazardous wastes, air pollution, water pollution, radiation, and noise pollution.

- Widespread recognition of the growing problem of environmental pollution officially occurred in 1970, with the celebration of the first Earth Day and the establishment of the Environmental Protection Agency (EPA).

- A number of significant pieces of federal legislation have been passed to protect our land, air, and water from further contamination, including the Resource Conservation and Recovery Act; the Comprehensive Environmental Response, Compensation, and Liability Act; the Clean Air Act; the Clean Water Act; and the Safe Drinking Water Act.

- Progress has been made in cleaning up our air, water, and even abandoned hazardous waste sites. However, there is still a great deal of work to do.

- Greater effort is needed by communities and individuals to increase the levels of recycling, source reduction, and resource conservation if we are to leave a healthy environment to future generations.

REVIEW QUESTIONS

1. Why are there more environmental problems today than ever before?

2. What are the primary sources of solid waste? Why are municipal wastes such a problem?

3. What piece of federal legislation deals with "cradle-to-grave" regulation of solid hazardous waste?

4. Define the following terms—*sanitary landfill, combustion, recycling,* and *source reduction.* Provide one advantage and one disadvantage for each process.

5. Define the term *hazardous waste* and give several examples.

6. How is a secured landfill different from a sanitary one?

7. The Superfund was part of what legislation? What is the Superfund used for?

8. What is the Number 1 source of air pollution?

9. In what forms can air pollutants be found?

10. What are the six criteria air pollutants?

11. What is the Pollutant Standard Index (PSI)?

12. Outline the process and conditions that result in acid rain.

13. How does the greenhouse effect result in global warming?

14. Why is the ozone layer thinning?

15. What relationship is there between photochemical smog and thermal inversion?

16. Why was the Clean Air Act so important to the United States?

17. Name six indoor air pollutants.

18. What is meant by *sick building syndrome*?

19. What makes water so important to life?

SCENARIO: ANALYSIS AND RESPONSE

As you know from reading this chapter, the problem Mary and Tom face is not so uncommon. The National Priority List (NPL) associated with the Superfund legislation has over 1,300 known hazardous waste sites that still need to be cleaned up.

1. Knowing what you now know about polluted water, what could Mary and Tom have done before purchasing their house to try to ensure against such a problem?

2. If you were confronted with the problem that Mary and Tom now face, how would you handle it?
3. Would you continue to live in the home, or would you move?
4. If you planned to sell the house, would you tell the realtor or prospective buyers about the problem?
5. Is it fair that Mary and Tom are faced with this problem? Name five things you could do to help prevent such a problem in the future.

---

20. What is the difference between point source and non-point source pollution?

21. How does the Clean Water Act and its amendments help to protect the water supply?

22. What is the Safe Drinking Water Act?

23. What is the purpose of municipal wastewater treatment?

24. What is a septic system?

25. What is radiation?

26. What types of human behavior increase exposure to radiation?

27. What types of radiation are dangerous to humans? Why?

28. How have humans benefited from radiation?

29. What is noise?

30. What are decibels? What do they measure?

31. What level of government passes the most noise ordinances?

Does your state/community have a clean indoor air act? If it does, briefly describe it.

Does your community have a noise ordinance? If so, briefly describe it.

What is the most recent piece of legislation your community has enacted to protect the environment? Do you agree with it? Why or why not?

2. Write a one-page paper describing either your support for or opposition to (a) nuclear power plants or (b) strengthening the Safe Drinking Water Act.

3. In a one-page paper, identify what you feel to be the Number 1 waste or pollution problem faced by the United States and then detail your rationale for feeling this way.

4. For two weeks, watch a television weather program that mentions the Pollutant Standard Index (PSI). During that two-week period, chart the PSI in a graph form and identify the major pollutant for each day.

5. During the next week, create a list of at least 10 things you could have done to conserve the water you use.

ACTIVITIES

1. In order for all of us to be better stewards of our environment, we need to be aware of how our community handles various important environmental issues. Find the answers to the following questions about your community and state:

How does your community dispose of solid waste?

How far do you live from a secured landfill? What is the closest community to it?

Where does your community get its water? If you personally get your water from a well, when was the last time the water was evaluated?

Where is the closest nuclear power plant to your home? What are you supposed to do in case of an accident?

COMMUNITY HEALTH ON THE WEB

The Internet contains a wealth of information about community and public health. Increase your knowledge of some of the topics presented in this chapter by accessing the Jones and Bartlett Publishers Web site at **health.jbpub.com/communityhealth/5e** and follow the links to complete the following Web activities.

• Environmental Protection Agency
• The Health Effects Institute
• The Office for Solid Waste and Emergency Response

REFERENCES

1. Miller, G. T. (2004). *Living in the Environment: Principles, Connections, and Solutions,* 13th ed. Pacific Grove, CA: Brooks/Cole-Thomson Learning.

2. Environmental Protection Agency (2004). *Municipal Solid Waste: Basic Facts.* Available at http://www.epa.gov/epaoswer/non-hw/muncpl/facts.htm.

3. Chiras, D. D. (2002). *Environmental Science: Creating a Sustainable Future,* 6th ed. Sudbury, MA: Jones and Bartlett Publishers.

4. Environmental Protection Agency (2004). *Municipal Solid Waste: Recycling.* Available at http://www.epa.gov/epaoswer/non-hw/muncpl/recycle.htm.

5. Environmental Protection Agency (2004). *MSW Programs.* Available at http://www.epa.gov/epaoswer/non-hw/muncpl/programs.htm.

6. Environmental Protection Agency (2004). *Treat, Store and Dispose of Waste.* Available at http://www.epa.gov/epaoswer/osw/tsd.htm.

7. U.S. Department of Health and Human Services (2000). *Healthy People 2010: Understanding and Improving Health,* 2nd ed. Washington, DC: U.S. Government Printing Office.

8. Environmental Protection Agency (2004). *Air Trends: Six Principal Pollutants.* Available at http://www.epa.gov/airtrends/sixpoll.html.

9. Moeller, D. W. (1997). *Environmental Health.* Cambridge, MA: Harvard University Press, 93.

10. National Institute for Occupational Safety and Health (1991). *Environmental Tobacco Smoke in the Workplace: Lung Cancer and Other Health Effects* (HHS pub. no. NIOSH 91-108). Cincinnati, OH: Author.

11. Spengler, J. D. (1991). "Sources and Concentration of Indoor Air Pollution." In J. M. Samet and J. D. Spengler, eds., *Indoor Air Pollution: A Health Perspective.* Baltimore, MD: Johns Hopkins University Press, 33–67.

12. Lioy, P. J. (1989). *Info Sheet: Indoor Air Pollution.* Piscataway, NJ: Environmental and Occupational Health Sciences Institute.

13. Environmental Protection Agency (2004). *Groundwater Basics.* Available at http://www.epa.gov/seahome/groundwater/src/basics.htm.

14. Steward, J. C. (1990). *Drinking Water Hazards: How to Know If There Are Toxic Chemicals in Your Water and What to Do If There Are.* Hiram, OH: Envirographics.

15. Sierra Club (2004). *Politics and Issues Watch: George W. Bush & Clean Water.* Available at http://www.sierraclub.org/wwatch/cleanwater/index.asp.

16. Environmental Protection Agency (2004). *Drinking Water Contaminant Candidate List.* Available at http://www.epa.gov/OGWDW/ccl/cclfs.html.

17. Cunningham, W. P., M. A. Cunningham, and B. W. Saigo (2005). *Environmental Science: A Global Concern,* 8th ed. New York: McGraw-Hill.

Chapter 16

The Impact of Environment on Human Health

Chapter Objectives

After studying this chapter you will be able to:

1 Define the terms *environmental health* and *environmental hazard.*

2 Explain the relationship between environmental sanitation, sanitary engineers, and the prevention of waterborne disease outbreaks.

3 Explain the meaning of waterborne, foodborne, and vectorborne diseases and give an example of each.

4 Define the term *vector* and give examples.

5 Define *pest, pesticides, target organism,* and *persistent* and *nonpersistent pesticides.*

6 Explain the benefits and risks of using pesticides.

7 Define *environmental tobacco smoke, mainstream smoke, sidestream smoke,* and *passive smoking.*

8 Describe the legislation in place to deal with environmental tobacco smoke.

9 Describe the sources of lead in the environment and the progress made in reducing lead levels in the United States.

10 Define *ionizing radiation* and give examples.

11 Explain the dangers of radon gas.

12 Explain how human activities have increased the risk of skin cancer by altering the environment.

13 Explain the relationship between psychological hazards and loss of health and give an example.

14 Describe the state of population growth in the world.

15 Interpret the relationships among population growth, the environment, and human health.

16 Outline some solutions to population growth.

17 Define natural disaster and describe two agencies involved in disaster preparedness, response, and recovery.

SCENARIO

Pam and Gary were numb when their physician told them that the laboratory tests indicated that Gary had prostate cancer. Numb yes, shocked no, for Gary had served in Vietnam with the 151st Airborne Infantry Rangers in 1968–1969. During that time, his entire unit had been exposed to the herbicide Agent Orange, the defoliant used in Vietnam and Laos to eliminate enemy hiding places by destroying their crops. Agent Orange, comprised of an equal mixture of 2,4-D (2,4-dichlorophenoxyacetic acid) and 2,4,5-T (2,4,5-trichlorophenoxyacetic acid), was named for the bright orange stripes on the steel drums in which it was contained. Later it was found that the 2,4,5-T was contaminated with an extremely toxic compound known as dioxin. Gary was aware that a number of other men in his unit had been diagnosed with cancer in the past couple of years, but he thought that somehow maybe the dreaded disease might have passed him by. Prior to the diagnosis Gary had suffered from rashes, and his skin always seemed dry.

INTRODUCTION

Environmental health is the study and management of environmental conditions that affect the health and well-being of humans. **Environmental hazards** are those factors or conditions in the environment that increase the risk of human injury, disease, or death. Regardless of whether the environment contributes a little or a lot to disease, the tragedy is that all environment-induced disease is highly preventable.[1] Both individuals and communities can contribute to the elimination of environmental health risks. Individuals can protect their own health and the health of those around them by making wise choices about their personal health behavior. Communities can limit their exposure to environmental hazards by adopting environmentally sound practices in the production, transport, storage, and disposal of hazardous wastes.

Environmental hazards can be biological, chemical, physical, psychological, or sociological. Some events, such as natural disasters or terrorist acts, can result in several types of environmental hazards. For example, a hurricane often causes physical hazards (high winds), followed by biological and chemical hazards (contaminated flood waters), and psychological and social hazards (fear and loss of homes and businesses). This chapter discusses each of these environmental conditions that poses a risk to human health.

environmental health the study and management of environmental conditions that affect the health and well-being of humans

environmental hazards factors or conditions in the environment that increase the risk of human injury, disease, or death

BIOLOGICAL HAZARDS AND HUMAN HEALTH

Biological hazards are living organisms (and viruses), or their products, that increase the risk of disease or death in humans. These may be animals (venomous snakes) or plants (toxic mushrooms), but they are usually viruses or microbes such as bacteria. Because the immediate source of many biological hazards is humans themselves, the improper handling of human waste and wastewater can jeopardize the health of the community.

Environmental sanitation is the practice of establishing and maintaining health and hygienic conditions in the environment. The protection of communities from biological hazards resulting from the mismanagement of wastewater or solid waste is the job of the **sanitary engineer.** Failure to maintain the integrity of the water supply can mean epidemics of **waterborne diseases,** illnesses and diseases transmitted through chemical or fecal contamination of drinking water. Environmental sanitation also includes protecting communities from unsafe food. The improper handling, storage, and service of food can result in outbreaks of **foodborne diseases.** Likewise, the overflow of wastewater into open fields and ditches or the mismanagement of solid waste near human habitation can result in outbreaks of **vectorborne diseases,** diseases transmitted by insects.

biological hazards living organisms (and viruses) or their products that increase the risk of disease or death in humans

environmental sanitation the practice of establishing and maintaining healthy or hygienic conditions in the environment

Table 16.1
Waterborne Biological Hazards

Hazard	Agent	Disease
Viruses	Poliomyelitis virus	Polio
	Hepatitis A virus	Infectious hepatitis
Bacteria	*Vibrio cholerae*	Cholera
	Salmonella typhi	Typhoid fever
	Shigella spp.	Bacillary dysentery
	Leptospira spp.	Leptospirosis
Protozoans (parasites)	*Entamoeba histolytica*	Amoebic dysentery
	Giardia lamblia	Giardiasis
	Cryptosporidium parvum	Cryptosporidiosis

Source: Chin, J., ed. (2000). *Control of Communicable Diseases Manual*, 17th ed. Washington, DC: American Public Health Association.

sanitary engineer
environmental worker responsible for management of waste-water and solid waste for a community

waterborne disease
a disease transmitted through contamination of drinking water (for example, typhoid fever)

foodborne disease
a disease transmitted through the contamination of food (for example, salmonellosis)

vectorborne disease
a communicable disease transmitted by insects or other arthropods (for example, St. Louis encephalitis)

waterborne disease outbreak (WBDO)
a disease in which at least two persons experience a similar illness after the ingestion of drinking water or after exposure to water used for recreational purposes and epidemiologic evidence implicates water as the probable source of the illness

Waterborne Diseases

Waterborne diseases occur when water, contaminated with a disease agent, is consumed by a susceptible person. Waterborne disease agents include viruses, bacteria, parasites, and chemicals. Waterborne viral agents and the diseases they cause include poliomyelitis virus (polio) and hepatitis A virus (hepatitis). Waterborne bacteria and the diseases they cause include *Escherichia coli*, *Salmonella typhi* (typhoid fever), *Shigella* spp. (shigellosis or bacillary dysentery), and *Vibrio cholerae* (cholera). Waterborne parasites include *Entamoeba histolytica* (amebiasis or amoebic dysentery), *Giardia lamblia* (giardiasis), and *Cryptosporidium parvum* (cryptosporidiosis). Each of these diseases can be serious, and two in particular—typhoid fever and cholera—have killed thousands of people in single epidemics (see Table 16.1).

One of the earliest carefully documented cholera epidemics was the one that occurred in London, England, in 1849. This epidemic occurred before the discoveries of Louis Pasteur, during a period of time when most people thought that diseases were caused by malodorous vapors (miasmas) or, perhaps, by spirits. Dr. John Snow believed that water drawn from a particular city well was contaminated. After interviewing many sick and well people, he had the handle removed from the Broad Street pump; the cholera epidemic subsided. This event was so remarkable that the site has been preserved in modern-day London (see Figure 1.8).

A **waterborne disease outbreak (WBDO)** is an event in which at least two persons experience a similar illness after ingestion of drinking water or after exposure to water used for recreational purposes *and* epidemiologic evidence implicates water as the probable source of the illness.[2] In the case of chemical poisoning, a single case is considered an outbreak. WBDOs can be associated with drinking water, recreational water, or occupational water exposure. In recent years, the leading causes of WBDOs (in cases in which the cause was identified) have been bacteria and parasites.[2-4] During the 1999–2000 reporting period, the cause could only be determined in 56.4% of the outbreaks associated with drinking water. Where cause was determined, bacteria were most often the cause, followed by parasites, viruses, and chemicals. For outbreaks associated with recreational water, the cause was determined 74.6% of the time; the leading cause of WBDOs associated with recreational water was parasites (*Cryptosporidium*), followed by bacteria (*E. coli* and *Shigella*), and viruses (Figure 16.1). There were only two outbreaks associated with occupational exposure.

Waterborne disease outbreaks can be traced to individual wells or to a municipal water supply. Outbreaks associated with municipal water systems can become quite large. The largest WBDO ever reported in the United States occurred in Milwaukee, Wisconsin, in 1993. In that outbreak, 403,000 people became ill and 4,400 were hospitalized. The disease agent was identified as the parasite *Cryptosporidium parvum*. This outbreak occurred because of

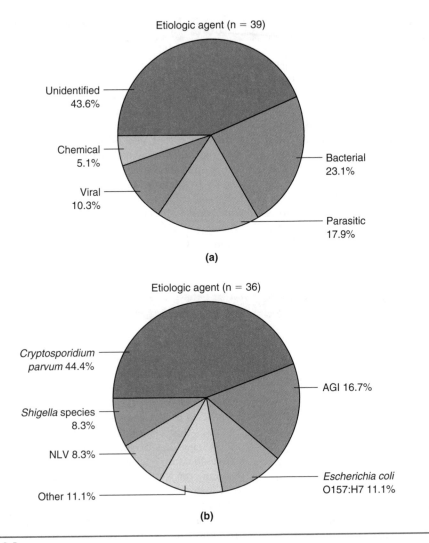

FIGURE 16.1

(a) Waterborne disease outbreaks associated with drinking water, by etiologic agent: United States, 1999-2000.
(b) Waterborne disease outbreaks of gastroenteritis associated with recreational water, by etiologic agent: United States, 1999-2000.

Note: AGI = acute gastrointestinal illness of unknown etiology; NLV = Norwalk-like virus. The "Other" category included outbreaks caused by *Campylobacter jejuni, Giardia lamblia,* and *Escherichia coli* O121:H19 and one mixed *Shigella/Cryptosporidium* outbreak.

Source: Centers for Disease Control and Prevention (2002). "Surveillance for Waterborne-Disease Outbreaks—United States, 1999-2000." *MMWR,* 51(SS-8): 1-28.

a breakdown in the city's water treatment plant.[4] (Refer to Chapter 15 for a summary of municipal water treatment.)

Waterborne disease outbreaks resulting from excessive levels of fluoride, copper, and nitrates can also occur. In one outbreak during 1993-1994, nitrate poisoning was associated with miscarriages (see Box 16.1).[4] In 1997-1998, two outbreaks of copper poisoning were reported in Florida.[3]

Public health laws that set standards for water and wastewater treatment facilities and plumbing are a community's first line of defense against such epidemics. While WBDOs occur from time to time in the United States, they occur much less frequently than in countries with

---

BOX 16.1

NITRATE POISONING IN INDIANA TRACED TO A LEAKING HOG FARM WASTE PIT

Two episodes of nitrate poisoning, associated with eight miscarriages, were reported in Indiana in the mid-1990s. In the first episode, three women who lived within a mile of each other reported a total of six miscarriages during 1993 and 1994. All three women drank water from private wells on their premises and all three wells tapped the same aquifer, which was probably contaminated by a leaking waste pit on a nearby hog farm. The well water had high nitrate-nitrogen levels, 2 to 3 times the EPA's maximum contaminant level (MCL). No other toxic substances were found in the water. All three women delivered full-term babies after changing to nitrate-free drinking water. During that same period, five women who lived in the same geographical area and who had wells with nitrate levels below the EPA's MCL had five normal pregnancies.[4]

Many states and local communities are being confronted by the establishment of large-scale hog operations in areas that were once occupied by family farms. State regulations, originally passed to protect the family farmer, often shield these large-scale hog operations from stricter regulation. The waste pits on these large hog farms sometimes contaminate nearby water supplies. Is your state or local community experiencing such a problem? What community approaches might be effective in correcting this problem?

BOX 16.2

TEN GREAT PUBLIC HEALTH ACHIEVEMENTS, 1900–1999: FLUORIDATION OF DRINKING WATER

From Toothless Grins to Pearly Whites

At the beginning of the twentieth century, tooth decay was rampant, and because no effective preventive measures existed, tooth extraction was routine. Now, thanks to water fluoridation, combined with other dental health advances, adults in the United States are retaining most of their teeth thoughout their lifetime.

In 1901, soon after establishing his dental practice in Colorado Springs, Colorado, Dr. Frederick S. McKay noted an ususual permanent brown stain on the teeth of many of his patients. He concluded that something in the public water supply was probably responsible. McKay also observed that teeth affected by this condition seemed to be less susceptible to dental caries.

In 1931, Dr. H. Trendley Dean, a U.S. Public Health Service Dental Officer, conducted pioneering research into the relationship between fluoride and dental caries. His research laid the groundwork for community water fluoridation in the United States.

In 1945, Grand Rapids, Michigan, became the first city in the world to fluoridate its drinking water. The caries rate among Grand Rapids children born after fluoride was added to the water supply dropped 60%. This finding revolutionized dental care and resulted in tooth decay being preventable for most people.

Water fluoridation is relatively inexpensive in the United States. The benefits of fluoridation are available, on average, for little more than $0.50 per person per year, and even less in large communities.

The documented effectiveness of community water fluoridation in preventing dental caries prompted rapid adoption of this public health measure in cities throughout the United States. In the 1960s, the U.S. Public Health Service provided funding, technical expertise, and leadership to promote and establish fluoridation programs throughout the Nation. The federal government continues to promote water fluoridation worldwide.

---

developing economies, where safe drinking water is at a premium. Wars and natural disasters can further disrupt normal water supplies, resulting in epidemics of waterborne diseases.

One of the most significant achievements in public health during the last century occurred not by removing harmful elements from community drinking water, but by adding something to it. Fluoridation of community drinking water is a major factor responsible for the decline in dental caries (tooth decay) in the United States since 1950 (see Box 16.2). At first, caries reduction rates of 50% to 70% were reported. More recently, the reduction among adolescents has averaged 25%. Because fluoride has appeared in other products, such as toothpaste and mouthwashes, the difference in rates of caries between those who receive

BOX 16.3	HEALTHY PEOPLE 2010 OBJECTIVE: REDUCE OUTBREAKS OF INFECTIONS CAUSED BY KEY FOODBORNE BACTERIA

10-2.   Reduce outbreaks of infections caused by key foodborne bacteria.

Target and baseline:

Objective	Reduction in Infections Caused by Foodborne Bacteria	Number of Outbreaks per Year 1997 Baseline	Number of Outbreaks per Year 2010 Target
10-2a.	*Escherichia coli* O157:H7	22	11
10-2b.	*Salmonella* serotype Enteritidis	44	22

Target setting method: 50% improvement.

Source: Foodborne Disease Outbreak Surveillance System, CDC, NCID.

For Further Thought

Outbreaks of *E. coli* O157:H7 have been associated with undercooked ground beef. How do you make sure that you are protecting yourself and your guests when you cook hamburgers at home?

---

fluoridated water and those who do not has declined. By 1992, 144 million people were receiving fluoridated water, at an average cost of 31 cents per person per year. The savings from prevention of dental caries attributable to fluoridation was estimated for the period 1979–1989 at $39 billion (1990 dollars), a savings per person that in some communities reached $53 per person per year.[5]

Foodborne Diseases

One way in which humans interact with their environment is by ingesting bits of it. The act of eating is, in effect, a way of bringing biological hazards into intimate contact with the tissues that line the intestinal tract. "More than 200 known diseases are transmitted through food. In these cases, food is the vehicle; and the agents can be viruses, bacteria, parasite's toxins, metals, and prions."[6] Symptoms of foodborne illness range from mild to severe, and organs involved can include stomach and intestines, liver, kidneys, and brain and nervous system. Foodborne diseases cause between 6 and 81 million cases of illness and up to 9,000 deaths each year in the United States.[6] A majority of these cases are never reported to the Centers for Disease Control and Prevention (CDC).

The CDC defines a **foodborne disease outbreak (FBDO)** as the occurrence of two or more cases of a similar illness resulting from the ingestion of food.[7] During the five-year period 1993–1997, only 878 (32%) of the 2,751 FBDOs reported to the CDC had a known etiology. These outbreaks accounted for 50,788 (59%) of the 86,058 infections reported.[7] Among the outbreaks for which the causative agent was established, bacterial pathogens caused 75% of the outbreaks and 86% of the cases. *Salmonella* serotype enteritidis accounted for the largest number of outbreaks, cases, and deaths, but *E. coli* O157:H7 was also responsible for multistate outbreaks that were associated with consumption of undercooked or raw ground beef. One of the food safety objectives of *Healthy People 2010* is to reduce outbreaks of infections caused by key foodborne bacteria by half (see Box 16.3). Chemicals were the cause of 17% of outbreaks (1% of cases) in which the cause was determined, viruses for 6% of outbreaks (8% of cases), and parasites for 2% of outbreaks (5% of cases) (see Figure 16.2).[7]

foodborne disease outbreak (FBDO) the occurrence of two or more cases of a similar illness resulting from the ingestion of food

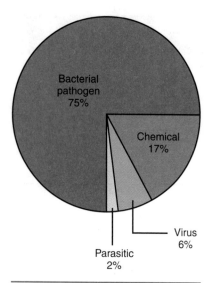

FIGURE 16.2

Foodborne disease outbreaks with known etiology by cause: United States, 1993–1997.

Source: Centers for Disease Control and Prevention (2000)."Surveillance for Foodborne-Disease Outbreaks—United States, 1993–1997." *MMWR,* 49.

sanitarians
environmental workers responsible for the inspection of restaurants, retail food outlets, public housing, and other sites to ensure compliance with public health codes

vector
a living organism, usually an insect or other arthropod, that can transmit a communicable disease agent to a susceptible host (for example, a mosquito or tick)

The leading factors that were found to contribute to FBDOs during 1993–1997 were improper holding temperatures and inadequate cooking of food.[7] Other factors that often contribute to FBDOs are poor personal hygiene of preparers, contaminated equipment, and obtaining food from an unsafe source (such as shellfish from polluted waters).

Almost any food can serve as a vehicle of transmission for a foodborne disease agent. The vehicle of infection for more than half of the cases is unknown. In some outbreaks, multiple foods are incriminated. Delicatessens, cafeterias, and restaurants are reported nearly twice as often as homes as places where the contaminated food is eaten. Also, more cases occur in the summer months than during any other season.[7,8] More and more of our foods are imported. Currently, 38% of the fruits, 12% of the vegetables, and 9% of the meats and poultry Americans consume each year are imported. Foodborne illness has been increasingly related to imported foods.[9]

To protect the public from foodborne diseases requires the coordinated efforts of federal, state, and local health agencies. At the federal level, the CDC, under its Emerging Infections Program, has established the Foodborne Diseases Active Surveillance Network (FoodNet) to provide better data on foodborne diseases. FoodNet tracks nine foodborne diseases in eight catchment areas with a combined surveillance population of 29.5 million people.[10] The CDC coordinates these surveillance activities with officials from the U.S. Department of Agriculture's Food Safety and Inspection Service, the Food and Drug Administration's Center for Food Safety and Applied Nutrition, and with the respective state epidemiologists.

A recent report analyzed the success rate for investigating and reporting FBDOs in FoodNet catchment areas during 1998–1999. The results were disappointing. In 71% of the outbreaks, no confirmed etiology (cause) was found, and in 46% of the outbreaks, no suspected food was identified. This study illustrates the difficulty of epidemiological and disease control work in the absence of adequate resources.[11]

Enforcing state regulations at the local level are **sanitarians,** also known as registered environmental health specialists. Hired by local health departments, these sanitarians inspect restaurants and other food-serving establishments (such as hospitals, nursing homes, churches, and schools), temporary and seasonal points of food service (such as those at fairs and festivals), and retail food outlets (grocery stores and supermarkets) to ensure that environmental conditions favorable to the growth and development of pathogens do not exist.

By enforcing food safety laws, public health officials protect the health of the community by reducing the incidence of FBDOs. In fact, safer and healthier foods has been one of the ten greatest achievements in public health in the twentieth century (see Box 16.4).[12] Guidelines for preventing foodborne disease transmission at home are simple and straightforward (see Box 16.5).

Vectorborne Diseases

Standing water, including runoff water from overflowing septic systems or overloaded sewer systems, and improperly handled solid waste are more than unsavory sights. They provide habitat for, and support the proliferation of, disease vectors. As discussed in Chapter 4, a **vector** is a living organism, usually an insect or other arthropod, that transmits microscopic disease agents to susceptible hosts. Examples of vectors and the diseases they transmit include mosquitoes (malaria, filariasis, and arthropodborne viruses—arboviruses), fleas (murine typhus and plague), lice (epidemic typhus), and ticks (Rocky Mountain spotted fever and Lyme disease) (see Table 16.2).

| BOX **16.4** | **TEN GREAT PUBLIC HEALTH ACHIEVEMENTS, 1900–1999: SAFER AND HEALTHIER FOODS** |

Food for Thought

Early in the twentieth century, contaminated food, milk, and water were responsible for many foodborne diseases, including typhoid fever, tuberculosis, botulism, and scarlet fever. In the first half of the century, scientific discoveries and public health policies, such as food fortification programs, led to large reductions in diseases caused by nutritional deficiency. More recently, the focus of many public health nutrition programs shifted to the prevention and control of chronic disease, such as cardiovascular disease and obesity, through nutrition.

After the characteristics and sources of foodborne diseases were identified, public health professionals began advocating control of those diseases through technology and safer food-handling procedures, including:

- Handwashing
- Better sanitation
- Refrigeration
- Pasteurization
- Pesticide application
- Reduction of foodborne pathogens
- Better animal care and feeding
- Safer food processing

Prompt refrigeration inhibits bacterial growth, thus reducing the risk for disease.

One notable discovery that reduced disease was the process invented by Louis Pasteur—pasteurization.

New foodborne pathogens have emerged in the United States during the past 20 years as a result of changes in agricultural practices and in food-processing operations and the globalization of the food supply. Seemingly healthy food animals can be reservoirs for human pathogens.

Pesticides have played an important role in increasing crop yields, decreasing food costs, and enhancing the appearance of food. However, without proper controls, the residues of some pesticides remaining on foods also create potential health risks.

| BOX **16.5** | **GUIDELINES FOR PREVENTING FOODBORNE ILLNESSES** |

1. Cook thoroughly raw food from animal sources.
2. Wash raw vegetables thoroughly before eating them.
3. Keep uncooked meats separate from vegetables and from cooked foods and ready-to-eat foods.
4. Avoid raw (unpasteurized) milk or foods made from raw milk.
5. Wash hands, knives, and cutting boards after each handling of uncooked foods.

Source: Centers for Disease Control and Prevention (2000). "Multistate Outbreak of Listerosis—United States, 2000." *MMWR,* 49(50): 1129–1130.

Table 16.2
Vectorborne Biological Hazards

Hazard	Agent	Vector	Disease
Virus	SLE virus	Mosquito	St. Louis encephalitis
	LaCrosse	Mosquito	LaCrosse encephalitis
Rickettsiae	*Rickettsia typhi*	Flea	Murine typhus
	Rickettsia rickettsii	Tick	Rocky Mountain spotted fever
	Ehrlichia chaffeensis	Tick	Ehrlichiosis
Bacteria	*Yersinia pestis*	Flea	Bubonic plague
	Borrelia burgdorferi	Tick	Lyme disease
Protozoa	*Plasmodium* spp.	Mosquito	Malaria
Nematodes	*Wuchereria bancrofti*	Mosquito	Filariasis (elephantiasis)

Source: Chin, J., ed. (2000). *Control of Communicable Diseases Manual,* 17th ed. Washington, DC: American Public Health Association.

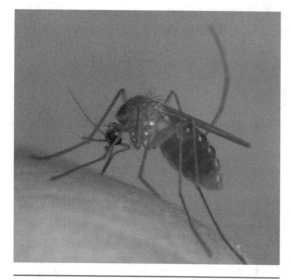

FIGURE 16.3

The northern house mosquito (*Culex pipiens*) is the most important vector of St. Louis encephalitis and West Nile virus in the eastern United States.

vectorborne disease outbreak (VBDO)
the occurrence of two or more cases of a vectorborne disease

Lyme disease
a systemic, bacterial, tickborne disease with symptoms that include dermatologic, arthritic, neurologic, and cardiac abnormalities

Mosquito larvae require standing water in which to complete their development. The improper handling of wastewater or inadequate drainage of rainwater provides an ideal habitat for mosquitoes and increases the risk for a **vectorborne disease outbreak (VBDO).** Of particular concern in this regard is the northern house mosquito, *Culex pipiens* (see Figure 16.3). *Culex pipiens* is the most important vector of St. Louis encephalitis (SLE) in the eastern United States. In California, the SLE virus is transmitted by another mosquito species, *Culex tarsalis,* which proliferates in mismanaged irrigation water. SLE is a disease to which the elderly are particularly susceptible. Those at greatest risk live in unscreened houses without air conditioning.

Culex pipiens also transmits West Nile virus (WNV), which first appeared in New York in 1999, where it caused 62 human cases of disease, including 7 deaths.[13] An excellent example of the global nature of emerging infectious diseases, WNV had caused outbreaks of encephalitis in Algeria (1994), Romania (1996–1997), the Democratic Republic of the Congo (1998), and Russia (1999) before arriving in the United States.[14] Once established, WNV spread rapidly in the United States. In 2002, 4,156 human cases, including 284 deaths, were reported from 39 states.[13] In 2003, an additional 9,858 cases, including 262 deaths, were reported from 45 states and the District of Columbia.[15] The WNV story underlines the importance of both proper environmental sanitation and active surveillance for vectorborne diseases.

Another species of mosquito that thrives on environmental mismanagement in the north-central and eastern United States is the eastern tree hole mosquito, *Aedes triseriatus.* While the natural habitat for this mosquito is tree holes, it flourishes in water held in discarded automobile and truck tires. It is estimated there are two billion used tires discarded in various places in the United States today, and two million more discarded tires are added to the environment each year. In the eastern United States, *Aedes triseriatus* is the vector for LaCrosse encephalitis, an arbovirus that produces a serious and sometimes fatal disease in children.

Improperly discarded vehicle tires are also the favored habitat of another vector, the Asian tiger mosquito, *Aedes albopictus.* Since 1985, when this species was first discovered in the United States (in Houston, Texas), it has been reported in 866 counties in 26 states.[16] The tiger mosquito arrived in the United States in used tires imported from Japan. *Aedes albopictus* has been called a "super vector" because it can transmit about 10 diseases to humans, including the viruses that cause LaCrosse encephalitis and dengue fever. Larvae of the Asian tiger mosquito can develop in water held in almost any artificial container, including discarded cups and plastic wrap. So far, two pathogenic arboviruses have been isolated from *Ae. albopictus* in the United States—the eastern equine encephalomyelitis virus and the Cache Valley virus.

In 1998, yet another Asian species of mosquito, *Aedes japonicus,* was detected in the United States. While no human cases of disease have been traced to *Ae. japonicus* in the United States thus far, the species has been shown to be a good vector of West Nile virus under laboratory conditions.[17]

Improper management of solid waste—such as occurs at open dumps, ill-managed landfills, and urban slums—fosters the expansion of rat and mouse populations. These rodents are hosts for fleas, which transmit murine typhus, a rickettsial disease characterized by headache, fever, and rash. If the rodent population should decline rapidly because of disease or a successful rodent control program, these fleas could come into contact with humans and spread the disease directly to them. Diseases of animals that are transmissible to humans, such as murine typhus, are referred to as *zoonoses*.

Seemingly harmless interactions with the environment can have unintended consequences. For example, white-tailed deer were decimated throughout much of the Midwest and eastern United States during the nineteenth century. As they declined in numbers, their predators and parasites vanished too. Reintroduced in the 1930s and protected from hunting by strict regulations, white-tailed deer populations became well established. Modern farming practices, which result in field after field of corn, soybeans, or other nutritious crops interspersed with wooded areas, resulted in deer populations large enough to reach pest status in some parts of the Midwest. As deer populations have increased, so have populations of the blacklegged tick, *Ixodes scapularis*. Sometimes called the deer tick, *I. scapularis* is the vector of **Lyme disease** caused by the bacterial spirochete *Borrelia burgdorferi* (see Figure 4.5). Lyme disease is currently the most commonly reported vectorborne disease in the United States. Between 1992 and 1998, a total of 88,967 cases of Lyme disease was reported to the CDC by 49 states and the District of Columbia, with the number increasing from 9,896 in 1992 to 16,802 in 1998. In 2002, 23,763 cases were reported, bringing the total number of cases reported since 1982 to 157,000.[18]

CHEMICAL HAZARDS AND HUMAN HEALTH

Chemical hazards are those that result from the mismanagement of chemicals. Not all people react to chemicals in the same way; some people are especially susceptible, whereas others are not. One fact is clear: Children are much more vulnerable to chemical assaults than adults. Although chemicals have provided modern society with innumerable benefits, they can have a deleterious impact on human health when mismanaged. This section examines three common sources of chemical exposure that could negatively affect health, namely, pesticides, environmental tobacco smoke, and lead.

Pesticides

The term **pest** refers to any organism (plant, animal, or microbe) that has an adverse effect on human interests. Some common examples are weeds in your vegetable garden, termites in your house, and mold on your shower curtain. **Pesticides** are natural or synthetic chemicals that have been developed and manufactured for the purpose of killing pests. In the United States, there are more than 25,000 different pesticide products that contain more than 600 pest-killing chemicals.[19] It has been estimated that without the use of chemical insecticides, American agricultural production would decrease by 30%. Because of this, it seems certain that pesticides will be present in our environment for the foreseeable future.

While chemical companies market pesticides to control a particular pest, most of them in fact kill a wide range of organisms. The pest organism against which the pesticide is applied is referred to as the **target pest** or **target organism** (see Table 16.3). All other organisms in the environment that may also be affected are called **nontarget organisms.** For example, most weed killers will not only kill the weeds, but also (nontarget) flowers and ornamental plant vegetation. Similarly, it is not uncommon for domestic animals to be poisoned and killed by rodenticides (rat poison). Overexposure to these chemicals can have adverse effects on human health.

The two most widely used types of pesticides are **herbicides** (pesticides that kill plants) and **insecticides** (pesticides that kill insects). It is also from these two types of pesticides that

---

chemical hazards
hazards caused by the mismanagement of chemicals

pest
any organism—a multicelled animal or plant, or a microbe—that has an adverse effect on human interests

pesticides
synthetic chemicals developed and manufactured for the purpose of killing pests

target organism (target pest)
the organism (or pest) for which a pesticide is applied

nontarget organisms
all other susceptible organisms in the environment, for which a pesticide was not intended

herbicide
a pesticide that kills plants

insecticide
a pesticide that kills insects

Table 16.3
Types of Pesticides

Type of Agent	Target Pest to Be Destroyed
Acaricides/miticides	Ticks/mites
Bactericides	Bacteria
Fungicides	Fungi, molds
Herbicides	Weeds, plants
Insecticides	Insects
Larvicides/grubicides	Insect larvae
Molluscicides	Snails, slugs
Nematocides	Worms
Rodenticides	Rats, mice

most human pesticide poisonings occur. The two groups at highest risk for pesticide poisoning are young children and the workers who apply the pesticides. Many of these persons live on farms or are engaged in farm work. Poisonings occur when the pesticides are consumed orally, inhaled, or when they come in contact with the skin. The majority of children poisoned by pesticides consume them orally. These are frequently unintentional poisonings that occur when pesticides are left within reach of children. Most adult poisonings occur because of careless practice. Examples include eating food without washing hands after handling pesticides, mouth-siphoning to transfer pesticides from one container to another, applying pesticides while one's skin is exposed, or spilling the pesticide on one's body.

In agricultural settings, poisonings can occur when agricultural workers misuse pesticides. For example, illiterate workers or those who do not read English may enter sprayed fields too soon because of the inability to read product directions or posted warning signs. Their employers may even tell them to enter the field too soon, and the workers' children may be with them.

Exposures may be acute (single exposure) or chronic (low-level exposure over an extended period of time). The effects of poisoning depend on many things, including the characteristics of the person exposed, the kind of pesticide, and the type and length of exposure. Some signals of poisoning are headaches, weakness, rashes, fatigue, and dizziness. More serious effects include cancer, mutations, birth defects, respiratory problems, convulsions, coma, and death.

A great deal of money and effort have been spent looking for the "ideal" pesticide for this or that purpose. The ideal pesticide has been characterized by Enger and Smith as one that would (1) be inexpensive, (2) kill only the target organism, (3) break down rapidly, and (4) break down into harmless materials.[20] Developing the ideal pesticide is an illusive goal, but a number of safe, effective, and useful pesticides have been developed. Pesticide development, like pharmaceutical (drug) development, is expensive because it requires years of research and testing.

Among the first modern pesticides developed were insecticides known as *chlorinated hydrocarbons*. The most famous example of this group is dichloro-diphenyl-trichloroethane (DDT). DDT and its relatives are very stable chemical compounds; that is, they are persistent in the environment. On the one hand, this was helpful because one did not have to make repeated treatments. It has been said that DDT has saved more lives than any other chemical developed by man by killing such disease vectors as lice, mosquitoes, and flies. On the other hand, its persistence meant that the chemical remained in the environment and even accumulated in organisms such as fish and birds that fed on the insects. Therefore, its use was eventually banned in the United States because of this problem. Another problem with DDT is the fact that it is a broad-spectrum insecticide—it kills any and all insects with which it comes into contact.

HEALTHY PEOPLE 2010 OBJECTIVE: REDUCE PESTICIDE EXPOSURES THAT RESULT IN VISITS TO A HEALTH CARE FACILITY

Target: 13,500 visits per year.

Baseline: 27,156 visits to health care facilities were due to pesticides in 1997. (A total of 129,592 pesticide exposures were documented in 1997.)

Target setting method: 50% improvement.

Pesticide exposures include those involving disinfectants, fungicides, herbicides, insecticides, moth repellants, and rodenticides, as defined by EPA. The American Association of Poison Control Centers surveillance covers approximately 93% of the U.S. population.

Source: Toxic Exposure Surveillance System (TESS), American Association of Poison Control Centers.

For Further Thought

Are there any pesticides stored in your house? Are they stored properly and out of the reach of children?

Source: Healthy People 2010.

Beginning in the 1960s, a new generation of pesticides arrived on the market called organophosphates. These pesticides were less persistent, breaking down into harmless products within weeks. The best-known organophosphate pesticide is Malathion, a relatively safe and widely used insecticide. In the 1970s, even less-persistent chemicals were developed, the carbamates. These chemicals break down in days or hours. The best example is carbaryl, which is still in use today. While today's pesticides are much safer for the environment, they are still not species-specific, and some have a higher acute toxicity to humans and other mammals than DDT.

While there is no doubt that pesticides have provided significant benefits to society, they can be dangerous if used or stored improperly. The victims are often children. In 1998 alone, 73,260 children were involved in common household pesticide-related poisonings or exposures in the United States.[21] An EPA survey revealed that 47% of all households with children under the age of 5 had at least one pesticide stored in an unlocked cabinet less than four feet off the ground (i.e., within the reach of children).[21]

The immediate solutions to the problems of pesticide poisoning and environmental quality are better education about the safe storage and proper application of pesticides, better regulation of pesticides, and better compliance by the homeowner to ensure that the products are used in accordance with instructions on the label. One of the *Healthy People 2010* objectives is to reduce pesticide exposures that result in visits to a health care facility (see Box 16.6).

Environmental Tobacco Smoke

Approximately 22.8% (46.2 million) of adult Americans smoke cigarettes.[22] As a result, many nonsmokers are exposed to environmental tobacco smoke. As noted in Chapter 15, *environmental tobacco smoke (ETS)*, also known as *secondhand smoke*, includes both sidestream smoke and mainstream smoke. The process of inhaling ETS is referred to as *passive smoking.*

The association between ETS and adverse health effects has been demonstrated in a number of different epidemiological studies.[23-25] These studies provide evidence that adults exposed to ETS have an increased relative risk of lung cancer and possibly heart disease.[23] In addition, the studies show that about 50% of all American children 5 years of age and under have been exposed to ETS from prenatal maternal smoking and/or sidestream smoke from household members after their birth (see Figure 16.4). Such exposure has been shown to increase the risk

FIGURE 16.4

Too many children are exposed to significant levels of environmental tobacco smoke.

of adverse prenatal consequences and postnatal health conditions in infants. Specifically, this exposure has been associated with intrauterine growth retardation, low birth weight, preterm delivery, respiratory tract infections, and behavioral and cognitive abnormalities.[23]

Even though the research to date does not indicate a cause-effect relationship between ETS and ill health, a large body of evidence indicates that ETS is detrimental to human health. It is known that tobacco smoke contains about 4,000 substances, many of which have carcinogenic and mutagenic properties. The obvious solution to eliminate the increased health risks associated with ETS is to eliminate exposure to ETS. Though many people do their best to avoid ETS, it is not always possible. In fact, many individuals who report no exposure to ETS have low concentrations of cotinine (a metabolite of nicotine) in their urine, indicating they have indeed been exposed.[25] Such evidence led the EPA to issue a report in 1993 classifying ETS as a group A carcinogen (known human carcinogen). In that report, the EPA stated that exposure to ETS is responsible for approximately 3,000 lung cancer deaths per year in non-smoking adults, 35,000 to 40,000 deaths from heart disease in people who are not current smokers, and 150,000 to 300,000 lower respiratory tract infections in American children younger than 18 months of age.[26,27]

Educational programs have been helpful in getting nonsmokers and smokers alike to understand the hazard of ETS. As a result, many nonsmokers attempt to avoid ETS, and many smokers have become more courteous about asking those around them for permission to smoke. At the same time, there are many smokers who believe that smoking whenever and wherever they wish is a right, not a privilege. It is these smokers who necessitate regulations against smoking in certain areas. Such regulations can originate at any level of government.

BOX 16.7	**PROTECT INDOOR AIR: NO SMOKING IN BARS AND TAVERNS**

In California, under existing law, smoking of tobacco products in an enclosed space at a place of employment is prohibited, with certain exceptions. Among the exceptions are bars, taverns, and gaming clubs. These exceptions were suspended on January 1, 1998, "unless and until Occupational Safety and Health Standards Board or Environmental Protection Agency adopts standards for reducing permissible employee exposure to environmental tobacco smoke to an exposure level that will prevent anything other than insignificantly harmful effects to exposed persons."*

This law means that waitresses, waiters, bartenders, and others who are employed in bars, taverns, and gaming clubs do not have to breathe environmental tobacco smoke for an eight-hour shift. Instead, they can work in a smoke-free environment like most other workers. Does your state protect workers employed in bars, taverns, and gaming clubs?

*AB 297, Gaming clubs: bars and taverns: smoking. Available at http://www.sen.ca.gov/htbin/ca-billpage?AB/297/gopher_root2:[bill.current.ab.from0200.ab0297].

For example, a federal regulation now prohibits smoking on all domestic air flights. Forty-nine states and the District of Columbia have some restriction on smoking in public places; Alabama has none. Of the 49 states with regulations, 45 restrict smoking in government workplaces and 25 have extended those limitations to private workplaces.[22] California has one of the strictest standards; it prohibits smoking in virtually any place of employment (see Box 16.7). Many communities throughout the United States have adopted local ordinances, which regulate smoking in public places when state laws do not. It is anticipated that the EPA ruling on ETS as a carcinogen will have a ripple effect across the country and will increase the number of smoke-free public places.

In addition, many employers are now creating policies (administrative laws) that restrict or prohibit smoking in the workplace, on workplace grounds, and/or in company-owned vehicles. Overall, 70% of the American workforce worked under a smoke-free policy in 1999.[27] Some of the smoking regulations are better than others. For example, many restaurants provide seating areas that are "no-smoking sections," but they are only an arm's length away from the smoking sections. Some employers prohibit smoking in common areas, but allow it in individual offices.

Regulating smoking behavior, even though it makes perfectly good health sense, can cause hard feelings and much anger between smokers and nonsmokers. If regulation is going to be adopted, it should be jointly developed by representatives of all those affected. Voluntary regulation often works best (see Figure 16.5).

Lead

Lead is a naturally occurring mineral element that is found throughout the environment and occurs in a variety of industrial products, including electric batteries, pipe, solder, paint and plastic pigments, and leaded gasoline. Its industrial usefulness notwithstanding, lead can adversely and chronically affect human health. Lead poisoning is chronic in nature. The list of health problems that can occur is lengthy and includes anemia, birth defects, bone damage, depression of neurological and psychological functions, kidney damage, learning disabilities, miscarriages, and sterility.[28]

Humans are exposed to lead primarily by ingestion and inhalation. Those who are at greatest risk of lead poisoning are young children who may inadvertently ingest lead, adults whose jobs bring them in contact with lead, and people of all ages who live in homes with water pipes made of or soldered with lead.

lead
a naturally occurring mineral element found throughout the environment and used in large quantities for industrial products

FIGURE 16.5

Environmental tobacco smoke is now considered a group A carcinogen.

Lead poisoning is the most significant and prevalent disease of environmental origin among American children.[29] The CDC estimates that approximately 434,000 children aged 1 to 5 years residing in America have blood lead levels (BLLs) that exceed the recommended level of 10 micrograms of lead per deciliter of blood.[30] The major source of lead exposure for these children is dust and chips of lead paint in their homes (see Figure 16.6). It is estimated that there are approximately 24 million housing units in the United States that still contain dangerous levels of lead-based paint and that more than 4 million of these dwellings are homes to children.[30] Children are much more susceptible to the effects of lead than adults. It is estimated that as much as 50% of the lead ingested by young children is absorbed, compared with only 10% in adults.

The federal government banned lead-based paints for use in housing in 1978 and completed the elimination of lead from gasoline in 1995. As a result of these actions, there has been significant improvement in the BLLs of the Nation's children. However, there is room for further improvement. One of the *Healthy People 2010* objectives is to eliminate elevated BLLs in children (see Box 16.8).[31]

Occupational exposure to lead is the major source of lead intake for adults. Lead is smelted for industrial use in larger quantities than any other heavy toxic metal. Though lead has many industrial uses, the most notable is in storage batteries. Lead exposure in the workplace often occurs through inhalation.

People of all age groups are exposed to lead if they consume water from lead pipes or pipes connected with lead solder. Lead pipes and solder can become corroded, and dissolved lead particles can be carried by the water. The EPA has estimated that about 40 million

FIGURE 16.6
Lead poisoning from paint dust continues to be a problem in the United States.

Americans who live in homes built before 1930 are drinking water containing more than the legally permissible level of lead (20 parts per billion). Around 1930, copper replaced lead as the metal of choice for water pipes. Federal laws now restrict the use of lead in pipe (no more than 8% lead in brass fittings) and solder (no more than 0.02% lead) in the installation and repair of public water systems. Some local governments have banned lead plumbing components altogether in drinking water systems.

It should also be noted that some well water used for drinking has been contaminated with lead by the inappropriate disposal of lead-containing materials such as old automobile batteries or solvents containing lead. Prior to passage of the laws governing the disposal of toxic substances, it was very common for the toxic substance to end up in dumps or landfills where it could leak into the groundwater.

The solution to preventing lead poisoning includes several strategies—education, regulation, and prudent behavior. Educational efforts to inform people of the dangers of lead in paint have been in effect for a number of years, and for the most part they seem to have been well received, even though there is still an unacceptable number of children being poisoned in this manner. The efforts to educate parents need to continue. National, state, and local laws have been useful in abating the lead poisoning problem. On the national level, the Lead-Based Paint Poisoning Prevention Act of 1971 initiated a national effort to identify children with lead poisoning and to abate the sources in the environment. Passage of the Resource Conservation and Recovery Act (RCRA) in 1976 and the Comprehensive Environmental Response,

BOX 16.8 HEALTHY PEOPLE 2010 OBJECTIVE: ELIMINATE ELEVATED BLOOD LEAD LEVELS IN CHILDREN

Target: 0%.

Baseline: 4.4% of children aged 1 to 6 years had blood lead levels exceeding 10 μg/dL during 1991–1994.

Target setting method: Total elimination.

Children Aged 1 to 6 Years, 1991–1994	Children with Blood Lead Levels Greater Than or Equal to 10 μg/dL			
	Residing in All Housing	Residing in Housing Built:		
		Before 1946[*]	1946 to 1973[*]	After 1973[*]
	Percent			
TOTAL	4.4	8.6	4.6	1.6
Race and ethnicity				
American Indian or Alaska Native	DSU	DSU	DSU	DSU
Asian or Pacific Islander	DSU	DSU	DSU	DSU
Asian	DNC	DNC	DNC	DNC
Native Hawaiian and other Pacific Islander	DNC	DNC	DNC	DNC
Black or African American	11.5	22.7	13.2	3.3
White	2.6	6.6	1.9	1.4
Hispanic or Latino	DSU	DSU	DSU	DSU
Mexican American	4.0	13.0	2.3	1.6
Not Hispanic or Latino	4.2	DNA	DNA	DNA
Black or African American	11.2	21.9	13.7	3.4
White	2.3	5.6	1.4	1.5
Gender				
Female	3.3	7.1	2.8	1.5
Male	5.5	9.6	6.6	1.7
Family income level				
Low	1.9	4.1	2.0	0.4
High	1.0	0.9	2.7	0

DNA = Data have not been analyzed; DNC = data have not been collected; DSU = data are statistically unreliable.

Source: National Health and Nutrition Examination Survey (NHANES), CDC, NCHS.

For Further Thought

While significant progress has been made in reducing BLLs in children through the reformulation of gasoline, it may be more difficult to find and treat the remaining 4.4% of children whose blood levels exceed the target level. Do you think this objective can be achieved?

Compensation, and Liability Act (CERCLA) in 1980 helped to regulate the disposal of lead-based products. Also at the federal level, the Lead Contamination Control Act of 1988 contributed to controlling lead poisoning. This act authorized the CDC to provide grants to state and local agencies for comprehensive programs to (1) screen infants and children for elevated BLLs, (2) ensure referral for medical and environmental intervention for infants and children who have been lead poisoned, and (3) provide education to parents and children about childhood lead poisoning.[32]

While significant progress has been made by the United States to reduce BLLs in children, such is not the case elsewhere in the world. The prevalence of elevated BLLs in Chinese children 1 to 6 years of age has been estimated at 38%, while that for Russian school-aged children at 58%.

Thus, it is not unusual to find elevated BLLS in children adopted from these countries as well as other Asian and Eastern European countries.[33]

The CDC has begun collaborating with other countries to eliminate childhood lead poisoning worldwide. So far, collaboration efforts are underway with Mexico, China, and India.[34]

PHYSICAL HAZARDS AND HUMAN HEALTH

There are a number of physical hazards in the environment that can negatively affect human health. They include high temperature, equipment and environmental design, and radiation. Two of the most pervasive physical hazards involve radiation from radon gas and ultraviolet light. As discussed in Chapter 15, *radiation* is the energy released when atoms are split or decay naturally from less stable to more stable forms. The energy, which can be thought of as either waves or particles, can damage the cells that make up living tissue. This damage occurs by a process called *ionization,* the removal of electrons from atoms in the molecules that are part of the living tissue. These molecular changes can result in biochemical lesions that can cause a mutation or cell death. On the skin, these can appear as burns, but the damage also can be internal. If the damage is severe enough, the organism will die.

Radon Contamination

Radon (radon-222) is a colorless, tasteless, odorless gas that is formed during an intermediate step in the radioactive decay process of uranium-238, a natural element that is found in most soil and rock but is more common in some places than in others. Radon gas has the ability to travel miles underground and rise to the earth's surface far away from any source of uranium. When it escapes the earth's crust outdoors, it quickly disperses harmlessly in the atmosphere. However, if it seeps into buildings occupied by humans, it can become a health hazard. It enters buildings through cracks in the foundation walls and floors, joints, openings around sump pump drains, loose-fitting pipes, and porous building materials, where it can then build up to harmful levels.[19] Such harmful levels are most likely to occur in unventilated lower levels of homes and buildings.

> **radon**
> a colorless, tasteless, odorless gas formed by the radioactive decay of uranium-238

Radon becomes attached to dust particles that are then inhaled and may be deposited on lung tissues. This exposes the tissue to ionizing radiation, thereby substantially increasing the risk of lung cancer. A case-control study of residential radon exposure and lung cancer published in 2000 reported a 50% excess lung cancer risk among women exposed to radon in their homes, even when exposure was at the minimum EPA action level of 4 pCi/L (picocuries per liter).[35] In fact, long-term exposure to radon is estimated to be the second leading cause of lung cancer—second only to smoking—causing between 3,000 and 32,000 lung cancer deaths annually.[36]

Like all other health problems related to environmental hazards, excessive exposure to radon can be prevented. The amount of radon in a home needs to be checked, and if levels are excessive, steps need to be taken to prevent its entry into the home. Radon levels can be tested by using an easy-to-use, relatively inexpensive test (about $25–$250 per test). "Do it yourself" kits are available in most communities and are sometimes sold in hardware stores. Local health department personnel can usually help you locate one. Once the test has been administered, the kit is returned to the manufacturer for analysis. The average radon level in homes in the United States is 1.5 pCi/L of air (see Figure 16.7). If a home has a reading higher than 4 pCi/L, steps should be taken to reduce the level. Such steps would include filling all cracks in the foundation and walls of a basement or crawl space; creating a barrier between the earth and home, by such means as pouring a concrete floor over a dirt-floor crawl space; and digging a new well if the radon is coming in with the water supply. Some of these steps can be expensive. Most homes with high radon levels can be fixed for $800 to $2,000.[36]

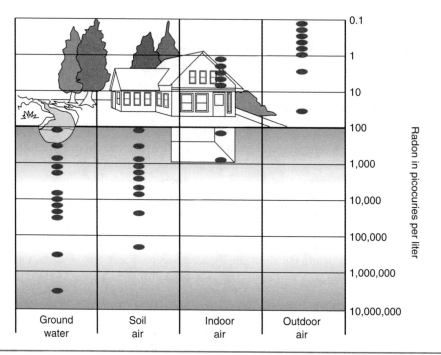

FIGURE 16.7
Radon levels in groundwater, soil, air, and indoor and outdoor air can vary dramatically.

Ultraviolet (UV) Radiation

ultraviolet (UV) radiation radiation energy with wavelengths 0–400 nm

Another source of ionizing radiation is the sun, yet millions of Americans think nothing of exposing (and overexposing) themselves to this form of radiation. Many actually seek it out in the mistaken belief that a tan body is a healthy body (see Figure 16.8). Sunshine comprises energy in many wavelengths, including visible light, heat, and **ultraviolet (UV) radiation.** UV radiation includes energy at wavelengths between 0 and 400 nanometers (nm). UV radiation between 290 and 330 nm, called UV-B, causes most of the harm to humans. In recent years, with the destruction of the ozone layer, the quantity of UV-B radiation reaching the earth has been increasing.[19]

Epidemiological studies have found an association between UV-B, or ionizing, radiation and skin cancer. For example, there is more skin cancer in those living closer to the equator if they are not protected by darker skin. Also, most skin cancer appears on the exposed body parts (i.e., arms, legs, head, and neck).

Each year over 1,000,000 new cases of skin cancer are reported in the United States, and, in recent years, the incidence rate of skin cancer has been increasing about 3% per year.[19] The vast majority of these cases are the highly curable *basal cell* and *squamous cell carcinomas*. This is the most common form of cancer. The most serious and least common skin cancer is *malignant melanoma*. More than 55,000 new cases of this cancer are diagnosed every year in the United States, and each year about 7,900 patients die of melanoma. This type of skin cancer is the most dangerous because of its ability to grow and spread quickly. However, like the other skin cancers, melanoma is curable if discovered and treated early.[27]

Solutions for dealing with this physical hazard are simple. The first is for people to reduce their risk of exposure, and the second is to seek early treatment if cancer is suspected. One can reduce the risk of exposure by staying out of the sun or by covering the skin with clothing or commercial sunscreens. Sunscreens work by absorbing, reflecting, or scattering ultraviolet light, thereby reducing the amount that reaches the skin.

FIGURE 16.8
Skin cancer is the prevalent type of cancer in the United States.

The key to discovering whether treatment is warranted is to practice monthly skin self-examination. Basal and squamous cell carcinomas often appear as a pale, waxlike, peely nodule or a red, scaly, sharply outlined patch. A physician should check either of these abnormalities, or the sudden change in a mole's appearance. Melanomas often start as small mole-like growths. The simple ABCD rule from the American Cancer Society outlines warning signs of melanoma.[27]

A is for *asymmetry* (half of the mole does not match the other half).

B is for *border irregularity* (the edges are ragged, notched, or blurred).

C is for *color* (the pigmentation is not uniform).

D is for *diameter* greater than 6 millimeters (any sudden or progressive change in size should be of concern).

PSYCHOLOGICAL HAZARDS AND HUMAN HEALTH

Psychological hazards can be just as important as biological, chemical, and physical hazards in the determination of human health. However, the precise effects of psychological hazards on human populations are difficult to quantify. Among the health problems associated with psychological hazards are hypochondriasis, depression, hysteria, and stress. (For more information on the effects of stress on health, refer to Chapter 11.)

An important psychological hazard today is international terrorism. Indeed, it has been stated that the primary purpose of terrorist acts, aside from the relatively few casualties that usually occur, is to produce a psychological state of fear, stress, and hysteria. Many Americans experienced one or more of these psychological conditions in the aftermath of the World Trade Center (WTC) attack that occurred in New York City on September 11, 2001 (see Figure 16.9).

FIGURE 16.9

The September 11, 2001, terrorist attacks on the World Trade Center resulted in fear, stress, and hysteria among some of those who witnessed these events at close range. Others developed post-traumatic stress disorder one to two months after the attack.

This terrorist attack was unique because it *did* cause a large number of deaths (2,726) and because it caused an unprecedented environmental assault on Lower Manhattan. At least 10,000 New Yorkers have suffered short- or long-term health ailments from exposure to WTC-generated air contaminants.[37] Longitudinal studies of firefighters and rescue workers have confirmed a positive relationship between intensity and duration of exposure to air pollutants and the severity of pulmonary symptoms. These symptoms included onset of cough, wheeze, shortness of breath, and bronchial hyperreactivity more than two and one-half years following the disaster.[38] Among the materials in the air after the collapse of the towers were cement dust, glass fibers, asbestos, lead, aromatic hydrocarbons, and organochlorine compounds.

A study to determine the psychological effects of the WTC attacks of September 11 on Manhattan residents found that 20% of those living near the WTC had symptoms consistent with post-traumatic stress disorder (PTSD) 5 to 8 weeks after the attack. Nearly 10% of those interviewed suffered from depression, which occurred most often in those who had suffered losses as a result of the attack.[39] Clearly, psychological hazards are an important community health concern.

SOCIOLOGICAL HAZARDS AND HUMAN HEALTH

Living around other people can create a number of sociological hazards that can impact human health. It is known that noise, overcrowding, traffic jams, isolation, lack of privacy, and crowds can influence human health. As in the case of psychological hazards, the exact impact of these hazards on human health is unknown.

Although sociological hazards alone can create health problems, it is more likely for them to be found in combination with other environmental hazards. For example, the loud music created by a band could very well be harmless in a rural area, but it could create a serious problem in a crowded housing project in the middle of a city. In order to demonstrate the impact of sociological problems on human health, we will discuss population growth.

Population Growth

A population is defined as a group of individuals of the same species occupying a given area.[40] In this section, we focus on the human species and the area it inhabits—earth. Specifically, we will examine the growth of this population and the impact that growth has on health.

The Principles

The growth of a population can be attributed to three factors—its birth rate, its death rate, and migration. However, because we are discussing the human population on our entire planet, migration is not a factor. Population growth can be illustrated by an S-curve (see Figure 16.10). Such a curve consists of three phases: the lag phase, the exponential phase, and the stable equilibrium phase. During the **lag phase,** the growth is slow because there are relatively few reproducing individuals and there is little difference between the death rate and the birth rate. The **exponential phase** is characterized by a birth rate that is greater than the death rate, caused by more than one generation producing offspring. When the birth rate and death rate are equal, we have **zero population growth,** or a stable **equilibrium phase.** Prior to movement into the stable equilibrium phase, a J-curve is formed (see Figure 16.11). When a population grows in a J-curve pattern, the environment will eventually put it into an equilibrium phase because the resources (food, water, shelter, etc.) to support such growth are limited and thus will not allow the population to grow any further. The maximum population size that can be supported by available resources (air, water, shelter, etc.) is referred to as the **carrying capacity** of the environment.[19]

The Facts

In examining the population growth of the human species, one could say its growth followed the J-curve pattern through most of the twentieth century. The world's 6 billionth human inhabitant was born during the first half of 1999. But during the past three decades, the rate of world population growth began to decline. Currently, projections are that the number of years required for the population to add one billion more people will increase (see Figure 16.11). While the world population growth rate will continue to decline (see Figure 16.12), the world population will continue to grow during the twenty-first century although somewhat more slowly (see Figure 16.13). The 2002 growth rate was about 1.2% or about 74 million people per year.[41] This is the equivalent of adding one new Germany to the world's population each year.[42] At this rate, the U.S. Census Bureau projects that world population will reach 9.1 billion by the year 2050, an increase of 45% over the 2002 size.[41]

lag phase
the initial phase of the population growth S-curve when growth is slow

exponential phase
the middle phase of the population growth S-curve when the birth rate is greater than the death rate

zero population growth (ZPG)
when the birth and death rates for a given population are equal

equilibrium phase
the last phase of the population growth S-curve when the birth and death rates are equal

carrying capacity
the maximum population size that can be supported by available resources (air, water, shelter, etc.)

FIGURE 16.10

A theoretical population curve—an S-curve.

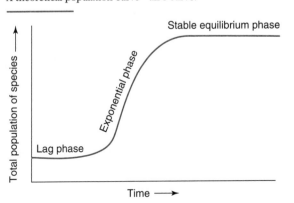

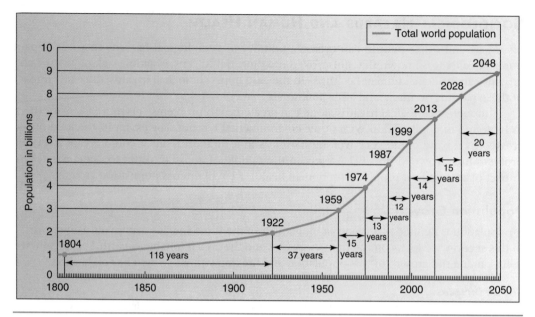

FIGURE 16.11

World population growth in historical perspective between 1750 and 2050, a typical J-shaped curve.

Source: United Nations (1995) and the U.S. Bureau of the Census, International Data Base.

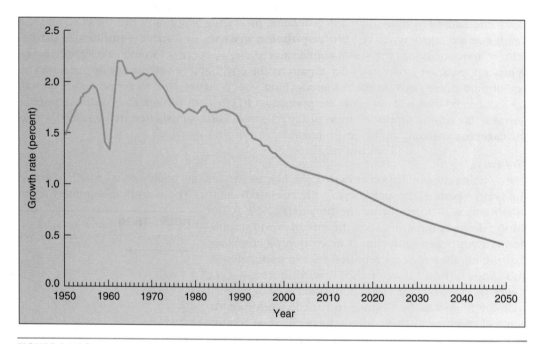

FIGURE 16.12

World population growth rate between 1950 and 2050.

Source: United States Department of Commerce, Bureau of the Census (2004). Available at www.census.gov/ipc/www/img/worldgr.gif.

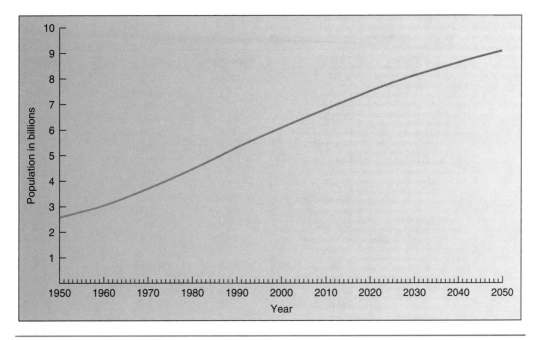

FIGURE 16.13
World population: 1950 to 2050.

Source: United States Department of Commerce, Bureau of the Census (2004). Available at
www.census.gov/ipc/www/img/worldpop.gif.

About 80% of the world's population lives in the world's less developed countries (LDCs), and virtually all of the world's population increase between now and 2050 will occur in these countries.[41] The largest percentage of growth during the next 45 years (2005–2050) is expected to occur in sub-Saharan Africa. Only one-third the size of China in 1950, sub-Saharan Africa was one-half the size of China in 2002, and is projected to surpass China in size by 2050.[41] By 2050, only the United States, among the more developed countries (MDCs), will remain on the list of the top 10 most populous countries; this will be due, in large part, to immigration. Whereas the growth rate remains high for the LDCs as a whole, the growth rate for the MDCs has fallen quite low. In many MDCs, fertility rates are below replacement levels (the level at which children born would just replace those persons lost to mortality).[41]

The Issues

While exponential world population growth is no longer occurring in absolute terms, world population growth continues to be substantial, and it is at a rate that is unsustainable if we wish to maintain the quality of life and health we enjoy today. In this chapter, we have discussed some of the ramifications of overpopulation. These include the prospects of global warming, acid rain, bulging landfills, depletion of the ozone layer, increasing crime rates, increasing vulnerability to epidemics and pandemics, smog, exhaustion or at least contamination of soils and groundwater, and growing international tensions. To these might be added the degradation of arable land, land that can be cultivated to grow crops. Between 1990 and 2000, about 610 million hectares were degraded.[43] Also, there will be a dwindling of natural resources for energy, housing, and living space—especially in large cities. Since 1950, the urban population has more than tripled. It is estimated that three-fourths of the current population growth is urban. In 1975, there were only five megacities (cities of more than 10 million

Table 16.4
Megacities of the World: 1975, 2000, and 2012 (Population in Millions)

1975	Population	2000	Population	2015	Population
Tokyo	19.8	Tokyo	26.4	Tokyo	26.4
New York	15.9	Mexico City	18.1	Bombay	26.1
Shanghai	11.4	Bombay	18.1	Lagos	23.2
Mexico City	11.2	São Paulo	17.8	Dhaka	21.1
São Paulo	10.0	Shanghai	17.0	São Paulo	20.4
		New York	16.6	Karachi	19.2
		Lagos	13.4	Mexico City	19.2
		Los Angeles	13.1	Shanghai	19.1
		Calcutta	12.9	New York	17.4
		Buenos Aires	12.6	Jakarta	17.3
		Dhaka	12.3	Calcutta	17.3
		Karachi	11.8	Delhi	16.8
		Delhi	11.7	Metro Manila	14.8
		Jakarta	11.0	Los Angeles	14.1
		Osaka	11.0	Buenos Aires	14.1
		Metro Manila	10.9	Cairo	13.8
		Beijing	10.8	Istanbul	12.5
		Rio de Janeiro	10.6	Beijing	12.3
		Cairo	10.6	Rio de Janeiro	11.9
				Osaka	11.0
				Tianjin	10.7
				Hyderabad	10.5
				Bangkok	10.1

Source: Hinrichsen, D., and B. Robey (2000). *Population and the Environment: The Global Challenge,* Population Reports, *28*(3), 12. Baltimore, MD: Johns Hopkins School of Public Health, The Information and Knowledge for Optimal Health (INFO) Project.

residents) in the world; now there are 19. By 2015, there will be 23 megacities with only two of them in the United States (see Table 16.4).[43]

Energy usage and world population are really two sides of the same coin. It is easy for people in the MDCs to lay the blame on people living in LDCs, where overpopulation is a more acute problem. But people living in the MDCs are using up the finite supply of the world's fossil energy faster at a very high rate. For example, the twenty richest countries consume nearly 80% of the natural gas, 65% of the oil, and 50% of the coal produced each year.[40]

The Solutions

Most experts agree that the world population is approaching the maximum sustainable limit. However, no one knows what the ultimate population size will be. There are some encouraging signs. The world population growth rate was over 2% just 30 years ago; it is now just 1.2%.[41] Although there are still great concerns with the population growth rates in parts of the Middle East and Africa, some developing countries have succeeded in slowing growth. For example, the average number of children born to a Mexican woman has plunged from seven to just 2.5 in the past 30 years.[42]

The so-called humane means of limiting population growth include (1) various methods of conception control such as the oral contraceptive pill, physical or chemical barrier methods, or sterilization (tubal ligation and vasectomy); (2) birth control methods such as intrauterine devices, legalized abortion, and morning-after pills; and (3) social policies such as financial incentives and societal disincentives for having children, as is the practice in China's one-child family program. While some of these methods are unacceptable to certain people, all are proactive solutions to the mounting population problem. The alternative is to allow exponential population growth to continue until it declines naturally, by way of famine, epidemic diseases, and perhaps warfare. Nature's way will require a good deal more environmental deterioration, social disintegration, poverty, and human suffering. The choice is still ours.

SITE AND LOCATION HAZARDS AND HUMAN HEALTH

In Chapter 15, we outlined some natural and human-made site and location situations that can be hazardous to humans. To further explain the hazards to human health that site and location may bring, we have chosen to discuss natural disasters.

Natural Disasters

Natural disasters include those geophysical and meteorological events (disaster agents) that greatly exceed normal human expectations in terms of magnitude or frequency and cause significant injury to individuals and damage to their property. Human health can be adversely affected by a disaster even before it occurs. Knowledge of an impending disaster can cause stress. Such stress can produce serious health problems in those who are unable to control their reaction to the situation. During the event, health can again be affected because of the physical damage causing both injuries and deaths. After a natural disaster, because of the remaining biological, sociological, psychological, and physical conditions, a variety of needs may exist. The primary needs of people after a natural disaster usually include food, water, shelter, health care, and clothing. The availability and quality of these items can dictate the impact of the disaster on human health.

Hurricane Floyd, which came ashore during September and October 1999, provides an example. Floyd, extending 300 miles with sustained wind of 96 to 110 miles per hour, made landfall in North Carolina, dropping up to 20 inches of rain in eastern regions of the state. At least 52 deaths were associated directly with the storm in North Carolina. There were also 59,398 emergency department visits.[44]

In what ways was Hurricane Floyd a community health problem for the communities it struck? First, there were the injuries and deaths directly associated with the destructive force of the hurricane's wind and water. Second, many of those who survived uninjured found themselves without adequate food, water, shelter, or clothing. Much of the food in the area had become contaminated or ruined, so that grocery stores and restaurants were unable to meet the needs of the residents. Third, survivors were left in a community in which important health services such as water supply and sewage systems were inoperable. Thus, human waste and contaminated water posed serious public health problems; a source of pure water had to be supplied quickly. Fourth, many people were left without their medications. Finally, because of the destruction of homes, motels, and health care facilities (hospitals, nursing homes, etc.) and the lack of transportation out of the area, shelter also became a problem. Comparing the first week following Hurricane Floyd with the first week in September 1998, significant increases were reported for suicide attempts, dog bites, febrile illnesses, dermatitis, and basic medical needs (e.g., oxygen, medication refills, dialysis, and vaccines). One month after Hurricane Floyd there were more reports of arthropod bites, diarrhea, violence, and asthma than during the same period in 1998.[44]

The Nation's official emergency response agency is the **Federal Emergency Response Agency (FEMA).** FEMA's mission is to lead America to prepare for, prevent, respond to, and recover from disasters with a vision of "A Nation Prepared."

While the origins of FEMA can be traced back nearly 200 years, it was then President Jimmy Carter who signed the executive order in 1979 merging many of the separate disaster-related responsibilities into one agency. In March 2003, FEMA was placed in the Department of Homeland Security, where it is part of the Emergency Preparedness and Response Directorate.

Federal Emergency Response Agency (FEMA) the Nation's official emergency response agency

FIGURE 16.14
The mission of the Federal Emergency Response Agency (FEMA) is to lead America to prepare for, prevent, respond to, and recover from disasters with a vision of "A Nation Prepared."

Today, FEMA has 2,600 regular employees supplemented by nearly 4,000 stand-by disaster assistant employees (see Figure 16.14).[45] Often FEMA works in partnership with other organizations that are part of the nation's emergency management system, including state and local emergency management agencies, 27 other federal agencies, and the American Red Cross. The FEMA Web site (www.fema.gov) provides links to a vast array of information, reports, and publications that can help individuals and communities prepare for emergencies.

The key to recovery from any disaster lies in a community's ability to mobilize resources to meet the needs of the people following a disaster. In the United States, the American Red Cross (ARC) has taken on the role of organizing such efforts. (See Chapter 2 for further discussion of the ARC.) "The American Red Cross, a humanitarian organization led by volunteers and guided by its Congressional Charter and the Fundamental Principles of the International Red Cross Movement, will provide relief to victims of disaster and help people prevent, prepare for, and respond to emergencies."[46]

While most of the disasters the ARC responds to are natural, the terrorist attack of September 11, 2001, stands as a visible exception (see Figure 16.15). The ARC received more than $1 billion in donations from people all over the world. The ARC placed all of this money in the Liberty Disaster Relief Fund for the use of those affected by the terrorist attack. By the end of 2003, the ARC had spent more than $853 million to help thousands of individuals and families throughout the world who were directly affected by the September 11 terrorist attacks.[46] The ARC's September 11 Recovery Program (SRP) continues to help those impacted regain their self-sufficiency. Services include assistance accessing mental health and health care services, health insurance, family support services, family information and support sessions, and financial assistance.

FIGURE 16.15
The American Red Cross offers many different support services.

Each year the ARC responds to more than 67,000 emergencies—from small emergencies such as apartment fires to large ones such as earthquakes and floods.[46] About 85% of all persons trained in disaster relief activities are ARC volunteers.

CHAPTER SUMMARY

- Environmental health is the study and management of environmental conditions that affect our health and well-being.

- The environmental factors and conditions that can affect human health are numerous, and many remain to be identified.

- Environmental hazards can be classified as biological, chemical, physical, psychological, social, or as site and location hazards.

- We come into contact with biological and chemical hazards through the water we drink, the food we eat, and the air we breathe.

- The way communities manage their environment can influence the level of vector populations and, hence, the incidence of vectorborne diseases.

- Chemical hazards include pesticides, environmental tobacco smoke, and lead.

- Radon and ultraviolet radiation are invisible physical hazards that have serious health consequences such as lung cancer and skin cancer.

- Psychological hazards can affect the health of community members.

- Worldwide population growth constitutes a potential sociological hazard for all.

- Natural disasters are unpredictable site and location hazards that can profoundly disrupt community health services and put citizens at risk.

- The Federal Emergency Response Agency (FEMA) and the American Red Cross (ARC) are two agencies that help communities prepare for, prevent, respond to, and recover from disasters.

SCENARIO: ANALYSIS AND RESPONSE

Please take a moment to reread the scenario at the beginning of this chapter. Then reflect on the questions that follow.

1. At the present time, the U.S. government acknowledges that there is conclusive evidence that Agent Orange exposure is related to specific diseases, and it compensates Vietnam veterans who are affected. Those diseases include three types of cancer (Hodgkin's disease, non-Hodgkin's lymphoma, and soft tissue sarcoma) and two other types of disorders (chloracne—a disfiguring skin disorder—and a metabolic disorder called porphyria cutanea tarda). The government does not compensate for prostate cancer. Even though science cannot prove it, do you believe Agent Orange caused Gary's cancer? Why or why not?

2. Because of the adverse health conditions of many Vietnam veterans, a group of veterans filed suit against the seven U.S. chemical companies that produced Agent Orange. Before the case went to trial, the companies agreed to place $180 million into a fund that would be used to compensate victims and their families. The companies also denied any liability and stated they created the herbicide using the military's specifications. Do you feel these companies should be held responsible? Why or why not? Do you feel the U.S. government should be held responsible? Why or why not?

3. Do you feel that Gary was the victim of an environmental hazard (the chemical, Agent Orange), a sociological hazard (the war), neither, or both? Explain your response.

REVIEW QUESTIONS

1. Define the following terms—*environmental health, environmental hazard,* and *environmental sanitation.*

2. Explain the differences between waterborne, foodborne, and vectorborne diseases and give an example of each.

3. How do sanitarians (registered environmental health specialists) protect your health?

4. What are chemical hazards and how are they detrimental to human health?

5. What is a pest? What are pesticides?

6. In what ways do pesticides pose a threat to human health?

7. How would you describe the ideal pesticide?

8. What does the term *persistence* mean with regard to pesticides? Give an example of a persistent and a non-persistent pesticide.

9. Explain the differences among environmental tobacco smoke, sidestream smoke, and mainstream smoke.

10. What is passive smoking?

11. To date, how has environmental tobacco smoke been regulated?

12. Who is at the highest risk for lead poisoning?

13. What are the most common ways to get lead poisoning?

14. What can be done to reduce the number of lead poisoning cases?

15. How is radon formed?

16. Why is radon such a concern?

17. How does ultraviolet radiation pose a health risk?

18. Why do you think there are so many cases of skin cancer each year in the United States?

19. Explain the ABCD rule of melanomas.

20. Explain how psychological hazards can adversely affect one's health.

21. Explain population growth using the S- and J-curves.

22. What percentage of the population growth is occurring in the more developed countries (MDCs)? In the less developed countries (LDCs)? What does such growth mean to all humans?

23. How close do you think the world is to reaching its carrying capacity?

24. Explain the role of the Federal Emergency Response Agency (FEMA) and contrast it with the role of the American Red Cross (ARC).

ACTIVITIES

1. Make arrangements to "shadow" a sanitarian from a local health department for at least half a day. Record and summarize the tasks in which he or she is involved and be sure to include your notes of all the tasks that were performed when you were with the sanitarian. Then, write a two-page paper answering the following:

   What professional training has the sanitarian completed to be qualified for this work?

   What role does this person play in protecting the community's health?

   What other tasks does the sanitarian routinely perform that he or she did not do on the day you visited?

   Would you like to be a sanitarian after you graduate? Why or why not?

2. Make arrangements to interview a director of environmental health in a local health department. Find answers to the following questions and summarize these answers in a two-page paper.

   What are all the tasks this division of the health department carries out?

   What is the primary environmental health problem of your community? Why is it a problem? How is it being dealt with?

   If they inspect restaurants, which ones have the best sanitation practices?

   What is an average day like for a health department sanitarian?

3. Interview at least three different farm workers. Ask if they know anyone who has ever been poisoned by a pesticide. Find out how each poisoning happened, ask if it could have been prevented, and find out what happened to the person who was poisoned. Write the results of your findings in a two-page paper.

4. Visit three different restaurants in your community. Ask to speak with the manager or assistant manager about the smoking policy in the restaurants. Find out what the policy is, who determined the policy, why it was created, and what happens if someone violates it. Write the results of your findings in a two-page paper.

5. Call your local health department and find out what kind of efforts have been made to eliminate lead poisoning. Ask about education programs and possible state or local laws. Also, find out if the health department will test for lead in the water and paint. If they will, ask about the procedures they use to do so. Write the results of your findings in a two-page paper.

6. Survey five of your friends by asking them the following questions. Once the interviews are complete, write a two-page paper summarizing their responses.

Do you lie out in the sun or go to tanning booths? If so, how often? Are you concerned about skin cancer?

What are the risk factors for skin cancer?

What is meant by the ABCD rule of melanoma?

Is tan skin more important to you than not getting cancer? If so, why?

7. Is radon gas a problem in your area of the country? If so, find out to what extent it is a problem and what percentage of the dwellings are contaminated. Also, obtain a home test kit and use it in the place where you live. In a two-page paper, report the extent of the problem in your community and the results of the test on your dwelling. Then project what your risk of disease from radon would be. (Note: If you are not sure where to get a radon test kit, contact your local health department.)

8. Go to the student union on your campus to conduct a survey of those who use the building. Ask the following questions of at least 25 people (do not interview people in only one part of the building; get responses from people in the food service areas, the lounges, bookstore, etc. Be sure to include students, faculty, and student union employees).

   Are you a student, faculty member, or staff member?

   Do you use tobacco in any form? If yes, what do you smoke or chew? How much?

   Do you believe people should be allowed to smoke in this building? Why or why not?

   Do you think smoking is a right or a privilege?

   Are you in favor of a total ban on smoking on this campus? In all buildings? In offices? In residence halls?

   After you have collected the data, summarize it in a written paper, and report any trends you find. Be sure to compare the answers of students to faculty and to staff.

9. Write a three-page position paper on one of the following questions. Make sure you cite references to support your position.

   Should the United States be concerned with worldwide population growth?

   Should the United States develop government policy to slow its population growth?

   What is the best means for controlling population growth in any country?

10. Find an issue of a weekly news magazine (e.g., *Newsweek, Time*) or visit the FEMA Web site (www.fema.gov) to find information on a recent natural disaster (e.g., earthquake in California in January 2004, flooding in Massachussetts in April 2004, or, the tornado and severe storm in Iowa in May 2004). Read all the stories covering the disaster and then write a two-page paper identifying what you believe to be the major community health concerns that resulted from the disaster and why.

COMMUNITY HEALTH ON THE WEB

The Internet contains a wealth of information about community and public health. Increase your knowledge of some of the topics presented in this chapter by accessing the Jones and Bartlett Publishers Web site at **health.jbpub.com/communityhealth/5e** and follow the links to complete the following Web activities.

- Environmental Hazards and Health Effects
- The Foodborne Diseases Active Surveillance Network
- Zero Population Growth

REFERENCES

1. Landrigan, P. J. (1992). "Commentary: Environmental Disease—A Preventable Epidemic." *American Journal of Public Health,* 82(7): 941-943.

2. Centers for Disease Control and Prevention (2002). "Surveillance for Waterborne-Disease Outbreaks—United States, 1999-2000." *MMWR,* 51(SS-8): 1-28.

3. Centers for Disease Control and Prevention (2000). "Surveillance for Waterborne-Disease Outbreaks—United States, 1997-1998." *MMWR,* 49(SS-4): 1-35.

4. Centers for Disease Control and Prevention (1996). "Surveillance for Waterborne-Disease Outbreaks—United States, 1993-1994." *MMWR,* 45(SS-1): 1-33.

5. Centers for Disease Control and Prevention (1999). "Achievements in Public Health, 1900-1999: Fluoridation of Drinking Water to Prevent Dental Caries." *MMWR,* 48(41): 933-940.

6. Mead, P. S., L. Slutsker, V. Dietz, L. F. McCaig, J. S. Bresee, C. Shapiro, P. M. Griffin, and R. V. Tauxe (1999). "Food-Related Illness and Death in the United States." *Emerging Infectious Diseases,* 5(5): 607-621.

7. Centers for Disease Control and Prevention (1996). "Surveillance for Foodborne-Disease Outbreaks—United States, 1988-1992." *MMWR,* 45(SS-5): 1-66.

8. Centers for Disease Control and Prevention (2000). "Surveillance for Foodborne-Disease Outbreaks—United States, 1993-1997." *MMWR,* 49(SS-1): 1-62.

9. American Public Health Association (1999). *Food Safety. Fact Sheet.* Available at http://www.apha.org/legislative/factsheets/fs.foodsafe.htm.

10. Centers for Disease Control and Prevention (2001). "Preliminary FoodNet Data on the Incidence of Foodborne Illnesses—Selected Sites, United States, 2000." *MMWR,* 50(13): 241-246.

11. Jones, T. F., B. Imhoff, M. Samuel, P. Mshar, K. G. McCombs, M. Hawkins, V. Deneen, M. Cambridge, and S. J. Olsen (2004). "Limitations to Successful Investigation and Reporting of Foodborne Outbreaks: An Analysis of Foodborne Disease Outbreaks in FoodNet Catchment Areas, 1998-1999." *Clinical Infectious Diseases,* 38(Suppl 3): S297-S302.

12. Centers for Disease Control and Prevention (1999). "Achievements in Public Health, 1900-1999: Safer and Healthier Foods." *MMWR,* 48(40): 905-913.

13. Centers for Disease Control and Prevention, Office of Communications (8 July 2003). "CDC Confirms Nation's First Human Case of West Nile in 2003 [Press Release]." Available at http://www.cdc.gov/od/oc/media/pressrel/r030708.htm.

14. Centers for Disease Control and Prevention, Division of Vector-Borne Infectious Diseases (2004). "West Nile Virus: Background—Virus History and Distribution." Available at http://www.cdc.gov/ncidod/dvbid/westnile/background.htm.

15. Centers for Disease Control and Prevention, Division of Vector-Borne Infectious Diseases (2004). "West Nile Virus: Statistics, Surveillance, and Control." Available at http://www.cdc.gov/ncidod/dvbid/westnile/surv&control.htm.

16. Centers for Disease Control and Prevention, Division of Vector-Borne Infectious Diseases (2000). "Information on *Aedes albopictus.*" Available at http://www.cdc.gov/ncidod/dvbid/arbor/albopic_new.htm.

17. Centers for Disease Control and Prevention, Division of Vector-Borne Infectious Diseases. "Information on *Aedes japonicus.*" Available at http://www.cdc.gov/ncidod/dvbid/arbor/japonicus.htm.

18. Centers for Disease Control and Prevention, Division of Vector-Borne Infectious Diseases (2004). "Lyme Disease: Epidemiology." Available at http://www.cdc.gov/ncidod/dvbid/lyme/epi.htm.

19. Miller, G. T. (2004). *Living in the Environment: Principles, Connections, and Solutions,* 13th ed. Pacific Grove, CA: Brooks/Cole-Thompson Learning.

20. Enger, E. D., and B. F. Smith (1992). *Environmental Science: A Study of Interrelationships,* 4th ed. Dubuque, IA: Wm. C. Brown.

21. Environmental Protection Agency (2000). *For Your Information: Pesticides and Child Safety. Prevention, Pesticides and Toxic Substances* (7506C 735-F-93-050). Washington, DC: Author.

22. American Lung Association, Epidemiology and Statistics Unit (2003). "Trends in Tobacco Use." Available at http://www.lungusa.org/.

23. Overpeck, M. D., and A. J. Moss (1991). *Children's Exposure to Environmental Cigarette Smoke Before and After Birth* (HHS pub. no. PHS-91-1250). Washington, DC: U.S. Government Printing Office.

24. U.S. Environmental Protection Agency (1993). *Respiratory Health Effects of Passive Smoking: Lung Cancer and Other Disorders* (EPA/600/6-90/006f). Washington, DC: U.S. Government Printing Office.

25. U.S. Department of Health and Human Services (1991). *Environmental Tobacco Smoke in the Workplace* (HHS [NIOSH] pub. no. 91-108). Washington, DC: U.S. Government Printing Office.

26. Environmental Protection Agency (1992). *Respiratory Health Effects of Passive Smoking: Lung Cancer and Other Disorders* (EPA/600/6-90/006). Washington, DC: U.S. Government Printing Office.

27. American Cancer Society (2003). *Cancer Facts and Figures—2003.* Atlanta, GA: Author.

28. Chiras, D. D. (2001). *Environmental Science: Creating a Sustainable Future,* 6th ed. Sudbury, MA: Jones and Bartlett Publishers.

29. Silbergeld, E. K. (1997). "Preventing Lead Poisoning in Children." *Annual Review of Public Health,* 18: 187-210.

30. Centers for Disease Control and Prevention, National Center for Environmental Health (2004). "About Childhood Lead Poisoning." Available at http://www.cdc.gov/nceh/lead/about/about.htm.

31. U.S. Department of Health and Human Services (November 2000). *Healthy People 2010: Understanding and Improving Health,* 2nd ed. Washington, DC: U.S. Government Printing Office.

32. Centers for Disease Control and Prevention (1992). "Implementation of the Lead Contamination Control Act of 1988." *MMWR,* 41(17): 288-290.

33. Centers for Disease Control and Prevention (2000). "Elevated Blood Lead Levels Among Internationally Adopted Children—United States, 1998." *MMWR,* 49(5): 97-100.

34. Centers for Disease Control and Prevention (2000). *National Center for Environmental Health Fact Book 2000.* Available at http://www.cdc.gov/nceh.

35. Field, R. W., C. F. Lynch, et al. (2000). *Residential Radon and Lung Cancer Case-Control Study.* Available at http://www.cheec.uiowa.edu/misc/radon.html.

36. Nichols, G. (1999). "The Ebb and Flow of Radon." *American Journal of Public Health,* 89(7): 993-994.

37. Nordgren, M. D., E. A. Goldstein, and M. A. Izeman (2002). "The Environmental Impacts of the World Trade Center Attacks: A Preliminary Assessment." Available at http://www.nrdc.org/air/pollution/wtc/wtcinx.asp.

38. National Institutes of Health, National Institute of Environmental Health Sciences (2004). "New Research Outlines Public Health Consequences of World Trade Center Disaster [News Release]." Available at http://www.nih.gov/news/pr/may2004/niehs-03.htm.

39. Galea, S., J. Ahern, H. Resnick, D. Kilpatrick, M. Bucuvalas, J. Gold, and D. Vlahov (2002). "Psychological Sequelae of the September 11 Terrorist Attacks in New York City." *New England Journal of Medicine,* 346(13): 982-987.

40. Cunningham, W. P., M. A. Cunningham, and B. Saigo (2005). *Environmental Science: A Global Concern,* 8th ed. New York: McGraw-Hill.

41. U.S. Census Bureau (2004). *Global Population Profile: 2002* (International Population Reports WP/02). Washington, DC: U.S. Government Printing Office.

42. Kluger, J. (2000). "The Big Crunch." *Time* (Special Edition), Earth Day 2000: 44-47.

43. Hinrichsen, D., and B. Robey (Fall 2000). *Population and the Environment: The Global Challenge* (Population Reports, Series M, 15). Johns Hopkins University School of Public Health, Population Information Program.

44. Centers for Disease Control and Prevention (2000). "Morbidity and Mortality Associated with Hurricane Floyd—North Carolina, September-October 1999." *MMWR,* 49(17): 369-372.

45. Federal Emergency Management Agency (2004). "About FEMA." Available at http://www.fema.gov/about/history.shtm.

46. American Red Cross (2004). "Disaster Services." Available at http://www.redcross.org/.

Chapter 17

Injuries as a Community Health Problem

Chapter Objectives

After studying this chapter you will be able to:

1 Describe the importance of injuries as a community health problem.

2 Explain why the terms *accidents* and *safety* have been replaced by the currently more acceptable terms *unintentional injuries, injury prevention,* and *injury control* when dealing with such occurrences.

3 Briefly explain the difference between intentional and unintentional injuries and provide examples of each.

4 List the four elements usually included in the definition of the term *unintentional injury*.

5 Summarize the epidemiology of unintentional injuries.

6 List strategies for the prevention and control of unintentional injuries.

7 Explain how education, regulation, automatic protection, and litigation can reduce the number and seriousness of unintentional injuries.

8 Define the term *intentional injuries* and provide examples of behavior that results in intentional injuries.

9 Describe the scope of intentional injuries as a community health problem in the United States.

10 List some contributing factors to domestic violence and some strategies for reducing it.

11 List some of the contributing factors to the increase in violence related to youth gangs and explain what communities can do to reduce this level of violence.

12 Discuss intervention approaches for preventing or controlling intentional injuries.

SCENARIO

Peter decided to mow the lawn before his ball game. He felt he could complete the task in less than an hour. He checked and filled the gas tank, started the mower, and began mowing. In one corner of the yard, he found it easier to pull the lawnmower backward rather than to push it forward. Peter had done this many times, without incident. This time, he tripped over a stump and lost his balance. In attempting to regain his balance, he pulled harder on the mower, causing it to run over his foot.

Instantly he experienced a severe sharp pain and automatically jerked his foot back, but it was too late; the mower blade had cut through Peter's shoe and big toe! Peter quickly turned off the mower and hobbled to the house. As he prepared to go to the emergency room at the local hospital, he was angry with himself as he thought about how his carelessness had caused his injury and might eventually lead to losing his toe.

INTRODUCTION

This chapter first defines and then examines the scope, causes, and effects on the community of both unintentional and intentional injuries. It also reviews approaches to the prevention and control of injuries and injury deaths.

Definitions

The word **injury** is derived from the Latin word for "not right."[1] Injuries result from "acute exposure to physical agents such as mechanical energy, heat, electricity, chemicals, and ionizing radiation interacting with the body in amounts or at rates that exceed the threshold of human tolerance."[2] In this chapter we discuss both **unintentional injuries,** injuries judged to have occurred without anyone intending that harm be done (such as those that result from car crashes, falls, drownings, and fires), and **intentional injuries,** injuries judged to have been purposely inflicted, either by another or oneself (such as assaults, intentional shootings and stabbings, and suicides).

The term *accident* has fallen into disfavor and disuse with many public health officials whose goal it is to reduce the number and seriousness of all injuries. The very word *accident* suggests a chance occurrence or an unpreventable mishap. Yet, we know that many, if not most, accidents are preventable. The term *unintentional injury* is now used in its place. Similarly, the rather vague term *safety* has largely been replaced by **injury prevention** or **injury control.** These terms are inclusive of all measures to prevent injuries, both unintentional and intentional, or to minimize their severity.

There are four significant characteristics of unintentional injuries: (1) they are unplanned events, (2) they usually are preceded by an unsafe act or condition (hazard), (3) they often are accompanied by economic loss, and (4) they interrupt the efficient completion of tasks.

An **unsafe act** is any *behavior* that would increase the probability of an unintentional injury. For example, driving an automobile while being impaired by alcohol or operating a power saw without eye protection is an unsafe act (see Figure 17.1). An **unsafe condition** is any *environmental factor* (physical or social) that would increase the probability of an unintentional injury. Icy streets are an example of an unsafe condition. Unsafe acts and unsafe conditions are **hazards.** While hazards do not actually *cause* unintentional injuries (an alcohol-impaired person may reach home uninjured, even over icy streets), they do increase the probability that an unintentional injury will occur.

injury
physical damage to the body resulting from mechanical, chemical, thermal, or other environmental energy

unintentional injury
an injury that occurred without anyone intending that harm be done

intentional injury
an injury that is purposely inflicted, either by the victim or by another

injury prevention (control)
an organized effort to prevent injuries or to minimize their severity

FIGURE 17.1

An unsafe act is a behavior that increases the probability of an injury. Should this person be wearing eye protection?

unsafe act
any behavior that would increase the probability of an injury occurring

unsafe condition
any environmental factor or set of factors (physical or social) that would increase the probability of an injury occurring

hazard
an unsafe act or condition

Cost of Injuries to Society

Injuries are costly to society in terms of both human suffering and economic loss. Injuries are a leading cause of death and disability in the world. An estimated 5.8 million people died from injuries in the world in 1998.[3] This is nearly 16,000 people each day. Each year, nearly 150,000 Americans die from **fatal injuries,** making it the fifth leading cause of death in the United States. Specifically, in 2001, there were 157,078 injury deaths that accounted for 6.3% of all deaths among residents of the United States.[4,5] Of these deaths, 101,537 (64.6%) were classified as unintentional injury deaths, 30,622 (19.5%) as suicides, and 20,308 (12.9%) as homicides. A total of 4,241 (2.7%) injury deaths were of undetermined intent, and 413 (0.3%) were classified as resulting from legal intervention (see Figure 17.2).

Deaths are only a small part of the total cost of injuries. Worldwide, 16% of the world's burden of disease can be attributed to injuries.[3] In the United States, there were 39.4 million injury-related visits to hospital emergency departments and 11.1 million injury-related visits to hospital ambulatory medical outpatient departments, for a total of 50.5 million medically attended injury-related episodes in 2001.[6,7] Of these injuries, an estimated 20 million were **disabling injuries,** injuries that restricted normal activity beyond the day of injury (see Figure 17.3).[8]

In addition to the human suffering caused by injuries are the economic costs. It has been estimated that injury-attributed medical expenditures make up about 10.3% of all medical expenditures annually; in 2000, that amounted to $117 billion. The figure of 10.3% is similar to the percentages of expenditures for other public health concerns, such as overweight and obesity (9.1%) and smoking (6.5% to 14.4%).[9] The true economic burden of injuries is much greater than this estimate because it does not include value of life lost to

FIGURE 17.2

Injury deaths: United States, 2001.

Source: Anderson, R. N., A. M. Miniño, L. A. Fingerhut, M. Warner, J. A. Heinen (2004). "Deaths: Injuries, 2001." *National Vital Statistics Reports,* 52(21): 1–86.

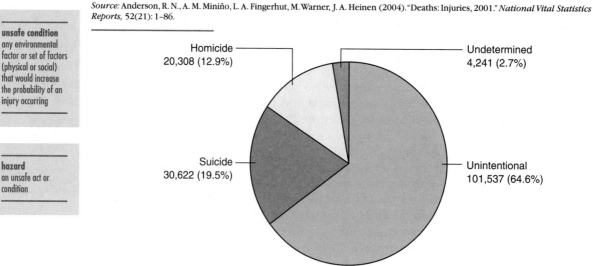

Homicide
20,308 (12.9%)

Undetermined
4,241 (2.7%)

Suicide
30,622 (19.5%)

Unintentional
101,537 (64.6%)

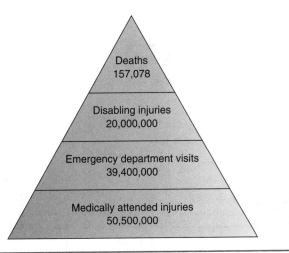

FIGURE 17.3
Burden of injury: United States, 2001.

Sources: Anderson, R. N., A. M. Miniño, L. A. Fingerhut, M. Warner, J. A. Heinen (2004). "Deaths: Injuries, 2001." *National Vital Statistics Reports,* 52(21): 1–86; McCaig, L. F., and C. W. Burt (2003). *National Ambulatory Medical Care Survey: 2001 Emergency Department Summary* (Vital and Health Statistics, no. 335). Hyattsville, MD: National Center for Health Statistics; Hing, E., and K. Middleton (2003). *National Ambulatory Medical Care Survey: 2001 Outpatient Department Summary* (Vital and Health Statistics, no. 338). Hyattsville, MD: National Center for Health Statistics; National Safety Council (2003). *Injury Facts.* Itasca, IL: Author.

Table 17.1
Leading Causes of Years of Potential Life Lost (YPLL) and Number of Deaths for Leading Causes of Death, United States, 2000

Disease or Condition	Age-Adjusted YPLL Before Age 75 (per 100,000 population)	Number of Deaths
Cancer	1,674	553,091
Injury	1,628	144,015
Heart disease	1,253	710,760
Stroke	223	167,661
Chronic lower respiratory diseases	188	122,009
Diabetes mellitus	178	69,301
Human immunodeficiency virus disease	174	14,478
Chronic liver disease and cirrhosis	164	26,552
Influenza and pneumonia	87	65,313

Sources: Freid, V. M., K. Prager, A. P. MacKay, and H. Xia (2003). *Chartbook on Trends in the Health of Americans. Health, United States.* Hyattsville, MD: National Center for Health Statistics; Miniño, A. M., E. Arias, K. D. Kochanek, S. L. Murphy, and B. L. Smith (2002). "Deaths: Final Data for 2000." *National Vital Statistics Reports,* 50(15): 1–120.

premature mortality, loss of patient and caregiver time, and nonmedical expenditures such as insurance costs, property damage, litigation, decreased quality of life, and disability. In 2002, it was estimated that the economic impact of fatal and nonfatal unintentional injuries alone amounted to $586 billion.[8]

Injuries contribute to premature deaths (deaths that occur before reaching the age of one's life expectancy) in the United States. In terms of years of potential life lost before 75 years of age (YPLL-75), unintentional injuries rank third. However, when one considers all injuries, both intentional and unintentional, then injuries are the second leading cause of YPLL-75 after cancer. Leading causes of YPLL-75 and number of deaths for various causes of death are shown in Table 17.1.[10,11]

fatal injury
an injury that results in one or more deaths

disabling injury
an injury causing any restriction of normal activity beyond the day of the injury's occurrence

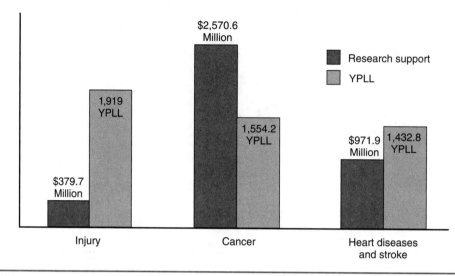

FIGURE 17.4

Average number of years of potential life lost (YPLL) versus the federal research investment.

Source: Bonnie, R. J., C. E. Fulco, and C. T. Liverman, eds. (1999). *Reducing the Burden of Injury: Advancing Prevention and Treatment.* Institute of Medicine, Committee on Injury Prevention and Control. Washington, DC: National Academy Press. Used with permission from the National Academies Press for the National Academy of Sciences.

It is important to understand that federal funding for health research is not allocated on a cost-per-death basis. The federal investment for injury research is only about one-seventh of that for cancer research and one-third of that for research on heart diseases and stroke (see Figure 17.4).[12]

Injuries place a special burden on our emergency departments because they are the leading cause of such visits, making up more than one-third of the total visits. There were an estimated 39.4 million injury-related emergency department (ED) visits during 2001, or 14.1 visits per 100 persons per year. This made up 36.6% of all ED visits in 2001. Included in this total were 400,000 visits related to self-inflicted injuries. Seventy-two percent of all emergency department injury visits are for unintentional injuries.[6]

UNINTENTIONAL INJURIES

Unintentional injuries are the cause of nearly two-thirds of all injury deaths in the United States and rank as the fifth leading cause of deaths in the United States (see Table 3.8). Motor vehicle crashes are the leading cause of unintentional injury deaths. In 2001, motor vehicle crashes resulted in 42,443 deaths, or 41.8% of all unintentional injury deaths. The second leading cause of unintentional injury deaths that year was falls, which accounted for 15,019 deaths, or 14.8% of all unintentional injury deaths; third was unintentional poisonings, which accounted for 14,078 deaths, or 13.9% of the total.[4] An estimated $268 billion was lost in wages and productivity, and $107 billion was incurred in medical expenses, $89 billion in insurance administration costs, and $71 billion in motor vehicle damage.[8] Clearly, unintentional injuries constitute a major community health problem. One of the *Healthy People 2010* objectives is to reduce the rate of unintentional injuries from nearly 35 per 100,000 population in 1998 to 17 per 100,000.[13]

BOX 17.1	HEALTHY PEOPLE 2010 OBJECTIVE: REDUCE DEATHS CAUSED BY MOTOR VEHICLE CRASHES

Target and baseline

Objective	Reduction in Deaths Caused by Motor Vehicle Crashes	1998 Baseline	2010 Target
15.15a	Deaths per 100,000 population	15.6*	9.2
15.15b	Deaths per 100 million vehicle miles traveled	1.6	0.8

*Age adjusted to the year 2000 standard population.

For Further Thought

In 1999, drivers between 15 and 20 years old made up just 6.8% of the licensed drivers but were involved in 14.7% of fatal crashes. Do you think that issuing graduated driver's licenses to new drivers is a solution? If not, how would you suggest states respond to this problem?

Source: Healthy People 2010.

Types of Unintentional Injuries

There are many types of unintentional injuries. The majority occur as a result of motor vehicle crashes, falls, poisonings, drownings, suffocation, fires and burns, and firearms. These are discussed briefly here.

Motor Vehicle Crashes

More people die from unintentional injuries associated with motor vehicle crashes than any other type of injury. In 2002, there were more than 6.3 million police-reported motor vehicle crashes, including nearly two million injury crashes. There were an estimated 2.9 million people injured and 42,815 people killed. Fatal injury rates per 100 million vehicle miles traveled (VMT) have declined every year since 1995. A majority of those killed were drivers (66%), followed by passengers (30%), pedestrians (3%), and pedalcyclists (2%).[14] One of the Nation's *Healthy People 2010* objectives is to reduce the deaths caused by motor vehicle crashes from 15.6 per 100,000 (1.6 deaths per 100 million vehicle miles traveled) to 9.2 deaths per 100,000 population (0.8 deaths per 100 million vehicle miles traveled) (see Box 17.1).[13]

Falls

The second leading cause of unintentional fatal injuries is falls, which resulted in 15,764 deaths in 2001.[4] Falls were the leading cause of injury-related emergency department visits in 2001, with 7.8 million visits.[6] Falls can occur from one surface level to another (like stairs), or on the same level. More than half the 17,000 or more deaths resulting from falls each year are from falls that occur at home. Falls account for one-third of all deaths from unintentional injuries that occur at home.

Falls disproportionately affect elders. In the United States, approximately 40% of elders (adults 65 years of age and older) fall each year. Falls are the leading cause of both nonfatal and fatal injury among elders, and the number one reason for ED visits among this population. Sixty-two percent of all nonfatal-injury ED visits by elders were attributed to falls.[15] In 2001, 11,746 elders died from fall-related injuries.[4]

Poisonings

Poisonings are the third leading cause of unintentional injury deaths in the United States and the second leading cause of deaths from injuries sustained at home. In 1999, poisonings accounted for 14,078 deaths.[4] Poisoning deaths include deaths from drugs, medicines, and toxic foods such as mushrooms and shellfish, as well as deaths from commonly recognized poisons. Four-fifths of these poisoning deaths occurred at home, where poisonings are the leading cause of injury deaths.[8]

Other Types of Unintentional Injuries

Other leading causes of unintentional injury deaths in 2001 were suffocation (5,555), fires and burns (3,309), drowning (3,281), and firearms (802). All other types of unintentional injury deaths numbered about 17,050 in 2001.[4]

Epidemiology of Unintentional Injuries

Unintentional injuries are a major community health concern because they account for a disproportionately large number of *early* deaths in our society. However, deaths are only a part of the human toll; incapacitation is another significant aspect of the problem. One in six hospital days can be attributed to unintentional injuries. As mentioned earlier, medical costs from unintentional injuries run into the billions of dollars annually. Many of these injuries, such as head and spinal cord injuries, result in long-term or permanent disabilities that can affect individuals and their families for years.

Some of the factors that describe where, when, and to whom unintentional injuries occur are discussed in the following sections. In addition to describing the occurrence of injuries by person, place, and time, we include a discussion of alcohol and other drugs as risk factors in unintentional injuries.

Person

Unintentional injuries resulting in death and disability occur in all age groups, genders, races, and socioeconomic groupings. However, certain groups are at greater risk for injury than others.

Age

After the first year of life, unintentional injuries become the leading cause of death in children. They are the leading cause of death in the following age groups: 1–4, 5–14, 15–24, and 25–34 years of age. They are the second leading cause of death in the 35- to 44-year age group (after cancers) and the third leading cause of death in the 45- to 54-year age group (after cancer and heart disease). Unintentional injuries account for 40% of the deaths in the 5- to 14-year age group; the percentage is higher for males (43%) than for females (35%).[5]

Nearly half of all deaths among older teenagers (15–19 years of age) are caused by unintentional injuries,[16] and about half of the 8 million emergency department visits each year by adolescents are due to injuries. The highest rate of injury-related visits to emergency departments for all types of injuries is by 15- to 24-year-old males (see Figure 17.5).[5]

Children and teenagers are at a higher than average risk of dying as a result of unintentional firearm injury. Unintentional fatal and nonfatal firearm-related injury rates are highest among persons aged 15–24 years, and these rates decrease consistently with age[17] (see Figure 17.6). Some people believe that childhood firearm deaths are a national tragedy in the United States. A child under 15 years of age is nine times more likely to die of an unintentional firearm injury in the United States than in the other 25 industrialized nations (see Figure 17.7).[18] Unintentional firearm injuries constitute an important public health problem. Two states, California and Florida, have enacted legislation making adults legally responsible for the inappropriate storage of firearms.

For all age groups except persons 80 years of age and older, motor vehicle crashes are the leading cause of unintentional injury deaths.[4,5] However, rates of involvement in crashes

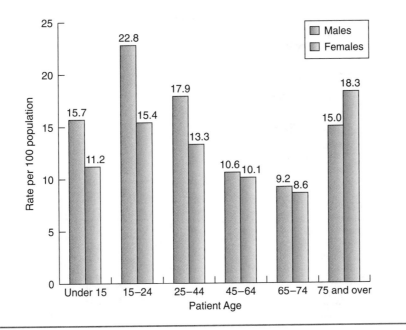

FIGURE 17.5

Rates of injury-related visits to emergency departments by age and sex, 2001.

Source: National Safety Council (2003). *Injury Facts.* Itasca, IL: Author. Used with permission.

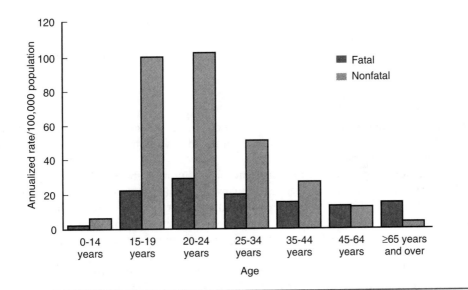

FIGURE 17.6

Fatal and nonfatal firearm-related injury rates, by age: United States, 1993–1998.

Source: Centers for Disease Control and Prevention (2001). "Surveillance for Fatal and Nonfatal Firearm-Related Injuries—United States, 1993–1998." *MMWR,* 50(SS-2): 1–34.

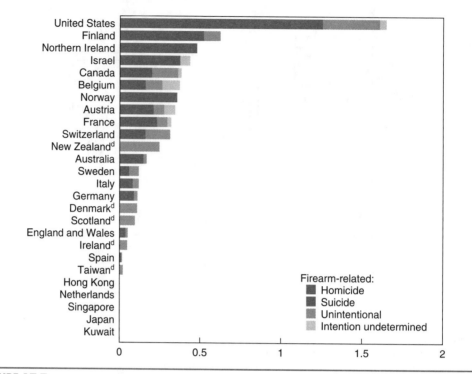

FIGURE 17.7

Rates[a] of firearm-related death[b] among children younger than 15 years in 26 industrialized countries.[c]

[a]Per 100,000 children aged <15 years and for 1 year during 1990–1995.

[b]Homicides by firearm (*International Classification of Diseases,* 9th Rev., codes E965.0–E965.4), suicides by firearm (E955.0–E955.4), unintentional deaths caused by firearm (E922.0–E922.9), and firearm-related deaths for which intention was undetermined (E985.0–E985.4).

[c]All countries classified in the high-income group with population = 1 million (5) that provided complete data. In this analysis, Hong Kong, Northern Ireland, and Taiwan are considered as countries.

[d]Reported only unintentional firearm-related deaths.

Source: Centers for Disease Control and Prevention (1997). "Rates of Homicide, Suicide and Firearm-Related Deaths among Children—26 Industrial Countries." *MMWR,* 46(5): 101–105.

resulting in fatal injuries in 2002 were the highest for drivers aged 16 to 20 (65 per 100,000 licensed drivers). This was twice the fatal injury involvement rate for all drivers (30 per 100,000 licensed drivers).[14]

Among elders (those 65 years of age and older), injuries are the eighth leading cause of death. Injury deaths would rank higher, but many elders die of other causes resulting from the aging process, such as heart disease, cancer, and stroke. An examination of the rates of death per 100,000 among elders reveals that elders have the highest unintentional injury death rate of any age group (92.6 per 100,000). For those 85 years and older, the injury death rate climbs to 276 per 100,000.[4]

Falls are the leading cause of unintentional injury deaths for those 80 years of age and older. At age 80, the death rate from falls surpasses that for motor vehicle crashes and accounts for more than half of the unintentional injury-related deaths of this age group.

Elders are at age-increased risk of dying in car crashes, too. A recent report published by the AAA Foundation revealed that drivers 65 years of age and older are almost twice as likely to die in car crashes as drivers aged 55 to 64. Drivers 75 and older were two and one-half times as likely to die, and drivers 85 and over were almost four times as likely to die in car crashes compared to drivers aged 55 to 64.[19]

Elders also experience high rates of nonfatal injuries. In 2001, approximately 2.7 million elders (935,556 men and 1,731,640 women) were treated for nonfatal injuries in EDs. Elders are three times more likely to hospitalized following an injury than those younger than 65.[15]

Gender
Statistics indicate that, at every age level, males are much more likely to become involved in a fatal unintentional injury than females. Overall, the ratio of male deaths to female deaths is nearly 2:1. In the 15- to 24- and 25- to 64-year age groups, males die from unintentional injuries at greater than three times the rate of their female counterparts. Although differences in unintentional injury death rates between the sexes decline with age, men retain a marginally higher rate even in the over-75-year age group. The type of unintentional fatality with the widest disparity is firearm injuries (86% males and 14% females); the type with the narrowest is falls (54% males and 46% females).[5]

Minority Status
In 2001, unintentional injuries and adverse effects were the leading cause of death for all ages through the 25- to 34-year age group in all racial and ethnic groups except for blacks. In this racial group, homicide and legal intervention replaced unintentional injuries as the leading causes of injury deaths for the 15–24 and 25–34 year age groups.[16] Age-adjusted death rates for unintentional injuries in 2001 were highest for the American Indian/Alaska Native population (44.6 per 100,000) and lowest for the Asian/Pacific Islander population (14.4 per 100,000). The white, non-Hispanic population had a rate of 37.0, while the Hispanic population had a slightly lower rate of 25.8 per 100,000 population.[16]

Place
Unintentional injuries occur wherever people are—at home, at work, or on the road. While more injuries occur at home, more injury deaths occur on the road.

Home
People spend more time at home than any other place, so it is not surprising that 41% of all unintentional injuries reported in the 1998 National Health Interview Survey were injuries that occurred in the home (see Figure 17.8).[5] Unintentional injuries in the home result from falls, burns, poisonings, accidental shootings and stabbings, and suffocation. Within the home, some areas are more dangerous than others. The presence of appliances (including stoves, toasters, mixers, and so on) and sharp knives in the kitchen makes this room one of the more dangerous in the house. Another location where many unintentional injuries occur, particularly to the very young and old, is on stairways. For children, the bathroom, garage, and basement are hazardous areas because of the drugs, cleaning agents, and other poisonous materials that are often stored in these areas. In the home, more people die in bedrooms, where they may be sleeping during a fire, than in any other room.

Highway
More than 15% of all injuries reported in the National Health Interview Survey in 1998 were sustained on streets, highways, and parking lots.[8] Although these venues rank second to the home as places for nonfatal injuries, they rank first for fatal injuries. Approximately 42% of all unintentional injury deaths are motor vehicle deaths (see Figure 17.9). Significant progress has been made in reducing the rate of motor vehicle–related deaths, from 22.5 per 100,000 population in 1980 to 14.9 per 100,000 in 2001.[14] This has been achieved through effective interventions, including increasing public awareness, education, legal proscriptions (such as child safety seats and safety belts), innovative vehicle and equipment designs, improved roadways, and enhanced medical systems.

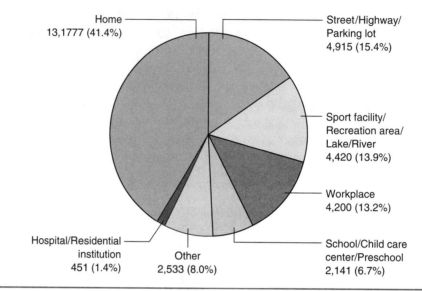

FIGURE 17.8

Number and percentage of injury episodes by place of occurrence: United States, 1998.

Source: National Safety Council (2003). *Injury Facts.* Itasca, IL: Author.

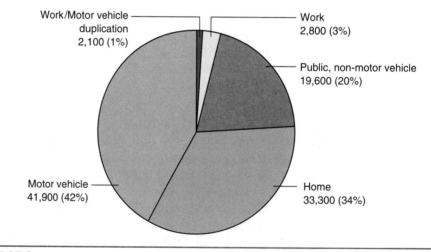

FIGURE 17.9

Unintentional injury deaths by class: United States, 2002.

Source: National Safety Council (2003). *Injury Facts.* Itasca, IL: Author. Used with permission.

Nonetheless, there are those who believe we could do a better job. One area of concern is the number of unlicensed or improperly licensed drivers on the highways. A five-year study (1993–1997) revealed that 20% of all fatal crashes—one in five—involves at least one improperly licensed driver. These are drivers with a license that is suspended, revoked, expired, cancelled, or denied. Nearly 4% of drivers involved in fatal crashes had no known license at all.[20]

| BOX **17.2** | TEN GREAT PUBLIC HEALTH ACHIEVEMENTS, 1900–1999: MOTOR VEHICLE SAFETY |

Bumper to Bumper and Curb to Curb . . . Driving Is Safer Now Than in 1900

Although more people are driving automobiles, traveling more miles, and driving at faster speeds than in 1900, driving is much safer now because of safer vehicles, highways, and drivers.

Since 1925, the annual death rate from motor vehicle travel has decreased 90%, despite the increase in miles traveled and the number of vehicles used per capita.

Approximately 85,000 American lives have been saved because of seat belts.

Using child safety seats has reduced the risk of infant death by 69% and of children aged 1 to 4 years by 47%.

Since 1987, community awareness and driving-while-intoxicated regulations have helped reduce alcohol-related traffic fatalities by 32%.

Recreation/Sport Area

The third most likely place to sustain an injury that results in a visit to an emergency department is a recreation or sports area, such as a soccer field, baseball diamond, or basketball court. Approximately 14% of injuries reported in the 1998 National Health Interview Survey occurred in these settings.[5]

Workplace

The workplace ranks fourth as a location where unintentional injuries frequently occur. About 13% of reported injuries occurred in the workplace.[8] As one might imagine, the risk of injury varies widely among different occupations. Among the most dangerous occupations are mining, farming (including logging), and construction. (For more information about workplace injuries, see Chapter 18.)

Time

During the twentieth century, there were declines for some types of unintentional injuries and increases for others. For example, motor vehicle deaths fell from 53,543 in 1969 to 42,815 in 2002. This reduction occurred despite the fact that Americans drove 2.7 times more miles in 2002 than they did in 1969. The fatality rate per 100 million vehicular miles traveled declined from 5.0 to 1.5 during that 33-year period.[14] This reduction in the death rate from motor vehicle crashes in the United States is one of the ten most significant public health achievements of the twentieth century (see Box 17.2).

Since 1975, unintentional deaths from drowning, fires, and burns have declined by more than half, and from firearms by two-thirds. However, deaths from falls, which declined significantly from 1975 to 1986, have begun to increase in the past few years, as the U.S. population ages. Deaths from poisonings have also increased since the late 1970s.[8]

There are seasonal variations in the incidence of some types of unintentional injuries, but these depend upon the types of injury. For example, 62% of all drownings occur in four months—May, June, July, and August—when more people take part in water sports. Conversely, 65% of all deaths due to fires and burns are recorded during the six months from November through April, when furnaces, fireplaces, wood-burning stoves, and electric and kerosene space heaters are most often in use.[8]

Motor vehicle crash rates per 100 million vehicle miles traveled in 2002 were highest during November and December. However, the highest fatal crash rate occurred in September.[14]

Motor vehicle–related deaths increase markedly at night. Fatalities also occur at a higher rate on weekends (Friday through Sunday). Although more fatal crashes occur on Saturdays, more crashes of all types occur on Fridays. The hours between midnight and 3 A.M. Saturdays and Sundays are the most dangerous three-hour periods to travel by car[14] (see Figure 17.10).

FIGURE 17.10
Approximately 50% of highway fatalities involve the use of alcohol.

Much publicity surrounds the number of motor vehicle deaths that occur during the following six major holiday periods: Memorial Day, Fourth of July, Labor Day, Thanksgiving, Christmas, and New Year. However, it has been shown that the number of crash-related deaths for these periods is not significantly different from the number occurring during nonholiday periods. However, the proportion of fatal crashes that are alcohol related is higher during holiday periods (about 50%) than during nonholiday periods (about 40%).[14]

Alcohol and Other Drugs as Risk Factors

An examination of the factors that contribute to intentional and unintentional injuries reveals that alcohol may be the single most important factor. This is certainly the case with fatal motor vehicle crashes, in which 41% of persons killed in traffic crashes in 2002 died in alcohol-related crashes. While 41% represents a significant decline from the 60% reported in 1982, it is still too high. There has also been a decline in the percentage of those killed in crashes who were intoxicated—that is, who had blood alcohol concentrations (BACs) that exceeded 0.08% (BAC > 0.08%)—from 53% in 1982 to 35% in 2002.[14]

The percentage of drivers in fatal crashes whose BAC exceeded the legal limit (0.08%) was 21% in 2002, but this percentage was four times higher at night than during the day. Alcohol was involved in 77% of the single-car crashes that occurred on a weekend night in which a 21-year-old or older driver was killed (see Figure 17.11). The percentage of drivers involved in fatal crashes whose BAC exceeded 0.08% was highest for drivers aged 21 to 24 years (39%) (see Figure 17.12), and twice as high for males as for females.[14] Fatally injured intoxicated drivers were six times more likely to have had a prior conviction for driving while intoxicated than fatally injured sober drivers.[21]

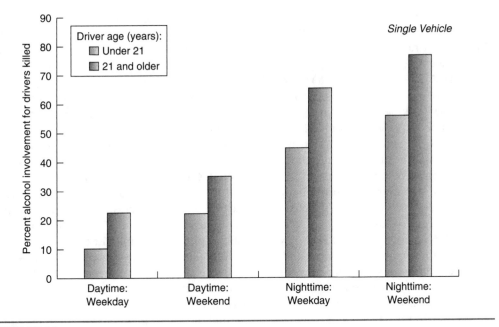

FIGURE 17.11

Alcohol involvement (BAC ≥ 0.01) for drivers killed, by driver age, time of day, and day of week.

Source: U.S. Department of Transportation, National Highway Traffic Safety Administration (2004). *Traffic Safety Facts 2002: A Compilation of Motor Vehicle Crash Data from the Fatality Analysis Reporting System and the General Estimates System* (DOT HS 809 620). Washington, DC: Author.

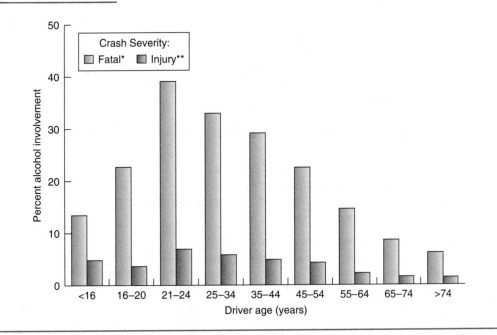

FIGURE 17.12

Percentage of driver alcohol involvement for fatal and injury crashes in 2002.

*For fatal crashes, alcohol involvement is a blood alcohol concentration (BAC) of 0.01 grams per deciliter or greater.
**For injury crashes, alcohol involvement is police-reported alcohol involvement.

Source: U.S. Department of Transportation, National Highway Traffic Safety Administration (2004). *Traffic Safety Facts 2002* (DOT HS 809 620). Washington, DC: Author.

Unfortunately, drivers are not the only persons killed in alcohol-related motor vehicle crashes. Motor vehicle crashes are the leading cause of death among children aged 1 year and older in the United States, and one in four deaths of child passengers aged 14 years and older involves alcohol use. Of the 2,355 children who died in alcohol-related crashes during the period 1997 to 2002, 1,588 (68%) were riding with drinking drivers.[22]

Alcohol use often contributes to motor vehicle injuries and deaths in another way. Safety-belt use by drinking drivers is lower than for their nondrinking counterparts, thus increasing the likelihood of a fatal outcome if there is a crash. In 1999, safety belts were used by only 19% of fatally injured *intoxicated* drivers, compared with 30% of fatally injured impaired drivers (with BAC levels between 0.01% and 0.09%) and 48% of fatally injured sober drivers.[21] Child passenger restraint use also decreases as the BAC of the driver increases. Of 1,409 child passengers with known restraint information who died while riding with drinking drivers (1997–2002), only 466 (32%) were restrained at the time of the crash. The likelihood that a child passenger restraint was used decreased with increases in drivers' BAC.[22] Passage of primary enforcement safety belt laws (laws that allow police to stop and ticket a driver solely because an occupant is unbelted) and stricter enforcement of these laws in all states could reduce child passenger deaths. Excessive drinking can also increase a pedestrian's chances of being killed by a motor vehicle. In 2002, more than one-third (33%) of pedestrians 16 years of age or older killed by motor vehicles were intoxicated.[14]

Alcohol has also been determined to be an important factor in other types of unintentional injuries and deaths, including aquatic-related deaths. Nearly half of those who drown have evidence of alcohol in their blood. Alcohol is also a major risk factor for boating fatalities. Alcohol involvement was reported in 39% of all boating fatalities in 2002.[23] A U.S. Coast Guard study estimates that boat operators with a BAC above 0.10% are more than 10 times as likely to be killed in a boating accident than boat operators with zero BACs.[24] In another study, it was found that nearly half of all boating fatalities occurred when vessels were not underway. This implies that while it is dangerous when the person who is operating the boat is drinking, it is also dangerous when passengers have been drinking.[25] Lastly, alcohol consumption lowers your chance of survival should you end up in the water. In a study conducted in Louisiana, alcohol and/or metabolites of an illicit drug were found in 60% of drowning victims aged 13 years or older.[26] Clearly, alcohol consumption and aquatic recreation are a dangerous combination.

Alcohol has also been shown to be a risk factor for bicyclists. More that one in three (37%) pedalcyclists killed in traffic crashes was killed in an alcohol-related crash.[14]

Prevention through Epidemiology

Sometimes it has been society's nature to wait until after a tragedy before correcting an existing hazard or dangerous situation. Most implementation of prevention activities related to injuries occurs only after costly disasters.

Early Contributors to Injury Prevention and Control

The first important efforts toward injury prevention and control began early in the twentieth century. Three of the most important contributors to early efforts at injury control were Hugh DeHaven, John E. Gordon, and William Haddon, Jr. Hugh DeHaven was a World War I combat pilot, who, after surviving a plane crash, dedicated his professional life to studying victims of falls in an effort to design ways to reduce the force of impact on a body. Many of his ideas have led to better design concepts, including structural adaptations to protect drivers and other occupants of moving vehicles. For example, today we have at our disposal the protection of safety belts, air bags, collapsible steering assemblies, and padded dashboards. Many of these safety devices built upon the early work of Hugh DeHaven.[27]

In 1949, John E. Gordon proposed that the tools of epidemiology be used to analyze injuries. Because of Gordon's work, a great deal was learned about risk factors, susceptible populations, and the distribution of injuries in populations.

model for unintentional injuries the public health triangle (host, agent, and environment) modified to indicate energy as the causative agent of injuries

William Haddon, Jr., was both an engineer and a physician and is often considered the founding father of modern injury prevention research.[27] He was an unrelenting proponent of the epidemiologic approach to injury control and insisted that the results of this work be used in the development of public policy. He was the foremost expert on highway safety in the 1960s and developed many successful countermeasures to reduce the number of unintentional highway injuries.

A Model for Unintentional Injuries

Until the 1950s, little progress occurred in the reduction of unintentional injuries and deaths. One reason for this was the failure to identify the causative agent associated with unintentional injuries. Chapter 4 discussed the public health model that describes communicable diseases in terms of the host, agent, and environment, arranged in a triangle. A similar **model for unintentional injuries** has been proposed. In this model, the injury-producing agent is *energy* (see Figure 17.13).

Examples of injury-producing energy are plentiful. A moving car, a falling object (or person), and a speeding bullet all have kinetic energy. When one of these moving objects strikes another object, energy is released, often resulting in injury or trauma. Similarly, a hot stove or pan contains energy in the form of heat. Contact with one of these objects results in the rapid transfer of heat. If the skin is unprotected, tissue damage (a burn) occurs. Electrical energy is all around us and represents a potential source of unintentional injuries. Even accidental poisonings fit nicely into the model that incorporates energy as the causative agent of injury. Cleansers, drugs, and medicines represent stored chemical energy which, when released inappropriately, can cause serious injury or death.

Prevention and Control Tactics Based upon the Model

Based upon the epidemiological model just described, there are four types of actions that can be taken to prevent or reduce the number and seriousness of unintentional injuries and deaths.[28] These four tactics are modified from those of Haddon.[29] The first is to prevent the accumulation of the injury-producing agent, energy. Examples of implementing this principle include reducing speed limits to decrease motor vehicle injuries, lowering the height of children's high chairs and of diving boards to reduce fall injuries, and lowering the settings on hot water heaters to reduce the number and seriousness of burns. In our electrical example, circuit breakers in the home prevent the accumulation of excess electrical energy.

The second type of action is to prevent the inappropriate release of excess energy or to modify its release in some way. Flame-retardant fabric that will not ignite is an example of such a prevention. Currently, there is a law that requires that such a fabric be used in the manufacture of children's pajamas. The use of automobile safety belts is another example. In this case, excess energy (movement of a human body) is released into the safety belt instead of into the car's windshield (see Figure 17.14). In the prevention of fall injuries, hand rails, walkers, and non-slip surfaces in bathtubs prevent the inappropriate release of kinetic energy resulting from falls.

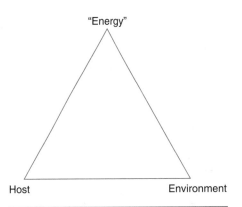

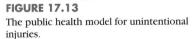

FIGURE 17.13
The public health model for unintentional injuries.

FIGURE 17.14
Safety belts prevent the inappropriate release of energy.

The third tactic involves placing a barrier between the host and agent. The insulation around electrical wires and the use of potholders and non–heat-transferring handles on cookware are examples of this preventive strategy. The use of sunscreen lotion and the wearing of a hat in the summer place a barrier between the sun's energy and you.

Finally, it is sometimes necessary or useful to completely separate the host from potentially dangerous sources of energy. Examples include the locked gates and high fences around electrical substations and swimming pools. At home, locking up guns and poisons provides protection against the likelihood of unintentional injury of young children.

Other Tactics

By viewing energy as the cause of unintentional injuries and deaths, it is possible to take positive steps in their prevention and control. There are still other actions that a community can take. First, injury-control education in the schools and in other public forums can be helpful. Second, improvements in the community's ability to respond to emergencies, such as encouraging the public to enroll in first aid and cardiopulmonary resuscitation (CPR) classes and expanding 911 telephone services, can limit disability and save lives. Third, communities can ensure that they have superior emergency and paramedic personnel by instituting the best possible training programs. The result will be improved emergency medical care and rehabilitation for the injured. Finally, communities can strengthen ordinances against high-risk behaviors, such as driving while impaired by alcohol, and then support their enforcement.

Community Approaches to the Prevention of Unintentional Injuries

There are four broad strategies for the prevention of unintentional injuries—education, regulation, automatic protection, and litigation.

Education

Injury prevention education is the process of changing people's health-directed behavior in such a way as to reduce unintentional injuries. Education certainly has a place in injury prevention. Many of us remember the school fire drill, lessons on bicycle safety, and the school crossing guard. Undoubtedly, millions of injuries were prevented in these ways. However, injury prevention education has its limitations. Figure 17.15 illustrates both the inefficiency of public education and the difficulties of measuring a successful outcome.

Regulation

The former 55-mile-per-hour national speed limit is an example of the power of **regulation**—the enactment and enforcement of laws to control conduct—as a means of reducing the number and seriousness of unintentional injuries. For years, motorists were advised to drive more responsibly. Public service announcements in the 1960s and 1970s informed audiences that "speed kills," and advised motorists not to "drink and drive." However, the highway death toll continued to mount until 1974, when then President Gerald Ford issued the national 55-mile-per-hour

injury prevention education
the process of changing people's health-directed behavior so as to reduce unintentional injuries

regulation
the enactment and enforcement of laws to control conduct

FIGURE 17.15

Attenuation of the effect of a public health education program.

Source: McLoughlin, E., C. J. Vince, A. M. Lee, et al. (1982) "Project Burn Prevention: Outcome and Implications," *American Journal of Public Health*, 72(3): 241–247. As presented in U.S. Congress, Office of Technology Assessment (February, 1988). *Healthy Children: Investing in the Future* (pub. no. OTA-H-345). Washington, DC: U.S. Government Printing Office.

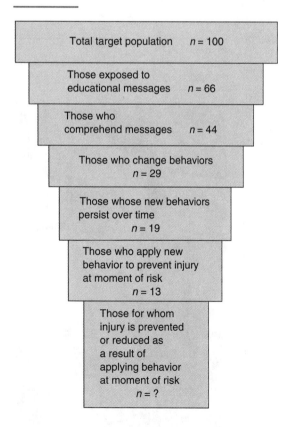

Total target population $n = 100$

Those exposed to educational messages $n = 66$

Those who comprehend messages $n = 44$

Those who change behaviors $n = 29$

Those whose new behaviors persist over time $n = 19$

Those who apply new behavior to prevent injury at moment of risk $n = 13$

Those for whom injury is prevented or reduced as a result of applying behavior at moment of risk $n = ?$

speed limit. Although the primary purpose of the slower speed limit was to conserve gasoline during the Arab oil embargo, more than 9,000 lives were saved as the number of motor vehicle deaths dropped from 55,511 in 1973 to 46,200 in 1974 because of the slower speeds.

State laws requiring child safety seats and safety belt use are another example of regulation to reduce injuries. Beginning in the 1980s, automobile child restraint and safety belt legislation spread across the United States. All states now have child passenger safety seat or restraint requirements for children, and all states except for New Hampshire have safety belt use laws for adults.[14] There is quite a bit of variation in the provisions of these laws from state to state with regard to enforcement, level of fines, seats of the vehicle covered (front seat or all seats), and type of vehicle covered (see Table 17.2).[14] Passage and vigorous enforcement of safety belt regulations are one reason why motor vehicle fatalities have declined in recent years. Regulation is often aimed not at the consumer, but at the industry. For example, beginning with the 1990 models, car makers were required to equip all passenger cars with safety belts or air bags.[30]

Another regulatory change that has helped reduce motor vehicle–related injuries is the lowering of the blood alcohol concentration at which a person is legally intoxicated to 0.08%. In 2004, Delaware became the final state to adopt this standard, which has now been adopted by all 50 states, Puerto Rico, and the District of Columbia.[31] A systematic review of the effectiveness of such laws has revealed that they decrease fatal alcohol-related motor vehicle crashes an average of 7%. This should save 400 to 600 lives per year nationally, and significantly decrease the number and seriousness of injuries.[32]

Inattention to the task of driving is the cause of many motor vehicle crashes. The authors of a recent report, *Distraction in Everyday Driving,* list the potentially distracting activities that drivers engage in while driving.[33] Drivers were found to be distracted 16% of the time with such activities as talking on a cell phone, eating, drinking, and adjusting the radio (see Table 17.3). As of mid-year 2004, relatively few states had regulations regarding the use of cell phones while driving, but this is an emerging highway safety issue and some states are gathering data on the role of cell phones in motor vehicle crashes.[34]

In a "free society," such as the one in which Americans live, there is a limit to how much can be accomplished through legislation. For example, it has been very difficult to reduce the number of firearm injuries in the United States through legislation because the National Rifle Association (NRA) has been able to lobby successfully against restrictions on gun ownership.

Another example of the difficulty of achieving a balance between personal freedoms and society's legitimate health interests is motorcycle helmet legislation. Studies show that helmet laws are associated with a 29% to 33% decrease in annual per capita motorcycle fatalities.[35] In 1975, all but two states required motorcyclists to use helmets. Beginning in 1976, states began to repeal these laws. By the end of 2002, only 20 states, Puerto Rico, and the District of Columbia required a helmet for all motorcyclists (see Table 17.4).[14]

The strategy of prevention through regulation can be difficult to implement. The idea of regulating health behavior grates against the individual freedom that Americans have come to expect. Why should someone be required to wear a safety belt? The answer to that is: For the good of the total public, to protect the resources, including human life, of the greater public. Others say, "It's my life, and if I choose to take the risk of dying by not wearing a safety belt, who should care?" That response is all well and good; but when life is lost, it affects many others, such as family members, friends, and co-workers, not just the deceased. This scenario would become worse if the person not wearing a safety belt does not die but becomes a paraplegic and a ward of the state. Many public resources then would have to be used.

At what point is some legislation enough? It is known that safety belts and air bags are good and effective, but so are helmets—at least they think so at the Indianapolis 500. So should people now work to pass a law that requires all automobile and truck drivers to wear helmets? How much legislated health behavior is enough?

Table 17.2
Key Provisions of Safety Belt Use Laws through August 2002

State	Enforcement	Fine ($)	Seats	Coverage Ages	Vehicles Exempted
AL	Primary	25	Front	6+	Designed for > 10 passengers; model year < 1965; exemptions for medical reasons, rural mail carriers, and paper delivery
AK	Secondary	15	All	16+	School bus
AZ	Secondary	10	All[a]	5+; under 5 = child seat	Designed for > 10 passengers; model year < 1972
AR	Secondary	25	Front	15+	School, church, or public bus; model year < 1968
CA	Primary	20	All	16+	None
CO	Secondary[b]	17	Front	17+	Passenger bus, school bus, farm tractor, implements of husbandry
CT	Primary	37	Front	4+; <16 all	Truck or bus > 15,000 lbs
DE	Secondary	20	Front	All	Postal service vehicles
DC	Primary	50[c]	All	16+	Seating > 8 people
FL	Secondary	30	Front	6+; 6-17 in rear	School bus, public bus, truck > 5,000 lbs
GA	Primary	15	Front	5+ must be restrained if in front; 5-17 if in rear	Designed for > 10 passengers; pickup
HI	Primary	45	Front (18+); all (4-17); under 4 = child seat	4+	Bus or school bus > 10,000 lbs
ID	Secondary	5	Front	4+	>8,000 lbs
IL	Secondary	25	Front (18+); all if driver and passengers < 18	6+; <6 = child seat or seat belt; <4 = child seat; 6+ but <16 = seat belt or child seat	None
IN	Primary	25	Front; all (4+ but <12)	4+; 4-11 in rear	Truck, tractor, RV
IA	Primary	25	Front	6+	None
KS	Secondary	10	Front	14+	Designed for > 10 people; truck > 12,000 lbs
KY	Secondary	25	All	Over 40 inches tall	Designed for > 10 people
LA	Primary	25	Front	13+	Designed for > 10 people; model year < 1981
ME	Secondary	25–50	All seats (18+); all 4-18; <4 = child seat		Manufactured without seat belts
MD	Primary	25	Front	16+	Historic vehicle
MA	Secondary	25	All seats; <5 and 40 lbs or less = child seat; 5+ but <12 = seat belt		Truck > 18,000 lbs; bus and taxi operators
MI	Primary	25	Front	4+; 4-15 in rear; <4 = child seat	Taxi, bus, school bus
MN	Secondary	25	Front; all (>3 but <11)	4+; 4-10 in rear	Farm pickup truck
MS	Secondary	25	Front	4+; 4-7 in rear	Farm vehicle; bus; exemptions for medical reasons and letter carriers
MO	Secondary	10	Front	4+; 4-15 in rear	Designed for > 10 people; truck < 12,000 lbs
MT	Secondary	20	All	4+	Specially licensed motor vehicles and vehicles that make frequent stops
NE	Secondary	25	Front[d]	6-15 in rear; <6 = child seat	Model year < 1973
NV	Secondary	25	All	5+	Taxi, bus, school bus
NH	No adult law	25	All	<18 only, primary law	School bus, vehicle for hire; model year < 1968
NJ	Primary	20[e]	Front; all (8-18 and >80 lbs); <8 and <80 lbs = child seat		None

			All Front (16+);all (<16); <4 = child seat	<18 (child seat or seat belt)	>10,000 lbs
NM	Primary	25[f]	All		>10,000 lbs
NY	Primary	50–100[g]	Front (16+);all (<16); <4 = child seat		Bus, school bus, taxi, emergency vehicle
NC	Primary	25	Front	16+	Designed for > 10 people
ND	Secondary[b]	20	Front	18+	Designed for > 10 people
OH	Secondary	25	Front	4+	None
OK	Primary	20	Front	All	Farm vehicle, truck, truck tractor, RV
OR	Primary	75	All	16+	Newspaper, mail, meter, transit vehicle[i]
PA	Secondary[j]	10	Front	4+	Truck > 7,000 lbs
RI	Secondary	50	All	>12; <6 must ride in rear	Manufactured before July 1, 1966; vehicles legally manufactured (under federal law) without seat belts; letter carriers; persons with physical/medical reasons, with a note from a licensed physician
SC	Secondary	10	All	6+	School bus, public bus; vehicle with no belts in rear seating areas
SD	Secondary[k]	20	Front	5+	Passenger bus, school bus
TN	Secondary	10	Front	4+	>8,500 lbs
TX	Primary	25–50	Front	<16 in rear	Designed for > 10 people, truck > 15,000 lbs, farm vehicle
UT	Secondary[l]	45	All	19+	None
VT	Secondary	10	All	13+	Bus, taxi
VA	Secondary	25	Front	16+	Designed for > 10 people, taxi
WA	Primary[m]	86	All	All	Designed for > 10 people
WV	Secondary	25	Front	9+; 9–17 in rear	Designed for > 10 people
WI	Secondary	10	All	4+; 4–15 in rear; <4 = child seat	Taxi, farm truck
WY	Secondary	25[n]	All	5+	Persons with physical/medical exemption documented by physician's signature; vehicles legally manufactured (under federal law) without seat belts; children riding in child seats as required by law
PR	Primary	50	All	All	None

[a] Ages 5–15, effective August 22, 2002.

[b] Primary enforcement for all positions if driver is under 17 years.

[c] Plus 2 points on license.

[d] All seats if driver holds provisional operators permit or school permit.

[e] $20 for seat belt violation; $10 to $25 for child seat violation.

[f] Plus 2 points on license.

[g] Plus 3 points on license. Front seat passengers 16 years and older can be fined up to $50, and drivers can be fined up to $100 for each passenger under 16 not wearing a seat belt.

[h] Primary enforcement for all positions if driver is under 18 years.

[i] Police/emergency vehicles exempted in some situations.

[j] Pennsylvania's fine is $10, but with court, EMS, judicial, and computer costs the ticket total is $51.50.

[k] Primary enforcement for all positions if occupant is under 18 years (South Dakota law effective July 1, 2001).

[l] Primary enforcement for all seating positions if occupant is under 19 years.

[m] Effective June 2002.

[n] Fine for driver is $25; fine for passengers over 12 years is $10.

Source: U.S. Department of Transportation, National Highway Traffic Safety Administration (2004). *Traffic Safety Facts 2002: A Compilation of Motor Vehicle Crash Data from the Fatality Analysis Reporting System and the General Estimates System* (DOT HS 809 620). Washington, DC: Author.

Table 17.3

Percentage of Drivers Engaging in Potentially Distracting Activities during 3 Hours of Driving, and Percentage Duration of These Activities When Their Vehicles Were Moving

Potential Distraction	% of Subjects	% of Total Driving Time
Talking on cell phone	30.0	
Answering cell phone	15.7	1.30*
Dialing cell phone	27.1	
Eating, drinking, spilling	71.4	1.45
Preparing to eat or drink	58.6	3.16
Manipulating music/audio controls	91.4	1.35
Smoking (includes lighting and extinguishing)	7.1	1.55
Reading or writing	40.0	0.67
Grooming	45.7	0.28
Baby distracting	8.6	0.38
Child distracting	12.9	0.29
Adult distracting	22.9	0.27
Conversing	77.1	15.32
Reaching, leaning, etc.	97.1	
Manipulating vehicle controls	100.0	3.78*
Other internal distraction	67.1	
External distraction	85.7	1.62

*Combined categories

Source: Stutts, J., J. Feaganes, E. Rodgman, C. Hamlett, T. Meadows, D. Reinfurt, K. Gish, M. Mercadante, and L. Staplin (2003). *Distractions in Everyday Driving.* Washington, DC: AAA Foundation for Traffic Safety. Used with permission of AAA Foundation.

Table 17.4

Status of State Motorcycle Helmet Use Requirements through December 2002

State	Original Law	Subsequent Action, Date(s), and Current Status
AL	11/06/67	Helmet use required for all riders.
AK	01/01/71	Repealed effective 7/1/76 except for persons under 18 yrs of age, and all passengers.
AZ	01/01/69	Repealed effective 5/27/76 except for persons under 18 yrs of age.
AR	07/10/67	Helmet use required for all riders. Repealed effective 8/1/97 except for riders under 21 yrs of age.
CA	01/01/85	Helmet use required by riders under 15½ yrs of age. Effective 1/1/92 helmet use required for all riders
CO	07/01/69	Repealed effective 5/20/77. No helmet use requirement.
CT	10/01/67	Not enforced until 2/1/74. Repealed effective 6/1/76. Effective 1/1/90 adopted requirement for helmet use by persons under 18.
DE	10/01/68	Repealed effective 6/10/78 except for persons under 19 yrs of age. Also requires that a helmet be carried on the motorcycle for persons 19 and older.
DC	10/12/70	Helmet use required for all riders.
FL	09/05/67	Repealed effective 7/1/2000 except for riders under 21 yrs old and those without $10,000 medical insurance covering injuries resulting from a motorcycle crash.
GA	08/31/66	Helmet use required for all riders.
HI	05/01/68	Repealed effective 6/7/77 except for persons under 18 yrs of age.
ID	01/01/68	Repealed effective 3/29/78 except for persons under 18 yrs of age.
IL	01/01/68	Repealed effective 6/17/69 after being declared unconstitutional by the state supreme court on 5/28/69. No helmet use requirement.
IN	07/01/67	Repealed effective 9/1/77. Effective 6/1/85 adopted requirement for helmet use by persons under 18.
IA	09/01/75	Repealed effective 7/1/76. No helmet use requirement.
KS	07/01/67	7/1/67 to 3/17/70 for all cyclists. 3/17/70 to 7/1/72 only for cyclists under 21 yrs of age. 7/1/72 to 7/1/76 for all cyclists. 7/1/76 to 7/1/82 applied only to persons under 16 yrs of age. After 7/1/82 applies only to persons under 18 yrs of age.
KY	07/01/68	Repealed effective 7/15/98 except for riders under 21 yrs old, riders operating with instruction permit, riders with less than 1 year experience, and/or riders not providing proof of health insurance. Insurance provision repealed effective 7/15/2000.
LA	07/31/68	Repealed effective 10/1/76 except for persons under 18 yrs of age. Readopted for all cyclists effective 1/1/82. Repealed effective 8/15/99 except for riders under age 18 and those without $10,000 medical insurance; proof of insurance policy must be shown to law enforcement officer upon request.

(continued)

Table 17.4 (continued)

State	Original Law	Subsequent Action, Date(s), and Current Status
ME	10/07/67	Repealed effective 10/24/77. Amended effective 7/30/80 to require use by riders under 15 yrs old, novices, and holders of learner's permits.
MD	09/01/68	Repealed effective 5/29/79 except for persons under 18 yrs of age. Effective 10/1/92 helmet use required for all riders.
MA	02/27/67	Helmet use required for all riders.
MI	03/10/67	Repealed effective 6/12/68. New law adopted effective 9/1/69. Helmet use required for all riders.
MN	05/01/68	Repealed effective 4/6/77 except for persons under 18 yrs of age.
MS	03/28/74	Helmet use required for all riders.
MO	10/13/67	Helmet use required for all riders.
MT	07/01/73	Repealed effective 7/1/77 except for persons under 18 yrs of age.
NE	05/29/67	Never enforced. Declared unconstitutional by state supreme court and repealed effective 9/1/77. Effective 1/1/89 helmet use required for all riders.
NV	01/01/72	Helmet use required for all riders.
NH	09/03/67	Repealed effective 8/7/77 except for persons under 18 yrs of age.
NJ	01/01/68	Helmet use required for all riders.
NM	05/01/67	Initial law applied only to cyclists under 18 yrs of age and to all passengers. Law requiring helmet use by all cyclists adopted effective 7/1/73. Repealed effective 6/17/77 except for persons under 18 yrs of age.
NY	01/01/67	Helmet use required for all riders.
NC	01/01/68	Helmet use required for all riders.
ND	07/01/67	Repealed effective 7/1/77 except for persons under 18 yrs of age.
OH	04/02/68	Repealed effective 7/1/78 except for persons under 18 yrs and first-year novices.
OK	04/27/67	4/27/67 to 4/7/69 helmet use required for all motorcyclists. From 4/7/69 to 5/3/76 for cyclists under 21 yrs of age. 5/3/76 for cyclists under 18 yrs of age.
OR	01/01/68	Repealed effective 10/4/77, except for persons under 18 yrs of age. Effective 6/16/89 helmet use required for all riders.
PA	09/13/68	Helmet use required for all riders.
RI	06/30/67	Repealed effective 5/21/76 except for passengers on motorcycles. Effective 7/1/92 helmet use required for operators under 21 yrs of age, all passengers, and first-year novices.
SC	07/01/67	Repealed for ages 21 and over effective 6/16/80. Required for riders under 18 yrs old.
SD	07/01/67	Repealed effective 7/1/77 except for persons under 18 yrs of age.
TN	06/05/67	Helmet use required for all riders.
TX	01/01/68	Repealed effective 9/1/77 except for persons under 18 yrs of age. Effective 9/1/89 helmet use required for all riders. Effective 9/1/97 helmets required for riders under 21, those who have not completed a rider training course, and those without $10,000 medical insurance.
UT	05/13/69	Helmets required only on roads with speed limits of 35 mph or higher. Effective 5/8/77 law changed to require helmet use only by persons under 18 yrs of age.
VT	07/01/68	Helmet use required for all riders.
VA	01/01/71	Helmet use required for all riders.
WA	07/01/67	Repealed effective 7/1/77. Effective 7/1/87 helmet use required for riders under 18. Effective 6/8/90 helmet use required for all riders.
WV	05/21/68	Helmet use required for all riders.
WI	07/01/68	Repealed effective 3/19/78 except for persons under 18 yrs of age and for all holders of learner's permits.
WY	05/25/73	Repealed effective 5/27/83 except for persons under 18 yrs of age.
PR	07/20/60	Helmet use required for all riders.

Summary: 20 states plus the District of Columbia and Puerto Rico require helmet use for all riders; 27 states require helmet use for certain riders; and 3 states do not require helmet use for riders.

Source: U.S. Department of Transportation, National Highway Traffic Safety Administration (2004). *Traffic Safety Facts 2002: A Compilation of Motor Vehicle Crash Data from the Fatality Analysis Reporting System and the General Estimates System* (DOT HS 809 620). Washington, DC: Author.

Automatic Protection

When engineered changes are combined with regulatory efforts, remarkable results can sometimes be achieved. The technique of improving product or environmental design to reduce unintentional injuries is termed **automatic (or passive) protection**.[28] A good example is child-proof safety caps (see Figure 17.16). Child-proof safety caps on aspirin and other medicine were introduced in 1972. By 1977, deaths attributed to ingestion of analgesics

FIGURE 17.16
Child safety caps are an example of automatic or passive protection.

and antipyretics had decreased 41%.[28] We are all familiar with automatic protection devices. Common examples include automatic shut-off mechanisms on power tools (such as lawn mowers), safety caps on toxic products, and the warning lights and sounds that remind us to buckle our safety belts in motor vehicles.

Litigation

When other methods fail, behavioral changes can sometimes come about through the courts. **Litigation**—lawsuits filed by injured victims or their families—has been successful in removing dangerous products from store shelves or otherwise influencing changes in dangerous behavior. Litigation against a manufacturer of unsafe automobile tires, for example, might result in safer tires. Lawsuits against bartenders and bar owners for serving alcohol to drunken customers, who have later injured other people, have produced more responsible server behavior at public bars. Alcohol-related deaths and injuries on college campuses have caused insurance companies to re-examine their liability insurance policies with fraternities and sororities. This has forced some of these organizations and the universities themselves to restrict the way alcohol is used. The outcome may be a drop in unintentional injuries on these campuses.

INTENTIONAL INJURIES

automatic (passive) protection the modification of a product or environment so as to reduce unintentional injuries

Intentional injuries, the outcome of self-directed and interpersonal violence, are a staggering community health problem in the United States. More than 50,000 people die, and millions of others receive nonfatal injuries each year, as a result of self-directed or interpersonal violence.[4] In 2000, an estimated 1.6 million persons were treated for nonfatal physical assault–related injuries in emergency departments (EDs). Although the physical assault rate was 77% higher for males than for females, the rate of ED visits for sexual assault–related injuries was five times higher for females. The highest injury rates for both males and females was for the 20- to 24-year age group. The injury rate for black males was about 4.6 times higher than the rate for non-Hispanic white males.[36]

Types of Intentional Injuries

litigation the process of seeking justice for injury through courts

The spectrum of violence includes assaults, abuse (child, spouse, and elder), rape, robbery, suicide, and homicide. In 2001, residents of the United States 12 years of age or older reported being victims in an estimated 5.7 million violent crimes. Stated another way, 25 of every 1,000 people in the United States were victims of violent crimes.[37] This is a significant decline from the 10.9 million violent crimes and a victimization rate of 52 per 1,000 people recorded in 1994.[37]

In 2001, homicide and legal intervention ranked as the thirteenth leading cause of death in the United States, accounting for 20,308 deaths.[4] Of these, nearly 3,000 deaths were the result of the terrorist attacks that occurred on September 11, 2001. The homicide rate in the United States is significantly higher than in other industrialized nations. One of the *Healthy People 2010* objectives is to reduce the homicide rate from the 1998 baseline of 6.5 per 100,000 to 3.0 per 100,000 people (see Box 17.3). In the 15- to 24-year age group, deaths from homicide and legal intervention numbered 5,297, and homicide and legal intervention were the second leading cause of death.[16]

BOX **17.3**	**HEALTHY PEOPLE 2010 OBJECTIVE: REDUCE HOMICIDES**

15-32.   Reduce homicides.

Target: 3.0 homicides per 100,000 population.

Baseline: 6.0 homicides per 100,000 population occurred in 1999 (age adjusted to the year 2000 standard population).

Target setting method: Better than the best.

Total population, 1999	Homicides (Rate per 100,000)			
	1999 Baseline	**2000**	**2001***	**Target 2010**
TOTAL	6.0	5.9	7.1	3.0
Race and Ethnicity				
American Indian or Alaska Native	9.1	6.8	6.8	3.0
Asian or Pacific Islander	3.0	3.0	4.2	3.0
Asian	DNC	DNA	DNA	3.0
Native Hawaiian or other Pacific Islander	DNC	DNA	DNA	3.0
Black or African American	20.1	20.5	21.2	3.0
White	3.8	3.6	4.9	3.0
Hispanic or Latino	7.6	7.5	8.2	3.0
Cuban	5.8	5.5	6.8	3.0
Mexican American	8.4	7.7	7.6	3.0
Puerto Rican	9.0	7.7	12.7	3.0
Not Hispanic or Latino	5.7	5.6	6.8	3.0
Black or African American, not Hispanic	20.7	21.1	21.7	3.0
White, not Hispanic	2.9	2.8	4.0	3.0
Gender				
Female	2.9	2.8	3.3	3.0
Male	9.1	9.0	10.8	3.0
Education Level (aged 25 to 64 years)				
Less than high school	16.4	17.1	16.4	NA
High school graduate	9.7	9.7	11.0	NA
At least some college	2.5	2.6	5.2	NA
Select Populations (not age adjusted)				
Children under 1 year	8.3	9.0	7.9	NA
Children aged 1 to 4 years	2.5	2.3	2.7	NA
Children aged 10 to 14 years	1.2	1.1	0.9	NA
Adolescents aged 15 to 19 years	10.4	9.5	9.4	NA
Persons aged 15 to 34 years	11.7	11.5	13.2	NA
Intimate partners aged 14 to 45 years (spouse, ex-spouse, boyfriend, girlfriend)	DNC	DNC	DNC	NA
Blacks or African Americans aged 15 to 34 years	43.6	44.4	45.6	NA
Females	11.8	10.8	10.4	NA
Males	77.4	80.0	82.5	NA
Hispanic males aged 15 to 34 years	24.8	24.2	25.7	NA

DNC = Data are not collected. DNA = Data have not been analyzed. NA = Not applicable.

Note: Age-adjusted to the year 2000 standard population.

*2001 homicide data include those killed in the terrorist attacks of September 11, 2001.

Sources: National Vital Statistics System (NVSS), CDC, NCHS; FBI Uniform Crime Reports, U.S. Department of Justice.

For Further Thought

Homicide rates have declined since 1993. What are some of the reasons for this? Do you think they will continue to decline if the economy worsens and unemployment rises?

What steps would you suggest to further lower homicide rates?

Sources: Healthy People 2010; CDC. Available at http://wonder.cdc.gov/.

During that same year (2001), suicide ranked as the eleventh leading cause of death, accounting for 30,622 deaths. Suicides account for about 20% of all injury deaths. Suicide among youth (15- to 24-year age group) numbered 3,971 and was the third leading cause of death in that age group in 2001.[4]

Interpersonal violence is a costly community health problem, not only because of the loss of life and productivity but also because of the economic cost to the community. Consider the community resources expended for each violent act. There are those of the police, the legal system, the penal system, emergency health care services, medical services, social workers, and many others. Clearly, this is a problem for which prevention is the most economic approach.

Epidemiology of Intentional Injuries

To better understand the problem of intentional injuries, it is instructive to look more closely at both the victims and the perpetrators of violence. Interpersonal violence disproportionately affects those who are frustrated and hopeless, those who are jobless and live in poverty, and those with low self-esteem. More violent acts, whether self-directed or directed at others, are committed by males. Firearms are increasingly involved in violent acts with ever-increasing fatal consequences. Abuse of drugs, especially alcohol, also contributes to the number of intentional injuries. Additionally, perpetrators of violent acts are more likely to have been abused or neglected as children or exposed to violence and aggression earlier in their lives.

Homicide, Assault, and Rape

Between 1991 and 2000, the homicide rate declined from 9.8 to 5.5 per 100,000 people.[38] In 2001 the rate increased to 7.1 per 100,000 because of the terrorist attacks of September 11. (Of the 2,957 death certificates issued, 2,922 were classified as homicides).[4] Preliminary data for 2002 place the rate at 5.9 per 100,000.[39] Both the upswing in the homicide rate prior to 1991 and the subsequent decline afterward resulted from large swings in the victimization rates of those less than 25 years of age. During that same period, the victimization rate for blacks was six times higher than for whites during some years.[40] Much of the increase in homicides could be traced to the use of handguns by juveniles involved in the distribution of crack cocaine.[40]

Research indicates a relationship between income level and risk for becoming a victim of violence. In 2001, persons in households with annual incomes less than $7,500 were nearly twice as likely as persons in households with incomes of $35,000 to $50,000 to become victim of violent crime.[37]

Males and blacks as well as the poor are more vulnerable to violence. Except for rape and sexual assault, every violent crime victimization rate is higher for males than for females. Males experienced violent crime at rates 18% higher than females, and they account for about three-fourths of all murder victims.[38] However, females were victims of rape and sexual assault 9 times more often than males. In 2001, 31 blacks, 25 whites, and 18 persons of other races per 1,000 were victimized. In 2001 there were 8.1 aggravated assaults per 1,000 black persons, 5.1 per 1,000 white persons and 2.6 per 1,000 persons of other racial categories.[37]

Overall, it is estimated that less than half of all violent crimes committed in 2001 were reported to police. Furthermore, only 39% of rapes or sexual assaults were reported to police.[37] This makes the acquisition of accurate statistics on rape and attempted rape difficult. Although reported offenders are usually strangers, 65% of all rapes and sexual assaults are committed by someone acquainted with, known to, or related to the victim.[37]

Suicide and Attempted Suicide

As previously indicated, more than 30,000 suicides are reported each year in the United States, accounting for one-fifth of all injury mortality. In 2001, 30,622 suicide deaths were reported. The suicide rate for men (17.6 per 100,000) was four times that for women (4.1 per 100,000).[4] The rates of suicide in young people (15 to 24 years of age) nearly tripled between 1950 and 1995 but have since declined to 9.9 per 100,000.[16,41] Those for the elderly have also declined in recent years. Suicide rates in older men, however, remain quite high. Senior men (65 years old and older) are seven times more likely to commit suicide than senior women.[41]

Firearm Injuries and Injury Deaths

Statistics on fatal and nonfatal firearm injuries include data covering both intentional and unintentional incidents. When one considers all firearm deaths—those that result from both intentional and unintentional acts—firearms are the second leading cause of injury deaths after motor vehicles and the leading cause of deaths due to traumatic brain injury.[4,8] In 2001, there were 29,573 firearm-related deaths. Of these, 16,869 (57%) were classified as suicide, 11,348 (38%) as homicide, 323 (1%) as resulting from legal intervention, and 231 (<1%) were of undetermined intent. Only 802 (2.7%) of all firearm fatalities were classified as unintentional deaths.[4] In 2001, firearms were used in 56% of all homicides, 55% of all suicides, and less than 1% of all unintentional injury deaths.[4] Males were six times more likely to die or be treated in a hospital emergency department for a gunshot wound than females.

At highest risk for homicide and suicide involving firearms are teenage boys and young men, aged 15 to 24 years (see Figure 17.6).[17] A national survey found that in 1999, 6% of 12- to 17-year-old boys had carried a handgun to school at least once in the past year.[42] Another national survey of youth carried out in 2001 reported that 5.7% of students (10.3% of males) in grades 9 to 12 had carried a gun to school on at least one of the 30 days preceding the survey.[43] The gun-toting behavior continues even in college. In a random sample of 10,000 undergraduate students, 4.3% reported that they had a working firearm at college, and 1.6% said they had been threatened with a gun while at college.[44] Despite these reports, death rates from firearms have declined in recent years. From 1993 to 2001, firearm death rates for 15- to 19-year-old males fell from 27.4 to 12.4 deaths per 100,000 people (a 55% drop), and for 20- to 24-year-old males, firearm death rates fell from 34.1 to 21.2 per 100,000 people (a 38% drop).[4,17]

When one compares the ratios of firearm-related fatalities to nonfatal injuries, the lethality of firearms becomes clear. When one looks at injuries from all causes, for each death, nine others are hospitalizations and 189 more are treated and released. When one looks at firearm-related injuries, for each death, only 1.2 people are hospitalized and one person is treated and released (Figure 17.17).[17]

As stated previously, motor vehicles and firearms are the Number 1 and Number 2 injury killers in the United States today. One barrier to preventing firearm injuries and deaths is the absence of a detailed, federally supported reporting system. Unlike the highly developed reporting system for motor vehicle crashes and crash injuries, there is no such system for firearm-related injuries. Such a system would provide the data necessary to focus prevention and control strategies on various aspects of the problem of firearm-related injuries. A system currently being piloted in several states is called the National Fatal Firearm Injury Reporting System (NFFIRS). NFFIRS is a collaborative effort being led by the National Firearm Statistics System of the Harvard School of Public Health's Injury Control Research Center and by the Firearm Injury Center of the Medical College of Wisconsin's Department of Emergency Medicine. Their goal is for NFFIRS to become adopted as the national data collection system for all 50 states, similar to the National Highway Traffic Safety Administration's Fatal Accident Reporting System.[45] An obstacle to the establishment of such a system is funding. Establishing and operating such a system in all 50 states would probably cost millions of dollars. Some view this as a reasonable expenditure given the fact that firearm injuries cost about $2.3 billion in medical costs alone in the United States each year.[46]

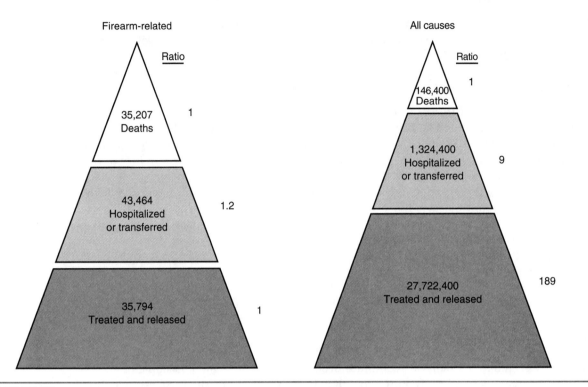

FIGURE 17.17

Injury pyramids for firearm-related injury versus all causes of injury: Firearm injuries are more deadly than other types of injuries.

Source: Centers for Disease Control and Prevention (2001). "Surveillance for Fatal and Nonfatal Firearm-Related Injuries—United States, 1993–1998." *MMWR,* 50(SS-2): 1–34.

Violence in Our Society and Resources for Prevention

A sixth-grade student brings a gun to school and kills a teacher and three students, a man is killed for "cutting" in line, and a child dies from punishment for breaking a rule at home. These are signs of the violent society in which Americans now find themselves living. Over the past few years, violence in America has increased. Many young people do not have the interest or skills to work out a solution to a conflict through verbal negotiation, and they resort to physical violence to resolve it. Some of these confrontations are gang-related, while others are simply individual actions. The availability of firearms in America makes violence all the more deadly, both for those in conflict and for innocent bystanders. In the next sections, we will discuss individual, family, and gang violence.

Individuals and Violence

A significant number of violent acts committed in the United States each year are committed by individuals who lack basic communication and problem-solving skills. Many of these people are not interested in resolving an argument through discussion or compromise. Instead, they are intent on "winning" their argument, by physical force if necessary. (After all, isn't that the way arguments are won in the movies?)

The availability and proliferation of firearms makes this approach particularly deadly. In 2001, homicide and legal intervention were the Number 1 cause of death for black Americans aged 15 to 24.[4] Unfortunately, violent confrontations often result in injuries and deaths not only for the victim, but also to others not directly involved in the confrontation.

Because of the level of violence, many schools and community organizations offer conflict resolution programs that teach youth alternative ways to resolve disagreements. These programs are designed for various grade levels and teach about the nature of conflicts, the harmful effects of violence, alternatives to violent behavior, and how to make safe decisions. Some of these programs, aimed specifically at reducing handgun-related violence, are listed in a report by the Office of Juvenile Justice and Delinquency Programs, United States Department of Justice. This report, *Promising Strategies to Reduce Gun Violence,* lists 60 of the more than 400 programs examined that were judged to be successful or "promising" at reducing gun violence.[47]

Family Violence and Abuse

One in every six homicides is the result of family violence. **Family violence** includes the maltreatment of children, intimate partner violence, sibling violence, and violence directed toward elder family members. Because children are our most important resources, and because being abused or neglected as a child increases one's risk for violent behavior as an adult, it is of paramount importance that society increase its efforts to intervene in cases of family violence. In recent years there has been increased attention paid to family violence, including violence against children and intimate partners. Between 1993 and 2001, the victimization rates for intimate partners and children declined. While some might credit this decline to improved efforts by the governmental and nongovernmental agencies involved with intervening and preventing violence among these groups, others would credit it to the strong economy during this period. Lower rates of unemployment mean better financial situations for families, lower levels of stress among family members, and fewer reports of domestic violence.

Child Maltreatment

Child maltreatment is an act or failure to act by a parent, caretaker, or other person as defined under state law that results in physical abuse, neglect, medical neglect, sexual abuse, emotional abuse, or an act or failure to act that presents an imminent risk of serious harm to a child. Also included are other forms of child maltreatment, such as child abandonment and congenital drug addiction. **Child abuse** can be physical, emotional, verbal, or sexual. Physical abuse is the intentional (nonaccidental) inflicting of injury on another person by shaking, throwing, beating, burning, or other means. Emotional abuse can take many forms, including showing no emotion, and the failure to provide warmth, attention, supervision, or normal living experiences. Verbal abuse is the demeaning or teasing of another verbally. Sexual abuse includes the physical acts of fondling or intercourse, nonphysical acts such as indecent exposure or obscene phone calls, or violent physical acts such as rape and battery. **Child neglect** is a type of maltreatment that refers to the failure by the parent or legal caretaker to provide necessary, age-appropriate care when financially able to do so, or when offered financial or other means to do so. Neglect may be physical, such as the failure to provide food, clothing, medical care, shelter, or cleanliness. It also may be emotional, such as the failure to provide attention, supervision, or other support necessary for a child's well-being (see Figure 17.18). Or, it may be educational, such as the failure to ensure that a child attends school regularly. Educational neglect is one of the most common categories of neglect, followed by physical, and then emotional neglect.

In 2002, 896,000 children under the age of 18 years were victims of abuse or neglect nationwide at a rate of 12.3 per 1,000 children. There has been a steady decline from the rate of reported child maltreatment since 1993, when the rate was 15.3 per 1,000 children (see Figure 17.19). Of the 896,000 children who were maltreated in 2002, 60% suffered neglect, 20% suffered physical abuse, 10% were sexually abused, and 7% were emotionally abused.[48] In 20% of all cases, other or additional types of maltreatment were reported, including abandonment,

family violence
the use of physical force by one family member against another, with the intent to hurt, injure, or cause death

child maltreatment
an act or failure to act by a parent, caretaker, or other person as defined under state law that results in physical abuse, neglect, medical neglect, sexual abuse, emotional abuse, or an act or failure to act that presents an imminent risk of serious harm to a child

child abuse
the intentional physical, emotional, verbal, or sexual mistreatment of a minor

child neglect
the failure of a parent or guardian to care for or otherwise provide the necessary subsistence for a child

FIGURE 17.18
Child neglect is the failure to provide care or other necessary subsistence for a child.

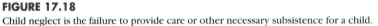

threats of harm to the child, and congenital drug addiction. The highest victimization rates were for the 0- to 3-year-old age group (16 maltreatments per 1,000 children), and these rates decline with age. Rates of many types of maltreatment are the same for males and females, but the sexual abuse rate for female children (1.6 female children per 1,000) was higher than the rate for male children (0.4 male children per 1,000). Victimization rates vary by race and ethnicity. In 2002, the lowest rates were for Asian/Pacific Islanders (3.7 children per 1,000), and the highest rates were for American Indian or Alaska Natives (21.7 children per 1,000) (see Figure 17.20). Children who had been victimized prior to 2002 were almost three times more likely be victimized again in the first six months of 2002 than children without a prior history of victimization.[48]

An estimated 1,400 children died of abuse or neglect in 2002, at a rate of approximately 1.62 deaths per 100,000 children. Three-fourths of the fatalities occurred in children under 4 years of age (see Figure 17.21). Maltreatment deaths were most often associated with neglect.[48]

Children who physically survive maltreatment may be scarred emotionally. "What happens to abused and neglected children after they grow up? Do the victims of violence and neglect later become criminals or violent offenders?"[49] In an attempt to answer these questions, researchers followed 1,575 child victims of abuse and neglect between 1967 and 1971. By the mid-1990s, 49% of the victims had been arrested for some type of nontraffic offense, compared with 38% of the control group (who shared other risk factors such as poverty). Eighteen percent had been arrested for a violent crime, compared with 14% in the control group. These differences were regarded as significant by the researchers. A key finding of the study was that neglected children's rates of arrest for violence were almost as high as

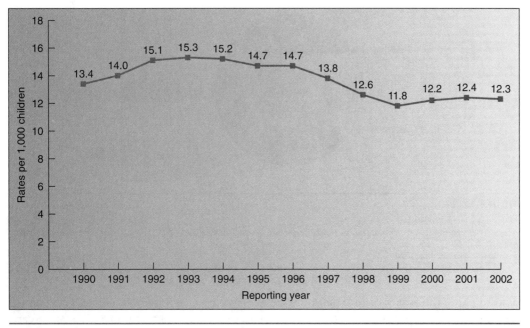

FIGURE 17.19

There has been a steady decline in the child maltreatment rates since 1993, when the rate was 15.3 victims per 1,000 children.

Source: U.S. Department of Health and Human Services, Administration on Children and Families (2004). *Child Maltreatment 2002.* Available at http://www.acf.hhs.gov/programs/cb/publications/cm02/index.htm.

physically abused children's. Another key finding was that black individuals who had been abused or neglected as children were being arrested at much higher rates than white individuals with the same background.[49]

Prevention of Child Maltreatment

One of the keys to protecting children from maltreatment is a system of timely reporting and referral to one of the many state and local child protective service (CPS) agencies. Anyone may make such a report (e.g., relative, neighbor, or teacher). In 2002, more than half of child abuse and neglect reports were received from professionals—people who came into contact with the victim through their jobs.[48] Signs of neglect are apparent to the trained professional, such as a teacher, a school nurse, or another community health professional. Signs of neglect include extremes in behavior, an uncared-for appearance, evidence of a lack of supervision at home, or the lack of medical care.

   "CPS agencies provide services to prevent future instances of child abuse or neglect and to remedy harm that has occurred as a result of child maltreatment."[48] These services are designed to increase the parents' child-rearing competence and knowledge of developmental stages of childhood. There may be an

FIGURE 17.20

In 2002, the lowest rates of child maltreatment were those for Asian/Pacific Islanders (3.7 victims per 1,000 children); the highest were those for American Indians or Alaska Natives (21.7 victims per 1,000 children).

Source: U.S. Department of Health and Human Services, Administration on Children and Families (2004). *Child Maltreatment 2002.* Available at http://www.acf.hhs.gov/programs/cb/publications/cm02/index.htm.

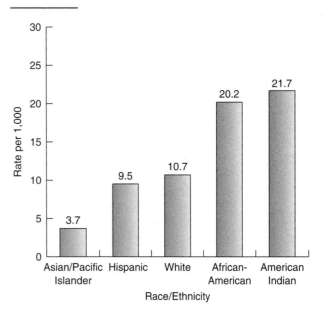

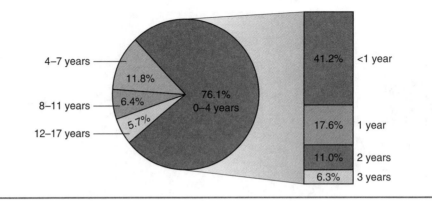

FIGURE 17.21

Percentage of child fatalities by age, 2002.

Source: U.S. Department of Health and Human Services, Administration on Children and Families (2004). *Child Maltreatment 2002.* Available at http://www.acf.hhs.gov/programs/cb/publications/cm02/index.htm.

assessment of the family's strengths and weaknesses, the development of a plan based on the family's needs, and post-investigative follow-up services. Services might include respite care, parenting education, housing assistance, substance abuse treatment, day care, home visits, counseling, and other services. The goal is to ensure the safety of the child or children.[48]

There are many useful sources of information and support for those interested in preventing child abuse and neglect. The *National Clearinghouse on Child Abuse and Neglect Information (NCCAN)* provides information, products, and technical assistance services to help professionals locate information related to child abuse and neglect and related child welfare issues (available at www.calib.com/nccanch/). Another source of information is the *Committee for Children.* Its mission is to promote the safety, well-being, and social development of children (available at www.cfchildren.org/cfcwho.htm). The *National Foundation for Abused and Neglected Children (NFANC),* created in 1992, is a nonprofit organization dedicated to the prevention of child abuse and neglect (available at www.gangfreekids.com/).

Intimate Partner Violence

intimate partner violence (IPV)
rape, physical assault, or stalking perpetrated by current or former dates, spouses, or cohabiting partners

Intimate partner violence (IPV) can be defined as rape, physical assault, and stalking perpetrated by current and former dates, spouses, and cohabiting partners (cohabiting meaning living together at least some of the time as a couple).[50] Each year between 2 and 3 million women and men are victimized by their intimate partners. Sometimes intimate partner violence is deadly. In 2000 1,247 women and 440 men were murdered by an intimate partner.[51] Nearly two-thirds of women who reported being raped, physically assaulted, or stalked since age 18 were victimized by a current or former husband, cohabiting partner, boyfriend, or date.[52] Injuries to women from intimate partner physical violence are underreported, but more than 500,000 women injured as a result of IPV require medical treatment each year. Women spend more days in bed, miss more work, and suffer more from stress and depression than men. The health care costs of intimate partner rape, physical assault, and stalking exceed $5.8 billion each year.[52]

One in four women residing in the United States has been physically assaulted or raped by an intimate partner; one of 14 men has reported such an experience.[52] Women are also more likely than men to be murdered by an intimate partner. In 2000, 33% of all women who were murdered were killed by an intimate partner, whereas fewer than 4% of male murder victims were killed by an intimate partner.[51] Each year, thousands of American children witness IPV within their families. Witnessing such violence is a risk factor for developing

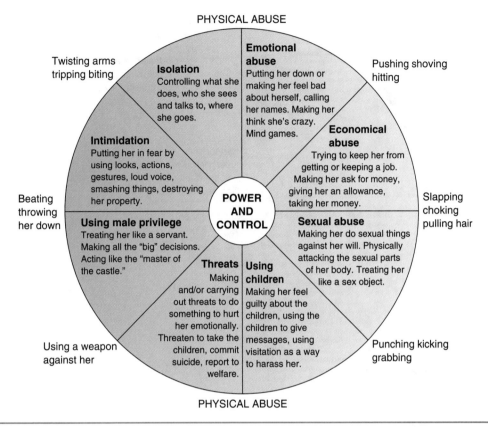

PHYSICAL ABUSE

FIGURE 17.22

The need for power and control characterize the abusive intimate partner.

Source: Domestic Abuse Intervention Project in Duluth, Minnesota, as reported in the *AHEC NEWS,* a publication of the Area Health Education Centers of Oklahoma, *AHEC News* (February, 1994), 2(1): 9. Used with permission.

long-term physical and mental health problems, including alcohol and substance abuse, becoming a victim of abuse, and perpetrating IPV.[52]

Despite the grim statistics just presented, the rates of victimization by an intimate partner have declined since 1993, when the rates were 9.8 per 1,000 for females and 1.6 per 1,000 for males. In 2001, these rates were 5.0 per 1,000 for females and 0.9 per 1,000 for males.

Risk factors for women who are likely to experience IPV include having a family income below $10,000, being young (19–29 years of age), and living with an intimate partner who uses alcohol or other drugs. Another risk factor is a previous episode of abuse. In a dysfunctional relationship, the male intimate partner may seek to exert power and control over his female intimate partner, resulting in a cycle in which violence recurs (see Figure 17.22). The *cycle of violence* depicts the progression of steps leading up to an attack or episode of violence and the restoration of calm. It also lists the factors that produce stress or contribute to a stressful family environment and lead to a violent episode, along with some of the abuser's characteristics (see Figure 17.23). A violent episode may result from the loss of a job, a divorce, illness, death of a family member, or misbehavior (actual or perceived) of children or an intimate partner. The likelihood that abuse will occur is greatly increased if alcohol has been consumed. While selected interventions aimed at one factor (for example, the abuser) might mitigate against family violence, community efforts to reduce violence should be both comprehensive, involving a variety of approaches, and coordinated among all agencies involved in order to be effective.

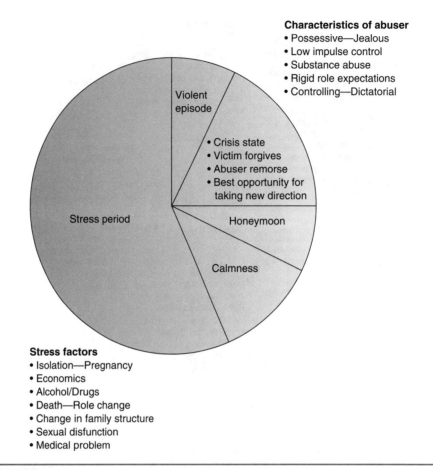

Characteristics of abuser
- Possessive—Jealous
- Low impulse control
- Substance abuse
- Rigid role expectations
- Controlling—Dictatorial

Violent episode

- Crisis state
- Victim forgives
- Abuser remorse
- Best opportunity for taking new direction

Stress period

Honeymoon

Calmness

Stress factors
- Isolation—Pregnancy
- Economics
- Alcohol/Drugs
- Death—Role change
- Change in family structure
- Sexual disfunction
- Medical problem

FIGURE 17.23
Cycle of violence.

Source: Domestic Violence Intervention Services, Inc., Tulsa, Oklahoma, as published in *AHEC NEWS,* a publication of the Area Health Education Centers of Oklahoma, *AHEC News* (February, 1994), 2(1): 8. Used with permission.

Prevention of Intimate Partner Violence

Prevention of intimate partner violence involves improvements in identifying and documenting cases of IPV and increasing access to services for victims and perpetrators of IPV and their children. Coordinating community initiatives strengthens the safety networks for high-risk individuals and families. Some communities have established a "Violence Coordinating Council" that holds monthly meetings to set an agenda and action plans for the community and to determine and clarify the roles and responsibilities of agencies and individuals. It is important for communities to develop and implement a coordinated response with strong advocates from criminal justice, victim services, children's services, and allied professions.[53] One of the important groups of allied professionals are health care providers. A guide to training materials and programs on IPV and sexual assault has been published by the National Center for Injury Control and Prevention, CDC.[54]

Violence in Schools

While schools are one of the safest places for children to spend their time, even rare acts of violence strike terror into parents, teachers, and the children themselves. Recent, highly publicized incidents of killings on school grounds have focused the Nation's attention on the question of just how safe (or unsafe) our nation's schools are. According to Principal Michael Durso of Springbrook High School, as quoted in the *Washingtonian* magazine, September 1997:[55]

> "No matter where you are, parents want their students to be safe and secure . . . that might even precede a quality education . . ." With drugs, gangs, and guns on the rise in many communities the threat of violence "weighs heavily on most principals' minds these days. . . . Anyone who thinks they are not vulnerable is really naïve."

The National Center for Educational Statistics (NCES) collected data to determine the "frequency, seriousness, and incidence of violence in elementary and secondary schools."[55] During the most recent year for which full data are available (1999–2000), 71% of U.S. public schools reported at least one crime incident, and one in five schools reported at least one serious violent crime (murder, rape, or other type of sexual battery, suicide, physical attack or fight with a weapon, or robbery). During that school year, 64% of public schools reported instances of physical attacks or fights without a weapon, 52% reported threats of physical attacks without a weapon, 51% reported vandalism, 46% reported theft or larceny, and 43% reported possession of a knife or sharp object. Six percent of public schools reported a student in possession of a firearm or explosive device, and 5% reported an attack or fight with a weapon. Only 2% reported sexual battery other than rape, and only 1% reported rape or attempted rape.[55] The incidence of violence is higher in middle and high schools than in elementary schools and higher in schools that report serious discipline problems than in schools that do not. While it seems as though the incidence of violent behavior in schools is high, the rates of behaviors that contribute to violence, such as weapon carrying, actually declined between 1991 and 2001.[43,56]

While multiple homicide events, like the one at Columbine High School, capture newspaper headlines and are lead stories on the evening news, the fact is that the odds of suffering a school-associated violent death are less than one in a million. Furthermore, less than 1% of the more than 1,350 children nationwide who were murdered or committed suicide in the first half of the 1997–1998 school year were at school (on school property, at a school-sponsored event, or on the way to or from school or a school-sponsored event).[57] The nature of crime away from school is far more serious than at school.

Most schools try do deal with violence problems by instituting zero tolerance policies toward serious student offenses. These policies, defined as school or district policy mandating predetermined consequences for various student offenses, have recently come under fire because administering such policies sometimes leads to somewhat ridiculous outcomes. In 2000, almost all schools (97%) also utilized some type of security measures, such as visitor sign-ins, closed campuses (at lunch), drug sweeps, and random metal detectors. About 7% of public schools had stringent security, such as daily or random metal detectors. Most schools reported having some type of formal violence-prevention or violence-reduction program or effort. Sixty-six percent train staff in violence prevention practices.[55]

Safe Schools/Healthy Students Initiative

The *Safe Schools/Healthy Students Initiative* is a unique grant program jointly administered by the U.S. Departments of Education, Health and Human Services, and Justice.[58] The program promotes a comprehensive, integrated problem-solving process for use by communities in addressing school violence. It is hoped that this initiative and others like it will address the problem of violence in schools. Steps in the process are:

1. Establishing school–community partnerships
2. Identifying and measuring the problem
3. Setting measurable goals and objectives
4. Identifying appropriate research-based programs and strategies
5. Implementing programs and strategies in an integrated fashion

6. Evaluating the outcomes of programs and strategies
7. Revising the plan on the basis of evaluation information

The initiative requires comprehensive, integrated community-wide plans to address at least the following six elements:

1. Safe school environments
2. Prevention and early intervention programs that address violence and the use of alcohol and other drugs
3. School and community mental health preventive and treatment intervention services
4. Early childhood psychosocial and emotional development programs
5. Education reforms
6. Safe school policies

Youth Violence After School

While violence in schools has grabbed the headlines, the real problem area is violence after school. Fewer and fewer children have a parent waiting for them at home after school. While many youths are able to supervise themselves and their younger siblings responsibly after school or are engaged in sports or other after-school activities, some are not. Statistics show that serious violent crime committed by juveniles peaks in the hours immediately after school (see Figure 17.24). Also, during these after-school hours, juveniles are most likely to become victims of crime, including violent crimes such as robberies and aggravated assaults. This is because at this unsupervised time, youth are more vulnerable to exploitation, injuries, and even death.[59]

For communities that want to become involved in reducing the problem of youth violence, the federal government has a variety of resources. One of these is *Best Practices of Youth Violence Prevention: A Sourcebook for Community Action*.[60] In addition, the federal government has established a Web site, www.afterschool.gov, that provides resources for communities that wish to develop after-school programs for youths. The Web site provides links to successful after-school programs, ideas for after-school activities, and Web sites for youths to visit after school.

FIGURE 17.24

Serious violent crime committed by juveniles peaks in the hours immediately after school.

Source: United States Department of Justice, Office of Justice Programs, Office of Juvenile Justice and Delinquency Prevention (1999). *Violence after School. 1999 National Report Series, November 2000.* Washington, DC: Author.

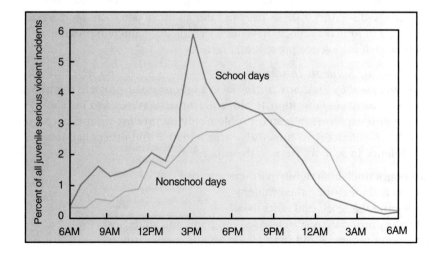

Violence in Our Communities

Youth gangs and gang violence contribute to the overall level of violence in the community and are a drain on community resources.

Youth Gang Violence

While most young women and men in the United States grow up subscribing to such American ideals as democracy, individualism, equality, and education, others do not. Many of those who do not are economically disadvantaged and have lost faith in society's capacity to work on their behalf. Some of these seek refuge and reward in organized subculture groups of youngsters who feel similarly disenfranchised.

One popular subculture structure is the **youth gang,** a self-formed association of peers bound together by mutual interests, with identifiable leadership and well-defined lines of authority. Youth gangs act in concert to achieve a specific purpose, and their acts generally include illegal activities and the control over a particular territory or enterprise. Types of illegal activities in which gang members participate include larceny/theft, aggravated assault, burglary/breaking and entering, and street drug sales.

A recent survey of a representative sample of 3,018 law enforcement agencies revealed youth gang activity in 40% of the districts under their jurisdiction. This is a significant decline since 1996, when 53% of jurisdictions reported youth gang activity. An estimated 24,500 gangs were active in the United States in 2000. Gang activity is more prevalent in cities with a population of 25,000 or greater. There were more than 750,000 active gang members in 2000.[61]

> **youth gang**
> an association of peers, bound by mutual interests and identifiable lines of authority, whose acts generally include illegal activity and control over a territory or an enterprise

Costs to the Community

Youth gangs and youth-gang-related violence present an enormous drain on the law enforcement resources of a community beyond the injuries and injury deaths that result from their activities. Pressured to "do something," field officers may be pulled from other duties and not replaced. If additional police are hired, it can cost the community $50,000 per year per officer. Next, there is the additional need to strengthen the prosecutor's office if the operation is to be effective. In short, the suppression of gangs by law enforcement is costly for communities, often depleting resources for other needed community improvements. Another problem is vandalism and the defacing of public and private buildings by gang-related graffiti. This money spent repairing damage and erasing graffiti could be used to hire teachers or to support educational activities.

Community Response

Many communities have responded effectively to the increased violence resulting from gang-related activity. Perhaps the best approach is a multifaceted effort involving law enforcement, education, diversion activities, and social services support. Suppression of gang activity by law enforcement is justified because many gang-related activities—such as selling illicit drugs, carrying and discharging weapons, and defacing property—are illegal. Education of children, teachers, parents, and community leaders is another facet of gang-related violence prevention. Just as there are drug abuse prevention curricula in schools, there are now anti-gang awareness programs in some schools. Diversion activities, including job opportunities and after-school activities such as enrichment programs, sports, and recreation, can reduce the attractiveness of less wholesome uses of free time. Sports and recreational activities have long been touted as a healthy outlet for pent-up physical energy. It seems logical to assume that young persons who participate in such activities would be less likely to become involved in destructive, violent behavior (see Figure 17.25).

Federal Government's Response

In 1993, two important pieces of federal legislation were passed and signed into law: the Brady Handgun Violence Prevention Act and the National Child Protection Act of 1993. The "Brady Bill" was signed with great fanfare by then President Bill Clinton, who stated that "Americans are finally fed up with violence that cuts down another citizen with gunfire every

FIGURE 17.25
Adequate recreational opportunities for youth can reduce violence in a community.

20 minutes" (see Figure 17.26). The Brady Handgun Violence Prevention Act (PL 103-159), implemented in February 1994, was aimed at reducing interstate gun trafficking and requires a five-day waiting period and a background check on all handgun buyers.[62] One of the purposes of the waiting period is to allow time for state and local police to run background checks on the purchasers, some of whom might be legally barred from owning a handgun because of a criminal record.

In addition to the Brady Law, which established national restrictions on the acquisition of firearms and ammunition from federal firearms licensees, there are other laws that attempt to regulate firearms. At least 50 studies have been carried out to determine the effects of firearm laws on preventing violence. A recent task force report reviewed 51 such studies to determine whether there was sufficient evidence to determine that firearm laws do prevent violence in the community. The task force "found insufficient evidence to determine the effectiveness of any of the firearms laws or combinations of laws reviewed on violent outcomes."[63] The task force noted, however, that their finding did not mean there was evidence of ineffectiveness. Thus, it remains to be proven whether or not firearm laws can be effective in reducing firearm-related violence.

The National Child Protection Act, meanwhile, encourages states to require a fingerprint-based national background check on individuals seeking employment in the child care field. The Violent Crime Control and Law Enforcement Act of 1994 subsequently amended this act to also include those seeking employment with the elderly and disabled.

The Office of Justice Programs offers a variety of programs to state and local agencies aimed at reducing intentional violence. Included are programs to empower communities (Community Prosecution, Safe Schools Initiative, Safe Start, Weed and Seed, and Offender Reentry). There are also programs aimed at breaking the cycle of drug abuse and crime (the

FIGURE 17.26
On November 30, 1993, President Clinton signed into law the Brady Bill, as James Brady looked on. James Brady suffered a disabling firearm injury during an assassination attempt on President Reagan in 1981.

Drug Free Communities Program, the Drug Prevention Demonstration Program, and Enforcing Underage Drinking). Other programs combat family violence, violence against women, and violence on college campuses. Still others address youth violence and protect and support victims of crime. The purpose of these programs is to support communities in their efforts to reduce intentional violence and violence-related injuries.[64]

In conclusion, intentional injuries resulting from interpersonal violence remain a national as well as a community concern. Significant resources are available at the federal level (from the Departments of Health and Human Services and Justice) to help states and local communities reduce the number and seriousness of violence-related injuries. It is up to each concerned citizen to make sure that his or her own community is taking advantage of these resources.

CHAPTER SUMMARY

- Injuries are the fifth leading cause of death in the United States.

- Unintentional and intentional injuries represent a major community health problem, not only because of the loss of life but also because of the lost productivity and the increase in the number of disabled Americans.

- Unintentional injuries are unplanned events that are usually preceded by an unsafe act or condition. They are often accompanied by economic loss, and they interrupt the efficient completion of a task.

- Most unintentional injuries occur in the home; most fatal unintentional injuries occur on the highway.

- Unintentional injuries occur across all age groups; however, they are the leading cause of death for younger Americans.

- Motor vehicle accidents are the leading cause of unintentional injury deaths, followed by falls, poisonings, drownings, suffocations, and fires and burns.

- Males and minority groups suffer proportionately more unintentional injuries.

- Prevention and control of unintentional injuries and fatalities can be instituted based upon a model in which energy is the causative agent for injuries.

- There are also four broad strategies that can prevent unintentional injuries—education, regulation, automatic protection, and litigation. Together, these

SCENARIO: ANALYSIS AND RESPONSE

Please take a moment to reread the scenario at the beginning of this chapter. Then reflect on the questions that follow.

1. How does the description of the unintentional injury fit the definition provided in the chapter? Can you identify each element of the definition as it pertains to this particular scenario?

2. Think about the four approaches to the prevention of unintentional injuries (education, regulation, automatic protection, and litigation). Provide an example of how each of these four approaches could prevent another similar injury from occurring.

strategies may be used to reduce the numbers and seriousness of unintentional injuries in the community.

- Intentional injuries are the outcome of self-directed or interpersonal violence.

- The spectrum of violence includes assaults, abuse (child, spouse, and elder), rape, robbery, suicide, and homicide.

- Minorities and youths are at highest risk for injury or death from an intentional violent act.

- Family violence, including child maltreatment, intimate partner violence, and elder abuse, is a serious and pervasive community health problem.

- Widely publicized lethal violence in schools has once again focused national attention on violence in our schools. However, schools remain a relatively safe place for the Nation's youth.

- Youth violence, including youth gang violence, grew in the 1990s but has since declined, in part because of federal, state, and local initiatives to address this problem.

- Significant resources are available at the federal level (from the Departments of Health and Human Services and Justice) to assist state and local community agencies in reducing the number and seriousness of violence-related injuries.

REVIEW QUESTIONS

1. List the ways in which injuries are costly to society and quantify the costs in terms of the United States.

2. Identify the leading types of unintentional injury deaths and the risk factors associated with each type of death.

3. Why have the terms *accident* and *safety* lost favor with injury prevention professionals?

4. What is a hazard? Do hazards cause accidents? Explain your answer.

5. What types of injuries are most likely to occur in the home, and in which rooms are they most likely to occur?

6. Characterize injuries from the following activities by time—motor vehicle driving, swimming, and heating the home.

7. How does alcohol consumption contribute to unintentional injuries?

8. Summarize the contributions of Hugh DeHaven, John E. Gordon, and William Hadden, Jr., to injury prevention and control.

9. Describe the epidemiological model for injuries and provide three examples of how energy causes injuries.

10. For each of your examples from Question 9, explain how the injury could have been prevented using prevention and control tactics.

11. List four broad strategies for the reduction of unintentional injuries and give an example of each.

12. Identify the different types of violent behavior that result in intentional injuries.

13. Describe the cost of intentional injuries to society.

14. Define family violence and give some examples.

15. Explain the difference between child abuse and child neglect. List some contributing factors to these phenomena. What is intimate partner violence?

16. How safe are our schools? How are schools responding to safety concerns?

17. What is a youth gang? Why are they attractive to some youths? How can communities compete for youths' attention?

18. Describe the best ways in which communities can respond to youth gang violence.

19. What is the Brady Law? Is it working?

ACTIVITIES

1. Obtain a copy of a local newspaper and find three stories dealing with unintentional injuries. Provide a two- or three-sentence summary of each article and then provide your best guess of (a) what the unsafe act or condition that preceded the event was, (b) what the resulting economic loss or injury was, and (c) what task was not completed.

2. Make an appointment and interview the director of safety on your campus. Find out what the most prevalent unintentional injuries are on campus, what strategies have been used to deal with them, and what could be done to eliminate them.

3. With guidance from your course instructor, conduct a random survey of safety belt use at your campus. Collect the data in such a manner that you can compare the results between school employees and students. Then, analyze your results and draw some conclusions.

4. Survey your home, apartment, or residence hall and create a room-by-room list of the unsafe conditions that may exist. Then, create a strategy for changing each condition.

5. Using a local newspaper, locate three articles that deal with violence. For each article: (a) provide a two-sentence summary, (b) identify and describe the victim and the perpetrator, (c) identify what you feel was the underlying cause of the violence, and (d) offer a suggestion as to how the violence could have been avoided or prevented.

6. Make an appointment with an officer of the local police department to interview him or her about violent crime in your hometown. Write a two-page summary of your interview and include answers to the following questions: (a) What is the Number 1 violent crime? (b) What is the law enforcement department doing to control violent crime? (c) Does the city have a comprehensive program against crime? (d) What can the typical citizen do to help reduce violence?

7. Write a two-page paper on what the typical citizen can do about violence.

8. Think about the public health triangle model of disease (agent, host, and environment) and gang violence. Describe in writing who or what represents each of these factors. What steps can be taken to reduce gang-related violence using this public health model? List the steps explaining each one.

COMMUNITY HEALTH ON THE WEB

The Internet contains a wealth of information about community and public health. Increase your knowledge of some of the topics presented in this chapter by accessing the Jones and Bartlett Publishers Web site at **health.jbpub.com/communityhealth/5e** and follow the links to complete the following Web activities.

- National Center for Injury Prevention and Control
- Family Violence Prevention Fund
- Children's Safety Network

REFERENCES

1. Baker, S. P. (1989). "Injury Science Comes of Age." *Journal of the American Medical Association, 262*(16): 2284-2285.

2. National Center for Health Statistics (1997). *Health, United States, 1996-97 and Injury Chartbook* (HHS pub. no. PHS 97-1232). Hyattsville, MD: Author.

3. Krug, E. G., G. K. Sharma, and R. Lozano (2000). "The Global Burden of Injuries." *American Journal of Public Health, 90*(4): 523-526.

4. Anderson, R. N., A. M. Miniño, L. A. Fingerhut, M. Warner, and J. A. Heinen (2004). "Deaths: Injuries, 2001." *National Vital Statistics Reports, 52*(21): 1-86.

5. Arias, E., R. N. Anderson, K. Hsiang-Ching, S. L. Murphy, and K. D. Kochanek (2003). "Deaths: Final Data for 2001." *National Vital Statistics Reports, 52*(3): 1-116.

6. McCaig, L. F., and C. W. Burt (2003). *National Ambulatory Medical Care Survey: 2001 Emergency Department Summary* (Vital and Health Statistics, no. 335). Hyattsville, MD: National Center for Health Statistics.

7. Hing, E., and K. Middleton (2003). *National Ambulatory Medical Care Survey: 2001 Outpatient Department Summary* (Vital and Health Statistics, no. 338). Hyattsville, MD: National Center for Health Statistics.

8. National Safety Council (2003). *Injury Facts*. Itasca, IL: Author.

9. Centers for Disease Control and Prevention (2003). "Medical Expenditures Attributable to Injuries—United States, 2000." *MMWR, 53*(1): 1-4.

10. Freid, V. M., K. Prager, A. P. MacKay, and H. Xia (2003). *Chartbook on Trends in the Health of Americans. Health, United States.* Hyattsville, MD: National Center for Health Statistics.

11. Miniño, A. M., E. Arias, K. D. Kochanek, S. L. Murphy, and B. L. Smith (2002). "Deaths: Final Data for 2000." *National Vital Statistics Reports, 50*(15): 1-120.

12. Bonnie, R. J., C. E. Fulco, and C. T. Liverman, eds. (1999). *Reducing the Burden of Injury: Advancing Prevention and Treatment.* Washington, DC: National Academy Press.

13. U.S. Department of Health and Human Services (2000). *Healthy People 2010: Understanding and Improving Health,* 2nd ed. Washington, DC: U.S. Government Printing Office.

14. U.S. Department of Transportation, National Highway Traffic Safety Administration (2004). *Traffic Safety Facts 2002: A Compilation of Motor Vehicle Crash Data from the Fatality Analysis Reporting System and the General Estimates System* (DOT HS 809 620). Washington, DC: Author.

15. Centers for Disease Control and Prevention (2003). "Public Health and Aging: Nonfatal Injuries Among Older Adults Treated in Hospital Emergency Departments—United States, 2001." *MMWR, 52*(42): 1019-1022.

16. Anderson, R. H., and B. L. Smith (2003). "Deaths: Leading Causes for 2001." *National Vital Statistics Reports, 52*(9): 1-88.

17. Centers for Disease Control and Prevention (2000). "Surveillance of Fatal and Nonfatal Firearm-Related Injuries—United States, 1993-1998." *MMWR, 50*(SS-2): 1-34.

18. Centers for Disease Control and Prevention (1997). "Rates of Homicide, Suicide and Firearm-Related Deaths among Children—26 Industrial Countries." *MMWR, 46*(5): 101-105.

19. Griffin, L. I., III (2004). *Older Driver Involvement in Injury Crashes in Texas, 1975-1999.* Washington, DC: AAA Foundation for Traffic Safety.

20. Griffin, L. I., and S. DeLaZerda (2000). *Unlicensed to Kill.* Washington, DC: AAA Foundation for Traffic Safety.

21. U.S. Department of Transportation, National Highway Traffic Safety Administration (2000). *Traffic Safety Facts 1999* (DOT HS 809 100). Washington, DC: Author.

22. Centers for Disease Control and Prevention (2004). "Child Passenger Deaths Involving Drinking Drivers—United States, 1997-2002." *MMWR, 53*(4): 77-79.

23. United States Department of Homeland Security, United States Coast Guard (2003). *Boating Statistics 2002* (Commandant pub. no. P16754.16). Available at http://www.uscgboating.org/statistics/accident_stats.htm.

24. United States Department of Transportation, United States Coast Guard (2000). *Boating Statistics 1999.* (Commandant pub. no. P16754.13). Available at http://www.uscgboating.org/statistics/accident_stats.htm.

25. Howland, J., G. S. Smith, T. Mangione, R. Hingson, W. DeJohg, and N. Bell (1993). "Missing the Boat on Drinking and Boating." *Journal of the American Medical Association,* 270(1): 91-92.

26. Centers for Disease Control and Prevention (2001). "Drowning—Louisiana, 1998." *MMWR,* 50(20): 413-414.

27. Lescohier, I., S. S. Gallagher, and B. Guyer (1990). "Not by Accident." *Issues in Science and Technology,* 6: 35-42.

28. Centers for Disease Control (1982). "Unintentional and Intentional Injuries—United States." *MMWR,* 31(18): 240-248.

29. Haddon, W. (1980). "Advances in the Epidemiology of Injuries as a Basis for Public Policy." *Public Health Reports,* 95(5): 411-421.

30. U.S. Department of Transportation, National Highway Traffic Safety Administration, National Center for Statistics and Analysis (1996). *Traffic Safety Facts* (US DOT HS 808 649). Washington, DC: Author.

31. U.S. Department of Transportation, National Highway Traffic Safety Administration (2004). "All U.S. States Now Have .08 BAC Laws, with Passage of Legislation in Delaware [Press release]." Available at http://www.nhtsa.dot.gov/.

32. Centers for Disease Control and Prevention, Community Guides Branch (2004). "Effectiveness of 0.08% Blood Alcohol Concentration (BAC) Laws." Available at http://www.thecommunityguide.org/mvoi/mvoi-alc-08-laws.pdf.

33. Stutts, J., J. Feaganes, E. Rodgman, C. Hamlett, T. Meadows, D. Reinfurt, K. Gish, M. Mercadante, and L Staplin (2003). *Distractions in Everyday Driving.* Washington, DC: AAA Foundation for Traffic Safety.

34. Governors Highway Safety Association (May 2004). "Cell Phone Restrictions—State and Local Jurisdictions." Available at http://www.statehighwaysafety.org/html/state_info/laws/cellphone_laws.html.

35. Waller, P. F. (2002). "Challenges in Motor Vehicle Safety." *Annual Review of Public Health,* 23: 93-113.

36. Centers for Disease Control and Prevention (2001). "Nonfatal Physical Assault Related Injuries Treated in Hospital Emergency Departments—United States, 2000." *MMWR,* 51(21): 460-463.

37. Rennison, C. (2002). "Criminal Victimization 2001, Changes 2000-01 with Trends 1993-2001" (National Crime Victimization Survey no. NCJ 194610). Washington DC: U.S. Department of Justice, Bureau of Justice Statistics.

38. Fox, J.A., and M.W. Zawitz (2002). *Homicide Trends in the United States.* U.S. Department of Justice, Bureau of Justice Statistics. Available at http://www.ojp.usdoj.gov/bjs/homicide/homtrnd.htm.

39. Kochanek, M.A., and B. L. Smith (2004). "Deaths: Preliminary Data for 2002." *National Vital Statistics Reports,* 52(13): 1-48.

40. Blumstein, A., F. P. Rivara, and R. Rosenfeld (2000). "The Rise and Decline of Homicide—and Why." *Annual Review of Public Health,* 21: 505-541.

41. Centers for Disease Control and Prevention, National Center for Health Statistics (2000). *Health, United States with Adolescent Health Chartbook* (HHS pub. no. 00-1232). Hyattsville, MD.

42. U.S. Department of Health and Human Services, Substance Abuse and Mental Health Services Administration, Office of Applied Studies (2000). "The NHSDA Report: Youths Who Carry Handguns." Available at http://www.oas.samhsa.gov/.

43. Centers for Disease Control and Prevention (2002). "Youth Risk Behavior Surveillance—United States, 2001." *MMWR,* 51(SS-4): 1-64.

44. Miller, M., D. Hemenway, and H. Wechsler (2002). "Guns and Gun Threats at College." *Journal of the American College of Health,* 51(2): 57-65.

45. NFFIRS Workgroup (2000). *Uniform Data Elements: National Fatal Firearm Injury Reporting System,* Release 1.1. Sponsoring institutions: National Firearm Injury Statistics System, Harvard Injury Control Research Center, Harvard School of Public Health, Cambridge, MA, and the Firearm Injury Center, Department of Emergency Medicine, Medical College of Wisconsin, Milwaukee, WI.

46. Cook, P. J., B. A. Lawrence, J. Ludwig, and T. R. Miller (1999). "The Medical Costs of Gunshot Injuries in the United States." *Journal of the American Medical Association,* 282(5): 447-454.

47. U.S. Department of Justice, Office of Juvenile Justice and Delinquency Programs (February 1999). *Promising Strategies to Reduce Gun Violence* (NCJ pub. no. 173950). Available at http://ojjdp.ncjrs.org/pubs/gun_violence.

48. U.S. Department of Health and Human Services, Administration on Children and Families (2004). *Child Maltreatment 2002.* Available at http://www.acf.hhs.gov/programs/cb/publications/cm02/index.htm.

49. National Institute of Justice (1996). "The Cycle of Violence Revisited." Washington, DC: U.S. Department of Justice.

50. Tjaden, P., and N. Thoennes (2000). *Extent, Nature, and Consequences of Intimate Partner Violence: Findings from the National Violence Against Women Survey* (NCJ pub. no. 181867). Washington, DC: National Institute of Justice.

51. U.S. Department of Justice, Bureau of Justice Statistics (February 2003). *Crime Data Brief: Intimate Partner Violence, 1993-2001* (NCJ pub. no. 197838). Available at http://www.ojp.usdoj.gov/bjs/.

52. Centers for Disease Control and Prevention, National Center for Injury Control and Prevention (2004). "Intimate Partner Violence: Fact Sheet." Available at http://www.cdc.gov/ncipc/factsheets/ipvfacts.htm.

53. Meuer, T., A. Seymour, and H. Wallace (2001). "Domestic Violence." In A. Seymour, M. Murray, J. Sigmon, M. Hook, C. Edmunds, M. Gaboury, and G. Coleman, eds. (2001). *2000 National Victim Assistance Academy.* Washington, DC: Office for Victims of Crime.

54. Osattin, A., and L. M. Short (1998). *Intimate Partner Violence and Sexual Assault: A Guide to Training Materials and Programs for Health Care Providers.* Atlanta, GA: Centers for Disease Control and Prevention.

55. U.S. Department of Education, National Center for Education Statistics (2004). *Crime and Safety in America's Public Schools: Select Findings from the School Survey on Crime and Safety* (NCES pub. no. 2004-370). Washington, DC: Author.

56. Brener, N. D., T. R. Simon, E. G. Krug, and R. Lowry (1999). "Recent Trends in Violence-Related Behaviors among High School Students in the United States." *Journal of the American Medical Association,* 282(5): 440-446.

57. Small, M., and K. D. Tetrick (2001). "School Violence: An Overview." *Juvenile Justice,* 8(1): 3-12.

58. U.S. Department of Education (1999). *1999 Annual Report on School Safety.* Washington, DC: Author.

59. U.S. Department of Justice, Office of Juvenile Justice and Delinquency Prevention (November 1999). *Violence after School* (1999 National Report Series). Washington, DC: Author.

60. Thornton, T. N., C. A. Craft, L. L. Dahlberg, B. S. Lynch, and K. Baer (2000). *Best Practices of Youth Violence Prevention: A Sourcebook for Community Action.* Atlanta, GA: Centers for Disease Control and Prevention.

61. Egley, A., Jr. (February 2002). "National Youth Gang Survey Trends from 1996 to 2000." *OJJDP Fact Sheet* no. 3. Available at http://www.iir.com/nygc/.

62. Hunt, T. (1993). "Brady Bill Becomes Law." *The Muncie Star,* 1.

63. Centers for Disease Control and Prevention (2003). "First Reports Evaluating the Effectiveness of Strategies for Preventing Violence: Firearm Laws—Findings from the Task Force on Community Preventive Services." *MMWR,* 52(RR-14): 11-20.

64. U.S. Department of Justice, Office of Justice Programs (2004). "Community-Based Programs." Available at http://www.ojp.usdoj.gov/.

Chapter 18

Safety and Health in the Workplace

Chapter Outline

Scenario

Introduction
Scope of the Problem • Importance of Occupational
Safety and Health to the Community

**History of Occupational Safety and Health
Problems**
Occupational Safety and Health in the United States
before 1970 • Occupational Safety and Health Act of
1970

**Prevalence of Occupational Injuries, Diseases,
and Deaths**
Overview of Recent Trends in Workplace Injuries and
Illnesses • Unintentional Injuries in the Workplace
• Prevention and Control of Unintentional Injuries in
the Workplace • Workplace Violence: Intentional
Workplace Injuries • Occupational Illnesses and
Disorders

**Resources for the Prevention of Workplace
Injuries and Diseases**
Occupational Safety and Health Professionals
• Occupational Safety and Health Programs

Chapter Summary

Scenario: Analysis and Response

Review Questions

Activities

Community Health on the Web

References

Chapter Objectives

After studying this chapter, you will be able to:

1 Describe the scope of the occupational safety and
health problem in the United States and its importance to the community.

2 Identify some of the pioneers in the prevention of
occupational injuries and disease.

3 Provide a short history of state and federal legislation on occupational safety and health.

4 Explain the difference between occupational
injuries and occupational diseases and give several
examples of each.

5 Discuss the types of injuries that frequently occur
in the workplace and describe their occurrence
with regard to person, place, and time.

6 Briefly describe broad strategies for preventing
injuries in the workplace.

7 Identify the different types of occupational illnesses and disorders and list some of the causative
agents.

8 Outline some general strategies for controlling
these diseases.

9 List several occupational safety and health professions and describe what the professionals in each
of these do.

10 List and briefly describe several occupational
safety and health programs for the workplace.

SCENARIO

At first Jen was exited about her new job. Now that she had turned 21, she was permitted to work in the Terrace Lounge and Restaurant where alcohol was served and the tips were excellent. She politely resigned from her job as a waitress at another restaurant where she had worked for more than two years. That restaurant, which enjoyed a clientele primarily of seniors, did not serve alcohol and had a no-smoking policy. She looked forward to working at the Terrace because she believed that she would make as much in tips in two nights as she made all week at her old job. This increase in earnings would help her buy many of the things she wanted for her baby, which was due in six months.

That was two months ago. Now she was wondering whether she really liked working at the Terrace. The problem was all the cigarette smoke. Her mother was the first to notice that her clothes smelled smoky. But Jen had also noticed the effects of working in the lounge. Her eyes always burned at the end of a night's work and lately her throat burned too. She had started to take her 10-minute breaks outside to enjoy a few breaths of clean air.

Then, she had begun to think about the effects of the inhaled cigarette smoke on the health of her baby. During her first checkup with the doctor after she realized she was pregnant, she had been asked whether she smoked. She had proudly answered, "No." But now she wondered, "Could working in such a smoky environment be harmful to my baby?" She hated the thought of having to quit this job because she was making good money, and her manager was very complimentary of her work.

INTRODUCTION

Globally, there are more than 2.6 billion workers and the workforce is growing continuously. Approximately 75% of these workers are in developing countries, where workplace hazards are more severe. Each year there are as many as 250 million occupational injuries resulting in 330,000 fatalities.[1] If one includes occupational illnesses, an estimated 1.1 million people worldwide die each year. Annually, an estimated 160 million new cases of work-related diseases occur worldwide. All of these estimates are almost certainly below the actual figures because the reports from many areas of the world are unreliable.[2]

The number of civilian Americans employed in the labor force is approximately 144.9 million.[3] After home, Americans spend the next largest portion of their time at work; thus, safe and healthy workplaces are essential if America is to reach its health objectives by 2010. It is not always easy to distinguish between the terms *occupational injury* and *occupational illness* or *disease*. However, it is generally accepted that an **occupational disease** is any abnormal condition or disorder, other than one resulting from an occupational injury, caused by factors associated with employment. It includes acute or chronic illnesses or disease that may be caused by inhalation, absorption, ingestion, or direct contact. An **occupational injury** is any injury, such as a cut, fracture, sprain, amputation, etc., that results from a work-related event or from a single, instantaneous exposure in the work environment.[4]

occupational disease
an abnormal condition, other than an occupational injury, caused by an exposure to environmental factors associated with employment

Scope of the Problem

Each day in the United States, on average, 15 workers die from an injury sustained at work. Although even one worker death is one too many, it is instructive to note that the work-related fatality rates in America have declined significantly over the past 100 years. In 1912, an estimated 18,000 to 21,000 work-related unintentional injury deaths occurred, a death rate of 21 per 100,000 workers.[5] In 2002, there were 5,524 such deaths, and the death rate for occupational injury deaths had fallen to below 4 per 100,000 workers.[6]

A total of 4.7 million nonfatal injuries and illnesses were reported in private industry workplaces during 2002, resulting in a rate of 5.3 cases per 100 equivalent full-time workers.

occupational injury
an injury that results from exposure to a single incident in the work environment

A total of 1.4 million injuries and illnesses in private industry required recuperation away from work beyond the day of the incident in 2002. The vast majority of these events, 4.4 million, were classified as injuries; about 294,500 were classified as illnesses.[7]

Even though more workplace injuries are reported than workplace illnesses, the estimated number of deaths is higher for workplace illnesses. For example, a 2000 study estimated that for each worker who died from a workplace injury in the United States, eight workers died from work-related diseases.[8]

Although significant progress has been made in reducing morbidity and mortality in the workplace in the United States, the U.S. occupational fatality rate is not the lowest among the highly developed nations. Five members of the European Union—Sweden, Great Britain, Denmark, Finland, and Germany—have lower occupational fatality rates than the United States.[9]

Occupational injuries and illnesses are an economic issue, too. It has been estimated that workplace injuries and deaths cost $146.6 billion in 2002, including $74 billion in lost wages and productivity, $27.7 in medical expenses, $26.3 billion in administrative costs, and other costs. Thus, each worker in America must produce $1,060 in goods or services just to offset the cost of work-related injuries.[5]

Importance of Occupational Safety and Health to the Community

Because of the grim statistics previously stated, it is important to recognize how occupational and community health problems are linked. The population of those working in industry is a subset of the population of the larger community in which the industry is located. Workers, usually the healthiest people in the community, are exposed in the course of their jobs to specific hazardous materials at the highest concentrations. It is in the factory that the most accurate exposure and health data are available for extrapolation to the general community. Most pollutants for which safe exposure levels have been adopted are workplace materials for which occupational exposures were studied first.

Hazardous agents in the workplace affect not only workers but also those outside the worksite. This can occur through soil and groundwater contamination with solids and liquids or air pollution with industrial gases and dusts. It can also occur through clothing and vehicle contamination, as in the case of asbestos workers whose wives and children became exposed to asbestos from these sources. It is important to note that the general population, which includes children, the elderly, and pregnant women, is more sensitive to exposure to pollutants than the workforce.

Another way that industries and their communities share health problems is in the instance of an industrial disaster. Examples include the Three Mile Island (Pennsylvania) nuclear reactor near-meltdown in the United States in 1979, the Bhopal tragedy in India in 1984, and the Chernobyl nuclear catastrophe in the Ukraine in 1986. In these cases, the risk of exposure to a chemical or nuclear energy source, which was originally limited to the workplace, became a community-wide risk.

Finally, it is important to recognize the workers themselves as a community, with common social problems and environmental risks. The failure to recognize the community nature of occupational groups and to monitor chronic conditions such as dermatitis, headaches, blood pressure, or blood chemistries has been a major weakness in our conventional approach to occupational health problems.

HISTORY OF OCCUPATIONAL SAFETY AND HEALTH PROBLEMS

Occupational risks undoubtedly occurred even in prehistoric times, not only during hunting and warfare, but also in more peaceful activities such as the preparation of flint by knapping. The discovery of flint heaps suggests that even these earliest of workers may have been at risk for silicosis (dust in the lungs).

An extensive historical review of occupational safety and health problems from early Egyptian times to the present day has been published.[10] The first of these milestones occurred in 1561 with George Agricola's treatise on mining, *De Re Metallica,* which emphasized the need for ventilation of mines. In 1567, the work of Philippus Aureolus Theophrastus Bombastus von Hohenheim, also known as Paracelsus, was published under the title *On the Miners' Sickness and Other Miners' Diseases.* These were the first significant works describing specific occupational diseases. The first work on occupational diseases in general was Ramazzini's *Discourse on the Diseases of Workers,* which appeared in 1700.[11,12] In this chapter, we will concentrate only on recent events in the United States and make only brief references to earlier milestones.

Occupational Safety and Health in the United States before 1970

The Industrial Revolution, which began in Britain in the eighteenth century, soon spread to continental Europe and then to the United States. Factors creating and driving the Industrial Revolution were the substitution of steam and coal for animal power, the substitution of machines for human skills, and other advances in industrial technology. These changes resulted in the rise of mass manufacturing, the organization of large work units such as mills and factories, and eventually the exposure of masses of workers to new hazards. Although mining remained the most dangerous form of work, there were soon other unsafe occupations, such as iron smelting and working in cotton mills and textile factories (see Figure 18.1).

FIGURE 18.1

Cotton mills in the late nineteenth century offered little protection from injuries.

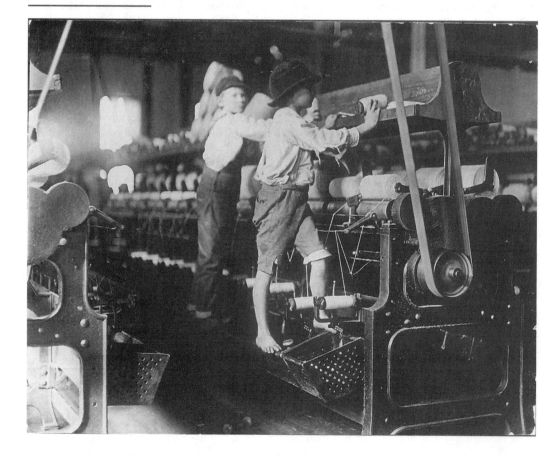

The recognition of the need to reduce workplace injuries began long before any attention was paid to workplace diseases. The earliest efforts of those responsible for inspecting workplaces were aimed primarily at the sanitation and cleanliness of workplaces. They soon became concerned with equipment safeguards and tending to those who had become injured or ill at work.[12] These efforts, while much needed and appreciated, did little to improve the overall health of the workforce.

State Legislation

The first official responses to new hazards in the workplace did not occur until 1835, when Massachusetts passed the first Child Labor Law, and later in 1867, when it created a Department of Factory Inspection to enforce it (see Figure 18.2). Under this law, factories were prohibited from hiring children less than 10 years of age.[13] At this time the federal government was concerned only with working conditions of federal employees. In 1877, Massachusetts passed the first worker safety law aimed at protecting textile workers from hazardous spinning machinery.[14]

In 1902, Maryland became the first state to pass any kind of workers' compensation legislation. In 1908, Congress, at the insistence of President Theodore Roosevelt, finally enacted the first of several **workers' compensation laws;** this first law covered certain federal employees. Over the next 40 years, all states and territories eventually enacted some type of workers' compensation legislation, beginning with New York in 1910 and ending with Mississippi in 1948.[10] So ended the first wave of reform in occupational safety and health. With the exception of several other legislative efforts, little progress was achieved during the first half of the century in protecting workers from injuries in the workplace, and almost nothing was done about occupational illnesses.

workers' compensation laws
a set of federal laws designed to compensate those workers and their families who suffer injuries, disease, or death from workplace exposure

FIGURE 18.2

Before child labor laws were passed, many children worked long hours at dangerous jobs such as mining.

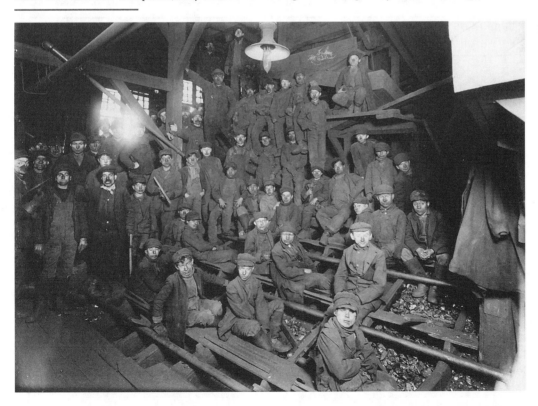

FIGURE 18.3

Alice Hamilton (1869-1970) was a pioneer in occupational safety and health in America.

There was one exception. Alice Hamilton (1869-1970) was a strong proponent of occupational health and a true pioneer in this field (see Figure 18.3). Over her 40-year career in occupational health, she led crusades to reduce poisonings from heavy metals such as lead and mercury. She investigated silicosis in Arizona copper mines, carbon disulfide poisoning in the viscose rayon industry, and many other industrial health problems.[13]

In spite of Hamilton's efforts, progress in occupational health legislation was slow in the first half of the twentieth century. Occupational diseases were by and large ignored. There was some safety legislation, such as the Coal Mine Safety Act of 1952. Beginning in the 1960s, some people began to take a closer look at the various state workers' safety and workers' compensation laws. It then was discovered that in most states, legislation was a fragmentary patchwork of laws; some states had good laws, but many had inadequate legislation. Many of the laws had failed to keep up with new technology or with inflation. Some groups of workers, including agricultural workers, were not covered at all by legislation. Other problems were the division of authority among various departments within state governments, fragmented record keeping, and inadequate administrative personnel.[15]

Federal Legislation

In 1884, the federal government created a Bureau of Labor, in 1910 the Federal Bureau of Mines, and in 1914 the Office of Industrial Hygiene and Sanitation in the Public Health

Table 18.1
Highlights of Federal Occupational Safety and Health Legislation

Year	Legislation
1908	Federal Workmen's Compensation Act—limited coverage
1916	Federal Highway Aid Act
1926	Federal Workmen's Compensation Act—amended to include all workers
1927	Federal Longshoremen's and Harbor Workers' Compensation Act
1936	Walsh-Healey Public Contracts Act
1952	**Coal Mine Safety Act**
1958	Federal Longshoremen's and Harbor Workers' Compensation Act—amended to include rigid safety precautions
1959	Radiation Standards Act
1960	Federal Hazardous Substances Labeling Act
1966	National Traffic and Motor Vehicle Safety Act
1966	Child Protection Act—banned hazardous household substances
1967	National Commission on Product Safety created
1968	Natural Gas Pipeline Safety Act
1969	Construction Safety Act
1969	Child Protection Act—amended to broaden the coverage
1969	Coal Mine Health and Safety Act
1970	**Occupational Safety and Health Act**

Service. In 1916, Congress passed the Federal Employees' Compensation Act, which provided federal employees compensation if injured while on the job.[14] Quite a few important laws were passed between 1908 and 1970 (see Table 18.1), but the two most comprehensive laws were the Coal Mine Health and Safety Act of 1969 and the **Occupational Safety and Health Act of 1970 (OSHAct),** also known as the Williams-Steiger Act in honor of Senator Harrison A. Williams, Jr., and Congressman William A. Steiger, who worked for passage of the act. At the time the act was passed, 14,000 workers died each year on the job. Since its passage, the act has served to raise the consciousness of both management and labor to the problems of health and safety in the workplace.

Occupational Safety and Health Act of 1970

The purpose of the Occupational Safety and Health Act of 1970 is to ensure that employers in the private sector furnish each employee "employment and a place of employment which are free from recognized hazards that are causing or likely to cause death or serious physical harm."[14] Furthermore, employers were henceforth required to comply with all occupational safety and health standards promulgated and enforced under the act by the **Occupational Safety and Health Administration (OSHA),** which was established by the act.

Also established by the OSHAct was the **National Institute for Occupational Safety and Health (NIOSH),** a research body now located in the Centers for Disease Control and Prevention of the Department of Health and Human Services. NIOSH is responsible for recommending occupational safety and health standards to OSHA, which is located in the Department of Labor.

The OSHAct contains several noteworthy provisions. Perhaps the most important is the employee's right to request an OSHA inspection. Under this right, any employee or any employee representative may notify OSHA of violations of standards or of the general duty obligation (to provide a safe and healthy workplace) by the employer. Under the act, the employee's name must be withheld if desired, and the employee or a representative may accompany the OSHA inspectors in their inspection. By another provision of the OSHAct,

Occupational Safety and Health Act of 1970 (OSHAct) comprehensive federal legislation aimed at ensuring safe and healthful working conditions for working men and women

Occupational Safety and Health Administration (OSHA) the federal agency located within the Department of Labor and created by the OSHAct that is charged with the responsibility of administering the provisions of the OSHAct

National Institute for Occupational Safety and Health (NIOSH) a research body within the Department of Health and Human Services that is responsible for developing and recommending occupational safety and health standards

individual states can regain local authority over occupational health and safety by submitting state laws that are and will continue to be as effective as the federal programs.[14]

PREVALENCE OF OCCUPATIONAL INJURIES, DISEASES, AND DEATHS

In this section, a brief overview of current trends in workplace injuries and illness is followed by a discussion of the occurrence and prevalence of work-related injuries and work-related diseases.

Overview of Recent Trends in Workplace Injuries and Illnesses

Since 1992, there has been a decline in the number of workplace injuries and illnesses reported in private industry. There were 4.7 million injuries and illnesses reported in 2002, resulting in a rate of 5.3 cases per 100 equivalent full-time workers per year. Approximately 2.5 million of these injuries and illnesses were cases with days away from work.[7] The majority of the 4.7 million injuries and illnesses (4.4 million) were injuries. About 294,500 new, non-fatal cases of occupational illnesses were reported in private industry in 2002. This figure does not include long-term latent illnesses, which are often difficult to relate to the workplace and therefore are underreported.[6]

The industries with the highest rates of nonfatal injuries and illnesses per 100 full-time workers in 2002 were manufacturing (7.2), construction (7.1), and agriculture, forestry, and fishing (6.4). Finance, insurance, and real estate had the lowest nonfatal injury and illness rates (see Figure 18.4).[7,16] Workplace injury and illness rates and cases with and without lost work-days have declined steadily since 1992 (see Figure 18.5).[17]

FIGURE 18.4

Nonfatal workplace injury and illness incidence rates by industry division, 2002.

Source: Bureau of Labor Statistics (2003). *BLS Charts of Workplace Injury and Illness Incidence Rates, 2002.* Available at http://www.osha.gov/oshstats/work.html.

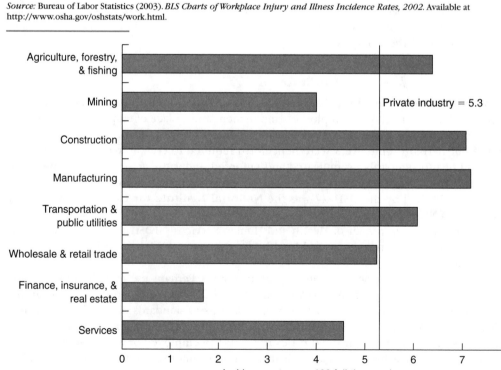

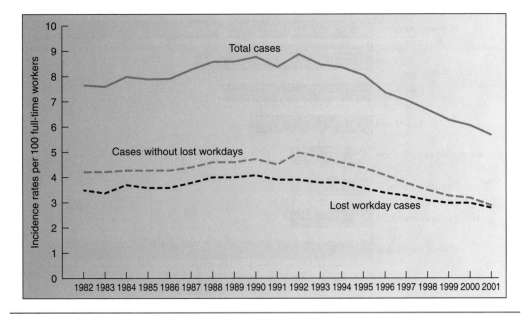

FIGURE 18.5

Workplace injury and illness incidence rates by type of case, 1982 to 2001.

Source: Bureau of Labor Statistics (2003). "Workplace Injuries and Illnesses in 2001." Available at http://www.bls.gov/iif/home.html.

Unintentional Injuries in the Workplace

Unintentional injuries in the workplace include minor injuries (such as bruises, cuts, abrasions, and minor burns), and major injuries (such as amputations, fractures, severe lacerations, eye losses, acute poisonings, and severe burns). Statistics on injuries and injury deaths are available from several sources, including the National Center for Health Statistics (NCHS), the National Safety Council (NSC), the Bureau of Labor Statistics (BLS), and the National Institute for Occupational Safety and Health (NIOSH). For this reason, estimates of the number of occupational injuries and injury deaths vary. However, beginning in 1992, the NSC adopted the figures published by BLS reports, including its *Census of Fatal Occupational Injuries (CFOI)*. The BLS reports are the source of figures used in this text.[6,7,16,17]

Fatal Work-Related Injuries

In 2002, according to the *CFOI,* there were 5,524 fatal work-related injuries, or about 15 per day.[6] This is the lowest number since the BLS began publishing the *CFOI* in 1992. Highway incidents continued to lead the way, with 1,372 deaths (25% of the total); followed by falls, with 714 fatal injuries (13%); homicides, with 609 deaths (11%); worker struck by object or equipment, with 506 deaths (9%); worker struck by vehicle, with 356 deaths (6%); non-highway transport, with 327 deaths (6%); and other events, with 1,540 deaths (30%) (see Figure 18.6).

Virtually all types of fatal workplace injuries decreased from 2001 to 2002. An exception was exposure to harmful substances or environments, which increased 8%. This category includes exposure to temperature extremes and electrocutions. Workplace-associated homicides have declined 44% since 1994, when 1,080 workplace homicides were reported.

The industries with the highest rate of fatal occupational injuries per 100,000 employees are mining (23.5) and agriculture (22.7). The industries with the lowest fatal injury rates are finance (1.0), services (1.7), and retail trade (2.1).[6]

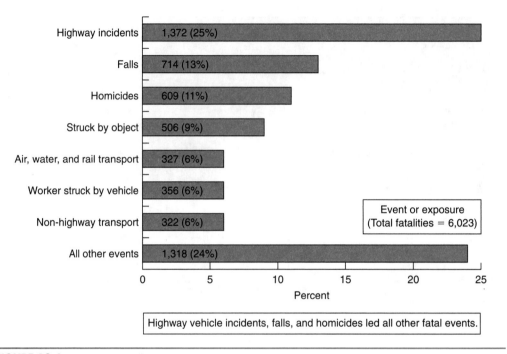

FIGURE 18.6

The manner in which workplace fatalities occurred, 2002.

Source: Bureau of Labor Statistics. *National Census of Fatal Occupational Injuries, 2002.* Available at http://www.bls.gov/iif/oshcfoi1.htm.

Nonfatal Work-Related Injuries

In 2001, an estimated 3.5 million occupational injuries and illnesses were treated in emergency departments.[5] The most common types of injuries and illnesses in private industry that required time away from work in 2001 were sprains and strains (43.6% of all such injuries), followed by bruises and contusions (8.9%), cuts and lacerations (7.5%), fractures (7.0%), multiple fractures (3.5%), carpal tunnel syndrome (1.7%), heat burns (1.6%), tendonitis (0.9%), chemical burns (0.6%), and amputations (0.6%).[18] However, the most disabling injury or illness was carpal tunnel syndrome, which resulted in a median of 25 days away from work (see Figure 18.7). Finally, the part of the body involved in the most cases with days away from work is the back, which accounted for almost one-fourth of all occupational injuries and illnesses.[18] The average cost of a disabling workplace injury was calculated at $33,000 in 2002.[5] One set of the *Healthy People 2010* objectives is to reduce work-related injuries that result in medical treatment, lost time from work, or restricted work activity (see Box 18.1).

Characteristics of Workers Involved in Work-Related Injuries

Differences in injury and injury death rates are often related to the age and gender of the worker. Injury death rate differences also occur between those of different income levels and races.

Age

Young workers aged 16 to 19 years accounted for 6.9 million (5.1%) of all employed workers in 2001, but accounted for just 3% of the 1.5 million injury and illness cases involving days away from work. Workers aged 16 to 17 and 18 to 19 years have the lowest workplace fatality rates of any age group (1.1 and 2.2 per 100,000 of workers, respectively). The lower injury, illness, and fatality rates for these groups may reflect the types of employment today's young people find: Fewer are finding jobs in manufacturing and more are finding employment in the service industry.[18]

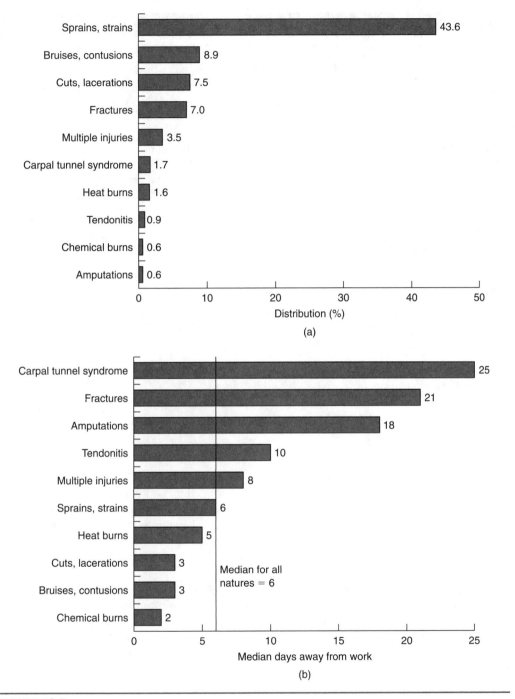

FIGURE 18.7

Characteristics of occupational injuries or illnesses. (a) Distribution of occupational injury and illness cases with days away from work in private industry by nature of injury or illness, 2001. (b) Median days away from work due to occupational injuries or illnesses in private industry by nature of injury or illness, 2001.

Source: National Institute for Occupational Safety and Health (2004). *Worker Health Chartbook, 2004.* Available at http://www.cdc.gov/niosh/pubs.html.

HEALTHY PEOPLE 2010: OBJECTIVES

20.2. Reduce work-related injuries resulting in medical treatment, lost time from work, or restricted work activities.

Target setting method: 30% improvement. (Better than the best will be used when data are available.)

Data sources: Annual Survey of Occupational Injuries and Illnesses, DOL, BLS; National Electronic Injury Surveillance System (NEISS), CPSC.

Target and baseline:

Objective	Reduction in Work-Related Injuries Resulting in Medical Treatment, Lost Time from Work, or Restricted Activity	1998 Baseline (unless noted)	2002* Status	2010 Target
		Injuries per 100 Full-Time Workers Aged 16 Years and Older		
20-2a.	All industry	6.2	5.0	4.3
20-2b.	Construction	8.7	6.9	6.1
20-2c.	Health services	7.9 (1997)	6.9	5.5
20-2d.	Agriculture, forestry, and fishing	7.6	6.0	5.3
20-2e.	Transportation	7.9 (1997)	5.8	5.5
20-2f.	Mining	4.7	3.4	3.3
20-2g.	Manufacturing	8.5	6.4	6.0
20-2h.	Adolescent workers	4.8 (1997)	—	3.4

*Due to revised OSHA reporting requirements, data are not comparable to those for previous years.

For Further Thought

The target is a 30% reduction in work-related injuries. What do you think the effect of a strong economy would have on reaching this goal? A weak economy? Do you think higher gasoline prices would make it easier or harder to achieve this objective?

Sources: U.S. Department of Health and Human Services (2000). *Healthy People 2010: Understanding and Improving Health,* 2nd ed. Washington, DC: U.S. Government Printing Office, November 2000; Centers for Disease Control and Prevention (2004). "Data 2010." Available at http://wonder.cdc.gov/data-2010/.

The service industry is also a major employer for older workers (workers aged 65 and older). However, older workers have the highest occupational fatality rates of any age group, 11.5 per 100,000 (see Figure 18.8). Older workers also have an increased burden of workplace injury and illness cases resulting in days away from work. The median number of days away from work following an injury was 14 for older workers, compared with 4 days for workers aged 16 to 19 years (see Figure 18.9).[18]

One group of workers that is of special concern is children. An estimated 70% to 80% of teens have worked for pay at some time during their high school years; 50% of employed youths work more than 15 hours during the school week. One in six works more than 25 hours during the school week. Although some level of employment may be desirable, studies show that teens who work more than 20 hours a week do worse academically and are more likely to abuse drugs and alcohol. There are other dangers, too. Every 30 seconds, a young worker under the age of 18 is injured in the workplace, and every five days a teenager dies because of a workplace injury.[19]

At particular risk are those youth who are employed in violation of child labor laws. An estimated 148,000 youth are illegally employed during an average week in the United States. This figure does not include the roughly 800,000 youth aged 6 to 17 years who are working as migrant and seasonal farmworkers.[19] A child labor survey found 6,015 child labor violations in the 33 states reporting violations in 2002. The top violations were hours violations, work permit and paperwork violations, and prohibited machinery/activities/industry violations.[20]

Youth employment peaks during summers, when an estimated 5.5 million youths find jobs. Young workers are at particular risk for injury because (1) they may not be trained to

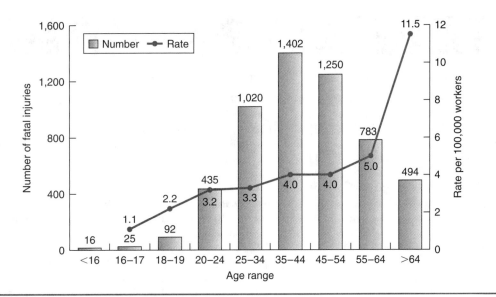

FIGURE 18.8

Number and rate of fatal occupational injuries by age of worker, 2002.

Source: National Institute for Occupational Safety and Health (2004). *Worker Health Chartbook, 2004.* Available at http://www.cdc.gov/niosh/pubs.html.

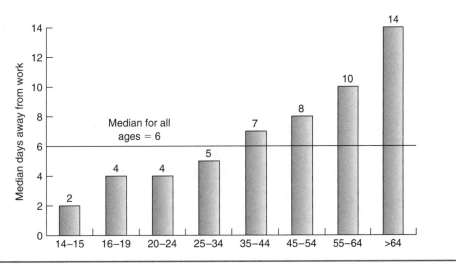

FIGURE 18.9

Median days away from work due to occupational injury or illness in private industry by age, 2001.

Source: National Institute for Occupational Safety and Health (2004). *Worker Health Chartbook, 2004.* Available at http://www.cdc.gov/niosh/pubs.html.

perform the assigned task, (2) they may not be adequately supervised, (3) they lack experience and maturity needed to perform assigned tasks and to recognize hazards, and (4) they may be unaware of child labor laws aimed at protecting them. The most dangerous types of work for youth are (1) agriculture, (2) retail trades, especially at night and handling cash, (3) transportation, and (4) construction. Box 18.2 provides recommendations for protecting the safety and health of young workers.[21]

| BOX 18.2 | HAZARDOUS WORK FOR ADOLESCENTS AND PRACTICAL STEPS FOR PROTECTING THEIR SAFETY AND HEALTH |

Work Too Hazardous for Adolescents

- Working in or around motor vehicles
- Operating tractors and other heavy equipment
- Working in retail and service industries where there is a risk of robbery-related homicide
- Working on ladders, scaffolds, roofs, or construction sites
- Continuous manual lifting or lifting of heavy objects

Recommendations

Young Workers

Young workers should take the following steps to protect themselves:

1. *Know about and follow safe work practices.*
   - Recognize the potential for injury at work.
   - Follow safe work practices.
   - Seek information about safe work practices from employers, school counselors, parents, state labor departments, and the Department of Labor (DOL). Visit www.youthrules.dol.gov, or call 1-866-4-USWAGE.
2. *Ask about training:* Participate in training programs offered by your employer, or request training if none is offered.
3. *Ask about hazards:* Don't be afraid to ask questions if you are not sure about the task you are asked to do. Discuss your concerns with your supervisor or employer first.
4. *Know your rights:* Be aware that you have the right to work in a safe and healthful work environment free of recognized hazards. Visit www.osha.gov/sltc/teenworkers/index.html.
   - You have the right to refuse unsafe work tasks and conditions.
   - You have the right to file complaints with DOL when you feel your rights have been violated or your safety has been jeopardized.
   - You are entitled to workers' compensation for a work-related injury or illness.
5. *Know the laws:* Before you start work, learn what jobs young workers are prohibited from doing. State child labor laws may be more restrictive than federal laws, and they vary considerably from state to state. Visit www.youthrules.dol.gov or call 1-866-4-USWAGE.

Employers

Employers should take the following steps to protect young workers:

1. *Recognize the hazards.*
   - Reduce the potential for injury or illness in young workers by assessing and eliminating hazards in the workplace.
   - Make sure equipment used by young workers is safe and legal. Visit www.dol.gov/dol/topic/youthlabor/hazardousjobs.htm or call 1-866-4-USADOL.
2. *Supervise young workers.*
   - Make sure that young workers are appropriately supervised.
   - Make sure that supervisors and adult coworkers are aware of tasks young workers may or may not perform.
   - Label equipment that young workers cannot use, or color-code uniforms of young workers so that others will know they cannot perform certain jobs.
3. *Provide training.*
   - Provide training in hazard recognition and safe work practices.
   - Have young workers demonstrate that they can perform assigned tasks safely and correctly.
   - Ask young workers for feedback about the training.
4. *Know and comply with the laws:* Know and comply with child labor laws and occupational safety and health regulations that apply to your business. State laws may be more restrictive than federal laws, and they vary considerably from state to state. Post these regulations for workers to read. For information about federal child labor laws, visit www.dol.gov/dol/topic/youthlabor/index.htm or call 1-866-4-USADOL. Links to state labor offices are available at www.iisa.net or www.youthrules.dol/gov/states.htm (1-866-4-USWAGE). Information about OSHA regulations that apply to workers of all age is available at www.osha.gov.
5. *Develop an injury and illness prevention program:* Involve supervisors and experienced workers in developing a comprehensive safety program that includes an injury and illness prevention program and

BOX
18.2   (CONTINUED)

a process for identifying and solving safety and health problems. OSHA consultation programs are available in every state to help employers identify hazards and improve their safety and health management programs. Visit www.osha.gov/oshprogs/consult.html.

Educators

Educators should take the following steps to protect young workers:

1. *Talk to students about work:* Talk to students about safety and health hazards in the workplace and students' rights and responsibilities as workers.

2. *Ensure the safety of school-based work experience programs:* Ensure that vocational education programs, school-to-work, or Workforce Investment Act partnerships offer students work that is allowed by law and is in safe and healthful environments free of recognized hazards. All such programs should include safety and health training.

3. *Include worker safety and health in the school curriculum:* Incorporate occupational safety and health topics into high school and junior high curricula (e.g., safety and health regulations, how to recognize hazards, how to communicate safety concerns, where to go for help). Information is available from NIOSH at www.cdc.gov/niosh/pdfs/99-141.pdf [NIOSH 1999] or 1-800-35-NIOSH.

4. *Know the laws:* If you are responsible for signing work permits or certificates, know the child labor laws. State laws may be more restrictive than federal laws, and they vary considerably from state to state. Visit www.dol.gov/gol/topic/youthlabor/ResourcesforEducators.htm (or call 1-866-USADOL), www.youthrules.dol.gov (or call 1-866-4-USWAGE), or visit www.osha.gov/SLTC/teenworkers/index. html.

Parents

Parents should take the following steps to protect young workers:

1. *Take an active role in your child's employment.*
   • Know the name of your child's employer and your child's work address and phone number.
   • Ask your child about the types of work involved, work tasks, and equipment he or she uses at work.
   • Ask your child about training and supervision provided by the employer.
   • Be alert for signs of fatigue or stress as your child tries to balance demands of work, school, home, and extracurricular activities.

2. *Know the laws:* Be familiar with child labor laws. State laws may be more restrictive than federal laws, and they vary considerably from state to state. Don't assume that your child's employer knows about these laws. Visit www.dol.gov/dol/topic/youthlabor/ ParentsofYoung.htm (or call 1-866-4-USADOL), www.youthrules.dol.gov (or call 1-866-4-USWAGE), or www.osha.gov/SLTC/teenworkers/index.html.

3. *Be aware of young workers' rights:* Report unsafe working conditions or employment in violation of child labor laws to DOL. Young workers are eligible for workers' compensation benefits if injured on the job.

4. *Share information with other parents:* Studies have shown that most young workers and parents are not aware of the laws and rights of young workers.

Source: U.S. Department of Health and Human Services, Centers for Disease Control and Prevention, National Institute for Occupational Safety and Health (2003). *NIOSH Alert: Preventing Deaths, Injuries, and Illnesses of Young Workers* (DHHS [NIOSH] pub. no. 2003-128). Available at http://www.cdc.gov/niosh/topics/youth.

Gender

More than 63 million women are part of the American labor force. Since 1950, the labor force participation rate of women has nearly doubled, so that today more than half of all adult women work. In 2001, females made up 46.6% of the American workforce. Although males made up 53.4% of the workforce, they worked 58.7% of all the hours worked. Because they work more hours and because there are still some dangerous jobs filled predominantly by males, males accounted for nearly two-thirds (66.1%) of all the injury and illness cases involving days away from work.[18] Women die of work-related injuries at much lower rates than men. During the period 1980 to 1997, only 7% of those who died of an injury in the workplace were women. When figures are adjusted for the numbers of each sex in the workforce, the overall occupational death rate for men is over 9 times higher than for women (8.3 deaths per 100,000 for men, compared with 0.9 per 100,000 workers for women).[22] A significant portion of the difference results from men being employed in more dangerous jobs.

Industries with the highest fatality rates are the same for both men and women—mining, agriculture, construction, and transportation. While the number of homicides is higher among men, proportionally homicides are greater for women, accounting for almost half of women's job-related fatalities.[22]

Like men, the most frequent job-related injury by body part injured by women was the hand, wrist, or fingers. However, when the injury resulted in one or more days away from work, the leading cause was back injuries. Nine million women had back pain, and one-third attributed this pain to the workplace. In fact, more that half of women in blue collar or service occupations attributed their back pain to the workplace.[22]

Working women are more likely than nonworking women to receive certain health benefits such as workplace prenatal education (offered in 9% of workplaces), weight control programs (24%), and cancer education (23%). Women in the workforce are more likely to be covered by health insurance than nonworking women (73% versus 46%) and were more likely to have a Pap test within the past three years (83% versus 73%).[22] One group of disorders in which females make up a higher proportion of cases with days away from work is anxiety, stress, and neurotic disorders. In 2001, female workers accounted for 64.9% of these cases.[18]

Poverty and Race

Studies show that those living in counties where income is lower have significantly higher occupational death rates than those living in higher-income counties. In general, death rates for nonwhites are about 12% higher than for whites (5.6 per 100,000 versus 5.0 per 100,000).[23] However, machinery injury death rates for whites are twice those of blacks. Hispanics, which make up 10.9% of the workforce, experience 15.2% of all occupational fatalities.[18] Native Americans are at highest risk for death from explosions and falling objects. Asians have very low death rates for occupational injuries. Although they make up 4.7% of the workforce they experience only 2.5% of all occupational fatalities.[18] Occupational injury rates may reflect the types of employment in which workers find themselves.

Geographic Differences in Workplace Injuries

During 2000, occupational injury death rates were highest in Alaska (21 per 100,000 workers), followed by Wyoming, Montana, and Idaho.[18] Deaths from nonfarm machinery are higher in the mountain states, but deaths from farm machinery are higher in the north-central states. Work-related death rates from machinery, falling objects, electric current, and explosion are all higher in rural states. Within states, work-related deaths are higher in rural areas than in more urban areas.

Temporal Variations in Workplace Injuries

As mentioned previously, between 1912 and 2002 injury death rates among workers have declined 81% (from 21 per 100,000 workers to 4 per 100,000). During this period, the workforce in America has nearly quadrupled in size, and the amount of goods and services produced has increased ninefold.[5] These improvements in workplace safety have been considered one of the 10 greatest achievements in public health during the past century (see Box 18.3).

There is a seasonality to work-related deaths. Injury death rates from machinery, falling objects, electric current, and explosions are highest in the summer, when farming and construction work increase. Deaths from these causes are also more often reported during weekdays than on weekends, when, in general, more injury deaths occur.

Workplace Injuries by Industry and Occupation

Fatal and nonfatal occupational injury rates vary according to type of industry and type of occupation.

BOX 18.3   **Ten Great Public Health Achievements, 1900–1999: Safer Workplaces**

Saving Lives, Promoting Health, and Protecting Jobs

A Sharp Increase in the Workforce, but an Even Sharper Decline in Work-Related Deaths

At the beginning of the twentieth century, workers in the United States faced remarkably high risks to their health and safety. Today, despite a much larger workforce than ever before, work-related deaths have declined sharply. Identifying and correcting occupational health hazards has greatly reduced the health and safety risks for such occupations as construction workers, miners, and farmers.

From 1933 to 1997, according to the National Safety Council, work-related injuries declined 90%. And, although the workforce tripled during those years, deaths declined from 37 per 100,000 to 4 per 100,000 workers.

If today's workforce of approximately 130 million were at the same risk for dying from injuries as workers in 1933, an additional 40,000 workers would have died in 1997 from preventable events.

In the coal mining industry, for example, improvements in workers' enviromental health and safety have resulted in lower rates of fatal injury, which were once common among miners.

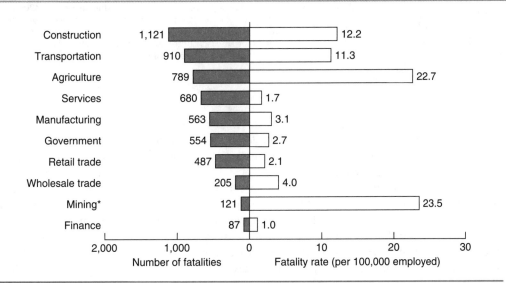

FIGURE 18.10

Numbers and rates of fatal occupational injuries by industry division, 2002.

*Includes all establishments categorized as Mining (Division B) in the *Standard Industrial Classification Manual,* 1987 edition, including establishments not governed by the Mine Safety and Health Administration (MSHA) rules and reporting, such as those in oil and gas extraction.

Rate = (Fatal work injuries/Employment) × 10,000 employed. Employment data were extracted from the 2002 Current Population Survey. The fatality rates were calculated using employment as the denominator; employment-based rates measure the risk for those employed during a given period of time, regardless of exposure hours.

Source: U.S. Department of Labor, Bureau of Labor Statistics (2003). *National Census of Fatal Occupational Injuries in 2002.* Available at http://www.bls.gov/iif/home.htm.

Fatal Occupational Injuries by Industry

Injury death rates vary by type of industry and occupation. In 2002, fatality rates per 100,000 workers were highest for mining (23.5), followed closely by agriculture (22.7), then construction (12.2), and transportation (11.3) (see Figure 18.10).[6] One of the *Healthy People 2010* objectives is to reduce deaths from work-related injuries for all industries. Mining, agriculture, construction, and transportation offer the best opportunity for improvement, and specific objectives have been proposed for these industries (see Box 18.4). When these data are

HEALTHY PEOPLE 2010: OBJECTIVES

20.1. Reduce deaths from work–related injuries.

Target setting method: Better than the best for 20-1a; 30 percent improvement for 20-1b, 20-1c, 20-1d, and 20-1e. (Better than the best will be used when data are available.)

Data source: Census of Fatal Occupational Injuries (CFOI), DOL, BLS.

Target and baseline:

Objective	Reduction in Deaths from Work-Related Injuries	1998 Baseline	2002 Status	2010 Target
		Deaths per 100,000 Workers Aged 16 Years and Older		
20-1a.	All industry	4.5	4.0	3.2
20-1b.	Mining	23.6	23.5	16.5
20-1c.	Construction	14.6	12.2	10.2
20-1d.	Transportation	11.8	11.3	8.3
20-1e.	Agriculture, forestry, and fishing	24.1	22.7	16.9

For Further Thought

The targets call for reducing deaths from work-related injuries by 30%. In which industry do you think the target will be reached first? Why?

Sources: U.S. Department of Health and Human Services (2000). *Healthy People 2010: Understanding and Improving Health,* 2nd ed. Washington, DC: U.S. Government Printing Office; Centers for Disease Control and Prevention (2004). "Data 2010." Available at http://wonder.cdc.gov/data2010/.

---

separated into more specific job categories, the highest job-related death rates for blue-collar workers are found among timber cutters and loggers (see Figure 18.11 and Table 18.2).

In the early 1990s, there was extensive media coverage of work-related homicides at U.S. Postal Service facilities. The phrase "Don't go postal on me," meaning don't become crazy or violent, is still heard occasionally. However, an examination of the occupational injury death rates for postal workers in the 1980s revealed that workplace injury death rates for postal workers were approximately 2.5 times lower than those for all workers combined.[24] A more recent study found that "'going postal' is a myth and a bad rap," and that postal workers are only one-third as likely as those in the national workforce to be victims of homicide at work. Some occupations are significantly more dangerous. For example, taxi drivers are 150 times likelier than letter carriers to be victims of homicide at work (31.54 versus 0.21 per 100,000).[25]

Nonfatal Occupational Injuries and Illnesses by Industry
A total of 4.7 million injuries and illnesses were reported in private industry workplaces during 2002, resulting in a rate of 5.3 cases per 100 equivalent full-time workers.[7] Goods-producing industries had higher rates than service-producing industries. Among goods-producing industries, manufacturing had the highest incidence rate in 1999 (7.2 cases per 100 full-time workers). In the service-producing industries, transportation and public utilities has the highest incidence rate (6.1 cases per 1,000 full-time workers). All 1999 incidence rates showed declines from 1998 levels.[7]

Agricultural Safety and Health
One particularly hazardous occupation is farming. Those working on farms are at considerable risk not just for injuries, but for lung diseases, noise-induced hearing loss, skin diseases, and certain cancers associated with chemical use and sun exposure. More than 3.1 million full-time workers are employed in agriculture and, if unpaid farm workers and family members are counted, the number is much higher. In 2002, 789 agricultural deaths were reported.[6]

FIGURE 18.11
Among the jobs with the highest fatality rates is logging.

Table 18.2
Top Ten Most Dangerous Jobs

Rank	Occupation	Fatality Rate*
1	Timber cutters/loggers	117.8
2	Fishers	71.1
3	Pilots and navigators	69.8
4	Structural metal workers	58.2
5	Drivers/Sales workers	37.9
6	Roofers	37.0
7	Electrical power installers	32.5
8	Farm occupations	28.0
9	Construction laborers	27.7
10	Truck drivers	25.0

*Selected occupations had a minimum of 30 fatalities in 2002 and 45,000 employed.

Source: Bureau of Labor Statistics.

In 2002, agriculture ranked second among major U.S. industries for work-related, unintentional injury fatality rates (see Figure 18.10).

A major contribution to farm-related fatalities is farm machinery, particularly farm tractors. For more than two out of five farm worker deaths, the source of the fatal injury was a tractor, and more than half of these deaths resulted from tractor rollovers. Rollover incidents are those in which the tractor tips sideways or backwards (especially when the tractor is improperly hitched), crushing the operator (see Figure 18.12). While all tractors manufactured since 1985 are fitted with seat belts and **rollover protective structures (ROPS),**

rollover protective structures (ROPS) factory-installed or retrofitted reinforced framework on a cab to protect the operator of a tractor in case of a rollover

FIGURE 18.12

The timing of events during rear rollovers of farm tractors.

Source: Centers for Disease Control and Prevention (1996). "Fatalities Associated with Improper Hitching to Farm Tractors—New York, 1991–1995." *MMWR*, 45(15): 307–311.

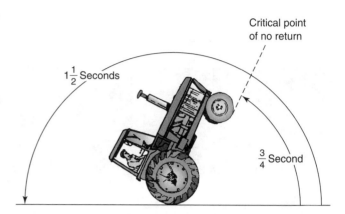

Critical point of no return

$1\frac{1}{2}$ Seconds

$\frac{3}{4}$ Second

many tractors in use in the United States lack this equipment. The effectiveness of ROPS in protecting the tractor operator was demonstrated by statistics collected in Nebraska, where only 1 (2%) of 61 persons operating ROPS-equipped tractors that rolled over died. These data compare favorably with a 40% death rate for the 250 persons involved in unprotected tractor rollover incidents. The single fatality in the ROPS-equipped tractor was not wearing a seat belt and was ejected from the ROPS-protected area.[26]

FIGURE 18.13

It is not unusual for farm boys under the age of 12 to be seen driving tractors.

A 1997 report confirmed that farm tractor rollovers continue to account for about 130 work-related deaths every year.[27] It was estimated that in 1993 only 38% of all tractors in the United States were equipped with ROPS. A survey found that the mean age of 63 tractors purchased by Iowa farmers in 1995 was 18 years and that only 40% had ROPS. The OSHA standard requiring ROPS be installed on all tractors is not actively enforced on farms with fewer than 11 employees, and family farms without other employees are exempt from OSHA regulations. NIOSH can promote ROPS use but has no authority to require their use.[27]

Another concern about farming is that it is one of the few industries in which the families of workers are also exposed to many of the same risks. Approximately 1 million children and adolescents less than 14 years of age reside in farm operator households, while another 800,000 children and adolescents live in households headed by hired farm workers. It is not unusual for farm boys under the age of 12 to be seen driving tractors (see Figure 18.13). Each year about 100 children are killed and 100,000 children and adolescents are injured in agriculture-related activities.[28] Many of those injured belong to the migrant workforce, where children as young as 12, 10, 8, and even 4 years of age can be found working in the fields. Testimony before the U.S. Senate Committee on Labor and Human Resources by Fernando Cuevas, Jr., paints a grim picture of migrant children (see Box 18.5).[29]

Of our 50 states, 48 rely heavily on migrant workers during the peak harvest season. These migrant workers have poor access to health care facilities; infant mortality is

COMMENTS OF A YOUNG FARM WORKER

"When I was younger it was all a game to me. But as I started getting older it became a job, and at the age of about 7 and 8, I was competing with my parents and my older sisters.... I was able to get out of the fields permanently at the age of 15 to try and get a decent education. I also became an organizer for the Farm Labor Organizing Committee at the age of 16, and I continue to see many, many young children working out in the fields at the same age that I was—4-, 5-, 6-, 7-, and 8-year-olds. They are still working out in the fields. I see it every year, up in Ohio, I see it down in Texas, I see it in Florida, I see it anywhere that we go and organize."

Source: Committee on Labor and Human Resources (August 12, 1992). *Childhood Labor Amendments* (report no. 102-230, to accompany Senate Bill 600). Washington, DC.

about 50 per 1,000 compared with the national average of about 7.2 per 1,000. In many cases, working conditions are hazardous, and water shortages require workers to drink water from irrigation ditches. Not only is such water unpurified, it is usually laden with agricultural chemicals and biological wastes. Migrant workers are also exposed to long hours in the sun, other unsanitary conditions, and numerous harmful pesticides from crop-dusting airplanes.

Prevention and Control of Unintentional Injuries in the Workplace

There are several principles that can point in the direction of controlling workplace injuries. These stem from the theory presented in Chapter 17, that injuries are the result of unintended exposure to energy in amounts that injure the body. As such, injuries on the job can be reduced by (1) eliminating or modifying the job to make it safer; (2) changing the work environment, physically or psychosocially, to make it less hazardous; (3) making machinery (including vehicles) safer; and (4) improving the selection, training, and education of the workers.[30,31] It is important to recognize that these strategies are listed in descending order of effectiveness. That is, eliminating or modifying a dangerous task is preferable to changing the work environment, safeguarding the machinery, or improving the selection and training of the worker.

National leadership in reducing the number and seriousness of workplace injuries and illnesses resides with OHSA and NIOSH. In an effort to chart the future course for research on workplace safety and health problems, NIOSH has developed a partnership with more than 500 public and private outside organizations and individuals. In 1996, NIOSH and its partners unveiled the National Occupational Research Agenda (NORA), a framework to guide occupational safety and health research into the twenty-first century. The NORA process resulted in a consensus on top research priorities and a goal of focusing "research in the areas with the highest likelihood of reducing the still significant toll of workplace illness and injury."[32]

Workplace Violence: Intentional Workplace Injuries

While only a small number of the incidents of workplace violence that occur each day make the news, some 1.7 million Americans are victims of workplace violence each year.[33] Many of us have heard about a teacher who was attacked by a student, a female worker who was sexually assaulted in the parking lot, a woman shot in her place of work by an irate boyfriend, or a pizza delivery man killed for a few dollars. In 2002, 609 homicides occurred in the workplace, making homicide the third leading cause of workplace fatalities behind highway incidents and falls and the second leading cause of workplace deaths among women.[6,34]

There are many reasons for workplace homicides and violence. Researchers have divided workplace violence into four categories:[35]

Criminal intent (Type I): The perpetrator has no legitimate relationship to the business or its employees and is usually committing a crime, such as robbery, shoplifting, and trespassing. This category makes up 85% of the work-related homicides.

Customer/Client (Type II): The perpetrator has a legitimate relationship with the business and becomes violent while being served. This category includes customers, clients, patients, students, and inmates. This category represents 3% of the work-related homicides.

Worker-on-worker (Type III): The perpetrator is an employee or past employee of the business who attacks or threatens another employee or past employee of the workplace. Worker-on-worker violence accounts for 7% of workplace homicides.

Personal relationship (Type IV): The perpetrator usually does not have a relationship with the business but has a personal relationship with the intended victim. This category, which includes victims of domestic violence assaulted or threatened at work, makes up just 2% of workplace homicides.

Data on nonfatal workplace violence are more difficult to obtain than data on workplace homicides. One estimate is that about 1.7 million people are victims of nonfatal workplace violence each year.[33] Assaults occur almost equally among men and women. Most of these assaults occur in service settings such as hospitals, nursing homes, and social service agencies. Forty-eight percent of nonfatal assaults in the workplace are committed by health care patients.[34]

Risk Factors

Risk factors for encountering violence at work are listed in Box 18.6. They include working with the public, working around money or valuables, working alone, and working late at night. Additionally, there are certain industries and occupations that put workers at particular risk. For workplace homicides, the taxicab industry has the highest risk at 41.4 per 100,000, nearly 60 times the national average rate of 0.70 per 100,000. Other jobs that carry a higher than average risk for homicide are jobs in liquor stores (7.5), detective and protective services (7.0), gas service stations (4.8), and jewelry stores (4.7). The workplaces that have the highest risk of nonfatal assault (and the highest percentage of all assaults that occurred) are nursing homes (27%), social services (13%), hospitals (11%), grocery stores (6%), and restaurants or bars (5%).[34]

Prevention Strategies

Prevention strategies for workplace violence can be grouped into three categories—environmental designs, administrative controls, and behavior strategies. Before these strategies can be implemented, a workplace violence prevention policy should be in place. Such a policy should clearly indicate a zero tolerance of violence at work. Just as workplaces have mechanisms for reporting and dealing with sexual harassment, they must also have a policy in place to deal with violence. Such a policy must spell out how such incidents are to be reported, to whom, and how they are to be addressed.

Environmental designs to limit the risk of workplace violence might include implementing safer cash handling procedures, physically separating workers from customers, improving lighting, and installing better security systems at entrances and exits. Administrative controls include staffing policies (having more staff is generally safer than having fewer staff), procedures for opening and closing the workplace, and reviewing employee duties (such as handling money) that may be especially risky. Behavior strategies include training employees in nonviolent response and conflict resolution and educating

BOX 18.6	FACTORS THAT INCREASE A WORKER'S RISK FOR WORKPLACE ASSAULT

- Contact with the public
- Exchange of money
- Delivery of passengers, goods, or services
- Having a mobile workplace such as a taxicab or police cruiser
- Working with unstable or volatile persons in health care, social services, or criminal justice settings
- Working alone or in small numbers

- Working late at night or during early morning hours
- Working in high-crime areas
- Guarding valuable property or possessions
- Working in community-based settings

Source: National Institute for Occupational Safety and Health (1996). "Violence in the Workplace: Risk Factors and Prevention Strategies." Available at www.cdc.gov/niosh/violrisk.html.

employees about risks associated with specific duties and about the importance of reporting incidents and adhering to administrative controls. Training should also include instruction on the appropriate use and maintenance of any protective equipment that may be provided.[33]

Occupational Illnesses and Disorders

Precise data on the number of cases of occupational illnesses are more difficult to acquire than data on injuries. It is more difficult to link illnesses to occupational exposure. Some illnesses that can result from occupational exposure (e.g., tuberculosis, cancer, and asthma) appear no different than those that result from exposure elsewhere. Also, there is usually a lengthy period of time between exposure and the appearance of disease, unlike injuries that are usually evident immediately. Nonetheless, estimates are possible and, in 1997, an estimated 429,800 nonfatal occupational illness cases were reported by the Bureau of Labor Statistics' **Survey of Occupational Injuries and Illnesses (SOII).**[36] Although this figure may seem high, it represents a decline from the more than 500,000 cases in 1994. In private industry, the highest incidence rates of nonfatal occupational illness occurred in the manufacturing sector.

> **Survey of Occupational Injuries and Illnesses (SOII)** an annual survey of injuries and illnesses from a large sample of U.S. employers (approximately 250,000) maintained by the Bureau of Labor Statistics in the Department of Labor

Types of Occupational Illnesses

Occupational diseases can be categorized by cause and by the organ or organ system affected. For example, repeated trauma is the cause, and the musculoskeletal system is the affected organ system. Exposure to asbestos is a cause of illness; the respiratory system, especially the lung, is the system affected.

Musculoskeletal Disorders

Musculoskeletal disorders are the most frequently reported occupational disorders. They include both acute and chronic injury to muscles, tendons, ligaments, nerves, joints, bones, and supporting vasculature. The leading type of musculoskeletal disorder was repeated trauma disorders (216,400), which made up 65% of all cases of nonfatal occupational illness in 2001.[18] Included in this category are carpal tunnel syndrome and noise-induced hearing loss. The Bureau of Labor Statistics reported an increase in rates for repeated trauma disorders from 5.1 per 10,000 full-time workers in 1984 to 41.1 in 1994. The rate then declined each year through 2001, when the rate was 23.8 per 10,000.[18]

Skin Diseases and Disorders

A total of 38,900 cases of occupational skin disorders were reported in 2001, less than half the number reported in 1974. Reported skin disorders included allergic and irritant dermatitis, eczema, rash, oil acne, chrome ulcers, and chemical burns. The highest incidences of occupational skin disorders were reported in agriculture, foresty, and fishing.[18] The skin may serve as the target organ for disease, or it may be the route through which toxic chemicals enter the worker's body.

pneumoconiosis
fibrotic lung disease caused by the inhalation of dusts, especially mineral dusts

coal workers' pneumoconiosis (CWP)
acute and chronic lung disease caused by the inhalation of coal dust (black lung disease)

asbestosis
acute or chronic lung disease caused by the deposition of asbestos fibers on lungs

silicosis
acute or chronic lung disease caused by the inhalation of free crystalline silica

Noise-Induced Hearing Loss

Noise-induced hearing loss is another form of repeated trauma. Approximately 30 million Americans are exposed to hazardous noise on the job, and an additional 9 million are at risk for hearing loss from other agents such as solvents and metals. Cases include workers with a permanent noise-induced hearing loss or with a standard threshold shift. Most of the cases were reported within manufacturing; within the manufacturing sector, 51% of the cases were associated with manufacturing.[18]

Respiratory Disorders

Occupational respiratory disorders are the result of the inhalation of toxic substances present in the workplace. The lungs, like the skin, can be both the target organ of disease and a portal of entry for toxic substances. Characteristic of occupational lung diseases are their chronic nature and the difficulty in early recognition (the latent period for such diseases may be 15 to 30 years). Also, there is the problem of multiple or mixed exposures in the home and the workplace.

Work-related asthma (WRA) is the most commonly reported occupational respiratory disease, even though estimates suggest that most cases are not recognized or reported as being work related. There is no estimate on how many cases of WRA occur nationwide. The highest percentage of cases occur among operators, fabricators, and laborers.[18]

One of the most important categories of lung diseases is **pneumoconiosis,** a fibrotic lung disease caused by the inhalation of dusts, especially mineral dusts. During the period 1968 through 1999, a total of 121,982 pneumoconiosis deaths were reported in U.S. residents.[18]

Types of pneumoconioses include coal workers' pneumoconiosis, asbestosis, silicosis, and byssinosis. The largest number of pneumoconiosis deaths were from coal workers' pneumoconiosis (CWP). **Coal workers' pneumoconiosis** (also called *black lung disease*), is an acute or chronic lung disease that is caused by inhaling coal dust (see Figure 18.14). Historically, deaths from CWP clearly outnumber all other types of pneumoconiosis deaths. During the period from 1987 to 1996, CWP made up 54% of all pneumoconiosis deaths.[36] However, deaths from CWP have declined during the last 30 years, from a high of 2,870 in 1972 to 1,003 in 1999.[18] No effective medical treatment is available for pneumoconiosis; therefore, primary prevention is essential.

Asbestos workers suffer from diseases that include **asbestosis** (an acute or chronic lung disease), lung cancer, and mesothelioma (cancer of the epithelial linings of the heart and other internal organs). In contrast to CWP, asbestosis deaths have increased from 77 in 1968 to nearly 1,265 in 1999.[18]

Workers in mines, stone quarries, sand and gravel operations, foundries, abrasive blasting operations, and glass manufacturing run the risk of **silicosis** (sometimes referred to as dust on the lungs) that is caused from inhaling crystalline silica. Silicosis deaths represent nearly 15% of all pneumoconiosis deaths in the United States. Mortality from silicosis has significantly declined in recent years from 1,157 in 1968 to 187 in 1999.[18]

Textile factory workers who inhale dusts from cotton, flax, or hemp often acquire **byssinosis** (sometimes called *brown lung disease*), an acute or chronic lung disease. In comparison with the other types of pneumoconiosis, byssinosis deaths are uncommon—fewer than 20 deaths are reported annually.

Other agents that can affect the lungs include metallic dusts, gases and fumes, and aerosols of biological agents (viruses, bacteria,

FIGURE 18.14

Mining is a dangerous occupation due to exposure to both injuries and disease.

and fungi). Health conditions that can result from exposure to these agents include occupational asthma, asphyxiation, pulmonary edema, histoplasmosis, and lung cancer.

Other Work-Related Diseases and Disorders

Other types of work-related illnesses and disorders are those that arise from poisonings and infections. Poisonings represented 1% of all nonfatal occupational illness cases in the SOII in 1997. Poisoning agents include heavy metals (including lead), toxic gases, organic solvents, pesticides, and other substances. Of all acute pesticide poisoning during 1993 to 1996, insecticides accounted for more than half. More than half (56%) of the cases of occupational illnesses related to pesticides in California occurred in agriculture.[36]

In 2002, 12.6 million people were employed by hospitals or in the health care industry in the United States, making up 9.3% of the employed workforce.[3] These workers are exposed to a variety of hazardous conditions, including infectious disease agents. Among the agents of concern are hepatitis B virus and human immunodeficiency virus (HIV). Health care workers are at risk if they become exposed to the blood or bodily fluids of patients or co-workers. The major route of exposure to these agents (82% of the cases) is percutaneous exposure (injuries through the skin) via contaminated sharp instruments such as needles and scalpels (see Figure 18.15). Exposure also occurs through contact with the mucous membranes of the eyes, nose, or mouth (14%), exposure to broken or abraded skin (3%), and through human bites (1%). Up to 800,000 percutaneous injuries occur annually, with an average risk of infection for HIV of 0.3% (3 per 1,000) and for hepatitis B of from 6% to 30%.[18] Health care workers are also at increased risk for acquiring other infectious diseases such as tuberculosis (TB); cases of TB in health care workers constitute about 3% of all TB cases.[36]

byssinosis
acute or chronic lung disease caused by the inhalation of cotton, flax, or hemp dusts (brown lung disease)

FIGURE 18.15
Health care workers are exposed to a variety of workplace hazards, including infectious diseases.

In 2001, more than 5,000 cases of anxiety, stress, or neurotic disorders with time away from work were reported in the SOII. This is about 0.6 cases per 10,000 workers. Half of these cases required 25 or more days away from work, and women constituted 65% of the cases.[18] The exposures most frequently associated with anxiety, stress, or neurotic disorders were "harmful substances (30%) and assaults or violent acts (13%)."[36]

As stated previously, there are any number of health problems that, while prevalent and serious, could be the result of dual or multiple exposures (workplace and home). Among these are cardiovascular diseases, cancers, and reproductive disorders. Perhaps a million or more workers are exposed to agents that can produce cancer, for example. However, there are no reliable estimates on the actual number of cancer deaths that can be traced directly to occupational exposure. Thus, we have discussed here only conditions generally accepted to be solely or predominantly related to work.

Prevention and Control of Occupational Diseases and Disorders

Preventing and controlling occupational diseases requires the vigilance of employer and employee alike and the assistance of governmental agencies. The agent-host-environment disease model discussed earlier in this book is applicable to preventive strategies outlined here. Specific activities that should be employed to control occupational diseases include identification and evaluation of agents, standard setting for the handling and exposure to causative agents, elimination or substitution of causative factors, engineering controls to provide for a safer work area, environmental monitoring, medical screenings, personal protective devices, health promotion, disease surveillance, therapeutic medical care and rehabilitation, and compliance activities.[37] Coordinated programs to monitor and reduce occupational hazards require professionally trained personnel. In a well-functioning program, these professionals work together as members of the occupational health and safety team.

RESOURCES FOR THE PREVENTION OF WORKPLACE INJURIES AND DISEASES

Community resources for the prevention of injuries and diseases attributable to the workplace include a variety of professional personnel and programs.

Occupational Safety and Health Professionals

The need for health professionals in the workplace is substantial. Among those with specialized training in their fields are safety engineers and certified safety professionals, health physicists, industrial hygienists, occupational physicians, and occupational health nurses.

Safety Engineers and Certified Safety Professionals

Approximately 400 academic institutions offer accredited programs that train occupational safety professionals. Many of these professionals will join the professional organization called the American Society of Safety Engineers (ASSE). "Founded in 1911, ASSE is the oldest and largest professional safety organization."[38] It has about 30,000 members who are involved in safety, health, and environmental issues in industry, insurance, government, and education. In spite of the name of this society, not all members are engineers. In fact, the background of the group is varied and includes a number of health educators.

Another recognizable group of trained professionals in this field is the Board of Certified Safety Professionals (BCSPs). This group is somewhat smaller; there are about 10,000 CSPs. "The Board of Certified Safety Professionals (BCSP) was organized as a peer certification board with the purpose of certifying practitioners in the safety profession."[39] Certification usually requires a bachelor's degree in engineering or in another scientific curriculum and the passing of two examinations.

FIGURE 18.16
Safety engineers prevent workplace injuries by detecting hazards.

Safety engineers and **certified safety professionals (CSPs)** design safety education programs, detect hazards in the workplace, and try to correct them (see Figure 18.16). Increased federal regulations have made the workload heavier for these occupational health professionals.

Health Physicists

Health physicists are concerned with radiation safety in the workplace. They monitor radiation within the work environment and develop plans for decontamination and coping with accidents involving radiation. It is estimated that there are approximately 11,000 health physicists in the United States. Many of these belong to the Health Physics Society, a 6,000-member, international scientific organization of professionals who are dedicated to promoting the practice of radiation safety.[40] An important certifying body of health physicists is the American Academy of Health Physics.[41]

Industrial Hygienists

Whereas the safety engineer or certified safety professional is primarily concerned with hazards in the workplace and injury control, the **industrial hygienist** is concerned with environmental factors that might cause illness. Examples of such factors might include poor ventilation, excessive noise, poor lighting, and the presence of hazardous substances.

It is estimated that there are 7,600 industrial hygienists practicing in the United States. Perhaps a third of them hold the title of Certified Industrial Hygienist (CIH), and many belong to the American Industrial Hygiene Association. To be certified requires a two-part written examination; the first part is given following one year of post-baccalaureate experience. The second is given after five years of professional activity. Many industrial hygienists belong to

safety engineer
a safety professional employed by a company for the purpose of reducing unintentional injuries in the workplace

certified safety professional (CSP)
a health and safety professional, trained in industrial and workplace safety, who has met specific requirements for board certification

health physicists
safety professionals with responsibility for developing plans for coping with radiation accidents

industrial hygienists
health professionals concerned with health hazards in the workplace and with recommending plans for improving the healthiness of workplace environments

the American Conference of Governmental Industrial Hygienists (ACGIH). This 5,000-member organization advances worker health and safety through education and the development and dissemination of scientific and technical knowledge through their publications.[42]

Occupational Physicians

The **occupational physician (OP)** or **occupational medical practitioner (OMP)** is a medical practitioner whose primary concern is preventive medicine in the workplace. Many OPs or OMPs belong to the American College of Occupational and Environmental Medicine (ACOEM), which represents more than 6,000 physicians specializing in the field of occupational and environmental medicine (OEM). "The American Board of Preventive Medicine (ABPM) recognizes and certifies qualified physicians in the medical specialty of occupational medicine. Approximately 2,200 physicians have been 'board certified' in occupational medicine within the United States."[43]

Because physicians are highly skilled and highly salaried occupational health professionals, only the largest companies maintain full-time OPs. Smaller companies may hire OPs on a part-time basis or as consultants.

Occupational Health Nurses

The role of the **occupational health nurse (OHN)** has changed over the years from running the company's medical department and first aid station to one of greater emphasis on health promotion and illness prevention. Because the OHN may be the only health professional employed in smaller plants, it is clear that if injury prevention and health promotion programs are to be offered, the job will fall to this individual.

The OHN must be a registered nurse (RN) in the state in which he or she practices. It is unlikely that these persons will have had much formal training in occupational health nursing prior to receiving their baccalaureate degrees because most nursing curricula do not provide much training in this area. However, the American Board of Occupational Health Nurses, Inc., established in 1972, now offers certifications. Requirements include many hours of continuing-education credits and five years' experience in the field of occupational health nursing. ABOHN is the only certifying body for occupational health nurses in the United States. More than 8,500 occupational health nurses have been certified by ABOHN.[44] Many OHNs belong to the American Association of Occupational Health Nurses (AAOHN), which was founded in 1942 and includes about 10,000 members.[45]

Occupational Safety and Health Programs

There are a number of programs that can be put in place in occupational settings to reduce injuries and diseases. These include pre-placement examinations, health maintenance programs, safety awareness programs, health promotion programs, investigation of accidents, stress management programs, employee assistance programs, and rehabilitation programs.

Pre-placement Examinations

The purpose of **pre-placement examinations** is to make sure that the worker fits the job. By selecting the employee who is the best physically and mentally qualified for a specific job, probabilities of job-related injuries or illnesses are minimized. Periodic evaluations are necessary to ensure that the selected individual continues to be physically and mentally qualified to carry out the job assignment. Examinations are also recommended for transferred and return-to-work employees. Sometimes a phasing in of these employees is desirable.

Occupational Disease Prevention Programs and Safety Programs

Occupational health services that facilitate preventive activities in the workplace include disease prevention programs and safety programs.

Disease Prevention Programs

Originally, occupational disease programs focused on controlling occupational diseases that one might succumb to from exposure in the work environment. Agents of concern were chemicals, radiation, and perhaps even psychological and social factors that could lead to sickness or disability. Gradually, these disease prevention efforts broadened into health maintenance programs and included the early detection and treatment of such diseases as hypertension, diabetes, obesity, and heart disease in order to keep employees healthier and on the job longer.

Safety Programs

Safety programs are those portions of the workplace health and safety program aimed at reducing the number and seriousness of unintentional injuries on the job. Each company needs to have a policy statement, safe operating procedures, a disaster plan, policies for hazard control, and policies for the investigation of injuries in the workplace. Provisions must be made for regular safety inspections of the workplace and for the maintenance of accurate records for each injury and for analysis of such records. Each safety program should include safety orientation and training programs and programs on first aid and cardiopulmonary resuscitation.

safety programs those parts of the workplace safety and health program aimed at reducing unintentional injuries on the job

Health Promotion Programs

Workplace health promotion began to evolve in the United States in the mid-1970s. **Health promotion programs (HPPs)** go beyond the idea of occupational health and beyond efforts to protect the worker from injury and disease in the workplace. Health promotion programs in the workplace usually consist of "health education, screening and/or intervention designed to change employees' behavior in a healthward direction and reduce the associated risks."[46]

The inclusion of workplace HPPs in the United States is driven by three major factors. The first is to promote the health of the employee. A healthy employee is a more productive employee. Such an employee is also more likely to use fewer health care dollars—the most rapidly growing cost of doing business today. The second major factor is the personal concern employers have for their employees. Corporations who provide HPPs for their employees show a personal concern for the employees and their families. This, in turn, increases employee morale. Third, workplace HPPs offer the potential of not only affecting the health of the workers and their families, but also the health of the corporation and the community.

Health promotion programs range in size from very modest programs that might include only hypertension screening to more comprehensive programs that offer cancer risk screening, nutrition, fitness, smoking cessation, stress management programs, and more. Generally, the objectives of these programs are to facilitate changes in behavior or lifestyle in order to prevent disease and to promote health.[46]

All indications are that HPPs will continue to grow. Corporations not only see them as a means to control health care costs and show a concern for the employees, but also as a means by which to recruit new employees and to retain the ones currently in the organization. (See Chapter 5 for more information on health promotion programs.)

health promotion programs (HPPs) health promotion programs in the workplace that include health education, screening, and/or intervention designed to change employees' health behavior and reduce risks associated with disease or injury

Employee Assistance Programs

Employee assistance programs (EAPs) are programs that assist employees who have substance abuse, domestic, psychological, or social problems that interfere with their work performance. These programs, which arrived at the workplace before HPPs, originally arose in response to occupational alcohol problems. EAPs provide help to employees with a variety of problems that affect their work performance. Whereas HPPs are primary prevention efforts, EAPs are secondary prevention or tertiary prevention efforts. They have as their goal the intervention and sometimes rehabilitation of employees with behavioral or other problems before such problems become costly for both the employer and employee.[46]

employee assistance programs (EAPs) workplace-based programs that assist employees who have substance abuse, domestic, psychological, or social problems that interfere with their work performance

CHAPTER SUMMARY

- After time spent at home, Americans spend the next largest portion of their time at work; thus, safe and healthy workplaces are essential if America is to reach its health potential.

- Every day approximately 15 people die from work-related injuries and many more people die of work-related diseases.

- Occupational health issues affect the quality of life economically as well as medically in communities in which workers live. Although occupational injuries and illnesses have been a long-standing concern of workers in America, rapid progress in reducing the number and seriousness of workplace injuries and illnesses became possible only after the passage of the Occupational Safety and Health Act (OSHAct) of 1970.

- The OSHAct established the Occupational Safety and Health Administration (OSHA) and the National Institute of Occupational Safety and Health (NIOSH) and required private industry to provide safe jobs and workplaces.

- The number and type of workplace injuries vary by person, place, time, and type of industry. Highway injuries are the leading cause of fatal work-related injuries. Falls and homicides are the second and third leading causes of workplace deaths.

- Nonfatal work-related injuries cost both employees and employers in terms of lost wages and lost productivity.

- Workplace violence affects 1.7 million workers in the United States each year, and homicide is the third leading cause of workplace fatalities.

- Work-related injuries can be controlled by applying a variety of injury prevention strategies, including eliminating a dangerous job, changing the work environment, using safer machinery, and improving the selection and training of workers.

- Work-related illnesses and disorders kill thousands of workers and former workers each year.

- The types of illnesses and disorders that can be attributed to workplace exposure are many, including musculoskeletal conditions, dermatological conditions, lung diseases, and cancers, among many others.

- Repeated trauma is the leading cause of work-related nonfatal illnesses.

- There are numerous resources to aid in the prevention of occupational injuries and diseases, including occupational health professionals and workplace injury and illness prevention programs and health promotion programs.

REVIEW QUESTIONS

1. Provide definitions of the terms *occupational injury* and *occupational disease* and give three examples of each.

2. In what ways are health problems in the workplace related to health problems in the general community?

3. How did the Industrial Revolution contribute to an increase in occupational health problems?

4. Who was Alice Hamilton? What did she do?

5. What were the deficiencies in state occupational safety and health laws in the early 1960s?

6. Discuss briefly the purpose of the Occupational Safety and Health Act of 1970 and outline its provisions.

7. What is OSHA and what does it do? What is NIOSH and what does it do?

8. What are some of the most frequently reported workplace injuries? Which are the leading causes of workplace injury deaths?

9. Which age group and gender of workers suffer the most occupational injuries? Which have the most fatal injuries?

10. Why is farming a particularly hazardous occupation? What are ROPS and how do they prevent deaths?

11. What are the risk factors for encountering violence in the workplace? Which occupation is at greatest risk for workplace homicides?

12. Outline some general control strategies that can reduce the number and seriousness of workplace injuries.

13. What is the most frequently reported occupational disorder?

14. What determines whether a musculoskeletal condition or skin condition should be considered an injury or a disease?

15. List four well-documented lung conditions that are related to occupational exposure. Name the occupations whose workers are at high risk for each of these conditions.

16. Why is it often difficult to prove that a disease or condition resulted from workplace exposure?

17. Outline some features of a workplace program to prevent or control occupational diseases. For each activity, indicate whether it is aimed at the agent, host, or environment aspect of the disease model.

18. List five health occupations that deal with worker safety and health. Describe their training and job assignments.

19. Name and describe four occupational safety and health programs.

20. What are some of the more common workplace health promotion activities offered today in the United States?

SCENARIO: ANALYSIS AND RESPONSE

Please take a moment to reread the scenario at the beginning of this chapter. Then reflect on the questions that follow.

1. If you were Jen, what would you do?
2. In 1998, California passed legislation protecting waitresses like Jen and bartenders by outlawing smoking in not only restaurants but also in bars. Do you support such legislation? How likely is it that your state legislature would pass a similar law?
3. Ambient smoke in a restaurant or bar is an example of situations that occur daily in the workplace.

Suppose you suspected that you were being exposed to a toxic agent where you worked. What would you do? Who would you contact? How could OSHA be of assistance?

4. Think about some of the jobs held by your fellow classmates. Do any of those jobs expose them to hazardous substances? Do any of the jobs students have put them at risk for injuries?

ACTIVITIES

1. Examine your local newspaper every day for a week for articles dealing with occupational injury or illness. Find three articles and, after reading them, provide the following: A brief summary, the resulting injury or disease, the cause of the injury or disease, and a brief plan for how the organization could eliminate the cause.

2. Interview an individual who works in the profession you wish to enter after graduation. Ask him or her to describe what he or she feels are the most prevalent injuries and illnesses connected with his or her job. Also ask about specific pre-service and in-service education the interviewee has had to protect against these problems. Finally, ask him or her to propose measures to limit future problems. Summarize your interview on paper in a two-page report.

3. If you have ever become injured or ill as a result of a job, explain what happened to you. In a two-page paper, identify the causative agent, how the injury could have been prevented, and what kind of training you had to prepare you for a safe working environment.

4. Go to the school library and research the injuries and diseases connected with your future profession. In a two-page paper, identify the major problems and what employers and employees should do about them and express concerns that you have about working in the profession due to these problems.

5. Visit any job site related to your future profession. At that site, find 10 things that employers and employees are doing to make it a safe work environment. List these 10 things briefly and explain the benefit of each one.

COMMUNITY HEALTH ON THE WEB

The Internet contains a wealth of information about community and public health. Increase your knowledge of some of the topics presented in this chapter by accessing the Jones and Bartlett Publishers Web site at **health.jbpub.com/communityhealth/5e** and follow the links to complete the following Web activities.

• National Institute for Occupational Safety and Health
• Occupational Safety and Health Administration
• American Industrial Hygiene Association

REFERENCES

1. World Health Organization (1997). *Occupational Health: The Workplace*. Available at http://www.who.int/peh/Occupational_health/occupational_health2.htm.

2. World Health Organization (1999). *Occupational Health: Ethically Correct, Economically Sound*. Available at http://www.who.int/inf-fs/en/fact084.html.

3. U.S. Bureau of the Census (2003). *Statistical Abstract of the United States—2003*. Available at http://www.census.gov/.

4. U.S. Department of Labor, Bureau of Labor Statistics. *BLS Glossary*. Available at http://www.bls.gov/bls/glossary.htm.

5. National Safety Council (2003). *Injury Facts*. Itasca, IL: Author.

6. U.S. Department of Labor, Bureau of Labor Statistics (2003). *National Census of Fatal Occupational Injuries in 2002*. Available at http://www.bls.gov/iif/home.htm.

7. U.S. Department of Labor, Bureau of Labor Statistics (2003). *Workplace Injuries and Illnesses in 2002*. Available at http://www.bls.gov/iif/home.htm.

8. National Institute for Occupational Safety and Health (2000). *Performance Highlights of the National Institute for Occupational Safety and Health* (HHS [NIOSH] pub. no. 2000-134). Cincinnati, OH: NIOSH Publications.

9. Health and Safety Executive (United Kingdom). "HSE Statistics." Available at http://www.hse.gov.uk/statistics/.

10. Felton, J. S. (1986). "History of Occupational Health and Safety." In J. LaDou, ed., *Introduction to Occupational Health and Safety.* Chicago: National Safety Council.

11. Rosen, G. (1958). *A History of Public Health.* New York: M.D. Publications.

12. LaDou, J., J. Olishifski, and C. Zenz (1986). "Occupational Health and Safety Today." In J. LaDou, ed., *Introduction to Occupational Health and Safety.* Chicago: National Safety Council.

13. Schilling, R. S. F. (1989). "Developments in Occupational Health." In H. A. Waldron, ed., *Occupational Health Practice.* Boston: Butterworths.

14. Ashford, N. A. (1976). *Crisis in the Workplace: Occupational Disease and Injury—A Report to the Ford Foundation.* Cambridge, MA: MIT Press.

15. Page, J. A., and M. W. O'Brien (1973). *Bitter Wages.* New York: Grossman.

16. U.S. Department of Labor, Bureau of Labor Statistics (2003). *BLS Charts of Workplace Injury and Illness Incidence Rates, 2002.* Available at http://www.osha.gov/oshstats/work.html.

17. U.S. Department of Labor, Bureau of Labor Statistics (2002). *Workplace Injuries and Illnesses in 2001.* Available at http://www.bls.gov/iif/home.htm.

18. National Institute for Occupational Safety and Health (2004). *Worker Health Chartbook, 2004.* Available at http://www.cdc.gov/niosh/pubs.html.

19. National Consumers' League (2003). "American Working Teens Fact Sheet." Available at http://nclnet.org/workingteens.htm.

20. Child Labor Coalition (2003). *2002 Child Labor State Survey Results.* Available at http://www.stopchildlabor.org/USchildlabor/childlaborUS.htm.

21. National Institute for Occupational Safety and Health (2003). *NIOSH Alert: Preventing Deaths, Injuries, and Illnesses of Young Workers* (HHS [NIOSH] pub. no. 2003-128). Available at http://www.cdc.gov/niosh/topics/youth/.

22. Wagener, D. K., J. Walstedt, L. Jenkins, et al. (1997). *Women: Work and Health* (HHS pub. no. PHS 97-1415). Hyattsville, MD: National Center for Health Statistics.

23. Centers for Disease Control and Prevention (2001). "Fatal Occupational Injuries—United States, 1980-97." *MMWR*, 50(16): 317-320.

24. Centers for Disease Control and Prevention (1994). "Occupational Injury Deaths of Postal Workers—United States, 1980-1989." *MMWR*, 43(32): 587-595.

25. The National Center on Addiction and Substance Abuse at Columbia University (2000). *The United States Postal Service Commission on a Safe and Secure Workplace.* New York: Author.

26. Centers for Disease Control and Prevention (1993). "Public Health Focus: Effectiveness of Rollover Protective Structures for Preventing Injuries Associated with Agricultural Tractors." *MMWR*, 42(3): 57-59.

27. Centers for Disease Control and Prevention (1997). "Use of Rollover Protective Structures—Iowa, Kentucky, New York, and Ohio, 1992-1997." *MMWR*, 46(36): 842-845.

28. National Institute for Occupational Safety and Health (1997). "NIOSH Facts: Health and Safety for Kids on the Farm." Available at http://www.cdc.gov/niosh/kidsag.html.

29. Novello, A. C. (1991). "A Charge to the Conference." Presented at the Surgeon General's Conference on Agricultural Safety and Health: Farm Safe 2000, Des Moines, IA.

30. National Institute for Occupational Safety and Health (1986). *Proposed National Strategies for the Prevention of Leading Work-Related Diseases and Injury: Severe Occupational Traumatic Injuries.* Cincinnati, OH: NIOSH Publications.

31. National Institute for Occupational Safety and Health (1986). *Proposed National Strategies for the Prevention of Leading Work-Related Diseases and Injury: Musculoskeletal Injuries.* Cincinnati, OH: NIOSH Publications.

32. National Institute for Occupational Safety and Health (2000). *National Occupational Research Agenda: Update, May 2000* (HHS [NIOSH] pub. no. 2000-143). Cincinnati, OH: NIOSH Publications.

33. National Institute for Occupational Safety and Health (2003). "Occupational Violence." Available at http://www.cdc.gov/niosh/injury/traumaviolence.html.

34. National Institute for Occupational Safety and Health (1997). "NIOSH Facts: Violence in the Workplace." Available at http://www.cdc.gov/niosh/violfs.html.

35. Injury Prevention Center, University of Iowa (2001). *Workplace Violence: A Report to the Nation.* Available at http://www.public-health.uiowa.edu/iprc/.

36. National Institute for Occupational Safety and Health (2000). *Worker Health Chartbook, 2000* (HHS [NIOSH] pub. no. 2000-127). Cincinnati, OH: NIOSH Publications.

37. National Institute for Occupational Safety and Health (1986). *Proposed National Strategies for the Prevention of Leading Work-Related Diseases and Injury: Lung Diseases.* Cincinnati, OH: NIOSH Publications.

38. American Society of Safety Engineers (2004). Information on this organization is available at http://www.asse.org.

39. Board of Certified Safety Professionals (2004). Information on this organization is available at http://www.bcsp.com.

40. Health Physics Society (2004). Information on this organization is available at http://www.hps.org.

41. American Academy of Health Physics (2004). Information on this organization is available at http://www.hps1.org/aahp.

42. American Conference of Governmental Industrial Hygienists (2004). Information on this organization is available at http://www.acgih.org.

43. American College of Occupational and Environmental Medicine (2004). Information on this organization is available at http://www.acoem.org.

44. American Board for Occupational Health Nurses, Inc. (2004). Information on this organization is available at http://www.abohn.org.

45. American Association of Occupational Health Nurses, Inc. (2004). Information on this organization is available at http://www.aaohn.org.

46. Lisle, J. R., and A. Newsome (1989). "Health Promotion and Counseling." In H. A. Waldron, ed., *Occupational Health Practice.* Boston: Butterworths.

Retrospective Studies: How to Calculate an Odds Ratio

Let us assume that you selected 100 lung cancer cases and 1,000 controls of the same age, sex, and socioeconomic status as the cases. Suppose 90 of 100 cases of lung cancer had been regular smokers, but only 270 of 1,000 controls smoked, an odds ratio could be calculated by the formula $(A \times D) \div (B \times C)$ where cases and controls are designated as follows:

		Disease Present	
		Yes	**No**
Risk Factor Present	Yes	A	B
	No	C	D

In our example:

		Disease Present	
		Yes	**No**
Risk Factor Present	Yes	90	270
	No	10	730

Substituting our data into the formula:

$[(90 \times 730) \div (270 \times 10)] = 65,700 \div 2,700 = 24.33$. Thus, lung cancer victims have 24.33 times greater probability of having been a smoker.

PROSPECTIVE STUDIES: HOW TO CALCULATE RELATIVE AND ATTRIBUTABLE RISK

Let us assume that in a cohort of 4,000 there were 1,000 smokers and 3,000 nonsmokers. If, after 20 years, cancer develops in 22 smokers (22 per 1,000) and in 6 nonsmokers (6 per 3,000 or 2 per 1,000), *relative risk* is the ratio of the incidence rates, 22 per thousand : 2 per thousand or 22:2 or 11 to 1.

Further, one can calculate an *attributable risk* by subtracting the deaths in the non-smoking group (2 deaths) from the number of lung cancer deaths in the smoking group (22 deaths). Thus, 20 deaths are attributable to smoking; the attributable risk is 20 per 1,000.

Appendix 2

Operational Definitions for the 1990 Census

American Indian, Eskimo, or Aleut Includes persons who classified themselves as such in one of the specific race categories identified below.

American Indian Includes persons who indicated their race as "American Indian," entered the name of an Indian tribe, or reported such entries as Canadian Indian, French-American Indian, or Spanish-American Indian.

Eskimo Includes persons who indicated their race as "Eskimo" or reported entries such as Arctic Slope, Inupiat, and Yupik.

Aleut Includes persons who indicated their race as "Aleut" or reported entries such as Alutiiq, Egegik, and Pribilovian.

Asian or Pacific Islander Includes persons who reported in one of the Asian or Pacific Islander groups listed on the questionnaire or who provided write-in responses such as Thai, Nepaili, or Tongan.

Asian Includes "Chinese," "Filipino," "Japanese," "Asian Indian," "Korean," "Vietnamese," and "Other Asian."

Chinese Includes persons who indicated their race as "Chinese" or who identified themselves as Cantonese, Tibetan, or Chinese American. In standard census reports, persons who reported as "Taiwanese" or "Formosan" are included here with Chinese. In special reports on the Asian or Pacific Islander population, information on persons who identified themselves as Taiwanese are shown separately.

Filipino Includes persons who indicated their race as "Filipino" or reported entries such as Philipino, Philipine, or Filipino-American.

Japanese Includes persons who indicated their race as "Japanese" and persons who identified themselves as Nipponese or Japanese-American.

Asian Indian Includes persons who indicated their race as "Asian Indian" and persons who identified themselves as Bengalese, Bharat, Dravidian, East Indian, or Goanese.

Korean Includes persons who indicated their race as "Korean" and persons who identified themselves as Korean-American.

Vietnamese Includes persons who indicated their race as "Vietnamese" and persons who identified themselves as Vietnamese-American.

Cambodian Includes persons who provided a write-in response such as Cambodian or Cambodia.

Hmong Includes persons who provided a write-in response such as Hmong, Laohmong, or Mong.

Laotian Includes persons who provided a write-in response such as Laotian, Laos, or Lao.

Thai Includes persons who provided a write-in response such as Thai, Thailand, or Siamese.

Other Asian Includes persons who provided a write-in response of Bangladeshi, Burmese, Indonesian, Pakistani, Sri Lankan, Amerasian, or Eurasian.

Pacific Islander Includes persons who indicated their race as "Pacific Islander" by classifying themselves into one of the following race categories or identifying themselves as one of the Pacific Islander cultural groups of Polynesian, Micronesian, or Melanesian.

Hawaiian Includes persons who indicated their race as "Hawaiian" as well as persons who identified themselves as Part Hawaiian or Native Hawaiian.

Samoan Includes persons who indicated their race as "Samoan" or persons who identified themselves as American-Samoan or Western Samoan.

Guamanian Includes persons who indicated their race as "Guamanian" or persons who identified themselves as Chamorro or Guam.

Other Pacific Islander Includes persons who provided a write-in response of a Pacific Islander group such as Tahitian, Northern Mariana Islander, Palauan, Fijiian, or a cultural group such as Polynesian, Micronesian, or Melanesian.

Black Includes persons who indicated their race as "black or Negro" or reported entries such as African-American, Afro-American, black Puerto Rican, Jamaican, Nigerian, West Indian, or Haitian.

White Includes persons who indicated their race as "white" or reported entries such as Canadian, German, Italian, Lebanese, Near Easterner, Arab, or Polish.

Other race Includes all other persons not included in "white," "black," "American Indian, Eskimo, or Aleut," and "Asian or Pacific Islander" race categories described above. Persons reporting in the "Other race" category and providing write-in entries such as multiracial, multiethnic, mixed, interracial, Wesort, or a Spanish/Hispanic origin group (such Mexican, Cuban, or Puerto Rican) are included here.

Hispanic origin Of Hispanic origin are those who classified themselves in one of the specific Hispanic origin categories listed on the questionnaire— "Mexican," "Puerto Rican," or "Cuban"—as well as those who indicated that they were of "other Spanish/Hispanic" origin. Persons of "Other Spanish/Hispanic" origin are those whose origins are from Spain, the Spanish-speaking countries of Central or South America or the Dominican Republic, or they are persons of Hispanic origin identifying themselves generally as Spanish, Spanish-American, Hispanic, Hispano, Latino, and so on.

Note: These definitions were taken directly from U.S. Dept. of Commerce (1990). *Census of Population and Housing, Summary Population and Housing, Characteristics, United States.* Washington, DC: U.S. Government Printing Office.

Appendix 3

Revised Operational Definitions for 1997*

American Indian or Alaska Native   A person having origins in any of the original peoples of North and South American (including Central America), and who maintains tribal affiliation or community attachment.

"Alaska Native" should replace the term "Alaskan Native."

Alaska Native should be used instead of Eskimo and Aleut.

Asian   A person having origins in any of the original peoples of the Far East, Southeast Asia, or the Indian subcontinent including, for example, Cambodia, China, India, Japan, Korea, Malaysia, Pakistan, the Philippine Islands, Thailand, and Vietnam.

Native Hawaiian or Other Pacific Islander   A person having origins in any of the original peoples of Hawaii, Guam, Samoa, or other Pacific Islands.

Hispanic or Latino   A person of Cuban, Mexican, Puerto Rican, South or Central American, or other Spanish culture or origin, regardless of race. The term, "Spanish origin," can be used in addition to "Hispanic or Latino."

*Federal programs had until January 1, 2003 to adopt these revised standards.

Source: Office of Management and Budget, *Revisions to the Standards for the Classification of Federal Data on Race and Ethnicity.* Available at: http://www.whitehouse.gov/wh/eop/omb/html/fedreg/ombdir15.html.

Self-Assessment Checklist Promoting Cultural Diversity and Cultural Competency

SELF-ASSESSMENT CHECKLIST FOR PERSONNEL PROVIDING SERVICES TO CHILDREN WITH SPECIAL HEALTH NEEDS AND THEIR FAMILIES

This checklist was developed by HRSA's Maternal and Child Health Bureau/Children with Special Health Needs component of the National Center for Cultural Competence. It is for personnel providing health services and supports to children with special health needs and their families and is intended to heighten the awareness and sensitivity of personnel to the importance of cultural diversity and cultural competence in human service settings. The checklist provides concrete examples of the kinds of values and practices that foster such an environment. *Directions: Select A, B, or C for each item listed below.*

A = Things I do frequently   B = Things I do occasionally   C = Things I do rarely or never

Physical environment, materials, and resources

___1. I display pictures, posters, and other materials that reflect the cultures and ethnic backgrounds of children and families served by my program or agency.

___2. I ensure that magazines, brochures, and other printed materials in reception areas are of interest to and reflect the different cultures of children and families served by my program or agency.

___3. When using videos, films, or other media resources for health education, treatment, or other interventions, I ensure that they reflect the cultures of children and families served by my program or agency.

___4. When using food during an assessment, I ensure that meals provided include foods that are unique to the cultural and ethnic backgrounds of children and families served by my program or agency.

___5. I ensure that toys and other play accessories in reception areas and those which are used during assessment are representative of the various cultural and ethnic groups within the local community and the society in general.

Communication styles

___6. For children who speak languages or dialects other than English, I attempt to learn and use key words in their language so that I am better able to communicate with them during assessment, treatment, or other interventions.

___7. I attempt to determine any familial colloquialisms used by children and families that may impact on assessment, treatment, or other interventions.

___8. I use visual aids, gestures, and physical prompts in my interactions with children who have limited English proficiency.

___9. I use bilingual staff or trained volunteers to serve as interpreters during assessment, meetings, or other events for parents who would require this level of assistance.

___10. When interacting with parents who have limited English proficiency I always keep in mind that:

    ___* limitations in English proficiency is in no way a reflection of their level of intellectual functioning.

    ___* their limited ability to speak the language of the dominant culture has no bearing on their ability to communicate effectively in their language of origin.

    ___* they may or may not be literate in their language of origin or English.

___11. When possible, I ensure that all notices and communiqués to parents are written in their language of origin.

___12. I understand that it may be necessary to use alternatives to written communications for some families, as word of mouth may be a preferred method of receiving information.

Values and attitudes

___13. I avoid imposing values that may conflict or be inconsistent with those of cultures or ethnic groups other than my own.

___14. In group therapy or treatment situations, I discourage children from using racial and ethnic slurs by helping them understand that certain words can hurt others.

___15. I screen books, movies, and other media resources for negative cultural, ethnic, or racial stereotypes before sharing them with children and their parents served by my program or agency.

___16. I intervene in an appropriate manner when I observe other staff or parents within my program or agency engaging in behaviors that show cultural insensitivity or prejudice.

___17. I understand and accept that family is defined differently by different cultures (e.g., extended family members, fictive kin, godparents).

___18. I recognize and accept that individuals from culturally diverse backgrounds may desire varying degrees of acculturation into the dominant culture.

___19. I accept and respect that male–female roles may vary significantly among different cultures (e.g., who makes major decisions for the family, play and social interactions expected of male and female children).

___20. I understand that age and life cycle factors must be considered in interactions with individuals and families (e.g., high value placed on the decisions of elders or the role of the eldest male in families).

___21. Even though my professional or moral viewpoints may differ, I accept the family/ parents as the ultimate decision makers for services and supports for their children.

___22. I recognize that the meaning or value of medical treatment and health education may vary greatly among cultures.

___23. I accept that religion and other beliefs may influence how families respond to illnesses, disease, and death.

___24. I recognize and accept that folk and religious beliefs may influence a family's reaction and approach to a child born with a disability or later diagnosed with a disability or special health care needs.

___25. I understand that traditional approaches to disciplining children are influenced by culture.

___26. I understand that families from different cultures will have different expectations of their children for acquiring toileting, dressing, feeding, and other self-help skills.

___27. I accept and respect that customs and beliefs about food, its value, preparation, and use are different from culture to culture.

___28. Before visiting or providing services in the home setting, I seek information on acceptable behaviors, courtesies, customs, and expectations, that are unique to families of specific cultures and ethnic groups served by my program or agency.

___29. I seek information from family members or other key community informants, which will assist in service adaptation to respond to the needs and preferences of culturally and ethnically diverse children and families served by my program or agency.

___30. I advocate for the review of my program's or agency's mission statement, goals, policies, and procedures to ensure that they incorporate principles and practices that promote cultural diversity and cultural competence.

There is no answer key. However, if you frequently responded "C", you may not necessarily demonstrate values and engage in practices that promote a culturally diverse and culturally competent service delivery system for children and families.

For more information contact: Tawara D. Goode, Georgetown University Child Development Center UAP. Adapted from "Promoting Cultural Competence and Cultural Diversity in Early Intervention and Early Childhood Settings" (Revised 1999).

Source: U.S. Department of Health and Human Services (2000). "Promoting Cultural Diversity and Culture Competency." Office of Minority Health, *Closing the Gap,* January, pp. 6–7.

Glossary Terms

absorption field The element of a septic system in which the liquid portion of waste is distributed.

accreditation The process by which an agency or organization evaluates and recognizes an institution as meeting certain predetermined standards.

acculturated The cultural modification of an individual or group by adapting to or borrowing traits from another culture.

acid rain Both wet and dry acidic deposits, which occur both within and downwind of areas that produce emissions containing sulfur dioxide and oxides of nitrogen (also called acid deposition).

Activities of Daily Living (ADLs) Eating, toileting, dressing, bathing, walking, getting in and out of a bed or chair, and getting outside.

acute disease A disease in which the peak severity of symptoms occurs and subsides within three months of onset, usually within days or weeks.

Administration on Aging An operating division of the Department of Health and Human Services designated to carry out the provisions of the Older Americans Act of 1965.

Administration for Children and Families An operating division of the Department of Health and Human Services that coordinates programs which promote the economic and social well-being of families, children, individuals, and communities.

adolescents and young adults Individuals between the ages of 15 and 24 years.

adult day care programs Daytime care provided to seniors who are unable to be left alone.

affective disorder Mental disorder characterized by a disturbance of mood, either depression or elation (mania); for example, bipolar disorder, major depression.

aftercare The continuing care provided to former drug abusers or drug dependent persons.

age pyramid A conceptual model that illustrates the age distribution of a population.

age-adjusted rates Rates used to make comparisons of relative risks across groups and over time when groups differ by age structure.

aged The state of being old.

ageism Prejudice and discrimination against the aged.

Agency for Healthcare Research and Quality (AHQR) An operating division of the Department of Health and Human Services that has the responsibility of overseeing health care research.

Agency for Toxic Substances and Disease Registry (ATSDR) An operating division of the Department of Health and Human Services created by Superfund legislation to prevent or mitigate adverse health effects and diminished quality of life resulting from exposure to hazardous substances in the environment.

agent (pathogenic agent) The cause of the disease or health problem; the factor that must be present in order for the disease to occur.

aging The physiological changes that occur normally in plants and animals as they grow older.

air pollution The contamination of the air by gases, liquids, or solids that interfere with the comfort, safety, or health of living organisms.

airborne disease A communicable disease that is transmitted through the air (e.g., influenza).

Alcoholics Anonymous (AA) A fellowship of recovering alcoholics who offer support to anyone who desires to stop drinking.

alcoholism A disease characterized by impaired control over drinking, preoccupation with drinking, and continued use of alcohol despite adverse consequences.

alien   A person born in and owing allegiance to a country other than the one in which he or she lives.

allied health care professionals   Health care workers who provide services that assist, facilitate, and complement the work of physicians and other health care specialists.

allopathic providers   Independent health care providers whose remedies for illnesses produce effects different from those of the disease. These people are doctors of medicine (MDs).

ambulatory care facilities   Free-standing health care facilities that provide a wide and rapidly expanding array of services.

American Cancer Society   A voluntary health agency dedicated to fighting cancer and educating the public about cancer.

American Health Security Act of 1993   The comprehensive health care reform introduced by then President Clinton, but never enacted.

amotivational syndrome   A pattern of behavior characterized by apathy, loss of effectiveness, and a more passive, introverted personality.

amphetamines   A group of synthetic drugs that act as stimulants.

amplitude   The loudness or intensity of sound measured in decibels.

anabolic drugs   Compounds, structurally similar to the male hormone testosterone, that increase protein synthesis.

analytical study   A type of epidemiological study aimed at testing hypotheses (e.g., case/control study, cohort study).

anthroponosis   A disease that infects only humans.

aquifers   Underground water reservoirs.

asbestos   A naturally occurring mineral fiber that has been identified as a class A carcinogen by the Environmental Protection Agency.

asbestosis   Acute or chronic lung disease caused by the deposit of asbestos fibers on lungs.

assisted-living facility   "A special combination of housing, personalized supportive services and health care designed to meet the needs—both scheduled and unscheduled—of those who need help with activities of daily living" (see Chapter 9, reference 34).

attack rate   A special incidence rate calculated for a particular population for a single disease outbreak and expressed as a percent.

automatic (passive) protection   The modification of a product or the environment in such a way as to reduce unintentional injuries.

bacteriological period   The period in public health history from 1875 to 1900 during which the causes of many bacterial diseases were discovered.

barbiturates   Depressant drugs based on the structure of barbituric acid; for example, phenobarbital.

behavioral health care services   The managed care term for mental health and substance abuse/dependence care services.

benzodiazapines   Nonbarbiturate depressant drugs; examples: Librium, Valium.

binge drinking   Consuming five or more alcoholic drinks in a row.

biogenic pollutants   Airborne biological organisms or their particles or gases or other toxic materials that can produce illness.

biological hazards   Living organisms (and viruses), or their products, that increase the risk of disease or death in humans.

biosphere   The zone of the earth where life is found, including parts of the atmosphere, earth, surface and ground water, and the oceans and their sediments.

bioterrorism   The threatened or intentional release of biological agents for the purpose of influencing the conduct of government or intimidating or coercing a civilian population to further political or social objectives.

bipolar disorder   An affective mental disorder characterized by distinct periods of elevated mood alternating with periods of depression.

birth rate   See *natality rate*.

blood alcohol concentration (BAC)   The percentage of concentration of alcohol in the blood; a BAC of 0.08% or greater is regarded as the legal level of intoxication in all states.

Bloodborne Pathogen Standard   A set of regulations promulgated by OSHA that sets forth the responsibilities of employers and employees with regard to precautions to be taken concerning bloodborne pathogens in the workplace.

bloodborne pathogens   Disease agents, such as HIV, that are transmissible in blood and other body fluids.

body mass index (BMI)   The ratio of weight (in kilograms) to height (in meters, squared). To calculate in pounds and inches, divide (weight in pounds)/2.20 by [(height in inches)/32.27]^2.

bottom-up community organization   Organization efforts that begin with those who live within the community affected.

brownfields   Abandoned gas stations, industrial plants, and commercial worksites, most of which are contaminated with hazardous chemicals.

Bureau of Alcohol, Tobacco, Firearms and Explosives (ATF) The federal agency in the Department of Justice that regulates alcohol, tobacco, firearms, and explosives.

Bureau of Indian Affairs (BIA) The original federal government agency charged with the responsibility for the welfare of Native Americans.

byssinosis Acute or chronic lung disease caused by the inhalation of cotton, flax, or hemp dusts; those affected include workers in cotton textile plants (sometimes called brown lung disease).

capitation See *prepaid health care*.

carcinogens Agents, usually chemicals, that cause cancer.

care-manager One who helps identify the health care needs of an individual but does not actually provide the health care services.

care-provider One who helps identify the health care needs of an individual and also personally performs the caregiving service.

carrier A person or animal that harbors a specific communicable disease agent in the absence of discernible clinical disease and serves as a potential source of infection to others.

carrying capacity The amount of resources (air, water, shelter, etc.) of a given environment necessary to support a certain-sized population.

case fatality rate (CFR) The percentage of cases of a particular disease that result in death.

case/control study (retrospective study) An epidemiological study that seeks to compare those diagnosed with a disease (cases) with those who do not have the disease (controls) for prior exposure to specific risk factors.

cases People afflicted with a disease.

categorical programs Those programs available only to people who can be categorized into a specific group based on disease, age, family means, geography, or other variables.

cause-specific mortality rate (CSMR) An expression of the death rate due to a particular disease; the CSMR is calculated by dividing the number of deaths due to a particular disease by the total population and multiplying by 100,000.

census The enumeration of the population of the United States that is conducted every ten years; begun in 1790.

Center for Mental Health Services (CMHS) The federal agency, housed within the Department of Health and Human Service's Substance Abuse and Mental Health Services Administration, whose mission it is to conduct research on the causes and treatments for mental disorders.

Centers for Disease Control and Prevention (CDC) One of the operating divisions of the Public Health Service; charged with the responsibility for surveillance and control of diseases and other health problems in the United States.

Centers for Medicare and Medicaid Services The federal agency responsible for overseeing Medicare, Medicaid, and the related quality assurance activities.

cerebrovascular disease (stroke) A disease in which the blood supply to the brain is interrupted.

certified safety professional (CSP) A health and safety professional, trained in industrial and workplace safety, who has met specific requirements for board certification.

chain of infection A model to conceptualize the transmission of a communicable disease from its source to a susceptible host.

chemical hazards Hazards caused by the mismanagement of chemicals.

chemical straitjacket The concept of a mental patient's behavior being restrained or subdued by a drug (chemical) such as Thorazine instead of by a physical straitjacket.

child abuse The intentional physical, emotional, verbal, or sexual mistreatment of a minor.

child maltreatment The act or failure to act by a parent, caretaker, or other person as defined under state law that results in physical abuse, neglect, medical neglect, sexual abuse, or emotional abuse, or an act or failure to act that presents an imminent risk of serious harm to the child.

child neglect The failure of a parent or guardian to care for or otherwise provide the necessary subsistence for a child.

childhood diseases Infectious diseases that normally affect people in their childhood (e.g., measles, mumps, rubella, and pertussis).

children Persons between 1 and 14 years of age.

chiropractor A nonallopathic, independent health care provider who treats health problems by adjusting the spinal column.

chlorofluorocarbons (CFCs) A family of chemical agents used in industry for such items as propellants, refrigeration, solvent cleaning, and insulation.

chlorpromazine The first and most famous antipsychotic drug introduced in 1954 under the brand name Thorazine.

chronic disease A disease or health condition that lasts longer than three months, sometimes for the remainder of one's life.

citizen initiated community organization See *bottom-up community organization*.

Clean Air Act (CAA) (P.L. 88-206) A 1963 law that provided the federal government with authority to address interstate air pollution problems.

Clean Water Act (CWA) (P.L. 92-500) A 1972 law that provided the federal government with authority to ensure water quality by controlling water pollution; first known as Federal Water Pollution Control Act Amendments.

club drugs A general term for those illicit drugs, primarily synthetic, that are most commonly encountered at night clubs and "raves." Examples include MDMA, LSD, GHB, GBL, PCP, ketamine, Rohypnol, and methamphetamines.

coal workers' pneumoconiosis (CWP) Acute and chronic lung disease caused by the inhalation of coal dust (sometimes called black lung disease).

coalition "Formal, long-term alliance among a group of individuals representing diverse organizations, factors, or constituencies within the community who agree to work together to achieve a common goal" (see Chapter 5, reference 15).

cocaine The psychoactive ingredient in the leaves of the coca plant, *Erythoxolyn coca*.

cognitive-behavioral therapy Treatment based on learning theory in which a patient learns adaptive skills through rewards and satisfaction.

cohort A group of people who share some important demographic characteristic—year of birth, for example.

cohort study (prospective study) An epidemiological study in which a cohort is selected, classified on the basis of exposure to one or more specific risk factors, and observed into the future to determine the rates at which disease develops in each class.

co-insurance Portion of insurance company's approved amounts for covered services that the beneficiary is responsible for paying.

combustion (incineration) The burning of solid wastes.

combustion by-products Gases and other particles generated by burning.

communicable disease (infectious disease) An illness due to a specific communicable agent or its toxic products, which arises through transmission of that agent or its products from an infected person, animal, or inanimate reservoir to a susceptible host.

communicable disease model A visual representation of the interrelationships of agent, host, and environment—the three entities necessary for communicable disease transmission.

community A group of people who have common characteristics; communities can be defined by location, race, ethnicity, age, occupation, interest in particular problems or outcomes, or other common bonds.

community analysis A process by which community needs are identified.

community building "[A]n orientation to community that is strength based rather than need based and stresses the identification, nurturing, and celebration of community assets" (see Chapter 5, reference 3).

community capacity "Community characteristics affecting its ability to identify, mobilize, and address problems" (see Chapter 5, reference 5).

community diagnosis See *community analysis*.

community health The health status of a defined group of people and the actions and conditions, both private and public (government), to promote, protect and preserve their health.

community mental health centers Local agencies, initially built with federal funding, that provide the community members with mental health services.

community organizing "A process through which communities are helped to identify common problems or goals, mobilize resources, and in other ways develop and implement strategies for reaching their goals they have collectively set" (see Chapter 1, reference 12).

community participation "A process of involving people in the institutions or decisions that affect their lives" (see Chapter 5, reference 6).

Community Support Program A federal program that offers financial incentives to communities to develop a social support system for the mentally ill.

complementary/alternative medicine (CAM) Diagnosis, treatment, and/or prevention that complements mainstream medicine by contributing to a common whole, by satisfying a demand not met by orthodoxy or by diversifying the conceptual framework of medicine (see Chapter 13, reference 29).

composting The natural, aerobic biodegradation of organic plant and animal matter to compost.

Comprehensive Drug Abuse Control Act of 1970 (Controlled Substances Act) The central piece of legislation that regulates controlled substances (drugs subject to abuse).

Comprehensive Environmental Response, Compensation, and Liability Act (CERCLA) (Superfund) A 1980 law created by the federal government primarily to clean up abandoned hazardous waste sites.

congregate meal programs Community-sponsored nutrition programs that provide meals at a central site, such as a senior center.

continuing care Long-term care for chronic health problems, usually including personal care.

continuing-care retirement communities (CCRCs) Planned communities for elders that guarantee a lifelong residence and health care.

controlled substances Drugs regulated by the Comprehensive Drug Abuse Control Act of 1970, including all illegal drugs and many legal drugs that can produce dependence.

coordinated school health program "An organized set of policies, procedures, and activities designed to protect and promote the health and well-being of students and staff which has traditionally included health services, healthful school environment, and health education. It should also include, but not be limited to, guidance and counseling, physical education, food service, social work, psychological services, and employee health promotion" (see Chapter 6, reference 3).

co-payment A negotiated set amount the insured will pay for a certain service after paying the deductible.

core functions of public health Health assessment, policy development, and health assurance.

coronary heart disease (CHD) A noncommunicable disease characterized by damage to the coronary arteries, which supply blood to the heart.

cosmic radiation That radiation which comes from outer space and the sun.

criteria pollutants The most pervasive air pollutants in the United States.

crude birth rate An expression of the number of live births per unit of population in a given period of time. For example, the crude birth rate in the United States in 1999 was 14.5 births per 1,000 population.

crude death rate (CDR) An expression of the total number of deaths (from all causes) per unit of population in a given period of time. For example, the crude death rate in the United States in 1999 was 877.0 per 100,000 population.

crude rate A rate in which the denominator includes the total population.

cultural and linguistic competency A set of congruent behaviors, attitudes, and policies that come together in a system, agency, or among professionals that enables effective work in cross-cultural situations.

culturally sensitive Having respect for cultures other than one's own.

curriculum Written plan for instruction.

cycles per second (cps) A measure of sound frequency.

death rate See *mortality rate*.

decibels (dB) A measure of sound amplitude.

deductible The amount of expense that the beneficiary must incur before the insurance company begins to pay for covered services.

deinstitutionalization The process of discharging, on a large scale, patients from state mental hospitals to less restrictive community settings.

demography (demographers) The study of a population and those variables bringing about change in that population.

Department of Health and Human Services (HHS) The largest federal department in the United States government, formed in 1980 and headed by a secretary who is a member of the president's cabinet.

depressant A psychoactive drug that slows down the central nervous system.

desalinization The process used to remove salt from salt water.

descriptive study An epidemiological study that describes an epidemic with respect to person, place, and time.

designer drugs Mind-altering drugs, synthesized in clandestine laboratories, that are similar to but structurally different from known controlled substances.

diagnosis-related groups (DRGs) A procedure used to classify the health problems of all Medicare patients when they are admitted to a hospital.

direct transmission The immediate transfer of an infectious agent by direct contact between infected and susceptible individuals.

disability-adjusted life expectancy (DALE) The number of healthy years of life that can be expected, on average, in a given population.

disability-adjusted life years (DALYs) A measure for the burden of disease that takes into account premature death and years lived with disability of specified severity and duration. One DALY is one lost year of healthy life.

disabling injury An injury causing any restriction of normal activity beyond the day of the injury's occurrence.

diseases of adaptation Diseases that result from chronic exposure to excess levels of stressors that elicit the General Adaptation Syndrome.

disinfection The killing of communicable disease agents outside the host, on counter tops, for example.

drug A substance other than food or vitamins that, upon entering the body in small amounts, alters one's physical, mental, or emotional state.

drug abuse Use of a drug despite the knowledge that continued use is detrimental to one's health or well-being.

drug abuse education Providing information about the dangers of drug abuse, changing attitudes and beliefs about drugs, providing skills necessary to abstain from drugs, and ultimately changing drug abuse behavior.

drug (chemical) dependence A psychological and sometimes physical state characterized by a craving for a drug.

Drug Enforcement Administration (DEA) The federal government's lead agency with the primary responsibility for enforcing the Nation's drug laws, including the Controlled Substances Act of 1970.

drug misuse Inappropriate use of prescription or nonprescription drugs.

drug use A non-evaluative term referring to drug taking behavior in general; any drug-taking behavior.

Earth Day Annual public observance for concerns about the environment; the first was held April 22, 1970.

ecology Interrelationship between organisms and their environment.

elderhostel Education programs specifically for seniors, held on college campuses.

elderly (or elder) Individuals over 65 years of age.

elderly support ratio The support ratio that includes only the elderly.

electroconvulsive therapy (ECT) A method of treatment for mental disorders involving the administration of electric current to induce a coma or convulsions.

employee assistance program (EAP) That aspect of a workplace drug program devoted to assisting employees in recovering from their alcohol or other drug problems.

empowered community "One in which individuals and organizations apply their skills and resources in collective efforts to meet their respective needs" (see Chapter 5, reference 7).

end-of-life practice Health care services provided to individuals shortly before death.

endemic disease A disease that occurs regularly in a population as a matter of course.

environment All the external conditions, circumstances, and influences surrounding and affecting the growth and development of an organism or community of organisms.

environmental hazards Factors or conditions in the environment that increase the risk of disease or death in humans.

environmental health The study and management of environmental conditions that affect the health and well-being of humans.

Environmental Protection Agency (EPA) The federal agency primarily responsible for setting, maintaining, and enforcing environmental standards.

environmental sanitation The practice of establishing and maintaining healthy or hygienic conditions in the environment.

environmental tobacco smoke (ETS) Tobacco smoke in the ambient air.

epidemic An unexpectedly large number of cases of disease in a particular population for a particular time period.

epidemic curve A graphic display of the cases of disease according to the time or date of onset of symptoms.

epidemiologist One who practices epidemiology.

epidemiology The study of the distribution and determinants of diseases and injuries in human populations.

equilibrium phase Last phase of the population growth S-curve, when the birth and death rates are equal.

eradication The complete elimination or uprooting of a disease (e.g., smallpox eradication).

etiology The cause of a disease (e.g., the etiology of mumps is the mumps virus).

evaluation Determining the value or worth of the objective of interest.

evidence-based practices Ways of delivering services to people using scientific evidence that shows that the services actually work.

exclusion A condition that is written into a health insurance policy indicating what is not covered by the policy.

exclusive provider organization (EPO) Similar to a preferred provider organization but with fewer providers and stronger financial incentives. See *preferred provider organization (PPO)*.

experimental study An epidemiological study carried out under controlled conditions, usually to determine the effectiveness of a vaccine, therapeutic drug, or surgical technique.

exponential phase Middle phase of the population growth S-curve, when the birth rate is greater than the death rate.

Family and Medical Leave Act Federal legislation that provides up to a 12-week unpaid leave to men and women after the birth of a child, an adoption, or an event of illness in the immediate family.

family planning The process of determining the preferred number and spacing of children in one's family and choosing the appropriate means to achieve this preference.

family violence The use of physical force by one family member against another, with the intent to hurt, injure, or cause death.

fatal injury An injury that results in one or more deaths.

fatality rate See *mortality rate*.

Federal Emergency Response Agency (FEMA) The nation's official emergency response agency.

Federal Water Pollution Control Act Amendments See *Clean Water Act*.

fee-for-service A method of paying for health care in which a bill (fee) is paid after the care (service) is rendered.

fertility rate The number of live births per 1,000 women of childbearing age (15–44 years).

fetal alcohol syndrome (FAS) A group of abnormalities that may include growth retardation, abnormal appearance of face and head, and deficits of central nervous system function including mental retardation in babies born to mothers who have consumed heavy amounts of alcohol during their pregnancies.

fetal deaths Deaths in utero with a gestational age of at least 20 weeks.

fight or flight reaction An alarm reaction that prepares one physiologically for sudden action (heart rate, blood pressure, and respiration increase).

fixed indemnity The maximum amount an insurer will pay for a certain service.

Food and Drug Administration (FDA) An operating division of the Department of Health and Human Services that regulates all food, over-the-counter and prescription drugs, medical devices, and cosmetics.

foodborne disease A disease transmitted through the contamination of food.

foodborne disease outbreak (FBDO) The occurrence of two or more cases of a similar illness resulting from the ingestion of food.

formaldehyde (CH$_2$O) A water-soluble gas used in aqueous solutions in hundreds of consumer products.

formative evaluation The evaluation that is conducted during the planning and implementing processes to improve or refine a program.

full-service hospitals Hospitals that offer services in all or most of the levels of care defined by the spectrum of health care.

functional limitations Difficulty in performing personal care and home management tasks.

gag rule Regulations that bar physicians and nurses in clinics receiving federal funds from counseling clients about abortions.

gatekeepers Those who control, both formally and informally, the political climate of the community.

General Adaptation Syndrome (GAS) The complex physiological responses resulting from exposure to stressors that can in time result in health deficits.

geriatrics The branch of medicine that deals with the structural changes, physiology, diseases, and hygiene of old age.

gerontology The study of aging, from the broadest perspective.

global warming The gradual increase in the earth's surface temperature.

government hospital A hospital that is supported and managed by governmental jurisdictions.

governmental health agency (or official health agencies) Health agencies that are part of the governmental structure (federal, state, or local) and that are funded primarily by tax dollars.

grass-roots community organizing A process that begins with those affected by the problem/concern.

greenhouse gases Atmosphere gases, principally carbon dioxide, the CFCs, methane, and nitrous oxide, that are transparent to visible light but absorb infrared radiation (heat).

groundwater Water located under the surface of the ground.

group model HMO An HMO that contracts with a multispecialty group practice.

hallucinogens Drugs that produce profound distortions of the senses.

hard-to-reach population Those in a priority population that are not easily reached by normal programming efforts.

hazard An unsafe act or condition.

hazardous waste "A solid waste or combination of solid wastes which—because of its quantity, concentration, or physical, chemical, or infectious characteristics—may (A) cause or significantly contribute to an increase in mortality or an increase in serious irreversible, or incapacitating reversible, illness; or (B) pose a substantial present or potential hazard to human health or the environment when improperly treated, stored, transported, or disposed of, or otherwise managed." (*Note:* This definition was taken from the Resource Conservation and Recovery Act of 1976.)

health A dynamic state or condition that is multidimensional in nature and results from a person's adaptations to his or her environment; it is a resource for living and exists in varying degrees.

health education "Any combination of planned learning experiences based on sound theories that provide individuals, groups, and communities the opportunity to acquire information and the skills to make quality health decisions" (see Chapter 5, reference 19).

health maintenance organizations (HMOs) Groups that supply prepaid comprehensive health care with an emphasis on prevention.

health physicist A safety professional with responsibility for monitoring radiation within a plant environment, developing instrumentation for that purpose, and developing plans for coping with radiation accidents.

health promotion "Any planned combination of educational, political, environmental, regulatory, or organizational mechanisms that support actions and conditions of living conducive to the health of individuals, groups, and communities" (see Chapter 5, reference 19).

health promotion program (HPP) A program aimed at improving the health of the priority population through changes in behavior and lifestyle.

health resources development period The period in public health history from 1900 to 1960; a time of great growth in health care facilities.

Health Resources and Services Administration (HRSA) An operating division of the Department of Health and Human Services established in 1982 to improve the nation's health resources and services and their distribution to underserved populations.

Healthy People 2010 The third set of health goals and objectives for the United States that defines the nation's health agenda and guides its health policy.

healthy school environment "The promotion, maintenance, and utilization of safe and wholesome surroundings, organization of day-by-day experiences and planned learning procedures to influence favorable emotional, physical and social health" (see Chapter 6, reference 26).

herbicide A pesticide designed specifically to kill plants.

herd immunity The resistance of a population to the spread of an infectious agent based on the immunity of a high portion of individuals.

home health care Care that is provided in the patient's residence for the purpose of promoting, maintaining, or restoring health.

home health care services Health care services provided in the patient's place of residence (home or apartment).

homebound A person unable to leave home for normal activities such as shopping, meals, or other activities.

hospice care A program of palliative and support care services providing physical, psychological, social, and spiritual care for dying persons, their families, and other loved ones by a hospice worker (see Chapter 13, reference 14).

Hospital Survey and Construction Act of 1946 (Hill-Burton Act) Federal legislation that provided substantial funds for hospital construction.

host A person or other living animal that affords subsistence or lodgment to a communicable agent under natural conditions.

hypercholesterolemia High levels of cholesterol in the blood.

hypertension A chronic condition characterized by a resting blood pressure reading of 140/90 mm of mercury or higher.

illegal alien An individual who entered this country without permission.

illicit (illegal) drugs Drugs that cannot be legally manufactured, distributed, bought, or sold, and that lack recognized medical value.

immigrant Individuals who migrate to this country from another country for the purpose of seeking permanent residence.

impairments Defects in the functioning of one's sense organs or limitations in one's mobility or range of motion.

implementation Putting a planned program into action.

incidence rate The number of new cases of a disease in a population-at-risk during a particular period of time, divided by the total number in that same population.

incubation period The period of time between exposure to an infectious agent and the onset of symptoms.

independent practice association (IPA) model HMO An HMO in which individual physicians contract with the HMO to provide care for a certain number of enrollees.

independent providers Health care professionals with the education and legal authority to treat any health problem.

Indian Health Service (IHS) An operating division of the Department of Health and Human Services whose goal is to raise the health status of the American Indian and Alaska Native to the highest possible level by providing a comprehensive health services delivery system.

indirect transmission Communicable disease transmission involving an intermediate step; for example, airborne, vehicleborne, or vectorborne transmission.

indoor air pollution The buildup of undesirable gases and particles in the air inside a building.

industrial hygienist A health professional concerned with health hazards in the workplace, including such things as problems with ventilation, noise, and lighting; also responsible for measuring air quality and recommending plans for improving the healthiness of work environments.

infant death (infant mortality) Death of a child under one year of age.

infant mortality rate The number of deaths of children under one year of age per 1,000 live births.

infection The lodgment and growth of a virus or microorganism in a host organism.

infectious disease See *communicable disease*.

infectivity The ability of a pathogen to lodge and grow in a host.

informal caregiver One who provides unpaid care or assistance to one who has some physical, mental, emotional, or financial need that limits his or her independence.

inhalants Breathable substances that produce mind-altering effects; for example, glue.

injury Physical harm or damage to the body resulting from an exchange, usually acute, of mechanical, chemical, thermal, or other environmental energy that exceeds the body's tolerance.

injury prevention (control) An organized effort to prevent injuries or to minimize their severity.

injury prevention education The process of changing people's health-directed behavior in such a way as to reduce unintentional injuries.

insecticides Pesticides designed specifically to kill insects.

Instrumental Activities of Daily Living (IADL) Measure of more complex tasks such as handling personal finances, preparing meals, shopping, doing homework, traveling, using the telephone, and taking medications.

intensity Cardiovascular work load measured by heart rate.

intentional injury An injury that is judged to have been purposely inflicted, either by the victim or another.

intern A first-year resident.

internal radiation Radiation in the human body that occurs as a result of ingesting food or inhaling air.

intervention An activity or activities designed to create change in people.

intimate partner violence (IPV) Rape, physical assault, or stalking perpetrated by current or former dates, spouses, or cohabiting partners, with cohabiting meaning living together at least some of the time as a couple.

isolation The separation of infected persons from those who are susceptible.

Joint Commission on Accreditation of Healthcare Organizations (JCAHO) The predominant organization responsible for accrediting health care facilities.

labor-force support ratio A ratio of the total number of those individuals who are not working (regardless of age) to the number of those who are.

lag phase Initial phase of the population growth S-curve, when growth is slow.

law enforcement The application of federal, state, and local laws to arrest, jail, bring to trial, and sentence those who break drug laws or break laws because of drug use.

leachates Liquids created when water mixes with wastes and removes soluble constituents from them by percolation.

lead A naturally occurring mineral element found throughout the environment and produced in large quantities for industrial products.

licensed practical nurse (LPN) Those prepared in one- to two-year programs to provide nontechnical bedside nursing care under the supervision of physicians or registered nurses.

life expectancy The average number of years a person from a specific cohort is projected to live from a given point in time.

limited (restricted) care providers Health care providers who provide care for a specific part of the body; for example, dentists.

limited-service hospitals Hospitals that offer only the specific services needed by the population served.

litigation The process of seeking justice for injury through courts.

lobotomy Surgical severance of nerve fibers of the brain by incision.

long-term care Different kinds of help that people with chronic illnesses, disabilities, or other conditions need to deal with the circumstances that limit them physically or mentally.

low-birth-weight infant An infant that weighs less than 2,500 grams, or 5.5 pounds, at birth.

Lyme disease A systematic, bacterial, tickborne disease with symptoms that include dermatologic, arthritic, neurologic, and cardiac abnormalities.

mainstream tobacco smoke The smoke of burning tobacco inhaled and exhaled by the smoker.

major depression An affective disorder characterized by a dysphoric mood, usually depression, or loss of interest or pleasure in almost all usual activities or pastimes.

majority Those with characteristics that are found in over 50% of a population.

malignant neoplasm Uncontrolled new tissue growth resulting from cells that have lost control over their growth and division.

managed behavioral health care organizations (MBHOs) Managed care providers who specialize in providing mental health care services.

managed care Health plans that integrate the financing and delivery of health care services to covered individuals by means of arrangements with selected providers to furnish comprehensive services to members; explicit criteria for the selection of health care providers; significant financial incentives for members to use providers and procedures associated with the plan; and formal programs for quality assurance and utilization review.

marijuana Dried plant parts of *Cannabis sativa*.

maternal, infant, and child health The health of women of childbearing age from pre-pregnancy, through pregnancy, labor and delivery, and the postpartum period and the health of the child prior to birth through adolescence.

maternal mortality The death of a woman while pregnant or within 42 days of termination of pregnancy, irrespective of the duration and the site of the pregnancy, from any cause related to or aggravated by the pregnancy or its management but not from accidental or incidental causes.

maternal mortality rate Number of mothers dying per 100,000 live births in a given year.

Meals on Wheels program A community-supported nutrition program in which prepared meals are delivered to elders in their homes, usually by volunteers.

median age The age at which half of the population is older and half is younger.

Medicaid A national health insurance program for the poor.

Medicare A national health insurance program for people 65 years of age and older, certain younger disabled people, and people with permanent kidney failure.

Medigap Private health insurance to supplement Medicare benefits—that is, to fill in the gaps of Medicare.

mental disorder Deficiency in one's psychological resources for dealing with everyday life, usually characterized by distress or impairment of one or more areas of functioning.

mental health Emotional and social well-being, including one's psychological resources for dealing with the day-to-day problems of life.

mental hygiene movement A movement by those who believed that mental illness could be cured if identified and treated at an early stage; proponents were Adolph Meyer and Clifford Beers.

mental illness A collective term for all mental disorders.

Mental Retardation Facilities and Community Mental Health Centers (CMHC) Act of 1963 (Community Mental Health Act of 1963) A law that provided federal funds directly to communities to assist in the building and funding of community mental health centers.

metastasis The spread of a disease, such as cancer, by the transfer of cells by means of the blood or lymphatics.

methamphetamine The amphetamine drug most widely abused.

methaqualone An illicit depressant drug.

methcathinone (cat) An illicit, synthetic drug, similar to the amphetamines, that first appeared in the United States in 1991.

migration Movement of people from one country to another.

minority groups Subgroups of the population that consist of less than 50% of the population.

minority health The morbidity and mortality of American Indians/Alaska Natives, Asian Americans and Pacific Islanders, black Americans, and Americans of Hispanic origin in the United States.

mixed model HMO A hybrid form of a health maintenance organization.

model for unintentional injuries The public health triangle (host, agent, and environment) modified to indicate energy as the causative agent of injuries.

modern era of public health The era of American public health that began in 1850 and continues today.

modifiable risk factor Factors contributing to the development of a noncommunicable disease that can be altered by modifying one's behavior or environment; for example, cigarette smoking is a modifiable risk factor for coronary heart disease.

moral treatment Treatment for mental illness in eighteenth and nineteenth centuries, based on belief that mental illness was caused by moral deterioration.

morbidity rate The rate of illness in a population.

mortality (fatality) rate The rate of deaths in a population.

multicausation disease model A visual representation of the host, together with various internal and external factors that promote and protect against disease.

municipal solid waste (MSW) Waste generated by individual households, businesses, and institutions located within municipalities.

narcotics Drugs similar to morphine that reduce pain and induce a stuporous state.

natality (birth) rate The rate of births in a population.

National Alliance for the Mentally Ill (NAMI) A national voluntary health agency that advocates for the mentally ill.

National Ambient Air Quality Standards (NAAQSs) Standards created by the EPA for allowable concentration levels of outdoor air pollutants.

National Electronic Telecommunications System (NETS) The electronic reporting system by which state health departments send health records to the Centers for Disease Control and Prevention (CDC).

National Institute of Mental Health (NIMH) The agency of the National Institutes of Health whose mission is to conduct research on the causes of and treatments for mental disorders.

National Institute for Occupational Safety and Health (NIOSH) A research body within the Centers for Disease Control and Prevention, Department of Health and Human Services, that is responsible for developing and recommending occupational safety and health standards.

National Institute on Drug Abuse (NIDA) The federal government's lead agency for drug abuse research; part of the National Institutes of Health.

National Institutes of Health (NIH) The research division of the Department of Health and Human Services. It is part of the Public Health Service.

National Mental Health Association (NMHA) A national voluntary health association that advocates for mental health and for those with mental illnesses; it has 600 affiliates in 43 states.

natural hazards Conditions of nature that increase the probability of disease, injury, or death of humans.

needs assessment The process of collecting and analyzing information to develop an understanding of the issues, resources, and constraints of the priority population, as related to the development of health promotion programs.

neonatal deaths (neonatal mortality) Deaths occurring during the first 28 days after birth.

neonatologist A medical doctor who specializes in the care of newborns from birth to two months of age.

net migration The population gain or loss resulting from migration.

network model HMO An HMO that contracts with more than one medical group practice.

neuroleptic drug A drug that reduces nervous activity; another term for antipsychotic drug.

noise pollution Excessive sound; unwanted sound.

nonallopathic providers Independent providers who provide nontraditional forms of health care.

noncommunicable disease (noninfectious disease) A disease not caused by a communicable agent, and that thus cannot be transmitted from infected host to susceptible host.

nonphysician practitioners (NPPs) Clinical professionals who practice in many of the areas similar to those in which physicians practice, but who do not have an MD or DO degree (see Ch. 13, ref. 1).

nonpoint source pollution All pollution that occurs through the runoff, seepage, or falling of pollutants into the water.

nontarget organisms All other susceptible organisms in the environment, for which a pesticide was not intended.

notifiable diseases Infectious diseases for which health officials request or require reporting for public health reasons.

occupational disease Any abnormal condition or disorder, other than one resulting from an occupational injury, caused by an exposure to environmental factors associated with employment.

occupational health nurse (OHN) A registered nurse whose primary responsibilities include prevention of illness and promotion of health in the workplace.

occupational injury An injury that results from exposure to a single incident in the work environment (e.g., cut, fracture, sprain, amputation).

occupational physician (OP) or occupational medical practitioner (OMP) A medical practitioner (doctor) whose primary concern is preventive medicine in the workplace.

Occupational Safety and Health Act of 1970 (OSHAct) Comprehensive federal legislation aimed at assuring safe and healthful working conditions for working men and women.

Occupational Safety and Health Administration (OSHA) The federal agency located within the Department of Labor and created by the OSHAct that is charged with the responsibility of administering the provisions of the OSHAct.

odds ratio A probability statement about the association between a particular disease and a specific risk factor, often the outcome of a retrospective (case/control) study.

Office of National Drug Control Policy (ONDCP) The headquarters of America's drug control effort, located in the executive branch of the federal government, and headed by a director appointed by the President.

official health agency See *governmental health agency*.

old Those 65 years of age and older.

old old Those 75 to 84 years of age.

Older Americans Act of 1965 Federal legislation to improve the lives of elders.

oldest old Those 85 years of age and older.

operationalize (operational definition) To provide working definitions.

osteopathic providers Independent health care providers whose remedies emphasize the interrelationships of the body's systems in prevention, diagnosis, and treatment.

over-the-counter (OTC) drugs (nonprescription drugs) Drugs (except tobacco and alcohol) that can be legally purchased without a physician's prescription (e.g., aspirin).

ownership A feeling that one has a stake in or "owns" the object of interest.

ozone layer Ozone gas (O_3) found in the stratosphere.

pandemic An outbreak of disease over a wide geographical area, such as a continent.

parity The concept of equality in health care coverage for people with mental illness and those with other medical illnesses or injuries.

passive smoking The inhalation of environmental tobacco smoke by nonsmokers.

pathogenicity The capability of a communicable agent to cause disease in a susceptible host.

peer counseling programs School-based drug education programs in which students discuss alcohol and other drug-related problems with other students.

pest Any organism—multicelled animal or plant, or microbe—that has an adverse effect on human interests.

pesticides Synthetic chemicals developed and manufactured for the purpose of killing pests.

phasing in Implementation of an intervention with small groups prior to its implementation with the entire priority population.

philanthropic foundation An endowed institution that donates money for the good of humankind.

photochemical smog A secondary air pollutant created when primary pollutants react with oxygen and sunlight.

physical dependence Drug dependence in which discontinued use results in the onset of physical illness.

physician-hospital organizations (PHOs) Various agreements between physicians and hospitals to form units to negotiate with insurers as managed care organizations.

pilot test Presentation of the intervention to just a few individuals, who are either from the intended priority population or from a very similar population.

placebo A blank treatment (e.g., a sugar pill).

pneumoconiosis Fibrotic lung disease caused by the inhalation of dusts, especial mineral dusts.

point-of-service (POS) option An option of a health maintenance organization plan that allows enrollees to be at least partially reimbursed for selecting a health care provider outside the plan.

point source epidemic curve An epidemic curve depicting a distribution of cases that can all be traced to a single source of exposure.

point source pollution Pollution that can be traced to a single identifiable source.

Pollutant Standard Index (PSI) A scale developed by the EPA which relates air pollutant concentrations to health effects.

polydrug use Concurrent use of multiple drugs.

population health The health status of people who are not organized and have no identity as a group or locality and the actions and conditions to promote, protect, and preserve their health.

population-at-risk Those in the population who are susceptible to a particular disease or condition.

population-based public health practice Incorporates interventions aimed at disease prevention and health promotion, specific protection, and case findings.

postneonatal deaths (postneonatal mortality)
Deaths that occur between 28 days and 365 days after birth.

pre-existing condition A medical condition that had been diagnosed or treated usually within six months before the date a health insurance policy goes into effect.

preferred provider organization (PPO) An organization that buys fixed-rate (discount) health services from providers and sells them (via premiums) to consumers.

premature infant One born following a gestation period of 38 weeks or less, or one born at a low birth weight.

prenatal health care (prenatal care) One of the fundamentals of a safe motherhood program, which includes three major components: risk assessment, treatment for medical conditions or risk reduction, and education. Prenatal health care should begin before pregnancy when a couple is considering having a child and continue throughout pregnancy.

prepaid health care A method of paying for covered health care services on a per-person premium basis for a specific period of time prior to service being rendered. Also referred to as capitation.

pre-placement examination A physical examination of a newly hired or transferred worker to determine medical suitability for placement in a specific position.

prevalence rate The number of new and old cases of a disease in a population in a given period of time, divided by the total number of that population.

prevention The planning for and taking of action to forestall the onset of a disease or other health problem before the occurrence of undesirable health events.

preventive care Care given to healthy people to keep them healthy.

priority population (audience) Those whom a program is intended to serve.

primary medical care The provision of integrated, accessible health care services by clinicians who are accountable for addressing a large majority of personal health care needs, developing a sustained partnership with patients, and practicing in the context of family and community.

primary prevention Preventive measures that forestall the onset of illness or injury during the prepathogenesis period.

private (proprietary) hospitals For-profit hospitals.

pro-choice A medical/ethical position that holds that women have a right to reproductive freedom.

pro-life A medical/ethical position that holds that performing an abortion is an act of murder.

problem drinker One for whom alcohol consumption results in personal, economic, medical, social, or any other type of problem.

professional nurse A registered nurse holding a bachelor of science degree in nursing (BSN).

program planning A process by which an intervention is planned to help meet the needs of a priority population.

Program Support Center An operating division of HHS established in 1995 to provide cost effective, efficient, and responsive administrative support to the HHS and other federal agencies.

propagated epidemic curve An epidemic curve depicting a distribution of cases traceable to multiple sources of exposure over time.

proportionate mortality ratio (PMR) The percentage of overall mortality in a population that can be assigned to a particular cause or disease.

prospective pricing system (PPS) One in which providers are paid predetermined amounts of money per procedure for services provided.

prospective study An epidemiological study that begins in the present and continues into the future for the purpose of observing the development of disease (e.g., cohort study).

providers Those individuals educated to provide health services, such as physicians, dentists, nurses, etc.

psychoactive drugs Mind-altering drugs; drugs that affect the central nervous system.

psychological dependence A psychological state characterized by an overwhelming desire to continue use of a drug.

psychopharmacological therapy Treatment for mental illness that involves medications.

psychotherapy A treatment methodology based on the Freudian concept of emotional release (catharsis), sexual conflict resolution, and subconscious drives.

public health The health status of a defined group of people and the governmental actions and conditions to promote, protect, and preserve their health.

public health professional A health care worker who works in a public health organization.

Public Health Service (PHS) An agency in the Department of Health and Human Services (HHS) that is comprised of eight of the 12 operating divisions of HHS.

public hospitals Hospitals that are supported and managed by governmental jurisdictions.

public policy The guiding principles and courses of action pursued by governments to solve practical problems affecting society.

quarantine Limitation of freedom of movement of those who have been exposed to a disease and may be incubating it.

quasi-governmental health organizations Organizations that have some responsibilities assigned by the government but operate more like voluntary agencies; for example, the American Red Cross.

radiation Energy released when an atom is split or naturally decays from a less stable to a more stable form.

radon A naturally occurring radioactive gas that cannot be seen, smelled, or tasted; it is formed by the radioactive decay of uranium-238.

rate The number of events (cases of disease) that occur in a given period of time.

recycling The collection and reprocessing of a resource after use so it can be reused for the same or another purpose.

reform phase of public health The period of public health from 1900 to 1920, characterized by social movements to improve health conditions in cities and in the workplace.

refugee A person who flees one area or country to seek shelter or protection from danger in another.

registered nurse (RN) An associate or baccalaureate degree—prepared nurse who has passed the state licensing examination.

regulation The enactment and enforcement of laws to control conduct.

rehabilitation center A facility in which restorative care is provided following injury, disease, or surgery.

relative risk A statement of the relationship between the risk of acquiring a disease when a specific risk factor is present and the risk of acquiring that same disease when the risk factor is not present.

resident A physician who is training in a specialty.

residues and wastes Unwanted by-products of human activities.

Resource Conservation and Recovery Act of 1976 (RCRA) A federal law that sets forth guidelines for the proper handling and disposal of solid and hazardous wastes.

respite care Planned short-term care, usually for the purpose of relieving a full-time informal caregiver.

restorative care Care provided to patients after a successful treatment or when the progress of a incurable disease has been arrested.

retirement communities Residential communities that have been specifically developed for those in their retirement years.

retrospective study An epidemiological study that looks into the past for clues to explain the present distribution of disease.

risk factors Factors that increase the probability of disease, injury, or death.

Roe v. Wade A 1973 Supreme Court decision that made it unconstitutional for state laws to prohibit abortions.

Rohypnol (flunitrazepam) A depressant in the benzodiazepine group that has achieved notoriety as a date rape drug.

rollover protective structures (ROPS) Factory-installed or retrofitted reinforced framework on a cab to protect the operator of a tractor in case of a rollover.

Safe Drinking Water Act (SDWA) A 1974 federal law that instructed the EPA to set maximum contaminant levels for specific pollutants in drinking water.

safety engineer A health and safety professional, sometimes with an engineering background, employed by a company for the purpose of reducing unintentional injuries in the workplace.

safety programs Those parts of the workplace health and safety program aimed at reducing unintentional injuries on the job.

sanitarians Environmental workers responsible for inspection of restaurants, retail food outlets, public housing, and other facilities to assure compliance with public health codes.

sanitary engineer Environmental worker responsible for management of wastewater and solid waste for a community.

sanitary landfill A waste disposal site located on land suited for this purpose and upon which solid waste is spread in thin layers and covered with a fresh layer of soil.

school health coordinator A professional at the district (or school) level responsible for management and coordination of all school health policies, activities, and resources (Chapter 6, reference 17).

school health council Individuals from a school or school district and its community who work together to provide advice on aspects of the school health program (Chapter 6, reference 8).

school health education "Planned, sequential, K–12 curriculum that addresses the physical, mental, emotional and social dimensions of health. The curriculum is designed to motivate and assist students to maintain and improve their health, prevent disease, and reduce health-related risk behaviors" (Chapter 6, reference 20).

school health policies Written statements that describe the nature and procedures of a school health program.

school health services Health services provided by school health workers to appraise, protect, and promote the health of students and school personnel.

scope Part of the curriculum that outlines what will be taught.

secondary medical care Specialized attention and ongoing management for common and less frequently encountered medical conditions, including support services for people with special challenges due to chronic or long-term conditions.

secondary prevention Preventive measures that lead to early diagnosis and prompt treatment of a disease or injury to limit disability and prevent more severe pathogenesis.

secondhand smoke Environmental tobacco smoke (ETS); tobacco smoke in the ambient air that can be inhaled.

secured landfill A double-lined landfill located above the flood plain and away from fault zones, equipped with monitoring pipes for seepage, used primarily for hazardous waste.

self-help support groups Groups of concerned citizens who are united by a shared interest, concern, or deficit not shared by other members of the community; Alcoholics Anonymous, for example.

self-insured organization One that pays the health care costs of its employees with the premiums collected from the employees and the contributions made by the employer.

senior centers Facilities where elders can congregate for fellowship, meals, education, and recreation.

septic tank A watertight concrete or fiberglass tank that holds sewage; one of two main parts of a septic system.

sequence Part of the curriculum that states in what order the content will be taught.

sick building syndrome A term to describe a situation in which the air quality in a building produces generalized signs and symptoms of ill health in the building's occupants.

sidestream tobacco smoke The smoke that comes off the end of burning tobacco products.

silicosis Acute or chronic lung disease caused by the inhalation of free crystalline silica; those affected include workers in mines, stone quarries, sand and gravel operations, and abrasive blasting operations.

sliding scale fee A fee based on ability to pay.

sludge A semi-solid mixture of solid waste that includes bacteria, viruses, organic matter, toxic metals, synthetic organic chemicals, and solid chemicals.

smokeless tobacco (spit tobacco) Snuff and chewing tobacco.

Social Security Administration (SSA) An independent federal agency that administers programs that provide financial support to special groups of Americans.

socioeconomic status A demographic term which takes into consideration the combination of social and economic factors.

solid waste Solid refuse from households, agriculture, and businesses, including garbage, yard waste, paper products, manure, excess stone generated from mining, and building material scraps.

solid waste management The collection, transportation, and disposal of solid waste.

sound-level meter Instrument used to measure sound.

source reduction A waste management approach entailing the reduction or elimination of use of materials that produce an accumulation of solid waste.

Special Supplemental Food Program for Women, Infants, and Children See *WIC*.

specialty hospital A hospital that provides mainly one type of medicine, is for-profit, and is owned at least in part by the physicians who practice in it.

specific rate A rate of a specific disease in a population or the rate of events in a specific population (e.g., cause-specific death rate, age-specific death rate).

spectrum of health care delivery The array of types of care—from preventive to continuing, or long-term, care. It comprises six levels of care.

spiritual era of public health A time during the Middle Ages when the causation of communicable disease was linked to spiritual forces.

staff model HMO A health maintenance organization that hires its own staff of health care providers.

standard of acceptability A comparative mandate, value, norm, or group.

State Children's Health Insurance Program (SCHIP) A title insurance program under the Social Security Act that provides health insurance to uninsured children.

stimulant A drug that increases the activity of the central nervous system; for example, methamphetamine.

student assistance programs (SAPs) School-based drug education programs to assist students who have alcohol or other drug problems.

Substance Abuse and Mental Health Services Administration (SAMHSA) An operating division of the Department of Health and Human Services whose stated mission is the reduction of the incidence and prevalence of alcohol and other drug abuse and mental disorders, the improvement of treatment outcomes, and the curtailment of the consequences of mental health problems for families and communities.

sudden infant death syndrome (SIDS) Sudden unanticipated death of an infant in whom, after examination, there is no recognized cause of death.

summative evaluation The evaluation that determines the impact of a program on the priority population.

Superfund legislation See *Comprehensive Environmental Response, Compensation, and Liability Act.*

Supplemental Security Program of the Social Security Administration that provides cash benefits to elderly, blind, and disabled Americans with minimal resources.

support ratio A ratio that compares the number of individuals whom society considers economically productive (the working population) to the number of those it considers economically unproductive (the nonworking or dependent population).

surface water Water that is found on the earth's surface (e.g., oceans, rivers, streams, ponds, lakes, etc.).

Survey of Occupational Injuries and Illnesses (SOII) An annual survey of injuries and illnesses from a large sample of U.S. employees (approximately 250,000) maintained by the Bureau of Labor Statistics in the Department of Labor.

Synar Amendment A federal law that requires states to set the minimum legal age for purchasing tobacco products at 18 years and that requires states to enforce this law.

synesthesia Impairment of mind (by hallucinogens) characterized by a sensation that senses are mixed (e.g., seeing sounds and hearing images).

tardive dyskinesia Irreversible, involuntary, and abnormal movements of the tongue, mouth, arms, and legs which can result from long-term use of certain antipsychotic drugs such as chlorpromazine.

target organism (target pest) The organism for which a pesticide is applied.

terrestrial radiation Radiation that comes from radioactive minerals within the earth.

tertiary medical care Specialized and technologically sophisticated medical and surgical care for those with unusual or complex conditions (generally no more than a few percent of the need in any service category).

tertiary prevention Measures aimed at rehabilitation following significant pathogenesis.

thermal inversion Condition that occurs when warm air traps cooler air at the surface of the earth.

third-party payment system A health insurance term indicating that bills will be paid by the insurer (the government or private insurance company) and not the patient (first party) or the health care provider (the second party).

Thorazine See *chlorpromazine.*

Title X A portion of the Public Health Service Act of 1970 that provides funds for family planning services for low-income people.

tolerance Physiological and enzymatic adjustments that occur in response to the chronic presence of drugs, reflected in the need for ever-increasing doses to achieve a previous level of effect.

top-down funding A method of funding in which funds are transmitted from the federal or state government to the local level.

total support ratio The support ratio that includes both youth and elderly.

transinstitutionalization The process by which patients from one type of public institution, a mental hospital for example, end up in a different institution, such as a nursing home or jail, because of changes in federal policy.

treatment An activity or activities designed to create change in people.

ultraviolet (UV) radiation Radiation energy with wavelengths ranging from 0 to 400 nm.

unintentional injury An injury judged to have occurred without anyone intending that harm be done.

unmodifiable risk factors Factors contributing to the development of a noncommunicable disease that cannot be altered by modifying one's behavior or environment.

unsafe act Any behavior that would increase the probability of an injury occurring.

unsafe condition Any environmental factor or set of factors (physical or social) that would increase the probability of an injury occurring.

urbanization The process by which people come together to live in cities.

U.S. Census The enumeration of the population of the United States that is conducted every 10 years; begun in 1790.

utilization review or utilization management The analysis of provided health care for its appropriateness by someone other than the patient and provider.

vector A living organism, usually an arthropod, that can transmit a communicable disease agent to a susceptible host (e.g., mosquitoes, ticks, lice, fleas).

vectorborne disease A communicable disease transmitted by insects or other arthropods; for example, St. Louis encephalitis.

vectorborne disease outbreak (VBDO) The occurrence of two or more cases of a vectorborne disease.

vehicle Inanimate materials or objects, such as clothes, bedding, toys, hypodermic needles; or nonliving biological materials such as food, milk, water, blood, serum or plasma, tissues or organs, that can serve as a source of infection.

vehicleborne disease A communicable disease transmitted by nonliving objects; for example, typhoid fever can be transmitted by water.

visitor services A community social service involving one individual taking time to visit with another who is unable to leave his or her residence.

vital statistics Statistical summaries of vital records—records of major life events, such as births, deaths, marriages, divorces, and infant deaths.

volatile organic compounds (VOCs) Compounds that exist as vapors over the normal range of air pressures and temperatures.

voluntary health agency A nonprofit organization created by concerned citizens to deal with health needs not met by governmental health agencies.

voluntary (independent) hospital A nonprofit hospital administered by a religious, fraternal, or other charitable community organization.

wastewater The aqueous mixture that remains after water has been used or contaminated by humans.

water pollution Any physical or chemical change in water that can harm living organisms or make the water unfit for other uses.

waterborne disease A disease that is transmitted through contamination of water.

waterborne disease outbreak (WBDO) The occurrence of two or more cases of a similar illness resulting from the ingestion of drinking water or after exposure to water used for recreational purposes and epidemiological evidence that implicates water as the probable source of illness.

WIC (also known as the Special Supplemental Food Program for Women, Infants, and Children) A federal program sponsored by the United States Department of Agriculture designed to provide supplemental foods, nutrition and health education, and referrals for health and social services to improve the health of at-risk, economically disadvantaged women who are pregnant or are caring for infants and children under age five.

workers' compensation laws A set of federal laws designed to compensate those workers and their families who suffer injuries, disease, or death from workplace exposure.

World Health Assembly Body of delegates of the member nations of the World Health Organization.

World Health Organization (WHO) Most widely recognized international governmental health organization today. Created in 1948 by representatives of United Nations countries.

years of potential life lost (YPLL) The number of years lost when death occurs before the age of 65 or 75.

young old Those 65 to 74 years of age.

youth gang A self-formed association of peers, bound together by mutual interests, with identifiable leadership and well-defined lines of authority, who act in concert to achieve a specific purpose and whose acts generally include illegal activity and control over a territory or an enterprise.

youth support ratio The support ratio that includes only youth.

zero population growth (ZPG) A state in which the birth and death rates for a given population are equal.

zoonosis A communicable disease transmissible under natural conditions from vertebrate animals to humans.

Index

Photo Credits